INTERNATIONAL HUMAN RIGHTS LAW

INTERNATIONAL HUMAN RIGHTS LAW

EDITED BY

DANIEL MOECKLI
University of Zurich

SANGEETA SHAH
University of Nottingham

SANDESH SIVAKUMARAN
University of Nottingham

CONSULTANT EDITOR:

DAVID HARRIS
Professor Emeritus and Co-Director, Human Rights Law Centre,
University of Nottingham

OXFORD
UNIVERSITY PRESS

OXFORD
UNIVERSITY PRESS

Great Clarendon Street, Oxford ox2 6DP

Oxford University Press is a department of the University of Oxford.
It furthers the University's objective of excellence in research, scholarship,
and education by publishing worldwide in

Oxford New York

Auckland Bangkok Buenos Aires Cape Town Chennai
Dar es Salaam Delhi Hong Kong Istanbul Karachi Kolkata
Kuala Lumpur Madrid Melbourne Mexico City Mumbai Nairobi
São Paulo Shanghai Taipei Tokyo Toronto

Oxford is a registered trade mark of Oxford University Press
in the UK and in certain other countries

Published in the United States
by Oxford University Press Inc., New York

British Library Cataloguing in Publication Data

Data available

Typeset by Newgen Imaging Systems (P) Ltd., Chennai, India
Printed in Great Britain
on acid-free paper by

Ashford Colour Press Ltd, Gosport, Hampshire

ISBN 978-0-19-956025-7

5 7 9 10 8 6

OUTLINE CONTENTS

WHAT ARE HUMAN RIGHTS FOR?
THREE PERSONAL REFLECTIONS

PART I   FOUNDATIONS

PART II   INTERNATIONAL LAW

PART III   SUBSTANTIVE RIGHTS

PART IV   PROTECTION

PART V   LINKAGES

PART II   INTERNATIONAL LAW

PART III SUBSTANTIVE RIGHTS

PART IV   PROTECTION

PART V LINKAGES

PART VI   CHALLENGES

PREFACE

Human rights mean different things to different people. From the woman on the street to the UN High Commissioner for Human Rights, from the local human rights activist to the government official, each of us has a different conception of the origin, purpose, and function of human rights. To reflect this diversity of views, we have invited a range of practitioners and academics with different regional, theoretical, and professional backgrounds to contribute chapters to this textbook on their respective fields of expertise.

The book opens with personal perspectives on what human rights are for from three leading human rights practitioners. It then covers the key elements of a typical international human rights law course. Part I seeks to show how human rights have developed over time, how they can be justified, on what basis they may be criticized, and what they have to do with politics. Today, human rights are firmly located in international law and Part II explores the key international law aspects of human rights. Part III considers some of the rights guaranteed to individuals and groups by international human rights law. Part IV addresses the systems of human rights protection at the UN, regional, and national levels. Part V examines the linkages between international human rights law and two other areas of international law: international humanitarian law and international criminal law. Finally, the book concludes, in Part VI, with a consideration of some of the major challenges to the protection of human rights. For want of space, it is impossible to cover all substantive rights, protected groups, systems of protection, linkages, and challenges. This is not meant to reflect in any way the importance, or lack thereof, of the omitted issues.

Many people have supported us in various ways throughout the process of producing this textbook. We are particularly grateful to the contributors to the book for their enthusiasm and support, to our consulting editor, David Harris, for his guidance throughout the process, to Ioannis Athanasopoulos for his assistance with the abbreviations, and to Tom Young, Rekha Summan, and their team at Oxford University Press for steering us through the various editorial stages.

DM/SS/SS
Zurich/Nottingham, March 2010

NOTES ON CONTRIBUTORS

Ed Bates is a Lecturer at the University of Southampton. He is a co-author of Harris, O'Boyle, Warbrick, Bates, and Buckley, *The Law of the European Convention on Human Rights* (Oxford University Press, 2009) and author of *The Evolution of the European Convention on Human Rights* (Oxford University Press, forthcoming 2010).

Kevin Boyle is Professor of Law, University of Essex and was director of the University's Human Rights Centre until 2007. He was senior adviser to Mary Robinson, then UN High Commissioner for Human Rights, 2001–2. He is Chair of the International Council of Minority Rights Group and founding director of Article 19, the Global Campaign for Freedom of Expression. He has litigated before the European Court of Human Rights, including on freedom of expression cases.

Andrew Byrnes is Professor of International Law at the Faculty of Law, the University of New South Wales (UNSW), and Chair of the Management Committee of the Australian Human Rights Centre, UNSW. His chapter with Catherine Renshaw draws on research conducted as a part of two Australian Research Council-funded Linkage projects (LP0776639 and LP0989167) on national human rights institutions in the Asia Pacific, and economic, social, and cultural rights, respectively.

Christine Chinkin, FBA, is Professor of International Law, London School of Economics and Political Science, and William W. Cook Global Law Professor, University of Michigan Law School.

Andrew Clapham is Director of the Geneva Academy of International Humanitarian Law and Human Rights and a Professor of Public International Law at the Graduate Institute of International and Development Studies in Geneva. His publications include *International Human Rights Lexicon* with Susan Marks (Oxford University Press, 2005), *Human Rights Obligations of Non-State Actors* (Oxford University Press, 2006), and *Human Rights: A Very Short Introduction* (Oxford University Press, 2007).

Fons Coomans holds the UNESCO Chair in Human Rights and Peace at the Department of International and European Law of Maastricht University. He is also the coordinator of the Maastricht Centre for Human Rights, and Senior Researcher at the Netherlands School of Human Rights Research. His research focuses on economic, social, and cultural rights and international human rights monitoring procedures.

Robert Cryer is Professor of International and Criminal Law at the University of Birmingham. He teaches international law, criminal law, and international criminal law.

Marie-Bénédicte Dembour is Professor of Law and Anthropology at the University of Sussex. She has published widely, including most prominently in the field of human rights a monograph entitled *Who Believes in Human Rights? Reflections on the European Convention* (Cambridge University Press, 2006). She is currently the holder of a Leverhulme Major Research Fellowship to work on a project entitled 'Migrants have human rights too! Critical perspectives on the Strasbourg case law'.

Asbjørn Eide is former Director and presently Professor Emeritus at the Norwegian Center for Human Rights at the University of Oslo. He has been Torgny Segerstedt Professor at the University of Gothenburg, Sweden, visiting professor at the University of Lund, and is adjunct professor at the College of Law, American University in Washington. He is author and editor of several books and numerous articles on human rights, and was for 20 years an expert member of the UN Sub-Commission on Promotion and Protection of Human Rights.

Malgosia Fitzmaurice is Professor of Public International Law at the Department of Law, Queen Mary, University of London. She specializes in international environmental law, the law of treaties, water law, and indigenous peoples law and published widely on all these subjects. In July 2001, she was invited to deliver keynote lectures on 'International Protection of the Environment' at the Hague Academy of International Law.

Steven Greer is Professor of Human Rights in the School of Law, University of Bristol. He studied Law at the University of Oxford, Sociology at the London School of Economics, and has a PhD in Law from the Queen's University of Belfast. In addition to the University of Bristol, he has taught at Queen's Belfast and at the Universities of Sussex, Hannover, and Wollongong. His many publications range over the fields of criminal justice, human rights, and law and terrorism, and his most recent book, *The European Convention on Human Rights: Achievements, Problems and Prospects* (Cambridge University Press, 2006), was short-listed with two other titles for the Hart Socio-Legal Book Prize 2008.

Christof Heyns is Dean and Professor of Human Rights Law at the University of Pretoria Faculty of Law.

Sarah Joseph is a Professor of Law at Monash University, Melbourne, and Director of the Castan Centre for Human Rights Law. She has published many articles and books on human rights, including *The International Covenant on Civil and Political Rights: Cases, Materials, and Commentary* (co-author) (Oxford University Press, 2004).

Magnus Killander is Head of Research at the Centre for Human Rights at the University of Pretoria Faculty of Law.

Stephen P. Marks is the François-Xavier Bagnoud Professor of Health and Human Rights at the Harvard School of Public Health, where he directs the Program on Human Rights in Development. He also teaches human rights in the Faculty of Arts and Sciences at Harvard College and is chair of the High-Level Task Force on the Implementation of the Right to Development under the authority of the UN Human Rights Council. Among his recent publications are *Development as a Human Right: Legal, Political and Economic Dimensions* (co-editor) (Harvard University Press, 2010) and *Human Rights Cities: Civic Engagement for Societal Development* (co-author) (PDHRE, 2008).

Robert McCorquodale is the Director of the British Institute of International and Comparative Law and Professor of International Law and Human Rights at the University of Nottingham.

Frédéric Mégret is an Assistant-Professor at McGill University's Faculty of Law, and the holder of the Canada Research Chair in the Law of Human Rights and Legal Pluralism. He holds a PhD from the Université de Paris I and the Geneva Graduate Institute of International Studies.

Julie Mertus, a Professor and Co-Director of the Ethics and Peace program at American University, has worked in the field on human rights for numerous governmental and non-governmental organizations, including UNHCR, USAID, the Norwegian government, the Open Society Institute, Women for Inclusive Security and the Women's Commission for Refugee Women and Children. A prolific writer, her books include *Bait and Switch: Human Rights and U.S. Foreign Policy* (Routledge, 2008) (named 'human rights book of the year' by the American Political Science Association), *Human Rights Matters: Local Politics and National Human Rights Institutions* (Stanford University Press, 2008), *The United Nations and Human Rights* (Routledge, 2009), and *Kosovo: How Myths and Truths Started a War* (University of California Press, 1999).

Daniel Moeckli is an Oberassistent in Public Law at the University of Zurich and a Fellow of the University of Nottingham Human Rights Law Centre. His research and teaching focus on human rights law, both international and national, and constitutional law. He is the author of *Human Rights and Non-discrimination in the 'War on Terror'* (Oxford University Press, 2008).

James Nickel is Professor of Philosophy and Law at the University of Miami in Coral Gables, Florida. Nickel teaches and writes in human rights law and theory, constitutional law, jurisprudence, and political philosophy. He is the author of *Making Sense of Human Rights* (Wiley-Blackwell, 2006) and many articles in philosophy and law.

Michael O'Flaherty is Professor of Applied Human Rights and Co-director of the Human Rights Law Centre at the University of Nottingham. He is a member of the UN Human Rights Committee.

Dianne Otto is Director of the International Human Rights Law Program of the Institute for International Law and the Humanities (IILAH) at the University of Melbourne. Her research interests include peace and security issues, international economic and social rights, gender issues in human rights and development, international human rights NGOs, and the domestic implementation of international legal obligations. Dianne has been active in a number of human rights NGOs including Women's Rights Action Network Australia (WRANA), Women's Economic Equality Project (WEEP) in Canada, and International Women's Rights Action Watch Asia Pacific (IWRAW-AP) in Malaysia.

Jo M. Pasqualucci is a Professor of Law at the University of South Dakota. She earned her JD at the University of Wisconsin and her SJD in International and Comparative Law at George Washington University Law School. She clerked at the Inter-American

Court of Human Rights and is the author of *The Practice and Procedure of the Inter-American Court of Human Rights* (Cambridge University Press, 2003) and several articles on the Inter-American human rights system.

David Reidy, JD, PhD, is Lindsay Young Associate Professor of Philosophy and Adjunct Associate Professor of Political Science at the University of Tennessee. He has published widely in political and legal philosophy. He has a special interest in the work of John Rawls.

Catherine Renshaw is Research Fellow, Faculty of Law, the University of New South Wales (UNSW), and Director of the Australian Research Council-funded National Human Rights Institutions project of the Australian Human Rights Centre at UNSW.

Sir Nigel Rodley is Professor of Law and Chair of the Human Rights Centre at the University of Essex. From 1992 to 2001 he served as UN Commission on Human Rights Special Rapporteur on the question of torture. Since 2001 he has been a member of the UN Human Rights Committee. He is also a Commissioner of the International Commission of Jurists.

Martin Scheinin is, since 2008, Professor of Public International Law at the European University Institute in Florence. He also serves as the UN Special Rapporteur on human rights and counter-terrorism (2005–2011). He has a doctorate in law from the University of Helsinki (1991) and was from 1997–2004 a member of the UN Human Rights Committee and from 1998–2008 Director of the Institute for Human Rights at Åbo Akademi University.

Markus Schmidt is senior legal officer for the UN Office at Geneva. Until December 2009, he was senior human rights officer in the Office of the UN High Commissioner for Human Rights (OHCHR). He served as secretary of the Human Rights Committee from 2001 to 2005 and was team leader of the Petitions Unit of OHCHR from 2002 to 2009.

Sangeeta Shah is a Lecturer in the School of Law, University of Nottingham and a Member of the Human Rights Law Centre, University of Nottingham. She is the Recent Developments Editor of the *Human Rights Law Review*.

Sandesh Sivakumaran is a Lecturer in the School of Law and Member of the Human Rights Law Centre, University of Nottingham. He has worked at the International Court of Justice, the International Criminal Tribunal for the former Yugoslavia, and the Special Court for Sierra Leone.

Theo van Boven is Professor Emeritus of International Law at Maastricht University, the Netherlands. Over the years he has been closely associated with the human rights programme of the UN, notably as Director of Human Rights, member of the Commission and the Sub-Commission for Human Rights, member of the Committee on the Elimination of Racial Discrimination, and Special Rapporteur on Torture.

ABBREVIATIONS

AAA	American Anthropological Association
ACHPR	African Charter on Human and Peoples' Rights
ACHR	American Convention on Human Rights
ACommHPR	African Commission on Human and Peoples' Rights
ADHR	American Declaration of the Rights and Duties of Man
AJIL	American Journal of International Law
APRM	African Peer Review Mechanism
ASIL	American Society of International Law
AU	African Union
BBC	British Broadcasting Corporation
BGE	Bundesgerichtsentscheid (Swiss Federal Supreme Court decision)
BYIL	British Year Book of International Law
CAT	Committee Against Torture
CDDH	Steering Committee for Human Rights
CEDAW	Convention on the Elimination of All Forms of Discrimination against Women
CEDAW-OP	Optional Protocol to CEDAW
CEJIL	Center for Justice and International Law
CERD	Committee on the Elimination of Racial Discrimination
CESCR	Committee on Economic, Social and Cultural Rights
CHR	UN Commission on Human Rights
CIDA	Canadian International Development Agency
CPPEVAW	Inter-American Convention on the Prevention, Punishment and Eradication of Violence Against Women
CRC	Convention on the Rights of the Child
CRPD	Convention on the Rights of Persons with Disabilities
CRPD-OP	Optional Protocol to the CRPD
CSCE	Conference on Security and Cooperation in Europe
CTC	Counter-Terrorism Committee
CUP	Cambridge University Press
DANIDA	Danish International Development Agency
DFID	UK Department for International Development
DPKO	UN Department of Peace-keeping Operations
DRC	Democratic Republic of Congo
EACJ	East African Court of Justice
EC	European Community
ECHR	European Convention on Human Rights
ECJ	European Court of Justice
ECOMOG	Economic Community of West African States Monitoring Group

ECOSOC	UN Economic and Social Council
ECOSOCC	Economic, Social and Cultural Council of the African Union
ECOWAS	Economic Community of West African States
ECPT	European Convention for the Prevention of Torture and Inhuman or Degrading Treatment or Punishment
ECSR	European Committee of Social Rights
EEC	European Economic Community
EHRLR	European Human Rights Law Review
EHRR	European Human Rights Reports
EIA	Environmental Impact Assessment
EJIL	European Journal of International Law
ELJ	European Law Journal
EPO	European Patent Office
EU	European Union
EWCA	England and Wales Court of Appeal
EWHC	England and Wales High Court
FAO	Food and Agriculture Organization of the UN
FARC	Revolutionary Armed Forces of Colombia
FRA	Fundamental Rights Agency
FRY	Federal Republic of Yugoslavia
G-20	The Group of Twenty
GA	General Assembly of the UN
GDR	German Democratic Republic
HDCA	Human Development and Capability Association
HHRJ	Harvard Human Rights Journal
HICP	Highly Indebted Poor Countries
HLR	Harvard Law Review
HMSO	Her Majesty's Stationery Office
HRBA	Human Rights-Based Approach
HRC	Human Rights Committee
HR Council	UN Human Rights Council
HRLJ	Human Rights Law Journal
HRLR	Human Rights Law Review
HRQ	Human Rights Quarterly
IACtHR	Inter-American Court of Human Rights
IACommHR	Inter-American Commission on Human Rights
ICC	International Criminal Court
ICCPR	International Covenant on Civil and Political Rights
ICCPR-OP1	Optional Protocol to the ICCPR
ICCPR-OP2	Second Optional Protocol to the ICCPR
ICERD	International Convention on the Elimination of All Forms of Racial Discrimination
ICESCR	International Covenant on Economic, Social and Cultural Rights

ICESCR-OP	Optional Protocol to the ICESCR
ICLQ	International and Comparative Law Quarterly
ICJ	International Court of Justice
ICRC	International Committee of the Red Cross
ICRMW	International Convention on the Protection of the Rights of All Migrant Workers and Members of Their Families
ICTR	International Criminal Tribunal for Rwanda
ICTY	International Criminal Tribunal for the former Yugoslavia
IDC	International Disability Caucus
IDEA	International Development Ethics Association
ILC	International Law Commission
ILM	International Legal Materials
ILO	International Labour Organization
IMF	International Monetary Fund
INSC	Supreme Court of India
IR	International Relations
IRA	Irish Republican Army
IRRC	International Review of the Red Cross
JCSL	Journal of Conflict and Security Law
JHR	Journal of Human Rights
JICJ	Journal of International Criminal Justice
KFOR	Kosovo Force
KLA	Kosovo Liberation Army
LGBT	Lesbian, Gay, Bisexual and Transgender
LJIL	Leiden Journal of International Law
LNOJ	League of Nations Official Journal
LTTE	Liberation Tigers of Tamil Eelam
LQR	Law Quarterly Review
MCC	Millennium Challenge Corporation
MDGs	Millennium Development Goals
MJIL	Michigan Journal of International Law
MINURCAT	UN Mission in the Central African Republic and Chad
MINUSTAH	UN Mission in Haiti
MLR	Modern Law Review
MONUC	UN Mission in the Democratic Republic of Congo
NAACP	National Association for the Advancement of Colored People
NATO	North Atlantic Treaty Organization
NEPAD	New Partnership for Africa's Development
NGO	Non-Governmental Organization
NHRIs	National Human Rights Institutions
NJIL	Nordic Journal of International Law
NPMs	National Preventive Mechanisms
NQHR	Netherlands Quarterly of Human Rights

Nuremberg IMT	Nuremberg International Military Tribunal
NYUJILP	New York University Journal of International Law and Politics
OAS	Organization of American States
OAU	Organization of African Unity
ODIHR	Office for Democratic Institutions and Human Rights
OECD	Organisation for Economic Co-operation and Development
OHCHR	Office of the UN High Commissioner for Human Rights
OJLS	Oxford Journal of Legal Studies
OPT	Occupied Palestinian Territory
OSCE	Organization of Security and Co-operation in Europe
OUP	Oxford University Press
PACE	Parliamentary Assembly of the Council of Europe
PAP	Pan-African Parliament
PCIJ	Permanent Court of International Justice
PKK	Kurdistan Workers' Party
PL	Public Law
PLD	Pakistan Legal Decisions
PRSPs	Poverty Reduction Strategy Papers
PRWA	Protocol of the Rights of Women in Africa
PSC	Peace and Security Council
Rec des Cours	Recueil des Cours de l'Académie de Droit International
RECs	Regional Economic Communities
SADC	Southern African Development Community
SCSL	Special Court for Sierra Leone
SSR	Soviet Socialist Republic
Tokyo IMT	Tokyo International Military Tribunal
UDHR	Universal Declaration of Human Rights
UK	United Kingdom
UKHL	United Kingdom House of Lords
UN	United Nations
UNAMA	UN Mission in Afghanistan
UNAMI	UN Nations Mission in Iraq
UNCAT	Convention against Torture and Other Cruel, Inhuman or Degrading Treatment or Punishment
UNCAT-OP	Optional Protocol to UNCAT
UNDAT	UN Declaration against Torture
UNDP	UN Development Programme
UNECE	UN Economic Commission for Europe
UNESCO	UN Educational, Scientific and Cultural Organisation
UNFPA	UN Population Fund
UNICEF	UN Children's Fund
UNIFEM	UN Development Fund for Women
UNMIK	UN Interim Administration Mission in Kosovo

UNMIS	UN Mission in Sudan
UPR	Universal Periodic Review
USA	United States of America
USC	United States Code
USSR	Union of Soviet Socialist Republics
VCLT	Vienna Convention on the Law of Treaties
WGC	Working Group on Communications
WGS	Working Group on Situations
WHO	World Health Organization
WLR	Weekly Law Reports
WTO	World Trade Organization
YJIL	Yale Journal of International Law

TABLE OF INTERNATIONAL INSTRUMENTS

TABLE OF CASES

International

WHAT ARE HUMAN RIGHTS FOR? THREE PERSONAL REFLECTIONS

NAVANETHEM PILLAY

UNITED NATIONS HIGH
COMMISSIONER FOR HUMAN RIGHTS

The editors of this textbook on international human rights law asked me to provide some thoughts on the question 'What are human rights for?' and to do so from the perspective of personal experience. I will begin by noting that I count myself among the lucky ones—those who against the odds of multiple discrimination based on gender, race, and social class, came to enjoy the benefits of civil and political liberties, as well as economic, social, and cultural rights.

I was born a non-white in apartheid South Africa. My ancestors were sugarcane cutters. My father was a bus driver. We were poor.

At age 16 I wrote an essay which dealt with the role of South African women in educating children on human rights and which, as it turned out, was indeed fateful. After the essay was published, my community raised funds in order to send this promising, but impecunious, young woman to university. My people perhaps did not know that a right to education actually existed and that it was enshrined in international law; but they believed in education. They understood that it creates paths out of poverty and discrimination.

Despite their efforts and goodwill, I almost did not make it as a lawyer, because when I entered university during the apartheid regime everything and everyone was segregated. The registrar actually discouraged me from becoming a lawyer. He argued that I could not expect white secretaries to take instructions from a person of my background. However, I persevered. After my graduation I sought an internship, which was mandatory under the law; but then as a black woman I had to fight against multi-layered forms of discrimination and barriers. Finally, it was a black lawyer who agreed to take me on board, but he first made me promise that I would not become pregnant. And when I started a law practice on my own, it was not out of choice but because no one would employ a black woman lawyer.

Yet, in the course of my life, I had the privilege to see and experience a complete transformation in my country. South Africa now has one of the strongest constitutions in the world, and while it struggles, as many countries do, to turn legal rights into reality, watching such amazing change over a single decade and through a relatively peaceful evolution gives me great hope. Indeed, I offer a living testimony of rights realized.

Against this background it is no surprise that when I read or recite Article 1 of the Universal Declaration of Human Rights, I intimately and profoundly feel its truth. The article states that: 'All human beings are born free and equal in dignity and rights. They are endowed with reason and conscience and should act towards one another in a spirit of brotherhood.' These words resonate today as widely and as movingly as they did in 1948 when the Universal Declaration came into being. They affirmed the force of ideas and a vision of respectful and peaceful coexistence in the aftermath of utter brutality and destruction. The Universal Declaration's words speak with timeless and unalterable force of both the power of rights and of our kinship in rights.

THE POWER OF RIGHTS AND OUR KINSHIP IN RIGHTS

The power of rights made it possible for an ever-expanding number of people, people like myself, to claim freedom, equality, justice, and well-being. All human rights—civil, political, economic, social, and cultural—were recognized as inherent and inalienable entitlements of all people, rather than privileges magnanimously bestowed upon them or denied to them at the caprice of the powerful.

The language of human rights makes manifest the relationship between fundamental freedoms and social justice, and the connection of these elements with peace and security. It is reflected in a wide and growing legal architecture, as well as advocacy vehicles for the promotion and protection of all rights.

Today, dedicated international, regional, and national mechanisms, including the UN Office of the High Commissioner for Human Rights and the UN Human Rights Council with its independent experts, have been put in place to be both the custodians and the monitors of human rights, to promote and protect all these rights. Civil society everywhere promotes vigilance of rights implementation with growing capacity and influence.

The protective canvas of human rights jurisprudence and implementing mechanisms recognizes the natural and social bonds of human destiny everywhere, that is, our kinship in rights. It empowers all of us to claim our entitlement to a life of dignity, our right to count and be counted irrespective of our ancestry, gender and colour, status and creed.

Human rights underpin the aspiration to a world in which every man, woman, and child lives free from hunger and protected from oppression, violence, and discrimination, with the benefits of housing, healthcare, education, and opportunity. A human rights approach shines a light over the critical vulnerabilities of individuals and groups at risk of abuse. It engages them as active participants and generators of change. For the opposite of marginalization, discrimination, and neglect is not only equality in rights and opportunities, but also the ability to make one's voice heard and to be counted.

Such participation requires the twin freedoms of expression and association. All over the world, the growth of organized civil society, as well as of a combative press that speaks truth to power, testifies to the vitality and enduring appeal of these principles. Indeed, information and the freedom to organize and express views openly are vital for good policy making and the measurable implementation of human rights policies. This encapsulates the global culture of human rights towards which we strive.

Yet for too many people in the world, human rights remain an unfulfilled promise, as the political will to give effect to states' human rights obligations lags lamentably behind their pledges. We live in a world where crimes against humanity are ongoing, where mass rape and murder continue with impunity, and where the most basic economic rights critical to survival are not realized and often not even accorded the high priority they warrant.

The UN Secretary-General noted that the recent food emergencies, degradation of the natural environment, current economic crisis, and the unrest that they engender all underscore that those who are at the frontlines of hardship are also likely to be the victims of the ripple effects of human rights violations.

GIVING EFFECT TO RIGHTS: MECHANISMS AND RESPONSIBILITIES

The challenge for all of us—states, international organizations, and civil society—remains in implementing human rights and ensuring that they are given effect without ranking them. The question is: how?

To begin to answer it, I will tap into the wisdom of Eleanor Roosevelt, leader of the Universal Declaration process, who once said, 'Where, after all, do universal human rights begin? … In small places, close to home.' Until these rights touch the lives of every man, woman, and child everywhere, our work is not done.

The years to come are crucial for sowing the seeds of an improved international partnership that, by drawing on individual and collective resourcefulness and strengths, can meet the global challenges of poverty, discrimination, conflict, scarcity of natural resources, recession, and climate change.

In defeating fear and want and in dissuading potential perpetrators from committing human rights violations, we can be assisted not only by existing human rights and international humanitarian law, as well as existing institutions of justice, but also by innovative and evolving mechanisms.

In 2005, the world leaders at their summit created the UN Human Rights Council, an intergovernmental body which replaced the much-criticized UN Human Rights Commission, with the mandate of promoting 'universal respect for the protection of all human rights and fundamental freedoms for all'. The Council began its operations in June 2006. Since then, it has equipped itself with its own institutional architecture and has been engaged in an innovative process known as the Universal Periodic

Review (UPR). The UPR is the Council's assessment at regular intervals of the human rights record of all UN member states. With time, I am confident that the review will help effectively to change for the better the human rights situation on the ground. We should recognize that this initiative carries a promising potential and is taken very seriously.

In addition, at each session of the Council several country-situations are brought to the fore in addresses and documents delivered by member states, independent experts, and the Office of the High Commissioner for Human Rights. Civil society eagerly contributes to the Council's work. Indeed, the Council is one of the pre-eminent international fora, attracting hundreds of representatives from NGOs, as well as individuals, whose clout and proposals are reflected in the decision-making processes. The Council also offers them a venue to channel comments and reflections, concerns and grievances.

Further, unlike the previous Commission, the Council is virtually a standing body. The frequency of its meetings—both in formal and informal gatherings—creates more opportunities for honing operations and responses to both chronic human rights conditions and crises. Among the latter, the Council tackled the recent food emergencies and the economic downturn with the sense of urgency they deserved. The assiduity of the Council's meetings may also help to build a firmer ground of understanding among the Council's members than sporadic interactions would permit.

If the Human Rights Council is the premier intergovernmental body for the promotion and protection of human rights, the Office of the High Commissioner for Human Rights, as part of the UN Secretariat, is their leading international advocate and independent champion.

As the UN Secretary-General noted, since its creation in 1993 the Office of the High Commissioner has grown to become a powerful driver of change. It has expanded dramatically, elevated the profile of human rights all over the world, provided expertise for capacity building both to states and within the UN system, and preserved the autonomy of judgement and scope of action that are indispensible to human rights work and advocacy.

Today, the Office of the High Commissioner is in a unique position to assist governments and civil society in their efforts to protect and promote human rights. The expansion of its field offices and its presence in more than 50 countries, as well as its increasing and deepening interaction with UN agencies and other crucial partners in government, international organizations, and civil society are important steps in this direction. With these steps we can more readily strive for practical cooperation leading to the creation of national systems which promote human rights and provide protection and recourse for victims of human rights violations.

Deterring the most flagrant human rights violations through the application of international criminal responsibility has also been a critical component of human rights advocacy. The International Criminal Court plays a central role in this regard. The Statute of the Court is a major step forward in that, for the first time, a major multilateral treaty unequivocally recognizes as war crimes acts committed in non-international armed conflicts. It is encouraging that an increasing number of states are signing and ratifying the Statute.

In the final instance, however, it is the duty of states, regardless of their political, economic, and cultural systems, to promote and protect all human rights and fundamental freedoms. Our collective responsibility is to assist states to fulfil their obligations and to hold them to account when they do not.

The roster of distinguished contributors to this textbook is very impressive. These experts will expand and clarify some of the thoughts that here I can only sketch. The readers of such an important contribution to human rights education are indeed in good hands.

KENNETH ROTH

EXECUTIVE DIRECTOR OF HUMAN RIGHTS WATCH

The modern state can be a source of both good and evil. It can do much good—protecting our security, ensuring our basic necessities, nurturing an environment in which people can flourish to the best of their abilities. But when it represses its people, shirks its duties, or misapplies its resources, it can be the source of much suffering.

International human rights law sets forth the core obligations of governments toward their people, prescribing the basic freedoms that governments must respect and the steps they must take to uphold public welfare. But the application of that law often differs from the enforcement of statutes typically found in a nation's law books.

In countries that enjoy the rule of law, the courts can usually be relied on to enforce legislation. The rule of law means that courts have the independence to apply the law free of interference, and powerful actors, including senior government officials, are expected to comply with court orders.

In practice, there is no such presumption in most of the countries where my organization, Human Rights Watch, works, and where international human rights law is most needed. The judges are often corrupt, intimidated, or compromised. They may not dare hold the government to account, or they may have been co-opted to the point that they do not even try, or the government may succeed in ignoring whatever efforts they make. It is worth noting that this problem is not limited to dictatorships or tyrannical governments. Even in functioning democracies, the courts do not always succeed in enforcing rights especially for the poor, the marginalized, and the unpopular. In those circumstances, the process of building political pressure through investigation, reporting and advocacy is often all we have. While it may not offer as simple a solution as a trip to the courthouse, it can still be quite powerful. Understanding how it works can be key to appreciating the significance of human rights law.

International human rights law should be seen as a backstop in such cases, a law of last resort when domestic rights legislation fails. Judicial enforcement is always welcome, but when it falls short, human rights law provides a basis that is distinct from domestic legislation for putting pressure on governments to uphold their obligations.

It is easy for many who live in rule-of-law countries to assume that the enforcement of rights is a purely judicial function. In fact, the government as a whole is responsible for defending rights; after all, the political branches of government, not the courts, sign and ratify human rights treaties. The pressure techniques developed by the human rights movement could theoretically be applied on behalf of any body of law, but international human rights law, with obligations that many governments are particularly prone to shirk, has been the context in which these techniques have been most refined.

The key to this enforcement pressure is exposure and shame. Human rights groups investigate and report on situations in which governments fall short of their obligations. The resulting publicity, through the media and other outlets, can undermine a government's standing and credibility, embarrassing it before its people and peers and generating pressure for reform. This reporting can also convince other governments and institutions to use their influence with the target government to promote change.

There is a different dynamic to this shaming process than to the enforcement of law in regular courts. Any law weakens when its dictates deviate too far from the public's moral judgements. Even judges in rule-of-law countries tend to be attentive to public opinion with respect to certain controversial issues.

But when it comes to enforcing the law through shaming rather than litigation, public morality plays an even more important role. To put it simply, there can be no shame if the public approves of the conduct in question. The law may say that certain governmental conduct is wrong, but if the public disagrees, if it applauds the conduct, the government will feel no pressure to comply with the law.

The law is not irrelevant to the shaming process. It helps to shape public morality, and thus to promote a sense of shame, particularly in areas, such as warfare, where the norms governing conduct might be complex. But it is important not to equate law and public morality, or to delude ourselves into thinking that the mere existence of a law translates into the type of extra-judicial pressure that human rights groups can generate.

Beyond documenting and reporting violations of human rights law, human rights groups thus must shape public opinion, to ensure that the exposure of government misconduct is met with opprobrium rather than approval. In part that is done by citing international law to convince the public of a global consensus about what is right or wrong in a given context. By presenting an issue in terms of rights, human rights groups help the public to develop a moral framework for assessing governmental conduct beyond public sentiment in any particular case or incident.

For example, many people might tend to believe that in an armed conflict, anything goes. International human rights law (as well as its sister body of law, international humanitarian law) makes clear that torture and other ill-treatment are prohibited, even in time of war. That is not necessarily an intuitive concept. But the unequivocal prohibition in international law helps to build a public morality that rejects all such mistreatment of detainees.

Or a public may feel that custom legitimizes the subordination of women. Human rights law provides an alternative moral framework to that custom and helps to build a public morality that finds such discrimination and inequality wrong.

For the law to play this role of moral instruction, it is not enough simply to recite it. When people's security or traditions are at stake, it takes more than a mere reference to the law to change the public's sense of moral propriety. Human rights groups must be creative in moving the public to embrace what the law demands.

One key to that effort is personifying the victim. When human rights abuses remain abstract—mere recitations of detention statistics or violated provisions of a penal code—it is far more difficult to mobilize public outrage than if the public can identify with the target of the abuse. The more compelling the story, the more likely there will be public outrage, whether about a political prisoner sentenced to a long prison term, a rape victim denied justice, or a child unable to obtain medical care despite adequate government resources. Here the media play an essential role in bringing the plight of these victims to the public's attention. Ideology, routine, or indifference can often be made to give way to human suffering made palpable.

Sometimes consequentialist arguments are required as well. After the September 11 attacks in the USA, many Americans were willing to contemplate torture because they thought it made them safer. It was not enough to ask Americans to identify with the primary victims—the foreign Muslim terrorist suspects, the supposed 'worst of the worst', because most Americans felt no such identity. But the public gradually rejected torture, in part out of a growing sense that it is not what the USA should stand for, but also, to a large degree, out of a growing belief that torture was making the public less safe by facilitating terrorist recruiters and discouraging the international cooperation needed to curb terrorism.

Sometimes the challenge is convincing the public to apply a broad concept to a particular situation. For example, international humanitarian law has long prohibited indiscriminate attacks, but few thought that this prohibition was violated by antipersonnel landmines or cluster munitions, even though these weapons are incapable of precise targeting of combatants. It took extensive factual reporting on the indiscriminate consequences of these weapons systems for the public to agree that their use was wrong. That public pressure, in turn, led governments to adopt treaties banning these weapons.

Sometimes it is difficult to convince a local public to disapprove of its government's conduct. In those cases, one option is to convince a more sympathetic external public to exert pressure indirectly, usually through its own government. Shaming is usually most powerful when the disapproving public is domestic. But even in the absence of domestic shame—for example, if a government succeeds in controlling its domestic media so that its public does not learn of its shameful conduct—surrogate publics can be a source of pressure. Any public whose views the target government cares about can play this surrogate role—because the target government fears that the surrogate public opinion might seep back home and influence domestic opinion, or because the surrogate public might influence its own government whose good graces matter to the target government.

Thus, the great challenge facing human rights groups is often less concerned with arguing the law's fine points or applying them to the facts of a case than with convincing the public that violations are wrong. That requires the hard work of helping the public to identify with the victim's plight, making the law come alive, and generating outrage at its violation with some public of relevance. When human rights law can be made to correspond with the public's sense of right and wrong, governments face intense pressure to respect that law. Shame can be a powerful motivator.

HINA JILANI

DIRECTOR OF AGHS LEGAL AID CENTER AND ADVOCATE OF THE SUPREME COURT OF PAKISTAN

What are human rights for? The answer seems fairly obvious to those who have spent many years striving to promote values and principles they consider essential for progress, peace, and social justice. Yet when asked to articulate a response to this question in a manner that connects concepts with the reality of everyday life, it becomes complex, with so many challenges emanating from different experiences determined by the political, social, and economic conditions in which the struggle for the promotion and protection of human rights is being conducted.

From the perspective of human rights defenders, support for human rights is essential to create the environment in which they are able to exercise the freedoms necessary to carry out their activities for advocacy, monitoring, and reporting on respect for human rights. For instance, the freedoms of expression, assembly, association, and access to information are indispensable for the defence of human rights. From the perspective of victims of violations, the human rights framework provides the essential components for effective remedies in the form of redress, compensation, and reparation, through institutions that are independent and impartial and adhere to the basic principles of human dignity, equality, and non-discrimination. The human rights framework also provides the standards that must be reached in order that rights can be realized through the combined medium of state responsibility and the rule of law. It is in this aspect that international law becomes most relevant to domestic legal frameworks by allowing people to have the same expectations from the law, national institutions, state policy, and methods of governance.

The truth of these arguments and fulfilment of these expectations will, nevertheless, only be borne out if individuals' experiences show that what human rights represent has enabled them to obtain justice or has protected them from harm to their dignity, security, or liberty. The abstract promotion of human rights seldom garners the credibility gained when human rights are put to the test and applied to concrete situations involving a quest for their realization.

Human rights defenders have a significant role to play in raising public support for human rights. Their actions and choices regarding the means of promoting human rights often determine popular perceptions about human rights. When called upon to respond to a situation concerning the promotion or protection of rights—individual or collective—human rights defenders are faced with the initial task of choosing the forum in which to raise their concerns. Their choices are largely dependent on their assessment of the surrounding environment, the efficacy of the tools available, and their own capacity to sustain action. As a lawyer and a human rights defender, I have frequently had to choose between political action, by way of advocacy or protest, and legal action, by seeking to assert rights through legal process.

One of the primary considerations in making that choice has always been: what is the best way of linking the search for justice, and the result achieved, to respect for human rights? Another consideration is how to maximize public consciousness about the interconnectedness of a public debate and the persons who suffer the consequences of human rights violations. In other words, 'giving the problem a human face' is more likely to result in the public relating directly to the issue at hand and having a stake in the outcome of the action taken. Sometimes, though, this may imply a complicated management of the role of a human rights defender as a lawyer *and* an activist, as it becomes necessary to take public action as well as to seek a judicial confirmation of rights on the same issue to maximize the impact of the campaign.

I recall our engagement in the 1980s with the pernicious and widespread practice of bonded labour in Pakistan. The human rights community began a public campaign to raise awareness of the issue and mobilize public opinion against the practice. While the process did take time to achieve a level of public sentiment that served as a pressure on the government and state institutions to take action, the objective was achieved and a public debate on the issue emerged from the campaign launched by human rights defenders. However, the public sentiment was focused on the moral wrongdoing in the practice but the essence of the rights to dignity, liberty, and security, and connected social and economic rights, was still not recognized as being at the core of the issue. Furthermore, although violations had been exposed, the practice of bonded labour persisted because of the failure of the government to respond with appropriate laws, policies, or enforcement mechanisms to eliminate the practice. It was through the courts that this was eventually achieved. A judgment of the Supreme Court of Pakistan spelled out the violations of fundamental freedoms and human rights that the practice entailed with reference to international human rights standards and constitutional guarantees, and laid down guidelines for legislation to outlaw the practice and the requirements for its effective enforcement. More importantly, several hundred petitions on behalf of bonded labourers raised the awareness of their rights amongst victims. This was instrumental in the formation of victim associations to protect their human rights as well as their rights under the law.

Where discrimination is inherent in social attitudes it becomes more difficult to strive for social justice for the more marginalized sections of the population on the basis of human rights. In many societies women's rights are not considered an inalienable part of human rights. Constitutional guarantees, even though prescribed, are often not applied to women's fundamental rights. In the context of Pakistan, I have found it more difficult to promote women's rights in the abstract and achieved better results when the plight of actual victims and the gross injustice and cruelty suffered by some of them was made visible through advocacy and litigation. The cumulative effect was more pronounced in terms of attitudinal changes and resulted in a slow, but very positive, change in public perception of the status and rights of women.

One particular case is that of a young woman at risk of 'honour killing', whose situation was given media exposure. More importantly, her case resulted in a landmark judicial decision which set the tone for state responsibility in holding non-state actors accountable for violating the rights to life, physical security, and liberty of women on misconceived notions of culture and harmful social practices.

It is these experiences that give convincing illustrations of why human rights principles and values matter in the struggle for human rights. If these principles are covered comprehensively in national laws, the potential for social justice increases. At the same time the international human rights system presents an option if national systems are flawed or unable to protect against violation of rights or to offer redress.

PART I

FOUNDATIONS

1

HISTORY

Ed Bates

SUMMARY

This chapter tells the story of the historical development of the concept of human rights and their status in international law. It is divided into three main sections. As the human rights story began on the domestic plane, the chapter starts by considering this. The focus is on the key developments since the seventeenth century, but in particular since the late eighteenth century. The chapter then turns to international law, examining it from the perspective of human rights over the period up to the Second World War. Finally, it focuses on the efforts to create international human rights law in the 1940s, culminating with the proclamation of the Universal Declaration of Human Rights in 1948.

1 INTRODUCTION

As an esteemed professor of international law and (later) international judge, Hersch Lauterpacht wrote in 1945: 'any attempt to translate the idea of an International Bill of the Rights of Man into a working rule of law is fraught with difficulties which disturb orthodox thought to the point of utter discouragement'.[1] The transformation of relations between a state and its nationals into international legal obligations by which the international community could derive a respectable and meaningful level of control and censure would, Lauterpacht argued, engender 'restrictions on sovereignty more far-reaching in their implications than any yet propounded in the annals of international utopias'.[2]

To be clear, Lauterpacht was firmly committed to the establishment of international human rights law, as his books of 1945 and 1950,[3] and his other work,[4] revealed. His 1945 study was published at a time when there were high hopes that there would soon be established an International Bill of Rights. It was a pioneering work as not only did

---

[1] Lauterpacht, *An International Bill of Rights of Man* (Columbia University Press, 1945) 9–10.
[2] Ibid, 14.   [3] Lauterpacht, *International Law and Human Rights* (Stevens and Sons, 1950).
[4] See Simpson, 'Hersch Lauterpacht and the Genesis of the Age of Human Rights' (2004) 120 *LQR* 49.

it address the substance of a proposed International Bill, but it also provided a detailed discussion of how it might be implemented and enforced at the international level. The dramatic quotations above were not intended to strike a pessimistic chord. Instead, the aim was to emphasize the extent of the task ahead for the international community. Lauterpacht was calling upon the international community, and leading states in particular, to face up to that task as the Second World War came to an end and plans for a 'new world order' started to take shape.

We will return to the successes and failures of the immediate post-war effort as regards international human rights law in Section 4, below. However, in order to obtain a better perspective on this, and the chapters that follow, we should trace the story of the protection of human rights, first, in domestic law and then in international law prior to 1945.

2 HUMAN RIGHTS ON THE DOMESTIC PLANE

Where should an analysis of the history of human rights begin?[5] One could go back several thousand years and find concepts related to human rights in ancient civilizations across the world, as with the Law Code of Hammurabi, created by the Babylonian king Hammurabi in the eighteenth century BC. The origins of human rights might also be traced back to various religious codes through the ages. By contrast, if the point of departure is the idea that human beings have natural rights, then the story commences at least as far back as the time of the Greek city states and the thinking of the Stoics.[6]

Finding a precise point of departure for 'a history of human rights' is an inherently controversial matter. It is probably quite unrealistic to credit any one culture, religion, or region of the world with the origins of human rights. Moreover, as a leading expert has put it, an attempt to do so would be 'politically charged'.[7] It inevitably risks privileging 'a particular world view' of human rights; it might be viewed as 'a way either to defend a specific status quo or value system against possible challenges'.[8] Two points must therefore be made at the outset. First, there are many different threads to the human rights idea as it exists today, and it is invidious to locate any one specific thread as *the* beginning. Second, the account that follows focuses especially on the origins of legal measures in the field of human rights. In that regard the first part of this chapter looks to the early developments in the Western world in particular, and to the extent that it might convey a Western bias, this is not the author's intention.[9]

From the perspective of legal measures championing the rights of the common person against the state, the starting point of the history of human rights is typically

---

[5] See Ishay, *The History of Human Rights: From Ancient Times to the Globalization Era* (University of California Press, 2004) ch 1; Ishay, *The Human Rights Reader* (Routledge, 2007) chs 1–4. For a useful 'timeline' on the history of human rights, see <http://www.udhr.org/history/timeline>.

[6] See n 3, ch 5.   [7] Ishay, n 5, xxii.   [8] Ibid.

[9] For much broader perspectives on the history of human rights, see n 5.

taken to be the Magna Carta of 1215. Yet this is somewhat erroneous. The Magna Carta resounds with statements that have since come to be celebrated: 'To none will we sell, to none deny or delay, right or justice'; and 'No freeman shall be taken, or imprisoned, or disseized, or outlawed, or exiled, or in any way harmed...save by the lawful judgment of his peers or by the law of the land.' But the rights to trial by jury and of habeas corpus for all were hardly established by the Magna Carta. It had little to do with the rights of the common man, and much to do with securing rights for powerful barons against an overbearing king of England. The enduring significance of the Magna Carta, and other similar documents of this age,[10] for the history of human rights lies in the fact that it has come to be seen as a starting point—the beginning of the limitation of absolute and arbitrary power of the sovereign. It therefore earns its place as the traditional point of departure in the story of how domestic law has addressed the enduring struggle of the individual against the tyranny and oppression of the state. This is a story that has lasted many centuries for some states and is still very much continuing in others.

We advance to the latter half of the seventeenth century for the next chapter in the overall story. The context was the English Civil War and the so-called 'Glorious Revolution', culminating in the Bill of Rights of 1689. Despite its name, that document was really a constitutional settlement that championed the sovereignty of Parliament. It set the seal on the absolute power of the Stuart kings after the myth of their 'divine power' had been debunked—in England at least, for it would last many more decades in France. So the bill of 1689 was no bill of rights in the sense that would be understood in modern democratic societies today.[11] Nonetheless it was the source of a limited number of defined rights, for example that 'cruel and unusual punishments [should not be] inflicted', which were applicable to all, at least in theory. Moreover, there were other important developments in this era such as the eradication of the practice of torture from the legal system of England in 1641 and the Habeas Corpus Act of 1679. The Bill of Rights of 1689 therefore saw the assertion of human liberty progress a stage further but, above all, its significance lay in its confirmation of a fundamental idea: that the absolute power of the state should be limited *for the sake of the individuals within it*. This idea had been prevalent in the contemporary writing of Thomas Hobbes and especially John Locke. And it deserves special emphasis since it is arguably the foundation stone upon which all progress in the field of human rights has been built.

2.1 THE ENLIGHTENMENT THINKERS

Hobbes' *Leviathan*,[12] published in 1651, soon after the beheading of Charles I, spoke of a world in which there was an imperative for absolute power; it was needed to keep society from the very type of disorder that had afflicted England in the 1640s. The

---

[10] eg the King's agreement with the Cortes of Leon (1188, Spain) and the Magnus Lagaboters Landslov (1275, Norway).

[11] For modern bills of rights, see Chapter 22, below.

[12] Many modern versions of the text are available, see eg Hobbes, *Leviathan* (OUP, 2009).

Leviathan world did not accept the idea of formal restraints on power. It envisaged few if any natural rights for the individual, for all were subservient to the ruler. A level of abuse on the part of the ruler vis-à-vis his subjects might almost be expected; it was the price to be paid for the greater collective gain for a society that was protected from the much greater evil of mass disorder. Having said this, the ruler was expected to exercise his authority responsibly, and in accordance with the laws of God and of nature, and in turn this placed theoretical restraints on his authority. Hobbes' *Leviathan* is therefore credited with introducing the concept of the 'social contract', that is, the idea that power to govern is to some extent derived from the consent of the governed.

However, it was Locke who carried this concept very much further, above all in his *Two Treatises of Government*,[13] published in 1690, shortly after the overthrowing of another English king in 1688 (James II) and the approval of the Bill of Rights by Parliament in 1689. Locke advocated the natural liberty and equality of human beings: '[m]an' was *born* with 'a title to perfect freedom, and an uncontrolled enjoyment of all the rights and privileges of the law of nature, equally with any other man, or number of men in the world'; he had '*by nature* a power... to preserve his property, that is, his life, liberty and estate, against the injuries and attempts of other men'.[14] Locke was therefore a strong advocate of natural rights, and in particular the right to property in the broad sense identified above, and, as he saw things, it was the state's duty to provide an environment in which such rights could flourish. His enduring contribution to the ideas that fuelled human rights thinking, however, lay in his theory of government, for it is in Locke that we see the origins of the idea of limited constitutional government and the fuller development of the idea of government by consent. Locke wrote that the 'end of government is the good of mankind', so rulers 'should be sometimes liable to be opposed, when they grow exorbitant in the use of their power, and employ it for the destruction, and not the preservation of the properties of their people'.[15] Within Locke's writing therefore were the seeds to the idea of modern democratic governance, although how much Locke expounded the democratic ideal through the idea of government by consent should not be exaggerated. He did not advocate universal suffrage and was, after all, writing in the seventeenth century when the right to vote remained a privilege of very few in England. But it is surely Locke we recall first when we read the following paragraph from the preamble to the Universal Declaration of Human Rights (UDHR) of almost three hundred years later: 'Whereas it is essential, if man is not to be compelled to have recourse, as a last resort, to rebellion against tyranny and oppression, that human rights should be protected by the rule of law'.

On the continent of Europe, the major historical contribution to ideas concerning the state and its relationship with the individual came in the eighteenth century. Authors such as Baron de Montesquieu (*The Spirit of Laws*, 1748), Jean-Jacques Rousseau (*The Social Contract*, 1762), Voltaire (*Philosophical Dictionary*, 1769), and Immanuel Kant (*On the Relationship of Theory to Practice in Political Right*, 1792)

---

[13] See eg Laslett (ed), *Locke: Two Treatises of Government* (CUP, 1988).
[14] Ibid, ch VII, para 87 (emphasis added).   [15] Ibid, ch XIX, para 229.

were leading figures in a movement which was later called 'the Enlightenment'. Montesquieu's contribution remains best known for his thoughts on the structures of government and his emphasis on the separation of powers. Rousseau advanced the theory of the 'social contract', but justice cannot be done in a few sentences here to the immense contribution made by him and others. It must suffice to say that the essence of all these philosophers' thinking was to place a new importance on the intrinsic value of man in society. There was thus further emphasis on the idea that everyone was born with certain natural rights which no authority could take away. This thinking was the intellectual force behind the French Declaration of the Rights of Man and Citizen (1789), but of course its impact was felt far beyond France. Indeed as one author has neatly put it:

Natural rights were the cutting edge of the ax of rationalization that toppled many of the inherited medieval traditions of eighteenth-century Europe. They were part of that general aspiration toward bringing peace and order to the world that lead Immanuel Kant to think that royal dynasties were the cause of war, and that a world of republics would bring a peaceful era to mankind.[16]

2.2 HUMAN RIGHTS TRANSFORMED INTO POSITIVE LAW

It was, however, in the 'new world' where the 'ax of rationalization' first achieved practical effect in a constitutional document. Locke's influence was unmistakable, and immortalized, in the US Declaration of Independence of 1776. That document listed grievances against George III and inspired the successful prosecution of the American War of Independence. Its opening words are now infamous:

We hold these truths to be self-evident, that all men are created equal, that they are endowed by their Creator with certain unalienable Rights; that among these are Life, Liberty and the pursuit of Happiness. That to secure these rights, governments are instituted among men, deriving their just powers from the consent of the governed; that whenever any form of government becomes destructive of these ends, it is the right of the people to alter or to abolish it, and to institute new government, laying its foundation on such principles and organizing its powers in such form, as to them shall seem most likely to effect their safety and happiness.

Even before Thomas Jefferson and others penned these words on 4 July 1776, the process of drafting the constitutions of the newly independent individual states in what would become the United States of America was well underway. In 1776, five would be drafted so as to enshrine the protection of human rights, and by 1783 all states would have done so in one form or another. Probably the most celebrated example was the Virginia Declaration of Rights of 12 June 1776, regarded by many as the first 'proper' bill of rights. Its first article proclaimed that 'all men are by nature equally free and independent, and have certain inherent rights, of which, when they enter

---

[16] Minogue, 'The History of the Idea of Human Rights' in Laqueur and Rubin (eds), *The Human Rights Reader* (Meridian, 1977) 11.

into a state of society, they cannot, by any compact, deprive or divest their posterity; namely, the enjoyment of life and liberty, with the means of acquiring and possessing property, and pursuing and obtaining happiness and safety'. The Virginia Declaration then set out the idea of government by consent ('all power is vested in, and consequently derived from, the people') and separation of powers ('the legislative and executive powers of the state should be separate and distinct from the judicative'), before listing a number of human rights including, for example, basic due process rights and freedom of expression ('the freedom of the press is one of the greatest bulwarks of liberty and can never be restrained but by despotic governments').

Events in France would help to ensure that the end of the eighteenth century was a defining time in the history of human rights. The years 1789–91 stand out above all. The French Revolution swept away any notions of absolute monarchical power, replacing it with the philosophy of the French Declaration of the Rights of Man and Citizen. With this Declaration on 26 August 1789, the French National Assembly pronounced that 'ignorance, forgetfulness, or contempt of the rights of man' were 'the sole causes of public misfortunes and of the corruption of governments'. It therefore:

resolved to set forth in a solemn declaration the natural, inalienable, and sacred rights of man, in order that such declaration, continually before all members of the social body, may be a perpetual reminder of their rights and duties; in order that the acts of the legislative power and those of the executive power may constantly be compared with the aim of every political institution and may accordingly be more respected; in order that the demands of the citizens, founded henceforth upon simple and incontestable principles, may always be directed towards the maintenance of the Constitution and welfare of all.

Article 16 French Declaration provided a classic formulation of the link between institutional limitations on state power and protecting human rights: 'Any society', it proclaimed, 'in which no provision is made for guaranteeing rights or for the separation of powers, has no Constitution.'[17]

Today, a study of the French Declaration would form a good starting point for any course on human rights and, no doubt, stimulate much debate. The Declaration defined 'liberty' as 'the power to do whatever is not injurious to others'. It followed that 'the enjoyment of the natural rights of every man has for its limits only those that assure other members of society the enjoyment of those same rights'. According to the Declaration 'such limits may be determined only by law'. A flavour of what followed may be gleaned from paragraphs in the Declaration setting out due process rights such as the presumption of innocence and to the effect that free speech was 'one of the most precious of the rights of man', so 'every citizen may speak, write, and print freely', 'subject to responsibility for the abuse of such liberty in cases determined by law'. More generally the Declaration profoundly announced that: 'The law has the right to forbid only actions which are injurious to society. Whatever is not forbidden by law may not be prevented, and no one may be constrained to do what it does not prescribe.'

---

[17] See also the *French Declaration of the Right of Man and Citizen* of 1793, a redraft of the 1789 text with an added emphasis on the principle of equality.

Against this background, the US Constitution of 1789 might, at first sight, have been regarded as a disappointment. There was no grand statement about the theory of government along the lines of the Declaration of Independence. Moreover, it provided for the protection of just a few rights; for example, the right to trial by jury (Article III, Section 2) and a right of habeas corpus, not to be suspended unless 'in cases of rebellion or invasion the public safety may require it' (Article I, Section 9). However, in 1791 the first ten amendments to the Constitution came into force having been ratified by three-quarters of the states. The (US) Bill of Rights, as it became known, began in now celebrated tones: 'Congress shall make no law respecting an establishment of religion, or prohibiting the free exercise thereof; or abridging the freedom of speech, or of the press; or the right of the people peaceably to assemble and to petition the government for a redress of grievances.' Among other things, the bill included the famous right to bear arms (Amendment II), protection from unreasonable search and seizure (Amendment IV), various protections relating to due process and fair trial (Amendments V and VI), and a prohibition on 'cruel and unusual punishments' (Amendment VIII). It should be added, however, that at this stage such rights were to be protected only at the federal level. It was in the individual constitutions of the states, with their own bills of rights, that the expression of the rights of man was really seen in the USA in the late eighteenth century.

These comments on the French and US experiences would not be complete without paying tribute to the work of Thomas Paine. Paine's 1776 work *Common Sense* set out the case for US democracy in the lead up to 4 July 1776. In 1791–2 he published *The Rights of Man*, which was in part a response to Edmund Burke's attack on the French Revolution. But he also subjected England's constitutional arrangements to severe criticism: 'government without constitution, is power without a right'. *The Rights of Man*, perhaps the first book ever to use the phrase 'human rights',[18] is said to have sold over 250,000 copies, making it a huge bestseller in today's terms. Paine did not invent the human rights thinking that was distilled into the landmark documents referred to above. But as Louis Henkin has observed, his writing 'did much to spread and root' the idea of human rights: 'he provided us a theology and a terminology, guiding principles as well as blueprints'.[19] Paine remains revered in the USA, as was evidenced when he was quoted by President Obama in his inauguration speech in 2009. But he remains little known in his native England where, in his lifetime, he was considered as a dangerous revolutionary and convicted of seditious libel.[20]

2.3 NINETEENTH-CENTURY CHALLENGES TO NATURAL RIGHTS

The French Declaration and the US Bill of Rights were landmarks in the history of human rights for they transformed the philosophy espoused by the likes of Locke and

---

[18] See Lauren, *The Evolution of International Human Rights: Visions Seen* (University of Pennsylvania Press, 1998) 20.
[19] Henkin, *The Rights of Man Today* (Stevens and Sons, 1978) 135.   [20] Lauren, n 18, 21.

Rousseau, and the thinking behind natural rights, into positive law. Nonetheless, during the nineteenth century the idea of natural rights came under attack from a new generation of philosophers.

The critics were led by Jeremy Bentham who famously criticized the idea of natural, God-given rights obtained by virtue of birth as 'nonsense upon stilts'.[21] His point was that natural rights counted for nothing on their own. To mean something, they required the protection of the law; so the real issue for Bentham, expounding a very British 'rights and remedy' approach to things, was what the law actually protected. As he famously put it: 'from real law come real rights; but from imaginary laws, from laws of nature, fancied and invented by poets, rhetoricians, and dealers in moral and intellectual poisons, come imaginary rights'.[22] For Bentham natural rights were dangerous since they fuelled revolutions such as those in France and so ultimately caused great social damage, hence the title of his famous work *The Anarchical Fallacies* (1843). Criticism of this type had already been made by another Englishman at the very time of the French Revolution. In his *Reflections on the Revolution of France*, Burke attacked the French Declaration as a 'monstrous fiction'. It inspired 'false ideas and vain expectations into men destined to travel in the obscure walk of laborious life' and had 'serve[d] to exaggerate and embitter that real inequality, which it can never remove'.[23]

The nineteenth century also saw an altogether different type of opposition to natural rights in the writing of Karl Marx. His 1844 work *On the Jewish Question* asked what use the French Declaration would be for Jews such as himself. As he saw it, it was found completely wanting for in reality the rights of man were the privileged rights of the bourgeoisie. According to Marx, rights were for egotistical men; they did not truly free the individual at all.[24]

As shown in Chapter 3, the longer term legacy of Bentham's and Marx's attacks on natural rights and the perspective they offer to contemporary thinking on human rights is still keenly debated today.

2.4 DOMESTIC PROTECTION OF HUMAN RIGHTS TODAY

We have seen, then, that for domestic law the human rights story really began in the seventeenth and eighteenth centuries. History will record the tribute to be paid to the visionaries of that age, such as Locke and Rousseau, many of whom were treated as dissidents at the time. The Bill of Rights of 1689, and in particular the American Declaration of Independence (1776), the French Declaration of the Rights of Man and Citizen (1789), and the US Bill of Rights (1791) were milestones in constitutional history, curtailing the sovereign power of the state in various ways, including by reference to the basic rights of the individual. This constitutional model certainly caught on as was evident by the constitutional arrangements secured in the Netherlands in

---

[21] See Chapter 3, below.
[22] Waldron (ed), *Nonsense upon Stilts: Bentham, Burke and Marx on the Rights of Man* (Routledge, 1987) 69.
[23] Burke, *Reflections on the Revolution in France* (Rivington, 1868) 46.   [24] See Chapter 3, below.

1798, Sweden in 1809, Spain in 1812, Norway in 1814, Belgium in 1831, Liberia in 1847, Sardinia in 1848, Denmark in 1849, and Prussia in 1850. In fact, it has been suggested that over 80 per cent of national constitutions adopted between 1778 and 1948 provided a human rights guarantee in one form or another, and that between 1949 and 1975 the figure was 93 per cent.[25] That this upward trend continued was evident in the 1990s with the new constitutions of those states which were formerly part of the Soviet Union.

As we look back on the achievements secured in the eighteenth century via the French and US settlements, one should be careful to keep them in perspective. They were certainly landmarks, but it would be wrong to exaggerate the practical effects that they had at the time. Indeed one does not have to look far in French and US history to see that in practical terms the idea of human rights had made only relatively limited headway at this stage—at least, that is, compared to how we would view things today. The inferior position of women both in society generally and in law stirred women's rights campaigners such as Mary Wollstonecraft (*Vindication of the Rights of Women*, 1792). Moreover, at this stage the idea of judicial protection of human rights was virtually non-existent. The French Declaration had been incorporated as the first part of the formal French Constitution in 1791, but it was not enforceable by the courts at that time. As Lauren observed, the French Declaration, 'reflected far more vision than reality'. It 'emerged not out of long tradition or wide-spread experience or inclusive election, but rather out of... revolution and had to be nurtured in the face of overwhelming opposition'.[26]

The USA was quite exceptional in that judicial protection of constitutional safeguards came in 1803 with the US Supreme Court's watershed decision in *Marbury v Madison*, holding that it had an inherent power of judicial review by which it could even declare acts of Congress unconstitutional.[27] Nonetheless, this was of limited use for individuals in human rights terms, for at this stage the Bill of Rights was an instrument that applied overwhelmingly at the federal, not the individual state, level. Of course, the individual state constitutions guaranteed rights, as noted above, but slavery was flourishing in many such states in the late eighteenth century and would continue to do so for decades into the nineteenth century. In fact, when the controversy about slavery was reaching its peak, the contribution made by the US Supreme Court served to perpetuate the practice. In *Dred Scott v Sandford* in 1857, it ruled that the Bill of Rights protected the right of slaveholders to their property, which included slaves and that, in effect, Congress had acted illegally by outlawing slavery in Northern states.[28] Neither slaves, 'nor their descendants, were embraced... [by] the Constitution',[29] the Court held. That is, they had no protection under the Bill of Rights. It would take a civil war and further amendments to the Constitution to secure the abolition of slavery in the 1860s. And it would take the better part of the next century

---

[25] Van Maarseveen and van der Tang, *Written Constitutions: A Computerized Comparative Study* (Oceana, 1978) 191–5.

[26] n 18, 32.   [27] 1 Cranch 137 (1803).   [28] 60 US 353 (1857).   [29] Ibid, Taney, J.

for the Supreme Court to finally start to use the Bill of Rights to attack grossly unfair and discriminatory practices suffered by the black population of certain states. The breakthrough case was *Brown v Board of Education*[30] of 1954 bringing an end to the 'separate but equal' doctrine previously upheld by the Court in *Plessy v Ferguson*.[31]

The point of this digression is not to single out the practice of the USA in any way. If this chapter were to attempt to provide even the broadest of overviews of the failures of other states to protect human rights over the same timeframe, it would no doubt run into dozens of pages. What has been said in the previous paragraph, however, provides a very useful perspective on the next section, which looks at the international protection of human rights.

It helps us to understand how very recent the protection of human rights is by domestic courts and by reference to bills of rights in the overall story of the history of human rights. In the UK, for example, there existed a long tradition of Parliament and the courts protecting the rights of individuals by various statutes and under the common law. But only in 2000, with the entry into force of the Human Rights Act 1998, did the UK obtain something akin to a modern bill of rights encompassing judicial protection of a select number of human rights against the acts of public authorities, albeit not against parliamentary acts.[32] In France, the 1958 Constitution refers in its preamble to the French people's commitment to the Declaration of 1789, but only a limited challenge to the authority of the legislature is possible via the *Conseil Constitutionnel*. Finally, the USA is without doubt the most celebrated exponent of the judicial protection of human rights. Yet only since around 1925 has the Supreme Court begun to use the Bill of Rights more widely to protect the rights of individuals against encroachments by the individual states themselves. Indeed, the story of human rights protection by the Supreme Court is overwhelmingly a post-Second World War phenomenon.[33]

Table 1.1 Human rights on the domestic plane: key dates

1215	Magna Carta
1689	English Bill of Rights
1776	US Declaration of Independence
	Virginia Declaration of Rights
1789	French Declaration of the Rights of Man and Citizen
	US Constitution
1791	US Bill of Rights

[30] 347 US 483 (1954).   [31] 163 US 537 (1896).   [32] See Human Rights Act 1998, ss 3 and 4.
[33] In 1935–6 only two of the 160 signed written opinions of the Supreme Court covered 'basic human freedoms', but by 1979–80 the ratio had increased to 80 out of 149. See Abraham and Perry, *Freedom and the Court* (OUP, 1998) 5.

The perspective we might take with us as we turn to the story of the *international* protection of human rights is therefore this: how incredibly grand the idea of an International Bill of Rights must have been in the 1940s when it was first proposed.

3 HUMAN RIGHTS ON THE INTERNATIONAL PLANE BEFORE THE SECOND WORLD WAR

Even if within domestic law there was a greater recognition of individual human rights by the start of the twentieth century, this was certainly not the case for international law. Prior to the 1940s there was no real conception in international law of the idea that one state had a right to interfere in the sovereign affairs of another state as regards how it treated its own citizens. International law was virtually a blank canvas as far as the protection of human rights was concerned. We say this from the perspective of a basic definition of human rights as the rights owing to human beings by nature of their humanity. Historically, international law could touch on or address the plight of human beings only in very limited ways.

For example, the inkling of the idea of certain minimal rights for certain human beings was present in customary international law in the guise of the doctrine of 'diplomatic protection', or the treatment of aliens. This doctrine has deep historical roots. It basically requires a state to treat foreigners in accordance with an 'international minimum standard' of protection,[34] at least as regards life, liberty, property, and protection from manifest denial of justice, regardless of how the state treats its own nationals. The point to note, then, is that the protection concerned is not afforded to the individuals as human beings, but because they are nationals of a foreign state. Moreover, it falls to that foreign state, not the individual, to pursue the enforcement of any claims. In the absence of such support, historically the foreigners concerned had no one to speak for them. As such they were placed in the same position as the nationals of the host state, for the traditional, pre-war position of customary international law was that it simply had nothing to say about the way that a state could treat its own nationals.

3.1 INTERNATIONAL HUMANITARIAN LAW AND THE ABOLITION OF THE SLAVE TRADE

Of course, states could enter into legal relations with each other motivated by a desire to relieve human suffering in certain ways. In this regard an apparently compassionate dimension to international law had been evident in the nineteenth century, first with the movement towards the abolition of the slave trade and, second, with the first steps that were taken in the field of international humanitarian law.

---

[34] See Shaw, *International Law* (CUP, 2008) 824–5.

The second of these is addressed in Chapter 23 and all that need be said here is that the nineteenth century saw increasing international activity which expressed a concern with the plight of the individual subjected to the ravages of war—prisoners of war and soldiers above all. The founding father of this movement was Henry Dunant, who was so shocked by scenes of the wounded and vanquished he witnessed at the Battle of Solferino (1859) that he later helped to establish the International Committee of the Red Cross. The Geneva Conventions of the mid-nineteenth century soon followed, while the Hague Conventions were opened for signature at the start of the twentieth century. Perhaps the most significant achievements of this sector of international law from the perspective of human rights, however, were secured with the Geneva Conventions of 1949 and the Additional Protocols thereto.

The nineteenth century also saw remarkable progress in the abolition of the slave trade. Slavery became illegal in England in 1771 after *Somersett's case*.[35] The UK and the USA subsequently passed legislation at the start of the nineteenth century to outlaw the trade of slaves within their own jurisdictions, which included the British colonies. Yet international action was required to abolish the trade altogether, and here progress was slow. Despite the campaigning efforts of figures such as William Wilberforce, the best that could be achieved by the major European states at the Congress of Vienna (1815) was a mere declaration expressing a commitment to the abolition of the slave trade. There then followed more than half a century in which the British made great diplomatic efforts to secure dozens of bilateral treaties with trading nations principally in the European and Latin American regions, and other agreements with native chiefs from the African coast. In each instance there was an agreement to abolish the slave trade but also, where relevant, various measures of enforcement were provided for. Typically, the treaties provided for the inspection of ships if there was a suspicion that a merchant vessel was engaging in illicit activity. The abolition of the slave trade was therefore one of the earliest, if not the first, human rights related British foreign policy initiatives. This period also witnessed the establishment of Anti-Slavery International, the oldest human rights NGO in the world; its origins go back to 1839.[36]

The list of states committed to abolishing the trade slowly grew, but a sufficient global consensus on abolition of the slave trade did not emerge until the last decades of the nineteenth century. Only in 1885 did the Conference on Central Africa, held in Berlin, see in its General Act a commitment by states 'to help in suppressing slavery, and especially the slave trade' and their recognition that 'trading in slaves is forbidden in conformity with the principles of international law as recognised by the Signatory Powers'. Five years later, negotiations in Brussels saw the conclusion of the 1890 General Act, which included an Anti-Slavery Act ratified by 18 states stipulating specific measures for countering slavery and the slave trade. By this stage the great majority of states had made slavery illegal in their own jurisdictions. The experience of the USA, with President Lincoln's Emancipation Proclamation of 1863, is known

---

[35] 20 State Trials 1.   [36] For further details see <http://www.antislavery.org>.

best. Yet even after the US Civil War, Cuba and Brazil maintained domestic slavery into the 1880s.

In the twentieth century, the international abolition of the slave trade and slavery was taken up by the League of Nations, the key international organization established after the First World War with the principal objective of maintaining peace and stability in the world. There followed the International Convention on the Abolition of Slavery and the Slave Trade of 1926. The declared aim of this treaty was 'the complete suppression of slavery in all its forms and of the slave trade by land and sea'. There have been further international agreements since.

The international effort toward the abolition of the slave trade and slavery provides some interesting general lessons for students of international human rights law. The abolition of the trade evidenced why international law, in the form of bilateral treaties, was needed to improve the protection of individuals when the activities of more than one state were involved. But it also demonstrated that general international agreements may only follow a consensus being reached across a sufficient number of states, and that this may take a considerable time to achieve. The abolition of slavery itself inevitably required action on the part of the individual states—in some cases prompted, no doubt, by the growing body of international opinion encouraging them to do so. State practice in this field became so clearly defined that the prohibition of slavery became part of customary international law. Hence an absolute prohibition on 'slavery and servitude' passed without controversy into the main post-Second World War human rights documents, with images of Nazi concentration camps still fresh in the mind.[37] Finally, however, it would be wrong to assume that such documents have in themselves magically abolished slavery and servitude (and forced labour) in all its forms.[38] The creation of international standards for the protection of human rights may be one thing; their actual implementation and enforcement is another.

3.2 THE PROTECTION OF MINORITIES AND THE LEAGUE OF NATIONS

Resuming our analysis of the position of international law with respect to human rights before 1945, the protection of minorities should now be discussed. Here we need to recall the pre-Second World War stance of international law whereby, in effect, states had free rein to abuse their own citizens behind their own borders. Indeed, stories of oppression directed toward national and religious minorities in particular fill many pages of our history books.

The first, rather sporadic, efforts to provide a level of protection for religious minorities may be traced back to the end of the Thirty Years War with the Treaty of

[37] See UDHR, Art 4. See also International Covenant on Civil and Political Rights, Art 8; European Convention on Human Rights, Art 4; American Convention on Human Rights, Art 6; African Charter on Human and Peoples' Rights, Art 5.

[38] Slavery persists, for example, in the form of human trafficking. For contemporary forms of forced labour, see eg *Siliadin v France* (2006) 43 EHRR 16.

Westphalia (1648) and, subsequently, those of Utrecht (1713) and Berlin (1878).[39] But
it was not until the early twentieth century that international law saw a much more
organized, institutionalized approach to the minorities issue. It was prompted by the
end of the First World War and in particular the significant redrawing of the political map of parts of Europe. This involved, for example, the restoration of Poland and
for some states, Germany in particular, a rather radical redrawing of their boundaries. Given how mixed the population was in parts of Europe, no matter how those
boundaries were (re)shaped, the result was that a significant number of minorities
found themselves displaced. As Tomuschat has described it, 'ethnic Hungarians found
themselves all of a sudden in Romania or Czechoslovakia, ethnic Germans became
Polish citizens, and, on the other hand, ethnic Poles continued to live in Germany'.[40]

President Wilson is reported to have said at the Paris Peace Conference of 1919, '[n]
othing...is more likely to disturb the peace of the world, than the treatment which
might in certain circumstances be meted out to the minorities'.[41] It being recognized
then that Europe's peaceful future could be jeopardized by the abuse of minorities by
the dominant majority, arrangements were made to try to safeguard against this. As
part of the various peace settlements ending the First World War, nine states[42] were
required to enter into specific treaty obligations for the protection of minorities and,
between 1921 and 1923, a further five[43] were required to settle upon similar arrangements as a condition of their membership of the League of Nations. The arrangements
were complex and here we will identify only three main aspects.[44]

First, the individual peace treaties required that as part of their constitutional
arrangements respective states should provide basic guarantees of protection as to
life, liberty, and equality before the law for all inhabitants within their borders. There
were also more specific guarantees which were particularly relevant for minorities
including, for example, provisions guaranteeing the enjoyment of freedom of religion,
use and recognition of minority languages, and various freedoms in the field of education. Second, when the League of Nations was set up, the Council of the League of
Nations was mandated to make arrangements for the supervision of the aforementioned obligations at the international level. The states which were subjected to the
treaty arrangements acknowledged that the guarantees constituted 'obligations of
international concern' for the League of Nations, albeit only insofar as they affected

[39] See Ezejiofor, *Protection of Human Rights under the Law* (Butterworths, 1964) 35–8.
[40] Tomuschat, *Human Rights: Between Idealism and Realism* (OUP, 2008) 18.
[41] Ezejiofor, n 39, 38.
[42] The treaties were concluded between 1919 and 1923. Czechoslovakia, Greece, Poland, Romania, and
Yugoslavia entered into specific minority treaty arrangements with the Principal and Allied Powers. For
Austria, Bulgaria, Hungary, and Turkey special chapters were inserted into the General Peace Treaties.
Additionally special chapters were inserted into the German Polish Convention concerning Upper Silesia,
and for the Memel Territory.
[43] Declarations undertaking to protect the rights of minorities were made by Albania, Estonia, Finland,
Latvia, and Lithuania.
[44] The classic account is De Azcarate, *League of Nations and National Minorities* (trans Broke) (Carnegie,
1945). See also Simpson, *Human Rights and the End of Empire* (OUP, 2001) 121–45.

persons belonging to racial, religious, or linguistic minorities, and therefore not for individuals forming part of the majority population. Third, oversight and possible measures of implementation with respect to the aforementioned obligations were envisaged. Arrangements were put in place to allow members of the minorities to directly petition the Council of the League about actual or potential infractions of the obligations.[45] If a petition was not settled, then the Permanent Court of International Justice was given competence to adjudicate upon the dispute. In fact, this occurred on only one occasion in a dispute concerning Germany and Poland regarding minority schools in Upper Silesia.[46] However, the Court could also deliver advisory opinions upon a request from the Council, and there were a small number of these, the most well known of which concerned the treatment of Greek minorities in Albania.[47]

Details of the successes and failures of these minority treaties can be found elsewhere.[48] Our concern here is to reflect on their significance from an historical perspective. So what should we say about these treaties today?

An extreme view might be that the treaties were not really about human rights at all, given that they applied only to certain geographical areas and that the petitions system developed by the League of Nations depended on status (belonging to a national minority). A sceptic would also point out that the motive for the creation of the treaties was not so much the protection of the minorities for humane reasons, but for the broader aim of regional stability.

A less cynical perspective would point to the significant advances made by the treaties. For the first time, international law imposed on the sovereign states concerned certain obligations to treat their inhabitants in certain ways—a stark contrast to the 'blank canvas' position noted above. Equally radical for its time was the idea of institutionalized oversight of such obligations, especially the notion that individuals could petition international organs, potentially challenging the actions of their own national authorities. In this way the treaties started to challenge the orthodox view that individuals simply could not be the subjects of international law. Such notions had underpinned Oppenheim's confident dismissal, in 1905, of the contention that 'the law of nations' guaranteed individuals 'at home and abroad the so-called rights of mankind' (alleged to be 'the right of existence, the right to protection of honour, life, health, liberty and property, the right of practicing [sic] any religion one likes, the right of emigration, and the like'). Such rights, it had been argued, 'cannot enjoy such guarantee, *since the Law of Nations is a law between States, and since individuals cannot be subjects of this Law*'.[49]

---

[45] Such arrangements were the product of procedures settled upon by the League itself. Only the treaty concerning Upper Silesia actually conferred a right of petition, although Finland was also obliged to forward petitions in relation to the Aaland Islands.

[46] *Rights of Minorities in Upper Silesia*, PCIJ Rep Series A No 15 (1928).

[47] *Minority Schools in Albania case*, PCIJ Rep Series A/B No 64 (1935).

[48] See n 44 and MacCartney, 'League of Nations' Protection of Minority Rights' in Luard (ed), *The International Protection of Human Rights* (Thames and Hudson, 1967) 22, 34–7.

[49] Oppenheim, *Treatise on International Law, Vol I, Peace* (1905) 346 (emphasis added).

Such a view had prevailed as far as most states were concerned when the Covenant of the League of Nations was concluded in 1919. As its preamble recited, the main aim of that organization was 'to promote international co-operation and to achieve international peace and security'. Talk that all states should protect minorities along the lines of the minority treaties was quickly dismissed; therefore no guarantees for the protection of individuals generally were imposed on states after the First World War. Quite simply, outside the discrete context of the minority treaties, the notion that international bodies could or should have an influence on how the state treated its own nationals was not developed at the general level at this stage. Hence, governments and the League of Nations made little attempt to intervene in what would today be seen as the human rights abuses that occurred in countries such as Germany, the Soviet Union, and Italy in the lead up to the Second World War. As Luard once put it, this was not because people did not care, rather:

The assumptions of national sovereignty were almost everywhere still accepted. Regulations restricting freedom of the press, of speech and assembly, imprisonment for political offences, persecution on racial grounds, all these things were deplored and denounced. But it was widely accepted that they were ultimately the sole responsibility of the legal government of the territory in question: and not therefore matters over which foreign individuals or governments could legitimately take action.[50]

4 HUMAN RIGHTS ON THE INTERNATIONAL PLANE AFTER THE SECOND WORLD WAR

And here, over an acre of ground, lay dead and dying people. You could not see which was which, except perhaps by a convulsive movement, or the last quiver of a sigh from a living skeleton, too weak to move. The living lay with their heads against the corpses, and around them moved the awful ghostly procession of emaciated, aimless people, with nothing to do, and no hope of life, unable to move out of your way, unable to look at the terrible sights around them... Babies had been born here, tiny wizened things that could not live. A mother, driven mad, screamed at a British sentry to give her milk for her child, and thrust the tiny mite into his arms and ran off, crying terribly. He opened the bundle, and found the baby had been dead for days. This day at Belsen was the most horrible of my life.[51]

These were the words of Richard Dimbleby reporting for the BBC at the time of the liberation of the Nazi concentration camp in Belsen. Such human rights atrocities, and countless others committed during the Second World War, were a galvanizing force

---

[50] Luard, 'The Origins of International Concern over Human Rights' in Luard, n 48, 21. The League of Nations did take some notable steps in the fields of anti-slavery law, refugee law, and trafficking in drugs.

[51] Richard Dimbleby, BBC News (13 May 1945), available at: <http://news.bbc.co.uk/1/hi/in_depth/4445811.stm>.

that would help to ensure a new approach for international law after 1945 as regards the rights of the individual. They would prompt the first steps towards a modern international law of human rights.

The first proposals for an international code of human rights can be traced at least as far back as 1929, when in New York the Institute of International Law adopted 'An International Declaration of the Rights of Man'. Soon after the outbreak of war, the British author HG Wells campaigned for a Declaration of Rights; his book *HG Wells on the Rights of Man* sold well in the UK and 'in an act of utter optimism'[52] the war ministry had German translations dropped on the advancing German forces on the continent. Also dropped were leaflets from the White Rose Movement—a body made up of a small group of students and some academics at the University of Munich. In 1942–3 they courageously produced and distributed a series of leaflets in defiance of the Nazi regime, calling for democracy in Germany and for the protection of certain fundamental rights in a new Europe. Six of the student authors and one academic were captured by the Gestapo in 1943; they were summarily tried and executed.[53]

Back in January 1941, in his message to Congress, US President Roosevelt spoke of a world founded on 'four essential human freedoms' ('freedom of speech and expression', 'freedom of every person to worship God in his own way', 'freedom from want', and 'freedom from fear'). Later that year, on 14 August, Roosevelt and the British Prime Minister Winston Churchill proclaimed the Atlantic Declaration; they hoped to see a world where 'the men *in all lands* may live out their lives in freedom of fear and want'.[54] This was followed in 1942 by the Declaration of the United Nations. Not to be confused with the UN Charter of some three years later, the Declaration of 1942 was signed by 47 alliance states all prepared to subscribe to the principle that 'complete victory over their enemies [was] essential to defend life, liberty, independence and religious freedom, and to preserve human rights and justice in their own lands as well as in other lands'. 'Human rights' and democracy therefore became one of the moral bases upon which the Second World War was fought; Churchill even spoke of a time when the world's struggle ended with 'the enthronement of human rights'.[55] Passages such as these were quoted by Lauterpacht in his 1945 book, referred to above, as he looked forward to the post-war world.

So what happened when the conflict finally ended? To what extent were these lofty ambitions realized in the war-shattered world?

4.1 CRIMES AGAINST HUMANITY

A very important step was taken in 1945 when the victorious powers decided that the major war criminals of the German Third Reich should be brought to justice. The Four-Power Agreement of 8 August 1945 provided for the establishment of the

---

[52] Robertson, *Crimes Against Humanity* (Penguin, 2006) 28.

[53] See Dumbach and Newborn, *Sophie Scholl and the White Rose* (Oneworld, 2006).

[54] 35 AJIL (1941), Supplement, 191, principle six (emphasis added).

[55] *The Times* (30 October 1942), quoted by Lauterpacht, n 1, 6.

International Military Tribunal for the Prosecution and Punishment of Major War Criminals of the European Axis (Nuremberg Tribunal). The crimes in question were primarily those of planning and waging a war of aggression and the committal of war crimes, but they also included 'crimes against humanity'. The Nuremberg Tribunal eventually interpreted these crimes in a rather restrictive way. Nonetheless, the concept of such crimes was very significant for international human rights law, for it realized the possibility of international accountability and punishment for appalling crimes committed against individuals. More detailed discussion of the Nuremberg Tribunal can be found in Chapter 24.

4.2 THE UN CHARTER

The main focus of the immediate post-war story for international human rights law concerned the attempts made to create legal instruments protecting human rights. Of course, this meant securing agreement on what that concept actually covered. The framing of the Charter of the UN in San Francisco in 1945 was the obvious starting point in this endeavour. Its preamble stated that the peoples of the United Nations were:

determined to save succeeding generations from the scourge of war, which twice in our life-time has brought untold sorrow to mankind, and to reaffirm faith in fundamental human rights, in the dignity and worth of the human person, in the equal rights of men and women and of nations large and small . . .

With the framing of the UN Charter, therefore, human rights had finally become a subject of official concern for the international community. Nonetheless, Article 2(7) UN Charter, the 'domestic jurisdiction' clause,[56] cast something of a shadow over this, while the six references to 'human rights' in the main body of the Charter itself did not appear to commit member states to very much.[57] At most, members of the UN would be required to 'promote' human rights in accordance with Article 55(c) read with Article 56. There had been proposals to go further than this; Chile and Cuba, for example, had been prepared to accept provisions in the Charter to guarantee *specified* rights, and there had been a Panamanian proposal to include a bill of rights in the Charter. But this was all far too ambitious for the majority of states which thwarted such proposals given the radical implications they had for state sovereignty. This was an inauspicious beginning. However, there remained hope that a more faithful consummation of the place of human rights in the new world order would follow. After all, President Truman's address to the San Francisco conference, which had concluded the Charter, had spoken of an International Bill of Rights 'acceptable to all the nations

---

[56] Art 2(7) reads (in part): 'Nothing contained in the present Charter shall authorize the United Nations to intervene in matters that are essentially within the domestic jurisdiction of any state . . .'.
[57] See Arts 1, 13, 55, 56, 62(2), 68, and 76. See also the preamble to the Charter.

involved' to follow soon, one which would be 'as much part of international life as our own Bill of Rights is a part of our Constitution'.[58]

4.3 THE UNIVERSAL DECLARATION OF HUMAN RIGHTS

In 1946 the UN Commission on Human Rights was instituted and given the task of working on an International Bill of Rights. The task, to create a human rights instrument applicable to all states and peoples across the globe, threw up a series of difficult philosophical and political questions.[59]

Even before the Commission began its work, the politics of international human rights protection had become apparent, but by 1947 'human rights' was rapidly becoming an ideological weapon in the war of words between East and West.[60] So the idea of an International Bill of Rights was an attractive one in principle, but there were major difficulties when it came to putting in place concrete measures, especially international legal obligations.

The Commission quickly decided that the International Bill should have three parts: a declaration, a convention containing legal obligations, and 'measures of implementation', that is, a system of supervision and control. A drafting committee of eight members (from Australia, Chile, China, France, Lebanon, the UK, the USA, and the Soviet Union) was appointed to formulate the declaration. Its chair was Eleanor Roosevelt. The UDHR was subsequently formulated from an initial outline produced by John Humphrey, as well as a British draft.[61] Following many sessions of the drafting committee and approval by the plenary Commission, on 10 December 1948, the UDHR was proclaimed by 48 states in the UN General Assembly. Indeed, the years 1948–9 proved to be remarkable ones for human rights standard-setting. The Convention on the Prevention and Punishment of the Crime of Genocide[62] was opened for signature on 11 December 1948 and the four Geneva Conventions in 1949.

The UDHR had been accepted by the General Assembly without any dissenting votes, although there had been eight abstentions from the six communist states which were then members of the UN (Byelorussian SSR, Czechoslovakia, Poland, Ukrainian SSR, USSR, and Yugoslavia), plus Saudi Arabia and South Africa. The 48 states had nevertheless backed the UDHR as a 'common standard of achievement for all peoples and all nations'. Eleanor Roosevelt famously told the General Assembly that the Declaration 'might well become the *Magna Carta* of all mankind'. Yet as she herself was quick to acknowledge, in her capacity as a US representative, the basic character of the UDHR had to be kept in mind. It was not, she stressed, a treaty; it did not 'purport to be a statement of law or of legal obligations'. Similarly, most of the delegates at

[58] UN Information Organisation, Documents of the UN Conference on International Organisation (1945), Vol I, 717, cited by Sohn, *The United Nations and Human Rights* (Oceana Publications, 1968) 55.

[59] Lauren, n 18, 219.   [60] Ibid, 228.

[61] See Humphrey, *Human Rights and the United Nations: A Great Adventure* (Transnational Publishers, 1984) 42–3.

[62] See Chapter 24, below.

the General Assembly were ready to applaud the UDHR, but quick to deny that it had legal force. In fact the emphatic and repeated denials that the UDHR had legal force were probably part of the efforts that were necessary for its acceptance by the 48 states in the first place.[63]

Writing less than two years after the UDHR had been proclaimed, Lauterpacht dismissed it as being of 'controversial moral authority'.[64] He was not alone in his criticism of the Declaration. Events, it seemed, had confirmed that states had failed to rise to the challenge foreseen by Lauterpacht in his 1945 book. From the perspective of 1950, Lauterpacht's disappointment can be appreciated. No International Bill of Rights was secured in the 1940s. Moreover, in 1950 the prospects for the remainder of the bill looked bleak. It took until 1954 for the UN Commission to complete the drafts of what would become the International Covenant on Civil and Political Rights (ICCPR) and the International Covenant on Economic, Social and Cultural Rights (ICESCR). However, they would not be opened for signature until 1966 and it would take until 1976 before they entered into force for the 35 states that were prepared to ratify them. The drafting history of the two Covenants reveals the many compromises and amendments that were necessary to secure their acceptability to the members of the UN, especially as the size of that organization grew significantly in the post-colonial era. A similar point may be made about the relatively weak enforcement regimes that were eventually agreed for both treaties. They revealed how unrealistic it had been in the mid-1940s to assume that classic features of state sovereignty could be pushed aside easily when it came to establishing an effective International Bill of Rights.

Table 1.2 Human rights on the international plane: key dates

1941	Roosevelt's Four Freedoms speech
1942	Declaration of the United Nations
1945	UN Charter
1948	Universal Declaration of Human Rights
	Convention on the Prevention and Punishment of the Crime of Genocide
1949	Four Geneva Conventions
1966	ICCPR and ICESCR opened for signature
1976	ICCPR and ICESCR enter into force

5 CONCLUSION

More than 60 years on from when Eleanor Roosevelt unveiled the UDHR, it seems that her description of it as a possible Magna Carta for mankind was most apt. After all, it was noted above that the document of 1215 was but the start of the story of the

---

[63] Moskowitz, *Human Rights and World Order* (Stevens and Sons, 1959) 79.
[64] Lauterpacht, n 3, 279. He was highly critical of the leading nations for their limited achievements. See ibid, 397–408.

domestic protection of human rights. Can the same comment not be made for the UDHR today with respect to the international protection of human rights?

As the subsequent chapters in this book will reveal, the rights protected by the UDHR, and the two Covenants more generally, which today have been ratified by a large majority of states, have become part of a body of international law the scope, breadth, and general significance of which would have been impossible to predict in the late 1940s. And if these are the achievements of only the last 60 years, then what further progress can we expect in this century and beyond?

Of course, none of this is to suggest that things are anywhere near perfect today. We know that serious human rights violations occur across the globe every day. We may nevertheless compare the situation now with that existing before 1945. Today, there are international legal obligations that restrain how a sovereign state may treat individuals within its jurisdiction. This is now a matter for legitimate international concern, and international human rights law represents the standard by which the conduct of states may be judged. Today, even the most authoritarian of regimes would not publicly oppose the principle that their citizens have certain fundamental rights, even though the actions of many such governments may not always faithfully uphold such ideals. Certainly much more needs to be done to see the proper enforcement of the international standards that have been created. But here we may recall the words of Lauterpacht; the history of human rights law, both at the domestic and the international level, confirms that '[t]he vindication of human liberties does not begin with their complete and triumphant assertion at the very outset'. Rather, 'it commences with their recognition in *some* matters, to *some* extent, for *some* people, against *some* organ of the State'.[65] The story of the history of human rights is, therefore, most certainly an ongoing one.

FURTHER READING

HENKIN, *The Rights of Man Today* (Stevens and Sons, 1978).

HUMPHREY, *Human Rights and the United Nations: A Great Adventure* (Transnational Publishers, 1984).

ISHAY, *The History of Human Rights: From Ancient Times to the Globalization Era* (University of California Press, 2004).

—— *The Human Rights Reader* (Routledge, 2007).

LAUREN, *The Evolution of International Human Rights: Visions Seen* (University of Pennsylvania Press, 2003).

ROBERTSON, *Crimes Against Humanity* (Penguin, 2006).

ROBERTSON and MERRILLS, *Human Rights in the World* (Manchester University Press, 1996) ch 1.

SIMPSON, *Human Rights and the End of Empire* (Oxford University Press, 2001) especially chs 2–5.

TOMUSCHAT, *Human Rights: Between Idealism and Realism* (Oxford University Press, 2008) ch 2.

---

[65] Lauterpacht, n 1.

USEFUL WEBSITES

Avalon Project: Documents in Law, History and Diplomacy (many of the 'constitutional' documents referred to in this chapter are available on this site): <http://avalon.law.yale.edu>

Official UN website on the UDHR, with links to audiovisual materials on the UDHR: <http://www.ohchr.org/EN/UDHR/Pages/introduction.aspx >

2

PHILOSOPHY

James W Nickel and David A Reidy

SUMMARY

This chapter explains the contemporary idea of human rights and surveys some attempts by philosophers to provide systematic justifications for such rights. It first sets out what human rights are, considers whether human rights need a special justification, and provides an overview of different approaches to explaining the foundations of human rights. It then discusses in detail the theories of human rights offered by three important philosophers: Alan Gewirth, James Griffin, and John Rawls.

1 INTRODUCTION

Human rights advocates make strong claims. They assert that all people everywhere have high-priority, specific, and duty-imposing rights—such as the right to freedom of peaceful assembly, the right to a fair trial, and the right to education. Puzzled and sceptical people often challenge these strong claims, demanding explanation and justification. Philosophers have responded by giving explanations of what human rights are, how they function, and how they are grounded. This chapter presents three such human rights theories.[1]

Section 2 explains the nature of human rights, explores the idea that they need to be justified, and gives an account of their philosophical foundations. Section 3 presents Alan Gewirth's view that human rights are grounded in the demands that a self-conscious human agent would inevitably make on others and, as a matter of logical consistency, impose on herself as well. Section 4 presents James Griffin's view that human rights can be given a coherent and determinate sense if we ground them in the universal good of functioning human autonomy. Section 5 presents John Rawls's view that human rights are best understood in light of the various purposes they serve within

---

[1] For comprehensive overviews, see Fagan, 'Human Rights', *Internet Encyclopedia of Philosophy*, <http://www.iep.utm.edu/hum-rts/>. See also Nickel, 'Human Rights' in Zalta (ed), *The Stanford Encyclopedia of Philosophy (2009)*, <http://plato.stanford.edu/archives/spr2009/entries/rights-human/>.

the foreign policies of just states, especially the purposes of marking the conditions and limits of reciprocal recognition between states and of coercive international actions.

We focus on these three theorists because their views both continue to attract considerable attention and indicate the range of justificatory approaches to human rights. Rawls's approach is decidedly political and in that sense a departure from more traditional attempts to ground the justification of human rights in basic propositions of moral philosophy. Griffin's and Gewirth's approaches are more traditional than Rawls's. But Griffin and Gewirth affirm and appeal to different moral philosophies. Griffin takes a broadly teleological view of human rights according to which human rights are justified by reference to what is substantively good for humans. Gewirth takes a broadly anti-teleological, or deontological, view according to which human rights are justified by reference to considerations other than what is substantively good for humans—for example, the commitments a practical agent must logically affirm insofar as she understands herself to be a practical agent.

2 THE NATURE AND FOUNDATIONS OF HUMAN RIGHTS

2.1 WHAT ARE HUMAN RIGHTS?

When people today think or talk about human rights they usually have in mind the sorts of rights found in the Universal Declaration of Human Rights (UDHR) and subsequent treaties. These are political rights in the sense that they are directed mainly to states and prescribe what their institutions should and should not do. They are not primarily interpersonal rights, although they include some rights that persons (and other non-state actors) can violate, such as rights against torture, slavery, and discrimination. Further, these rights are numerous (several dozen) and specific, not abstract and generic like John Locke's rights to life, liberty, and property.[2] They can be organized into seven families:

1. security rights that protect people against crimes such as murder, massacre, torture, and rape;
2. due process rights that protect against abuses of the legal system such as imprisonment without trial and excessive punishments;
3. fundamental freedoms in areas such as thought, expression, and assembly;
4. rights of political participation such as protesting and voting;
5. equality rights that guarantee equal citizenship, equality before the law, and non-discrimination;

---

[2] Locke, *Second Treatise of Government* (1689). See Chapter 1, above.

6. social rights that guarantee subsistence, basic healthcare, and education; and

7. minority and group rights that protect individuals and groups against genocide, persecution, discrimination, inequality, and deprivation of territory.

Most of the rights contained in the UDHR were subsequently incorporated into treaties. However, the idea of human rights as justified moral rights binding on states regardless of international law (or their own national law) continues to play an important role in human rights theory and practice.

Human rights are, first and foremost, rights. Accordingly they have the structure of rights. For every right, there is a *rightholder*, the party (or parties) who has the right. And so too for human rights. It is often said that for any human right, all human persons are the rightholders. But this is not quite right. Human rights that are minority or group rights are not held by all persons. And human rights to political participation are not held by infants. Still, as a general matter, human rights are rights held by all living human persons irrespective of their national, religious, ethnic, gender, racial, or other distinguishing identities.

Every right has an *object*—what the right is a right to. Rights focus attention on their objects. The object of the right to freedom of association is free association, or the absence of governmental restraints on association. Specifying the object of a human right is not always easy. For example, Article 27 UDHR concerns the human right to participate freely in the cultural life of the community. It is difficult to specify the object of this right.

There is also for every right an *addressee*—the party or parties who are directed to do something about making available to the rightholder the object of the right. Most human rights are primarily addressed to states. But, of course, states are complex entities made of many parts, each of which may be directed to do different things. For example, the right to freedom of assembly directs the legislature not to pass laws prohibiting peaceful assembly, the police not to interfere with peaceful assembly, the courts to take reasonable steps to secure persons peacefully assembling from interference by others, and so on. When a state fails to act as required by a human right, the right may direct backup addressees to act. For example, if a state fails to act as required by the human right to subsistence, other states or international organizations or even individual persons may be directed to act in various ways. Some human rights are addressed to multiple and co-equal addressees. For example, the right to asylum directs all states to provide asylum to those seeking asylum from persecution. Of course, so long as one state provides asylum, the right is fulfilled.

Every right has a normative *content*. It specifies the normative position of the addressees and rightholders in relation to the object. The normative content of most human rights is complex, involving the affirmation or denial of duties, and the power or lack of power to alter the rights or legal status of others. Consider the right not to be tortured. At its core is the claim each person has not to be tortured and the duty each person has not to torture others. The right not to be tortured is also a right that, unlike, say, one's right to a piece of property, cannot be waived. Now consider the right to marry. At its core is neither a claim each person has to be married nor a duty each person has to marry others. Rather, at its core is the idea that no person has a duty to propose marriage to another or to consent to a marriage proposal from another but that every person has the power to alter his or her legal status by joining with another, through reciprocal consent, in marriage. The right to marry also imposes on the state a duty not to try to prevent persons from marrying for reason of race, nationality, or religion. That is, it vests each person with a claim to be free of discriminatory state action with respect to marriage.

Most rights, including many human rights, have *exceptions*. For example, the right to freedom of association does not prevent the state from outlawing criminal organizations and conspiracies. Exceptions are typically specified either in the object of the right (what the right is a right *to*) or in the normative content of the right (the normative relations the right establishes between the rightholder and addressee).

Human rights generally have a high priority or *weight*. They are important enough to prevail in competition with many—perhaps most—other moral considerations. For example, human rights can generally trump considerations of economic efficiency and national pride. This is not to say, however, that human rights are generally absolute.

The more fully the foregoing elements (rightholder, object, addressee, normative content, any exceptions, weight) are specified, the more determinate the right. A human right is vague or abstract to the extent these elements are left unspecified. For example, the formulation of the right to life in the European Convention on Human Rights identifies several exceptions (that is, types of justifiable killings)[3] and accordingly is less abstract than the formulation in the UDHR which clearly contemplates but mentions no such exceptions.[4] Of course, a right that is specified without any exceptions or qualifications because none are accepted is not vague or abstract but is determinate, at least with respect to exceptions and qualifications.

Most human rights deal with contemporary problems and institutions and thus cannot plausibly be thought of as holding for all time. Human beings in ancient Greece had no right to social security. And human beings in pre-legal societies had no right to a fair trial. Human rights, as contemplated by the UDHR and contemporary human rights discourse and practice, protect people today against familiar sorts of abuses, typically by states, of their dignity, agency, and most important interests. They are concerned with abuses such as massacre, torture, unfair trials, denials of freedom of assembly, and the unavailability of education. They often presuppose contemporary political institutions such as formal criminal trials, electoral systems, and state-funded education.

2.2 DO HUMAN RIGHTS NEED SOME SPECIAL SORT OF JUSTIFICATION?

Human rights are a central part of international law today. Therefore, one might think that human rights raise no special moral or philosophical issues. After all, their existence and role within international law can be settled by simply consulting the relevant

---

[3] European Convention on Human Rights, Art 2.   [4] UDHR, Art 3.

legal documents and judicial decisions. We can still wonder about the moral merits or philosophical foundations of existing human rights law, just as we might wonder about those of any other area of existing law. But, it could be argued, there are no special moral or philosophical issues raised by human rights.

There is a modest and a less modest response to this view. The modest response simply says that 'no special issues' does not imply 'no issues'. The moral merits and philosophical foundations of all areas of law are worth examining. International human rights, as with other areas of law, should not go unexamined or untheorized.

The less modest response says that human rights, unlike other areas of law, have several distinctive features that make them more controversial and more philosophically challenging. These features include:

- Human rights claim to apply everywhere and to trump contrary cultural and political practices. Consider the human right to political participation. What sort of consideration, if any, could be both strong enough and general enough to justify a human right to political participation in the face of so many longstanding national traditions of authoritarian rule, each of which will have its own ideas about the values that justify it?

- At least some human rights purport to be binding whether or not a state recognizes them in its domestic laws or through the ratification of human rights treaties. This suggests that at least some human rights are universal moral rights that bind states and individuals apart from and prior to domestic or international law. But how should we understand such rights? What is their relationship to legal rights or to existing institutions and practices?

- The international community may use coercive measures, such as economic sanctions and military interventions, to deal with gross violations of human rights. Such measures invade national sovereignty and risk both wounding national pride and threatening international peace. Are human rights, or *all* human rights, strong enough to justify taking on these costs of their coercive enforcement?

2.3 WHAT ARE THE FOUNDATIONS OF HUMAN RIGHTS?

According to a theory of knowledge known as 'foundationalist epistemology', people have available to them non-inferentially justified beliefs that provide foundational grounds for inferentially justified beliefs. (One way a belief might be non-inferentially justified is by being self-evident.)[5] If human rights have a foundation of this sort, it might explain in one fell swoop their universality, moral urgency, and atypical enforcement. A conception of human rights as universal moral rights would be foundationalist in this sense if it derived human rights from some self-evident point that

---

[5] See Fumerton, 'Foundationalist Theories of Epistemic Justification' in Zalta (ed), n 1, <http://plato.stanford.edu/archives/fall2008/entries/justep-foundational/>.

either is, or should be, common to all moral codes and cultures on earth. For example, it might be supposed that it is simply self-evident that certain sorts of killings are very serious moral wrongs, or that the value of human life is very great, and then proceed inferentially to justify a human right to life (specifying the object of the right, the rightholder, the duties the right imposes on others, and so on) as a universal moral right. The pattern of justification here would be 'foundationalist'—it would proceed from foundations known non-inferentially to a superstructure of further knowledge known by inference.

Many contemporary theorists of human rights do not mean to offer philosophical foundations in this strong sense of self-evident foundations. They mean only to provide good reasons for accepting human rights, without asserting that the reasons are self-evident or non-inferentially known. They may doubt the existence of any foundational truths justified non-inferentially, or see their primary task as limited to providing people sceptical of, or puzzled by, human rights with good reasons to affirm them. If this is their task, it is more important that the reasons they draw on be reasons others accept than that they be foundational in the sense of self-evident.

A theorist may not intend to justify human rights by appeal to a foundational self-evident truth and yet still proceed in a way that appears to be foundationalist. For example, John Rawls rejects a foundationalist view of human knowledge, at least when it comes to morality. He maintains that all moral beliefs are known inferentially and that our beliefs are maximally justified when they are all in 'reflective equilibrium' with one another. In principle, any belief, and thus any theory, is vulnerable to being overturned by another belief or theory; nothing is self-evident or self-justifying. For this reason, among others, Rawls rejects foundationalist justifications for moral claims, including claims about human rights. Nevertheless, he often makes use of foundationalist patterns of argument for expository purposes. He cites 'root' or 'fundamental' ideas or ideals—for example, of society as a fair system of cooperation, or of persons as rational, reasonable, free, and equal—which he then arranges in such a way as to support more specific conclusions about social justice and human rights. But Rawls does not claim or think that these fundamental notions are non-inferentially known or self-justifying. They are justified, like all moral beliefs, insofar as they are in 'reflective equilibrium' with all our other beliefs.[6]

Various traditions within moral philosophy are capable of generating accounts of the foundations or justification of human rights. Although it is impossible in the brief space available here to give an adequate account of all these traditions, we offer some brief sketches and a few references.

Human rights would be easier to understand if they were straightforward claims that certain things are good or bad (for example, freedom is good; torture is bad) or even that certain things are in general right or wrong (torture is wrong; assisting others in need is right). But what they say is more complicated. The right to life says, inter

---

[6] See Daniels, 'Reflective Equilibrium' in Zalta (ed), n 1, <http://plato.stanford.edu/archives/fall2008/entries/reflective-equilibrium/>.

alia, that each person has a particular claim that her life be respected and protected and, correlatively, that the state has a particular duty to provide that respect and protection. As this example suggests, human rights involve duties (and other 'deontic' elements such as permissions and immunities) between particular agents. Justifying these duties and explaining how they come to govern the relations between particular agents involves appealing to more than what is generally good or bad or right or wrong. Two main approaches to justifying human rights can be distinguished: teleological and deontological theories.

2.3.1 Teleological theories

We often explain and justify duties by showing that they promote, or are required by, some good. For example, we explain the duty to follow the directions given by traffic lights in terms of the good of reducing injuries and fatalities. This pattern of reasoning, explaining and justifying rights and duties by reference to some good or goods, is typically referred to as 'teleological'. *Utilitarian* and *consequentialist* theories, in their pure forms, use this teleological pattern alone to explain *all* moral duties. They say that rights and duties are justifiable if adopting and complying with them promotes some good more than do their normative alternatives. Rights and duties are ultimately to be explained and justified in terms of their role in promoting intrinsic (basic or non-instrumental) goods.

Consequentialist and utilitarian theories identify one or more intrinsic goods that provide the source of all justifications of actions, policies, and norms. Utilitarianism, in its many forms, identifies the good as human happiness or welfare. It holds that norms are justified when compliance with them maximizes aggregate or average happiness or welfare. Consequentialist theories differ from utilitarianism in not defining the good exclusively in terms of happiness or welfare. Some consequentialist theories are pluralistic in the sense that they identify more than one intrinsic good. And some consequentialists hold that it is neither necessary nor desirable always to maximize the good in order rationally to promote it.[7] But like utilitarians, consequentialists justify deontic norms, including rights, teleologically, by appealing to the good or goods they promote.

It is sometimes said that consequentialists and utilitarians cannot *really* justify rights, including human rights, because the logic of their position commits them to authorizing or even requiring the violation of rights when that is what best or most rationally promotes happiness or welfare. But this is a superficial objection.[8] Very few people think of human rights as absolute, and most think that what best or most rationally promotes happiness or welfare is at least sometimes relevant to the specification of the object of a right and the duties it imposes. In any case, there are many consequentialist and utilitarian defenders of human rights. They include the well-

---

[7] On the variety of consequentialist views, see Sinnott-Armstrong, 'Consequentialism' in Zalta (ed), n 1, <http://plato.stanford.edu/archives/fall2008/entries/consequentialism/>.

[8] See also Chapter 3, below.

known utilitarian John Stuart Mill, who saw genuine duty-generating rights arising in regard to goods such as security that were 'the most necessary of necessaries', as well as a number of contemporary utilitarians and consequentialists.[9] What is true is that consequentialists and utilitarians have a hard time accounting fully for the particularist relational nature of many rights. In the end, the relationship between a rightholder and the addressee is, for the consequentialist or utilitarian, something determined and justified instrumentally. That is, the rightholder and the addressee stand in the particular normative relationship specified by the right in question not because of anything they directly and particularly owe to one another but because that relationship best generally promotes happiness or welfare (or whatever instrinsic good is taken to be fundamental).

Natural law theories of rights are teleological, but not utilitarian or consequentialist. They hold that humans naturally pursue certain intrinsic goods that are knowable as intrinsic goods through reason and that these goods provide the most basic reasons humans have for action. They then explain natural law and natural rights by reference to, or as required by, these goods. But they take a wider view than consequentialists and utilitarians of the relationship between rights and the goods in terms of how they are justified. For example, natural law theorists may justify rights as constitutive of or essential to the expression or acknowledgement of a good rather than as simply instrumental to its being maximized or promoted. So, there is a right to life because the preservation of human life is a very weighty good, and to act directly and intentionally against that good is almost always to fail to express or acknowledge its great weight. Natural law theories differ from consequentialist and utilitarian theories in another way. They typically include as intrinsic goods certain moral relationships as well as the common good of a community beyond the mere aggregation of the good of each individual (for example, the just, virtuous, or faithful community). This often leads them to affirm rights or limitations on rights that consequentialists or utilitarians reject (for example, a natural law theorist might deny a right to homosexual marriage that a consequentialist or utilitarian would affirm) and it sometimes provides them with a basis from which to derive the apparently intrinsic, particularist, relational nature of many rights.[10]

2.3.2 Deontological theories

In contrast to teleological approaches to human rights, deontological (or anti-teleological) approaches do not attempt to derive all duties and other deontic norms, and thus human rights, from a conception of the good. Instead, they appeal from the beginning to some basic or fundamental consideration(s) other than the good, such as a duty.

---

[9] See Bentham, *The Principles of Morals and Legislation* (1789) and Mill, *Utilitarianism* (1861) ch 5. See also Lyons, *Rights, Welfare, and Mill's Moral Theory* (OUP, 1994); Sumner, *The Moral Foundations of Rights* (OUP, 1987); and Talbott, *Which Rights Should be Universal* (OUP, 2005).

[10] See Murphy, 'The Natural Law Tradition in Ethics' in Zalta (ed), n 1, <http://plato.stanford.edu/archives/fall2008/entries/natural-law-ethics/>.

For example, *divine command theories* take the duty to obey God as basic or fundamental. There is an important strand in thinking about human rights that suggests that they are somehow given by God. For example, the US Declaration of Independence of 1776 declared: 'We hold these truths to be self-evident, that all men are created equal, that they are endowed by their Creator with certain unalienable Rights, that among these are Life, Liberty and the pursuit of Happiness.' Those subscribing to divine command theories may hold that human rights can be known by divine revelation, the careful use of human reason, or both. But they will typically hold that, even if they can be *known* through the careful use of human reason alone, human rights exist and are binding because they were prescribed by a benevolent divine lawgiver. Further, they will typically hold that while God's benevolence may assure us that honouring human rights will serve our good, human rights are neither defined nor justified by reference to our good. Instead, they are defined and justified by reference to God's will or commands. In this respect, divine command theories depart from the teleological pattern of justification. They define and justify rights not by reference to considerations of the good, but of God's command or will and our duty to obey it. This is true for both human rights and for moral rights more generally. For example, a particular husband and wife have the rights they have in marriage because God so commanded or willed. Divine command theories typically hold that human rights were given by God long ago and for all time. Accordingly they must define and justify human rights in very general and abstract terms and without presupposing contemporary institutions. To justify contemporary human rights, which are numerous and specific rather than few and abstract, divine command theories need to explain how to make the transition from the broad and few to the specific and many.[11]

Believers may assure themselves of the metaphysical and moral status of human rights by rooting them in God's commands. But in a theologically diverse world, appealing to God's commands is a poor strategy for public justification. Billions of people do not believe in the God found in Christianity, Islam, and Judaism. Many believe in no God at all. Yet the vast majority of non-believers are reasonable and many are ready to affirm and honour human rights, provided they are given a justification addressed to them.

Instead of appealing to God's will, deontological theories may appeal to a basic notion of right relations between persons, for example the ideal of reciprocal recognition and respect. Immanuel Kant (1724–1804) is perhaps the most well-known proponent of a deontological approach to rights. Kant thought of morality as a system of categorical imperatives or duties we must fulfill regardless of our desires. At the centre of this system was a most basic command or duty: the Categorical Imperative. Kant characterized the Categorical Imperative in several ways. But one important characterization is in terms of respect for persons as ends in themselves. The Categorical Imperative commands us, regardless of our desires, to respect others always as ends

---

[11] See Waldron, *God, Locke, and Equality: Christian Foundations in Locke's Political Thought* (CUP, 2002) and Wolterstorf, *Justice: Rights and Wrongs* (Princeton University Press, 2007).

in themselves and never to treat them merely as means to our own ends. We may, of course, use the baker's work as a means to enjoy a sandwich, but we may not treat the baker as if she were merely an instrument or machine. We must act towards her in ways that recognize and respect her humanity.[12] On Kant's view, our duty to recognize and respect the humanity or moral personality of others is inseparable from our own humanity or moral personality. And our duty to recognize and respect the humanity or moral personality of others is sometimes expressed in the form of human rights. Thus, Kant justifies human rights by reference to a fundamental categorical command, thought to be a condition and expression of our own humanity or moral personality, to treat all persons as moral equals within a single moral community.

Contemporary deontological theories typically acknowledge that considerations of the good must play a role in the justification of rights and duties. But they deny that rights and duties can be justified entirely by reference to considerations of the good. They insist that some other moral consideration—perhaps a fundamental duty to obey God, perhaps an ideal of reciprocal recognition and respect between persons—always plays a fundamental role in the justification of rights and duties generally and human rights in particular.

As the theories of Gewirth, Griffin, and Rawls discussed below illustrate, while plausible contemporary accounts of human rights typically lean in a teleological or deontological direction, they rarely fit fully and neatly in one or the other category. Instead, they draw together teleological and deontological elements in a distinctive and fruitful way. Further, as the three theories show, few plausible contemporary accounts of human rights argue from a claim about the one true, universal, and complete moral code to a claim about human rights. Given the depth, ubiquity, and intractability of reasonable disagreement over the existence and content of any one true, universal, and complete moral code, and the need for a public justification for human rights, it makes more sense to try to justify human rights by appeal to more limited and less controversial claims.

3 GEWIRTH'S ARGUMENT FOR HUMAN RIGHTS TO FREEDOM AND WELFARE

Alan Gewirth (1912–2004) constructed a simple but grand argument for universal human rights.[13] The argument attempts to rely solely on unassailable facts about humans and requirements of logical consistency. It has 11 steps. If the argument turns out to be sound, it is of tremendous importance.

[12] See Johnson, 'Kant's Moral Philosophy' in Zalta (ed), n 1, <http://plato.stanford.edu/archives/fall2008/entries/kant-moral/>.
[13] Gewirth, *Reason and Morality* (University of Chicago Press, 1978); *Human Rights: Essays on Justification and Application* (University of Chicago Press, 1982); *The Community of Rights* (University of Chicago Press, 1996). The version of Gewirth's argument discussed here is derived from *The Community of Rights*, 8–30.

The general idea of Gewirth's argument is simple. It is that insofar as you claim, as you inevitably will, that others must respect your freedom and well-being, you commit yourself to respecting the freedom and well-being of others. We can imagine Professor Gewirth engaging in dialogue with a student who claims not to believe in human rights. He says to the student, 'In order to live you're going to have to be an agent, someone who acts to achieve various ends. Isn't that so?' The student agrees that this is inescapable. Professor Gewirth then notes that successful agency is far from easy and will require the restraint and assistance of others. He suggests that the student must therefore see her freedom and well-being as valuable and demand that it be respected by everyone. The student agrees. Professor Gewirth then reminds the student that there is nothing distinctive about her in this respect; she is in exactly the same situation as everyone else. Accordingly, consistency requires her to recognize that other agents will make the same demands and that if her claims are valid, so too are theirs. Gewirth's point is not that she must respect the freedom and well-being of others in order to induce them or give them reason to respect her freedom and well-being. His point is rather that as a matter of logical consistency or reason she must respect the freedom and well-being of others just as soon as she formulates the demand that they respect her freedom and well-being. Gewirth holds that 'right-claims arise logically . . . out of the concern of all human beings, as prospective . . . agents, that the . . . necessary conditions of their . . . successful action be protected'.[14] Gewirth does not derive human rights from considerations of the general good; he derives them from the conditions of human agency and the logical structure of reason.

Gewirth's argument begins from the perspective of the self-aware human agent who faces many choices and needs to act. When such a person deliberates and acts there can be attributed to him a statement of the form:

(1) I do X for end or purpose E.[15]

Since all normal humans engage in self-conscious action on at least some occasions, this starting point is nicely universal.

The second premise is that this agent must regard her end, E, as good. From (1) the agent logically must accept:

(2) E is good.

The agent need not commit to E as defining or constituting the good; it is enough if E has for the agent 'some value sufficient to merit his trying to attain it'.

From these modest beginnings the third premise takes a large step. [S]ince freedom and well-being are the proximate necessary conditions of the agent acting to attain any of his purposes and thus any good, the agent, having accepted (2), must also accept:

(3) My freedom and well-being are necessary goods.

---

[14] *The Community of Rights*, n 13, 16.   [15] For the steps of the argument, see ibid, 16–19.

From the point of view of any agent acting to attain any of her purposes and thus any good, freedom and well-being are not optional goods it would be nice to have—they are necessary. If they were not necessary then agents would not be committed logically to claiming them as a matter of right.

From (3) Gewirth moves to a practical prescription that the agent must accept:

(4) I must have freedom and well-being.

Notice that here we are still within the perspective of a particular agent who is considering what successful action and choice will require. The prescription is prudential, or rooted solely in self-, not moral, interest. But while expressing only a prudential prescription, this premise is not merely saying that freedom and well-being are nice. Rather, it is saying that they are things one *must* have—they are prudentially imperative.

Gewirth moves directly from (4) to:

(5) I have rights to freedom and well-being.

That is, Gewirth claims that the prudential self-interested rational agent who 'must have' freedom and well-being will herself assert a right, or as he calls it, a 'prudential right-claim', to freedom and well-being. Here the language of rights makes its first appearance. But it is not yet fully a moral language, for the agent in question has not yet found herself logically compelled to commit to the rights of others. That is, (5) expresses a claim each agent logically must make about her own rights and thus the duties of others; it expresses no claim that she logically must make about the rights of others and thus her own duties. And so (5) is not yet a moral claim. To get to a moral claim about rights, more argument is needed.

Many who have gone along with his argument up until (4) will feel uneasy about the move from (4) to (5) simply because they do not see how one can get a claim about rights, even if only a prudential claim about *my* rights, out of a claim about necessary goods. How does the recognition that one has a compelling need for freedom and well-being lead necessarily to the assertion that one has or must claim rights to them?

Gewirth has an argument to reassure us that the step from (4) to (5) is valid. He gives it in steps 6 to 8, which follow a pattern of argument known as *reductio ad absurdum*. This pattern begins by assuming the falsity or negation of what one hopes to prove and continues by showing that a contradiction (absurdity) follows from that assumption. To prove X, one assumes not-X and shows that this assumption leads to a contradiction. If not-X leads to a contradiction, then we must reject not-X. But that means we must affirm X which is, of course, what we wanted to prove. Since Gewirth wants to prove that any agent committed to (4) must also be committed to (5), he begins by assuming for purposes of argument that there is an agent committed to (4) but also to the negation or falsity of (5), that is, to:

(6) I do not have any right to freedom and well-being.

But, Gewirth argues, if this agent does not have any right to freedom and well-being (that is, if premise 6, which is the negation of (5), is true), then it follows that other persons have no general duty to refrain from removing or interfering with this agent's freedom and well-being. They are morally free to limit the agent's freedom or diminish her well-being. And this means that it is permissible that the agent not have freedom and well-being. This, then, gives us premise 7.

(7) It is permissible that I not have freedom and well-being.

But (7) contradicts (4), which holds that freedom and well-being are things the agent must have. Since (7) followed from denying (5), Gewirth concludes, it is inconsistent to endorse (4) but deny (5). Since we already have good reason to endorse (4), we must, to be consistent, affirm (5). So we conclude that having affirmed (4) we have reason also to affirm (5), which brings us to premise 8, which is just a restatement of (5):

(8) I have rights to freedom and well-being.

This is a clever argument. But we worry that it equivocates on the word 'must' in premise 4. When our agent asserts in (4) that she 'must' have freedom and well-being, is she really asserting that it is *impermissible* for others to fail to respect her freedom and well-being, that others have a duty to respect her freedom and well-being? Is this what follows from premises 1 to 3? She must be asserting something like this as what follows from premises 1 to 3. Otherwise (4) will not logically conflict with (7). But it seems unlikely that the 'must' in (4) is properly understood to mean 'impermissible'. It is just not possible to infer from premises 1 to 3 anything about the duties of others. The 'must' in (4), then, is better understood to mean something like 'anything else would be a disaster' or 'anything else would make it impossible for me to act effectively'. But if that is what the 'must' in (4) means, then there is no logical inconsistency in affirming (4) and in affirming what (7) claims, namely that others have no duty not to remove or interfere with my freedom or well-being. And if there is no logical inconsistency, then steps 6 to 8 fail to close the gap between premises 4 and 5 and Gewirth's overall argument for human rights to freedom and well-being fails.

Let us assume that steps 6 to 8 do succeed in closing the gap between premises 4 and 5. In step 9, Gewirth summarizes what he thinks he has established thus far:

(9) I have rights to freedom and well-being because I am a prospective purposive agent.

From (9) Gewirth moves, in another large step, to premise 10. It universalizes (9) by attributing generic rights to freedom and well-being to every agent. Since all other agents are in exactly the same position as our agent, consistency requires that our agent 'logically must accept':

(10) All prospective purposive agents have rights to freedom and well-being.

Once this step of universalization is completed we have justified abstract moral rights to freedom and well-being 'because the agent is now committed to taking favorable account of the interests of other persons as well as of himself'.

The final step in the argument issues a generic prescription for action:

(11) Act in accord with the generic rights of your recipients as well as of yourself.

Gewirth calls this the 'Principle of Generic Consistency'. It is an abstract moral principle requiring that each person 'respect the freedom and well-being of all other persons'. The overall argument moves from concern for the necessary goods of oneself as an agent to commitment to equal rights for all.

Steps 6 to 8 are not the only potential weak point in the argument. Consider the transition from (9) to (10), from:

(9) I have rights to freedom and well-being because I am a prospective purposive agent.

to:

(10) All prospective purposive agents have rights to freedom and well-being.

This step proceeds on the principle that if a person A in situation S concludes that he has a right to X, then consistency requires that person A recognize that any other person, say B, who is in exactly the same situation S, has the same right to X. This principle is sound so long as there are no relevant differences between persons in the same situation. But what if there are relevant differences, or more to the point, what if person A thinks there are? Person A may think he is in the same situation as person B, but that he is relevantly different from B because of his ethnicity or ancestry or because of his biological sex. He may think that he has a right to X in situation S not because he is a purposive agent, but because he is the right kind of purposive agent or person.

Gewirth has a ready reply to this worry. Recall that premises 1 to 4 rely on no special features of persons to establish (5). If person A agrees to each of premises 1 to 4, she will have committed herself to having a right to freedom and well-being simply because she is a person capable of purposive agency. But then she must logically recognize that every person capable of purposive agency may claim exactly the same right.

Of course, not all human beings are purposive agents—for example, the severely cognitively impaired or infants. It is not clear how to extend Griffin's argument so that it establishes rights for human beings who are not purposive agents.

Another difficulty with these final steps in Gewirth's argument is that the rights Gewirth universalizes in step 10 are prudential rights claims. That is, (9) refers to rights in the sense of the rights I must necessarily claim for myself simply out of self-interest. Universalizing (9) would seem to give us only the claim that we must recognize that every purposive agent will necessarily claim rights for herself out of self-interest. But this claim is not the same as Gewirth's (10). Premise 10 claims that we must recognize that every person *has* rights to freedom and well-being. It suggests a moral claim about the rights of others rooted in an awareness of their moral status or dignity as purposive agents, not just a logical recognition of the fact that we cannot hold that they ought not claim for themselves what we claim for ourselves.

If Gewirth succeeds in establishing that there are generic human rights to freedom and well-being, then the next step is to derive specific rights from them. For example, from the generic right to freedom we can derive freedom of religion or assembly. And from the generic right to well-being we can derive the right to education. Gewirth believes that he can derive as moral rights most of the rights in the UDHR, including economic and social rights.[16]

Gewirth's justification for human rights is fascinating. From principles of logic and a few hard-to-dispute facts about human agents and their situation he derives two generic human rights, and then from these, the familiar list of more determinate human rights. But the argument is also controversial and not obviously successful.

It is hard to decide whether Gewirth is a teleological natural law theorist or a deontologist. The former classification is suggested by the fact that he starts with the self-conscious human agent naturally oriented towards and able to know certain things as good(s) and ends up with universal rights and duties. Those who would classify Gewirth as a deontologist might emphasize that he does not start from a general, unconditional, and substantively rich claim about the good for humans. Instead, he starts from the fact or inevitability of self-conscious action (practical agency), the conditions necessary to it (arrived at by way of something like a transcendental argument), and the logical demands of consistency and universality that one cannot avoid insofar as one exercises one's practical agency through reason. Put this way, his starting points, and the general thrust of his position, appear to be more deontological than teleological.

4 GRIFFIN ON AUTONOMY AND HUMAN RIGHTS

Griffin shares Gewirth's view that human rights, as universal moral rights, are grounded in the human capacity to choose and act. He proposes that we reconstruct the idea of human rights by tying our conception of it to a single very important interest of all humans, namely developing and exercising their capacity to choose, evaluate, deliberate, plan, revise, and pursue through action their own course in life. Griffin refers to the object of this interest as 'normative agency', 'autonomous agency', and 'personhood'. He thinks that from this interest he 'can generate most of the conventional list of human rights'.[17] He believes that grounding human rights in this universal good will bring unity and coherence to the theory and practice of human rights. Griffin's approach seems to be teleological: he reasons from a universal good for humans (normative agency) to human rights.

Griffin divides the good of normative agency into three parts. The first is the good of developing, using, and maintaining the capacity to make choices and plans ('autonomy'). The second is the good of being able to pursue what one has chosen ('liberty'). The third is the good of having the material resources minimally sufficient to be able to pursue what one has chosen ('minimal provision' or welfare).[18] Autonomy, liberty,

---

[16] Gewirth, *Human Rights: Essays on Justification and Application*, n 13.
[17] Griffin, *On Human Rights* (OUP, 2008) 33.   [18] Ibid, 159.

and welfare are goods that characteristically enhance the quality of life to a very high degree. Accordingly, they generate 'claims on us not to destroy them, and within limits, to protect and promote them'.[19] Human rights, as universal moral rights, express and embody these claims.

Corresponding to this division, there are abstract human rights to: (1) autonomy, (2) liberty, and (3) minimum material provision. More specific human rights fall under one or the other of these abstract headings. We wonder why the list of abstract rights does not include two others: equality and security. Griffin may think that all rights falling under the abstract headings of equality and security may be derived from those falling under his three headings of autonomy, liberty, and minimum material provision. But it is not obvious, for example, how to derive the rights constitutive of equal treatment under the law.

Practicalities matter too in the derivation of specific rights. Practicalities here refer to general facts, neither historically nor geographically relative, about the human condition and human societies. Their role as a second justificatory foundation for human rights is to make it possible, without appealing to positive acts of legislation or adjudication, to move from the good of normative agency to a more fine-grained specification of human rights.[20]

Seeing all human rights as rooted in the good of normative agency (and practicalities) is Griffin's proposed means of remedying the 'intolerable degree of indeterminacy of sense'[21] with which he thinks the idea of human rights as universal moral rights is afflicted, an indeterminacy that has led to a proliferation of human rights claims in recent decades. Nevertheless, he affirms a fairly robust list of human rights. In his view, human rights as universal moral rights include most of the rights in the UDHR as well as a wide variety of interpersonal moral rights.

Griffin's failure to include equality rights as a distinct family of human rights reflects his general ambivalence toward rooting human rights in considerations of fairness or equality. Although Griffin recognizes that today's conception of human rights has strong egalitarian dimensions, particularly in its commitments to equal treatment under the law, to an equal distribution of rights, and to non-discrimination, he is sceptical of the tendency to turn human rights into a strongly egalitarian project. For the most part, Griffin insists that human rights concern a moral minimum or floor, not the distribution of goods above that floor.

Still, Griffin endorses welfare rights at levels above 'subsistence' as a necessary means of ensuring that everyone has the material resources necessary to develop and exercise normative agency.[22] He also endorses funding or implementing these rights through progressive or redistributive taxation. Here, at the level of implementation, Griffin concedes that the values of equality, fairness, or reciprocity may play an important role in shaping human rights. But he insists that it does not follow from the fact that these values play an important role in guiding the implementation of a human right that they also play an important role in grounding a human right

---

[19] Ibid, 185.   [20] Ibid, 37–8, 192.   [21] Ibid, 143.   [22] Ibid, 39–44, 144–5, 162, 176–87.

or a family of human rights. He says that it would be 'a non sequitur to move from a value's being indispensable in working out these implications of human rights to its being foundational to the notion of a human right itself'.[23] Still, it is hard to see how to avoid substantial reliance on these values when completing the justification of human rights. The idea that human rights are universal and are to be enjoyed without discrimination seems to require foundational support from some principle of human equality.

Griffin's abstract right to liberty does not imply specific moral rights to every kind of action, or even to every harmless action. Rights to drive the wrong way down one-way streets or to refuse to wear a necktie are said not to follow from the generic right to liberty. What the abstract human right to liberty requires is for all people to have access to broadly useful paths for pursuing plausible conceptions of a worthwhile life. Following Griffin's view, human rights must often be balanced against other weighty moral concerns. They do not function generally as 'moral trumps'. These other weighty moral concerns may include the demands of justice, efficiency, or the common good.[24] This is an ample menu of grounds for rejecting or qualifying liberties that are candidates to be human rights.

Griffin denies that tie wearing and smoking are valuable or important enough to form a major component of a worthwhile life, so he rejects any liberty right to engage in these activities. But he believes that having a family and children is a major component of a worthwhile life. He is prepared, therefore, to affirm for same-sex couples a human (liberty) right to family and children: '[I]f there are same-sex couples who want to form some sort of union and raise children—who want, that is, to have the rich, stable, recognized, respected relations that are at the heart of most people's conceptions of a worthwhile life—and ... there are no social institutions to allow it, then we should create one or other form of them.'[25] Griffin argues that restricting the liberty of homosexuals in the areas of family relations and children has too large an impact on their ability to pursue worthwhile lives: 'What is at stake for same-sex couples are several of the most important components of a good life available to human beings.'[26] As this illustrates, Griffin's fundamental test of whether free access to an option is required by human rights is not ultimately whether the option is general or specific but whether denying access to it seriously impairs access to 'the most important components of a good life'.

If the justification of human rights to liberty depends on judgements about the most important components of a good life for human beings, it is reasonable to worry that these judgements will carry a large subjective component. Griffin believes that a good life for human beings must include access to the visual arts, but many people care little for art. Griffin believes that plausible views of human nature and society help to reduce subjectivity, but we wonder if they can eliminate most of it.

---

[23] Ibid, 41–3.   [24] Ibid, 164, 168, 235.   [25] Ibid, 163–4.   [26] Ibid.

Human rights are universal, in Griffin's view, because all 'normal' adult humans are capable of autonomous agency at a level above the basic threshold at which it becomes a great and universal human good. Infants and very young children and those who suffer from very serious and permanent cognitive ability may not be so capable, of course. Griffin explicitly denies that they have human rights, though he insists that their lives are protected by other weighty moral considerations.

But here Griffin's refusal to take the values of equality, fairness, or reciprocity seriously at the level of justification again causes difficulty. Contemporary human rights practice is committed to equality of human rights in spite of very large variations in levels of the capacity for autonomy among humans within the normal range. Given these variations, we could allocate rights to liberty to adults in a manner proportionate to their capacity for autonomy (after all, we do something like this with children). But we do not find this acceptable and it is not part of contemporary human rights practice. Instead we give equal rights to liberty to all adults above a certain threshold, notwithstanding their differences above the threshold. But if normative agency is our only concern, then Griffin's threshold conception of human rights (according to which everyone above the threshold gets equal rights) is not obviously superior to a proportional conception (according to which persons above the threshold get rights proportional to the degree they exceed the threshold). Griffin needs, it seems, to appeal at the level of foundational justification to some notion of equality, or fairness, or reciprocity, to justify his preference for a threshold conception.

Griffin seems to be some sort of teleological natural law theorist. He starts with the objective value or good of our practical agency. The development and exercise of our normative agency is, he thinks, a good we all recognize and must respect. It is not simply that one recognizes one's own normative agency as good; one recognizes the good of the development and exercise of normative agency wherever and whenever. Griffin's argument for rights proceeds from conjoining that good with timeless and universal practicalities regarding human nature and human societies and then reasoning to more determinate applications in local, contingent conditions (getting us rights such as the right to a free press).

Still, there are deontological aspects to Griffin's view. Griffin draws on independent considerations of fairness or equality or reciprocity to justify various features of human rights, including their universality. This seems to introduce a deontological element, though Griffin is eager to restrict its role to the 'shaping of human rights' rather than their justification. Further, Griffin seems at times to be engaged in the Kantian project of explaining what respect for persons means and requires.

Gewirth and Griffin both attempt to work out and justify a conception of human rights as universal moral rights by starting from moral ground common to all interpersonal moralities. Only when it comes to implementation do they consider the extension of human rights to the institutional setting of international relations. John Rawls, who we consider next, takes a very different approach. He begins with the institutional setting of international relations and grounds human rights in international morality.

5 JOHN RAWLS AND THE LAW OF PEOPLES

John Rawls (1921–2002) offered an account of human rights in *The Law of Peoples*.[27] Rawls is best known for his liberal-egalitarian-democratic theory of social justice, first presented in his highly influential *A Theory of Justice* and then elaborated in *Political Liberalism*.[28] With his theory of social justice at the national level in hand, Rawls attempted in *The Law of Peoples* to identify the moral principles that ought to guide international political and economic relations. He undertook to articulate and justify these principles as part of a 'political conception of right and justice' applicable to international law and relations and worked out from the perspective of a just state—that is, a constitutional democracy that respects individual liberty, provides equal opportunity, secures a basic economic minimum for all, and limits social and economic inequalities. His account of human rights belongs to this 'political conception of right and justice'.[29]

Rawls recognizes that justice sets a more demanding standard for a state to meet than is set by human rights. A state may secure human rights yet still be unjust in important ways. Indeed, it may secure human rights and still fail to secure other rights required by justice. So, like Gewirth and Griffin, Rawls holds that human rights are a subset of the rights secured in and by a just state. Rawls explains this difference by reference to the distinctive roles played by human rights within international relations. In particular, human rights restrict the justifying reasons for coercive intervention and war and constitute a necessary condition of a state's status recognition and respect as a full and equal member of the international order in good standing.[30] This emphasis on the political roles played by human rights within international relations is a distinctive feature of Rawls's view.

It is useful to identify three senses of 'human rights' in *The Law of Peoples*. The first sense is human rights proper. Human rights proper are those rights that limit the internal autonomy of all states and provide justifying reasons within international relations for coercive intervention and war. States that honour human rights proper have a right against coercive intervention by other states. And states that deliberately violate them in a major way have no rightful claim to recognition and respect within the international legal and political order. Rawls restricts human rights proper to those found in, or clearly implied by, Articles 3 to 18 UDHR and the conventions on genocide and apartheid.[31] So, broadly, they include the rights to life, liberty (including liberty of conscience), personal property, and formal equality. But they do not

---

[27] (Harvard University Press, 1999).
[28] *A Theory of Justice* (Clarendon Press, 1972); *Political Liberalism* (Columbia University Press, 1993).
[29] See n 27, 169–75.   [30] Ibid, 79–80, 90.   [31] Ibid, 80.

include, for example, the rights to freedom of expression or to participate and have non-discriminatory access to positions in government.

The second sense of human rights is human rights proper plus modest rights of political participation. States that honour these rights merit status recognition and respect as full and equal members of the international order. However, their violation provides no justification for coercive intervention or war. States need not secure all liberal democratic political participation rights, but they must guarantee such non-trivial political participation rights as the rights to express dissent, to petition the government, to receive reasoned justifications for official state action, and so on.

The third sense of human rights is human rights as understood originally in the UDHR, as goals or ambitions that all peoples have good reason to take on, through treaties or other voluntary undertakings in the international system. They include the full range of rights associated with liberal democracy and specify a further ideal of the just state. Human rights in this sense play a role within the non-coercive and peaceful politics and diplomacy of states recognized and respected as full and equal members of the international order.

How does Rawls arrive at this view? In *A Theory of Justice* Rawls set out his account of the principles that should govern the cooperation between persons in the national context. He developed and deployed his contractualist idea of a unanimous agreement persons enter into as a matter of rational choice in an 'original position'.[32] This original position argument asks what principles rational and informed persons concerned to advance their basic interests through social cooperation, but also made impartial by not knowing what their natural abilities or initial place in society will be, could unanimously accept to govern the society in which they will live. Rawls argues that rational and informed persons so situated would agree on two principles of justice. The first requires a fully adequate scheme of equal basic rights and liberties that is compatible with the same scheme for all. The second requires that social and economic inequalities are attached to positions and offices open to all under conditions of fair equality of opportunity and work to the advantage of those least advantaged more than all other available systems of social and economic inequalities.[33]

Rawls argues that individual rights and liberties may be adjusted to one another to improve the scheme of equal basic rights and liberties overall. But, he asserts, persons placed in an original position will insist that the equal basic rights and liberties required by the first principle are never to be sacrificed in order to meet the demands of fair equality of opportunity, economic efficiency, national security, or a wide range of other political values. Rawls refers to the two principles of (national) justice and the original position argument in favour of them as 'justice as fairness'. According to 'justice as fairness', only constitutional liberal democracies are just states.

Rawls's theory of justice has a teleological dimension. The principles of justice must promote fundamental human interests. But they must do so fairly. Fundamental to

---

[32] *Political Liberalism*, n 28, 22–8.
[33] *A Theory of Justice*, n 28, 60–90. See also *The Law of Peoples*, n 27, 50.

Rawls's theory of justice is the idea that the right relationship between persons is always one of reciprocity. Thus, deontological elements are an indispensable and fundamental part of the Rawlsian scheme. The same is true when we move to thinking of international justice and human rights.

Rawls approaches the question of international justice, and hence human rights, from the point of view of a just state concerned to identify the principles that ought to govern its relations with other just states. He does so in part because there is no world government that forms all peoples into a single nation, with one currency, one system of property, a global executive and legislature, and so on. Another reason for proceeding in this way is that Rawls thinks a just state or 'people' possesses—through its citizens and officials—the moral capacities essential to reasonable cooperation. Rawls's theory of international justice sets out a reasonable 'law of peoples' that is to govern cooperative international relations.

In working up his account of the 'law of peoples', Rawls develops a second 'original position' argument. Its purpose is to provide just societies with a reasonable framework for thinking about the principles that ought to govern their international cooperation. It asks what principles just societies, moved only by their own interests (for example, to preserve their political independence, to keep their territory secure, to prosper economically), but made impartial (by not knowing, for example, their level of development, or geographical size, or economic power) could unanimously accept to govern their interactions on the global stage. In this way, it enables just societies to identify principles of cooperation that treat each and all of them fairly as full and equal members of the international order.

Rawls argues that just societies or 'peoples' could reasonably and unanimously accept the following eight principles to govern their relations.

1. Peoples are free and independent, and their freedom and independence are to be respected by other peoples.
2. Peoples are to observe treaties and undertakings.
3. Peoples are equal and are parties to the agreements that bind them.
4. Peoples are to observe a duty of non-intervention.
5. Peoples have a right of self-defence, but no right to instigate war for reasons other than self-defence.
6. Peoples are to honour human rights.
7. Peoples are to observe certain specified restrictions in the conduct of war.
8. Peoples have a duty to assist other peoples living under unfavorable conditions that prevent their having a just or decent political and social regime.[34]

Rawls refers to these principles, and the overall pattern of argument for them, as 'the law of peoples'. Rawls's argument for the law of peoples, and thus for the conception

[34] n 27, 35–8.

of human rights belonging to it, is contractualist, internationalist, and political. These characteristics mark significant contrasts with the approach to human rights taken by Gewirth and Griffin.

The law of peoples includes a commitment to human rights in principle 6. It is tempting to suppose that because the law of peoples expresses principles of international justice that any just state could reasonably accept, the human rights referred to in principle 6 must be simply the rights common to all just states, that is, the rights common to all liberal democracies. But Rawls denies this. As seen above, he holds that 'human rights proper' are limited to the rights found in Articles 3 to 18 UDHR and the conventions on genocide and apartheid. What explains these features of Rawls's view? Why would just states, liberal democracies, settle on such standards? Why would they not specify human rights as the rights associated with liberal democracy? After all, for Rawls every just state is a liberal democracy.

Here is one way to understand Rawls's reasoning. As they specify the law of peoples and, within it, human rights, just states will attend to the fact that human rights play the three distinct roles described above in international relations. While they will certainly agree to treat the rights associated with liberal democracy as human rights in the third sense, that is, as specifying goals or ambitions voluntarily pursued within the international order, they will not agree to treat them as human rights in the second or first sense. To treat them as human rights in the second sense would be equivalent to claiming that to merit status recognition and respect as a full and equal member of the international order, a state must first constitute itself as a liberal democracy. But what would be the basis for this claim? There is no reason to think that a state must be liberal and democratic to honour those aspects of the law of peoples (observing treaties, avoiding war, and so on) unrelated to human rights. So the only question is whether states either not liberal or not democratic necessarily treat their own members in ways that would make it unreasonable for just states, that is liberal democracies, to accord them status recognition and respect as full and equal members in the international order. Rawls thinks that non-liberal or non-democratic states do not necessarily so treat their own members. He conjectures that there may be 'decent, well-ordered peoples', either non-liberal or non-democratic or both and hence by his lights unjust, that treat their own members in ways that would make it reasonable for just states to accord them status recognition and respect within the international order. 'Decent, well-ordered peoples' in Rawls's sense subscribe to and enforce a public conception of social justice oriented by a conception of the common good shared by many of their members and, accordingly, secure 'human rights proper'. Rawls thinks that it would be reasonable for just states to extend status recognition and respect to decent, well-ordered peoples, so described.

Human rights provide only one part of a complete theory of justice, whether domestic or international. They specify floors beneath which legal, political, social, economic, military, diplomatic, and cultural relations, institutions, and practices may not sink. But they also permit a great deal of variation above the floors they set. Both socialist and capitalist states can satisfy human rights in the first and second sense discussed above. And both are free to take on further human rights commitments in the third sense. And there are various ways in which the global economy and international institutions might be arranged consistent with human rights in each of these senses. To be sure, human rights require a global economy that does not encourage the impoverishment of populations or facilitate the ambitions of kleptocratic warlords. And they require international capacities for coercive humanitarian intervention (to enforce human rights proper) and for non-coercive aid and assistance (to bring about a world within which all regimes are either decent or just). But above this floor, human rights permit a great deal of variation when it comes to the structure of the international order and the conduct of particular states within it.

Rawls's approach to human rights has been criticized on several grounds. Many have complained that his list of human rights proper is simply too impoverished to be taken seriously. They have argued that there are a number of human rights not recognized as human rights proper that ought to be coercively enforced worldwide—though perhaps not through military intervention. Others have complained that the categories and distinctions central to Rawls's approach are too stylized to shed much light on, or provide much direction to, human rights within existing international law and practice. They have pointed out that according status recognition and respect to states within international relations is not an all or nothing affair and is, in any case, itself a form of soft coercion; that states which are neither liberal nor democratic seem rarely to be decent or well-ordered; and that human rights are as tied up with an emerging cosmopolitan morality within global civil society as they are with the norms recognized and honoured by just states in their international relations.[35] Still others have objected to Rawls's political and internationalist approach, holding that to provide a complete account of human rights, Rawls must explain how they morally link up with the interests or agency or rationality of individual persons. That is, the critics charge that Rawls needs to address the questions addressed by Gewirth and Griffin.

6 CONCLUSION

Three contemporary philosophical conceptions of human rights have been surveyed. Gewirth and Griffin each theorize human rights as moral rights justified by reference to a moral conception of the nature or good of persons claimed to be universally true. They each offer theories with the potential, at least, to satisfy those who hunger for deep, comprehensive, moral foundations for human rights. Rawls, on the other hand, offers a 'political' conception of human rights. Of course, he too theorizes human rights as moral rights, but not as general moral rights in the fashion of Gewirth or Griffin. Instead, Rawls views human rights as moral rights tied explicitly from the start to the political domain of international relations and international law, giving special emphasis to the relationship between human rights and justified coercion (or, alternatively, justified toleration) within international

[35] See Martin and Reidy (eds), *Rawls's Law of Peoples: A Realistic Utopia?* (Wiley-Blackwell, 2006) 263–77.

relations. Gewirth and Griffin reject this approach. For them, the requirements of international tolerance do not define what human rights are, although those considerations may bear on the application or implementation of human rights. Human rights themselves, for Gewirth and Griffin, are determined by moral considerations prior to and independent of the practical political question of coercion (or toleration) within the international order.

All three theorists surveyed in this chapter are 'liberals' in the sense that they have a strong commitment to individual liberty. All give a central place in their theories to the interest in effective and autonomous choice and action. And all are committed to a conception of human rights that includes fundamental freedoms such as freedom of conscience, expression, and assembly—although Rawls's commitments in this area are less robust than Gewirth's and Griffin's. On the other hand, the values of fairness and reciprocity play a larger role in Rawls's account of human rights. Just as Rawls justifies his account of the liberal democratic rights necessary to a just state by reference to an ideal of fair cooperation reciprocally affirmed by free and equal citizens, so too he justifies his account of the human rights necessary to a just international order by reference to an ideal of fair cooperation reciprocally affirmed by free and equal peoples (whether just or decent).

Like most contemporary human rights theorists, Gewirth, Griffin, and Rawls are each committed to including at least minimal economic and social rights as genuine human rights. And Rawls argues that just and decent states have a duty to assist 'burdened' societies—societies unable to fulfil basic human rights, including basic economic and social rights—in becoming well-ordered states within which basic human rights are fulfilled.

Philosophical debates over human rights have advanced considerably in recent decades. While there are still important disagreements, there is today general (though still not universal) philosophical agreement that there are human rights; that they include rights both negative and positive, and both political and economic; and that they are among the weightiest moral considerations bearing on the choices we make as we act in an increasingly interconnected world.

FURTHER READING

DONNELLY, *Universal Human Rights in Theory and Practice* (Cornell University Press, 2002).

FINNIS, *Natural Law and Natural Rights* (Clarendon Press, 1979).

GOULD, *Globalizing Democracy and Human Rights* (Cambridge University Press, 2004).

KYMLICKA, *Liberalism, Community, and Culture* (Clarendon Press, 1989).

NICKEL, *Making Sense of Human Rights* (Wiley-Blackwell, 2006).

NUSSBAUM, *Women and Human Development: The Capabilities Approach* (Cambridge University Press, 2000).

POGGE, *World Poverty and Human Rights: Cosmopolitan Responsibilities and Reforms* (Polity Press, 2002).

SEN, *Development as Freedom* (Oxford University Press, 2001).

SHUE, *Basic Rights: Subsistence, Affluence, and US Foreign Policy* (Princeton University Press, 1996).

THOMSON, *The Realm of Rights* (Harvard University Press, 1992).

WOLTERSTORF, *Justice: Rights and Wrongs* (Princeton University Press, 2007).

USEFUL WEBSITES

Stanford Encyclopedia of Philosophy: <**http://plato.stanford.edu/**>

Internet Encyclopedia of Philosophy: <**http://www.iep.utm.edu/**>

3

CRITIQUES

Marie-Bénédicte Dembour

SUMMARY

Whether they are conceived as the rights that every human being *has*, thus 'naturally' setting limits to the legitimate action of states and others, or as principles of good political action which society *agrees* to adopt and follow, human rights have always been subjected to intense and perceptive critiques. This chapter reviews six such critiques, deriving from realist, utilitarian, Marxist, particularist (cultural relativist), feminist, and postcolonial theoretical perspectives. The first three critiques emerged in reaction to the (successive) French Declarations of the Rights of Man of the late eighteenth century; the last three were fully developed in reaction to the International Bill of Rights enacted after the Second World War. Each of these critiques reveals a gap between what human rights claim to be or achieve, on the one hand, and what human rights are or do in practice, on the other. The question arises as to whether this gap is bridgeable. The critiques answer this question in various ways.[1]

1 INTRODUCTION

Do human rights embody the promise of a solution to problems of bad governance? Not necessarily so. There always have been and continue to be persuasive critiques of the concept of human rights. This chapter reviews six such critiques, emanating respectively from realist, utilitarian, Marxist, particularist (cultural relativist), feminist, and, finally, postcolonial theoretical perspectives.

Before understanding a critique, the concept it is critiquing first needs to be understood. This is not the context, however, to discuss in detail what human rights are.[2] Suffice it to say here that this chapter is written with the understanding that human rights orthodoxy has been moving from conceiving human rights as a given ('natural

---

[1] Parts of this chapter draw upon *Who Believes in Human Rights?: Reflections on the European Convention* © Marie-Bénédicte Dembour (CUP, 2006) extracts reproduced with permission.

[2] But see Chapter 2, above.

school') to conceiving them as values and principles which are agreed upon ('deliberative school'). For ease of terms, the natural school will be referred to as the 'old orthodoxy' and the deliberative school as the 'new orthodoxy', even though this terminology may suggest that the understanding of human rights at any one time is clearly set. It is not. Human rights are a highly contested concept.[3]

In one way or another, each of the six critiques reviewed in this chapter points to a gap between the promise that every human being enjoys a number of fundamental rights and a world where human rights violations abound and many people are excluded from the enjoyment of human rights; that is, a gap between the human rights ideal and practice. Why is there such a gap? Two rather different answers are possible. The gap can be thought to exist *either* because the practice has, so far, failed to live up to the theory, but without this affecting the validity of the concept of human rights, *or* because human rights cannot be what they are said to be, making the concept invalid. In other words, critiques of human rights can either require human rights to be true to their word or reject them as constructed on unsound premises. These two positions correspond to what will be called in this chapter the practical and the conceptual critiques of human rights.

Practical critiques conceive of problems with human rights as demanding that a better practice be elaborated. The problems that such critiques identify are various and include, in a non-exhaustive list, the existence of double standards in the application of human rights, the fact that powerful non-state actors largely remain outside the human rights compass, the relative neglect of economic and social rights, the status of collective rights, the implications of environmental degradation, overzealous responses to the terrorist threat, and so on.[4] Practical critiques accept the idea of human rights, but demand that human rights be made to work better in the face of challenges. Crucially, they do not suggest that the concept is irretrievably defective. They 'simply' ask for the gap between what the concept promises and what it delivers to be closed, believing that human rights must and *can* be improved.

In contrast, conceptual critiques conceive of the concept of human rights as fundamentally flawed. They regard problems of bad governance as requiring a solution that lies outside the human rights logic. For them, human rights are not the best way to try to implement the ideas of justice, equality, and humanity which human rights supposedly stand for; better ways have to be found. Obviously those who embrace these views are not *against* human rights in the sense that their aim is not to call for the supposed binary opposite of human rights, namely, violations of human rights. Rather, their view is that the route towards emancipation need not, and perhaps even, *should not*, take the form of human rights.

The critiques reviewed in this chapter have both conceptual and practical variants. To complicate matters further, they often overlap. At the risk of caricature, but

---

[3] See further Dembour, 'What are Human Rights? Four Schools of Thought' (2010) 32 *HRQ* 1.
[4] Some of these problems are discussed in Chapters 25–8, below.

in order to introduce them, an attempt can be made to encapsulate each of them in one sentence. Realists reject the idea that human rights are natural, simply existing out there to be recognized and implemented; they argue that human rights cannot be 'above' or 'beyond' the state but necessarily originate from and are enmeshed within the state. Utilitarians, seeking the common good, oppose the granting of individual rights regardless of the consequences for the common good; they think it is impossible for human rights to be absolute and/or inalienable. Marxists view rights as sustaining the bourgeois order and thus feeding oppression by privileging a particular class to the detriment of the oppressed majority. Particularists object to the idea that moral judgements can be made that hold true across cultures; they call for tolerance of practices that are not comprehensible within the dominant perspective and denounce what they see as the inherent imperialism of human rights, which are not universal but the product of the society which has created them. Feminists attack human rights' pretence of equality and neutrality by observing that rights, which have generally been defined by men, largely bypass the interests and concerns of women; they dispute the idea that human rights are gender-neutral. Postcolonial theorists link human rights to imperialism; they observe that the International Bill of Rights was developed outside any concern for the inequities arising from the colonial situation and that the rise of human rights in political discourse has not signalled an end to inequality.

These critiques encompass variants which dismiss the concept of human rights altogether. When they are conceptual, the critiques tend to hold the human rights logic to be defective in at least four respects. First, the human rights logic is said to present the concept as universal, while the claim that human rights are relevant to all human beings across time and space is not credible in the face of human history. Second, the logic is criticized for celebrating the individual to the neglect of solidarity and other social values. Third, the human rights logic is found to be derived from an abstract reasoning about 'man' which is ill-equipped to assess both the reality of political life and the requirements of social justice. Fourth, the human rights logic is denounced for being oblivious to the way it directly participates in sustaining power relationships and thus fails to produce equality.

For some thinkers, there is a very close connection—almost a conflation—between human rights and liberalism, understood as the political philosophy that either holds that government should interfere as little as possible in the lives of its citizens or signifies, more broadly, 'an order in which the state exists to secure the freedom of individuals on a formally egalitarian basis'.[5] For example, Jack Donnelly refuses to say of the USA that they are a liberal society because they do not realize the very high human rights benchmarks he associates with a liberal society.[6] At the opposite end of such a conflation, it is increasingly common for scholars to bemoan the 'hijacking' of human

---

[5] In a definition borrowed from Brown, 'Neo-Liberalism and the End of Liberal Democracy' (2003) 7 *Theory and Event* 6.

[6] Donnelly, *Universal Human Rights in Theory and Practice* (Cornell University Press, 1989) 68 and 73.

rights by liberalism.[7] This position might suggest that conceptual critiques of human rights necessarily stand opposed to or outside liberalism. However, it is possible to oppose the concept of human rights (as understood under the old orthodoxy) on liberal grounds. A resounding illustration is provided by Jeremy Bentham, a utilitarian firmly belonging to the liberal tradition, who, as we shall now see, famously qualified human rights as 'nonsense upon stilts'.[8]

2 EARLY CRITIQUES

2.1 THE REALIST CRITIQUE

Considering the old orthodoxy which viewed human rights as a given, it is not surprising that human rights have typically first been *declared* before being turned into conventional law. This practice can be traced back to the two French Declarations of the Rights of Man and the Citizen of the eighteenth century (French Declarations) and, in the contemporary era, the 1948 Universal Declaration of Human Rights (UDHR) (which was directly inspired by the French Declarations). Why is there this tradition of 'declaring' rights? In contemporary international law it is, of course, important to distinguish between a declaration, which has no binding force, and a convention, which has binding force for those states that have ratified it. This crucial distinction, however, cannot have been the reason why the French National Assembly entitled the document it adopted in 1789 'Declaration'. The preamble of the Declaration spoke of the need to 'set forth in a solemn declaration, the natural, inalienable, and sacred rights of man'. It purported to have done this 'in the presence and under the auspices of the Supreme Being'. Clearly, the intention was to spell out the belief that human rights were being *declared* rather than created. This idea is also found in the UDHR, albeit more implicitly, in line with the fact that an exact convergence on the foundations of human rights was, in the more plural context of the UN, lacking. The UDHR laconically refers to a 'faith in fundamental human rights'.[9]

The implications of believing that human rights pre-exist any legislative or social recognition have been helpfully spelled out by Louis Henkin: 'Implied in one's humanity, human rights are inalienable and imprescriptible: they cannot be transferred, forfeited, or waived; they cannot be lost by having been usurped, or by one's failure to exercise or assert them.'[10] This is another way of saying that human rights are 'natural', existing irrespective of social recognition and so discoverable through reason. These

---

[7] See eg Douzinas, *Human Rights and Empire: The Political Philosophy of Cosmopolitanism* (Routledge-Cavendish, 2007) 24; Stammers, *Human Rights and Social Movements* (Pluto, 2009).

[8] Bentham, 'Anarchical Fallacies. An Examination of the Declaration of the Rights of the Man and the Citizen Decreed by the Constituent Assembly in France' in Bentham, *Selected Writings on Utilitarianism* (Wordsworth, 2000) 381, 405.

[9] Preambular para 5.　　[10] Henkin, *The Age of Rights* (Columbia University Press, 1990) 2.

assumptions were at the core of the old human rights orthodoxy. But they have not been without their detractors. Among these is what is referred to here as the realist critique of human rights, which stresses the man-made origin of human rights and argues that they are not obvious at all.

For present purposes, Jeremy Bentham, popularly known as the father of utilitarianism, can be qualified as a realist. His virulent critique of the 1789 French Declaration argued: '[F]rom *real* laws come real rights; but from *imaginary* laws, from laws of nature, fancied by poets, rhetoricians, and dealers in moral and intellectual poisons, come *imaginary* rights, a bastard brood of monsters, "gorgons and chimeras dire".'[11] For Bentham, it was clear that the French Declaration was 'nonsense upon stilts' and the rights it declared imaginary. Not only did these rights not exist, but making people believe they existed was dangerous, for their inevitable disrespect would lead to discontent, and possibly in turn, insurrection. Bentham's critique was published under the title 'Anarchical Fallacies', which said it all. The Declaration was *conceptually* fallacious—a nonsensical flow of words amounting to nothing more than a bundle of contradictions. It also presented a *practical* problem as the promise of rights that could not be respected in practice invited a perpetual overthrowing of political institutions. As far as Bentham was concerned, the rights proclaimed in the Declaration were a 'mere effusion of imbecility'.[12] For him, the way to deal with abusive government was to induce the legislator to change the law, not to call for its abandonment in the name of non-existent natural rights.

Bentham argued that the rights of the French Declaration, if taken literally, meant nothing. For example, he noted that, contrary to what the Declaration stated, human beings are obviously not born equal. In Bentham's opinion, the drafters of the Declaration were constantly oscillating between a utopian world, where all men would be equal, and the real world, where they clearly were not. This led them to use ambiguous wording, for example to use 'can' instead of 'ought' (as in 'every man can do this' instead of 'every man ought to be able to do this').[13] If the rights of the Declaration were not to be taken literally, then they still meant nothing as they would need to be given limits. For example, Article 10 guaranteed freedom of expression and religion. However, it accepted exceptions governed by public order considerations. Bentham derided: 'Disturb the public order?—what does that mean? Louis XIV need not have hesitated about receiving an article thus worded into his code.'[14] Of liberty, he said:

Suppose a declaration to this effect—no man's liberty shall be abridged in any point. This, it is evident, would be an useless extravagance, which must be contradicted by every law that came to be made. Suppose it to say—no man's liberty shall be abridged, but in such points as it shall be abridged in, by the law. This, we see, is saying nothing: it leaves the law just as free and unfettered as it found it.[15]

---

[11] n 8, 458 (original emphases).   [12] Ibid, 441.   [13] Ibid, 402 and 393.
[14] Ibid, 435.   [15] Ibid, 387.

Giving or recognizing supposedly 'natural', 'superior', 'inalienable', 'fundamental' rights which can then be defeated through legislation amounts to *nothing*. Bentham concluded: 'Look to the letter, you find nonsense—look beyond the letter, you find nothing.'[16]

Bentham's critique was very much directed at the old human rights orthodoxy, which regarded human rights as natural—a given. For a realist critique of human rights in their new, increasingly dominant conception—as agreed upon through a deliberative process—one can turn to International Relations (IR). IR realism holds the state as the key actor on the international scene, and one which always follows its own interests.[17] According to one of its long dominant variants, the state does whatever is required to ensure its own survival and, what is more, acts morally when it does as, in this pursuit, it should not be guided by private morality. The idea that political ethics should be brought into line with private ethics is thought 'not only ill-advised but also irresponsible:...not only mistaken intellectually but also fundamentally wrong morally'.[18] In this perspective, given the ill-advisability of cooperation with other states that by definition also follow their own interests and cannot be trusted, *raison d'état* (literally, reason of state, an idea linked to realpolitik) is a fundamental concept and state sovereignty a chief concern. Human rights have no real place.

Not all IR realist scholars are of the persuasion described above. For some, that states are unwilling to act in ways which restrict their power is an empirical fact, but not a moral precept. Starting from the observation that states cling to power as much and as long as they can, these scholars argue that if states act in apparently immoral ways, it is because it is in their interests to do so, not because they (should) follow a public morality different from the one governing relations between individuals. Realism, in this variant, is not a moral vision but an inescapable fact. These realists are wary of the idea that states might ever truly approach a document such as the UDHR as 'a common standard of achievement for all peoples and all nations'—whatever its preamble asserts. They would be quick to point out how human rights law is yet another sphere where states play their power games, as evidenced by reservation clauses and derogations which let them off the hook or the double standards they apply.[19] At best, then, human rights provide protection akin to a sandbag, holding back the bulk of the water/government's arbitrariness and oppression—for as long as the tide/repressive impulse is not too strong.

Like all 'isms', realism can mean many things. What the realisms of Bentham and IR have in common is that, taking a realistic look at the world, they reject the idea that human rights could somehow exist 'above' or 'aside from' the state. For them, human rights belong to the imagination of utopian dreamers. In Bentham's case, this is because the French Declaration did not provide a positive legal framework which made the declared rights real. In the case of today's realists, it is because they do not

---

[16] Ibid, 397.   [17] Jackson and Sørensen, *Introduction to International Relations* (OUP, 1999) 96.

[18] Ibid, 77.

[19] See eg Mertus, *Bait and Switch: Human Rights and US Foreign Policy* (Routledge, 2004).

believe that states wish to submit to either the spirit or the letter of the human rights declarations and conventions that are supposedly now guiding the international community.

2.2 THE UTILITARIAN CRITIQUE

Bentham, a towering figure of the utilitarian movement, dismissed the predecessor of human rights (the rights of man) as 'nonsense upon stilts'. Does this mean that utilitarianism is irretrievably opposed to human rights? Yes and no. On the one hand, the logic of utilitarianism is such that it cannot accept the idea of absolute and inalienable rights, which at first sight seems central to human rights orthodoxy—at least in its old version. On the other hand, individual rights being obviously conducive to the happiness of a great number of individuals, utilitarianism can act as a strident defender of human rights. Why these two apparently contradictory positions coexist requires understanding the nature of both utilitarianism and human rights orthodoxy.

Utilitarianism is the ethical philosophy that posits that an action must be judged morally by reference to the welfare (utility) it produces. It holds that the good act is the one that maximizes happiness. Such a philosophy is consequentialist: it judges actions by reference to their consequences. Before deciding on a course of action, utilitarianism demands that the action's likely effects on various interests be considered and weighed. In other words, it does not believe in *a priori* judgements as to the value of some good (in the sense of an interest worthy of protection) over other goods.

The trade-offs that utilitarianism never rules out have led its detractors to intimate that it allows the individual to be sacrificed to the collective interest. One healthy person, so the argument goes, could be killed under utilitarianism for the benefit of a number of people who depend for their survival on the transplant of various organs. In a similar vein, an innocent could be found guilty in order to defuse a riotous situation when his condemnation would appear to facilitate a return to peace and order. These kinds of scenarios, however, are more often than not put forward by thinkers who oppose utilitarianism. Self-declared utilitarians observe that they are unlikely to present themselves in the clear-cut form imagined by their detractors.[20] Utilitarians are quick to note that repeated sacrifices of individuals would immediately generate a substantial decrease in general happiness because of the sense of insecurity it would foster across the population.

Many utilitarians are thus wary of the concept of individual sacrifice for the collective good which utilitarianism supposedly supports. Nonetheless, it remains that utilitarianism does not accept the idea that some rights are absolute and inalienable. By contrast, this idea is at the core of (the old) human rights orthodoxy. To understand the crucial difference between these two positions, one must understand what makes a right absolute.

---

[20] Häyri, *Liberal Utilitarianism and Applied Ethics* (Routledge, 1994) 80.

For a right to be absolute, the corresponding duty to which it gives rise must be expressed in a negative form. Let us take the example of the right to be free from torture, one of the few rights to be considered absolute in human rights orthodoxy. To respect this right, it might be thought that governments must do one thing and one thing only: *refrain from* inflicting torture. Clearly, this is a negative duty: that of *not acting* in a certain way. If this reasoning is followed, there is only one way to respect the right not to be tortured; hence its infringement is easy to establish (at least in principle). Now, rights which are not absolute are relative. Their respect is relative to many things; it is never easy, in the sense of clear-cut, to establish when they are, in fact, respected. A standard example of relative rights is economic and social rights. Their respect requires the state to provide education, healthcare, and so on, that is, *to act* in a certain way. Endless discussions can be had as to whether a state has done enough to fulfil its positive obligations in that respect. A positive obligation is by nature unclear, in the sense of never strictly defined.

Logically, only a negative obligation can give rise to an absolute right. In turn, thinking in these terms entails categorical reasoning. To return to the example of the prohibition of torture, human rights orthodoxy considers torture to be intrinsically wrong: it considers that torture is and always will be wrong, whatever the circumstances. This is based on deontological philosophy, which holds that some things have an intrinsic, categorical, not-consequential value.[21]

By contrast, utilitarianism is a consequentialist theory which evaluates the morality of an action by reference to its consequences. Utilitarianism does not ask, 'Is this wrong?' but, 'Is this *causing* wrong?' It does not hold anything to have intrinsic value as such. A utilitarian cannot rule out, once and for all, the possibility that one day utility will require a right to be set aside in order to further the collective good. This is true in particular of the right to be free from torture, even though it is difficult to imagine *sound* utilitarian reasoning justifying it easily. It is worth stressing in this respect that the would-be convincing scenario of the ticking bomb is not very convincing at all: the police would know everything, including who has the vital information, except for the single element of where the bomb is—how likely is this? Even if this unlikely scenario were to happen in practice, there would still be strong utilitarian arguments against the use of torture, including the corrupting effect of having to train officials to inflict it.[22] Having said this, it remains that the consequential logic of utilitarianism makes it ill-fitted to defend human rights in all cases. Does this mean that there is an unbridgeable divide between utilitarianism and human rights orthodoxy?

In many ways, utilitarianism and human rights have in practice always been largely compatible. A long tradition within utilitarianism, going back to John Stuart Mill, has never stopped to defend human rights for being conducive to the common good. Allan Gibbard argues, from a self-avowed utilitarian perspective, that rights contribute to

---

[21] See Chapter 2, above.   [22] Brecher, *Torture and the Ticking Bomb* (Blackwell, 2007) ch 2.

good institutional design.[23] Conversely, starting from the other end of the relationship, the human rights orthodoxy has always been replete with utilitarian considerations, as the numerous possible limitations of human rights in the name of public consid- erations (such as public order, health, or morality) and the concept of proportional- ity (requiring different interests to be balanced), central to human rights law, readily demonstrate.[24] More generally, the old human rights orthodoxy has had to give way: while its emphasis on clear-cut negative rights should have generated a relatively well- delimited list of 'core' rights,[25] what has happened instead is a continual identification of 'new' rights as well as a recognition that positive obligations attach to *all* rights— including the right to be free from torture, which also entails action by the state, such as appropriate training of the police force, for its full implementation.[26]

The compatibility between human rights and utilitarianism is arguably deepening today as human rights orthodoxy increasingly slides from 'natural' logic into 'delib- erative' mode. The latter tends to regard human rights as guiding principles of good governance (rather than firm entitlements). It conceives of human rights as being agreed upon, the result of a consensus most evident in the development of interna- tional human rights law, rather than constituted as a universal given which exists outside social recognition. The 'deliberative' orientation of the new orthodoxy makes it possible for some thinkers to refer explicitly to utilitarian considerations (admit- tedly alongside other ones) in order to justify human rights.[27] This would have been unthinkable under the old orthodoxy. The divide between utilitarianism and human rights is ceasing to be the great chasm once intimated both by 'the father of utilitarian- ism' (as Bentham came to be known) and by human rights defenders. Having said this, it remains relatively rare for human rights to be defended today from a perspective which is conspicuously utilitarian in its inspiration.

2.3 THE MARXIST CRITIQUE

For Karl Marx, far from being nonsense, the French Declaration was problematic because it made too much sense in the political order of the so-called 'free state' which had followed the French Revolution but had not succeeded in emancipating man. (Marx did not think much about women.)

Marx's essay 'On the Jewish Question', written at the tender age of 23, was implacable in its critique of the French Declaration of the Rights of Man and the Citizen of 1791. The essay denounced the rights of man as being 'nothing but the rights of the member of civil society, i.e. egoistic man, man separated from other men and the community'.[28]

---

[23] Gibbard, 'Utilitarianism and Human Rights' in Paul, Miller Jr, and Paul (eds), *Human Rights* (Blackwell, 1984) 92.

[24] See Chapter 6, below.

[25] Dembour, *Who Believes in Human Rights? Reflections on the European Convention* (CUP, 2006) 87. See also Chapter 8, below.

[26] See Chapter 10, below.   [27] Nickel, *Making Sense of Human Rights* (Blackwell, 2007) 58–61.

[28] 'On the Jewish Question', reproduced in McLellan, *Karl Marx: Selected Writings* (OUP, 2000) 46, 60.

The right to liberty, the young Marx argued, was the right to do anything which does not harm others, that is, the liberty of man 'as an isolated monad...withdrawn into himself'; the right to private property was the right to enjoy and dispose of one's possessions 'arbitrarily, without regard for other men, independently from society, the right of selfishness'. The right to equality represented nothing else but access to liberty as described above; the right to security provided the guarantee of egoism.[29] Marx concluded: 'Thus none of the so-called rights of man goes beyond egoistic man, man as he is in civil society, namely an individual withdrawn behind his private interests and whims and separated from the community. Far from the rights of man conceiving of man as a species-being, species-life itself, society, appears as a framework exterior to individuals.'[30]

A question mark has been raised on the value to be assigned to Marx's early writings in Marxist theory. Marx's early work grappled with philosophy and was explicitly interested in discussing the nature of man; his mature work was devoted to the 'scientific' study of material conditions, leading him to identify the 'laws of motion' of capitalism and to elaborate a theory of history as progress through stages conditioned by society's attained level of productivity and the requirements of increase. While Louis Althusser forcefully rejected the relevance of Marx's 'pre-scientific' writings, Erik Fromm relied on these early works to develop a humanist interpretation of Marxism and denounce the claims of 'scientific Marxism', especially as propounded in the Soviet Union.

If the absence of a break in Marx's works is accepted, 'On the Jewish Question' appears recognizably Marxian in its denunciation of human alienation. The essay cautions that man is not yet free in the free state.[31] While it recognizes that political emancipation may have been achieved, it argues that this falls short of human emancipation. The rights granted in the political state newly created in France supposedly endow man with freedom; but, in fact, they alienate him. Why? Because they split the 'citizen' from the 'bourgeois' in the individual. The 'citizen' part of man corresponds to the public self and belongs to the political state; the 'bourgeois' part corresponds to the private self and belongs to civil society.[32] In the political state, Marx argues, man is condemned to lead a double life. This is the more serious since the citizen (the part where man regards himself as a communal being) is put at the service of the bourgeois (the part where man acts as a private individual and leads an egoistic life). Man is thus alienated from his true self which is to be a species-being where the individual interest corresponds to everyone else's interest.

'On the Jewish Question' can also be read in the light of the concept of ideology which Marx developed fully in his later work. As an ideology, the rights declared in France announce and guarantee man's liberty. However, what they really do is to mask and sustain the inequality and oppression characteristic of capitalist society. Applying this reading to the contemporary era, the anthropologist Talal Asad urges us to 'examine critically the assumption that...human rights always lead in an emancipatory

---

[29] Ibid.   [30] Ibid, 61.   [31] Ibid, 51.   [32] Ibid, 53; see also 57.

direction, that they enable subjects to move beyond controlling power into the realm of freedom'.[33] In Asad's view, the language of human rights 'articulates inequalities in social life'.[34] It is therefore doubtful that the human rights project could bring about 'practical equality and an end to all suffering'.[35]

That real emancipation cannot be expected through human rights is an idea that was explicitly stated in 'On the Jewish Question'. Marx believed that true emancipation would come through the establishment of a society where man would be able to 'take the abstract citizen back into himself and ... become a species-being', recognizing his own forces as social forces.[36] Under communism, he believed, the institutions of state, law, and property would have withered away. The political state—and its declaration of the rights of man and citizen—represented a necessary stage in the progression towards communism. But it was only a step. In Marx's words: 'Political emancipation is of course a great progress. Although it is not the final form of human emancipation in general, it is nevertheless the final form of human emancipation inside the present world order.'[37]

History has shown that Marx's belief in the establishment of a communist society true to his words was ridiculously naive. Not surprisingly perhaps given the utopian character of his project, Marx failed to indicate anywhere in his work how the transformation from bourgeois man to species-being would be achieved. He did mention 'a political transition period in which the state [could] be nothing but the revolutionary dictatorship of the proletariat',[38] but without working out its details. Taken as a political programme, Marx's writings were at best hollow, at worst dangerous. Had they had little impact, this would not have mattered much. But Marx, who died in 1883, inspired revolutions and dictatorships throughout the world, starting in 1917 in what became the Soviet Union. The most appalling acts were committed in the twentieth century in the name of Marxism and communism. It is probably disingenuous to criticize a thinker for ideas that have been used in a way that he could not have imagined and to hold him partly, if unwillingly, responsible for the Stalinist gulag. But many did exactly that. At the same time, during the Cold War, others continued to profess their faith in Marxism, refusing to acknowledge the terror which Marxist ideas, taken to a logical extreme, could inspire.

There were exceptions. For example, the British Marxist historian EP Thompson did not end *Whigs and Hunters*, his study of the eighteenth century 'Black Act',[39] with a conventional Marxian conclusion. This would have been that 'law is an instrument of brute force by which the ruling class consolidates and reinforces its hegemony'.[40] In an afterword which made him controversial in Marxist circles, Thompson stated instead that the rule of law is an 'unqualified human good'.[41] This qualification was

---

[33] Asad, 'What Do Human Rights Do? An Anthropological Enquiry' (2000) 27 *Theory and Event* 40.
[34] Ibid, 43.   [35] Ibid, 57.   [36] n 28, 64.   [37] Ibid, 54.
[38] Marx, 'Critique of the Gotha Programme' reproduced in McLellan, n 28, 610, 611.
[39] Thompson, *Whigs and Hunters: The Origins of the Black Act* (Allen Lane, 1975).
[40] Cole, '"An Unqualified Human Good": EP Thompson and the Rule of Law' (2001) 28 *J Law & Soc* 177, 181.
[41] Thompson, n 39, 266.

spurred by his disturbing experience of the Soviet regime which had led him to resign his membership of the Communist Party in 1956. Thompson wanted to stress the 'very large difference...between arbitrary extra-legal power and the rule of law [which] may disguise the true realities of power, but, at the same time,...may curb that power and check its intrusions'.[42] He declared the rule of law—to which he would likely have readily associated human rights law—'a cultural achievement of universal significance'.[43] This attracted the ire of many fellow Marxist thinkers.

It could be asked, 'Who were/are the true Marxists?' This question is controversial, with one person often accusing another of abusing Marxism. What is not disputed, however, is that the way Marx analysed power relationships and examined how things are not as they seem left a mark on all the social sciences. This is clear, in particular, in respect of the human rights critiques reviewed below.

3 MORE RECENT CRITIQUES

3.1 THE CULTURAL RELATIVIST OR PARTICULARIST CRITIQUE

The universal versus cultural relativist debate can be said to have been spurred by discussions generated by the UDHR. In 1947, the year before the UDHR was adopted, the American Anthropological Association (AAA) addressed a 'Statement on Human Rights' to the UN Commission on Human Rights, which was drafting it.[44] The Statement asked: 'How can the proposed Declaration be applicable to all human beings, and not be a statement of rights conceived only in terms of the values prevalent in the countries of Western Europe and America?'[45] It argued for the need to seek respect for the individual both as individual and as member of 'his' society (at a time when feminist concerns were still very much out of public consciousness). Bearing in mind the cultural destruction heralded by colonialism, imperialism, and the very establishment of the USA (not least in respect of native Americans), it called for 'respect for the cultures of differing human groups'.

The AAA Statement was right in arguing that the formulation of human rights cannot but derive from a particular culture. The UDHR is replete with concepts, such as legal personality (Article 6), nationality (Article 15), and protection against unemployment (Article 23), which are simply not known to most human societies. The concept of human rights itself is not incontrovertible in humankind's repertoire. If the Statement rightly cautioned that no declaration could ever manage to identify universal human rights valid for all humankind across time and space, it was nonetheless problematic in other respects. It treated culture as a static and homogeneous 'thing' rather than the

---

[42] Ibid, 265.   [43] Ibid.
[44] See 'Statement on Human Rights' (1947) 49 *American Anthropologist* 539.
[45] Ibid.

dynamic and contested process that anthropologists have now demonstrated culture always is.[46] Moreover, it lent itself to be taken to call for the respect of any cultural trait, simply because of its cultural nature; which is ethically unacceptable. In other words, the Statement bore the mark of cultural relativism, the core tenet of US anthropology in the 1920s and 1930s which, with time, increasingly came to appear untenable.

But what do we mean by 'cultural relativism'? The theory is founded on the double observation that moral systems are embedded in culture and that different cultures produce different moralities. However, to become an 'ism', ethical inferences must be derived from these (assuredly sound) empirical observations. What are these inferences? According to its detractors, cultural relativism would dictate tolerance of any culturally embedded moral system on earth, perhaps even any morality. However, whether self-declared cultural relativists hold this position is doubtful.[47]

Recognizing that different societies hold different values need not logically lead to the conclusion that all these different values and practices must be tolerated. The observation that cultures produce different moral norms does not say anything about the respective value of these norms.[48] Despite this, and no doubt also due to excessive formulations by its proponents, cultural relativism came to be denigrated for demanding that the intolerable be tolerated. The doctrine is even said to have been an embarrassment to anthropologists, because of the indifference and/or inaction which it advocated.[49] It has also been criticized for lending itself to abuse, allowing those in power to make spurious or disingenuous cultural arguments in pursuit of their own political ends.[50] Undoubtedly, cultural relativism, like other theories, has been abused, and the last point must indeed be conceded. This, however, should not detract from appreciating what the doctrine offers.

In the words of anthropologist Elvin Hatch, the 'good side' of relativism is that it highlights the difficulty of 'establishing reasonable and general grounds for making moral judgments about the actions of others' and the 'strong tendency among the more powerful peoples of the world to use their own standards, or standards favourable to them, in their relations with others'.[51] Put more simply, the doctrine acts as a counterpart to the arrogance and abusive effect of universalism. This is vital, given the imperialism which has accompanied and still accompanies human rights enunciation and practice.

The universality of human rights is *not* a fact. At best, human rights universal*ism* is a theory. It is a worthwhile project, directed at discussing, agreeing upon, and practising principles of governance which should benefit all individuals equally, but which

---

[46] Cowan, Dembour, and Wilson (eds), *Culture and Rights: Anthropological Perspectives* (CUP, 2001).

[47] See eg Herskovits, *Cultural Relativism: Perspectives in Cultural Pluralism* (Random House, 1972) 64.

[48] Renteln, 'Relativism and the Search for Human Rights' (1988) 90 *American Anthropologist* 56, 64.

[49] Engle, 'From Skepticism to Embrace: Human Rights and the American Anthropological Association from 1947–1999' (2001) 23 *HRQ* 536. For a more nuanced view, see Goodale, *Surrendering to Utopia: An Anthropology of Human Rights* (Stanford University Press, 2009) ch 2.

[50] Pollis, 'Cultural Relativism Revisited: Through a State Prism' (1996) 18 *HRQ* 316.

[51] Hatch, 'The Good Side of Relativism' (1997) 53 *J Anthropological Research* 371, 372.

also has a dark side which it would be either disingenuous or naive not to recognize. This dark side includes the inherent danger not to respect the ways of others, if not an active collusion in their destruction. Universalists too often assume that they are on firm ground in making judgements about others. They can easily end up imposing their ways on others for no other reason than sheer dominant position, without even realizing this, so full are they of their good intentions. By contrast, instead of saying 'we know best' or 'we know', relativism poses the question, 'What do we know?'

Universalism has a good side—the elaboration of minimal common standards—but it also has a bad side—arrogance. Similarly, relativism has a good side—respect for different ways—but it also has a bad side—inaction or indifference. Let us think about the implications of this conceptual matrix with a concrete example. In 1994, an 18-year-old US citizen was sentenced in Singapore to six lashes for spray-painting parked cars.[52] Let us first judge the caning abhorrent, assaulting the dignity of the young man. If so, universalism should be applauded for making it possible to condemn the punishment, while relativism would show only its bad side by calling for inaction when resistance is called for. Another assessment, however, is to say that the caning is a legitimate part in the disciplinary framework put in place in a society largely different from ours. If so, universalism would be showing its bad side by condemning the practice while it is relativism which should be welcome for letting the punishment be. What some regard as an expression of the good side of relativism is *always* regarded by others as an expression of its bad side, and the same is true of universalism (see Table 3.1). Applying the conceptual matrix to concrete situations and deciding which position is which is rarely easy; nor is it uncontroversial.

Table 3.1 The universalism vs relativism matrix

	Universalism	Relativism
Good side	Respect for common standards	Respect for difference
	(caning is abhorrent)	*(caning is OK)*
Bad side	Arrogance	Indifference
	(caning is abhorrent)	*(caning is OK)*

Wishing the controversy away will not do. It arises *every time* common standards are predicated, whatever the limits of the constituency—the whole world, a regional system, a nation, a village. Establishing common standards is never completely unproblematic because minimal common standards are never entirely common. However small the relevant constituency, it always stands in the way of more peculiar, or particular, norms.

Universalism cannot exist independently of its opposite, most aptly named 'particularism'. (Etymologically, what is not universal is special, specific, or particular;

[52] Hubbard, 'Singapore shrugs off uproar over "barbaric" flogging', *The Independent* 2 April 1994.

what is not relative is absolute. Using the word 'particularism' presents the further advantage of avoiding both the possibly reifying tone of the reference to 'culture' and the embarrassment of the faint moral position commonly associated with 'cultural relativism'.) It is in opposition to practices that appear abhorrent that universal norms are being set, and it is by reference to local particularities that these universal norms are implemented. The reverse is true. Particularism does not exist independent of universalism. As moral beings concerned with ethics, we are not just beings of culture but respond to what could be termed the call of universalism. This is to say that we are always somewhere between the ideal represented by universalism (which should be recognized as an ideal) and the reality of our being embedded in culture (which is inescapable). We are bound to oscillate between the two positions in a pendulum-like motion.[53]

The debate between universalism and particularism is not primarily concerned with the reaction by the rest of the world to something which originated in the West. Its essence is to capture the difficult and always controversial accommodation of unity and diversity in mankind. While the debate was obviously pertinent under the old orthodoxy where human rights were conceived as a given, it remains relevant under the new orthodoxy. The reason why the debate cannot be put to rest once and for all is that we do not have a choice between being either universalists or particularists: we must be both at the same time. Similarly, human rights law must accommodate both positions—whether it does so explicitly or not. (This contributes to an explanation of, for example, the development of the doctrine of the margin of appreciation in the European Convention system whereby the European Court of Human Rights often asserts that local authorities are in principle in a better position than an international court to assess local requirements.) Properly understood, the particularist critique is less a critique than a corrective to the ever-possible excesses of universalism. These excesses remain a danger under the new human rights orthodoxy, for the human rights values supposedly agreed upon at any given level (international, regional, or national) rarely derive from a consensus as broad as believed by those who unreservedly declare their commitment to them.

3.2 THE FEMINIST CRITIQUE

In 1789, the first article of the French Declaration proudly stated: 'Men are born and remain free and equal in rights.' One year later, Olympe de Gouges asserted in a 'Declaration of the Rights of Woman', of her own making: 'Women are born free and remain equal to men in rights.'[54] This stance did not go down well. On 3 November

---

[53] Dembour, 'Following the Movement of the Pendulum: Between Universalism and Relativism' in Cowan *et al.*, n 46, 56.

[54] De Gouges's Declaration is reproduced in Ishay (ed), *The Human Rights Reader: Major Political Writings, Essays, Speeches and Documents. From the Bible to the Present* (Routledge, 1997) 140–7. My translation of Art 1 is slightly different from that of Ishay, who offers: 'Woman is born free and lives equal to man in her rights.'

1793, de Gouges was guillotined—like a man—for having forgotten the virtues of her sex and inappropriately sought to become a statesman. A feminist critique of human rights was then largely silenced, but it has now become vigorous. Can the argument that human rights remain predominantly male in their conception and implementation be dismissed in an age when women, especially in the West, have successfully fought for the rights to vote, be educated, manage their property, open a bank account, exercise a profession, receive equal pay for equal work, keep their nationality upon marriage with a foreign man, and so on? The answer is a resounding no. The affirmation in law of women's entitlement to equal rights is assuredly a momentous achievement. While it must be celebrated, it should not lead to complacency. Feminist analyses demonstrate human rights law to have been and continue to be male-oriented.

Before turning to these analyses, it is worth pondering what feminism is. As noted above, virtually all 'isms' have more than one variant. This is certainly the case with feminism, of which the variants are so pronounced that for someone to declare herself—and possibly, though more rarely, himself—a feminist does not say much about her position. One can nonetheless tentatively speak of feminism in the singular. Janet Halley has identified its components as follows:

First, to be feminism, a position must make a distinction between m and f. Different feminisms do this differently: some see men and women; some see male and female; some see masculine and feminine.... And secondly, to be a feminism..., a position must posit some kind of subordination as between m and f, in which f is the disadvantaged or subordinated element. At this point feminism is both descriptive and normative... Feminism is feminism because, as between m and f, it carries a brief for f.[55]

Feminism is a way of looking at the world, seeing it as organized along gendered lines which benefit men, and trying to change it so that women are empowered. In the human rights field, feminist critique has taken a long time to be expressed—or, perhaps more accurately, to be heard. For two centuries, the vibrant and clear message sent by Olympe de Gouges in her Declaration of 1790 remained dormant in human rights scholarship. In the last 30 years, however, feminist critiques of human rights have become inescapable. In 1989, a working bibliography on women's international human rights contained a mere 142 publications and a list of 15 international governmental and NGOs and other sources of information; by 2003, it included approximately 700 articles and 246 links to websites.[56] No doubt the increase has continued to be exponential.

The feminist critique to which human rights have increasingly been subjected does not mean that an agreement has emerged as to what constitutes, and what should be done in respect of, a human rights situation analysed as problematic for women. This is because there are many different ways of being a feminist. Following an admittedly limited, but nonetheless useful, classification followed in various synthesizing works,

---

[55] Halley, 'Take a Break from Feminism?' in Knop (ed), *Gender and Human Rights* (OUP, 2004) 57, 61.
[56] Knop, 'Introduction' in ibid, 1.

this section discusses the liberal, woman's voice, radical, and postmodern strands of feminism.

At the core of the *liberal* feminist strand is the assumption that women are equal to men, with the consequence that women must not in principle be excluded from the rights enjoyed by men—and vice versa. In other words, liberal feminism asks for liberalism to be true to its fundamental intuition that everyone must have their rights guaranteed. Laws that explicitly guarantee, or implicitly endorse, the principle of sex and gender equality constitute its great achievement. Today, this principle is for the most part accepted. However, assessing what it requires in the practice of actual rights is riddled with difficulties. The implementation of a feminist liberal agenda is a far from straightforward matter, the more so since liberal feminism is concerned not simply with the formal allocation of rights but also with the under-representation of women in politically and socially significant positions, as well as their over-representation among the poor.

'But why should a woman want to be treated like a man?', asks a second strand of feminism. In 1982, the book *In a Different Voice* contrasted the logical, abstract, deductive reasoning favoured by boys to the emotional, concrete, and contextual reasoning favoured by girls.[57] Its author, the social psychologist Carol Gilligan, concluded that the masculine model of an 'ethic of rights' is not universal and called for the feminine model of an 'ethic of care' to be valued. Her book established the feminist strand generally known as cultural feminism but referred to here, after Gilligan's title, as *woman's voice* feminism. This strand of feminism has clear implications for human rights. As with other areas of law, human rights law tends to look at individuals as individuals, to decontextualize situations, and to be confrontational; it accordingly has—so the woman's voice argument goes—nothing or little to offer to women who are 'naturally' inclined to think their problems through contextually, for example by assessing the implications of any possible solution for the people for whom they care (including, but not only, their children). Human rights law should either be rejected, or at the very least transformed, in order to accommodate the female way of thinking and acting.[58]

For the leading *radical* feminist Catharine MacKinnon, however, getting women to think of themselves as carers is, in itself, a male trick. The problem is not whether women are equal or different to men; the problem is that men subordinate women. The key issue is women's oppression, whereby men reduce women to their sexuality and use them as sexual objects. In MacKinnon's phrase, 'Man fucks woman: subject, verb, object.'[59] The aim of the radical feminist movement, led in law by MacKinnon, is therefore the empowerment of women—even those who are not aware of the continual sexual oppression to which men subject them because of 'false consciousness'. MacKinnon

[57] Gilligan, *In a Different Voice: Psychologist Theory and Women's Development* (Harvard University Press, 1982).

[58] See eg Hardwig, 'Should Women Think in Terms of Rights?' (1984) 94 *Ethics* 441.

[59] MacKinnon, *Feminism Unmodified: Discourses on Life and Law* (Harvard University Press, 1987) 71. See also her *Toward a Feminist Theory of the State* (Harvard University Press, 1989).

asks that women become women on their own terms: feminism 'unmodified'. One can again immediately see the implications of this strand of feminism for our subject. Far from being neutral, human rights theory and law are on the whole made by men for men. They do not adequately address women's concerns, such as sexual violence in the home, and rely on concepts, such as the public-private dichotomy, which tend to perpetuate men's sexual subordination of women.

In contrast to the strands reviewed above, the important point for *postmodern* feminism is that the situation of one woman is not that of another, so that no woman can speak for all women.[60] Postmodern feminists are therefore well placed to deconstruct the categories of 'woman' and 'gender'. They listen to the 'Other', thus exploring rather than explaining. This leaves them without a definite agenda, for they do not claim to know how to put the world right. Instead, they offer a critique which does not take one definite direction. Their aim is to understand how we come to make sense of the world, including ourselves. Meta-narratives are distrusted, myths debunked, basic concepts questioned. Postmodernism goes hand in hand with a sceptical attitude and a drive to go beyond appearances. This, in particular, is true of human rights and human rights law, which cannot be taken at face value.

The theoretical framework presented above is simplistic. Feminist scholars are not necessarily encompassed by it nor do they all fit neatly within its four categories. Nonetheless, this section should have indicated that there are many ways in which feminists will wish to challenge the human rights orthodoxy, both in its old and new guises.

3.3 THE POSTCOLONIAL CRITIQUE

It is often remarked that it was the atrocities of the Second World War that brought into being the international human rights bill. Some would be ready to thank, admittedly not without irony, Hitler and Stalin for this gift.[61] Others bitterly note that it took the suffering of whites to force the powers that be into action; by comparison, slavery and colonialism left the world indifferent.[62] The postcolonial critique teases out the implications of this observation. At its core is the argument that there were, and continue to be, direct connections between the Enlightenment universalizing project and the history of European and Western conquest. A mild postcolonial critique of human rights shows human rights, as a child of the Enlightenment, not to have been completely immune to the colonial logic which long governed the world. Deeper critiques go further than this and argue that human rights are, to this day, irretrievably entrenched in a colonial logic.

The term 'postcolonial' has been used in many different ways. It emerged first to denote the condition that succeeded the formal passing of colonial rule, but soon

---

[60] See eg Mohanty, 'Under Western Eyes: Feminist Scholarship and Colonial Discourses' (1988) 30 *Feminist Review* 61.

[61] Sieghart, *The Lawful Rights of Mankind: An Introduction to the International Legal Code of Human Rights* (OUP, 1985) 38.

[62] Mutua, *Human Rights: A Political and Cultural Critique* (University of Pennsylvania Press, 2002) 16.

came to denote a variety of theoretical perspectives. The three towering figures of postcolonialism in its theoretical form are commonly recognized to be the late Edward Said, Gayatri Spivak, and Homi Bhabha, three scholars of southern origin who have pursued an academic career in the West and grappled with the question of how the postcolonial subject can understand and overcome the condition of having been born into the abjection of colonialism. Said forever changed the way we look at representation with the publication in 1978 of *Orientalism*: after this book, the way we (academics, journalists, novelists, film makers, common people) represent (study, report, discuss, portray, talk about) the 'Other' could never again appear as a neutral exercise.[63] Spivak asked: 'Can the Subaltern Speak?', directly pointing at the mutedness suffered by those who are not in a position to speak/be heard.[64] More optimistically, Bhabha's development of the concept of 'hybridity' (meaning mixture) seems to promise the possibility of finding a space where we shall be able to speak of Ourselves and Others.[65]

Postcolonialism is many different things. What these things have in common is a commitment 'to critique, expose, deconstruct, counter and (in some claims) to transcend, the cultural and broader ideological legacies and presences of imperialism'.[66] In this phrasing, imperialism is understood as the source of power at the receiving end of which are the colonized, in their physical but also cultural and mental self; colonialism is not understood as pertaining exclusively to the formal colonial era—it existed in the past and continues to exist today under many guises. Postcolonialism is committed to a double task: revealing how the colonial logic imbibes ideas and behaviours, even ones which seemingly have nothing to do with colonialism, and trying to make it possible to hear the experiences of the colonized.

How does this relate to human rights? Listen to Makau Mutua, born 'in a part of colonial Africa that the British had named Kenya'.[67] Mutua recalls how colonialism stripped him of his identity, forcing him to take a Christian name to enter the Church, and then argues:

There was a basic assumption that Christianity was *superior* to, and better than, any African spirituality. It was presented as a cultural package. What is interesting are the parallels between Christianity's violent conquest of Africa and the modern human rights crusade. The same methods are at work and similar cultural dispossessions are taking place, without dialogue or conversation. The official human corpus, which issues from European predicates, seeks to supplant all other traditions, while rejecting them. It claims to be the only genius of the good society.[68]

[63] Said, *Orientalism* (Routledge and Kegan Paul, 1978).
[64] Spivak, 'Can the Subaltern Speak?' in Nelson and Grossberg (eds), *Marxism and the Interpretation of Culture* (University of Illinois Press, 1998).
[65] Bhabha, *The Location of Culture* (Routledge, 1994).
[66] In a formulation borrowed from Sidaway, 'Postcolonial Geographies: An Exploratory Essay' (2000) 24 *Progress in Human Geography* 591, 594.
[67] Mutua, n 62, x.   [68] Ibid, xi (original emphasis).

Contrary to its claims of being inclusive, the idea of human rights was always an exclusionary concept—as Marx and feminists such as de Gouges had perceived from the start. Postcolonial perspectives broaden these early critiques by showing how the supposedly universal and all-encompassing liberal tradition in which human rights were developed nurtured stark differences between 'us' and 'them' on the basis of arguments about civilization, cultural backwardness, and racial superiority. The Enlightenment figure of 'the individual', bearer of human rights, suddenly appears to be full of the arrogance of the West, rather than neutral and innocent. Moreover, even if the presumed existence of an essential difference between us and them is no longer referred to in the explicit language used in the formal colonial era, this arrogance is not something of the past but something which carries on, albeit in new forms. The conduct of international relations in the post-Cold War era has been characterized as follows:

'We' of the West are not inefficient, corrupt or dependent on a benevolent international society for our existence. 'We' are the unquestioned upholders of human rights. 'We' attained positions of privilege and authority as a result of our capacities. "We' of the West are different from 'them'. 'Their' fate could not befall 'us'. 'They' can succeed only if 'they' become more like 'us'. . . . The North is constituted vis-à-vis the South as modern, efficient, competent. The South is constituted as its lack, its other. . . . The incapacity to exercise agency in the same manner as the Western 'self' is repeatedly inscribed in the identity of non-Western 'other'.[69]

The 'civilizing mission' was at the very heart of colonialism's justification and remains so in the deployment of new imperial forms. The bringing of law, and rights, and gender equality are some of its key elements. But the overall achievements of human rights are dubious in the face of continual oppression, hurry for wars, rampant poverty, persistent inequalities in trade, lack of attention to the consequences of global warming, and, more generally, rejection of the 'Other'. In this light, trumpeting the rise of human rights as 'one of the great civilising achievements of the modern era'[70] appears problematic. Postcolonialism asks, 'Is there a sense in which human rights have been "civilizing"?'

A postcolonial critique intimates that the human rights logic has all too often led to the annihilation of the 'Other'. This has occurred not only in respect of their identity—for example through 'assimilation' and the imposition of a Christian name as in Mutua's experience—but also in their physicality—still holding true when, among other current atrocities taking place in the world, wars conducted in the name of human rights entail 'collateral damage' which refer to the death of the 'Other'. There is also a whole spectrum of exclusionary discourse and practices, which the treatment of the deemed illegal or suspected terrorist migrant—barred from entry,

---

[69] Doty, *Imperial Encounters: The Politics of Representation in North-South Relations* (University of Minnesota Press, 1996) 162.

[70] Gearty, *Can Human Rights Survive?* (CUP, 2006) 1.

detained, deported, subjected to extraordinary rendition, tortured, or simply left to die—exemplifies today.

The crucial question for postcolonial critiques therefore is, 'Can human rights be redeemed?' Most seem unwilling to reject human rights outright. In the words of Ratna Kapur: 'We "cannot not want" human rights. Rights are radical tools for those who have never had them. Human rights seems a preferable, though a flawed ideal, to no rights at all.'[71] According to her, 'the centering of excluded subjects, excluded zones and excluded histories can bring the project back to a space of greater optimism and lesser despair'.[72] This, however, is easier said than done. This is to say that the post-colonial critique hits at the new—not to mention the old—human rights orthodoxy very hard. Those ready to see that a colonial logic remains pertinent in understanding today's world would all agree that managing 'to give the human rights body a soul'[73] is a challenge which, if at all successful, will need to be taken up over and over again, rather than being met once and for all.

4 CONCLUSION

Human rights accounts are generally celebratory and triumphalist. This is so much the case that a student can take a course entirely devoted to human rights without ever being introduced to some of the critiques reviewed above. Admittedly, it has become politically incorrect for human rights tutors not to refer, at least in passing, to the feminist critique. A lack of formal reference to the IR realist critique is not very dam-aging, given that most students are attuned to its suggestions. This may also largely be true of the utilitarian perspective: students perceive immediately, especially in the context of the war on terror, its relevance (and difficulties). Grasping the implications of the Marxist critique is already more difficult. And is it not irresponsible to relegate the particularist (cultural relativist) critique to something worthy of discussion only if time allows, which it apparently does not (in a manifestation of what I have called elsewhere 'the footnote 10 phenomenon')?[74] As for the postcolonial critique, its neglect is even more staggering: this critique is hardly mentioned in human rights courses, leaving not only the 'Other' but also those in the privileged world moved by the idea of a social justice project more disempowered than if they had been made aware of the critique.

Such silences are unfortunate because all the critiques reviewed in this chapter (as well as others) are worth pondering. They each make important points. Some critiques

---

[71] Kapur 'Human Rights in the 21st Century: Take a Walk on the Dark Side' (2006) 28 *Sydney LR* 665, 682.

[72] Ibid, 687.   [73] In a paraphrase of Kapur's concluding sentence, ibid.

[74] Dembour, n 53, 72.

are more profound than others that can be, and indeed have already been, absorbed in human rights theory. Bentham's objection to the rights of man as 'imaginary' falls in the face of the new orthodoxy and the constant definition, re-definition, and implementation of 'real' rights. The utilitarian perspective is capable of being accommodated in the new orthodoxy—as has already started to happen.[75] In a different mode, this is also the case of the particularist (cultural relativist) critique which has been argued in this chapter to be in need of being constantly considered by human rights theory and practice, thus hopefully making it possible to keep in check the possible excesses of universalism.

The other human rights critiques that have been reviewed are less easily absorbed. The Marxist critique remains as pertinent as ever, pointing as it does to the exclusion that the human rights discourse continues to encompass. This insight penetrates the critiques that have been developed in the last decades. Radical feminists, some IR realists, and some postcolonial theorists posit that human rights will *never* be able to live up to the promises it makes, so that it is hardly a project worth pursuing.[76] Others, again found across a broad theoretical spectrum that includes realism, feminism, and postcolonialism, are less extreme in their critique and argue that human rights has contradictory effects, which make it an inherently ambiguous project/discourse, sometimes worth pursuing and sometimes not.[77] Still others believe in the intrinsic value of human rights but call for them to be/become true to themselves, which in their view means doing the protest work that brought them into being in the first place.[78]

FURTHER READING

BAXI, *The Future of Human Rights* (Oxford University Press, 2006).

BHAMBRA and SHILLIAM (eds), *Silencing Human Rights: Critical Engagements with a Contested Project* (Palgrave, 2009).

CAMPBELL, *Rights: A Critical Introduction* (Routledge, 2006).

DEMBOUR, *Who Believes in Human Rights? Reflections on the European Convention* (Cambridge University Press, 2006).

DOUZINAS, *Human Rights and Empire: The Political Philosophy of Cosmopolitanism* (Routledge, 2007).

---

[75] See eg Nickel, n 27.

[76] See Brown, '"The Most We Can Hope For ...": Human Rights and the Politics of Fatalism' (2004) 103 *South Atlantic Quarterly* 451.

[77] See eg Cowan, 'Ambiguities of an Emancipatory Discourse: The Making of a Macedonian Minority in Greece' in Cowan *et al.*, n 46, 152; Bhambra and Shilliam, 'Introduction: "Silence" and Human Rights' in Bhambra and Shilliam (eds), *Silencing Human Rights: Critical Engagements with a Contested Project* (Palgrave, 2009) 1, 9; Nash, *The Cultural Politics of Human Rights: Comparing the US and UK* (CUP, 2009) vii.

[78] See eg Douzinas, n 7; Stammers, n 7; Bowring, *The Degradation of the International Legal Order? The Rehabilitation of Law and the Possibility of Politics* (Routledge-Cavendish, 2009).

KAPUR, 'Human Rights in the 21st Century: Take a Walk on the Dark Side' (2006) 28 *Sydney LR* 665–87.

MERTUS, *Bait and Switch: Human Rights and US Foreign Policy* (Routledge, 2004).

MUTUA, *Human Rights: A Political and Cultural Critique* (University of Pennsylvania Press, 2002).

NASH, *The Cultural Politics of Human Rights: Comparing the US and UK* (Cambridge University Press, 2009).

STAMMERS, *Human rights and Social Movements* (Pluto Press, 2009).

WALDRON (ed), '*Nonsense upon Stilts*': *Bentham, Burke and Marx on the Rights of Man* (Methuen, 1987).

4

POLITICS

Julie Mertus

SUMMARY

This chapter explores the interrelationship between human rights and politics. Using the anti-racism movements at the time of the creation of the UN Charter as a case study, the chapter first shows how the anti-racism agenda was informed by the struggle for international human rights and, in turn, how international human rights norms and practices were shaped by the anti-racism agenda. Next, the chapter examines the political terrain for human rights. By examining the campaign for the rights of people with disabilities, it suggests that different conceptions of power can be promoted through human rights politics. Finally, the chapter looks at the importance of human rights in two pressing areas of international politics: inclusion in peace accords and as justification for military intervention.

1 INTRODUCTION

The story of human rights and politics can be told through many ideological and disciplinary lenses but, ultimately, it concerns itself with power and the relationships through which power is negotiated for political gain. In this sense, the manner in which both the aggrieved and the transgressor frame issues as rights—a complex process that has been referred to as 'rights-talk'—is deeply political.[1]

Rights-talk is useful for individuals and groups recovering from human wrongs, as well as for social justice advocates concerned with empowering communities to realize their human potential. For individuals and their advocates, human rights and politics are intertwined and mutually reinforcing. Strong politics make for strong rights and the consistent and even-handed application of human rights makes for consistent and even-handed politics. It is through political processes that individuals assert the validity of their claims against states and it is a matter of politics when states respond,

---

[1] See eg Perry, *The Idea of Human Rights* (OUP, 1998); Ignatieff, *The Rights Revolution* (Anansi Press, 2000).

honouring some claims and denying others. While individuals may quibble with each other and with states over the existence and content of human rights, there is general agreement over the importance of opening doors to participation in the political arena in which rights compete with other ideas and, at times, with each other. To deny individuals and collectives the ability to frame their claims in terms of human rights presents a great injustice.

Rights-talk has proved useful for states also. States seize on rights-talk as the *lingua franca* of the civilized world. Both states that accuse others of human rights violations and those that are accused turn to human rights, and the panoply of institutions created for the promotion, protection, and preservation of rights, for help in making their position heard and understood. For states, rights-talk is like the euro: it is acceptable as currency almost everywhere, although the exchange rate and cost of transaction vary considerably, at times appearing so high that it is not worth the trouble. Human rights, like the euro, can be experienced as essential components of unity or, alternatively, as impositions from the outside.

The idea of human rights, and the institutions charged with promoting this idea, are imperfect political instruments. However, currently they are the most accepted measures available.[2] The entry of rights-talk into politics has left its mark on the considerations that state actors (such as diplomats negotiating peace agreements) and non-state actors (such as NGOs) employ when making, implementing, monitoring, and enforcing public policies.

2 THE INTERRELATIONSHIP BETWEEN HUMAN RIGHTS AND POLITICS

The acceptance of human rights in politics has provoked major changes in the political thinking and behaviour of both rulers and the ruled, and in so doing has left its imprint on human rights theory and practice. First, the successful development of human rights as a political idea involved a major shift in both how rulers perceived their subjects and how individuals perceived themselves. Second, the creation of political space for human rights promotion and protection required openness to challenges by individuals and groups demanding inclusion. The progressive development of both these changes in thinking will be discussed in turn.

2.1 CHANGES IN THINKING ABOUT THE RULER/RULED RELATIONSHIP

In feudal times, individuals were born into circumstances that determined their degree of freedom. Moving out of one class and into another was rare and difficult.

---

[2] See generally Risse, Ropp, and Sikkink (eds), *The Power of Human Rights* (CUP, 1999).

People were owned by, or at least controlled by, lords and kings: their masters. Under the feudal arrangement, the word 'right' was closer in meaning to our present under-standing of 'property'. 'Individuals and groups had rights to do various things—to hold markets, to graze animals on specific common lands—but these rights were spe-cific to them as individuals. They did not enjoy them because they were citizens, still less because they were human beings.'[3] Royalty in medieval society granted 'rights' to peasants and, in return, collected monies and young men for their armies. There was no real 'bargained for exchange' as peasants had no bargaining power.[4] It was the duty of peasants to honour the king's demands, and his discretion in setting these demands was virtually unlimited. This arrangement worked in favour of those peasants seeking security, because the king was willing to provide security for peasants, from threats both inside and outside the kingdom. In return, very little was expected other than obedience from peasants, who were identified not as individuals with dreams and desires of their own, but by their position within their society.[5]

In sharp contrast, the logic of human rights blasts these notions apart by mak-ing individuals the subject of their own lives. 'Agency', 'bodily integrity', 'empathy', 'dignity', and 'participation' are all concepts encouraged by human rights. Accepting these concepts required a radical rethinking of rulers' relationships to their subjects as well as individuals' relationships with one another.

Consider the following. For a long time, people used to gather in town squares for exhibitions of pain and suffering. They cheered on the hangman as he prepared the noose for the poor fellow who was already almost dead, having been nailed to a cross and put on display. They watched attentively while a man's body was stretched on the rack, listening for the sound of bones cracking. They sang while the women accused of witchcraft were tied to stones and tossed into a well. Today, although torture and cruel and inhuman punishment certainly occurs, it is, by and large, carried out clan-destinely—and it is publicly condemned. Why? Because human rights presume an individual's right to bodily integrity, and today people want to think of themselves as being on the side of human rights. To believe in human rights in modern times means to shut down the torture chamber in the town square. Contemporary human rights politics insists that individuals view one another as equally morally worthy of enjoy-ing the same set of rights.

2.2 DEMANDS FOR INCLUSION: THE ANTI-RACISM MOVEMENT

The idea and practice of human rights has long informed the demands of racial minor-ities and, at the same time, anti-discrimination campaigns have helped to shape the idea and practice of human rights. The international nature of human rights held promise in situations in which actions at the state level had failed.[6] The debate in the

---

[3] Harrison and Boyd, *Understanding Political Ideas and Movements* (Manchester University Press, 2003) 122.
[4] Ibid.   [5] See eg Hunt, *Inventing Human Rights* (WW Norton, 2008).
[6] See eg Sherwood, '"There is No New Deal for the Blackman in San Francisco": African Attempts to Influence the Founding Conference of the United Nations, April–July 1945' (1996) 29 *Intl J African Historical*

mid-1940s over the UN Charter's human rights provisions initially appeared to give racial minorities a 'powerful podium' from which to address their concerns as human rights issues.[7] Before they could reach the podium, however, their ability to participate was obfuscated by an unlikely nemesis: Eleanor Roosevelt.

Eleanor Roosevelt has been championed for her strong leadership on human rights and, in particular, her support of anti-racism movements.[8] A different story, however, is described in more recent scholarly accounts of these events.[9] This research exposes Eleanor Roosevelt as a well-intentioned, but tightly controlled, advocate who relented to political pressure emanating from Washington to keep the discussion of racism and colonialism separate and as far off the UN agenda as possible. For her, this meant more than simply not addressing racism or colonialism. It meant 'using her chairmanship and influence to manipulate the human rights treaties in ways that would shield the United States from UN scrutiny' and that prevented human rights from becoming a 'viable force' at home.[10]

Eleanor Roosevelt's orders from Washington permitted her to support a small list of civil and political rights while blocking progress on economic and social rights. For the anti-racism movement this was disastrous. US anti-racism advocates at the UN Charter negotiations in San Francisco in 1945 knew that without economic and social rights, civil liberties rested, at best, on quicksand. Yet, in the mid-1940s in the USA supporting economic rights was a risky proposition. Any group or individual fighting for economic rights risked being branded communist and effectively shut down.[11] Afraid of losing what little political leverage it had, the most powerful US anti-racism group, the National Association for the Advancement of Colored People (NAACP), muted their demands for economic and social rights and pulled back from the international stage to the apparent safety of a narrow, US-focused, civil rights agenda.[12]

The NAACP and its consultants at the UN Charter negotiations also were skittish on the topic of colonialism. Highly organized Nigerian graduate students met individually with state delegates and pressed for the words 'independence' and 'freedom' to be added to the UN Charter, along with a specific provision on the human rights dimensions of colonialism. As with economic rights, however, the time was not ripe for discussing colonial rule. Outsides the confines of the Charter negotiations, tensions were rising between Washington and Moscow.[13] Among those accused of breaching human rights during colonial occupations were the main US allies who stood together against the Soviet Union. The USA did not want to lose the support of any of these

Studies 71; Cmiel, 'The Emergence of Human Rights Politics in the United States' (1999) 86 *J American History* 1231.

[7] Tyson, 'Robert F Williams, "Black Power", and the Roots of the African American Freedom Struggle' (1999) 85 *J American History* 540, 550–1.

[8] See eg Glendon, *A World Made New: Eleanor Roosevelt and the Universal Declaration of Human Rights* (Random House, 2001).

[9] Anderson, *Eyes off the Prize: The United Nations and the African American Struggle for Human Rights, 1944–1955* (CUP, 2003); Normand and Zaidi, *Human Rights at the UN: The Political History of Universal Justice* (Indiana University Press, 2007).

[10] Anderson, n 9, 4.   [11] Ibid.   [12] Ibid, 6.   [13] Tyson, n 7, 51.

allies—or change the positioning of military aircraft that were located within striking distance of Moscow. Thus, the USA began what would become a major theme in its foreign policy for years to come: ignoring human rights abuses committed by avowed anti-communists.

A two-part deal was struck between the USA and colonial states. First, the names of the individual colonized states would not be mentioned by name in the UN Charter. Second, the USA would support adding a provision to the UN Charter that for decades proved to be elastic enough to present an effective roadblock to human rights enforcement. Article 2(7) UN Charter provides: 'Nothing contained in the present Charter shall authorize the United Nations to intervene in matters which are essentially within the domestic jurisdiction of any state.' This anti-intervention provision appeased racist politicians in the USA. They read the provision as complementary to their 'states' rights' movement, which argued that in a federal system such as the USA issues like race relations were matters to be decided on a local basis. Wearing federalism as a shield, the US delegation at the UN Charter negotiations rejected the NAACP's demand that the US government acknowledge and address the ill-effects of racism in the USA.

Ignored at the UN Charter negotiations, the NAACP attempted to file its own petition with the UN two years later, in 1947. That petition squarely linked racism to US foreign policy, declaring: 'It is not Russia that threatens the United States as much as Mississippi, not Stalin or Molotov, but Bilbo and Rankin.'[14] The petition went on to condemn the denial of human rights to minorities of African descent in the USA. Not surprisingly, the NAACP petition went nowhere. Frustrated from its experience and fearful of being accused of being communist supporters, the NAACP almost completely withdrew from the global campaign for international human rights, situating itself instead as an 'American organization' concerned with US civil rights.[15] It was Eleanor Roosevelt who, despite being on the NAACP's board of directors, led the drive against the organization's petition. At the same time, she worked to block a complaint to the UN concerning racial discrimination and related human rights abuses in South Africa. In so doing, she accepted the 'slippery slope' argument: if the South Africa complaint succeeded, it would set a dangerous precedent that could ultimately lead to a UN investigation of the condition of African Americans in Alabama and even the invasion of UN-commanded forces—the ultimate fear of the 'states' rights' supporters.[16] For advocates of the rights of racial minorities, the door to inclusion slammed shut. Prying it open would require a new strategy based on empowerment and coalition building (that is, religious and racial minorities working together over common concerns). Political organizing on race issues had left its mark on human rights—and human rights left its mark on politics.

---

[14] Senator Theodore Bilbo and Congressman John E Rankin, both of Mississippi, were two prominent, controversial figures who have been called 'racists' by historians of that era. See Anderson, n 9, 103.
[15] Ibid, 6.   [16] Ibid, 4.

3 POWER AND THE POLITICAL TERRAIN FOR HUMAN RIGHTS

The efforts of strong states to control where, when, and how human rights standards are established and implemented (as in the example discussed above) represents one type of power that is used by both friends and foes of human rights. This 'power over' is control by sanction, or fear of sanction. Peace agreements, treaty negotiations, meeting agendas, and trade talks are dominated by this form of power. In contrast, 'power with' is collective power through organization, solidarity, and joint action. This section examines how different kinds of power function in human rights politics. It begins by outlining the different types of power and then offers an example of both these types of power: the international disability rights movement.

3.1 'POWER OVER'

The 'power over' scenario captures the direct and indirect ways in which states bind themselves to international human rights norms and compete with one another as human rights friend or foe. The traditional 'power over' tactic is also employed by NGOs with their strategy of 'naming, blaming, and shaming' to promote human rights. Many human rights advocates use this as their mantra. They engage in monitoring and fact finding in order to document independently, accurately, and persuasively what is happening on a particular human rights issue or in a particular geographic region. They then name the specific human rights provisions implicated and the human rights violator(s), blame the responsible party (or parties), and prompt remedial action though shaming.[17]

The naming of human rights violators is one result of two decades of standard setting. Today, a host of treaties and declarations spell out the parameters of specific rights, and the content of human rights is further defined in the rulings of international adjudicative bodies. Advocates have become increasingly sophisticated in incorporating such standards into their strategies for determining responsibility for violations.

These efforts, however, are insufficient for realizing human rights. Experience demonstrates that these international adjudicative bodies are only as good as the domestic institutions supporting them.[18] Domestic institutions facilitate compliance with international human rights norms both directly and indirectly. Human rights advocates would do well to direct their advocacy at the domestic bodies charged with promotion and enforcement, such as national human rights institutions

---

[17] See eg Clark, *Diplomacy of Conscience: Amnesty International and Changing Human Rights Norms* (Princeton University Press, 2001); Pack, 'Amnesty International: An Evolving Mandate in a Changing World' in Hagerty and Siobhan (eds), *Human Rights: An Agenda for the 21st Century* (Cavendish, 1999).

[18] See eg Mertus, *Human Rights Matters: Local Politics and National Human Rights Institutions* (Stanford University Press, 2008). See also Lord and Stein, 'The Domestic Incorporation of Disability Human Rights and the UN Convention on People with Disabilities' (2008) 83 *Washington LR* 449.

(independent human rights monitoring and reporting organizations established by the state, but with a mandate to be independent of both the state and civil society organizations).[19] Institutions of the state also work indirectly to support international human rights norms by promoting and protecting the norms and practices inherent in liberal, rights-observing democracies. Good illustrations of this phenomenon worldwide include the promotion of independent judiciaries, free and fair elections, multi-party systems, and freedom of the press. It is through participation in such activities and exchanges that both states and NGOs learn political etiquette, that is, the boundaries of acceptable behaviour, and acquire the information and skills necessary for future engagement with that particular institution and human rights bodies generally.[20]

Those seeking to uphold human rights face particularly difficult challenges when many of the worst individual violators are concealed within the skirt folds of state sovereignty as many of the new armed conflicts are intra-state.[21] In recent years, new international courts, truth commissions, and other fact-finding bodies have tried to expose these violators. However, there are limits to the effectiveness of this approach. The 'naming, blaming, and shaming' triad cannot be applied effectively to non-state violators of human rights, such as guerrilla groups in intra-state conflicts. These non-state violators are not looking for international approval. In fact, they might even appreciate being credited with fear-inspiring human rights atrocities. Moreover, the approach fails to challenge the structure of international relations which permits, and in some cases even reinforces, the social, political, and economic sources of oppression. By not addressing many of the root causes of conflict, the 'power over' approach provides insubstantial, temporary solutions at best.

3.2 'POWER WITH'

'Power with' approaches replace competition with coordination, and focus on creating networks for information exchange, solidarity, and encouragement. 'Participation facilitates individuals' discovering who they are and what they want', opine Bachrach and Botwinick, who emphasize that 'in periods of social strife, . . . their sense of solidarity and group empowerment is nurtured and developed' as well.[22] Also known as 'social empowerment', 'power with' uses a vision of equality and self-knowledge to advance civil, political, economic, social, and cultural rights:

---

[19] See generally Mertus, ibid. See also Chapter 22, below.

[20] Apodaca, *Understanding US Human Rights Policy* (Routledge, 2006) xix.

[21] Hafner-Burton, 'Sticks and Stones: Naming and Shaming the Human Rights Enforcement Problem' (2008) 62 *International Organization* 689.

[22] Bachrach and Botwinick, *Power and Empowerment: A Radical Theory of Participatory Democracy* (Temple University Press, 1992) 31.

Social Empowerment is a process by which people reclaim their power, the power to shape their own lives and to influence the course of events around them. They use their power against oppression and exclusion, and for participation, peace and human rights.[23]

The old feminist adage 'the personal is political' is turned on its head for this strategy, as the political is personal for those seeking empowerment. Power is embedded in particular institutions, networks, knowledge, and resources. 'Empowerment is also about locating our own resources, discovering what other resources are available, and learning to use them.'[24] Understood in this manner, empowerment goes hand in hand with the central claim of international human rights politics, 'denial of the means for a decent life and exclusion from a fair share in social goods and opportunities are to be grasped as forms of inhumanity'.[25] If the processes of empowerment are permitted to play themselves out, they will result in the redistribution of these resources to previously marginalized groups.

When accompanied by strong participation, 'power with' approaches can enhance the efficiency of 'power over' approaches. A good example of both types of power can be found in the campaign for the Convention on the Rights of Persons with Disabilities discussed below.

3.3 THE POLITICS OF DISABILITY RIGHTS

The second most quickly ratified treaty in history, the Convention on the Rights of Persons with Disabilities (CRPD) was adopted in 2006, opened for signature in 2007, and entered into force in 2008. A major victory for disability rights advocates, the adoption of the CRPD represents a classic 'power over' strategy: it is a form of coercion. States, once bound by the treaty's provisions, will be open to naming, blaming, and shaming of any violations they commit. In contrast, the approach chosen for advancing the creation and operation of the treaty is a good example of 'power with'. One popular slogan of the treaty campaign was: 'Nothing about us without us.'[26]

The International Disability Caucus (IDC), the official NGO coalition for the treaty negotiations, made a decision to present a unified movement, with consensus on every line and every issue. The disability community, however, is in fact extremely heterogeneous, with multiple possibilities for faction and friction, such as mental disability versus physical disability, visible disability versus invisible disability, stable conditions versus progressively disabling.[27] Some advocates had a long tradition of rights-based organizing, while others were first-time proponents. The many differences led one observer to wonder, 'do the disabled have a unifying group identity in the same way that other statutorily protected groups—say women or people of color—are said

---

[23] Kraft, '"Power with", not "power over"' [2009] *The Broken Rifle No 47 International,* available at: <http://www.wri-irg.org/node/2234>.

[24] Ibid.   [25] Marks and Clapham, *International Human Rights Lexicon* (OUP, 2005) 449.

[26] Charlton, *Nothing About Us Without Us: Disability, Oppression and Empowerment* (University of California Press, 1995).

[27] Stein, 'Disability and Identity' (2003) 44 *William and Mary LR* 907, 919.

to have?'[28] To some extent, the united front projected by the IDC was a sham, given the extensive differences in participants' needs and expectations, sparking numerous behind-the-scenes disagreements. Yet, advocates could agree on the foundational issues discussed in this chapter: the need to rethink one's relationship to the state, to open the doors for participation, and the importance of self-empowerment.

Until very recently, society 'viewed persons with disabilities through a medical model that considered "handicapped" individuals as naturally excluded from mainstream culture'.[29] This medical/charity view pathologized disabilities as an 'illness' in need of a cure.[30] Once branded as in need of protection, the disabled person was expected to be a passive, grateful recipient of goodwill. Persons with disabilities were regarded as being incapable of living as autonomous individuals.[31] There was little chance for self-advocacy; those who attempted to advocate for themselves were quickly put in their place.[32] Thus, to join the human rights community, the first step that persons with disabilities (and their advocates) needed to take was a rethinking of their relationship with the state and medical establishments. Like the peasant in medieval times, they needed to improve their self-image as human beings, equally worthy and entitled to human dignity. Unlike the townsperson who once passively watched their brother being tortured, they needed to believe that they were entitled to participate in decision making about their own care and the care of others. But the burden was not on them alone. The state and medical establishments had to begin treating them as subjects, not mere objects.

In contrast to the medical model, disability rights advocates have used a social model to fight for fair and equal treatment. Under the social model, disability is seen as a social construction. As disability advocate and scholar Wendell puts it, 'the entire physical and social organization of life' has been created with the able-bodied in mind. Society requires adaptation, not the person with a disability. A human rights approach to disability conceptualizes persons with disabilities as subjects of their own lives, active claimants of their rights.

The appropriate strategy for making human rights claims was hotly contested within the disability community.[33] On the one hand, disability rights advocates could remain a specialized, largely single-issue campaign. On the other hand, they could emphasize the legitimacy of their claims by seeking the embrace of the mainstream human rights movement. Once under the wing of the mainstream movement, disability rights would thrive, proponents of this approach opined. However, the new issues raised by disability advocates were susceptible to being buried in the large mainstream

---

[28] Lord, 'Disability Rights and the Human Rights Mainstream: Reluctant Gate-Crashers?' in Clifford (ed), *The International Struggle for New Human Rights* (University of Pennsylvania Press, 2008) 161.

[29] Stein and Stein, 'Beyond Disability Civil Rights' (2007) 58 *Hastings LJ* 1203, 1205.

[30] Williams, 'Theorizing Disability' in Albrecht *et al.* (eds), *Disability Studies* (Sage Publications, 2001) 123.

[31] See Lord, n 28.

[32] Rosenthal *et al.*, 'Implementing the Rights to Community Integration for Children Disabilities in Russia: A Human Rights Framework for International Action' (1999) 4 *Health and HR* 83, 89.

[33] See Lord, n 28.

organization of the UN. In addition, because they had little experience with disability issues, mainstream groups did not know where to begin. Nonetheless, the disability community (at least its most vocal and, ultimately, influential components) agreed that the integration of disability rights into the human rights movement would be achieved best through the development of a specialized treaty.

The drive for an international disability rights campaign is a good example of both 'power over' and 'power with'. The decision to take a unified stance and to advocate for a specialized treaty was 'power over' as it was coercive in nature—coercive of both the disability advocates and states that did not agree with the approach taken. But the campaign also illustrates 'power with'. The experience was transformative for many individuals with disabilities. They began to think of themselves differently. Whereas before they were recipients of charity, now they are global rights activists, demanding inclusion on all matters pertaining to their welfare. The development of human rights within the disability rights community opened space for new actors, working across what had been boundaries with different needs, interests, and demands. They made a point to be open and participatory, creating guides to enable even activists with the least knowledge of the UN to participate. Together, activists of many stripes used human rights to craft their demands for structural change and new patterns of individual-government interaction on disability issues.

4 ARMED CONFLICT AND HUMAN RIGHTS POLITICS

Human rights advocates eyed the end of the Cold War with great anticipation, but any hope that the end of the Cold War would mark the beginning of worldwide peace faded quickly. 'The removal of the equilibrium established by the dualism of the Cold War…left a political vacuum, opening the way to the resurgence of other pressures and antagonisms which have lain masked or latent beneath the artificial stability which an east-west balance tended to enforce.'[34] New armed conflicts erupted almost immediately, surprising political analysts with their intense brutality and especially their deliberate targeting of civilians for mass murder, rape, and torture. Two areas in which human rights figured prominently were: (1) peace agreements, where the inclusion of rights-talk was considered to be necessary to end war; and (2) humanitarian intervention, where rights-talk formed the justification for intervening.

4.1 PEACE AGREEMENTS

Since the end of the Cold War, human rights have become a central component of peace agreements, appearing particularly in those agreements that spell the end of

---

[34] Munro, 'Humanitarianism and Conflict in a post-Cold War World' (1999) 835 *IRRC* 463

internationalized armed conflicts, such as that which took place in Bosnia-Herzegovina. In former diplomat Chester Crocker's words, human rights have become 'part of the furniture' when it comes to peace negotiations.[35] The parties to peace negotiations, as well as the diplomats supporting their efforts, have come to expect that they will have to address human rights in their final agreement.

Creating quite a stir in the human rights community, in 1996, the *Human Rights Quarterly* published a sharply critical, anonymous article entitled 'Human Rights in Peace Negotiations'.[36] The author of that article cited several examples of peace agreements, but focused on the negotiations and accords pertaining to the armed conflicts in the former Yugoslavia, noting that the latter included 'some of the most extensive and far-reaching provisions on human rights to be found in any peace agreement ever'.[37] The author blamed the reports of human rights advocates for prolonging wars and causing additional deaths, as they documented the role of would-be peace negotiators in human rights abuses. The focus of peace talks, the anonymous author contended, should not be on idealistic human rights issues, but on pragmatic measures to stop the violence. 'The quest for justice for yesterday's victims of atrocities', the author declared, 'should not be pursued in such a manner that makes today's living the dead of tomorrow.'[38]

Gaer, a human rights advocate and diplomat, immediately rebuked these accusations.[39] According to her analysis, the anonymous author incorrectly placed blame for difficulties with peace accords on the human rights community. Instead, Gaer insisted, attention should be paid to the ineffectiveness of the political actors and of the political system as a whole. In fact, the inclusion of human rights guarantees in peace agreements has proven to be essential in cases such as the former Yugoslavia, where human rights abuses contributed to the outbreak, intensification, and prolongation of violent conflict. While Gaer supported the inclusion of human rights in peace accords, she also recognized the 'urgent need for negotiators to work with the human rights community to develop new, better strategies to address complex, often inconvenient realities and to uphold fundamental principles in their negotiations'.[40] The politics of human rights at the international level went beyond reporting of *past* violations and demanded greater attention to *future* enforcement.

Academic studies of human rights in peace agreements remain conflicted. According to Licklider, the empirical evidence does not fully support the push for human rights in talks to end internal armed conflicts.[41] While the inclusion of extensive human rights provisions in peace agreements may be helpful in some cases, it certainly should not be touted as a cure-all. Licklider calls for closer study on what

[35] Mertus, *Bait and Switch: Human Rights and US Foreign Policy* (Routledge, 2006) 26.
[36] Anonymous, 'Human Rights in Peace Negotiations' (1996) 18 HRQ 249. [37] Ibid.
[38] Ibid, 258.
[39] Gaer, 'UN-Anonymous: Reflections on Human Rights in Peace Negotiations' (1997) 19 HRQ 1.
[40] Ibid, 4–5.
[41] Licklider, 'Ethical Advice: Conflict Management vs. Human Rights in Ending Civil Wars' (2008) 7 J HR 376, 385.

elements of conflict situations, in fact, impact the achievement of sustainable peace.[42] In contrast, O'Flaherty is much more enthusiastic about the inclusion of human rights provisions, especially when they reflect the input of the human rights community.[43] Although many factors contribute to a successful peace process, on balance most commentators would agree that respect for human rights is often imperative.

4.2 HUMANITARIAN INTERVENTION

Just as diplomats use human rights as tools in peace processes, states have used human rights as a justification for armed intervention in other states, an action commonly referred to as 'humanitarian intervention'. This takes place when the international community forcibly interferes in the affairs of a state in order to prevent further widespread violations of human rights.[44] The basic premise of humanitarian intervention is that 'those who are suffering terribly should be helped if their host state is unwilling to do so'.[45] Pro-interventionists argue that international law in the past century has brought about the codification of human rights, yet still the assistance of third parties in the protection of human rights is sometimes warranted because states have not acted effectively to eradicate human rights violations. The end of the Cold War created 'a new dimension to the responsibility of the global community to take a direct hand in the resolution of disputes involving gross violations of human rights and which threaten to generate wider instability or unacceptable human suffering. This "right" of intervention, extending to a military option, challenges the hitherto cherished principle of national sovereignty.[46]

The rise in the number of humanitarian catastrophes since the end of the Cold War, combined with the high ranking of human rights as a global preference, has led to increased support for humanitarian intervention, among both political leaders and the general public. Whether this trend will continue depends largely on the ability of specific interest groups to draw attention to their cause. In his observations on the subject, Falk refers to the power of modern media around the globe in 'building public pressure to act in the face of severe humanitarian abuse'.[47] This evolution in global priorities and problems has pressured individual states, as well as the UN and regional collectives, to 'provide politically acceptable and logistically effective responses'.[48] Falk

[42] Ibid, 385–6.
[43] O'Flaherty, 'Sierra Leone's Peace Process: The Role of the Human Rights Community' (2004) 26 *HRQ* 29, 29–34.
[44] See generally Murphy, *Humanitarian Intervention: The United Nations in an Evolving World Order* (University of Pennsylvania Press, 1996).
[45] Hehir, *Humanitarian Intervention After Kosovo: Iraq, Darfur and the Record of Global Civil Society* (Palgrave, 2008) 5.
[46] Munro, n 34.
[47] Falk, 'Humanitarian Intervention after Kosovo' in Mertus and Helsing (eds), *Human Rights and Conflict: Exploring the Links between Rights, Law, and Peacebuilding* (United States Institute of Peace Press, 2006) 185.
[48] Ibid.

argues that humanitarian intervention can be a positive response to cases of mass violations of human rights and is well within the political toolbox of states with enough resources and political will to make it happen.

Seybolt's work on humanitarian military intervention does not deny the controversial nature of these decisions, but instead embraces a cautionary approach wherein 'skepticism is always in order about the need to use military force'.[49] Seybolt suggests important criteria meant to help political leaders to decide when the use of military force against a sovereign state in the service of human rights is justified.

- Is the cause just?
- Is the intervention intended to help the needy population?
- Has the UN or (less desirably) another intergovernmental body authorized the intervention?
- Is military force the last resort, all reasonable alternatives having been tried or considered?
- Is the intervention proportionate to the need?
- Is there a reasonable chance of success?[50]

Humanitarian intervention, along with peace negotiations, exposes the 'crucial connections between war and human rights'.[51] Human rights violations may be the cause of conflict, and as such the justification for intervention and a central issue to be addressed by diplomats negotiating peace. Alternatively, human rights abuses may be a consequence of war, exacerbated by military intervention, rendering peace talks more difficult. Accountability for human rights violations may arise as a key issue during peace negotiations, and humanitarian intervention factors into the ability to hold successful peace talks. Critics of human rights in peace agreements decry the unwillingness of human rights advocates to negotiate with purported war criminals, asserting that the resulting prolongation of conflict comes at a high price: civilian lives. Whether this price is too high to pay is a question raised by the practitioners of international politics balancing the often competing demands between peace and justice.

5 CONCLUSION

This chapter has introduced the complex interrelationship of politics and human rights. A sweeping, selective exploration into the genesis of rights-talk in politics, this chapter began with medieval times, when human rights atrocities were a form of entertainment and government control. The chapter fast-forwarded to the end of

---

[49] Seybolt, *Humanitarian Military Intervention: The Conditions for Success and Failure* (OUP, 2007) 267.
[50] Ibid, 269.
[51] Sriram, Martin-Ortega, and Hermann, *War, Conflict and Human Rights* (Routledge, 2009) 5.

the Second World War and the political negotiations over the inclusion of anti-racism provisions in the new UN Charter. The role played by Eleanor Roosevelt in anti-racism politics serves to suggest some of the limitations with reliance on the political sphere for the advancement of human rights. Fast-forwarding again to the present day, the discussion shifted to the international campaign for the rights of persons with disabilities, a highly successful movement that illustrates the different conceptions of power in human rights politics. The final section built on the lessons of the chapter as a whole, offering additional usages for human rights advocacy as brokered by diplomats in peace accords and as state justification for armed intervention. These examples support the argument that human rights are deeply political.

FURTHER READING

ANDERSON, *Eyes off the Prize: The United Nations and the African American Struggle for Human Rights, 1944–1955* (Cambridge University Press, 2003).

CLARK, *Diplomacy of Conscience: Amnesty International and Changing Human Rights Norms* (Princeton University Press, 2001).

HUNT, *Inventing Human Rights* (WW Norton, 2008).

IGNATIEFF, *The Rights Revolution* (Anansi Press, 2000).

LORD, 'Disability Rights and the Human Rights Mainstream: Reluctant Gate-Crashers?' in Clifford (ed), *The International Struggle for New Human Rights* (University of Pennsylvania Press, 2009).

MERTUS, *Bait and Switch: Human Rights and US Foreign Policy* (Routledge, 2008).

—— *Human Rights Matters: Local Politics and National Human Rights Institutions* (Stanford University Press, 2008).

NORMAND and ZAIDI, *Human Rights at the UN: The Political History* (Indiana University Press, 2007).

SRIRAM, MARTIN-ORTEGA, and HERMANN, *War, Conflict and Human Rights* (Routledge, 2009).

STEIN and LORD, 'Future Prospects for the United Nations Convention on the Rights of Persons with Disabilities' in Arnardóttir and Quinn (eds), *The UN Convention on the Rights of Person with Disabilities: European and Scandinavian Perspectives* (Brill, 2009).

USEFUL WEBSITES

Peace Agreements Database: <http://www.peaceagreements.ulster.ac.uk/>

Global Policy Forum, Humanitarian Intervention: <http://www.globalpolicy.org/qhumanitarianq-intervention.html>

PART II

INTERNATIONAL LAW

5

SOURCES

Christine Chinkin

SUMMARY

This chapter outlines the sources of international human rights law that are listed in Article 38(1) Statute of the International Court of Justice: treaties, custom, general principles of law, and, as subsidiary sources, judicial decisions and the writings of jurists. The chapter also considers how so-called 'soft law' instruments such as resolutions of the UN General Assembly and the work of human rights expert bodies may also be regarded as sources of human rights law.

1 INTRODUCTION

A source of law identifies what constitutes law, that is, how decision-makers can determine what instruments, practices, or policies constitute legally binding obligations as opposed to moral, political, or other social commitments. Sources of law provide us with the basis of legal obligation: they are 'really all about the provenance of norms'.[1] In practical terms, the sources of law tell us how new rules are made and existing rules are repealed or abrogated.

International human rights law is a specialist regime within general public international law. Its prescribed or *formal sources* are therefore the same as those for other subject areas of international law, such as international environmental law, trade law, or the law of the seas. Unlike national legal systems, international law lacks a central legislative body (comparable to a national parliament), an executive (a government), and a general court of compulsory jurisdiction. International law—and hence international human rights law—must therefore derive from other sources.

These are set out in Article 38(1) Statute of the International Court of Justice (ICJ Statute). This provision directs the judges of the International Court on where they should turn when deciding a dispute brought before them. However, Article 38 has

---

[1] Higgins, *Problems and Process: International Law and How We Use it* (OUP, 1994) 17.

long been accepted as providing the authoritative statement of the sources of international law. It states that the Court shall apply:

a. international conventions, whether general or particular, establishing rules expressly recognized by the contesting states;

b. international custom, as evidence of a general practice accepted as law;

c. the general principles of law recognized by civilized nations;

d. subject to the provisions of Article 59, judicial decisions and the teachings of the most highly qualified publicists of the various nations, as subsidiary means for the determination of rules of law.

As well as stipulating the formal sources of international law, this statement contains elements of both law-making and what are often termed material sources of law. *Law-making* is the 'how' of international law, the methods adopted by the relevant participants in the international arena through which international law is made.[2] The *material sources* of international law are the 'where' of international law: where to look for evidence of the content of a rule—the words of a treaty, the resolution of an international organization, a statement by the prime minister or foreign secretary to the House of Commons or UN General Assembly. Material sources are numerous and diverse.

These initial definitions do not indicate the complexity or diversity of contemporary international human rights law, which are reflected in contestations about its content and sources. Like other areas of international law, in the decades since 1945 international human rights law has grown exponentially and on an essentially ad hoc basis. There has been no overarching plan or design; rather it has developed through a range of processes and in response to demands from numerous participants. Human rights offer a vision of the 'good life' and engender an almost messianic zeal among their proponents. People seek to ground claims in the language of human rights so as to gain the 'high moral ground' against governments, against corporations, against faceless bureaucrats, against anyone that they deem to have violated their rights. To this end, multiple actors operating within an array of institutions—civil society activists, legal advocates, the media, individual lobbyists—draw on material far beyond the formal sources listed in Article 38(1) ICJ Statute and engage a variety of instruments and statements to bolster their arguments that a particular matter can be cast as a binding rule of international human rights law.

Human rights generate claims and counterclaims. Those against whom claims are made—primarily governments—seek to contain their human rights obligations within the formal sources of law to which they have agreed, while claimants may receive support from the growing body of specialist human rights experts mandated to monitor human rights compliance. There is no 'litmus test'[3] for determining claims of new rights or arbiter with comprehensive authority to make such decisions. The

[2] Boyle and Chinkin, *The Making of International Law* (OUP, 2007).
[3] Koskenniemi, 'Human Rights Mainstreaming as a Project of Power', available at: <http://www.iilj.org/courses/documents/Koskenniemi.pdf>.

sources of international human rights law and thus its substantive content are often hotly contested and, in the absence of any final authoritative global decision-maker, are likely to remain so.

This chapter first discusses the formal sources of international human rights law as set out in Article 38(1) ICJ Statute. It then examines other more contested sources so as to give a fuller picture of contemporary international human rights law.

2 FORMAL SOURCES

What we now regard as the international human rights story largely dates from the adoption of the UN Charter in 1945, although the underlying ideas are much older.[4] What has occurred since 1945 has been the legalization of human rights within global and regional institutional frameworks. Today, it is widely accepted that international human rights law is based on state consent as expressed through the forms outlined in Article 38(1) ICJ Statute.

This was not always the case. The idea of human rights derives its inspiration from multiple sources, including religious creed, natural law, and the nature of society. Natural law sources of rights have long been influential. They rest in the concept of a higher law than that made through human agency, although the content of such law must be mediated through the exercise of human reason.[5] A natural law basis for rights is incapable of empirical proof and its legitimacy rests upon societal agreement on what constitutes the common good, or on the exercise of power in its assertion. In the eighteenth century natural law theories evolved away from reliance on the state of nature through to concepts of the social contract, while in the nineteenth century positivist views based on state consent prevailed. Natural law was to some extent reinvigorated after the horrors of the Second World War and the judgments of the International Military Tribunals at Nuremburg and Tokyo revealed the potential moral abyss of excessive adherence to positivist law.

Nevertheless, although the UN Charter was adopted in a climate of revulsion at the extremism of some state law, the foundations of contemporary human rights law lie in positivist law, based on state consent. The primary way in which states express that consent is through the first instrumentality listed in Article 38(1), the negotiation and adoption of treaties.

3 TREATIES

International human rights law today primarily derives from international and regional treaties. An agreement between states may be termed a treaty, convention, charter, covenant, or pact. The chosen term does not denote any legal difference.

---

[4] See Chapter 1, above.   [5] See Chapter 2, above.

Generally only states can become parties to treaties but exceptionally other actors
may be authorized to become parties.[6] States are bound by the treaties to which they
have given formal consent, generally through ratification or accession. This is done by
the constitutionally appropriate state organ depositing an instrument of ratification
with the body so designated within the treaty, in the case of UN human rights treaties
generally the UN Secretary-General.[7] International human rights treaties are unlike
many other treaties in that they do not provide for a reciprocal exchange of rights and
duties between states parties.[8] Instead, by accepting the terms of such treaties, states
accept legal constraints upon their treatment of individuals within their territory and
subject to their jurisdiction.

3.1 THE PRINCIPAL TREATIES

The UN Charter provides the first guarantees of human rights and fundamental
freedoms within a global treaty, albeit in general and indeterminate language.[9] The
immediate follow up to the Charter was the adoption by the General Assembly of the
non-binding Universal Declaration of Human Rights (UDHR), in 1948, eventually
followed in 1966 by the adoption of two UN Covenants, the International Covenant on
Civil and Political Rights (ICCPR) and its First Optional Protocol and the International
Covenant on Economic, Social and Cultural Rights (ICESCR). These three instruments—the UDHR, ICCPR, and ICESCR—are often referred to as the International
Bill of Rights.

   There has since followed a large number of multilateral treaties that complement
the International Bill of Rights by adding new rights, by identifying categories of
people who are especially vulnerable to violations of their rights, and by refining the
obligations of those first treaties. The multilateral treaties that share some common
features are widely regarded as constituting the UN human rights treaty system. In
addition to the ICCPR and ICESCR, in chronological order these treaties are: the
International Convention on the Elimination of All Forms of Racial Discrimination,
1965 (ICERD); the International Convention on the Elimination of All Forms of
Discrimination Against Women, 1979 (CEDAW) and its Optional Protocol, 1999;
the Convention against Torture and Other Cruel, Inhuman or Degrading Treatment,
1984 (UNCAT) and its Optional Protocol, 2002; the International Convention on the
Rights of the Child, 1989 (CRC) and two Optional Protocols, 2000 (on the Involvement
of Children in Armed Conflict and on the Sale of Children, Child Prostitution and
Child Pornography); the International Convention on the Protection of the Rights

---

   [6] Convention on the Rights of Persons with Disabilities, Art 43 provides for regional integration organizations to do so.

   [7] Ratification is the name of the process where a state has previously signed the treaty text while the same
process is called accession in the case of a non-signatory state.   [8] See Chapter 6, below.

   [9] UN Charter, Art 1(3) provides that one of the purposes of the UN is '[t]o achieve international cooperation in...promoting and encouraging respect for human rights and for fundamental freedoms for all
without distinction as to race, sex, language, or religion'. See also Arts 55 and 56.

of All Migrant Workers and Members of their Families, 1990; the Convention on the Rights of Persons with Disabilities (CRPD), 2006 and its Optional Protocol, 2006; and the International Convention for the Protection of All Persons from Enforced Disappearance, 2006. An Optional Protocol to the ICESCR (OP-ICESCR) was adopted by the General Assembly in 2008.

The most important of the common features shared by the treaties comprising the UN human rights system is the establishment of specialist committees ('treaty bodies') in accordance with their terms.[10] Each committee, whose members serve in their personal capacity, monitors implementation of the relevant treaty and their work has been central to the development of international human rights law. No account of the sources of human rights law at the global level is complete without taking the work of the treaty bodies into account.

There are many other multilateral treaties that include human rights obligations but which do not have such monitoring mechanisms. Other treaties adopted by the General Assembly include the Convention on the Prevention and Punishment of the Crime of Genocide (1948), the International Convention on the Suppression and Punishment of the Crime of Apartheid (1973), and the Convention relating to the Status of Refugees (1951). Specialist bodies within the UN system have adopted important human rights treaties, notably the International Labour Organisation with respect to workers' rights and the UN Educational, Scientific and Cultural Organisation (UNESCO) on rights to education and information.[11] Human rights obligations for particular states may also derive from peace agreements, which now almost routinely incorporate existing human rights treaties or set out specific rights. For example, the Dayton Peace Accords, which terminated the armed conflict in Bosnia-Herzegovina, gives the European Convention on Human Rights (ECHR) priority over all other domestic law, incorporates certain specific rights enumerated in the Convention, and requires the state to become (or to remain) a party to listed UN and regional human rights instruments.[12]

Regional institutions have developed their own human rights systems through the adoption of treaties which are limited to states within the region. Today the ECHR, the American Convention on Human Rights (ACHR), and the African Charter on Human and Peoples' Rights are principal sources of human rights obligations for states parties.

3.2 THE IMPORTANCE OF TREATIES

Treaty law is indisputably the most significant source of international human rights law today. It has a number of advantages. Potentially a large number of states may become parties to a treaty, thereby accepting its provisions as binding legal obligations. After a somewhat slow start (the two UN Covenants each took ten years to receive the

[10] See Chapter 18, below.
[11] eg ILO Convention No 100, Equal Remuneration Convention, 1951; UNESCO Convention Against Discrimination in Education, 1960.
[12] Framework Agreement for Peace in Bosnia and Herzegovina, 1995.

required number of parties to come into force), the objective of widespread—ideally universal—adherence to the human rights treaties has been largely successful: there is no state that is not party to at least one UN human rights treaty. Widespread treaty adherence provides for a degree of uniformity between states in their understanding of the requirements of international human rights law, which undermines arguments of cultural or other specificity. Treaty ratification and accession also allow for certainty in identifying states parties and written texts set out the obligations accepted.

But there are also some downsides. The authority of a treaty as a source of law lies in states' consent to be bound. Some treaties may not be widely accepted, for example the Migrant Workers Convention has less than 50 states parties. Treaty language is open to differing interpretations, so states may agree to be bound by the same particular obligations but may differ on their precise meaning. Further, as an expression of their consent states may make reservations to their acceptance of a treaty. Allowing states to make reservations recognizes the many interests of over 190 states and that concessions may have been made during the negotiation process. But reservations also eat away at the integrity of the text and may undermine any serious obligation.[13]

3.3 REVITALIZING THE TREATY SYSTEM

It is evident that many human rights treaties are now relatively old. The International Bill of Rights was negotiated between 1945 and 1966 when the global, political, and economic environments were very different from those of today. There is a dilemma for the development of human rights law. On the one hand, the early conventions have acquired a significant authority and status but, on the other hand, they risk becoming outdated. While international law provides recognized procedures for treaty amendment,[14] the process risks dilution (or even rejection) of existing obligations. Other techniques have been sought for ensuring that the legal guarantees of human rights retain their relevance within a dynamic system. This entails the articulation of new rights as societal conditions demand them, the refinement of existing rights, and the enhancement of implementation mechanisms. A number of such techniques have been developed, which add to the richness of the sources of human rights law.

3.3.1 Additional protocols

One such technique comes directly within the ambit of treaty law and that is the adoption of additional protocols to an existing treaty. This has been done at both the UN and regional levels. An additional protocol is essentially a new treaty. States may select whether (and when) to become a party to a protocol in exactly the same way as they do for the main treaty. Protocols to the human rights treaties serve one of two functions: they either provide for rights not included within the original treaty or provide for new methods of enforcement.

---

[13] See Chapter 6, below.   [14] Vienna Convention on the Law of Treaties, 1969, Arts 39–41.

An example of the former is the Second Optional Protocol (OP2) to the ICCPR aiming at the abolition of the death penalty, adopted by the General Assembly in 1989. Abolition of the death penalty is controversial with its exponents claiming that capital punishment is contrary to the right to life while those committed to its use deny that this is the case. Article 6 ICCPR recognizes the continued existence of the death penalty. The adoption of OP2 allows each state to choose its legal stance on the subject. For those states that become a party, the protocol is the formal source of a legal obligation not to execute any person within their jurisdiction. Other states can remain parties to the ICCPR without accepting this additional obligation. Similarly, states parties to the CRC have the choice whether to accept additional legal obligations relating to the recruitment and use of children in armed forces and hostilities and to the economic and sexual exploitation of children. An unusual situation is that of the USA which has chosen to become a party to both Optional Protocols to the CRC, but not to the 'parent' Convention.

An example of the latter is the OP-ICESCR which was adopted by the General Assembly in December 2008. When it enters into force, it will make three new procedures available with respect to states parties to it: communications from an individual, or group of individuals, alleging violation of the ICESCR; inquiry into situations that appear to constitute a consistent pattern of gross or systematic violations of economic, social, and cultural rights within a state party; and inter-state complaints.

3.3.2 General comments

Another technique through which states' treaty obligations have arguably evolved is the adoption of general comments or recommendations on the part of treaty bodies, which set out their understanding of the treaty language. The status of such general comments, of which there are now many,[15] as a source of human rights law is uncertain. While general comments are readily cited by advocates as sources of human rights law, and may be relied upon by decision-makers, any assertion of legally binding effect must depend upon states' consent to their terms. Where a general comment clarifies treaty provisions it might be seen as a form of secondary treaty law, deriving its authority from the binding nature of the treaty and the implied consent of states to it. However, the treaty bodies have not been bestowed with law-making competence and in some instances states may consider a particular treaty body to have exceeded its competence. It must then be doubtful whether any such consent can be assumed.

Two examples illustrate the different possibilities. The CEDAW has no article directly addressing gender-based violence against women as a violation of women's human rights. In its General Recommendation 19, the CEDAW Committee asserted that the Convention did indeed prohibit such violence as a form of discrimination against women within the terms of Article 1. The Committee required states to include the measures they had taken to combat violence against women in their reports. States

---

[15] The human rights treaty bodies' general comments are collected annually in UN Doc HRI/GEN/1/ Rev.9 (Vol I).

have responded positively to this recommendation and have engaged in dialogue with the Committee on the issue. It seems that they have consented to an interpretation of the CEDAW that includes violence against women.

In contrast is the response of at least some states to the Human Rights Committee's General Comment on treaty reservations. The Committee asserted that the special nature of human rights treaties and its need to be able to perform adequately its monitoring tasks mean that it 'necessarily falls to the Committee to determine whether a specific reservation is compatible with the object and purpose of the [ICCPR]'.[16] This assertion has been challenged, in particular by the USA, the UK, and France.[17] State consent to the Human Rights Committee's interpretation of its role is thus lacking, at least in the case of these states. General comments may be considered as sources of human rights law where they are treated by states as coming within the terms of the treaty but this is less likely where the particular committee is considered to have overstepped its competence. A general comment may also become the basis of state practice, which leads on to the next source of international human rights law—customary international law.

4 CUSTOMARY INTERNATIONAL LAW

The second source of international law, and therefore also international human rights law, listed in Article 38(1) ICJ Statute is customary international law. While treaties are binding only on states that have chosen to become parties, custom is binding upon all states with limited exceptions.[18] A treaty may codify customary international law or come to be accepted as customary international law. It is then binding on all states as custom. Customary international law is unwritten. Just as there are regional human rights treaties there may also be regional customary law.[19]

The International Court of Justice has affirmed that customary international law—whether global or regional—comprises two components: an extensive and virtually uniform and consistent state practice and the belief that the practice is required by law (*opinio juris*),[20] rather than for some other reason such as diplomatic nicety or etiquette. But these two requirements are not easily applied, and determining the content of customary international law is strewn with practical and theoretical difficulties. The first problem is selecting from among the daily activities and statements made by states, those that constitute evidence of state practice. Places where one might look to

---

[16] HRC, General Comment 24, HRI/GEN/1/Rev.9 (Vol I) 210.

[17] See A/50/40, 126 (USA), 130 (UK); A/51/40, 104 (France).

[18] One exception is the so-called persistent objector rule. See Cassese, *International Law* (OUP, 2005) 162–3. The rule appears to have little application to human rights. Eg, South Africa persistently objected to the designation of apartheid as contrary to customary international law but was nevertheless held to be in violation. [19] *Asylum Case (Columbia v Peru)* [1950] ICJ Rep 266.

[20] eg *North Sea Continental Shelf Cases (FRG v Denmark) (FRG v The Netherlands)* [1969] ICJ Rep 3, para 77; *Continental Shelf (Libyan Arab Jamahiriya v Malta)* [1985] ICJ Rep 29, para 27.

discover evidence of custom include diplomatic correspondence, government policy statements, press releases, the opinions of government legal advisers, official manuals, and government comments on international drafting processes. In the context of human rights, other materials may be included such as the behaviours described in states' reports to the UN treaty bodies, material gathered for the Human Rights Council Universal Periodic Review process, and the work and documentation of national human rights institutions.

Two examples illustrate how some decision-makers have approached the task of deciding whether a customary rule of international law exists and some of the theoretical quandaries in so deciding. In *Filartiga v Peña-Irala*, a US judge had to decide whether torture is contrary to customary international law. The case was in 1980, four years before the adoption of the UNCAT. Judge Kaufman sought to find international consensus on the prohibition of torture. He looked to General Assembly resolutions (including the UDHR), 'numerous international treaties and accords', and their reiteration in municipal law, including the constitutions of over 55 states. In sum, he found evidence of state practice in 'the usage of nations, judicial opinions and the work of jurists'.[21]

In *R v Jones*, the House of Lords determined the crime of aggression to be established under customary international law. Lord Bingham referred to what he called the 'major milestones along the road leading to this conclusion'.[22] These included a mix of treaties and statements: a draft Treaty of Mutual Assistance in 1923 (which never came into force); descriptions by the League of Nations Assembly; a resolution of the Pan-American Conference (1928); the Charter of the International Military Tribunal, Article 6; decisions of the International Military Tribunal; General Assembly Resolutions dating from 1946; the work of the International Law Commission; and the Rome Statute of the International Criminal Court (1998). In neither of these cases did the judge have to decide when the rule of custom had emerged; it was sufficient that it had done so by the time of the litigation.

Two further issues emerge from these examples. The first issue is that treaties, including treaties that never came into force, were drawn upon as evidence of state practice. It might be argued that a treaty that has not come into force is evidence of what states have not accepted, rather than of what they have. Further, the practice of treaty parties is not evidence of state practice for the purpose of establishing a rule of custom because it must be assumed that such states are acting in accordance with their treaty obligations, not because they consider themselves bound by custom to do so.[23] They therefore lack the requisite *opinio juris*. States' reports to the treaty bodies are especially relevant for determining customary human rights law. Reports provide a wealth of information about a state's policies, practices, and legislation, including changes that can be traced through the multiple rounds of reporting that many states have now undergone. However, if states have changed their practices in response to

[21] 630 F2d 876 (2d Cir 1980).   [22] [2007] 1 AC 136.
[23] *North Sea Continental Shelf Cases*, n 20, para 76.

the concluding comments addressed to them by the relevant treaty bodies, this too must be viewed as action taken for treaty compliance, not as evidence of state practice for the purpose of establishing a rule of customary international law. Nevertheless, in terms of human rights policy, changed behaviour towards implementation is precisely the desired objective and if consistency in state practice can be identified it seems artificial to discount it as evidence of customary international law.

The second issue is the problem caused by the divergence between what states do and what states say. In *Filartiga*, Judge Kaufman noted that he had not been 'directed to any assertion by any contemporary state of a right to torture its own or another nation's citizens'.[24] But this optimistic statement is contradicted by reports of torture evidenced by human rights organizations. In 2007, Amnesty International documented cases of torture and other cruel, inhuman, or degrading treatment in more than 81 countries.[25] For evident policy reasons—the desire not to deny the existence of a rule of customary international law prohibiting torture—custom may be asserted by reference to states' words rather than the reality of their actions. As will be seen below, General Assembly resolutions are formally non-binding, but these statements are often used as evidence of *opinio juris*, overriding inconsistent practice.[26] Both Judge Kaufman and Lord Bingham in *R v Jones* referred to General Assembly resolutions in determining customary international law. The desire to hold states to their words, particularly when pronounced in the formal setting of the General Assembly, is especially strong where the conduct is 'violative of the basic concept of human dignity', which is at the core of human rights.[27]

Treaties and custom coexist and despite the wide adherence by states to human rights treaties, customary international law retains some considerable importance as a source of human rights law.[28] A claim of obligation under custom may be made against a state that has not become a party to a particular treaty, or which has made a reservation to a treaty provision as a state cannot reserve out of customary international law. A binding treaty may not yet have been concluded on the topic in question. Non-state actors that cannot be treaty parties may be held to be bound by rules of customary international law. In a number of states, including the UK, treaty law creates rights

[24] Filartiga, n 21, 884.

[25] Amnesty International, *State of the World's Human Rights* (2008). The 2009 Amnesty International *State of the World's Human Rights* report, recorded torture and other forms of ill-treatment in 14 of the G-20 countries.

[26] In the *Nicaragua* case, the ICJ found that, despite numerous examples of armed conflict, there was sufficient evidence of contrary *opinio juris* in General Assembly resolutions to support principles of customary law prohibiting the use of force and wrongful intervention: *Military and Paramilitary Activities in and against Nicaragua (Nicaragua v US)* [1986] ICJ Rep 14, paras 186–90. However, in *Legality of the Threat or Use of Nuclear Weapons* the ICJ considered that 'although those [General Assembly] resolutions are a clear sign of deep concern regarding the problem of nuclear weapons, they still fall short of establishing the existence of an *opinio juris* on the illegality of the use of such weapons': [1996] ICJ Rep 226, para 71.

[27] Schachter, 'International Law in Theory and Practice: General Course in Public International Law' (1982) 178 *Rec des Cours* 21, 334–8. In such instances Schachter considered that 'statements of condemnation are sufficient evidence of its illegitimacy under customary international law'.

[28] See Clapham, *Human Rights Obligations of Non-State Actors* (OUP, 2006) 85–6.

and obligations that can be relied on in national courts only if the treaty has been made part of national law through incorporating legislation. A state may thus become a party to a treaty but have failed to take the requisite action to allow it to be relied on within its own courts, as was the case in the UK before the passing of the Human Rights Act in 1998 to give domestic effect to the ECHR which it had ratified in 1951. It has still not taken such action with respect to the ICCPR or ICESCR. In contrast, customary international law may be accepted as the law of the land without any such act of incorporation.

5 JUS COGENS

A *jus cogens* norm is a 'peremptory norm of general international law...accepted and recognised by the international community of states as a whole as a norm from which no derogation is permitted and which can be modified only by a subsequent norm of general international law having the same character'.[29] *Jus cogens* norms or 'intransgressible principles of customary international law'[30] constitute the pinnacle of the hierarchy of sources of international law. They both limit states' freedom to enter into treaties by reference to fundamental values of the international community and bind all states regardless of whether they have ratified the treaties that contain them. They import notions of universally applicable norms into the international legal process.

Until relatively recently candidates for *jus cogens* norms were designated by commentators or scholars but had had relatively little application. Many of the norms most commonly asserted to have this status were those of human rights, including the prohibitions of genocide, slavery and the slave trade, murder/disappearances and torture, prolonged arbitrary detention, and systematic racial discrimination.[31] Indeed, it has been remarked that there is 'an almost intrinsic relationship between peremptory norms and human rights'.[32] Since the 1990s, international, regional, and national courts have recognized certain norms as *jus cogens*, including the prohibitions against torture,[33] genocide,[34] and fundamental rules of humanitarian law.[35] Such judicial recognition has an important symbolic effect, signifying the seriousness with which the international community regards certain behaviours. It also has practical consequences, including making illegitimate any national legislative,

---

[29] Vienna Convention on the Law of Treaties, Art 53.

[30] *Legality of the Threat or Use of Nuclear Weapons*, n 26, para 79.

[31] American Law Institute, *Restatement (Third) of the Foreign Relations Law of the United States* (1987) para 702.   [32] Bianchi, 'Human Rights and the Magic of Jus Cogens' (2008) 19 *EJIL* 491.

[33] eg *A and others v Secretary of State for the Home Department (No 2)* [2005] UKHL 71; *Prosecutor v Furundžija*, Judgment, IT-95-17/1-T, 10 December 1998 (ICTY); *Ould Dah v France*, App no 13113/03, Decision of 30 March 2009 (European Court of Human Rights).

[34] eg *Armed Activities on the Territory of the Congo* (New Application 2002) (*Democratic Republic of the Congo v Rwanda*) [2006] ICJ Rep 3, para 64.

[35] *Legality of the Threat or Use of Nuclear Weapons*, n 26, para 79.

administrative, or judicial act authorizing such acts, subjecting alleged perpetrators to universal criminal jurisdiction, and forbidding their exclusion from extradition under any political offence exemption.

States are bound by *jus cogens* norms whether or not they have expressly consented to them. For example, the 50 or so states that are not parties to the UNCAT remain subject to the prohibition of torture: they cannot derogate from it through international treaties, through local or special customs, or even 'through general customary rules not endowed with the same normative force'.[36] Although the grounding of *jus cogens* norms in fundamental interests of the wider international community overrides the requirement for individual state consent, the threshold is high. These norms must be accepted as such by the 'international community of states as a whole' indicating widespread general consent.

However, there remains controversy over which human rights norms have this status and over some of its implications. There is widespread agreement on the *jus cogens* quality of certain rights such as the prohibition of torture and genocide, but others that have been accepted by some bodies are more controversial, for example all forms of discrimination,[37] the death penalty for those under 18,[38] and the right to property.[39] With respect to the legal consequences of a determination of *jus cogens*, it seems that it does not override jurisdictional requirements. For example, the European Court of Human Rights as well as some domestic courts have held that the prohibition against torture does not deprive a foreign state of its immunity from jurisdiction before the national courts of another state, where it is accused of torture.[40]

6 GENERAL PRINCIPLES OF LAW

The meaning of 'general principles of law' as listed in Article 38(1)(c) ICJ Statute remains controversial and has had little practical application. One view is that this expression refers to principles found in most, if not all, national legal systems, such as notions of procedural fairness or equity, while another view is that they include 'general principles applicable directly to international legal relations',[41] for example the principle that treaties are binding upon states parties. In both cases, human rights are more likely to be applied as general principles rather than general principles constituting a source of human rights.

---

[36] *Furundžija,* n 33, para 153.

[37] *Juridical Conditions and Rights of Undocumented Migrants,* IACtHR Series A No 18 (2003) paras 82–110.

[38] Case 12.240, *Douglas Christopher Thomas v United States,* IACommHR Report No 100/03, OEA/Ser./L/V/II.114 Doc.70 rev.1 (2003) 790, para 52.

[39] The European Court of First Instance suggested this in *Kadi v Council of the EU and Commission of the EC* (T-315/01) [2005] ECR II-3649, 293, at least where there is arbitrary deprivation.

[40] *Al-Adsani v UK* (2002) 34 EHRR 11.

[41] Thirlway, 'The Sources of International Law' in Evans (ed), *International Law* (OUP, 2006) 128.

Simma and Alston have argued for greater use of general principles as a contemporary source of human rights law and that general principles derived from the international plane should be expanded:

Principles brought to the fore in this 'direct' way... would (and should) then percolate down into domestic fora, instead of being elevated from the domestic level to that of international law by way of analogy.[42]

General principles drawn from international arenas may be found in statements of consensus, such as those expressed at global summits, and in the resolutions of UN organs. Simma and Alston reason that this would retain the consensual basis of international law while overcoming many of the conceptual and practical problems of customary international law, in particular the need to prove state practice and *opinio juris*. However, it does not seem that their position has influenced decision-makers.

7 JUDICIAL DECISIONS

There is no dedicated international human rights court. However, a feature of the international legal system over the past few decades has been the proliferation of judicial bodies, many of which determine questions of human rights that arise before them. There is no hierarchy between these courts but their interaction has contributed to the dynamic quality of human rights law.

Article 38(1)(d) ICJ Statute provides that judicial decisions are 'subsidiary means' for determining rules of international law. The article does not clarify which courts it is referring to or the weight that should be given to judicial decisions. It does, however, refer to Article 59, which rejects any doctrine of precedent before the International Court of Justice.[43] The formal position is that international courts do not make law and that their decisions are binding only on the parties to the particular case and can be discounted in subsequent cases. However, this ignores the reality that through the interpretation and application of treaties and custom, judicial decisions elucidate and develop international law. In a decentralized legal system that lacks a legislature and where unwritten law is developed through the amorphous processes of state practice and *opinio juris*, judicial decision making carries great weight through exposition of the law. At the national, regional, and international levels courts play an especially important role in developing and moulding human rights law in accordance with changing social circumstances and understandings of rights.

---

[42] Simma and Alston, 'The Sources of Human Rights Law: Custom, *Jus Cogens* and General Principles' (1992) 12 *Australian YIL* 82, 102.

[43] Art 59 states that '[t]he decision of the Court has no binding force except between the parties and in respect of that particular case'.

7.1 INTERACTION AT THE INTERNATIONAL AND REGIONAL LEVELS

The International Court of Justice is the only international court with jurisdiction over all questions of international law, which includes issues relating to human rights.[44] It has, for example, asserted the applicability of human rights law in armed conflict and in occupied territories.[45] Other bodies may follow its lead. For example, the Human Rights Committee adopted a similar approach in its General Comment 31.[46] Although the Committee did not refer directly to the opinions of the International Court, it is likely that it sought to follow a similar path for the development of the law. Decisions of the International Court of Justice may also contribute to state practice where its decisions are followed by national courts, although there is no guarantee that this will be the case.

International human rights law and international criminal law are companion legal regimes and developments in one area may impact on the other, adding to the richness of the sources of each. Thus, international criminal courts may consider human rights law as a potential source of international criminal law. For example, the sources of the prohibition of torture, as a human rights violation, are customary international law, the ICCPR, and the UNCAT. The human rights definition of torture can be found in Article 1 UNCAT. Torture is also an international crime and the International Criminal Tribunal for the former Yugoslavia (ICTY) has had to determine whether the international crime of torture has the same definition as the human rights violation. The ICTY first looked to human rights law and accepted the UNCAT definition as customary international law.[47] It subsequently changed its stance and adapted the definition to suit its own context—armed conflict—and the requirement that it apply international humanitarian law.[48] The ICTY Appeals Chamber affirmed that the UNCAT definition remains important as customary international law when considering state responsibility—the domain of human rights—but not for individual criminal responsibility—the domain of international criminal law.[49]

Similarly, decisions of international criminal tribunals may be turned to by human rights courts as a subsidiary source of human rights law. For example, in *MC v Bulgaria* the European Court of Human Rights looked to the jurisprudence of the ICTY in determining that rape constituted torture contrary to Article 3 ECHR. While accepting that the ICTY was dealing with the particular context of rape in armed conflict,

---

[44] eg the former Permanent Court of International Justice made an important contribution to the understanding of equality and difference: *Minority Schools in Albania, Advisory Opinion*, PCIJ Series A/B No 64 (1935). Dissenting Judge Tanaka in the *South West Africa Cases* (second phase) [1966] ICJ Rep 6, 305–6 did likewise.

[45] *Legality of the Threat or Use of Nuclear Weapons*, n 26; *Legal Consequences of the Construction of a Wall in the Occupied Palestinian Territory* [2004] ICJ Rep 136.

[46] HRC, General Comment 31, HRI/GEN/1/Rev.9 (Vol I) 243, para 11.

[47] *Prosecutor v Mucić et al.*, Judgment, IT-96-21-T, 16 November 1998, para 459.

[48] *Prosecutor v Kunarac*, Judgment, IT-96-23-T and IT-96-23/1-T, 22 February 2001, paras 465 ff.

[49] *Prosecutor v Kunarac*, Judgment, IT-96-23 and IT-96-23/1-A, 12 June 2002, para 146.

the European Court considered that its jurisprudence 'reflected a universal trend' that was relevant to its own determination of rape as a human rights violation.[50] The decisions of international criminal courts may be a subsidiary source of human rights law, but their different legal focus means that there cannot be an automatic transposition between the two legal regimes.

7.2 INTERACTION BETWEEN NATIONAL COURTS

The same processes can be observed across national courts. Many states have adopted international human rights standards into their constitutions and legislation, requiring national courts to interpret and apply the relevant provisions. In some cases international human rights treaties are incorporated into national law, while in others language is simply taken from them. In either event, judges in different jurisdictions must interpret and apply similarly worded provisions and may look to each other's decisions in doing so. The jurisprudence of regional and national courts is authoritative only within their own legal system, but careful judicial analysis can be influential in the decision making by courts in other regions and states that are faced with comparable problems and must apply similar language. Judicial decisions can carry persuasive weight across national and regional boundaries and it is becoming commonplace for judges in one jurisdiction 'to refer extensively to the decision of the courts of foreign jurisdictions when interpreting human rights guarantees'.[51] Especially when deciding a novel point, judges may feel that drawing on a decision, or reasoning, of another court bestows legitimacy on their own judgment. Nevertheless, this process must not be taken for granted and research is required on specific issues to determine whether there is judicial consistency on a particular point and its extent. Where there is such consistency, it can be used as evidence of uniform state practice.

The reputation of certain courts, or the novelty of the point of human rights law under consideration, may give some decisions additional persuasive weight. They may also be used in advocacy and in writings and reports by human rights groups. For example, the decision of the House of Lords in the *Pinochet* case[52] has been widely cited and referred to. Similarly, the decisions of the South African Constitutional Court with respect to the understanding of economic and social rights have been influential.[53] The importance of this jurisprudence may have been enhanced because of the lack of judicial decision making on these rights at the international and regional levels: the Committee on Economic, Social and Cultural Rights historically has not had the

---

[50] (2005) 40 EHRR 20.

[51] McCrudden, 'A Common Law of Human Rights? Transnational Judicial Conversations on Constitutional Rights' (2000) 20 *OJLS* 499, 506.

[52] *R v Bow Street Metropolitan Stipendiary Magistrate, ex parte Pinochet Ugarte (No 3)* [1999] 2 WLR 827.

[53] *Government of the Republic of South Africa & Ors v Grootboom & Ors* 2000 (11) BCLR 1169; *Minister of Health v Treatment Action Campaign (TAC)* (2002) 5 SA 721 (CC).

competence to hear individual complaints, and the ECHR and ACHR are primarily focused on civil and political rights.

7.3 HUMAN RIGHTS LITIGATION

Human rights litigation is a comparatively new phenomenon but has rapidly evolved, thereby increasing the availability of argument, interpretation, and application of norms and enhancing the value of judicial decisions as a source of human rights law. Electronic information means that pleadings and decisions from numerous fora are readily available and accessible. Global networks of human rights activists devise litigation strategies, seek out test cases, and publicize successful claims so that similar arguments may be made elsewhere. There is now a body of judges and experts in global and regional institutions who regularly hear cases involving claims of violations of human rights. These are complemented by judges in national courts responsible for the judicial enforcement of human rights. They too form networks through bodies such as the International Bar Association, and can thus support and reinforce each other. They may attend training sessions on international human rights law. While they must all work within the constraints of their particular institution and legal framework, they face similar issues and may turn to the decisions of other bodies in determining their own approach. In all these ways judicial decision making fleshes out and develops international human rights treaties and custom and, thus, has a greater influence than might be expected of a 'subsidiary source' of human rights law.

8   WRITINGS OF JURISTS

Article 38(1)(d) ICJ Statute includes the 'teachings of the most highly qualified publicists' as another subsidiary source of international law. Within the international human rights system there are now a plethora of expert bodies and individuals who produce important reports and commentaries on a wide range of human rights issues. These include the UN Human Rights Council special procedures (Special Rapporteurs, fact-finding missions, working groups, expert meetings), the reports of the former Sub-Commission on Human Rights (now advisory council), human rights work of UN specialized agencies, and NGO reports such as those of Human Rights Watch and Amnesty International. Such works are often scholarly, well researched, and analytical. They are compiled for many purposes: to expose a particular violative practice, to provide an academic analysis of an issue, or to gain media attention. They may also consciously seek to develop human rights law, by bringing together examples of state practice and *opinio juris* and arguing that these are sufficiently consistent to found a new rule of custom, or to demonstrate the need for a treaty on the subject. Writings of this type are not binding and do not constitute a formal source of human rights law.

Nevertheless, the result is that there is a wealth of literature that may be understood as a subsidiary source. The persuasiveness of any one piece of writing depends upon the quality of research and analysis and the authority of the relevant institution or author. There may be deliberate strategies to enhance the authority of a particular piece of work, for example the growing practice of reports by multiple Special Rapporteurs.[54] As with judicial decisions, much depends on the use made of such works by states and other actors. Today, such works are more influential in developing human rights law than the writings of more traditional publicists referred to in Article 38(1)(d).

9 OTHER SOURCES

In addition to the formal sources of international law as spelled out in Article 38(1) ICJ Statute, other methods of developing human rights law must be identified.

9.1 WORK OF TREATY BODIES

The role of the UN treaty bodies in developing human rights law has been previously mentioned. The different activities of these bodies cut across the sources discussed above. The treaty bodies elucidate states' obligations under the various treaties through the adoption of general comments and concluding observations in response to states' reports. These might be described as secondary treaty law, in that state consent can be implied from their acceptance of the treaties and the authority of the expert committees. This is reinforced where states comply with the reporting requirements.

Some of the treaty bodies also have a form of quasi-judicial competence. This is the individual complaint or communication procedure, which is primarily a written procedure and concludes with a recommendatory decision by the relevant committee.[55] Can such decisions be regarded as judicial decisions under Article 38(1)(d)? On the one hand, they are non-binding and in many instances include only limited reasoning. On the other hand, the monitoring role accorded by treaty to the expert committees means that the opinions cannot be easily disregarded. The individual complaint procedure allows the treaty bodies to develop jurisprudence on the interpretation and application of the relevant convention and their opinions may be cited before decision-makers, or used as supporting evidence of current human rights law. The weight given to their output varies according to the strength of the argument, the esteem accorded to the particular committee, and the extent to which their work is in tune with other developments in human rights law.

---

[54] eg Situation of detainees at Guantánamo Bay, joint report of five holders of mandates of special procedures of the Commission on Human Rights, E/CN.4/2006/120 (27 February 2006).

[55] See Chapter 18, below.

9.2 RESOLUTIONS OF INTERNATIONAL INSTITUTIONS

An important omission from Article 38(1) ICJ Statute is resolutions of international institutions. Security Council resolutions adopted under UN Charter Chapter VII are binding on states parties, but have not been used as a source of human rights law. Of much greater significance are the numerous General Assembly resolutions which have widened the scope of human rights, set standards for states and non-state actors, and have provided aspirations and goals. Indeed, the foundational document of international human rights law—the UDHR—is in the form of a General Assembly resolution. Such non-binding instruments (often termed 'soft law') may be the basis for binding norms where they are declaratory of custom, or are subsequently transformed into a treaty or custom. The UDHR was followed, albeit 18 years later, by the ICCPR and ICESCR, treaties binding on states parties. It is also regarded by many commentators as having become customary international law. This transformation into formal sources, however, fails to indicate its own abiding authority and status.

The same pattern—resolution followed by treaty—has occurred in many other instances: the Declaration on Torture was followed by the UNCAT; many resolutions on the rights of the child were followed eventually by the CRC; resolutions on the rights of persons with disabilities were followed by the CRPD. In other cases no treaty has been adopted on the subject matter addressed in a General Assembly resolution. There has been no global treaty on the rights of minorities following the General Assembly Declaration on the Rights of Persons belonging to National, Ethnic, Religious and Linguistic Minorities. Even where a treaty has followed a resolution, it is unlikely that all states will become parties. Individuals may therefore wish to argue that the resolution has crystallized into customary international law. Criteria for determining that a resolution has become customary international law have been put forward. They include adoption of the resolution by consensus, the inclusion of normative language, and follow-up procedures—all factors that indicate states' consent to be bound.

Another way in which a non-binding resolution may be understood as a source of human rights law is where it provides an authoritative interpretation of a treaty. This was the approach taken by the Inter-American Court of Human Rights in considering the status of the American Declaration of the Rights and Duties of Man. The Court considered that for

member states of the Organization, the Declaration is the text that defines the human rights referred to in the [OAS] Charter...with the result that...the American Declaration is for these States a source of international obligations related to the Charter of the Organization....That the Declaration is not a treaty does not, then, lead to the conclusion that it does not have legal effect.[56]

The Inter-American Commission has accordingly determined that the USA has human rights obligations under the Declaration despite it not having become a party to the ACHR.

---

[56] OC-10/89, *Interpretation of the American Declaration of the Rights and Duties of Man within the Framework of Article 64 of the American Convention on Human Rights*, Series A No 10 (1989), paras 45–7.

9.3 OTHER FORMS OF SOFT LAW

Other forms of soft law include resolutions of the Human Rights Council, guidelines,[57] codes of conduct[58] and standards of behaviour,[59] and the final instruments of global summit meetings held under UN auspices. The latter have become noteworthy features of the international landscape since the 1990s. They have typically generated great energy through the establishment of a conference secretariat, wide participation, intensive preparations, lobbying, and intense (often heated) negotiations. They have culminated in declarations and programmes of action directed to states, intergovernmental organizations, and NGOs.[60] There have been follow-up procedures, normally at five-year intervals.

It is noticeable that many of these instruments are negotiated with as much care and attention to detail as binding texts and states also make reservations to them, undermining the formal position that they lack legal authority. The practical difference in impact between treaties and non-binding resolutions may not be great, especially where treaty language is imprecise and seems to deny legal obligation. For example, under Article 2 ICESCR, each state party undertakes to 'take steps...to the maximum of its available resources, with a view to achieving progressively the...rights recognized...by all appropriate means'. Words such as 'take steps', 'progressively', and 'appropriate means' lack clear legal content. As there was originally no right of individual complaint under the ICESCR, the treaty might be considered as imposing only a 'soft' obligation despite its legal form.[61] There are advantages to the 'soft' form: it may facilitate reaching a political consensus, bring an issue onto the international agenda, define the area of international concern, and provide guidelines for behaviour that may generate the requisite practice for a rule of customary international law. Judges and other decision-makers may turn to formally non-binding instruments in much the same way as treaties,[62] and there is often little distinction in terms of compliance.[63]

The example of violence against women illustrates how the different procedures of a specialist UN human rights treaty body, the CEDAW Committee, in conjunction

[57] eg Basic Principles and Guidelines on the Right to a Remedy and Reparation for Victims of Gross Violations of International Human Rights Law and Serious Violations of International Humanitarian Law, GA Res 60/147, 16 December 2005.

[58] eg Code of Conduct for Law Enforcement Officials, GA Res 34/169, 17 December 1979; Basic Principles on the Use of Force and Firearms by Law Enforcement Officials, 1990.

[59] eg Standard Minimum Rules for the Treatment of Prisoners, 1955.

[60] eg World Conference on Human Rights, Vienna, 1993; Fourth World Conference on Women, Beijing, 1995; and review conferences.   [61] See Chapter 8, below.

[62] eg in *R v Immigration Officer at Prague Airport, ex parte European Roma Rights Centre and Others* [2005] 2 WLR 1, the UK House of Lords referred to a range of formally non-binding documents, including a UN High Commissioner for Refugees *Handbook on Procedures and Criteria for Determining Refugee Status*; the Declaration on Territorial Asylum, 1967; American Law Institute, *Restatement of the Foreign Relations Law of the United States (Third)*; resolutions of the Committee of Ministers of the Council of Europe; reports of the International Law Association; HRC, General Comment 31; reports by the Inter-American Commission for Human Rights and UN Committee on the Elimination of Racial Discrimination; academic articles.

[63] Shelton (ed), *Commitment and Compliance: The Role of Non-Binding Norms in the International Legal System* (OUP, 2000).

with other non-binding processes, may work together to produce binding norms. The Committee has used its General Recommendation 19 on violence against women, its concluding observations on states parties' reports, an inquiry procedure,[64] and its decisions in individual complaints of brutal domestic violence sustained over many years,[65] to develop the understanding that gender-based violence is discrimination within the terms of the CEDAW and that states have an obligation to exercise due diligence to protect women from such violence, prosecute it, and punish it. The Committee's work has been reinforced by General Assembly resolutions,[66] resolutions of the Commission on Human Rights (and now Council), including the adoption of a mandate for a Special Rapporteur on the causes and consequences of violence against women, the final instruments of global conferences, and ongoing work by the General Assembly, including commissioning the Secretary-General to prepare an 'In-Depth Study on Violence against Women' and an annual report on implementation of its recommendations. In addition, the European Court of Human Rights has drawn upon such materials in determining that a state's 'failure to protect women against domestic violence breaches their right to equal protection of the law'.[67] These non-binding processes taken together have strong accumulative effect in determining that violence against women violates human rights law.[68] At the very least, these expressions by states of the wrongfulness of failing to prevent and punish such behaviour constitute considerable evidence of *opinio juris* of an international norm prohibiting violence against women, despite its continuing prevalence.

10 CONCLUSION

The formal sources of international human rights law derive from state consent: states negotiate and enter into treaties; custom is drawn from state behaviour and intent. However, this conclusion should be treated with some caution for two reasons. First, the requirement for state consent may be weakening through the turn to international community interests and values as in the concept of *jus cogens*. Long a theoretical concept that held little attraction for judges and decision-makers, *jus cogens* has been more widely appealed to since the 1990s. Second, human rights law speaks to people who appeal to its standards against what they regard as unwarranted state intrusion

---

[64] Report on Mexico produced by the CEDAW Committee under Article 8 of the Optional Protocol to the Convention, and reply from the Government of Mexico, CEDAW/C/2005/OP8/Mexico (27 January 2005).

[65] *Ms AT v Hungary*, CEDAW/C/36/D/2/2003 (26 January 2005); *Şahide Goecke v Austria*, CEDAW/C/39/D/5/2005 (6 August 2007); *Fatma Yildirim (deceased) v Austria*, CEDAW/C/39/D/6/2005 (6 August 2007).

[66] Most importantly the Declaration on the Elimination of Violence against Women, GA Res 48/104, 20 December 1993.   [67] *Opuz v Turkey*, App no 33401/02, Judgment of 9 June 2009.

[68] The only treaties on violence against women are the Inter-American Convention on the Prevention, Punishment and Eradication of Violence against Women, Belém do Pará, 1994 and the Protocol to the African Charter on Human and Peoples' Rights on the Rights of Women in Africa, 2003. See Chapter 16, below.

into their lives. It provides a language, a methodology, and techniques for challenging state action. Working as individuals and through human rights NGOs, they seek to influence the development of human rights law through a range of activities. The practice and statements of these non-state actors do not constitute formal sources of human rights law but they should not be ignored. NGOs have been the driving force in the negotiation of a number of treaties (for example the UNCAT, the CRC, and the CRPD) and their monitoring activities may influence state practice.

Contemporary human rights law is dynamic and evolving through claims for new rights, additional instruments, and practices. Decision-makers have a choice: they can be rigid and rely strictly on formal sources which they interpret narrowly; or they may interpret open-ended and indeterminate treaty language, or move beyond treaties to the range of other instruments that are out there to capture a wide range of behaviours and assert them to be contrary to international law.

FURTHER READING

ALVAREZ, *International Organizations as Law-Makers* (Oxford University Press, 2005).

BOYLE and CHINKIN, *The Making of International Law* (Oxford University Press, 2007).

CASSESE, *International Law* (Oxford University Press, 2005) chs 8–11, 19.

GOWLLAND-DEBBAS (ed), *Multilateral Treaty-Making* (Martinus Nijhoff, 2000).

INTERNATIONAL LAW ASSOCIATION, *Final Report of the Committee on Formation of*

Customary (General) International Law (2000) available at <http://www.ila-hq.org/en/committees/index.cfm/cid/30>.

ORAKHELASHVILI, *Peremptory Norms in International Law* (Oxford University Press, 2008).

THIRLWAY, 'The Sources of International Law' in Evans (ed), *International Law* (Oxford University Press, 2006).

USEFUL WEBSITES

For the work of the UN treaty bodies, see the website of the Office of the High Commissioner for Human Rights, Human Rights bodies: <**http://www.ohchr.org/EN/HRBodies/Pages/HumanRightsBodies.aspx**>

For human rights treaties, see the University of Minnesota human rights library: <**http://www1.umn.edu/humanrts/**>

6

NATURE OF OBLIGATIONS

Frédéric Mégret

SUMMARY

Human rights obligations have a special status in international law because they are, in some ways, fundamentally different from other international law obligations. States that ratify international human rights treaties are not primarily committing to respect human rights vis-à-vis other states, but vis-à-vis persons within their jurisdiction. This is what is sometimes known as the 'special character' of international human rights obligations and it has concrete implications. States must implement human rights domestically in particular ways, even though they may have a 'margin of appreciation' in doing so. When ratifying human rights treaties, states must be particularly careful of what reservations they make, as many reservations have been found to be incompatible with the 'object and purpose' of such treaties. Human rights obligations can be limited on the basis of certain needs justifiable in a democratic society, and can even be derogated from in very exceptional circumstances, but it is likely that a state cannot withdraw entirely from a human rights treaty if the treaty does not contain a clause on denunciation.

1 INTRODUCTION

What is the fundamental nature of human rights obligations? What does it mean to be bound by international human rights law? Obligations can be defined in terms of their duty-holders and their beneficiaries. In trying to assess the 'nature' of human rights obligations, this chapter will go beyond assessing duty-holders and beneficiaries in an attempt to understand what *sort* of obligations are involved. For example, are human rights obligations fundamentally unilateral or multilateral, reciprocal or non-reciprocal, temporal or eternal, conditional or unconditional, relative or absolute? The main idea in this chapter is that human rights obligations are in some ways radically distinct from other types of obligations existing under general international law.

Why does this matter and why should general international law be the standard of comparison? First, international human rights law is a branch of public international law. When human rights lawyers sought to internationalize the human rights project in the middle of the twentieth century, they had no choice but to draw on the body of law existing at the global level.[1] Only public international law could bind states 'from above' and change domestic practices. However, international law as a legal system is far from neutral. It comes with its own legal assumptions, preferences, and logic, some of which, as will be seen, might be at odds with the very idea and purpose of human rights. It must be remembered that, classically, international law was a law created by, between, and for states. Its cardinal concept was state sovereignty, and the typical source of obligation was state voluntarism (that is, states are only bound by those obligations to which they have consented). International law was, in a sense, dedicated to ensuring that state sovereignty and state voluntarism would not be undermined. It would be surprising, therefore, if these origins did not lead to some tensions with the human rights project, the goal of which is very much geared towards redefining sovereignty. Although the stark divide between public international law and international human rights law has lessened over time as the development of the former has been influenced by the growth of the latter, some tensions between these bodies of law remain.

The problem can be analysed as one of tension between substance and form, where ideally in any given legal system the two should be aligned. Substantively, the projects of public international law and international human rights law could not be more at odds. Human rights law is concerned with proclaiming and enforcing certain fundamental guarantees for individuals against the state. As such, it is both radical and revolutionary. The strict international protection of sovereignty is, in principle, largely incompatible with a strong stance in favour of human rights, in that human rights deal with issues that are largely domestic and traditionally considered to be part of states' exclusive purview.

Formally, human rights law, as it has emerged domestically, and general international law differ very significantly. International law is the slow maturing of ancient customary practice. It emphasizes states' obligations, and it is marked by a high degree of flexibility. Human rights law emerges from the proclamation of rights, usually in declarations. It outlines minimum rights with a strong principled component, and its focus is on the beneficiaries of obligations (individuals). However, the two have converged formally, at least to the extent that human rights obligations are typically given their binding character internationally by being recognized in international sources, such as custom and treaty.

Inevitably, this creates a tension between the *substance* of human rights, and the *form* they take, between the idea of rights as inherent to the human person and the fact that they only have traction internationally to the extent they are recognized in, especially, treaties. Historically, international law has been seen as neutral about results, essentially only offering states the means for a very basic interaction that safeguarded their sovereignty by allowing them to coexist. International norms have emerged

---

[1] See Chapter 1, above.

from consent between equals. The model for them was the *contract*, that is, an obligation based on reciprocity. In other words, the obligations of each party are entered into in exchange for the other party undertaking similar obligations, and each party is bound to the extent that the other respects its own obligations. Some of the implications of this included the fact that states could subscribe to whatever obligations they freely agreed to, modify the content of their obligations through consensus, and even under certain conditions cease to respect certain obligations. A further consequence was that international legal instruments only created obligations between states, at the expense of individuals who were considered mere 'objects' of international law, at best unintended and collateral beneficiaries of obligations undertaken by states. Although international law diversified in due course, regulating ever more areas of international life, it did and largely still does claim to lay the ground rules for all thematic branches of international law. For example, the Vienna Convention on the Law of Treaties (VCLT) is not interested in the particular content of treaties, whether they deal with trade, the environment, or diplomatic immunities; it lays down the same basic rules which apply to all treaties.

The problem is that the international law form—the particular expression international commitments take legally—is not substantively neutral and the substance of human rights does not always fit this form. The point has been made eloquently by Craven in the context of human rights treaties:

In human rights treaties the two elements of 'form' and 'function' appear to be fundamentally at odds with one another. On the one hand, the form in which the rights are expressed—the treaty—supposes that human rights are merely the incidental subject of a contractual bargain between states. Individual 'right-holders' are therefore simply the fortuitous beneficiaries of a regime that is otherwise concerned with promoting the rights and interests of states. The teleology of the regime on the other hand—focused as it is on individual or group 'human rights'—supposes that the treaties are quasi-constitutional in character.[2]

Historically, this has created a very significant conceptual and practical challenge for human rights lawyers: how can we avoid the human rights project being stultified, or even absorbed, by the language of traditional international law? The answer generally has been to redefine human rights obligations, particularly treaty obligations, as *special* in nature. Thus, human rights obligations are dependent on, and yet also crucially distinct from, the way in which international legal obligations typically operate. But this idea that human rights obligations are somehow 'special' needs to be grounded and explained, to understand exactly why this is so, and what the implications are.

This chapter will introduce the basic idea of what it means for a legal obligation to be described as 'special' in nature in international law (Section 2). It will then identify several key consequences that can be said to flow from this character in terms of implementing human rights obligations (Section 3), reservations (Section 4),

---

[2] Craven, 'Legal Differentiation and the Concept of the Human Rights Treaty in International Law' (2000) 11 *EJIL* 489.

limitations and derogations (Section 5), withdrawal (Section 6), and enforcement (Section 7).

2 THE 'SPECIAL CHARACTER' OF HUMAN RIGHTS OBLIGATIONS

Defining in general terms the 'special character' of human rights obligations is a difficult exercise. The fundamental idea is that international human rights obligations differ from normal international law obligations in that they deal with the obligations of states towards individuals rather than between states.

At a certain level, international human rights law is hardly a rejection of all the rules of public international law. As has been seen in Chapter 5, for example, there is no reason to think that the list of existing sources of the 'branch' that is international human rights law is entirely different from the 'trunk' of public international law. International human rights treaties borrow much from the traditional law of treaties, including the way treaties come into existence, the simple idea that states are bound by treaties they ratify (the *pacta sunt servanda* rule), and that states should discharge their obligations in good faith. Many of the key aspects of state responsibility (that is, what happens when a state violates its obligation), moreover, are applicable in the field of human rights. There is no reason to think that any of these rules apply in markedly different ways simply because the subject matter of a treaty is human rights.

However, there are also clearly some ways in which human rights obligations are different. A traditional treaty is one that creates rights and obligations between states, to the broad exclusion of any other actor, even if that other actor may objectively benefit from such arrangements. States typically *exchange* such rights and obligations, with a view to securing an advantage commensurate with their costs. Moreover, treaties are often quite strictly relational: states enter into treaties only with those states they want to enter into such treaties with. Finally, international law traditionally does not have a significant stake in the subject matter to which states commit (as opposed to the fact that they should honour whatever commitments they make).

Human rights treaties superficially borrow the idea of an agreement between states as the basis of international human rights obligations. But they are also strikingly different. They are agreements, typically between states, the beneficiaries of which are in fact third parties, namely 'all individuals within its [the state's] territory'.[3] Indeed, human rights treaties create rights specifically for individuals who are not normally subjects of international law generally or treaties specifically. To describe human rights treaties as contractual, moreover, would be profoundly misleading. It is wrong to say that states commit to respecting certain human rights obligations in exchange for other states doing the same. From a practical point of view, international human

---

[3] ICCPR, Art 2.

rights obligations are not as dependent on this idea of reciprocity as most ordinary treaties, where the interest of incurring an obligation will very quickly lapse if the other party or parties do not comply with their obligations. Finally, human rights lawyers think that human rights treaties have a substance that is inherently of a high normative worth, above and beyond states' consent to be bound by them.

All these differences are very important, because they have an impact on the way international human rights obligations are understood, administered, and interpreted. To capture what makes human rights different, human rights lawyers have forged the unique notion of the 'special character' of human rights obligations.[4] At first, the meaning of 'special character' was unclear. It seemed to be one of those 'catch-all' phrases that merely seemed to imply that ordinary rules of international law did not apply when it came to human rights. However, human rights bodies have refined the idea over the years to reflect what is distinctive about human rights.

The first reference to the special character of a human rights treaty occurred when the General Assembly sought an advisory opinion from the International Court of Justice on reservations to the Genocide Convention. The Court distinguished between ordinary treaties and those of a humanitarian or human rights character. In the case of the latter:

[T]he contracting States do not have any interests of their own; they merely have, one and all, a common interest, namely, the accomplishment of those high purposes which are the *raison d'être* of the convention. Consequently, in a convention of this type one cannot speak of individual advantages or disadvantages to States, or of the maintenance of a perfect contractual balance between rights and duties.[5]

The idea was that the Genocide Convention created something greater than the sum of each party's will. Moreover, there was a certain vertical element involved: states were not so much bargaining between each other horizontally, as solemnly committing themselves to a certain supranational standard of behaviour.

A similar approach was taken by the European Commission of Human Rights in 1961, when it affirmed that:

The obligations undertaken by the High Contracting Parties in the [European] Convention [on Human Rights] are essentially of an objective character, being designed rather to protect the fundamental rights of individual human beings from infringements by any of the High Contracting Parties than to create subjective and reciprocal rights for the High Contracting Parties themselves.[6]

In this context, 'objective' does not mean that the obligations in question are absolute or that they are scientifically proven. Rather, it should be understood in the legal meaning of not strictly dependent on the commitments of other states. Again, the

---

[4] This special character is most frequently adduced in the context of treaty obligations, but it also has an impact on how obligations emerging from other sources (eg customary international law) should be understood.

[5] *Reservations to the Genocide Convention* (Advisory Opinion) [1951] ICJ Rep 15, para 23.

[6] *Austria v Italy (Pfunders Case)* (1961) 4 *YB* 116, para 138.

idea is that, despite appearances of a treaty being concluded with other states, there is something relatively unilateral about states' adherence to a treaty like the European Convention on Human Rights (ECHR), even though some of the traditional benefits of treaties, such as getting other states to behave in a particular manner, retain a residual role.[7] States are better understood as making a solemn promise to the international community, and indeed to individuals within their jurisdiction.

The Inter-American Court of Human Rights has added its own views on the idea of special character. As the Court put it in one of its advisory opinions:

[M]odern human rights treaties in general, and the American Convention in particular, *are not multilateral treaties of the traditional type concluded to accomplish the reciprocal exchange of rights for the mutual benefit of the contracting States.* Their object and purpose is the protection of the basic rights of individual human beings irrespective of their nationality, both against the State of their nationality and all other contracting States. In concluding these human rights treaties, the States *can be deemed to submit themselves to a legal order within which they, for the common good, assume various obligations, not in relation to other States, but towards all individuals within their jurisdiction.*[8]

The special character of human rights suggests that states' human rights obligations are in some ways independent of their consent to be bound by them. Human rights obligations have a life of their own that takes over as soon as states have manifested their initial commitment to be bound. This is also linked to old claims about human rights pre-existing their legal recognition (the idea, for example, that rights exist 'in nature'). States are solemnly committing to something which they were already, at least morally or philosophically, obliged to recognize. Another way of putting it would be to say that becoming a party to a human rights treaty is *declaratory* of states' obligations rather than *constitutive* of them.

Moreover, the objective character of human rights obligations points to their *erga omnes* status. The International Court of Justice famously suggested that certain obligations may have an *erga omnes* character in that they were owed 'towards the international community as a whole' so that 'by their very nature, (they) are the concern of all States'.[9] What was a slightly puzzling obiter dictum in the international law context, has become relatively mainstream in the human rights environment, where it is understood that, precisely as a result of the special character of human rights obligations, each and every state (that is a party to the human rights system) has an interest in their enforcement. Indeed, it could be said that international human rights obligations have become a typical example of *erga omnes* obligations.

The ECHR has been described by the European Court of Human Rights as a 'constitutional instrument of European public order'.[10] The reference to this constitutional

---

[7] Ratification of a human rights treaty may be based on an expectation that other states will do the same.

[8] OC-2/82, *The Effect of Reservations on the Entry into Force of the American Convention (Arts 74 and 75)*, IACtHR Series A No 2 (24 September 1982) paras 29–30 (emphases added).

[9] *Barcelona Traction, Light and Power Company, Limited (Belgium v Spain)* (New Application: 1962) [1970] ICJ Rep 3, para 33.   [10] *Loizidou v Turkey* (Preliminary Objections) (1995) 20 EHRR 99, para 75.

character also underlines the extent to which international human rights treaties, perhaps especially regional ones, are part of governance structures and, beyond that, one of the normative foundations of political community (for example, that of the Council of Europe in the case of the ECHR). International human rights thus appear as the cement that binds groups of states together in a collective project that is domestic, transnational, and supranational.

Although the special nature of human rights obligations might at first appear to be a mere doctrinal construct, what is remarkable is the extent to which concrete consequences have flowed from this idea. In the sections that follow, we will see some of the manifestations of the special character of human rights obligations, and the considerable impact it has had on the enjoyment of human rights.

3 IMPLEMENTATION OF HUMAN RIGHTS OBLIGATIONS

Typically, under traditional international law the manner in which an obligation is supposed to be discharged is not specified. States simply have to do what they commit themselves to do, and considerable discretion is left as to the means by which they do so. When it comes to human rights, this traditional, laissez-faire, approach will not do. International human rights law has thus come up with a complex concept of how obligations are to be discharged. An entirely new vocabulary of obligations has emerged. Typically, states are supposed to 'respect and ensure rights to all individuals'.[11] However, this is a very broad obligation and in practice the UN human rights treaty bodies have adopted a tripartite typology of how human rights obligations should be secured. According to that typology, states must respect, protect, and fulfil human rights.

3.1 RESPECT

The duty to secure human rights is, perhaps first and foremost, a duty to 'respect' human rights. Thus, states have a negative obligation not to take any measures that result in a violation of a given right. They should not consciously violate rights, either through their organs (for example, parliament or the executive) or through their agents (such as, civil servants, the police, or the army).

3.2 PROTECT

In addition, and this phrase is becoming ever more important, states must 'protect' individuals from human rights violations. This means that the state needs to

---

[11] eg ICCPR, Art 2.

proactively ensure that persons within its jurisdiction do not suffer from human rights violations at the hands of third parties. This is much more akin to creating an environment in which rights are enjoyed. Of course, the state does not become liable for every adverse interference with individuals' rights by private actors. However, the state is liable for those failures that can be traced to its shortcomings in protecting individuals from other individuals, for example because it has adopted a law that made the violation possible, or because it has failed to do something that would have prevented the violation from happening.[12] This is known as the indirect horizontal effect of human rights. States have been found liable for failing to protect demonstrators from third parties,[13] for failing to protect an individual from murder despite the fact that the police knew the victim's life had been threatened,[14] and, in cases of domestic violence, for failing to provide adequate structures or legal protection to abused women.[15] As the Inter-American Court of Human Rights put it in the landmark case of *Velásquez Rodríguez v Honduras*, which involved the forced disappearance by unidentified abductors of a student activist:

An illegal act which violates human rights and which is initially not directly imputable to a State (for example, because it is the act of a private person or because the person responsible has not been identified) can lead to international responsibility of the State, not because of the act itself, but because of the lack of due diligence to prevent the violation or to respond to it as required by the [American] Convention..... [The state is liable when it] allows private persons or groups to act freely and with impunity to the detriment of the rights recognized by the Convention.[16]

3.3 FULFIL

The obligation to 'respect' human rights is a primarily negative one (to not actively violate rights). Treaty bodies, however, have long emphasized the existence of an obligation to 'fulfil' human rights, by which it is understood that states should proactively engage in activities that have as a consequence the greater enjoyment of rights. Some civil and political rights, such as the right to vote, are meaningless if the state does nothing to implement them. Similarly, the right to be free from torture entails not only an obligation not to torture but also an obligation to adopt all types of concrete measures to prevent and sanction torture.[17]

In formal terms, the obligation to fulfil involves an obligation on states to adopt appropriate laws that implement their international undertakings. This may involve incorporating the very rights protected by the international instrument into domestic law. However, treaty bodies, confronted with claims by states that rights were

---

[12] eg *X and Y v The Netherlands* (1986) 8 EHRR 235; *Young, James and Webster v UK* (1982) 4 EHRR 38. See also Chapter 7, below.   [13] *Plattform 'Ärzte für das Leben' v Austria* (1991) 13 EHRR 204.
[14] *Osman v UK* (2000) 29 EHRR 245; *William Eduardo Delgado Páez v Colombia*, CCPR/C/39/D/195/1985 (12 July 1990).   [15] *AT v Hungary* A/60/38 (Part I) Annex III (26 January 2005).
[16] *Velásquez Rodríguez v Honduras* (*Merits*), IACtHR Series C No 4 (29 July 1988), paras 172 and 176.
[17] See Chapter 10, below.

effectively protected simply because they were formally protected in the constitution, have insisted that the duty to secure human rights includes an obligation to adopt, not just legislative measures, but also 'judicial, administrative and educative and other appropriate measures',[18] and an obligation to organize the structure of the state apparatus in a way that ensures the full exercise of human rights.

In particular, the obligation to fulfil entails provision of a remedy, whether judicial or administrative, to all victims of human rights violations. In the *Velásquez Rodríguez* case, the Inter-American Court of Human Rights insisted that:

The State is obligated to investigate every situation involving a violation of the rights protected by the Convention. If the State apparatus acts in such a way that the violation goes unpunished and the victim's full enjoyment of such rights is not restored as soon as possible, the State has failed to comply with its duty to ensure the free and full exercise of those rights to the persons within its jurisdiction.[19]

Economic and social rights are the prime example of rights which entail a positive obligation to adopt specific measures and where 'not doing anything' is not an option. The obligation to fulfil has been understood in the context of the right to food as entailing both an obligation on states to *facilitate* individuals' ability to access resources and means to ensure their livelihood and an obligation to *provide* them with adequate food whenever they are unable to enjoy the right to food 'for reasons beyond their control'.[20] At its most general, the obligation to fulfil is considered to also involve an obligation to *promote* human rights, which means that states should adopt policies that promote rights, both domestically (for example, human rights education) and internationally (such as a foreign policy conducive to human rights).

In practice, the obligations to 'respect', 'protect', and 'fulfil' are closely interrelated issues and it may not always be easy to make a clear-cut distinction between these different aspects. Nevertheless, the typology is a helpful conceptual device to identify the various ways in which states can and must discharge their obligations under international human rights law.

3.4 MARGIN OF APPRECIATION

Whereas general international law obligations are typically not susceptible to fine-tuning by states, international human rights law has been at the forefront of efforts to develop a geographically and culturally plural notion of implementation. Particularly in the European context, there is no expectation of absolute uniform implementation, rather that a certain minimum standard should be achieved, while respecting the cultural, legal, and political specificity of each state. The European Court of Human Rights has pioneered the idea of states having a 'margin of appreciation' in how they

[18] HRC, General Comment 31, HRI/GEN/1/Rev.9 (Vol I) 243, para 7.
[19] *Velásquez Rodríguez*, n 16, para 176.
[20] CESCR, General Comment 12, HRI/GEN/1/Rev.9 (Vol I) 55, para 15.

implement their obligations, taking into account their historical, social, political, and legal specificities.

The margin of appreciation is the idea that, although states are bound by the same standards, they also have leeway in assessing what these standards imply domestically. As the European Court put it:

the main purpose of the Convention is 'to lay down certain international standards to be observed by the Contracting States in their relations with persons under their jurisdiction'. This does not mean that absolute uniformity is required and, indeed, since the Contracting States remain free to choose the measures which they consider appropriate, the Court cannot be oblivious of the substantive or procedural features of their respective domestic laws.[21]

This is often related to the jurisdictional notion that 'the machinery of protection established by the Convention is subsidiary to the national systems safeguarding human rights'.[22] The European Court does view the margin as 'go(ing) … hand in hand with a European supervision'.[23]

One rationale for the margin of appreciation is that states and domestic courts are better suited to assess local peculiarities and that there is simply too much uncertainty about how human rights are to be implemented for international supervision to exercise more than relatively minimal control. Issues of legitimacy also arise, as international bodies might provoke political backlash if they delve too deeply in matters that are seen as culturally specific.

The idea of the margin of appreciation is not universally accepted beyond the European context. The Human Rights Committee, in particular, has expressed scepticism about a 'margin of appreciation' in at least one context.[24] It has been criticized as leading to an excessively relativistic application of human rights that may even contain the seeds of the project's dissolution.

Nonetheless, margin of appreciation reasoning has featured prominently in cases involving sexual minorities,[25] corporal punishment,[26] and the place of religion in society,[27] to mention only a few examples. It contains both a temporal and a spatial dimension. Temporally, the margin of appreciation is something that can evolve over time in relation to a certain subject. For example, states parties to the ECHR may have had a considerable margin of appreciation 50 years ago when it came to criminalizing homosexuality, but the very same treaty today is interpreted in a radically different way that suggests that criminalizing same-sex relations between consenting adults is a violation of several rights. The spatial element to the margin of appreciation involves an assessment of the degree of consensus (a minimum common denominator) about

---

[21] *Sunday Times v UK* (1979–80) 2 EHRR 245, para 61.

[22] *'Belgian Linguistics' Case* (1979–80) 1 EHRR 241.

[23] *Kjeldsen, Busk Madsen and Pedersen v Denmark* (1979–80) 1 EHRR 711, para 49.

[24] *Länsman v Finland*, CCPR/C/52/D/511/1992 (30 October 1996).

[25] *Handyside v UK* (1979–80) 1 EHRR 737; *Frette v France* (2004) 38 EHRR 21; *Goodwin v UK* (2002) 35 EHRR 18.   [26] *Costello Roberts v UK* (1995) 19 EHRR 112.

[27] *Otto-Preminger-Institut v Austria* (1995) 19 EHRR 34; *Wingrove v UK* (1997) 24 EHRR 1, para 57; *'The Last Temptation of Christ' v Chile* (*Olmedo Bustos et al*), IACtHR Series C No 73 (5 February 2001), para 64.

a certain practice across member states. In the absence of such consensus and, more importantly, in the presence of divisions, the European Court will hesitate to impose on a minority (let alone a majority) of states a particular understanding of rights.

One of the consequences of this is that the margin of appreciation militates in favour of a conservative international assessment of rights. The European Court of Human Rights, for example, has often been less of a pioneer than a safe endorser of existing trends and developments. But on a more positive note, the margin of appreciation also reinforces the sense of human rights being rooted in a community of reference (which is also a community of interpretation), dynamic in time, and a product of a constant interaction between rights and ideas about society and justice.

4 RESERVATIONS

States may modify their obligations under international human rights treaties by entering reservations. This is one way in which states may limit their human rights obligations. Reservations are a particularly technical area of international law, but the study of this rather dry subject in the context of international human rights law is enlightening. A reservation is defined in Article 2 VCLT as a 'unilateral statement, however phrased or named, made by a State, when signing, ratifying, accepting, approving or acceding to a Treaty, whereby it purports to exclude or to modify the legal effect of certain provisions of the Treaty in their application to that State.' The aim of a reservation is to limit a state's obligations under a particular treaty. International law is not formalistic about what constitutes a reservation: it does not matter whether a state presents it as a 'general political statement' or a 'declaration of interpretation'. If the result is exclusion or modification of the legal effect of certain provisions, it will be considered a reservation.

In the international human rights context, states have availed themselves broadly of the possibility of reservations, both quantitatively and qualitatively. For example, as of October 2009, 38 of the 165 state parties to the International Covenant on Civil and Political Rights (ICCPR) had, between them, entered more than 200 reservations. A typical reservation is one whereby a state purports to interpret an internationally protected right only in accordance with its domestic, often constitutional or religious, law. For example, the USA has entered a reservation to the ICCPR that its obligations under Article 7, regarding the prohibition of torture and other cruel, inhuman, and degrading treatment, are to be interpreted in the light of its constitutional protections of rights.[28] A problematic reservation from some states has been to the effect that accession to a human rights treaty, such as the Convention on the Elimination of Discrimination Against Women (CEDAW), is 'subject to the general reservation that

---

[28] See US reservations, declarations, and understandings, International Covenant on Civil and Political Rights, 138 Cong Rec S4781-01 (2 April 1992).

such accession cannot conflict with the laws on personal status derived from Islamic Sharia'.[29]

There are, of course, valid reasons why a state may wish to enter reservations to human rights treaties. A state may generally be committed to human rights but have problems with one particular provision and therefore want to exclude or limit the application of that provision in order to be able to become a party to the treaty. The state may wish to inject a certain cultural understanding of a particular obligation or guard against an expansive interpretation by international human rights bodies by pre-empting the meaning of a particular provision. States may know in advance that part of their domestic law is incompatible with a provision of a treaty and nonetheless wish to ratify the treaty. This is something that human rights lawyers will want to encourage, as the process of making domestic law conform to the human rights treaty obligations could take a long time and ratification would be considerably delayed.

However, there is no doubt that reservations are problematic for international human rights law, even more so than they are for general international law. Of course, one might consider that reservations should be permitted to allow a state to become bound by at least some obligations. But human rights are clearly more of a 'package' than most international normative instruments. There is a very real tension between the idea of human rights and the notion that a state may, through reservations, pick and choose the obligations to which it wishes to be bound. It is the very universality of human rights and the whole point of international human rights treaties which is threatened if states do not agree to honour the same rights. Moreover, there is a sense that some states may 'free ride' human rights treaties, by obtaining the benefits broadly associated with being a party to them, whilst subscribing only to an eviscerated set of obligations. Finally, reservations also create problems of legal certainty, making it difficult for individuals to ascertain the exact scope of the rights they have been guaranteed.

Accordingly, human rights supervisory bodies have frequently deplored the abundance and scope of reservations, and urged states to repeal them. This is in itself a departure from ordinary international treaties, where few bodies are authorized or would see fit to criticize something that is largely seen as within a state's prerogative. International human rights law has also evolved specific notions of what reservations are permissible, who may decide on their permissibility, and what consequences flow from reservations.

4.1 PERMISSIBILITY

The general regime under Article 19 VCLT is that states may formulate reservations to a treaty, unless a reservation is prohibited by the treaty or, more problematically, is incompatible with the object and purpose of the treaty. Although Article 19

---

[29] Such is the wording of the Libyan reservation to the CEDAW.

is presented as authoritative, providing 'relevant guidance',[30] and some states have insisted that the general regime of international law is sufficient,[31] human rights bodies have nonetheless developed quite a specific approach to permissible reservations. Most human rights treaties neither allow nor specifically exclude reservations.[32] Therefore, most of the discussion has focused on whether certain reservations are compatible with the 'object and purpose' of the respective treaties.

One of the most important sources on the issue is the Human Rights Committee's general comment on reservations, General Comment 24, the very existence of which is an indication of how seriously the issue is taken by the UN treaty monitoring bodies. According to the Committee:

In an instrument which articulates very many civil and political rights, each of the many articles, and indeed their interplay, secures the objectives of the Covenant. *The object and purpose of the Covenant is to create legally binding standards for human rights* by defining certain civil and political rights and placing them in a framework of obligations which are legally binding for those States which ratify; and to provide an efficacious supervisory machinery for the obligations undertaken.[33]

The Human Rights Committee defines the object and purpose of the ICCPR very broadly. Moreover, the sheer interdependence of rights suggests that it will be difficult to make reservations to one right without altering the entire content of the obligations contained in a treaty. The Committee has also specifically excluded a number of reservations which it considers would be incompatible per se with the object and purpose of human rights treaties, such as those violating peremptory norms, customary international law, or non-derogable norms.

States may not make reservations relating to basic guarantees associated with the rights protected, such as the right to an effective remedy. Defined as 'supportive guarantees', these provisions are seen to provide 'the necessary framework for securing the rights in the Covenant and are thus essential to its object and purpose'.[34] In fact, they 'are an integral part of the structure of the Covenant and underpin its efficacy' so that to limit them would defeat the purpose of the ICCPR.[35] Finally, states cannot make reservations to institutional arrangements designed to supervise the implementation of treaties. For example, a state cannot become a party to one of the main treaties and make a reservation to the effect that it does not consider itself bound by the obligation to submit periodic reports to its supervisory body.

This leaves very few areas where reservations might be valid. The Human Rights Committee does give a few examples of reservations that would be considered acceptable, such as a reservation saying that communications can be heard by the Committee only after the entry into force of the ICCPR for the state party, or that communications

---

[30] HRC, General Comment 24, HRI/GEN/1/Rev.9 (Vol I) 210, para 6.

[31] See eg Observations on General Comment 24 (1996) 3 IHHR 261, para 4.

[32] There are a few exceptions. See eg Second Optional Protocol to the ICCPR, aiming at the abolition of the death penalty, Art 2(1); ECHR, Art 57.   [33] General Comment 24, n 30, para 7 (emphasis added).

[34] Ibid, para 11.   [35] Ibid.

cannot be examined if they are already being examined by a comparable international procedure. These reservations are procedural rather than substantive in nature.

Even where reservations are permitted, the Human Rights Committee has added a number of formal and substantive requirements to the type of reservations that can be made, pointing out for example that they must be 'specific and transparent', cannot be 'general' and must 'refer to a particular provision'. Moreover, states should 'take into consideration the overall effect of a group of reservations', and avoid committing to treaties only to the extent that these conform with their domestic law.[36]

The European Court of Human Rights has also considered invalid a number of reservations that were 'too vague or broad for it to be possible to determine their exact meaning and scope'.[37] In *Loizidou v Turkey*, for example, it found that the 'special character of the Convention as an instrument of European public order' meant that Turkey's attempt to exclude the application of the ECHR to Northern Cyprus by a reservation was invalid.[38]

The grounds for such limitations to the ability to make reservations are easily understandable. International human rights bodies have sought to protect international treaties from crippling reservations that lead to 'a perpetual non-attainment of international human rights standards'[39] and protect beneficiaries from uncertainty about the exact scope of their rights. Thus, the use of reservations is tightly constrained by numerous rules that suggest that the object and purpose of the human rights treaty would be defeated by selective assumption of human rights obligations.

4.2 RESPONSIBILITY FOR ASSESSMENT

In a typical international law scenario, the invalidity of reservations will be raised by other states parties. However, one can see how the dependence on state objections to reservations is problematic for the protection of human rights. In the human rights context, states are less likely to object to other states' reservations, for the simple reason that generally they are not impacted by these reservations. States have occasionally manifested their rejection of other states' reservations, but this is a haphazard process. In fact, as the Human Rights Committee has pointed out, the pattern is so unclear that it is not safe to assume that a non-objecting state thinks that a particular reservation is acceptable.[40]

These key differences have led the Human Rights Committee to opine that 'the operation of the classic rules on reservations is inadequate for the [ICCPR]'.[41] Consequently, a new rule has emerged in the human rights context, whereby a purely consensual approach to reservations (reservations are accepted or not) has been replaced by an increasingly axiological one (reservations are valid or not). States are asked to act as the guardians of the integrity of human rights treaties and judge whether reservations

---

[36] Ibid, para 19.   [37] *Belilos v Switzerland* (1988) 10 EHRR 466, para 55.
[38] *Loizidou v Turkey* (1997) 23 EHRR 513, para 43.   [39] General Comment 24, n 30, para 19.
[40] Ibid, para 17.   [41] Ibid.

are valid, rather than simply be the keepers of their own national interest. Moreover, human rights bodies, whether judicial or supervisory organs, have seen themselves as the defenders of the *ordre public* of international human rights law and raised issues of invalid reservations before actual disputes arise. The particular interest that the international community has in the integrity of human rights treaties necessitates that their legitimacy be maintained by a strong system of international supervision.

4.3 CONSEQUENCES

The consequences that flow from reservations are complex, particularly if reservations turn out to be invalid. This matter raises different problems for the treaty, the reserving state, and third states. There is a fundamental tension between, on the one hand, the desire to have as many states as possible ratify a treaty, thereby allowing it to enter into force as quickly as possible, and, on the other hand, the risk of a treaty's integrity being compromised by too many reservations.

As regards the effects of reservations on the entire treaty, Article 20(2) VCLT provides that only where 'it appears from the limited number of the negotiating States and the object and purpose of a treaty that the application of the treaty in its entirety between all the parties is an essential condition of the consent of each one to be bound by the treaty' do all state parties to a treaty need to accept a reservation. This would be typical of treaties between very few parties. However, international human rights treaties are the exact opposite, since they are intended to become universal. Therefore, reservations do not have to be accepted by all states for a human rights treaty to enter into force. This explains why so many human rights treaties have in fact entered into force despite considerable numbers of reservations.

The second question is what happens to reserving states. Under general international law, the position is that the reserving state becomes bound by the treaty if at least one other state accepts the reservation.[42] However, in the context of treaties of a humanitarian or human rights character, the International Court of Justice has held that states can in fact become party to a treaty even if other state parties object to its reservation:

The object and purpose of the Genocide Convention imply that it was the intention of the General Assembly and of the States which adopted it that as many States as possible should participate. The complete exclusion from the Convention of one or more States would not only restrict the scope of its application but would detract from the authority of the moral and humanitarian principles which are its basis. It is inconceivable that the contracting parties readily contemplated that an objection to a minor reservation should produce such a result.[43]

Not only is there an interest in states being bound as soon as possible, notwithstanding the reservations of a few, but the specific nature of human rights treaties suggests

---

[42] VCLT, Art 20(4)(c).   [43] *Reservations to the Genocide Convention*, n 5, para 24.

that approval by other parties should really be seen as a secondary matter. This was further clarified by the Inter-American Court of Human Rights. The Inter-American Commission asked the Court for an advisory opinion on whether the American Convention on Human Rights (ACHR) would enter into force as soon as the requisite number of states had ratified it, or whether ratifications accompanied by reservations should be considered complete only when at least one state had accepted them[44] (or, as the VCLT stipulates, all states parties had failed to object to them within a year of the ratification).[45] The Inter-American Court found that because of the special character of the ACHR as 'a multilateral legal instrument or framework enabling States to make binding unilateral commitments not to violate the human rights of individuals within their jurisdiction', it would enter into force regardless of whether any other state accepted reservations appended to an instrument of ratification as 'no useful purpose would be served by such a delay'.[46] In other words, states became bound the moment they deposited their instrument of ratification, notwithstanding the fact that their reservations were not accepted and might even be invalid. This again underlines the strictly non-relational character of human rights treaties.

One of the problems created by this approach is that the actual validity of reservations will only be examined at a later date. This can create complex issues of retroactive application when a reservation turns out to have been invalid all along. A state that has ratified a treaty with a reservation may insist that it ratified the treaty only on the basis of such a reservation and that if the latter is then found to be invalid, it is either not bound by the provision to which the reservation related or not bound by the treaty at all. The opposite stance is that invalid reservations are 'severable' from the commitment to be bound by a treaty so that the reservation can be 'quarantined' and the overall commitment to the treaty preserved. This last proposition was illustrated in the *Loizidou* case. The European Court of Human Rights held that Turkey's reservation excluding its activities in Northern Cyprus from the supervision of the European Court was invalid. The Court was then required to ascertain whether Turkey's broader recognition of jurisdiction was nonetheless valid. Under normal international law rules, the tendency would be to consider that the whole consent to the treaty had been contaminated by the invalidity of the reservation. Against Turkey's arguments, however, the Court considered that the reservation could be severed from the recognition of jurisdiction, so that Turkey would still be considered to have accepted the compulsory jurisdiction of the European Court. This was all the more so since, the Court argued, Turkey must have known at the time that its reservation was invalid, especially in view of protests by several state parties.[47]

Finally, the situation of the third state is perhaps the simplest. Under normal international law, a state that agrees to another state's reservation is bound in its relations with the other state by that reservation.[48] However, that is not a very helpful way of thinking about human rights treaties, for which it should not make a difference to

---

[44] *Effect of Reservations*, n 8.   [45] VCLT, Art 20(4)(c). [46] *Effect of Reservations*, n 8, para 33.
[47] *Lozidiou v Turkey*, n 10, para 96.   [48] VCLT, Art 20(4)(b).

states' commitment to individuals within their jurisdiction whether other states have sought to limit their ratification in any way. In particular, the fact that a state accepts another state's invalid reservation certainly does not make that reservation applicable between them. Similarly, a state that objects to another state's reservation, even on grounds of invalidity, cannot draw on this to then claim that it is not bound in its relations with the other state by the relevant provision, or that it is not bound at all by the relevant provision, or that it is not bound by the treaty at all. It should again make no difference for the entry into force of a human rights treaty that a state is objecting to a reservation, precisely because such a reservation cannot in any significant way be said to affect the interests of that state in the way normally understood in treaty law. For example, the UK could not say that it is not bound by the ECHR or its recognition of the European Court's jurisdiction simply because it objects to Turkey having limited its jurisdiction to its continental territory. One can see from such examples how the application of normal principles of international law to human rights treaties is almost nonsensical. As the Human Rights Committee put it:

Human rights treaties, and the [ICCPR] specifically, are not a web of inter-State exchanges of mutual obligations. They concern the endowment of individuals with rights. The principle of inter-State reciprocity has no place.[49]

Therefore a state is not released from its general obligation to abide by the ICCPR, merely because it disapproves of a reservation made by another state.

5 LIMITATIONS AND DEROGATIONS

Despite what is sometimes suggested, the vast majority of human rights are not absolute in the sense that they can never be limited. One of the only absolute rights is the right to be free from torture, which is absolute in the sense that no social goal or emergency can ever limit the categorical prohibition of torture. There are two ways in which human rights can be limited. First, some treaty provisions explicitly provide circumstances in which the enjoyment of a right may be limited. These are known as limitations. Second, states have the possibility of derogating from their obligations under some human rights treaties in a time of emergency when it might not be possible to secure respect for all human rights.

5.1 LIMITATIONS

Although human rights stipulate certain forms of minimum treatment, the nature of this minimum treatment will vary somewhat. This is especially the case when human rights do not operate in an 'either/or' fashion (to be tortured or not to be tortured), but

---

[49] General Comment 24, n 30, para 17.

where the question is the scope of a right (for example, the degree of privacy to which one is entitled). Human rights obligations inevitably raise tensions between individual and collective demands. To take an easy example, an individual who is imprisoned for having committed a crime following a fair trial cannot invoke a violation of his or her right not to be detained. It is understood that the right to liberty is limited by the exigencies of public order. Moreover, it is primarily for the state to define the framework of collective life that constrains certain rights, in ways that other states will have little cause to complain about (unlike a normal international treaty situation based on exact reciprocity).

Limitations do not grant states the ability to abuse rights; they simply define the actual scope of rights. Rights are limited in a number of ways. Sometimes, because a right is crucial—and all rights relating to integrity and security of the person are—permitted limitations will be spelled out in detail. This is the case for the right to life (which is limited by the possibility of imposing the death penalty, killings in armed conflict situations, and the use of reasonable force by law enforcement agents)[50] or the right to be free from detention (which is limited by, for example, the possibility of being sentenced to imprisonment for a criminal offence, pursuant to a fair trial).[51]

Some instruments contain a general limitation clause. The Universal Declaration of Human Rights (UDHR), for example, proclaims that: 'In the exercise of his rights and freedoms, everyone shall be subject only to such limitations as are determined by law solely for the purpose of securing due recognition and respect for the rights and freedoms of others and of meeting the just requirements of morality, public order and the general welfare in a democratic society.'[52] A similar formulation is used for specific provisions of the ICCPR. For example, Article 12(3) ICCPR provides limitations to the right to liberty of movement, providing that the right 'shall not be subject to any restrictions except those which are provided by law, are necessary to protect national security, public order (*ordre public*), public health or morals or the rights and freedoms of others, and are consistent with the other rights recognized in the Covenant.'[53] The possibility of such limitations has been confirmed by international and domestic case law, but subject to a tripartite test that ensures that the limitations are in conformity with human rights. Thus, limitations to rights have to be justified by the fact that they (1) are prescribed by law, (2) pursue a legitimate aim, and (3) are necessary in a democratic society.

5.1.1 Prescribed by law

The requirement that limitations be prescribed by law means that they must be based on laws as instruments adopted by parliament, not merely that they are 'part of the Law'.[54] This reading, confirmed by the Inter-American Court of Human Rights, is based on the notion that limitations should be adopted by legislatures. Given that limitations are those 'necessary in a democratic society', it is logical that they should

---

[50] See Chapter 10, below.   [51] See Chapter 14, below.   [52] UDHR, Art 29(2).

[53] See also ICCPR, Art 19 (freedom of expression), Art 21 (peaceful assembly), and Art 22 (freedom of association).

[54] OC-6/86, *The Word 'Laws' in Article 30 of the American Convention on Human Rights*, IACtHR Series A No 6 (9 May 1986).

be adopted by a legislative body rather than, for example, the executive. The requirement that limitations be stipulated in law also guarantees a certain foreseeability of
the law and the rights guaranteed. First, the law should be

adequately accessible: the citizen must be able to have an indication that is adequate in
the circumstances of the legal rules applicable to a given case. Secondly, a norm cannot be
regarded as a 'law' unless it is it is formulated with sufficient precision to enable the citizen
to regulate his conduct: he must be able—if need be with appropriate advice—to foresee, to
a degree that is reasonable in the circumstances, the consequences which a given action may
entail.[55]

Unfettered executive discretion, even if granted by the law, would not satisfy this
requirement.[56]

5.1.2 Legitimate aim

According to the European Court of Human Rights, a legitimate aim must be a 'pressing social need'.[57] A state cannot overturn human rights simply for idiosyncratic
policy preferences. Typically, pressing social needs are identified by human rights
treaties themselves as grounds for limitations of rights that are prima facie valid.
For example, the ICCPR mentions 'national security, public order (ordre public), public health or morals or the rights and freedoms of others'. These are then expanded
through interpretation by human rights bodies. The protection of democracy, pluralism, or secularism and a great many others have all been presented at various times as
being legitimate goals. It is interesting that human rights law, which is often presented
as being against the state, is also very much about legitimizing a certain state role.

5.1.3 Necessary in a democratic society

The limitation has to be necessary in a democratic society. It does not suffice to simply
allege a desirable social policy and then adopt a measure that is in fact not truly connected to that goal. Many laws that criminalized homosexuality, for example, which
were presented as in pursuance of the legitimate aim of maintaining good mores, were
struck down because they were not related to that goal at all, especially since they stigmatized homosexuality in the private sphere.[58]

The necessity test also implies that the relevant measure must be proportionate to
the goal sought. Proportionality involves a complex equation evaluating the importance of the social aim, the importance of the right guaranteed, and the degree of
encroachment. Certain rights are very inelastic to even the most important social
goals. Others will be more responsive to limitations. For example, the right to demonstrate will be quite sensitive to states' invocation of public order or the need to
protect the rights of others.

The onus to prove any limb of the test is typically on states, which cannot simply
claim that they know better. But by what standard are such limitations to be judged?

[55] *Sunday Times v UK*, n 21, para 49.   [56] *Hasan v Bulgaria* (2000) 24 EHRR 55.
[57] *Handyside v UK*, n 25, para 48.   [58] *Dudgeon v UK* (1983) 5 EHRR 573.

After all, what is necessary for some may be seen as perfectly abusive by others. Several human rights instruments suggest that the key threshold is that of a 'democratic society'. In other words, limitations are justified on all the grounds that have just been introduced, if they conform to what would be considered necessary in a 'democratic society'. This is certainly a standard that can be criticized as vague (not to mention the possible tensions between democracy and human rights), but at least such limitation clauses acknowledge that human rights are not simply about upholding absolutes but very often about the complex exercise of balancing individual rights against legitimate social priorities. Obviously, human rights should be taken seriously, but the emphasis is on state justification, transparency, and accountability, in circumstances in which states may otherwise gladly invoke the priority of politics over rights.

5.2 DEROGATIONS

The law of state responsibility in general international law traditionally contemplates that a defence of necessity is available to states in limited circumstances. However, international human rights treaties often have their own regime to deal with states of exception, known as the 'derogation' regime, which better takes into account the special character of human rights obligations.[59] Essentially, states are permitted to suspend some of their obligations under human rights treaties if a state of emergency requires them to do so. The consequence of recognizing states' power to derogate from human rights treaties in times of emergency is an increased regulation and supervision of such derogations by international organs. The regime applicable in situations of emergency is typically more constraining than for ordinary international law obligations.

First, a situation of public emergency under international human rights law needs to exist. It must be declared in advance, and its existence (and abrogation) notified to relevant authorities.[60] A situation of public emergency can only be invoked where there exists a threat to 'the life of the nation' itself. This is clearly a high threshold, and such a threat cannot be inferred from 'every disturbance or catastrophe'. Not even an armed conflict will automatically justify the recognition of a public emergency.[61] The European Court of Human Rights, for example, has described a public emergency under Article 15 ECHR as 'an exceptional situation of crisis or emergency which affects the whole population and constitutes a threat to the organized life of the community of which the State is composed.'[62]

Second, the public emergency should be invoked only insofar and for as long as is strictly necessary to return to a situation of normalcy. Indeed, 'the restoration of a state of normalcy where full respect for the [ICCPR] can again be secured must be the predominant objective of a State party derogating from the Covenant'.[63] In other words,

---

[59] eg ICCPR, Art 4; ECHR, Art 15; ACHR, Art 27. The ACHPR does not have a derogation regime. Other human rights treaties, such as the UNCAT or the Convention on Enforced Disappearances, do not have a derogation regime, but this is because they protect non-derogable rights.

[60] *Cyprus v Turkey* (1982) 4 EHRR 482, para 526.

[61] HRC, General Comment 29, HRI/GEN/1/Rev.9 (Vol I) 234, para 3.

[62] *Lawless v Ireland* (1979–80) 1 EHRR 15, para 28.   [63] HRC, General Comment 29, n 61, para 1.

human rights can be suspended only in order for the state to be able to guarantee them as soon as the danger has passed, not to achieve something that is in itself alien to human rights. Situations of public emergency come with various strict conditions concerning their temporary, necessary, and proportional nature. Derogations should specify their territorial[64] and temporal[65] reach, and can only be of an exceptional and temporary nature. A standard provision in several international human rights treaties, for example, is that emergencies should only be proclaimed 'to the extent strictly required by the exigencies of the situation'.

Third, situations of national emergency can only be invoked to suspend (at best) a limited set of so-called derogable rights. For example, it may be legitimate for a state confronting an armed conflict or a major natural catastrophe to suspend the right to demonstrate or the right to vote. Conversely, there are a number of 'non-derogable' rights that can never be suspended. The list varies slightly from treaty to treaty, but the ICCPR mentions the following provisions as non-derogable: Articles 6 (life), 7 (torture), 8(1) and (2) (slavery), 11 (imprisonment for failure to fulfil a contractual obligation), 15 (*nullum crimen sine lege*), 16 (recognition as a person under the law), and 18 (freedom of thought, conscience, and religion). Derogation measures, furthermore, should not be inconsistent with states' other obligations under international law and should not involve discrimination solely on the ground of race, colour, sex, language, religion, or social origin. The former means that states cannot use derogations to, for example, violate international humanitarian law or commit crimes against humanity. Even in situations of emergency, moreover, states are to provide remedies, particularly judicial guarantees, to individuals whose rights may have been violated.

This intense regulation of situations of emergency is designed to ensure that exceptional situations are not maintained indefinitely, which can have a catastrophic impact on rights. The Human Rights Committee, for example, has frequently deplored that some states have been operating under states of emergency for decades, leading to situations in which rights can be easily trampled.

6 WITHDRAWAL

In international law, withdrawal from a treaty under certain conditions is always an option and is generally known as the possibility of 'denouncing' a treaty. This is consonant with the fact that general international law is not particularly concerned

---

[64] eg as the European Court recognized in *Sakik and others v Turkey* (1998) 26 EHRR 662, the fact that Turkey had declared a state of emergency in Kurdistan did not mean that it was therefore in a similar state of exception in Northern Cyprus.

[65] This is particularly important in light of the tendency of states of emergency to prolong themselves far beyond what is strictly necessary. 'Sunset clauses', eg, should indicate the exact date or the occurrence of the event which will bring an end to the public emergency.

with the substantive content of obligations but with making sure that states adhere to whatever commitments they have made. The situation is more complicated when it comes to international human rights treaties. Withdrawals can have the effect of leaving populations legally vulnerable to violations, especially since supervisory machinery is often attached to substantive human rights commitments. The position of international human rights law on this matter is not entirely settled, but there appear to be two possibilities, depending on whether denunciation is explicitly anticipated by the relevant treaty.

Some international human rights instruments contain denunciation clauses. For example, Article 21 Convention on the Elimination of Racial Discrimination provides that '[a] State Party may denounce this Convention by written notification to the Secretary-General of the United Nations'. Similarly, the ECHR[66] and ACHR[67] also include denunciation clauses. It should be noted, nonetheless, that despite the existence of such provisions, straightforward withdrawal is quite unlikely.

Even though a state may do so for other alleged reasons, withdrawal from a human rights treaty is likely to be seen as an admission that a state is up to no good. Only two states have availed themselves successfully of the possibility of denouncing a human rights treaty, namely Greece, which denounced the ECHR from 1969 to 1974 following a military coup, and Trinidad and Tobago, which denounced both the Optional Protocol to the ICCPR, as well as the ACHR from 1998 to 1999. In both cases, the denunciations did not have retroactive effect, and therefore these states could not escape liability for violations committed prior to withdrawal, even if these violations only became known after the denunciation was deposited.

As regards human rights treaties that do not explicitly allow for denunciation, there is a view that denunciation is simply not an option. There is only one case to date of the issue being decided internationally, but it is an interesting and unusual one. In 1998, North Korea sought to withdraw entirely from the ICCPR, after becoming upset about the Human Rights Committee's criticism of its record. The question of whether this was possible was referred to the UN Secretary-General, as depository of the treaty, who promptly returned an opinion to the effect that states could not withdraw from the ICCPR. According to the Human Rights Committee's general comment on the issue, 'it is clear that the Covenant is not the type of treaty which, by its nature, implies a right of denunciation'.[68] Moreover, in what was quite a bold move, the Human Rights Committee went on to note that:

the rights enshrined in the Covenant belong to the people living in the territory of the State party. The Human Rights Committee has consistently taken the view, as evidenced by its long-standing practice, that once the people are accorded the protection of the rights under the Covenant, such protection devolves with territory and continues to belong to them, notwithstanding change in government of the State party.[69]

---

[66] Art 28.   [67] Art 44.   [68] HRC, General Comment 26, HRI/GEN/1/Rev.9 (Vol 1) 222, para 3.
[69] Ibid, para 4.

In other words, and in striking contrast to normal international law treaties, rights once recognized (rather than granted) cannot subsequently be withdrawn. This suggests a unique 'stickiness' to international human rights commitments, which cannot be undone even when states desire to do so formally. The Secretary-General did point out, however, that North Korea could withdraw from the ICCPR if all states parties agreed, obviously an unlikely prospect.

7 REMEDIES FOR VIOLATIONS OF HUMAN RIGHTS OBLIGATIONS

A typical way in which international law obligations are enforced, traditionally, is through termination, suspension, or even counter-measures by the party that considers that its legal interests have been violated.[70] This is understandable in an inter-state world in which the dominant model is contractual and where states are really only bound to the extent that other parties respect their part of the deal. It is also a consequence of the fact that quite often enforcement bodies will not be available, so that each state has to decide for itself whether obligations owed to it have been violated and whether one of these remedies is justified. This is what is sometimes known as the 'decentralized' enforcement of international law.

This is, of course, always problematic under classical international law, but it is arguably even more so when it comes to international human rights law. In fact, quite strikingly, Article 60 VCLT, which concerns counter-measures, is not applicable 'to provisions relating to the protection of the human person contained in treaties of a humanitarian character, in particular to provisions prohibiting any form of reprisals against persons protected by such treaties'.[71]

The idea is simple enough: whereas under general international law, it is reasonable that a violating state suffer the consequences of its unwillingness or inability to respect its obligations, the same cannot be said if it violates a human rights obligation, which is not primarily secured for the benefit of other states. Several scenarios are conceivable. For example, in a context where state A violates the human rights of citizens of state B on its territory, one can imagine that state B could cease to honour its human rights obligations vis-à-vis the citizens of state A. However, this would clearly run against the object and purpose of human rights treaties, the obligations of which are not primarily owed to other states parties even when it comes to their nationals. The International Court of Justice held that much when it affirmed that Bosnia could not have invoked a violation of the Genocide Convention by Yugoslavia as a rationale to violate the Convention itself.[72]

Even more nonsensical is the possibility that state A would cease to respect its international human rights obligations vis-à-vis its own nationals as a counter-measure to

---

[70] The possibility is anticipated by VCLT, Art 60.   [71] VCLT, Art 60(5).
[72] Separate Opinion of Judge Weeramantry, n 5.

state B not respecting its own obligations vis-à-vis persons within its jurisdiction. This would result in the state essentially punishing itself and would have no effect on the offender state. It would be absurd from a human rights point of view.

Non-execution is thus clearly not an adequate remedy in the case of human rights violations. Instead, international human rights law has evolved its own unique modes of enforcement that emphasize the role of supranational institutions and jurisdictions.

Because human rights obligations are primarily incurred by states vis-à-vis persons within their jurisdiction, the inter-state element in human rights enforcement has tended to recede. This has served to benefit the modes of enforcement that emphasize the role of both the international community and individuals.[73]

Nevertheless, inter-state procedures do exist for international human rights obligations. In theory, nothing prevents states from bringing cases before the International Court of Justice for violations of various international human rights instruments. They have certainly done so in relation to the Genocide Convention in the *Bosnia Genocide* case;[74] or sometimes indirectly as in the cases brought against the USA concerning foreign nationals who had been sentenced to capital punishment following violations of the Vienna Convention on Consular Relations on the part of the USA.[75] Several human rights instruments specifically envisage inter-state procedures, whether before regional courts or treaty bodies.[76]

Inter-state procedures provide evidence of the communal interest in the enforcement of a human rights guarantee. For example, the notion of *locus standi* (that is, standing to appear before a court or tribunal) has been developed to fit the concerns of international human rights law. Under traditional international law, the only agents able to invoke a breach of an obligation are those that were directly its beneficiaries and therefore directly affected by its breach. Third parties do not normally have a general interest in the law's enforcement such that they could bring a sort of *actio popularis*. The International Court of Justice famously considered that Liberia and Ethiopia did not have standing in the *South-West Africa* case because they could not adduce a violation of a specific interest.[77] However, because of the largely *erga omnes* character of human rights obligations, a third state *can* bring a case against a violating state even if none of its nationals were affected. It is assumed that states parties to human rights treaties are affected by a human rights violation committed by any state, even if it is against its own citizens.

This *erga omnes* nature of human rights obligations, incidentally, has implications not only for formal inter-state mechanisms but more generally for human rights foreign policy. By making human rights (regardless of where they may be violated) a

[73] See Chapters 18–21, below, for a detailed discussion.

[74] *Application of the Convention on the Prevention and Punishment of the Crime of Genocide (Bosnia and Herzegovina v Serbia and Montenegro)* [2007] ICJ Rep 108.

[75] *Case Concerning the Vienna Convention on Consular Relations (Germany v USA) (Request for the Indication of Provisional Measures: Order)* [1999] ICJ Rep 9.   [76] See eg ACHR, Art 44; ECHR, Art 24.

[77] *South-West Africa Cases (Ethiopia v South Africa; Liberia v South Africa) (Second Phase)* [1966] ICJ Rep 6.

matter of concern for all, human rights law profoundly redefines the notion of sovereignty and the internal affairs of states. Normatively this should make it more difficult for states to claim that other states that criticize their human rights record are meddling in their internal affairs (although in practice and politically, of course, it may not be that difficult to make such claims).

However, it should be said that resort to inter-state human rights procedures has in practice been very much the exception. There have been fewer than two dozen inter-state procedures before the European Commission and Court of Human Rights, while no inter-state dispute regarding a violation of a human rights treaty obligation has been referred to a UN treaty body. Instead, a number of important, innovative, *sui generis* mechanisms for enforcement have been pioneered in the international human rights field. First are various mechanisms through which states are required to provide periodic reports to international committees, outlining how they have complied with their treaty obligations. These mechanisms are described in more detail in Chapters 18 to 21, below, but it is interesting to note here that they create a situation where states, in contrast to the tradition in international law, have to report on their behaviour even if there has been no dispute or litigation. This undeniably reflects the higher interest of human rights in preventing violations, rather than simply adjudicating upon them. Second, and this must surely count as international human rights' greatest innovation in terms of enforcement, many instruments create a right of petition for individuals before international bodies (or at least the possibility of such a right if it is recognized by state parties). This is inconceivable in the inter-state context where the possibility of individuals, or even significant non-state actors, intervening before the International Court of Justice, for example, is never seriously entertained. There are relatively stringent conditions to appearing directly before international human rights bodies, but it is a remarkable characteristic of international human rights law that it allows individuals to directly sue their state at the international level.

8 CONCLUSION

This chapter has presented some key ways in which international human rights obligations differ from mainstream international law obligations. Human rights obligations may allow for a degree of flexibility in their application, but they are also highly binding, regardless of how other state parties conform to their duties. The root of the tension lies in the fact that human rights are intrinsically different in nature and belong to a very different history than general international law. Although typically expressed through treaties, human rights obligations norms have a logic of their own.

It is testimony to the flexibility of international law that it has adapted itself to this new subject matter, in the process changing many rules and practices. In return, human rights law has also significantly shaped the evolution of public international law, and contributed to redefine it less as a project of coexistence between equal states, and more as a common effort to achieve certain universal minimal standards of treatment of the individual.

FURTHER READING

GARDBAUM, 'Human Rights as International Constitutional Rights' (2008) 19 *EJIL* 749.

GOODMAN, 'Human Rights Treaties, Invalid Reservations, and State Consent' (2002) 96 *AJIL* 531.

HUMAN RIGHTS COMMITTEE, General Comment 24, HRI/GEN/1/Rev.9 (Vol I) 210.

—— General Comment 31, HRI/GEN/1/ Rev.9 (Vol I) 243.

KAMMINGA, 'State Succession in Respect of Human Rights Treaties' (1996) 7 *EJIL* 469.

KOJI, 'Emerging Hierarchy in International Human Rights and Beyond: From the Perspective of Non-Derogable Rights' (2001) 12 *EJIL* 917.

LIJNZAAD, *Reservations to UN-Human Rights Treaties: Ratify and Ruin?* (Martinus Nijhoff, 1995).

MOWBRAY, 'The Creativity of the European Court of Human Rights' (2005) 5 *HRLR* 57.

SHELTON, *Remedies in International Human Rights Law* (Oxford University Press, 1999).

7

SCOPE OF APPLICATION

Sarah Joseph

SUMMARY

A state is clearly not responsible for every act or omission which harms human rights, regardless of location. Therefore, it is necessary to examine the scope of application of a state's obligations under international human rights law. That is, when do human rights duties apply? This chapter first defines key concepts and identifies the duty-bearers and beneficiaries of human rights law. Then it explains the instances in which a state will be held responsible for the actions or omissions of particular persons or entities. Finally, it addresses the scope of the territorial application of a state's human rights duties.

1 INTRODUCTION

It is necessary to clarify some key concepts for the purposes of the discussion in this chapter: those of 'state responsibility' and 'jurisdiction'.

'State responsibility' refers to the circumstances in which a state will be held liable for the violation of its international obligations. For example, a state will be held to have breached international human rights law if an act or omission, which is wrongful under human rights law, is attributable to that state. The state will not be held in breach if the act or omission cannot be attributed to it.

The concept of 'jurisdiction' is very complex. It can refer, for example, to the circumstances in which a state is recognized under its own domestic law, or under international law, as having a right to prescribe and enforce its laws. In this chapter, it is used in a limited context to refer to a state's authority over a particular act or omission. The European Court of Human Rights has suggested that the notion of jurisdiction is 'primarily territorial': states have jurisdiction over their own territory and territories in which they exercise 'effective control'.[1] However, as discussed below, the broadest views of a state's jurisdiction extend it to acts and omissions over which a state

---

[1] *Bankovic et al. v Belgium et al.* (2007) 44 EHRR SE5, para 59.

exercises effective control, regardless of the control exercised by the state in the territory in which the act or omission takes place.

A state is not responsible under human rights law for every act or omission by any person that arises within its jurisdiction. However, a state's responsibility under human rights law is limited by its jurisdiction. That is, a state is not responsible for acts or omissions under human rights law that fall outside its jurisdiction.

2 WHO HAS HUMAN RIGHTS OBLIGATIONS?

States have duties under human rights treaties as they are party to them. No human rights treaty directly binds an entity other than a state. Under customary international law, the principal duty-bearers of human rights obligations are again states. There are rare exceptions under customary international law where entities other than states have direct human rights obligations. Examples include the duties not to perpetrate genocide, certain war crimes, or crimes against humanity.[2] In this chapter, the focus is on the scope of application of a state's duties under human rights treaties.[3]

3 WHO HAS HUMAN RIGHTS?

As noted directly above, states generally have duties under international human rights law. To whom are these duties owed? That is, who is recognized as a person with human rights under international human rights law?

Individuals within a state's jurisdiction are generally recognized as having human rights. For example, Article 2(1) International Covenant on Civil and Political Rights (ICCPR) requires states parties to respect and ensure the human rights of 'all individuals' within their territory and jurisdiction.

3.1 NON-NATIONALS

One does not have to be a national of a state in order to be able to claim human rights against that state. Numerous international human rights cases in many contexts have confirmed that non-nationals have human rights.[4] In most instances, they enjoy civil and political rights to the same extent as nationals.[5] However, rights of political participation, such as those found in Article 25 ICCPR, including the right to vote and stand for election, may legitimately be restricted to citizens. Similarly, non-citizens do

---

[2] See Joseph, *Corporations and Transnational Human Rights Litigation* (Hart, 2004) 48–9.

[3] See Chapter 25 for a discussion of the human rights duties of non-state actors.

[4] See eg *Gueye v France*, CCPR/C/35/D/196/1985 (6 April 1989); *A v Australia*, CCPR/C/59/D/560/1993 (30 April 1997); *Adam v Czech Republic*, CCPR/C/57/D/586/1994 (25 July 1996); and *Soering v UK* (1989) 11 EHRR 439.   [5] HRC, General Comment 15, HRI/GEN/1/Rev.9 (Vol 1) 189.

not have the same rights to enter or remain in a state as nationals,[6] though that is not to say that states have an absolute right under international human rights law to expel them. Due to their special vulnerability to deportation, non-nationals have unique procedural rights with regard to deportation under Article 13 ICCPR and similar provisions.

Under Article 2(3) International Covenant on Economic, Social and Cultural Rights (ICESCR), 'developing countries' are permitted to determine the extent to which they guarantee 'economic rights' to non-nationals, taking into account 'human rights and their national economy'. Economic rights have been defined by one commentator as those ICESCR rights 'that enable a person to earn a living or that relate to that process', that is, the employment rights in Articles 6 to 8 and perhaps Article 13(2)(e).[7] Article 2(3) has not been authoritatively interpreted by the Committee on Economic, Social and Cultural Rights. The Committee did not even mention Article 2(3) in its General Comment 18 on the right to work,[8] and it receives only the briefest of mentions and no explication in its General Comment 20 on non-discrimination.[9] Hence, the extent of developing states' discretion under Article 2(3) is unclear. Dankwa describes the provision as transitional, designed to permit post-colonial states to favour local people in employment to redress the balance in economies dominated by ex-patriot populations.[10] A report by the UN Special Rapporteur on the rights of non-citizens suggests that this 'exception to the general rule on equality' should be interpreted narrowly.[11]

3.2 THE UNBORN

Do human rights extend to the unborn? The American Convention on Human Rights (ACHR), in Article 4(1), is the only human rights treaty that explicitly contemplates life beginning from conception rather than birth, and thus seems to confer human rights on unborn children.[12] The European Court of Human Rights and the European Commission of Human Rights have found that a foetus is not a person protected by the right to life, and, in any case, its right would not automatically override the rights and interests of its mother. Accordingly, the European human rights bodies have found complaints brought on behalf of a foetus to be inadmissible.[13] In *Queenan v Canada*,

[6] See eg *Stewart v Canada*, CCPR/C/58/D/538/1993 (16 December 1996); *Canepa v Canada*, CCPR/C/59/D/558/1993 (20 June 1997).

[7] Dankwa, 'Working Paper on Article 2(3) of the International Covenant on Economic, Social and Cultural Rights' (1987) 9 *HRQ* 230, 240.

[8] CESCR, General Comment 18, HRI/GEN/1/Rev.9 (Vol 1) 139.

[9] CESCR, General Comment 20, E/C.12/GC/20.   [10] Dankwa, n 7, 246–9.

[11] Final report of the Special Rapporteur on the rights of non-citizens, E/CN.4/Sub.2/2003/23 (26 May 2003) para 19.

[12] The right to life in Art 4(1) applies 'in general, from the moment of conception'. See also Case 2141, *The Baby Boy Case*, IACommHR Res 23/81 (6 March 1981) Annual Report 1980–81.

[13] See *Vo v France* (2005) 10 EHRR 12; *Paton v United Kingdom* (1981) 3 EHRR 408; *H v Norway* (1992) 73 DR 155.

the Human Rights Committee found that a claim could not be brought on behalf of unborn children against the practice of abortion.[14]

3.3 ARTIFICIAL ENTITIES

Do artificial entities such as corporations and associations including NGOs have human rights? Corporations and associations have standing to make claims on their own behalf before the European Court of Human Rights. Examples include *Sunday Times v UK*,[15] a case concerning a media corporation's freedom of expression, and *Refah Partisi (The Welfare Party) v Turkey*,[16] a case concerning the rights of a political party. In contrast, the UN human rights treaties generally protect only individual rights. Though some rights can clearly be enjoyed in conjunction with other people, such as freedom of association in Article 22 ICCPR or minority rights in Article 27 ICCPR,[17] the only collective right recognized in the global treaty system is that of self-determination in Article 1 ICCPR and Article 1 ICESCR.[18] Corporations and other artificial entities do not have rights under the UN treaties.[19] Similarly, the Inter-American system is concerned with the rights of individuals,[20] though complaints may be submitted in respect of those rights by others, such as corporations or other artificial entities.[21]

However, restrictions on the rights of a corporation may, in some instances, inevitably impact severely on the rights of a person, such as a director or shareholder, such that that person may bring a claim of abuse of his or her own rights. *Singer v Canada* concerned a complaint by one Alan Singer about Quebec laws that banned businesses from advertising outdoors in a language other than French.[22] Canada responded that the real 'victim' of this limit to freedom of expression was Singer's company, Alan Singer Ltd, which owned the relevant business. The Human Rights Committee disagreed, noting that freedom of expression was 'inalienably linked to the person' and that person's 'freedom to impart information concerning his business in the language of his choice'.[23] It is likely that the Committee's decision was influenced by the fact that Singer's company was a small family business, such that breaches of its rights necessarily impacted on his enjoyment of those same rights. The same might not apply, for example, in regard to large listed companies.[24]

---

[14] *Queenan v Canada*, CCPR/C/84/D/1379/2005 (23 August 2005). Indeed, the HRC found the application of a prohibition on abortion to breach various rights in the ICCPR in *Huamán v Peru*, CCPR/C/85/D/1153/2003 (22 November 2005). [15] (1980) 2 EHRR 317.

[16] (2003) 37 EHRR 1. [17] HRC, General Comment 31, HRI/GEN/1/Rev.9 (Vol 1) 243, para 9.

[18] See Chapter 17, below.

[19] See eg *SM v Barbados*, CCPR/C/50/D/502/1992 (4 April 1994); *JRT and the WG Party v Canada*, CCPR/C/18/D/104/1981 (6 April 1983).

[20] ACHR, Art 2(1) clarifies that a person for the purposes of that Convention is a 'human being'.

[21] ACHR, Arts 1(2) and 44. See eg *Tabacalera Boqueron SA v Paraguay*, IACommHR Report 47/97 (16 October 1997) Annual Report 1997, paras 29 and 35. [22] CCPR/C/51/D/455/1991 (15 August 1994).

[23] Ibid, para 11.2.

[24] Joseph, Schultz, and Castan, *The International Covenant on Civil and Political Rights: Cases Commentary and Materials* (OUP, 2004) 69.

However, other cases before the Human Rights Committee, such as *SM v Barbados*[25] and *Lamagna v Australia*,[26] which have concerned allegations of the unfair treatment of small one-person companies, have been dismissed for want of personal jurisdiction. Emberland has criticized these decisions, particularly *Lamagna*, on the basis that the Committee adopted an overly formal approach to the issue at hand, leaving Ms Lamagna without any relevant human rights protection simply because she chose to use the corporate form to arrange her business affairs.[27] While Emberland does not recommend the conferral of rights on companies under the ICCPR, he recommends a less legalistic approach in the case of small businesses.

4 FOR WHICH ENTITIES IS A STATE RESPONSIBLE?

This section considers the responsibility of states under international human rights law for the acts of a person or entity. The key question is: when is an act or omission attributable to the state?

A state is clearly responsible under international human rights law for the actions of its organs, such as its executive, legislature, judiciary, and its bureaucracy.[28] Thus, breaches of human rights law may arise from actions taken by leaders, police officers, army, judges, administrative officers, and so on. States remain responsible for the actions of their agents even when they act beyond their authority, as long as they are purportedly acting in an official capacity.[29]

Provincial government entities in a federal state are treated as emanations of the national government for the purposes of international human rights obligations. A federal division of powers is not deemed to alter a state's human rights obligations at all.[30] For example, Tasmanian anti-gay legislation gave rise to a breach of the ICCPR by Australia in *Toonen v Australia*,[31] even though the national government neither enacted nor approved of the impugned laws. Indeed, the national government of Canada has been found in breach of the ICCPR on numerous occasions due to provincial laws, even though it lacks, in some instances, the domestic constitutional power to alter those laws.[32]

---

[25] n 19.   [26] CCPR/C/65/D/737/1997 (30 April 1999).

[27] Emberland, 'Corporate Veil in the Jurisprudence of the Human Rights Committee and the Inter-American Court and Commission of Human Rights' (2004) 4 *HRLR* 257, 272.

[28] See HRC, n 17, para 4. See also International Law Commission (ILC), Draft Articles on Responsibility of States for Internationally Wrongful Acts, A/56/10, ch IV.E.1, Art 4.

[29] See eg *Sarma v Sri Lanka*, CCPR/C/78/D/950/2000 (31 July 2003); see also Draft Articles, n 28, Art 7.

[30] See eg ICCPR, Art 50.   [31] CCPR/C/50/D/488/1992 (4 April 1994).

[32] See *Ballantyne et al. v Canada*, CCPR/C/47/D/385/1989 (5 May 1993); *Waldman v Canada*, CCPR/C/67/D/694/1996 (5 November 1999).

Thus, states are clearly responsible for actions of their organs. But to what extent, if at all, are they responsible for the actions of other persons or entities such as private actors, international organizations, or other states?

4.1 PRIVATE ACTORS

Governments are not the only threat to human rights. The right of non-discrimination, for example, is a very limited right if it has no impact in the private sector. According to the Draft Articles on State Responsibility, a state is responsible for the acts of a private actor if that actor is acting in a governmental capacity, or under its direction and control, or where it adopts a person's actions as its own.[33] Such situations might arise, for example, when private contractors carry out governmental functions.

Furthermore, the application of human rights within the private sphere is now well recognized in international human rights law.[34] Some human rights provisions, such as Article 20 ICCPR, explicitly require the regulation of private actors by the state.[35] The classical tripartite description of a state's human rights duties, that is, to respect, protect, and fulfil human rights, reveals a more general duty with regard to private actors. As part of a state's duty to protect a person's enjoyment of a human right, it must exercise due diligence by taking reasonable measures to prevent and punish actions by a private actor that prejudice the human rights of another. The Inter-American Court of Human Rights enunciated the duty in the following way in *Velasquez-Rodriguez v Honduras*:

An illegal act which violates human rights and which is initially not directly imputable to a State (for example, because it is the act of a private person or because the person responsible has not been identified) can lead to international responsibility of the State, not because of the act itself, but because of the lack of due diligence to prevent the violation or to respond to it as required by the [American] Convention.[36]

The Human Rights Committee explained in General Comment 31:

[T]he positive obligations on States Parties to ensure Covenant rights will only be fully discharged if individuals are protected by the State, not just against violations of Covenant rights by its agents, but also against acts committed by private persons or entities that would impair the enjoyment of Covenant rights in so far as they are amenable to application between private persons or entities. There may be circumstances in which a failure to ensure Covenant rights as required by article 2 would give rise to violations by States Parties of those rights, as a result of States Parties' permitting or failing to take appropriate measures

---

[33] Draft Articles, n 28, Arts 5, 8, and 11. The Draft Articles were drafted by the ILC, an expert group with a mandate under the UN Charter to develop and codify international law, over a number of decades, and adopted in 2001. Most aspects of the Draft Articles are recognized as customary international law.

[34] See Chapter 6, above.

[35] See also Convention on the Elimination of All Forms of Discrimination Against Women (CEDAW) Arts 6 and 11; and Convention on the Elimination of All Forms of Racial Discrimination (ICERD) Art 5.

[36] IACtHR Series C No 4 (29 July 1988) para 172.

or to exercise due diligence to prevent, punish, investigate or redress the harm caused by such acts by private persons or entities.[37]

In *Osman v UK*, the European Court of Human Rights confirmed that states have duties to do all that can reasonably be expected to prevent human rights abuses by private actors. The expectations upon a state increase if the state knows, or should know, that a person or entity poses a risk to another's enjoyment of human rights.[38]

The following are examples of this application of human rights within the private sphere. *A v UK* concerned a young boy who had been hit with a garden cane by his stepfather. The stepfather was acquitted of assault in the UK, where the court found he had merely engaged in 'reasonable chastisement'. The European Court found that the UK, in acquitting the stepfather in its courts, had failed properly to protect the boy's right to be free from inhuman and degrading treatment.[39] Various human rights bodies have held that states must take reasonable and effective measures to protect a person from domestic violence: failure to do so will result in violations of the rights of the person subjected to such violence, such as the right to life if the person is killed, or the right to be free from torture or other ill-treatment.[40] In *Lopez Ostra v Spain*, the European Court found that Spain had failed to take reasonable measures to prevent the spread of severe air pollution from a privately owned waste treatment plant, which breached the rights to privacy and family life of those who lived in the plant's vicinity.[41] Similarly, in *SERAC v Nigeria*, the African Commission on Human and Peoples' Rights found that Nigeria had failed to protect indigenous peoples in Ogoniland from prejudicial actions by an oil consortium, which breached the peoples' rights to health, property, housing, food, and freedom from forced deprivation of wealth and resources.[42]

4.2 INTERNATIONAL ORGANIZATIONS

To what extent, if at all, are states responsible for the actions of international organizations of which they are a member? *H v d P v Netherlands* concerned a complaint to the Human Rights Committee about the recruitment practices of the European Patent Office (EPO), an international organization to which the Netherlands was one of five member states.[43] The complaint was dismissed as it was aimed at the EPO and thus concerned issues beyond the jurisdiction of the Netherlands. However, the Committee has since stated that states are responsible for the actions of 'forces constituting a national contingent of a State party assigned to an international peace-keeping or peace-enforcement operation'.[44] One must therefore inquire as to when a

---

[37] n 17, para 8.   [38] (2000) 29 EHRR 245, para 116.   [39] (1999) 27 EHRR 611, 624.

[40] See eg *Opuz v Turkey*, App no 33401/02, Judgment of 9 June 2009; *AT v Hungary*, CEDAW/A/61/38/2006 (26 January 2005); *Goekce v Austria*, CEDAW/C/39/D/5/2005 (6 August 2007); *Yildirim v Austria*, CEDAW/C/39/D/6/2005 (6 August 2007). See also CEDAW, General Recommendation 19, HRI/GEN/1/Rev.9 (Vol II) 331.   [41] (1995) 20 EHRR 277.

[42] Communication No 155/96 (2002).   [43] CCPR/C/29/D/217/1986 (8 April 1987).

[44] n 17, para 10.

state's personnel are its own and when they are the responsibility of an international organization.

The European Court, in the joined cases of *Behrami and Behrami v France* and *Saramati v France, Germany and Norway*, found that complaints against various European states that had contributed personnel to peacekeeping forces in Kosovo (KFOR) and to the UN interim administration in Kosovo (UNMIK), in respect of certain acts (and omissions) of KFOR and UNMIK, were inadmissible *ratione personae*.[45] The Court found that the activities of KFOR and UNMIK were attributable to the UN Security Council. It went on to find that it was not competent to review the actions of states parties in respect of actions taken by their personnel on behalf of the UN as part of KFOR and UNMIK.

However, it appears that a state can be held responsible under human rights treaties for its own actions taken in order to implement a Security Council resolution and, by implication, other international obligations. In *Bosphorus v Ireland*, the European Court of Human Rights found a complaint regarding the seizure in Ireland of the applicant's leased aircraft to be admissible. The seizure took place pursuant to a ministerial decision that implemented an EC Council regulation which itself applied a Security Council resolution that had imposed sanctions on the Federal Republic of Yugoslavia. Ireland was bound under EC law to implement the regulation. The impugned actions were deemed to be those of Ireland and the complaint was admissible. However, no violation (of the right to property) was ultimately found. The Court found that there was a presumption that actions taken to implement international obligations as a member of an international organization were compatible with the European Convention on Human Rights (ECHR) if the relevant organization provided equivalent or comparable protection of the rights recognized in the ECHR.[46] The presumption can be rebutted where protection of ECHR rights is 'manifestly deficient'. The presumption was not rebutted in *Bosphorus*.

Sayadi and Vinck v Belgium was a case before the Human Rights Committee under the ICCPR.[47] Sayadi and Vinck were a married couple and officers in a charitable organization that was suspected of links with al-Qaida. The organization was placed on the UN Sanctions List, which purports to identify persons associated with terrorism and provide for sanctions against them. Within weeks of that listing, Belgium transmitted the couple's names to the Sanctions Committee of the Security Council, which duly placed them on the list too. As a result, their assets were frozen and their travel was restricted, prompting allegations by the couple of violations of various rights, such as their freedom of movement. Belgium argued the case was outside the competence of the Human Rights Committee, as it essentially concerned the actions of the Security Council, and measures taken to implement its resolutions.

The majority of the Human Rights Committee in *Sayadi and Vinck* found that it was 'competent to admit a communication alleging that a State party had violated rights

[45] (2007) 45 EHRR SE10.   [46] (2006) 42 EHRR 1, paras 155–6.
[47] CCPR/C/94/D/1472/2006 (29 December 2008). See also Chapter 26, below.

set forth in the Covenant, regardless of the source of the obligations implemented by the State party'.[48] A minority of Committee members found that the complaint was inadmissible, as they felt it essentially concerned the actions of the Security Council as well as Belgium's obligations to obey Security Council resolutions stemming from the UN Charter. The majority went on to find that Belgium had not in fact been required by Security Council resolutions to transmit the names, and that Belgium's actions had caused the listing of the couple. Belgium was therefore responsible for the detrimental effects of the listing and the consequent breaches of a number of human rights. The Committee's factual finding regarding the scope of Belgium's obligations under the Security Council resolutions (that is, that it was not *required* to transmit the names) meant that it did not ultimately have to decide if actions *necessarily* taken by a state in order to comply with a Security Council resolution were ultimately attributable to that state. The admissibility decision indicates that such actions are attributable to the state, though whether it might also mean the state is exonerated from a finding of violation of the ICCPR is uncertain.

In *Kadi and al Barakaat International Foundation v Council of the European Union*, the Grand Chamber of the European Court of Justice found that it was competent to review the validity of a European Council regulation which gave effect to the UN sanctions regime, and which had resulted in the freezing of the assets of the appellants.[49] By implication, the Court would therefore be able to review the compatibility of a measure with European Community (EC) law taken by an individual state if that measure was necessary to implement a Security Council resolution.[50] Ultimately, the Court found that the relevant Council regulation breached fundamental rights in EC law, so it made an order of annulment.

Bosphorus, *Sayadi and Vinck*, and *Kadi* indicate that a state can be held responsible for its own actions in implementing a Security Council resolution. By analogy, a state cannot escape responsibility for human rights violations by hiding behind inconsistent international obligations, including its obligations to an international organization of which it is a member.[51] However, *Behrami and Saramati* indicates that a state will not be held responsible for human rights violations by its personnel, such as its troops, if command of those people is given to an international body: those personnel are held to be beyond the jurisdiction of that particular state.

A state, which is a member of an international organization, is not per se responsible for the actions of that organization under international human rights law. Can a state be held responsible for its own actions within the organization, such as its votes, or even its decision to join a particular organization? The Committee on Economic, Social and Cultural Rights has stated, regarding the right to food, that states violate

---

[48] Ibid, para 7.2.

[49] Cases C-402/05 P and C-415/05 P, ECJ Judgment, 3 September 2008. See also Chapter 26, below.

[50] See Opinion of Advocate General Poiares Maduro in *Kadi v Council of the European Union and Commission of the European Communities*, 16 January 2008, para 30.

[51] *Bosphorus* and perhaps *Sayadi* indicate that measures that are necessary to implement such obligations will rarely be found in breach. See also *R (Al-Jedda) v Secretary of State for Defence* [2007] UKHL 58.

that right if they fail to take it into account 'when entering into agreements with other States or with international organisations'.[52] Therefore, for example, a state should take its ICESCR obligations into account when joining the World Trade Organization or signing a free trade deal with another state.[53] The Committee has also strongly implied that members of the Security Council must take ICESCR rights into account when imposing economic sanctions on a state.[54]

4.3 OTHER STATES

Finally, to what extent is a state responsible for the actions of another state? A state is responsible for those of its acts which expose a person to a violation of his or her rights by another state, where that breach was reasonably foreseeable at the time of the relevant act. The classic situation where such issues arise is in the context of refoulement: where a state deports a person to another state in circumstances where it should know that the individual will be tortured. States are thus under a duty not to put individuals into such situations. This duty is explicit in Article 3 of the Convention against Torture and Other Cruel, Inhuman or Degrading Treatment or Punishment (UNCAT).

In *Soering v UK*, the European Court of Human Rights found that the extradition of Soering, a young man accused of murder, to the USA would amount to inhuman and degrading treatment contrary to Article 3 ECHR.[55] This was because the UK would have knowingly exposed Soering to a real possibility of experiencing the death row phenomenon, that is, a prolonged period of time on death row characterized by mounting anguish at the inevitable prospect of death. *Agiza v Sweden* concerned the expulsion of a terrorist suspect, one Ahmed Hussein Agiza, from Sweden to Egypt.[56] He was transported to Egypt by US agents. Sweden was found to have violated Article 3 UNCAT by allowing Agiza to be transported from Sweden to Egypt where it could reasonably foresee that he would be tortured. Sweden also breached the prohibition on cruel, inhuman, and degrading treatment in Article 16 by handing Agiza over to US agents in Sweden, and apparently acquiescing in his inhuman and degrading treatment by US agents while he remained on Swedish soil prior to his removal to Egypt.[57] The Article 16 finding thus manifested a different type of responsibility of a state for the human rights violations of another state.

However, a sending state is not responsible for every human rights violation that it might foreseeably expose a person to in another state. The case law thus far indicates that states cannot deport a person in circumstances where he or she foreseeably

---

[52] CESCR, General Comment 12, HRI/GEN/1/Rev.9 (Vol 1) 55, para 19. See also CESCR, General Comment 14, HRI/GEN/1/Rev.9 (Vol 1) 78, para 39.

[53] See generally Howse and Teitel, 'Beyond the Divide: The Covenant on Economic, Social and Cultural Rights and the World Trade Organization' (Occasional Paper No 30, Friedrich Ebert Stiftung, 2007), available at <http://library.fes.de/pdf-files/iez/global/04572.pdf>.

[54] CESCR, General Comment 8, HRI/GEN/1/Rev.9 (Vol 1) 43, esp para 8. This statement also raises issues regarding the extraterritorial obligations of states, an issue which is discussed below.

[55] (1989) 11 EHRR 439.   [56] CAT/C/34/D/233/2003 (24 May 2005).

[57] Agiza was stripped, blindfolded, and hooded for his flight to Egypt by US agents.

faces violations of the right to life or the right to be free from torture and other cruel, inhuman, and degrading treatment. But could a state also be held liable under the ICCPR if it deported a person to a state where he or she might face another human rights violation, such as racial discrimination or an unfair trial? Such a complaint was an aspect of *Judge v Canada*. In that case the complainant alleged, inter alia, that his extradition from Canada to the USA would expose him to a breach of his right to appeal in criminal trials in Article 14(5) ICCPR.[58] The majority did not address the issue. In a separate opinion, Mr Solari-Yrigoyen found a breach of Article 14(5). Mme Chanet, in another separate opinion, stated that it was 'less obvious' that states should be held liable for abuses of rights other than the rights to life and freedom from torture foreseeably perpetrated by other states. In General Comment 31, the Human Rights Committee described the obligation not to deport as arising when deportation would give rise to a 'real risk of irreparable harm, such as that contemplated by articles 6 and 7 of the Covenant'.[59] It seems doubtful that many other human rights violations can be characterized as 'irreparable'.[60] It is, however, assumed that the obligations would be more extensive if the sending state somehow colluded with the receiving state in bringing about violations of those other rights.

5 WHERE DO HUMAN RIGHTS APPLY?

What is the territorial scope of a state's jurisdiction for the purposes of human rights law? Clearly, a state has jurisdiction over its own territory. For example, Article 2(1) ICCPR specifies the duties owed to individuals within a state's territory. What is the scope, if any, of a state's extraterritorial jurisdiction under human rights treaties?

Before moving on, it is important to set the limits of what is meant by 'extraterritorial jurisdiction'. Cases such as those concerning refoulement mentioned above involve intra-territorial acts which generate extraterritorial consequences. They do not involve instances of extraterritorial jurisdiction. The actual breach by the sending state in such cases arises at the time of its intra-territorial act of expelling the person, rather than when the receiving state perpetrates the anticipated human rights abuse (for example, an act of torture upon the deported person).

So, what about a state's responsibility outside its own territory? A state's obligations under the ICCPR are generally presumed to extend to its colonies unless it has made a contrary declaration at the time of ratification.[61] On the other hand, under Article

---

[58] CCPR/C/78/D/829/1998 (5 August 2002).   [59] n 17, para 12.

[60] See, however, *R (Ullah) v Special Adjudicator* [2004] UKHL 26, where the UK House of Lords indicated that non-refoulement may apply to prevent exposure to very serious breaches of other rights, such as one's right to freedom of religion.

[61] The HRC's decision in *Kuok Koi v Portugal*, CCPR/C/73/D/925/2000 (8 February 2002) seems somewhat confused on the matter, but on balance favours this conclusion. See Joseph, 'Human Rights Committee: Recent Cases' (2002) 2 *HRLR* 287, 287–95. See also ICCPR, Art 1(3).

56 ECHR, a state must specifically extend the application of the Convention to its dependent territories.

The various international human rights bodies seem to have adopted different approaches to the issue of extraterritorial application of rights. In particular, the UN treaty bodies and the Inter-American human rights bodies seem to have adopted a more expansive approach than the European Court of Human Rights. The Committee on Economic, Social and Cultural Rights may have adopted an even more lenient approach in relation to the types of extraterritorial duties a state might have.

5.1 ECHR

Article 1 ECHR states that '[t]he High Contracting Parties shall secure to everyone within their jurisdiction the rights and freedoms' in the Convention. No territorial limit is expressed therein. The extraterritorial application of the ECHR in certain circumstances was confirmed in *Loizidou v Turkey*[62] and *Cyprus v Turkey*[63] where the acts of the authorities in Northern Cyprus were held to be within Turkey's jurisdiction due to the 'effective control' exercised over those authorities by Turkey. Similarly, the actions of the authorities in the Transdniestrian separatist region in Moldova were held in *Ilascu v Moldova and Russia* to be within Russia's jurisdiction, due to Russia's 'effective authority, or at the very least decisive influence' over those authorities, due to its 'military, economic, financial and political support'.[64] It seems that this threshold of 'effective authority' over Transdniestrian authorities is similar, or even slightly lower, than the requirement of 'effective control' over a territory in *Loizidou*.[65]

Bankovic et al. v Belgium et al. concerned a complaint about the actions of North Atlantic Treaty Organization (NATO) troops in bombing Radio Television Serbia in Belgrade during the airstrikes against the Federal Republic of Yugoslavia (FRY) in 1999.[66] The complaint was issued against 17 European states that were members of NATO.[67] The European Court of Human Rights, in a decision of the Grand Chamber, concluded that the complaint was inadmissible for want of territorial jurisdiction. Extraterritorial jurisdiction was limited to instances where a respondent state is in 'effective control' of a particular territory through, for example, military occupation. The firing of missiles was not enough to establish such a level of control. Furthermore, the Court went on to state that the ECHR was a regional treaty confined to a particular 'legal space (*espace juridique*)',[68] of which the FRY was not part. It stated: 'The Convention was not designed to be applied throughout the world, even in respect of the conduct of Contracting States'.[69] *Bankovic* thus seemed to close the door on claims under the ECHR with regard to the behaviour of contracting states outside the area of

---

[62] (1997) 23 EHRR 513.   [63] (2002) 35 EHRR 30.   [64] (2005) 40 EHRR 46, para 392.

[65] Cerone, 'Human Dignity in the Line of Fire: The Application of International Human Rights Law during Armed Conflict, Occupation, and Peace Operations' (2006) 39 *Vanderbilt JTL* 1446, 1491.   [66] n 1.

[67] A separate issue regarding the responsibility of these states for NATO actions was not considered by the Court.   [68] n 1, para 80.

[69] Ibid.

the Council of Europe. However, cases before and after *Bankovic* have chipped away at this principle.

Öcalan v Turkey, decided soon after *Bankovic*, concerned the arrest of the leader of the Kurdistan Workers' Party (PKK), Abdullah Öcalan, by Turkish agents in Nairobi airport in Kenya and his blindfolded flight back to Turkey. The European Court found that Turkey had jurisdiction over the actions that took place at Nairobi airport and duly considered the complaint of unlawful detention in this regard.[70]

Issa v Turkey concerned an allegation of killings by Turkish soldiers in northern Iraq. The applicants argued that that area was under the effective control of Turkish troops. On the issue of the Convention's 'legal space', the European Court stated that if the deceased had been under the effective control of Turkey at the relevant time, 'it would follow logically that they were within the jurisdiction of Turkey (and not that of Iraq, which is not a Contracting State and clearly does not fall within the legal space (*espace juridique*) of the Contracting States'.[71] This argument renders the issue of 'legal space' irrelevant when a contracting state is in fact exercising 'effective control' over any area anywhere in the world. The Court also adopted a very broad concept of 'effective control' to include 'overall control' so that a contracting party did not have to exercise 'detailed control over the policies and actions of the authorities' in the relevant area.[72] The Court also stated:

[A] State may also be held accountable for violation of the Convention rights and freedoms of persons who are in the territory of another State but who are found to be under the former State's authority and control through its agents operating—whether lawfully or unlawfully—in the latter State... Accountability in such situations stems from the fact that Article 1 of the Convention cannot be interpreted so as to allow a State party to perpetrate violations of the Convention on the territory of another State, which it could not perpetrate on its own territory.[73]

Thus, according to *Issa*, effective control can arise when a state's agents have effective control over a person (or persons) rather than over a particular area. According to that reasoning, in the *Bankovic* case, the people who were in Radio Television Serbia were arguably under the control of NATO forces when the latter decided to target that building with airstrikes.[74]

The conflicting European jurisprudence was reviewed by the UK House of Lords in *Al Skeini v Secretary of State for Defence*. That case concerned a claim under the Human Rights Act 1998, which incorporates the ECHR into British law, concerning the deaths of six Iraqi civilians at the hands of British troops in Iraq. Five of the deceased had allegedly been killed by British forces in the streets of Basra, while the sixth was allegedly detained and mistreated before dying in British custody at a

---

[70] (2005) 41 EHRR 45. Ultimately, that particular complaint was not upheld.
[71] (2005) 41 EHRR 27, para 74.   [72] Ibid, para 70.   [73] Ibid, para 71.
[74] Ultimately, the Court in *Issa* could not find any evidence that the Turkish forces were in the area at the relevant time, so the case was dismissed for lack of evidence that the relevant events occurred within Turkish jurisdiction.

military base in Basra. The House of Lords, applying the principles in *Bankovic*, held that the UK did not have jurisdiction over the five street deaths. It interpreted the decision as confirming that the ECHR did not normally apply outside the area of the Council of Europe. Cases such as *Öcalan* were distinguished on the basis that they represented a discrete exception to the *Bankovic* principle, which applied in cases of 'forcible removal... effected with the full cooperation of the [relevant] foreign authorities'.[75] The House of Lords also agreed that an exception applied in respect of the sixth alleged victim: it held that persons detained by British personnel in a prison in Iraq were within British jurisdiction.[76] Lord Brown analogized such jurisdiction to that exercised in an overseas embassy or consulate.[77] *Issa*, a decision of a single chamber of the European Court, was sidelined as it could not be reconciled with the higher authority of the Grand Chamber in *Bankovic*.[78]

5.2 ACHR

Article 1(1) ACHR requires states to respect and ensure the rights to 'all persons subject to their jurisdiction', so, as with the ECHR, no territorial limit is expressed. In *Coard et al. v United States,* the Inter-American Commission on Human Rights found that the USA exercised jurisdiction over persons in Grenada during its 1983 invasion for the purposes of the American Declaration of Human Rights.[79] The USA is not a party to the ACHR and no jurisdictional clause is contained within the American Declaration. On the facts in *Coard*, it does not seem debatable that the USA had jurisdiction over the relevant persons. They were detained on a US military ship, and the USA arguably had effective control over Grenada at the time.[80] Nevertheless, neither fact was explicitly referenced in the Commission's decision. It found that people could come within US jurisdiction through the actions of US agents, namely the US military in Grenada.

Alejandre v Cuba concerned the shooting down of unarmed civilian aircraft by Cuban aircraft.[81] The case again concerned findings under the American Declaration, as Cuba was not a party to the ACHR. The Inter-American Commission found that Cuba had jurisdiction over the four deceased occupants of the airplanes. The shootings took place in international airspace, and two of the deceased were not Cubans. The only potential basis for jurisdiction lay 'in the relationship between the agents of Cuba and the victims in the circumstances at the time of the incident'.[82] Indeed, the

---

[75] [2007] UKHL 26, para 119.

[76] See also *Hess v UK* (1975) 2 DR 72, concerning UK responsibility for the detention of Rudolf Hess in Germany.

[77] n 75, para 132. See also *Bankovic*, n1, para 73; *X v Germany* (1965) 8 Eur Comm HR 158; *X v the United Kingdom* (1977) 12 Eur Comm HR 73.   [78] n 75, para 75.

[79] Case 10.951, IACommHR Report No 109/99 (29 September 1999).

[80] Cerone, 'The Application of Regional Human Rights Law Beyond Regional Frontiers: The Inter-American Commission on Human Rights and US Activities in Iraq', *ASIL Insights* (25 October 2005) 3.

[81] Case 11.589, IACommHR Report No 86/99 (29 September 1999).   [82] Cerone, n 80, 4.

control exercised over the victims seems analogous to that exercised by the ops over the victims in *Bankovic*.

imission indicated that the ACHR had similar extraterritorial application .ᵤ ᵤₑ American Declaration in *Saldano v Argentina*, stating that extraterritorial jurisdiction arose 'under certain circumstances for the acts and omissions of [state agents] which produce effects or are undertaken outside that State's own territory'.[83] It therefore appears that a lower threshold applies under the Inter-American human rights system compared to the European system with regard to the extraterritorial application of regional human rights law. However, the Inter-American bodies have not yet confronted the issue of whether Inter-American human rights law might be confined to the Inter-American 'legal space'.

5.3 AFRICAN CONVENTION ON HUMAN AND PEOPLES' RIGHTS

In *Democratic Republic of the Congo v Burundi, Rwanda, and Uganda*, the respondent states were found responsible by the African Commission on Human Rights for the actions of their occupying troops in the Democratic Republic of the Congo.[84] Indeed, the respondent states did not dispute the admissibility of the complaint on the grounds of extraterritoriality. The case seems a fairly clear instance of 'effective control' being exercised in an extraterritorial context.

5.4 ICCPR

The UN treaties are logically unaffected by the 'legal space' argument. While one might argue that regional treaties are presumed to apply only within a particular region, no such argument can apply to treaties with a global reach. Article 2(1) ICCPR requires states to respect and ensure ICCPR rights 'to all individuals within its territory *and* subject to its jurisdiction'.[85] Thus, the language of the ICCPR seems to limit a state's responsibility under the ICCPR to its territory. Nevertheless, the Human Rights Committee has confirmed the extraterritorial impact of the ICCPR in a number of cases. The Committee (and other UN human rights treaty bodies) have confirmed Israel's responsibility for human rights abuses in the Occupied Territories,[86] and the same for the USA regarding its detention camp in Guantánamo Bay in Cuba.[87] In numerous cases, such as *Montero v Uruguay*, states have been held responsible for the actions of their overseas consulates in unreasonably refusing to renew a passport.[88] In

---

[83] IACommHR Report No 38/99 (11 March 1999) para 17.
[84] Communication No 227/99 (May 2003).   [85] Emphasis added.
[86] See eg HRC, Concluding observations of the Human Rights Committee: Israel, CCPR/CO/78/ISR (21 August 2003). See also *Legal Consequences of the Construction of a Wall in the Occupied Palestinian Territory* (Advisory Opinion) [2004] ICJ Rep 36.
[87] See eg HRC, Concluding observations: US, CCPR/C/USA/CO/3 (15 September 2006).
[88] CCPR/C/18/D/106/1981 (31 March 1983).

Lopez Burgos v Uruguay, Uruguay was held responsible for the kidnap in Argentina of a man by its agents.[89]

In General Comment 31, the Human Rights Committee described the extraterritorial impact of the ICCPR as follows:

[A] State party must respect and ensure the rights laid down in the Covenant to *anyone within the power or effective control* of that State Party, even if not situated within the territory of the State Party.... This principle also applies to those within the power or effective control of the forces of a State Party acting outside its territory, regardless of the circumstances in which such power or effective control was obtained.[90]

Thus, the ICCPR and the ACHR seem to apply extraterritorially where an affected person is under the effective control of a state's agents, rather than only where an affected person is within territory that is effectively controlled by a state. The focus of the Committee in defining the extent of jurisdiction seems to be on the state's relationship with the relevant impugned act and the person affected, rather than its relationship with the territory where a relevant act takes place.

5.5 ICESCR

The extraterritorial scope of the ICESCR is more open to debate due to the current lack of case law under that treaty. Furthermore, the ICESCR does not contain a provision relating to jurisdictional or territorial scope.[91] Article 2(1) does, however, say that states must progressively realize ICESCR rights through steps taken individually 'and through international assistance and cooperation'. Those words seem to imply that states should at least refrain from actions which harm those rights abroad, as such measures are decidedly non-cooperative.

The International Court of Justice confirmed in its advisory opinion on the *Legal Consequences of the Construction of a Wall in the Occupied Palestinian Territory* that states have duties under the ICESCR to 'territories over which a State party has sovereignty and to those over which that State exercises territorial jurisdiction'.[92] Ultimately, the Court found that Israel had violated a number of rights in the ICESCR by building part of its wall in the Occupied Territory and, for example, hindering access to educational facilities, places of employment, health services, agricultural land, and sources of water. In *Democratic Republic of Congo v Uganda* the Court stated that states are responsible under international human rights treaties for acts done in the exercise of jurisdiction outside their territory, especially in occupied territories.[93] The *Wall* standard focused on territorial control (which Israel exercised over the West Bank), at least

[89] CCPR/C/13/D/52/1979 (29 July 1981). A similar decision arose in *Celiberti de Casariego v Uruguay,* CCPR/C/13/D/56/1979 (29 July 1981), concerning the kidnapping of a person from Brazil.

[90] n 17, para 10 (emphasis added).

[91] The new Optional Protocol to the ICESCR states in Art 2 that communications may be received on behalf of people 'under the jurisdiction of a State party'.   [92] n 86, paras 111–13.

[93] *Armed Activities on the Territory of the Congo (Democratic Republic of the Congo v Uganda)* (Judgment, Merits) [2005] ICJ Rep 168, para 216.

in respect of the ICESCR, while the *Congo* standard seemed to focus on extraterritorial acts with regard to all human rights treaties.

Given that extraterritorial jurisdiction under the ICESCR exists, one may readily assume that states are required to *respect* ICESCR rights outside their borders, that is, to refrain from harming such rights. In fact, the most important aspects of a duty to respect may arise with regard to intra-territorial acts which have an extraterritorial effect, rather than with extraterritorial acts as such. For example, the adoption by a state of protectionist measures within its territory will often cause harm to the right to work of those in export industries outside its territory. Indeed, a state's intra-territorial acts are more likely to impact detrimentally (or beneficially) on economic, social, and cultural rights abroad than civil and political rights. The comparable analysis is arguably that of the refoulement cases, meaning that harm amounts to a breach of ICESCR obligations if it is reasonably foreseeable. On the other hand, the connection between the state and the expelled person is clearer than in the case of an external person who suffers economic harm, as the impugned act of refoulement initially occurs while the person is within the state's territory, and the act is clearly aimed at that person such as to cause harm to his or her rights. Therefore, the crucial jurisdictional issue in this context concerns the identification of circumstances when a state owes persons outside its territory ICESCR obligations, such that it must avoid acts, whether occurring inside or outside its territory, that cause harm to their ICESCR rights. That is, the question may be more one of 'who has rights' rather than 'where did the impugned act occur'.

The Committee on Economic, Social and Cultural Rights has indicated that states parties also have duties to *protect* ICESCR rights in other states. For example, it stated in General Comment 15 on the right to water that states should take steps 'to prevent their own citizens and companies from violating the right to water of individuals and communities in other countries'.[94] On the other hand, experts at a series of workshops convened in 2006 under the auspices of the UN Special Representative on the issue of human rights and transnational corporations concluded that the existence of such duties remained an open question.[95] Such a duty is easier to maintain if a state is actively facilitating its corporations' overseas activities, such as through the provision of export credits.

The most controversial aspect of potential extraterritorial duties under the ICESCR relates to *fulfilling* ICESCR rights in other states. Such a duty would imply that rich states are obliged to provide aid to assist poorer countries. Rich states predictably resist such a characterization of their ICESCR duties. Such a duty is more evident in the words of the Declaration on the Right to Development,[96] as well as the Millennium

---

[94] CESCR, General Comment 15, HRI/GEN/1/Rev.9 (Vol 1) 97, para 33. See also CESCR, General Comment 19, HRI/GEN/1/Rev.9 (Vol 1) 152, para 54.

[95] See Report of the Special Representative of the Secretary-General on the issue of human rights and transnational corporations and other business enterprises, A/HRC/4/35/Add.2 (15 February 2007) 15.

[96] Declaration on the Right to Development, esp Art 4.

Development Goals.[97] For its part, the Committee has indicated that states have a duty to assist other states to provide international assistance when they are in a position to do so.[98] On the other hand, the parameters of such a duty are difficult to determine. When, precisely, would state X have a duty to a person in state Y to take positive actions to fulfil his or her rights? And when could that person's socio-economic deprivation be held to come within the responsibility of a particular external state?

5.6 OVERALL ASSESSMENT

Wilde has put forward a convincing argument that the focus on jurisdiction over a person, rather than territory, is the preferred determinant of when extraterritorial human rights responsibility arises. He claims, correctly, that a territorial focus inevitably discriminates against non-nationals, as states are far more likely to be in control of territory populated by nationals. Furthermore, that focus permits states to dictate that their agents behave on foreign soil in a manner that is not permitted under human rights law at home. Finally, the territorial approach might regrettably generate legal vacuums where no human rights law applies.[99]

Even the UK courts, which seemed so enamoured with *Bankovic* in *Al Skeini*, drove another chink into that case's armour in *Secretary of State for Defence v Smith* concerning the death of a British soldier from heatstroke in Iraq.[100] The Court of Appeal of England and Wales held that the UK had human rights duties towards its soldiers serving in Iraq under the ECHR. The Court found that it was not tenable that a UK soldier could be recognized as having such rights in certain areas, such as in a military base, military prison, or military hospital, but not while out in the field. Thus, the Court of Appeal held that a state's extraterritorial jurisdiction under the ECHR could attach to a person rather than an area when that person was a soldier, and perhaps any person, acting abroad as a servant of the state. *Smith* indicates that the rights of the NATO pilots in *Bankovic* came within the jurisdiction of their respective NATO states, while the rights of the people they were firing upon did not.

An issue arises as to the comprehensiveness of a state's extraterritorial human rights obligations. Within its territory, a state must respect, protect, and fulfil human rights. One might imagine that, extraterritorially, a sliding scale of duties might apply according to the degree of control a state has over a particular situation.[101] For example, the detainees in Guantánamo Bay are under the total control of the USA, and

[97] See Alston, 'Ships Passing in the Night: The Current State of the Human Rights and Development Debate seen through the Lens of the Millenium Development Goals' (2005) 27 *HRQ* 778. See also Charter of Economic Rights and Duties of States, Art 24.

[98] See eg CESCR, General Comment 3, HRI/GEN/1/Rev.9 (Vol 1) 7, para 14; CESCR General Comment 12, n 66, para 35; CESCR General Comment 15, n 94, para 38.

[99] Wilde, 'Legal "Black hole"? Extraterritorial State action and international treaty law on civil and political rights' (2005) 26 *Michigan JIL* 1, 25–8. See also *Lopez Burgos*, n 89, including the concurring opinion of Mr Tomuschat. [100] [2009] EWCA Civ 441

[101] Wilde, 'Triggering State Obligations Extraterritorially: the Spatial Test in Certain Human Rights Treaties' (2007) 40 *Israel LR* 503, 524.

therefore should be entitled to claim the full range of treaty rights against the USA, regardless of their Cuban location. On the other hand, one might assume that Israel's human rights responsibilities in Gaza are not as comprehensive since its withdrawal from that territory. While Israel is obliged to refrain from measures which harm rights in Gaza, it seems unlikely that Israel retains the same obligation to fulfil the right to education in Gaza, where educational facilities are essentially controlled by Hamas, an entity that is hostile to Israel. Similarly, while the victim in *Montero v Uruguay* could claim the right to freedom of movement against the Uruguayan consulate in Germany with regard to a refusal to renew his passport, Montero could not claim that the consulate was required to take measures to protect the full range of his rights while he was in Germany. When jurisdiction is tied to an act with respect to a person, rather than effective control over territory, 'it would seem that the individual is within the jurisdiction of that state only for the purposes of that act',[102] with the relevant act in *Montero*, for example, being the refusal to renew the passport.[103]

In *Bankovic*, where the concept of jurisdiction over an individual was rejected, the European Court of Human Rights denied that a state's obligations could 'be divided and tailored in accordance with the particular circumstances of the extra-territorial act in question'.[104] However, this 'all or nothing' approach seems unduly strict. There seems little difficulty, for example, in imposing a duty on states to respect human rights, and therefore refrain from actions which harm human rights outside their territory. On the other hand, the extent of extraterritorial positive obligations (to protect and fulfil) seem logically more dependent upon a greater degree of control over a situation. Indeed, the European Court seemed to depart from its strict *Bankovic* position in *Ilascu*, with regard to the scope of Moldova's human rights responsibilities on the facts of that case.

The complaint against Moldova in *Ilascu* concerned its jurisdiction over an area within its own territory, but where it plainly lacked control. Analogous situations include Cuba's responsibility for Guantánamo Bay and Cyprus's responsibility for Northern Cyprus. Does a state retain jurisdiction over such areas for human rights purposes? In *Ilascu*, the European Court conceded that Moldova did not have effective control over Transdniestria so the scope of its jurisdiction was reduced,[105] but it retained 'a positive obligation...to take diplomatic, economic, judicial or other measures that [were] within its power to take...to secure the rights guaranteed in the Convention'.[106] The concession that jurisdiction can be retained in a reduced form cuts against the Court's 'all or nothing' approach in *Bankovic* that jurisdiction is not divisible.

[102] Cerone, n 65, 1497.
[103] The impugned act in *Munaf v Romania*, CCPR/C/96/D/1539/2006 (21 August 2009) was that the Romanian embassy in Iraq wrongly released Munaf into the hands of the US embassy, where he was ultimately handed over to Iraqi authorities and charged with capital crimes. Ultimately, the claim of a breach of the right to life (and other rights) was not upheld, as Romania was found not to be in a position to have foreseen the events following its release of Munaf. [104] n 1, para 75.
[105] n 64, para 333.   [106] Ibid, para 331.

6 CONCLUSION

Generally, states owe human rights duties to individuals and groups within their juris-diction. However, the extent of a state's jurisdiction and responsibility for the purposes of its human rights treaty obligations are complex and evolving concepts. There would be huge lacunae in human rights protection if a state's jurisdiction and responsibility only arose in connection with its own acts and omissions within its own territory.

Therefore, human rights law has evolved to generate the concept of due diligence to ensure some accountability for human rights abuses in the private sphere. In contrast, the extent of state jurisdictional responsibility for the acts of international organiza-tions is less clear. *Kadi* is a strong decision of the European Court of Justice indicating that human rights obligations cannot be disregarded when implementing obligations under other areas of international law. The approach of the European Court of Human Rights, on the other hand, has been more deferential to other organizations, particu-larly the Security Council, while the Human Rights Committee's approach is not yet clear.

The scope of a state's human rights jurisdiction outside its territory is also unclear, with the European Court taking a more conservative approach than the UN treaty bodies, the Inter-American bodies, and perhaps the International Court of Justice. Under the narrower view epitomized by *Bankovic*, extraterritorial jurisdiction arises only when a state has effective control over territory. An additional consideration is whether, as indicated in *Bankovic*, the jurisdictional scope under regional treaties extends beyond their own regional space. *Bankovic* is, however, subject to a number of exceptions. Indeed, the number of exceptions, particularly taking into account *Issa* and the recent UK decision in *Smith*, is arguably reaching unwieldy levels. The broader view holds that jurisdiction arises when a state has effective control over the enjoy-ment of a particular right by an individual. This view has significant ramifications for the extraterritorial scope of the ICESCR, given the ubiquity of external economic impacts, and consequent effects on economic, social, and cultural rights, caused by state actions in today's interconnected global economy.

FURTHER READING

CERONE, 'Human Dignity in the Line of Fire: The Application of International Human Rights Law during Armed Conflict, Occupation, and Peace Operations' (2006) 39 *Vanderbilt JTL* 1446.

COOMANS and KAMMINGA (eds), *Extraterritorial Application of Human Rights* (Intersentia, 2004).

CRAVEN, 'The Violence of Dispossession: Extra-Territoriality and Economic, Social and Cultural Rights' in Baderin and McCorquodale (eds), *Economic Social and Cultural Rights in Action* (Oxford University Press, 2007).

Draft Articles on Responsibility of States for Internationally Wrongful Acts, A/56/10, ch IV.E.1.

KAMCHIBEKOVA, 'State Responsibility for Extraterritorial Human Rights Violations' (2007) 13 *Buffalo HRLR* 87.

KNOX, 'Horizontal Human Rights Law' (2008) 103 *AJIL* 1.

MCCORQUODALE and SIMON, 'Responsibility beyond Borders: State Responsibility for Extraterritorial Violations by Corporations under International Human Rights Law' (2007) 70 *MLR* 599.

SARI, 'Jurisdiction and International Responsibility in Peace Support Operations: the *Behrami* and *Saramati* cases' (2008) 8 *HRLR* 151.

SKOGLY, 'Extraterritoriality: Universal Human Rights without Universal Obligations?' in Joseph and McBeth (eds), *Research Handbook on International Human Rights* (Edward Elgar, 2010).

WILDE, 'Legal "Black Hole"?: Extraterritorial state action and international treaty law on civil and political rights' (2005) 26 *Michigan JIL* 739.

PART III

SUBSTANTIVE RIGHTS

8

CATEGORIES OF RIGHTS

Theo van Boven

SUMMARY

This chapter seeks to identify different categories of human rights, but in doing so recognizes the indivisibility, interdependence, and interrelatedness of all human rights. A first categorization distinguishes civil and political rights from economic, social, and cultural rights. This distinction is, however, increasingly contested and should not disguise the mutual relationship between these rights as essential conditions for the life and well-being of the human person. A second distinction is that between the rights of individuals and the rights of collectivities, in particular indigenous peoples. Collective rights offer parameters for the effective enjoyment of individual rights. A third distinction is that between core rights and other rights, raising the issue whether there is a ranking among human rights as to their fundamental nature. It is argued that basic substantive rights determining the life, survival, dignity, and worth of individuals and peoples may be considered as core rights. The chapter finally discusses the question whether 'new human rights' are emerging. It advises that this question be approached with caution and that human rights should be understood in an inclusive and newly focused manner, encompassing hitherto marginalized and excluded groups and human beings.

1 INTRODUCTION

There is a certain uneasiness about classifying human rights in different categories. Leading UN documents state that all human rights are *indivisible, interdependent, and interrelated*. Whatever categories of human rights one may have in mind—civil, political, economic, social, or cultural rights; individual or collective rights; core or non-core rights—intersections bear out that all rights are interlinked and that categories or classifications correspond more to conceptual premises than to realities. The relative inadequacy of human rights categories and classifications becomes evident when the focus is on the human being whose enjoyment of rights and freedoms depends on prevailing conditions of freedom from fear and freedom from want. Domestic and

olicies, insofar as they take into account the holistic nature of human
end human rights categorizations and classifications.

nprehensive and holistic nature of human rights was recognized by US
it Franklin D Roosevelt when, in his famous speech of 1941, he mentioned
essential freedoms' that must be guaranteed to all persons everywhere in the
rld: freedom of speech and expression, freedom of worship, freedom from want,
and freedom from fear.[1] This forward-looking four-freedoms message served as one
of the sources of inspiration for the UN International Bill of Rights and continues to
inspire policy-makers. For example, former UN Secretary-General Kofi Annan, in
his landmark report *In Larger Freedom: Towards Development, Security and Human
Rights for All*, drew extensively on the freedom from want and freedom from fear
paradigm.[2] A major thrust thereof is that development, security, and human rights are
not only interlinked, they also reinforce each other.[3] In order to attain larger freedom,
human rights must be an integral part of development and security policies. Even
though this chapter reviews various categories of human rights, this should neither
distract from the indivisibility of all human rights, nor from their comprehensive and
holistic nature.

2 CATEGORIES OF HUMAN RIGHTS

2.1 ECONOMIC, SOCIAL, CULTURAL RIGHTS/CIVIL, POLITICAL RIGHTS

Much attention has been given over the years to the distinction between, on the one
hand, *economic, social, and cultural rights* (such as the rights to an adequate standard
of living, education and work, dealt with in Chapters 11 and 13, below) and, on the
other, *civil and political rights* (such as the rights to life and integrity of the person,
the freedoms of thought, expression, association, and assembly, and the rights to liberty and a fair trial, dealt with in Chapters 10, 12, and 14, below).[4] There is indeed
a significant difference between the two as far as the nature of states parties' obligations under the International Covenant on Economic, Social and Cultural Rights
(ICESCR) and the International Covenant on Civil and Political Rights (ICCPR) are
concerned. While Article 2 ICESCR provides for the *progressive realization* of economic, social, and cultural rights and acknowledges the constraints due to limits of
available resources, the parallel Article 2 ICCPR prescribes the obligation to respect
and ensure all civil and political rights as an *immediate* obligation. Accordingly,
the Committee on Economic, Social and Cultural Rights has viewed the concept of

[1] Commager, *Documents of American History* (Crofts, 1946) 634.   [2] A/59/2005 (21 March 2005).
[3] See World Summit outcome document, GA Res 60/1 (24 October 2005) para 9.
[4] van Boven, 'Distinguishing Criteria of Human Rights' in Vasak and Alston (eds), *The International
Dimensions of Human Rights: Vol 1* (UNESCO/Greenwood Press 1982) 87.

progressive realization as a recognition that full realization of all economic, social, and cultural rights will generally not be achieved in a short period of time. Since progressive realization is an essential objective, not in the abstract but to the maximum of available resources, a question arises regarding how such an obligation of the state is to be interpreted in times of economic depression and shrinking resources as experienced at the end of the first decade of the twenty-first century. An essential bottom-line to be respected under all circumstances, even in times of shrinking resources, is that of non-discrimination which the Committee termed 'an immediate and cross-cutting obligation in the [ICESCR]'.[5]

Nevertheless, the Committee on Economic, Social and Cultural Rights has pointed out that, despite this difference, there are also significant similarities between the ICESCR and the ICCPR. In particular, the ICESCR imposes various obligations of *immediate effect*.[6] Thus, there are a number of provisions in the ICESCR that, as the Committee has pointed out in its General Comment 3, would seem to be capable of immediate application by judicial and other organs in many domestic legal systems. Among these are the elimination of discrimination (Articles 2(2) and (3)), the right to form and join trade unions and to strike (Article 8), protection of children and young persons from economic and social exploitation (Article 10(3)), equal remuneration for work of equal value without distinction of any kind (Article 7(a)(i)), the provision of free and compulsory primary education for all (Article 13(2)(a)), the liberty of parents to choose schools for their children, other than those established by public authorities (Article 13(3)), and the liberty of individuals and bodies to establish and direct educational institutions which conform to certain minimum standards (Article 13(4)).[7]

In addition to the difference between obligations of immediate effect and progressive realization, it is quite common to advance further criteria to distinguish civil and political rights from economic and social rights by contrasting the concept of freedom rights with that of welfare rights or by referring to duties of the state not to intervene as opposed to duties to take positive measures. Such distinctions are helpful but do not apply across the board insofar as there is no strict dividing line between civil and political rights on the one hand and economic and social rights on the other.

While the status of civil and political rights as human rights is largely uncontested, this is less true for economic, social, and cultural rights.[8] The latter are sometimes referred to as 'aspirations' phrased in terms of rights but without legal enforceability. The media, many NGOs, public officials, as well as public opinion generally understand human rights in terms of the right to life, the abolition of the death penalty, the prohibition of torture, the right to privacy, freedom of information and expression, freedom of religion or belief, and the right to vote and to be elected. The rights to food, healthcare, housing, and employment are considered much less part of the

---

[5] CESCR, General Comment 20, E/C.12/GC/20 (2009) para 7.
[6] CESCR, General Comment 3, HRI/GEN/1/ (Vol 1) 7, para 1.   [7] Ibid, paras 1 and 5.
[8] See Robinson, 'Advancing Economic, Social and Cultural Rights: The Way Forward' (2004) 26 *HRQ* 866; Roth, 'Defending Economic, Social and Cultural Rights: Practical Issues Faced by an International Human Rights Organization' (2004) 26 *HRQ* 63.

human rights package. However, this perception of human rights overlooks the comprehensive nature of the Universal Declaration of Human Rights (UDHR) and notably its Article 28, which provides that everyone is entitled to a social and international order in which the rights and freedoms set forth in the Declaration can be fully realized. Over the years, as the human rights discourse became part of processes towards widening categories of entitlements and beneficiaries and linking human rights to the promotion of peace, security, and sustainable development, as well as preserving a healthy environment, a comprehensive human rights approach has evolved, encompassing the broad and interlinked scale of civil, political, economic, social, and cultural rights.

2.2 RIGHTS OF INDIVIDUALS/RIGHTS OF COLLECTIVITIES

The same process has also had an impact on another traditional categorization of human rights, namely the distinction between *rights of individuals* and *rights of collectivities*. In the frame of reference of the UDHR and the international covenants, with their emphasis on human dignity and the worth and uniqueness of every human being, the focus is on the rights of every individual person. Of course, in many ways individual human beings live and work in community and partnership with other human beings, in family and similar relations, in the exercise of religion or belief, in educational settings, and in forming and joining trade unions. Yet it is the individual person, while part of social or cultural relations of a community nature, who is the beneficiary of rights.

The same construction has been used, at least in the UN terminology, where rights of peoples and minority groups, addressed in Chapter 17 below, are involved. Minorities, as collectivities, are not referred to as beneficiaries of rights. This is so that any separatist ambitions that they may pursue in the states where they live are not legitimized. Accordingly, the relevant provision of the ICCPR, Article 27 reads: 'In those States in which ethnic, religious or linguistic minorities exist, *persons belonging to such minorities* shall not be denied the right, in community with other members of their group, to enjoy their own culture, to profess and practise their own religion, or to use their own language.'[9] This provision is phrased in very restrained terms and avoids, at least in theory, the recognition of collective rights. Similarly, the UN Declaration on the Rights of Persons Belonging to National or Ethnic, Religious and Linguistic Minorities (1992) cautiously and consistently refers to 'persons belonging to minorities', thereby focusing on individuals rather than collectivities.

A different approach, one that is more collectivist or peoples-oriented, is to be found in the UN Declaration on the Rights of Indigenous Peoples (2007). The text of this declaration was negotiated over a period of more than 20 years with considerable input from indigenous peoples themselves. In the preamble of the Declaration,

---

[9] Emphasis added.

the rights of individuals and the rights of collectivities are brought together in a dialectical fashion by 'recognizing and reaffirming that indigenous individuals are entitled without discrimination to all human rights recognized in international law and that indigenous peoples possess collective rights which are indispensable for their existence, well-being and integral development as peoples'.[10] Throughout the text of the Declaration, rights are attributed to both indigenous peoples as well as to indigenous individuals, with the indigenous peoples as principal rights-holders and the express recognition of the right to self-determination as the cornerstone of their rights. Article 3 of the Declaration restates the wording of common Article 1 of the international covenants, applying it to the particular case of indigenous peoples: 'Indigenous peoples have the right to self-determination. By virtue of that right they freely determine their political status and freely pursue their economic, social and cultural development.' In many ways, the Declaration on the Rights of Indigenous Peoples brings together peoples' rights and individual rights in a spectrum of mutual relationship and reach. A good illustration of this is Article 7, which, echoing Article 3 UDHR, provides that 'indigenous individuals have the rights to life, physical and mental integrity, liberty and security of person', while at the same time making it clear, in language similar to the UN Declaration on the Right of Peoples to Peace (1984),[11] that 'indigenous peoples have the collective right to live in freedom, peace and security as distinct peoples'.

This collective dimension of the rights of peoples and populations, for present and future generations, recognizes that the realization and enjoyment of individual rights are conditioned by the attainment of peace, security, and development. The same notion is embodied in the right to self-determination, defined in terms of free determination of political status and free pursuance of economic, social, and cultural development. Peoples' right to self-determination is recognized as a leading and underlying principle for the enjoyment of civil, political, economic, social, and cultural rights and was therefore included in both international covenants as the first substantive provision. Against this background, the 1993 Vienna World Conference on Human Rights considered the denial of the right of self-determination as a violation of human rights.[12] Similarly, it is significant that the UN Declaration on the Right to Development (1986) places the individual and collective aspects of this right in a mutual relationship and seeks to link the conditions of life of the human person with the welfare and well-being of peoples.[13] Thus, the right to development is defined as an inalienable human right with the proviso that equality of opportunity for development is a prerogative both of nations and of individuals who make up nations. Further, the Declaration states that 'the human person is the central subject of development and should be the active participant and beneficiary of the right to development'.[14]

---

[10] GA Res 61/295 (13 September 2007) preamble.   [11] GA Res 39/11 (12 November 1984).
[12] Vienna Declaration and Programme of Action, A/CONF.157/23 (25 June 1993) para 2.
[13] GA Res 41/128 (4 December 1986).   [14] Ibid, Art 2(1).

2.3 ONE-DIMENSIONAL/COMPOSITE RIGHTS

As compared to rights such as freedom of expression or the right to a fair trial, the rights to self-determination and development, as well as the right to peace, are of a more complex nature. Therefore, they are often described as composite rights. The question may be asked what the legal significance of such rights is. While they condition the life and welfare of individual human beings, they are not rights inherent in the human person. Their realization depends on political, economic, social, and cultural policies deployed by national and international organs and institutions. These rights do not lend themselves to enforcement by legal authorities. Nevertheless, gross violations of the right to peace, the right to self-determination, or the right to development may, under given circumstances, incur state responsibility as well as civil responsibility of other major actors, or, if they amount to aggression, genocide, or crimes against humanity, even criminal responsibility of natural or legal persons. While these rights primarily represent major policy objectives of a national and international order, their legal implications are not without significance and may be tested in political or judicial settings in case of their breach or gross denial.

3 INTERDEPENDENCE AND INDIVISIBILITY
OF ALL HUMAN RIGHTS

The previous section identified different categories of human rights: civil and political rights as compared to economic, social, and cultural rights; rights of individuals as compared to rights of collectivities; one-dimensional rights as compared to rights of a composite nature. But it has also already been made clear that all these rights are intersected and interrelated. They condition each other, with the human person, as the UN Declaration on the Right to Development puts it, as 'the central subject' and 'beneficiary' of rights,[15] and, in the words of the preambles of the international covenants, with a focus on 'the ideal of free human beings enjoying freedom from fear and want'.

Against this background, the interdependence and indivisibility of all human rights, whether or not classified in various categories, has become a leading axiom in the international human rights discourse. A number of examples taken from UN instruments, statements, and practices can be advanced to underline this interdependence and indivisibility. The Proclamation of Teheran, adopted at the first world conference on human rights in 1968, stated that human rights and fundamental freedoms are indivisible.[16] The second world conference held in Vienna in 1993 stated with greater emphasis that '[a]ll human rights are universal, indivisible, and interdependent and interrelated'.[17] The outcome document of the 2005 World Summit reaffirmed this

---

[15] Ibid, Art 2(1).

[16] UN, *Compilation of International Instruments, Vol 1 (First Part)* (1993) 51–4, Art 13.

[17] n 12, para 5.

statement.[18] The General Assembly resolution of 2006 establishing the Human Rights Council again reaffirmed that 'all human rights are universal, indivisible, interrelated, interdependent and mutually reinforcing, and that all human rights must be treated in a fair and equal manner, on the same footing and with the same emphasis'.[19]

It may be argued that reiterating and reaffirming the same phrase does not necessarily make it a reality. Perhaps more convincing are the language and contents of specific legal instruments on non-discrimination and the rights of vulnerable persons and persons in need of special recognition and protection. Thus, the International Convention on the Elimination of All Forms of Racial Discrimination, the Convention on the Elimination of All Forms of Discrimination Against Women, the Convention on the Rights of the Child, the International Convention on the Protection of the Rights of All Migrant Workers and Members of Their Families, and the Convention on the Rights of Persons with Disabilities all recognize the full scope of human rights in a comprehensive interrelationship. Finally, as was noted above, it can be argued that the UN Declaration on the Rights of Indigenous Peoples is in its scope and wording the most far-reaching illustration of the interdependence and interrelatedness of all human rights, be they economic, social, cultural, civil, or political rights; rights of individuals or collectivities; or composite rights such as the right to self-determination and the right to development. More concretely, the interrelationship between economic, social, and cultural rights, on the one hand, and civil and political rights, on the other, may be demonstrated through Table 8.1, which illustrates how the former set of rights can be protected by invoking the latter—in other words, how economic, social, and cultural rights can be framed in terms of civil and political rights.[20]

Table 8.1 Indirect protection of economic, social, and cultural rights through civil and political rights

Invoked civil and political rights	Protected economic, social, cultural rights
Right to life	Rights to health, food, water, education
Freedom from torture/degrading treatment	Rights to health, housing
Right to private/family life and home	Rights to health, housing
Right to property	Right to social security, housing; collective right to ancestral land of indigenous people
Protection of the child	Rights to health, food, education
Freedom of movement, residence	Right to housing; collective right to ancestral land of indigenous people
Freedom of association	Right to form and join trade unions; rights to collective bargaining
Freedom from forced/compulsory labour	Right to work/to fair conditions of work

[18] n 3, para 13.   [19] GA Res 60/251 (3 April 2006) preambular para 3.

[20] This illustration is reproduced from International Commission of Jurists, *Courts and the Legal Enforcement of Economic, Social and Cultural Rights: Comparative Experiences of Justiciability* (2008) 72 (© Copyright International Commission of Jurists, 2008).

In line with the interdependence and indivisibility of all human rights, a significant evolution has occurred over the years towards the *enhanced status of economic, social, and cultural rights*. Thus, UN supervisory mechanisms and procedures, including those relating to violations of human rights, have progressively brought economic, social, and cultural rights on a par with civil and political rights. Further, while initially, after the entry into force of the ICESCR, the UN Economic and Social Council was entrusted with general monitoring tasks, it soon became clear that it lacked the capacity and expertise to carry out these tasks effectively. Therefore, the Council established a supervisory committee of independent experts, the Committee on Economic, Social and Cultural Rights, with similar tasks and responsibilities as the Human Rights Committee under the ICCPR. More recently, the UN General Assembly adopted an Optional Protocol to the ICESCR, which provides for the right to petition by individuals or groups of individuals claiming to be victims of a violation of any of the rights set forth in the Covenant by a state party that has accepted the Optional Protocol. This new legal instrument can be considered as a counterpart to the previously established Optional Protocol to the ICCPR. It will help to strengthen the legal protection of economic, social, and cultural rights by the development of case law which will enhance, domestically and internationally, the justiciability of economic, social, and cultural rights. Although the Optional Protocol to the ICESCR was finally, after lengthy and protracted negotiations, adopted without a vote, it did not attract unreserved support of the entire UN membership. A number of states would have preferred an *à la carte* instrument which would expressly allow states to select the rights they would accept as falling under the operation of the Protocol. This view however did not prevail and the Protocol therefore covers all the rights included in the ICESCR.

The same tendency of rendering a more prominent status to economic, social, and cultural rights is also apparent in the system of special procedures developed under the former UN Commission on Human Rights and now operating under the authority of the Human Rights Council. These special procedures with geographic or thematic mandates were established to respond to gross and consistent patterns of human rights violations. They initially concentrated on violations of civil and political rights, notably enforced disappearances, extrajudicial, summary, and arbitrary executions, torture and ill-treatment, arbitrary arrests and detention, freedom of religion or belief, and freedom of opinion and expression.[21] Gradually, however, during the last decade of the twentieth century and in later years, civil and political rights mandates were complemented by mandates in the area of economic, social, and cultural rights, notably dealing with the right to adequate housing, the right to food, human rights and extreme poverty, the right to physical and mental health, the right to education, and the right to water. Other thematic mandates dealing with contemporary forms of racism, indigenous people, minority issues, and the rights of migrants cover a whole range of human rights, not limited to civil and political rights or economic, social, and cultural rights.

---

[21] See Gutter, *Thematic Procedures of the United Nations Commission on Human Rights and International Law: In Search of a Sense of Community* (Intersentia, 2006).

A significant role in identifying and supporting the normative content of eco-nomic, social, and cultural rights was played by the Limburg Principles on the Implementation of the ICESCR, drawn up in 1986 by a group of experts.[22] The Limburg Principles were instrumental in helping to frame the conceptual work of the Committee on Economic, Social and Cultural Rights so as to clarify the obligations of states under the ICESCR, including their legal duties arising from violations of economic, social, and cultural rights. Ten years later, the Maastricht Guidelines on Violations of Economic, Social and Cultural Rights underscored the violations component by spelling out that violations can occur through both acts of commission and omissions by the state, and by providing guidance on states' responsibility for violations, the notion of victims, and remedies and other responses to violations.[23]

The focus on violations is linked with the issue of the *justiciability* of economic, social, and cultural rights. 'Justiciability' refers to the ability of an independent and impartial body to provide a remedy for individuals in case of a violation of a right.[24] The general comments by treaty bodies, notably the Committee on Economic, Social and Cultural Rights and the Committee on the Rights of the Child, have helped to define the content of economic, social, and cultural rights in view of their justiciability.[25] The Optional Protocol to the ICESCR will most likely contribute to a broader acceptance of the notion of justiciability of economic, social, and cultural rights.

4 CORE RIGHTS

While the principle of interdependence and indivisibility of all human rights has become axiomatic and largely uncontested, the issue remains whether certain human rights rank higher than other rights because they are more essential for the preser-vation of human life and the upholding of human dignity and human welfare. For instance, there is little doubt that the right to life and the prohibition of torture, enshrined in Articles 2 and 5 of the UDHR, are more fundamental or basic than the right to rest and leisure, set out in Article 24 of the same document. Widely ratified human rights instruments and their interpretation by judicial and quasi-judicial human rights bodies clearly indicate that certain human rights represent or embody core attributes of human life and human dignity, so that violations of these rights entail a special and imperative responsibility to prevent, to protect, and to remedy. The following examples illustrate that in international human rights law certain rights and

[22] (1987) 9 *HRQ* 121.   [23] (1998) 20 *HRQ* 691.
[24] See Coomans (ed), *Justiciability of Economic and Social Rights; Experiences from Domestic Systems* (Intersentia, 2006).
[25] n 5. See further Committee on the Rights of the Child, General Comment 5, HRI/GEN/1/ (Vol II) 421.

their protection rank particularly high on the scale of basic values of human life and existence and can thus be classified as core rights.[26]

Major human rights treaties, notably the ICCPR, the European Convention on Human Rights, and the American Convention on Human Rights, recognize a set of core rights from which no derogation is permitted, not even during times of public emergency. Thus, Article 4(2) ICCPR lists as non-derogable the right to life, the prohibition of torture or cruel, inhuman, or degrading treatment or punishment, the prohibition of slavery, the prohibition of imprisonment because of inability to fulfil a contractual obligation, the principle of legality in criminal law, the recognition of everyone as a person before the law, and the freedom of thought, conscience, and religion. In its General Comment 29, the Human Rights Committee has analysed the implications of Article 4 in detail.[27] It notes that the enumeration of non-derogable provisions is related to, but not identical with, the question whether certain human rights obligations have the nature of peremptory norms of international law (*jus cogens*) and recognizes that some of the non-derogable ICCPR rights also fall into that category, notably the right to life and the prohibition of torture or cruel, inhuman, or degrading treatment or punishment.

Core rights entail essential obligations on the part of states that have undertaken to respect, protect, and fulfil them. Such obligations are not limited to the field of civil and political rights but extend to economic, social, and cultural rights. Thus, the Committee on Economic, Social and Cultural Rights has stated in its General Comment 3 that 'a minimum core obligation to ensure the satisfaction of, at the very least, minimum essential levels of each of the [ICESCR] rights is incumbent upon every State party'.[28] For example, a state party in which a significant number of individuals are deprived of essential foodstuffs, essential primary healthcare, basic shelter and housing, or the most basic forms of education would, according to the Committee, prima facie be failing to discharge its obligations under the Covenant. The formulation of these core obligations relating to basic conditions of human life corresponds to the phrase in common Article 1(2) of both international covenants concerning the right of all peoples to self-determination that 'in no case may a people be deprived of its own means of subsistence'. Consequently, basic subsistence rights which determine the life, the dignity, and the well-being of individuals and peoples should be considered as core rights.

Furthermore, with the development of international criminal law through standard-setting and national and international adjudication, violations of internationally protected basic human rights may amount to crimes under international law, with the corresponding duty of states to carry out an effective and prompt investigation and to prosecute and punish the perpetrators.[29] Another corresponding duty involves the provision of effective remedies to victims, including reparation for harm suffered. As

---

[26] See also Seiderman, *Hierarchy in International Law: The Human Rights Dimension* (Intersentia, 2001).   [27] HRC, General Comment 29, HRI/GEN/1/ (Vol I) 234.
[28] n 6, para 10.   [29] See Chapter 24, below.

the Human Rights Committee has stated in its General Comment 31, these obligations arise notably in relation to those violations of ICCPR provisions that are recognized as criminal under domestic or international law, such as torture, summary and arbitrary killing, and enforced disappearance.[30] When such violations of the Covenant are committed as part of a widespread or systematic attack on a civilian population, they are crimes against humanity under Article 7 Statute of the International Criminal Court.[31] While the violation of all human rights entails legal consequences in terms of effective remedies, the violation of core rights requires legal action so as to combat impunity and to make reparations. Moreover, the evolving practice of international human rights bodies, notably the European Court of Human Rights, the Inter-American Court of Human Rights, and the Human Rights Committee, makes it abundantly clear that in cases where core rights such as the right to life and the right to be free from torture or ill-treatment are at stake, urgent preventive action by way of provisional or interim measures are called for in order to avoid irreparable harm to persons.[32]

Finally, the newly evolving doctrine of the Responsibility to Protect, set out in the outcome document of the 2005 UN World Summit, attributes special responsibility to protect populations from genocide, war crimes, ethnic cleansing, and crimes against humanity. This responsibility rests primarily with individual states but may also require collective action, through the UN, should national authorities manifestly fail to protect their populations from such crimes.[33] The doctrine of the Responsibility to Protect represents a common *opinio juris* in theory but still needs affirmation and implementation in practice. However, what is important for present purposes is that it implies that core rights and core values pertaining to the very existence and survival of populations may, in situations where national authorities are failing to respect these rights and values, prevail over invocations of national sovereignty.

5 NEW HUMAN RIGHTS?

It may be argued that the standard-setting or codification process of human rights was completed with the adoption and entry into force of the general and comprehensive human rights instruments, notably the international covenants and regional instruments such as the European Convention on Human Rights, the European Social Charter, the American Convention on Human Rights, and the African Charter of Human and Peoples' Rights. However, while a broad corpus of internationally recognized standards has taken shape in these instruments, the standard-setting process

---

[30] HRC, General Comment 31, HRI/GEN/1/ (Vol I) 243.   [31] Ibid.

[32] Rieter, *Preventing Irreparable Harm: Provisional Measures in International Human Rights Adjudication* (Intersentia, 2010).

[33] n 3, paras 138–40. See further Evans, *The Responsibility to Protect: Ending Mass Atrocity Crimes Once and For All* (Brookings Institution Press, 2008).

did not stop but continued progressively in order to respond to widely felt needs to further define the normative scope of basic rights and principles and to provide more explicit protection for vulnerable and marginalized people.

Examples of the further elaboration of the normative scope of human rights include instruments relating to the abolition of the death penalty, the prohibition of torture or cruel, inhuman, or degrading treatment or punishment, and the elimination of discrimination on the grounds of race, religion, and gender. More explicit protection of specific groups of people is envisaged in instruments relating to the rights of women, children, migrant workers, persons with disabilities, persons subjected to enforced disappearance, and indigenous peoples. These instruments do not define new rights but re-define and re-conceptualize existing human rights in order to make them more explicit and more inclusive and to extend their reach to persons in need of special care, attention, and protection. This is a dynamic process that involves the shaping of the normative content of rights and basic principles such as the best interests of the child, the absolute prohibition of gender-based violence, and the relevance of the right to self-determination.

Human rights treaty bodies, as authoritative interpreters and custodians of treaty norms, have drawn up general comments and recommendations so as to further define or refine the scope and reach of the human rights norms already embodied in legal instruments. Do treaty bodies thereby create new human rights norms? This would not seem to be the purpose and task of treaty bodies. Rather, the purpose of general comments and recommendations is to clarify the normative scope of human rights. For instance, in its General Comment 15, the Committee on Economic, Social and Cultural Rights made it clear that there is a right to water, although such a right is not explicitly referred to in the ICESCR.[34] The Committee did not proclaim this right as a new human right, but defined it as emanating from, and indispensable for, the realization of the right to an adequate standard of living and as inextricably related to the rights to the highest attainable standard of health, adequate housing, and adequate food.[35] Similarly, the Committee on the Elimination of Racial Discrimination, in its General Recommendations on the rights of indigenous peoples, on discrimination against Roma, on descent-based discrimination, and on discrimination against non-citizens,[36] clearly set out the relevance and the applicability of the International Convention on the Elimination of All Forms of Racial Discrimination with respect to groups of marginalized and vulnerable people. It did this, not by the creation of new rights, but by explaining the normative content and the implications of the Convention in support of these groups.

In the human rights discourse and campaigns entertained by proponents of a rights-based strategy on behalf of marginalized and excluded groups, claims are

---

[34] See Chapter 11, below.   [35] CESCR, General Comment 15, HRI/GEN/1/ (Vol I) 97, para 3.
[36] Committee on the Elimination of Racial Discrimination, General Recommendation XXIII, HRI/GEN/1/ (Vol II) 285, General Recommendation XXVII, HRI/GEN/1/ (Vol II) 289, General Recommendation XXIX, HRI/GEN/1/ (Vol II) 296, General Recommendation XXX, HRI/GEN/1/ (Vol II) 301.

often framed as being part of a 'struggle for new rights'.[37] The rights of children born of wartime rape, Dalits, lesbian, gay, bisexual, and transgender (LGBT) people, mentally and physically disabled people, people living with HIV/AIDS, and other stigmatized minorities are advocated under this label.[38] These campaigns have greatly contributed to awareness-building and the broadening and deepening of a rights-based approach in support of people who for long had been neglected and treated as outsiders or even outcasts. They constitute another step in the long process from exclusion and to inclusion, with due regard for the specific situation and the specific interests of the people concerned.

This newly developed reach of human rights has found expression in a series of new instruments and documents such as the Convention on the Rights of Persons with Disabilities, the General Recommendations of the Committee on the Elimination of Racial Discrimination on discrimination against Roma and descent-based discrimination, the General Recommendation of the Committee on the Elimination of Discrimination against Women on the avoidance of discrimination against women in national strategies for the prevention and control of AIDS, as well as the General Comment of the Committee on the Rights of the Child on HIV/AIDS and the rights of the child.[39] The statement on LGBT rights supported by 66 states and presented to the UN General Assembly in December 2008 is a further example illustrating this new human rights focus.[40] While in all these instances the focus and scope of human rights is newly defined and developed to underline their relevance and applicability to people hitherto neglected, ignored, or degraded, their basic thrust lies in the recognition that all people, without discrimination or exclusion, are entitled to the full benefit of all human rights, notably the right to be equal before the law and non-discrimination. It appears, therefore, that in these instances the term 'new human rights' is conceptually not called for. Instead, the better term might be 'newly focused human rights'. The concept of 'new human rights' should be approached with caution.

Attention may also be drawn to victims' rights in this context. Victims of gross human rights violations have been largely overlooked, both at the national and the international level. Only in recent decades, in particular in the context of transitional justice processes in societies scarred by serious crimes under international law, has there been some tentative movement towards the express recognition of victims' rights as a main condition for the attainment of reconciliation and justice.[41] This new emphasis on victims' rights is duly reflected in the UN Basic Principles and Guidelines on the Right to a Remedy and Reparation to Victims of Gross Violations of International Human Rights Law and Serious Violations of International

---

[37] See in particular Bob (ed), *The International Struggle for New Human Rights* (University of Pennsylvania Press, 2009).   [38] Ibid.

[39] Committee on the Elimination of Racial Discrimination, General Recommendation XXVII, n 36; Committee on the Elimination of Discrimination against Women, General Recommendation 15, HRI/GEN/1/ (Vol II) 327; Committee on the Rights of the Child, General Comment 3, HRI/GEN/1/ (Vol II) 398.

[40] See Chapter 15, below.   [41] van Boven, 'Reparative Justice: Focus on Victims' (2007) 25 *NQHR* 723.

Humanitarian Law (2005) (Reparation Principles).[42] This instrument is not intended to define new victims' rights but to identify mechanisms, modalities, procedures, and methods for the implementation of victims' rights.[43] Another normative document of particular relevance to transitional justice situations is the Updated Set of Principles for the Protection and Promotion of Human Rights Through Actions to Combat Impunity (2005) (Impunity Principles).[44] This document provides for the right to know, the right to justice, and the right to reparation, and guarantees of non-recurrence. Under the right to know, the inalienable right to know the truth figures prominently. This right has a collective dimension. Every people has the right 'to know the truth about past events concerning the perpetration of heinous crimes and about the circumstances and reasons that led ... to the perpetration of those crimes'.[45] But the right to truth also includes the right of victims and their families 'to know the truth about the circumstances in which violations took place and, in the event of death or disappearance, about the victims' fate'.[46] In line with the Reparation Principles and Impunity Principles, the new International Convention for the Protection of All Persons from Enforced Disappearance affirms the right of each victim to know the truth regarding the circumstances of the enforced disappearance, the progress and results of the investigation, and the fate of the disappeared person. Finally, it also spells out the right of victims to obtain reparation and prompt, fair, and adequate compensation.[47]

These normative developments raise the question of whether the right to know the truth, as a collective and individual right, qualifies as a 'new human right'. It may be argued in this connection that this right is a corollary of the freedom to seek, receive, and impart information and ideas of all kinds set out in Article 19(2) ICCPR. Technically speaking, this argument is correct, although it insufficiently appreciates the existential life and death dimensions that lie at the basis of the right to know the truth. Nevertheless, it can be argued that the right to know the truth is a basic principle that already forms part of existing human rights law. In fact, the International Convention for the Protection of All Persons from Enforced Disappearance gives support to this reasoning insofar as its preamble 'affirms' the right of any victim to know the truth.[48] Therefore, the right to know the truth should not be qualified as a 'new human right' as if it had only emerged recently. Such a classification would fail to do justice to efforts to seek and uncover the truth about many historical wrongs that still beleaguer past and present generations. Rather, there are good reasons to state, in consonance with the Impunity Principles, that there is an inalienable right to know the truth. This right is in need of recognition and renewed emphasis and is thus correctly affirmed in a legal document such as the International Convention for the Protection of All Persons from Enforced Disappearance.

---

[42] GA Res 60/147 (16 December 2005).   [43] Ibid, preambular para 7.
[44] E/CN.4/2005/102/Add.1, endorsed by UN Commission on Human Rights Res 2005/81 (21 April 2005).   [45] Ibid, Principle 2.
[46] Ibid, Principle 4.   [47] Art 24.   [48] Ibid, preambular para 8.

6 CONCLUSION

All human rights are indivisible, interdependent, and interrelated. This chapter fully subscribes to this postulate, not as a method to put all rights in a melting-pot where they lose their own distinct character, but as a means to reinforce the validity and impact of all rights. Classifying human rights in various categories—civil, political, economic, social, and cultural; individual and collective; one-dimensional and composite—is not as such a reduction of the indivisibility, interdependence, and interrelatedness of human rights. Such classifications or categorizations are not meant to store human rights in watertight compartments. Their merit lies in their capacity to operationalize human rights, to make rights and responsibilities more specific and transparent, with corresponding claims and obligations.

Neither does the maxim of indivisibility, interdependence, and interrelatedness of all human rights stand in the way of the notion of core rights as distinct from other human rights. It is true that the notion of core rights presumes a ranking or hierarchy of human rights. Such ranking is inherent in essential rights and entails corresponding core obligations on the part of states and non-state actors. It runs across all human rights categories and classifications, with the right to life, the inviolability of the human person, and the very existence of people as cornerstones.

It is self-evident that human rights, in whatever manner they are classified or subdivided, are the rights of individuals and collectivities. But it has been less obvious, under past and present policies and practices of exclusion and discrimination, that human rights are the inalienable rights of all members of the human family. The UDHR proclaimed human rights as the rights of all human beings and set into motion a major trend towards the inclusion of all people in human rights documents. It is in keeping with this trend to grant explicit recognition to people who had been, over the years and in many places if not everywhere, the subject of exclusion, discrimination, neglect, or treatment as inferiors. It was also in line with the same trend that the call was widely heard: women's rights are human rights, children's rights are human rights, indigenous rights are human rights, Roma rights are human rights, Dalits rights are human rights, and so on. International instruments with a specific focus on the human rights of particular categories of people were drawn up, most recently of persons with disabilities. Rather than labelling the rights of these persons as 'new human rights', they should be denominated as the rights of newly identified categories of people, as inclusive rights. In sum, categories of human rights are not abstract concepts. Human rights relate to all people, including categories of people who belong to the downtrodden, the disadvantaged, and the discarded in national and international society.

FURTHER READING

Bob (ed), *The International Struggle for New Human Rights* (University of Pennsylvania Press, 2009).

Coomans (ed), *Justiciability of Economic and Social Rights: Experiences from Domestic Systems* (Intersentia, 2006).

International Commmission of Jurists, *Courts and the Legal Enforcement of Economic, Social and Cultural Rights* (Geneva, 2008).

Nowak, *Introduction to the International Human Rights Regime* (Martinus Nijhoff, 2003).

OHCHR, *Report on the Right to the Truth*, A/HRC/12/19 (21 August 2009).

Seiderman, *Hierarchy in International Law: The Human Rights Dimension* (Intersentia, 2001).

Tomuschat, *Human Rights: Between Idealism and Realism* (Oxford University Press, 2008).

9

EQUALITY AND NON-DISCRIMINATION

Daniel Moeckli

SUMMARY

The international human rights system is founded on the idea that all human beings have the same set of fundamental rights. Accordingly, almost all general human rights instruments guarantee the right to equality and non-discrimination, and several specialized treaties provide protection against particular forms of discrimination. International human rights law prohibits discrimination in treatment (direct discrimination) as well as in outcome (indirect discrimination), regardless of whether it is intended or unintended. Yet it also acknowledges that it may sometimes be justified to classify people: differences in treatment or outcome are permissible as long as they pursue a legitimate aim in a proportionate manner. Indeed, the right to equality may *require* states to treat people differently in order to overcome historical patterns of disadvantage and achieve real equality.

1 INTRODUCTION

The notion that all human beings are equal and therefore deserve to be treated equally has a powerful intuitive appeal. It is one of the central ideals of the Enlightenment and at the heart of liberal theories of the state.[1] The US Declaration of Independence of 1776 famously proclaimed that 'all men are created equal', and today virtually every liberal democratic state guarantees equality in its constitution. The principle of equality and non-discrimination has gained a similarly important status in international law. It is included in the key human rights instruments and the Vienna Declaration and Programme of Action, adopted by the World Conference on Human Rights in 1993, describes it as 'a fundamental rule of international human rights law'.[2]

---

[1] See Chapter 1, above.   [2] A/CONF.157/23 (25 June 1993) para 15.

What this fundamental rule entails in practice, however, is difficult to establish. For, of course, no two human beings are equal in the sense that they are identical. We might be able to say that two people are equal in respect of some measurable characteristic ('they both weigh 82 kilograms'), but they will always be different in some other respects (income, political opinion, and so on). In order to apply the principle of equality we first need to define the relevant criterion in respect of which people should be judged to be alike or different. And even when two persons can be said to be alike, it might still be questionable whether they should always be treated equally. Furthermore, we need to decide what kind of equality we seek to achieve. Do we mean by equality that people should be treated identically? Or that they should be given the same opportunities? Or that they should be placed in the same position? Equality can be formulated in different ways, and deciding which concept of equality to use is not a question of logic but a political choice. In this sense, equality is an 'empty idea'[3]—it does not answer the questions of who are equals and what constitutes equal treatment. External values, not derivable from the concept of equality, are necessary to answer these questions.

The challenge, therefore, is to give substance to the abstract notion of equality by translating it into concrete legal formulations that make clear which forms of unequal treatment are legitimate because they are based on morally acceptable criteria and which ones are wrongful. This chapter explains how this challenge has been addressed in international human rights law.

Section 2 discusses what, in general terms, equality and non-discrimination can be interpreted to mean. Section 3 gives an overview of the different norms guaranteeing equality and non-discrimination in international human rights law. Section 4 explains the concepts of direct and indirect discrimination. Section 5 considers the requirements for a difference in treatment to be justified under international human rights law. Section 6 sets out the different sorts of obligations that the right to equality imposes on states, in particular their duty to take positive action to ensure everyone can enjoy this right.

2 THE MEANING OF EQUALITY AND NON-DISCRIMINATION

The terms 'equality' and 'non-discrimination' have often been used interchangeably and described as the positive and negative statement of the same principle: whereas the maxim of equality requires that equals be treated equally, the prohibition of discrimination precludes differential treatment on unreasonable grounds.[4] In recent years, however, there has been an increased emphasis on the positive

---

[3] Westen, 'The Empty Idea of Equality' (1982) 95 *Harvard LR* 537.

[4] eg OC-4/84, *Proposed Amendments to the Naturalization Provisions of the Constitution of Costa Rica*, IACtHR Series A No 4 (1984), Separate Opinion of Rodolfo E Piza, J, para 10 ('... it appears clear that the

formulation. This shift in terminology highlights that equality implies not only a negative obligation not to discriminate, but also a duty to recognize differences between people and to take positive action to achieve real equality. Thus, whereas 'non-discrimination' corresponds to the more limited concept of *formal equality*, usage of the term 'equality' stresses the need for a more positive approach aimed at *substantive equality*.

2.1 FORMAL EQUALITY

Formal equality refers to Aristotle's classical maxim according to which equals must be treated equally or, more precisely, likes must be treated alike.[5] This notion of equality as consistency focuses on the process rather than the outcome: equality is achieved if individuals in a comparable situation are treated equally, regardless of the result. The values underpinning formal equality are the liberal ideals of state neutrality and individualism, that is, the notion that the state should not give preference to any one group and that people should be treated exclusively on their individual merits and regardless of group membership.

However, as noted above, this idea of equality raises the question of when two cases can be said to be alike. It is inevitable that laws and government action classify persons into groups that are treated differently. Under a progressive taxation system, for example, people are treated differently according to their income. In states with a juvenile justice system, people are treated differently according to their age. These distinctions are generally seen as perfectly legitimate because they are based on morally acceptable grounds. Accordingly, at least in common language, the word 'discrimination' also has a positive connotation ('to discriminate between right and wrong'). But which differences in treatment are legitimate and which ones are not? The principle that likes should be treated alike does not, by itself, answer this question.

There are a number of other problems with the concept of equality as consistency.[6] First, since it is not concerned with the outcome, it does not matter whether two parties are treated equally well or equally badly. Thus, it is compatible with this understanding of equality that a city closes all its swimming pools rather than open its 'whites only' pools to black people ('levelling down').[7] Second, inconsistent treatment can only be demonstrated if the complainant can find a comparably situated person who has been treated more favourably. Yet for a woman in a low-paid position, for instance, it may be difficult to find a man doing the same job. Third, treating people apparently consistently regardless of their differing backgrounds may have a disparate impact on particular groups. A law which, in the famous words of Anatole France,

---

concepts of equality and non-discrimination are reciprocal, like the two faces of one same institution. Equality is the positive face of non-discrimination. Discrimination is the negative face of equality').

[5] Aristotle, *The Nicomachean Ethics of Aristotle* (1911) Book V3, paras 1131a–1131b.

[6] See Fredman, *Discrimination Law* (OUP, 2002) 7–11.   [7] See *Palmer v Thompson* 403 US 217 (1971).

'forbids the rich as well as the poor to sleep under bridges, to beg in the streets, and to steal bread' will in fact entrench inequality.[8]

2.2 SUBSTANTIVE EQUALITY

Proponents of a substantive conception of equality recognize that a merely formal notion of equality as procedural fairness can in fact perpetuate existing patterns of disadvantage. Drawing on values such as human dignity, distributive justice, and equal participation, they argue that equality must go beyond consistent treatment of likes. There are two main variants of substantive equality: equality of opportunity and equality of results.

According to the notion of equality of opportunity, true equality can only be achieved if people are not only treated equally but are also given the same opportunities. Like competitors in a race, everyone should be able to begin from the same starting point. Equality of opportunity requires the removal of barriers to the advancement of disadvantaged groups, such as upper age limits for employment that may disadvantage women with childcare responsibilities. According to a broader, substantive understanding of the concept, it may also require positive measures such as training. But equality of opportunity does not aim to achieve equality of outcome. Once the race has started, everyone is treated the same. Thus, while equality of opportunity is to some extent about redressing past discrimination, it also stresses individual merit.

Equality of results goes further than this and aims to achieve an equal distribution of social goods such as education, employment, healthcare, and political representation. It recognizes that removing barriers does not guarantee that disadvantaged groups will in fact be able to take advantage of available opportunities. Abolishing upper age limits, for example, does not, by itself, ensure that more women with childcare responsibilities will be able to apply for the respective jobs. Equality of results can be understood and achieved in different ways. In its strongest form, it explicitly aims to increase the representation of disadvantaged groups in educational institutions, employment, or public office through preferential treatment and quota systems.

These differing conceptions of equality find their reflection in different forms of legal regulation. Formal equality forms the conceptual basis of the requirement of equality before the law and prohibitions of direct discrimination, whereas prohibitions of indirect discrimination are supported by a substantive notion of equality (see Section 4, below for the distinction between direct and indirect discrimination). 'Affirmative action' programmes (see Section 6, below) can be justified on the basis of a substantive notion of equality, but they are incompatible with a formal conception of equality as consistency. In any jurisdiction, a range of regulations that reflect different conceptions of equality will be found; no legal system relies exclusively on simply one approach to equality.

---

[8] France, *Le Lys Rouge* (Calmann-Lévy, 1894) ch 7.

3 EQUALITY AND NON-DISCRIMINATION IN INTERNATIONAL LAW

The right to equality and non-discrimination gives concrete expression to the basic idea on which the whole international human rights system is founded: that all human beings, regardless of their status or membership of a particular group, are entitled to a set of rights. Since it underlies all other human rights, equality is often described not only as a 'right' but also as a 'principle'. The foundational significance of equality is reflected in the fact that it is proclaimed in the very first article of the Universal Declaration of Human Rights (UDHR): 'All human beings are born free and equal in dignity and rights'.

This section first gives an overview of the different sources of the right to equality and non-discrimination in international law. Next, it considers the scope of these norms: do they guarantee equality and non-discrimination only in the context of other human rights or across the board? Finally, the prohibited grounds of distinction are explored: which groups are protected against discrimination?

3.1 SOURCES

Article 1(3) of the UN Charter makes it clear that one of the basic purposes of the UN is the promotion of the equal guarantee of human rights for all without any distinction. Numerous instruments aimed at the realization of this notion have been adopted under the auspices of the UN. The general human rights instruments guarantee the right to equality and non-discrimination in several of their provisions: the UDHR in Articles 1, 2(1), and 7; the International Covenant on Civil and Political Rights (ICCPR) in Articles 2, 3, and 26; and the International Covenant on Economic, Social and Cultural Rights (ICESCR) in Articles 2(2) and 3. As far as the specialized human rights treaties are concerned, at least three of them are specifically devoted to addressing certain forms of discrimination: the International Convention on the Elimination of All Forms of Racial Discrimination (ICERD), the Convention on the Elimination of All Forms of Discrimination against Women (CEDAW), and the Convention on the Rights of Persons with Disabilities (CRPD). The Convention on the Rights of the Child (CRC) and the International Convention on the Protection of the Rights of All Migrant Workers and Members of Their Families (ICRMW) at least partly pursue the same objective and contain explicit provisions on equality and non-discrimination.[9] The only international human rights treaties without explicit non-discrimination clauses are the Convention against Torture and Other Cruel, Inhuman or Degrading Treatment or Punishment (UNCAT) and the International Convention for the Protection of All Persons from Enforced Disappearance.

---

[9] CRC, Arts 2 and 28; ICRMW, Arts 1(1), 7, 18, 25, 27, 28, 30, 43, 45, 54, 55, and 70.

The right to equality and non-discrimination is also guaranteed by all major regional human rights instruments: the African Charter on Human and Peoples' Rights (ACHPR) (Articles 2, 3, 18(3)–(4), and 28), the American Convention on Human Rights (ACHR) (Articles 1 and 24), the American Declaration of the Rights and Duties of Man (Article II), the Arab Charter on Human Rights (Articles 2, 9, and 35), the European Convention for the Protection of Human Rights and Fundamental Freedoms (ECHR) (Article 14 and Protocol No 12), and the Charter of Fundamental Rights of the European Union (Articles 20, 21(1), and 23). In addition, a range of specialized regional treaties, such as the Protocol to the African Charter on Human and Peoples' Rights on the Rights of Women in Africa and the Inter-American Convention on the Elimination of All Forms of Discrimination Against Persons with Disabilities, provide protection against particular forms of discrimination.

Finally, it is now widely acknowledged that, at the very least, the right to non-discrimination on the grounds of race, sex, and religion binds all states, irrespective of their ratification of human rights treaties, because it has become part of customary international law.[10] The Inter-American Court of Human Rights has gone further than this and held that also the guarantee against discrimination on other grounds, including language, political or other opinion, national, ethnic or social origin, nationality, age, economic situation, property, civil status, birth, or any other status, forms part of general international law and, indeed, is a norm of *jus cogens* that cannot be set aside by treaty or acquiescence.[11]

3.2 SCOPE: SUBORDINATE AND AUTONOMOUS NORMS

Non-discrimination provisions can be subdivided into subordinate and autonomous (or free-standing) norms. *Subordinate norms* prohibit discrimination only in the enjoyment of the rights and freedoms otherwise set forth in the respective instrument. An example of a subordinate norm is Article 2(1) ICCPR, which states:

Each State Party to the present Covenant undertakes to respect and to ensure to all individuals within its territory and subject to its jurisdiction the rights recognized in the present Covenant, without distinction of any kind, such as race, colour, sex, language, religion, political or other opinion, national or social origin, property, birth or other status.

Other subordinate norms include Article 2(1) UDHR, Article 2(2) ICESCR, Article 2(1) CRC, Article 7 ICRMW, Article 1 ACHR, Article 2 ACHPR, and Article 14 ECHR.[12] As the ECHR does not contain an autonomous norm in addition to its subordinate

---

[10] For race, see eg *South-West Africa Cases (Second Phase)* [1966] ICJ Rep 6, 293 and 299–300 (Tanaka, J dissenting); *Barcelona Traction (Second Phase)* [1970] ICJ Rep 3, 32. For the other grounds, see Shaw, *International Law* (CUP, 2008) 287 and references cited there.

[11] OC/18, *Juridical Condition and Rights of the Undocumented Migrants,* IACtHR Series A No 18 (2003) paras 100–1 and 173.4.

[12] ECHR, Art 14 reads: 'The enjoyment of the rights and freedoms set forth in this Convention shall be secured without discrimination on any ground such as sex, race, colour, language, religion, political or other opinion, national or social origin, association with a national minority, property, birth or other status.'

provision in Article 14, the jurisprudence of the European Court of Human Rights interpreting it is of particular importance. According to the European Court, in order to invoke Article 14, an applicant must show that the facts of the case fall 'within the ambit' of another substantive Convention right.[13] However, there is no need to show that there has been *a violation* of that Convention right. A measure that in itself is in conformity with the requirements of a given ECHR right, but is of a discriminatory nature, will violate that right *when read in conjunction with Article 14*. For example, it does not as such amount to a violation of Article 6 ECHR (the right to a fair trial) if a state fails to establish a system of appeals. However, when a state does establish such a system, then this is a matter falling within the ambit of Article 6, and there is a violation of that article read in conjunction with Article 14 if, without a legitimate reason, certain persons are given the right to appeal while others are denied it.

Article 7 UDHR, Article 26 ICCPR, Articles 2 and 5 ICERD, Article 24 ACHR, and Article 3 ACHPR, on the other hand, are *autonomous norms*: they guarantee non-discrimination not only in the context of other rights but in general. For example, Article 26 ICCPR provides:

All persons are equal before the law and are entitled without any discrimination to the equal protection of the law. In this respect, the law shall prohibit any discrimination and guarantee to all persons equal and effective protection against discrimination on any ground such as race, colour, sex, language, religion, political or other opinion, national or social origin, property, birth or other status.

The UN Human Rights Committee elaborated on the scope of this provision in *Broeks v The Netherlands*.[14] Mrs Broeks had been denied unemployment benefits on the basis of legislation that provided that married women could only claim benefits if they could prove that they were 'breadwinners'—a requirement that did not apply to married men. The Netherlands argued that Mrs Broeks could not rely on Article 26 ICCPR as it could only be invoked in the sphere of civil and political rights; Mrs Broeks' complaint, however, related to the right to social security, which was specifically provided for under the ICESCR. The Human Rights Committee rejected the government's argument, holding that it did not matter whether a particular subject matter is covered by the ICCPR or some other international instrument. It stressed that 'Article 26 does not merely duplicate the guarantees already provided for in Article 2' but instead 'prohibits discrimination in law or in practice in any field regulated and protected by public authorities'.[15] The Committee confirmed this finding in its General Comment 18.[16] Thus, states parties to the ICCPR have a general obligation neither to enact legislation with a discriminatory content nor to apply laws in a discriminatory way.

As noted above, the ECHR only contains a subordinate non-discrimination guarantee. This gap is partially addressed by Protocol No 12 to the ECHR. The Protocol,

---

[13] *Rasmussen v Denmark* (1984) 7 EHRR 371, para 29.   [14] CCPR/C/29/D/172/1984 (9 April 1987).

[15] Ibid, para 12.3.   [16] HRC, General Comment 18, HRI/GEN/1/Rev. 9 (Vol I) 195, para 12.

which entered into force in 2005 but has not been widely ratified so far, contains a non-discrimination guarantee that is not limited to the enjoyment of Convention rights.[17] However, this guarantee is still narrower than the general right to equality before the law and equal protection of the law under Article 26 ICCPR in that it only applies to the enjoyment of rights set forth by (national) law.

3.3 PROHIBITED GROUNDS OF DISTINCTION

Which grounds of distinction are unacceptable and should therefore be prohibited? There is no straightforward answer to this question as, depending on one's moral and political views, any criterion may be regarded as either relevant or irrelevant. There is certainly broad consensus today that normally a person's inherent characteristics such as race, colour, or sex are not acceptable criteria for differential treatment. In addition, grounds such as membership of a particular group, holding certain beliefs, and national or social origin are outlawed by most human rights treaties. But as is evident from a comparison between the ICCPR, adopted in 1966, and the ICRMW, adopted in 1990, what is seen as unacceptable can change over time: the ICRMW has considerably expanded the list of prohibited grounds by adding the criteria of conviction, ethnic origin, nationality, age, economic position, and marital status. Today, further criteria, including disability[18] and sexual orientation and gender identity,[19] would have to be added.

Equality and non-discrimination norms vary widely in their approaches to defining the prohibited grounds of distinction. A first type of norm provides for a *general guarantee of equality*, without specifying any particular prohibited grounds. Article 24 ACHR, for instance, simply states: 'All persons are equal before the law. Consequently, they are entitled, without discrimination, to equal protection of the law.' Such norms leave it to the relevant body to decide which distinctions are acceptable and which ones are not.

A second category of norms uses a diametrically opposed approach: these norms contain an *exhaustive list* of prohibited grounds. The CEDAW, for instance, prohibits only distinctions based on 'sex' (Article 1), the ICERD those based on 'race, colour, descent, or national or ethnic origin' (Article 1(1)), and the CRPD those based on 'disability' (Articles 1 and 5). Article 2(2) ICESCR, Article 2(1) CRC, and Article 1 ACHR contain lists that are much longer but still fixed (in the case of the ICESCR, 'race, colour, sex, language, religion, political or other opinion, national or social origin, property, birth or other status').

---

[17] Protocol No 12 to the Convention for the Protection of Human Rights and Fundamental Freedoms, Art 1 ('(1) The enjoyment of any right set forth by law shall be secured without discrimination on any ground such as sex, race, colour, language, religion, political or other opinion, national or social origin, association with a national minority, property, birth or other status. (2) No one shall be discriminated against by any public authority on any ground such as those mentioned in paragraph 1').   [18] See ICPRD.
[19] See Chapter 15, below.

Steering a middle course between these two extremes, there is a third category of norms which contain a list of prohibited grounds but one that is *open-ended*. For instance, Article 14 ECHR (as well as its Protocol No 12) prohibit 'discrimination on *any* ground *such as* sex, race, colour, language, religion, political or other opinion, national or social origin, association with a national minority, property, birth or other status'. Similarly, Article 2(1) UDHR, Articles 1(1) and 7 ICRMW, and Article 2 ACHPR provide for non-discrimination 'without distinction of *any* kind, *such as* ...' As a consequence, even distinctions made on grounds that are not explicitly listed may engage these provisions. The European Court of Human Rights sometimes does not even find it necessary to state the particular ground of distinction involved when considering a case under Article 14 ECHR.[20]

The text of Article 26 ICCPR ('discrimination on *any* ground *such as* race, colour, sex, language, religion, political or other opinion, national or social origin, property, birth or other status') suggests that this provision is also open-ended. Nevertheless, the Human Rights Committee has often been at pains to fit a particular distinction within one of the listed grounds, be it the specific ones or the broad rubric of 'other status'. Thus, it has found that the reference to 'sex' also includes 'sexual orientation'[21] and that 'other status' covers grounds such as nationality,[22] age,[23] and marital status.[24] But it has never clarified how it decides whether a difference in treatment comes within the reference to 'other status'. Its efforts to apply one of the listed grounds suggest that the Committee regards the list of Article 26 as exhaustive and it has accordingly stated that an applicant is required to show that the difference in treatment was based on one of the enumerated grounds.[25]

4 DIRECT AND INDIRECT DISCRIMINATION

At the heart of all non-discrimination norms is the formal equality requirement that likes should be treated alike. It is therefore clear that international human rights law prohibits direct discrimination (Section 4.1). But human right bodies and courts have acknowledged that the requirement of consistent treatment is not sufficient to achieve true equality: not only discriminatory treatment but also a discriminatory outcome (indirect discrimination) is prohibited (Section 4.2). Finally, it is important to note that international human rights law prohibits both intended and unintended discrimination (Section 4.3).

Whether there has been a difference in treatment or result is the first question that a court needs to assess when considering a discrimination claim under international

---

[20] See eg *Rasmussen v Denmark*, n 13, para 34.

[21] *Toonen v Australia*, CCPR/C/50/D/488/1992 (31 March 1994) para 8.7.

[22] *Gueye v France*, CCPR/C/35/D/196/1985 (3 April 1989) para 9.4.

[23] *Schmitz-de-Jong v The Netherlands*, CCPR/C/72/D/855/1999 (16 July 2001).

[24] *Danning v The Netherlands*, CCPR/C/OP/2 (9 April 1987).

[25] *BdB v The Netherlands*, CCPR/C/35/D/273/1988 (2 May 1989) para 6.7.

human rights law. Once a prima facie case of direct or indirect discrimination has been made out, the court must decide whether there is a justification for the difference in treatment or outcome. This second element of the test is discussed in Section 5 below.

4.1 DIRECT DISCRIMINATION

Direct discrimination occurs when a person, *on account of one or more of the prohibited grounds*, is treated less favourably than someone else in comparable circumstances. Thus, the complainant must show, first, that others have been treated better because they do not share the relevant characteristic or status and, second, that these others are in a comparable, or, in the terminology of the European Court of Human Rights, 'analogous'[26] or 'relevantly similar',[27] situation. In practice, international human rights bodies often tend to merge the comparability test with the test as to whether there is an objective justification for the difference in treatment, explained in Section 5 below.

A classic example of direct discrimination is when members of a certain ethnic group are denied access to a public facility, such as a swimming pool, which is open to everyone else. But most cases of direct discrimination are not as straightforward as this. More often, direct discrimination occurs covertly: the 'discriminator' will not admit that the difference in treatment was based on a prohibited ground, making it difficult for the complainant to provide sufficient evidence. Furthermore, as explained above, it may not always be easy to identify a person who is in a comparable situation. How can a woman establish pay discrimination when there are no men doing the same job?

4.2 INDIRECT DISCRIMINATION

Indirect discrimination occurs when a practice, rule, or requirement that is outwardly '*neutral*', that is, not based on one of the prohibited grounds of distinction, has a disproportionate impact on particular groups defined by reference to one of these grounds. Thus, although there is no difference in treatment, due to structural biases, treating unequals equally leads to unequal results.

The concept of indirect discrimination has its origins in US and European Community (EC) law but has now also found its way into the jurisprudence of international and regional human rights bodies. The Human Rights Committee recognized the possibility of indirect discrimination, albeit without explicitly referring to the concept, for the first time in *Singh Bhinder v Canada*.[28] The case concerned a Sikh who was dismissed from his employment with the Canadian Railway because he refused to comply with a legal requirement that safety headgear be worn at work, as his

---

[26] *Lithgow v UK* (1986) 8 EHRR 329, para 177.   [27] *Fredin v Sweden* (1991) 13 EHRR 784, para 60.
[28] CCPR/C/37/D/208/1986 (9 November 1989).

religion required him to wear only a turban. The Committee found that the legislation may amount to de facto discrimination: although it was neutral in that it applied to all persons without distinction, it disproportionately affected persons of the Sikh religion. (There was nevertheless no violation of Article 26 ICCPR as the safety headgear requirement was based on reasonable and objective grounds.) But only much later, in *Althammer v Austria*, a case concerning the abolition of household benefits that affected retired persons to a greater extent than active employees, did the Committee expressly refer to the concept of 'indirect discrimination':

The Committee recalls that a violation of article 26 can also result from the discriminatory effect of a rule or measure that is neutral at face value or without intent to discriminate. However, such indirect discrimination can only be said to be based on the grounds enumerated in Article 26 of the Covenant if the detrimental effects of a rule or decision exclusively or disproportionally affect persons having a particular race, colour, sex, language, religion, political or other opinion, national or social origin, property, birth or other status.[29]

Similarly, it was only in 2007 that the European Court of Human Rights, in its groundbreaking ruling in *DH and others v Czech Republic*, came up with an explicit definition of 'indirect discrimination'. Several Roma children had complained that the manner in which statutory rules governing assignment to schools were applied in practice resulted in the placement of a disproportionate number of Roma pupils in 'special schools' for children with 'mental deficiencies'. Referring to the definition of 'indirect discrimination' in EC law, the Grand Chamber of the European Court stated:

The Court has already accepted in previous cases that a difference in treatment may take the form of disproportionately prejudicial effects of a general policy or measure which, though couched in neutral terms, discriminates against a group.... In accordance with, for instance, Council Directives 97/80/EC and 2000/43/EC and the definition provided by ECRI [the European Commission against Racism and Intolerance], such a situation may amount to 'indirect discrimination', which does not necessarily require a discriminatory intent.[30]

The African Commission on Human and Peoples' Rights seems also to have recognized the concept of indirect discrimination when it found a violation of Articles 2 and 3 ACHPR in a case where legal remedies, even though guaranteed to everyone by law, were in practice 'only... available to the wealthy and those that can afford the services of private counsel'.[31]

4.3 DISCRIMINATORY INTENTION

In some legal systems, such as the USA, complainants need to show a discriminatory intention or purpose to establish discrimination.[32] There is no such requirement under

---

[29] CCPR/C/78/D/998/2001 (8 August 2003) para 10.2.

[30] App no 57325/00, Judgment of 13 November 2007, para 184.

[31] *Purohit and Moore v The Gambia*, Communication No 241/2001, 16th Activity Report (2002) paras 53–4.   [32] The leading case is *Washington v Davis* 426 US 229 (1976).

international human rights law, the reason why someone has been treated less favourably is irrelevant.

That both intended and unintended discrimination are prohibited under international law is apparent from the explicit definitions of discrimination contained in some of the human rights treaties. The ICERD defines discrimination as any distinction based on one of the listed grounds 'which has the purpose *or effect* of nullifying or impairing the recognition, enjoyment or exercise, on an equal footing, of human rights and fundamental freedoms'.[33] The CEDAW definition is almost identical.[34] The Human Rights Committee, in its General Comment on non-discrimination, has adopted the same definition for the purposes of the ICCPR[35] and has made it clear in its jurisprudence that discriminatory intention is not a necessary element of discrimination.[36] Equally, the European Court of Human Rights has indicated that discrimination under Article 14 ECHR may also relate to the *effects* of state measures.[37]

As is illustrated by the rulings in *Althammer* and *DH* described above, indirect discrimination is often equated with unintended discrimination. Conversely, it is normally assumed that where there is direct discrimination, there is a discriminatory intention. Although it is true that these concepts will often correlate, this is not always the case. There may be cases of direct discrimination—for example, the exclusion of pregnant women and mothers from certain types of work—where the intention is to protect the respective groups rather than to discriminate against them. On the other hand, a 'neutral' criterion such as a literacy test for job applicants may well be used as a pretext for excluding certain ethnic groups, amounting to intended indirect discrimination.

5 JUSTIFIED AND UNJUSTIFIED DISTINCTIONS

Once it is established that there has been a difference in treatment or outcome, the next question that needs to be answered is whether there is a justification for it. As explained above, it is to some extent inevitable that states classify people into different groups. The crucial question is whether there are objective and reasonable criteria for these distinctions. This section first explains the relevant test under international human rights law. Next, it explores what standard of review human rights bodies or courts apply to carry out this test. Finally, it considers matters concerning evidence and proof.

---

[33] Art 1(1) (emphasis added).   [34] Art 1.   [35] n 16, para 7.
[36] See eg *Simunek et al. v The Czech Republic*, CCPR/C/54/D/516/1992 (19 July 1995) para 11.7; *Adam v The Czech Republic*, CCPR/C/57/D/586/1994 (23 July 1996) para 12.7.
[37] *Case Relating to Certain Aspects of the Laws on the Use of Languages in Education in Belgium (Belgian Linguistics Case) (No 2)* (1968) 1 EHRR 252, para 10.

5.1 THE JUSTIFICATION TEST

The Human Rights Committee, in its General Comment on non-discrimination, has stressed that, for the purposes of the ICCPR, 'not every differentiation of treatment will constitute discrimination, if the criteria for such differentiation are reasonable and objective and if the aim is to achieve a purpose which is legitimate under the Covenant.'[38] But it is in the jurisprudence of the European Court of Human Rights that the criteria for distinguishing between justified and unjustified distinction have been most clearly articulated. The Court interpreted Article 14 ECHR for the first time in the *Belgian Linguistics Case* and has since repeatedly confirmed those conclusions:

[T]he Court, following the principles which may be extracted from the legal practice of a large number of democratic states, holds that the principle of equality of treatment is violated if the distinction has no objective and reasonable justification. The existence of such a justification must be assessed in relation to the aim and effects of the measure under consideration, regard being had to the principles which normally prevail in democratic societies. A difference of treatment in the exercise of a right laid down in the Convention must not only pursue a legitimate aim: Article 14 is likewise violated when it is clearly established that there is no reasonable relationship of proportionality between the means employed and the aim sought to be realised.[39]

This two-limb test, requiring that any difference in treatment must (1) pursue a legitimate aim and (2) be proportionate, is very similar to the test used in the context of other rights to assess the permissibility of limitations, described in Chapter 6, above. The test formulated by the European Court has been adopted, explicitly or implicitly, by most other human rights bodies. While the Human Rights Committee had originally failed to provide a clear and consistent explanation of what it means by 'reasonable and objective criteria', it has recently increasingly started to interpret these terms as requiring a legitimate aim and proportionality.[40] The Committee on the Elimination of Racial Discrimination and the Committee on Economic, Social and Cultural Rights have embraced the same approach,[41] as has the Inter-American Court of Human Rights.[42]

In terms of what exactly this test involves, its first limb will not usually be very difficult for states to meet: most distinctions can be argued to pursue some aim that qualifies as legitimate, for example the protection of public order or tailoring the education system to children's differing learning capabilities. More difficult to satisfy is the second element of the test, the proportionality requirement. This requirement reflects the basic notion that a fair balance ought to be struck between the interests of the community and respect for individual rights. A wide range of factors may need to be considered to assess proportionality, including the suitability of a distinction to achieve

---

[38] n 16, para 13.   [39] n 37, para 10.   [40] eg *Gillot v France*, A/57/40 (15 July 2002) para 13.2.

[41] CERD, Concluding observations: Australia, CERD/C/AUS/CO/14 (14 April 2005) para 24; CESCR, General Comment 20, E/C.12/GC/20, para 13.

[42] *Proposed Amendments to the Naturalization Provisions of the Political Constitution of Costa Rica*, n 4, paras 56–7.

the aim pursued, the availability of alternative means, and the question of whether the disadvantage suffered by the affected individuals or groups is excessive in relation to the aim. Whilst this assessment inevitably turns on the specific facts of a given case, international human rights bodies have been consistent in their characterization of certain reasons as not sufficient to justify differential treatment; these include, among others, mere administrative inconvenience,[43] existence of a longstanding tradition,[44] prevailing views in society,[45] or convictions of the local population.[46]

5.2 STANDARD OF REVIEW

The stringency with which human rights courts or bodies review the existence of a justification will vary according to a number of factors.

Most importantly, certain grounds of distinction are generally regarded as inherently suspect and therefore require particularly strict scrutiny. The grounds attracting the greatest degree of attention and most likely to be declared unjustified are race, ethnicity, sex, and religion. That *race* is among these 'suspect classifications' is indicated by the general acceptance of the prohibition of racial discrimination as forming part of customary international law, the widespread ratification of the ICERD, and the finding of the European Commission of Human Rights, later endorsed by the Court, that 'a special importance should be attached to discrimination based on race' and that it may amount to degrading treatment.[47] The Inter-American Commission on Human Rights also applies a strict standard of scrutiny to distinctions based on race.[48]

With regard to the related notion of *ethnicity*, the European Court has stressed that 'no difference in treatment which is based exclusively or to a decisive extent on a person's ethnic origin is capable of being objectively justified in a contemporary democratic society built on the principles of pluralism and respect for different cultures'.[49] That distinctions based on *sex* are particularly suspect is underlined by the wealth of international treaties addressing the problem of sexual discrimination, including the CEDAW.[50] The Inter-American Commission has stated that distinctions based on sex 'necessarily give rise to heightened scrutiny'[51] and the European Court has observed that 'very weighty reasons would have to be advanced before a difference in treatment on the ground of sex could be regarded as compatible with the [ECHR]'.[52] Finally, the suspect nature of distinctions based on *religion* can be concluded from the unanimous adoption by the General Assembly of the

---

[43] *Gueye v France*, n 22, para 9.5.
[44] *Müller and Engelhard v Namibia*, CCPR/C/74/D/919/2000 (26 March 2002) para 6.8.
[45] *Broeks v The Netherlands*, n 14.   [46] *Inze v Austria* (1988) 10 EHRR 394, para 44.
[47] *East African Asians v UK* (1973) 3 EHRR 76, paras 207–8; *Cyprus v Turkey*, App no 25781/94, Judgment of 10 May 2001, para 306.
[48] Case 11.625, *María Eugenia Morales de Sierra v Guatemala*, IACommHR Report No 4/01 (19 January 2001) para 36.
[49] *Timishev v Russia*, App nos 55762/00 and 55974/00, Judgment of 13 December 2005, para 58.
[50] See Chapter 16, below.   [51] *María Eugenia Morales de Sierra v Guatemala*, n 48, para 36.
[52] *Abdulaziz, Cabales and Balkandali v UK* (1985) 7 EHRR 471, para 78.

Declaration on the Elimination of All Forms of Intolerance and Discrimination Based on Religion or Belief[53] and the European Court's finding that '[n]otwithstanding any possible arguments to the contrary, a distinction based essentially on a difference in religion alone is not acceptable'.[54]

As far as other grounds of distinction are concerned, it is difficult to discern a consistent approach in international case law. The Human Rights Committee, for instance, has indicated that any distinction based on one of the grounds explicitly listed in Article 26 ICCPR 'places a heavy burden on the State party to explain the reason for the differentiation',[55] but that does not seem to mean that differential treatment on grounds other than race, sex, and religion are subject to the same intense scrutiny. The European Court, on the other hand, has suggested that also distinctions based on nationality and illegitimacy should be treated as inherently suspect.[56] Lists of suspect classifications are, in any event, not fixed but can change as international law on these matters develops. Given the recent emergence of new international norms against discrimination on grounds such as disability,[57] sexual orientation,[58] and age,[59] it seems likely that these classifications will soon be regarded as suspect, if they are not already regarded as such.

Apart from the ground of distinction, the intensity of review may also depend on a number of other factors. For example, most courts and human rights bodies tend to apply a lenient standard as far as matters of social or economic policy are concerned,[60] whereas classifications affecting fundamental individual interests entail particularly strict scrutiny.[61] Furthermore, it will generally be more difficult for states to justify direct rather than indirect discrimination. The Declaration of Principles on Equality, an important but non-binding document signed by numerous human rights and equality experts, states that 'direct discrimination may be permitted only very exceptionally'.[62]

5.3 EVIDENCE AND PROOF

According to established human rights jurisprudence, it is up to the individual complaining of discrimination to establish a difference in treatment or outcome, the ground of distinction, and the existence of comparably situated groups. Having done

---

[53] GA Res 36/55 (25 November 1981).   [54] *Hoffmann v Austria* (1993) 17 EHRR 293, para 36.

[55] *Müller and Engelhard v Namibia*, n 44, para 6.7.

[56] See *Gaygusuz v Austria* (1996) 23 EHRR 364, para 42 and *Inze v Austria*, n 46, para 41, respectively.

[57] See the CRPD.   [58] See Chapter 15, below.

[59] See UN Principles for Older Persons, GA Res 46/91 (16 December 1991).

[60] See eg *Oulajin and Kaiss v The Netherlands*, CCPR/C/46/D/406/1990 and 426/1990 (23 October 1992), individual opinion submitted by Committee members Herndl, Müllerson, N'Diaye, and Sadi, and *James v UK* (1986) 8 EHRR 123, para 46 (stating that 'the margin of appreciation available to the legislature in implementing social and economic policies should be a wide one').

[61] See eg *Dudgeon v UK* (1981) 4 EHRR 149, para 52.

[62] Equal Rights Trust, Declaration of Principles on Equality, available at <http://www.equalrightstrust. org/endorse/index.htm>, Principle 5.

so, the burden of proof shifts to the state to show that there is a justification for the distinction.[63]

In cases of alleged indirect discrimination, however, complainants may find it very difficult to prove that a neutral measure has a disproportionate impact on particular groups. Therefore, the European Court of Human Rights has held that less strict evidential rules should apply in these cases: 'statistics which appear on critical examination to be reliable and significant' may be sufficient prima facie evidence of indirect discrimination.[64] Thus, in *DH*, even though the statistical figures submitted by the applicants were contentious, the Court still thought that they revealed a dominant trend and thus accepted them as sufficient to establish a presumption of disproportionate numbers of Roma children being placed in 'special schools'. As a consequence, the burden of proof shifted to the government to show that there was a justification for the disparate impact of the legislation.[65]

DH demonstrates that statistical evidence may be of decisive importance to the outcome of cases of alleged indirect discrimination. Yet often the data required to establish a presumption that a measure has a discriminatory effect can, unlike in *DH*, only be collected by state authorities. The UN treaty bodies therefore regularly stress in their concluding observations that states have a duty to collect and analyse relevant statistical data, disaggregated by grounds of distinction.[66] Such a duty to gather information has also been included in the Declaration of Principles on Equality.[67]

6   POSITIVE ACTION

As with any other human right, the right to equality and non-discrimination entails state obligations of different types.[68] The *obligation to respect* requires states to refrain from any discriminatory action and to ensure that all their laws and practices comply with the right to non-discrimination. The *obligation to protect* imposes a duty on states to prevent discrimination by non-state actors. According to the consistent jurisprudence of the UN treaty bodies, this means that states must introduce comprehensive legislation prohibiting discrimination in fields such as employment, education, healthcare, housing, and the provision of goods and services. This conclusion is supported by various provisions in the respective human rights treaties themselves. Article 2(d) ICERD, for example, explicitly states that '[e]ach State Party shall prohibit and bring to an end, by all appropriate means, including legislation as required by circumstances, racial discrimination by any persons, group or organization'; the CEDAW contains a parallel provision in Article 2(e); and most treaties are scattered with norms requiring states to prohibit particular actions of private parties that are discriminatory or may

---

[63] Ibid, Principle 21. For the ECHR, see *Timishev v Russia*, n 49, para 57.
[64] *DH v Czech Republic*, n 30, para 188.   [65] Ibid, paras 191–5.
[66] See eg CEDAW Committee, Report on twenty-ninth session, A/58/38 (part II), para 134 (Brazil).
[67] Declaration of Principles on Equality, n 62, Principle 24.   [68] See Chapter 6, above.

contribute to discrimination, such as racial hate speech (Article 20 ICCPR, Article 4 ICERD, Article 13(5) ACHR), trafficking in women and exploitation of prostitution of women (Article 6 CEDAW), or racial discrimination with regard to employment, housing, or education (Article 5(e) ICERD).

However, an exclusively prohibitory approach is severely limited in that it focuses on discrimination understood as individual, isolated events that can be remedied through penalizing the perpetrators and compensating the victims. In fact discrimination is often the consequence of deeply embedded patterns of disadvantage and exclusion that can only be addressed through changes to social and institutional structures. Accordingly, it is now well established in international human rights law that it is not sufficient for states to have anti-discrimination legislation in place. Instead, they also have an *obligation to promote, guarantee, and secure* equality by taking proactive steps to eliminate structural patterns of disadvantage and to further social inclusion.[69] This obligation, often referred to as the duty to take 'positive action', may cover a huge variety of legislative, administrative, and policy measures, ranging from the restructuring of institutions to the provision of 'reasonable accommodation'[70] for individuals in particular circumstances, from educational campaigns to the use of public procurement to promote equality, and from the 'mainstreaming'[71] of equality issues in public policy to encouraging participation of affected groups in relevant decision-making processes.

One important aspect of 'positive action' are 'affirmative action programmes' or, as they are generally called in international law, *special measures of protection*. These are 'measures...aimed specifically at correcting the position of members of a target group in one or more aspects of their social life, in order to obtain effective equality'.[72] In their strongest form, such special measures involve the preferential treatment of members of a previously disadvantaged group over others in the allocation of jobs, university places, and other benefits (often referred to as 'positive' or 'reverse discrimination'). For example, when two equally qualified persons apply for a job, priority is given to the female applicant, or a certain number of university places are reserved for racial minorities.

Although such preferential treatment is clearly incompatible with a formal notion of equality, international human rights law permits it, thus recognizing that it may be

---

[69] See eg ICERD, Arts 2(1)(e), 2(2), and 7; HRC, General Comment 4, HRI/GEN/1/Rev. 9 (Vol I) 175, para 2; HRC, General Comment 18, n 16, paras 5 and 10; CEDAW, Arts 3 and 5; CERD, General Recommendation XXIX, HRI/GEN/1/Rev. 9 (Vol II) 296, paras 5, 6, 8, 9, 17, 33–5; Protocol to the African Charter on Human and Peoples' Rights on the Rights of Women in Africa, Arts 2(1)(d), 2(2), 3–24.

[70] For a definition of 'reasonable accommodation', see CRPD, Art 2.

[71] For 'gender mainstreaming', that is, the integration of a gender perspective in all legislation and public policies, see Report of the Fourth World Conference on Women, A/Conf.177/20 (1995), strategic objective H.2. The Protocol to the African Charter on Human and Peoples' Rights on the Rights of Women in Africa contains, in Art 2(1)(c), an explicit obligation of gender mainstreaming. See further Chapter 16, below.

[72] Progress report on the concept and practice of affirmative action by the Special Rapporteur of the Sub-Commission on the Promotion and Protection of Human Rights, E/CN.4/Sub.2/2001/15 (26 June 2001) para 7.

legitimate to prioritize the achievement of substantive equality over the requirement of consistent treatment. Article 1(4) ICERD, for example, provides:

Special measures taken for the sole purpose of securing adequate advancement of certain racial or ethnic groups or individuals requiring such protection as may be necessary in order to ensure such groups or individuals equal enjoyment or exercise of human rights and fundamental freedoms shall not be deemed racial discrimination, provided, however, that such measures do not, as a consequence, lead to the maintenance of separate rights for different racial groups and that they shall not be continued after the objectives for which they were taken have been achieved.

The CEDAW contains a similar provision in Article 4(1). For purposes of the ICCPR, the Human Rights Committee has made it clear that special measures are permissible as long as they meet the general justification test described above, that is, as long as they pursue a legitimate aim in a proportionate manner.[73] Proportionality in this context means, among other things, that the preferential treatment must be introduced for the benefit of genuinely disadvantaged groups, be temporary and cease once the objectives have been achieved, and not result in the maintenance of separate rights for different groups.

Not only does international human rights law permit, but to some extent it even *requires*, states to adopt special measures of protection. As the Human Rights Committee's General Comment on non-discrimination states:

[T]he principle of equality sometimes requires States parties to take affirmative action in order to diminish or eliminate conditions which cause or help to perpetuate discrimination prohibited by the Covenant. For example, in a State where the general conditions of a certain part of the population prevent or impair their enjoyment of human rights, the State should take specific action to correct those conditions. Such action may involve granting for a time to the part of the population concerned certain preferential treatment in specific matters as compared with the rest of the population.[74]

That states may need to adopt special measures has also been highlighted by the Committee on Economic, Social and Cultural Rights.[75] As far as racial groups and women are concerned, the duty follows from Article 2(2) ICERD and Article 3 CEDAW, respectively. At the regional level, the Inter-American Court of Human Rights has observed that 'States are obliged to take affirmative action to reverse or change discriminatory situations that exist in their societies to the detriment of a specific group of persons',[76] while the European Court has stressed that 'a failure to attempt to correct inequality through different treatment' may amount to a violation of the right to non-discrimination.[77]

[73] eg *Stalla Costa v Uruguay*, CCPR/C/30/D/198/1985 (9 July 1987) para 10; *Jacobs v Belgium*, CCPR/C/81/D/943/2000 (7 July 2004) para 9.5.   [74] n 16, para 10.
[75] eg CESCR, General Comment 16, HRI/GEN/1/Rev. 9 (Vol I) 113, paras 15 and 35.
[76] *Juridical Condition and Rights of the Undocumented Migrants*, n 11, para 104.
[77] *Stec and Others v UK*, App nos 65731/01 and 65900/01, Judgment of 12 April 2006, para 51.

7 CONCLUSION

The concept of equality and non-discrimination in international human rights law has evolved significantly since the adoption of the UDHR. Detailed legal standards have been drawn up and human rights bodies and courts have developed a rich jurisprudence, giving concrete substance to the notion of equality. Nevertheless, considerable gaps, inconsistencies, and uncertainties remain: the concept of indirect discrimination was developed in other jurisdictions and has only very recently been acknowledged by international human rights bodies; details of the justification test, such as the applicable standard of review and evidentiary rules, need further elaboration; and, as far as implementation at the national level is concerned, numerous states do not yet have comprehensive legislation to combat discrimination.

The most important challenge, however, is to ensure that every human being is in fact able to enjoy her or his right to equality. In a world in which the average income of the richest 20 per cent is about 50 times that of the bottom 20 per cent and the 500 richest people earn more than the poorest 416 million,[78] equal rights remain an unfulfilled promise for large sections of the population. Recent developments in international human rights law are evidence of a growing recognition that, while prohibitions of discrimination play a crucial role in achieving equality, states also have an obligation to proactively tackle structural patterns of disadvantage—in other words, that formal and substantive approaches to equality need to be combined. One key component of such a proactive strategy must be to ensure that all people can participate on an equal basis in all areas of economic, social, and political life, including in the very decisions on how equality should be realized.

FURTHER READING

ARNARDÓTTIR, *Equality and Non-discrimination under the European Convention on Human Rights* (Martinus Nijhoff, 2003).

BAYEFSKY, 'The Principle of Equality or Non-Discrimination in International Law' (1990) 11 *HRLJ* 1.

CHOUDHURY, 'Interpreting the Right to Equality under Article 26 of the International Covenant on Civil and Political Rights' [2003] *EHRLR* 24.

FREDMAN (ed), *Discrimination and Human Rights: The Case of Racism* (Oxford University Press, 2001).

——*Discrimination Law* (Oxford University Press, 2002).

LERNER, *Group Rights and Discrimination in International Law* (Martinus Nijhoff, 2003).

McCRUDDEN (ed), *Anti-Discrimination Law* (Ashgate, 2004).

McKEAN, *Equality and Discrimination under International Law* (Clarendon Press, 1983).

VANDENHOLE, *Non-Discrimination and Equality in the View of the UN Human Rights Treaty Bodies* (Intersentia, 2005).

[78] UN Development Programme, *Human Development Report 2005*, 36–7.

USEFUL WEBSITES

UN Committee on the Elimination of Racial Discrimination (CERD): <**http://www2.ohchr. org/english/bodies/cerd/**>

European Commission Against Racism and Intolerance (ECRI): <**http://www.coe.int/t/e/ human_rights/ecri/**>

Equal Rights Trust: <**http://www.equalrightstrust.org**>

10

INTEGRITY OF THE PERSON

Nigel S Rodley

SUMMARY

This chapter examines the right to be free from torture and cruel, inhuman, or degrading treatment or punishment and the right to life, arguably the core rights understood within the concept of integrity of the person. They also have a direct pedigree to the principle of respect for human dignity that is at the heart of the International Bill of Human Rights. The complex definitional issues of what constitutes torture and other ill-treatment are addressed, mainly in light of treaty definitions and case law of courts and other bodies charged with applying relevant treaties. The same approach is taken with respect to the right to life, where the central issues of the limits international law places on the death penalty and on the use of force by security forces and law enforcement officials are considered. Both rights are considered to be rules of customary international law and probably peremptory norms of international law (*jus cogens*).

1 INTRODUCTION

1.1 RESPECT FOR HUMAN DIGNITY

Respect for human dignity is the one explicit underlying principle of the International Bill of Human Rights. It is invoked in the first preambular paragraph of the Universal Declaration of Human Rights (UDHR) and the second preambular paragraphs of both the International Covenant on Economic, Social and Cultural Rights (ICESCR) and the International Covenant on Civil and Political Rights (ICCPR).

The prohibition of torture and cruel, inhuman, or degrading treatment or punishment ('torture and ill-treatment') and the right to life both have an immediate link to the principle of human dignity. Thus, the African Charter on Human and Peoples' Rights (ACHPR) places the prohibition of torture and ill-treatment in its Article 5 that guarantees 'respect of the dignity inherent in a human being'. In a more limited way, the analogous Article 5 of the American Convention on Human Rights (ACHR), after stating the basic prohibition on torture and ill-treatment, provides that all persons deprived of liberty are to be 'treated with respect for the inherent dignity of the human person'. A similar requirement is found in Article 10(1) ICCPR. While this is separate from Article 7 containing the prohibition of torture and ill-treatment, it has long been treated by the Human Rights Committee as intimately linked to Article 7.[1] With regard to the right to life, the first preambular paragraph of the Second Optional Protocol to the ICCPR (ICCPR-OP2), aiming at the abolition of the death penalty, affirms that abolition 'contributes to enhancement of human dignity'.

1.2 THE RIGHT TO INTEGRITY OF THE PERSON

The prohibition of torture and ill-treatment and the right to life are at the core of the notion of integrity of the person. Article 5 ACHR, for example, which guarantees the right to humane treatment, provides in its first paragraph: 'Every person has the right to have his physical, mental, and moral integrity respected.' The link between the right to humane treatment and personal integrity is established. The same is true for the link between the right to life and integrity of the person. Thus, Article 4 ACHPR stipulates the right of every human being 'to respect for his life and the integrity of his person'. Here the link is essential.

This chapter deals, first, with the right to be free from torture and ill-treatment (Section 2) and, then, with the right to life (Section 3).

2 THE RIGHT TO BE FREE FROM TORTURE AND ILL-TREATMENT

Article 5 UDHR provides: 'No-one shall be subjected to torture or to cruel, inhuman or degrading treatment or punishment.' Verbally inspired by the prohibition of 'cruel and unusual punishments' in the English and American Bills of Rights, the direct stimulus for this provision was Nazi Germany's use of torture. Related vivid concerns included the use of harmful and painful medical experiments, such as those conducted by the notorious Dr Josef Mengele. This breadth of concern explains the expansive, non-technical language of the prohibition.

While torture had been legal under certain circumstances in Europe from at least Roman times, it had been abolished virtually everywhere by the end of the eighteenth century.[2] Its re-emergence in the heart of Europe in a post-Enlightenment world was a matter for shock and felt to be an aberration. Accordingly, after the prohibition's inclusion in the UDHR, it found its way uncontroversially, in almost identical language, into the ICCPR and the principal regional treaties.

---

[1] HRC, General Comment 20, HRI/GEN/1/Rev.9 (Vol I) 200, para 2; General Comment 21, HRI/GEN/1/Rev.9 (Vol I) 202, para 3.

[2] Torture seems to have been alien to Islamic tradition from its beginnings, albeit not, in practice, to various governments claiming to apply Islamic law in their legal systems.

That this may not have been such an aberration became clear in the 1970s when Amnesty International published a report documenting the practice of torture in many countries from all regions of the world and led a campaign on the issue. Demonstrably in response to this campaign and a successor one in 1984–5,[3] the UN began sustained activities, first in the field of standard-setting, then in the area of developing an institutional response. There were also activities at the regional level to the same effect.

The product of the standard-setting is referred to in section 2.1 below. The institutional output has included the creation of the mandate of the UN Special Rapporteur on the question of torture, the UNCAT's establishment of the Committee against Torture under the UN Convention against Torture and Other Cruel, Inhuman or Degrading Treatment or Punishment (UNCAT), and a Sub-Committee on the Prevention of Torture created by the Optional Protocol to UNCAT (UNCAT-OP) (2002). The latter was inspired by the work of the European Committee for the Prevention of Torture and Inhuman or Degrading Treatment or Punishment that was put in place by the European Convention of the same name adopted by the Council of Europe in 1987.

2.1 SOURCES

The right to be free from torture and ill-treatment is guaranteed by the general universal and regional human rights treaties: Articles 7 and 10 ICCPR, Article 3 European Convention on Human Rights (ECHR), Article 5 ACHR, and Article 5 ACHPR. In addition, a human rights treaty specifically designed to ensure protection of the right to be free from torture and ill-treatment has been adopted: UNCAT. Key UN 'soft law' sources include the Standard Minimum Rules for the Treatment of Prisoners (1955), the Declaration on the Protection of All Persons from Being Subjected to Torture and Other Cruel, Inhuman or Degrading Treatment or Punishment (1975), the Code of Conduct for Law Enforcement Officials (1979), the Principles of Medical Ethics relevant to the Role of Health Personnel, particularly Physicians, in the Protection of Prisoners and Detainees against Torture and Other Cruel, Inhuman or Degrading Treatment or Punishment (1982), the Body of Principles for the Protection of All Persons under Any Form of Detention or Imprisonment (1988), and the Principles on the Effective Investigation and Documentation of Torture and Other Cruel, Inhuman or Degrading Treatment or Punishment (Istanbul Principles, 2000). There are also treaties in the field of international humanitarian law that prohibit torture, cruel treatment, inhuman treatment, and humiliating and degrading treatment.[4] As with the human rights treaties, the terms are undefined. Finally, there is international criminal law, which covers, among other aspects, crimes against humanity and war crimes. Torture and other forms of ill-treatment may amount to war crimes and, when committed as part of a widespread or systematic attack against a civilian population, crimes

---

[3] See Amnesty International, *Report on Torture* (1973) and *Torture in the Eighties* (1984).

[4] Geneva Convention I, Arts 12 and 50; Geneva Convention II, Arts 12 and 51; Geneva Convention III, Arts 17, 87, and 130; Geneva Convention IV, Arts 32 and 147; and Common Art 3 to all four Geneva Conventions, which is understood as reflecting the 'fundamental principles of international humanitarian law'. See Chapter 23, below.

against humanity. The case law of the International Criminal Tribunal for the former Yugoslavia and the International Criminal Tribunal for Rwanda, therefore, also provide helpful guidance in determining the normative content of the right to be free from torture and ill-treatment. Furthermore, the Rome Statute of the International Criminal Court (ICC Statute) has both codified crimes against humanity and war crimes and provided definitions for some components, including torture.[5]

2.2 LEGAL STATUS

There is no doubt that the prohibition of torture and other ill-treatment is a norm of customary international law. Relevant indications are: the fact that the rule is couched in absolute terms, brooking no exception (such as for public order or national security purposes, as allowed for in some rights, notably the freedoms covered in Chapter 12, below), not even the spurious 'ticking bomb' situation;[6] the non-derogability of the rule even in time of war or other public emergency;[7] and the fact that states do not claim a right to torture. One might also look to the prohibition in international humanitarian law and its criminal nature under international criminal law.

It seems also beyond peradventure that the prohibition of torture is a rule of *jus cogens*, a peremptory rule of international law which cannot even be modified by treaty.[8] It has been described as such by the European Court of Human Rights, the Inter-American Court of Human Rights, the Human Rights Committee, the Committee Against Torture, the International Criminal Tribunal for the former Yugoslavia, the International Law Commission, and the UK House of Lords.[9] It is worth noting that, not only has the influential American Law Institute long ago espoused this position, in its third Restatement of US Foreign Relations Law,[10] so has one of the controversial legal memoranda from the US Department of Justice that provided the basis for the temporary use of 'enhanced interrogation techniques' by US personnel of certain 'high value' detainees held in the context of the 'global war on terror'.[11] All that remains unsettled is whether the prohibition of other ill-treatment has the same status. The

---

[5] Arts 7 and 8.

[6] This posits the extremely hypothetical situation that a person in custody knows where a bomb that would cause great loss of life has been placed and the aim is to locate it and prevent it from going off. In reality, the person's knowledge will be doubtful and the person will be able to prevaricate until the bomb goes off, even in the unlikely event that a 'specialist' interrogation team is available.

[7] See case law listed in n 9. See also *Chahal v UK* (1997) 23 EHRR 413; *Saadi v Italy*, App no 37201/06, Judgment of 28 February 2008.   [8] See Chapter 5, above.

[9] See eg *Al-Adsani v United Kingdom* (2002) 34 EHRR 273, para 61; *Caesar v Trinidad and Tobago*, IACtHR Series C No 123 (11 March 2005); HRC, General Comment 29, HRI/GEN/1/Rev.9 (Vol I) 234, para 3; CAT, General Comment 2, HRI/GEN/1/Rev.9 (Vol I) 376 para 1; *Prosecutor v Furundzija* (1998), No 17-95-17/1, Trial Judgment, paras 153–7; International Law Commission, Draft Articles on State Responsibility, A/56/10, ch IV.E.2; *Regina v Bow Street Metropolitan Stipendiary Magistrate, ex parte Pinochet Ugarte (No 3)* [1999] UKHL 17.

[10] American Law Institute, Restatement of the Law: Restatement (Third) of the Foreign Relations Law of the United States, Vol II (1987) s 702.

[11] See Memorandum from Daniel P Levin to James B Comey (30 December 2004) 1 and n 2 available at <http://www.usdoj.gov/olc/18usc23402340a2.htm>.

American Restatement makes no distinction. Most of the other sources cited focus on torture, without necessarily excluding other ill-treatment.

2.3 COMPONENTS

We have seen that the prohibition of torture and cruel, inhuman, or degrading treatment or punishment was drafted broadly with a view to avoiding an overly technical or narrow approach. Indeed, international bodies have found an extensive range of practices to fall foul of it. For instance, in the late 1960s and early 1970s the UK refused to admit British nationals being deported from Uganda, resulting in their 'shuttle-cocking' between the two countries. In 1973, the (former) European Commission of Human Rights found the practice to violate Article 3 ECHR.[12] Another type of concern was highlighted when a team of UN Special Rapporteurs found that the widespread property destruction carried out by East Timorese paramilitaries in Dili engaged the prohibition of torture and ill-treatment.[13] Nevertheless, the earliest case law, especially by the European Commission of Human Rights and the European Court of Human Rights, started to break down the prohibition into its component limbs, mostly in connection with cases dealing with prisoners.

2.3.1 Definition of 'torture' and 'cruel, inhuman, and degrading treatment or punishment'

In the *Greek Case*, arising out of treatment inflicted on political opponents by the military regime that seized power in Greece in 1967, the European Commission distinguished between various kinds of ill-treatment. In particular, it characterized *falanga* (beatings on the soles of the feet) as 'torture *and* inhuman treatment' while it considered some extremely severe beating as 'torture *or* inhuman treatment'.[14]

The landmark case of *Ireland v UK* concerned the treatment by UK security forces of suspected Irish Republican Army (IRA) prisoners in Northern Ireland. Again the European Commission distinguished between treatment amounting to torture and other ill-treatment. While it assigned serious physical beatings to the category of inhuman treatment, it concluded that five special interrogation techniques amounted to torture. The five techniques were:

1) wall-standing: forcing the detainees to remain for periods of some hours in a 'stress position', spread-eagled against the wall, with their fingers put high above the head against the wall, the legs spread apart and the feet back, causing them to stand on their toes with the weight of the body mainly on the fingers;

2) hooding: putting a bag over the detainees' heads and, at least initially, keeping it there all the time except during interrogation;

---

[12] *East African Asians v UK* (1973) 3 EHRR 76.

[13] Joint report of the Special Rapporteurs on extrajudicial, summary or arbitrary executions, torture, and violence against women, A/54/660 (10 December 1999) paras 70–1. See also *Hajrizi Dzemajl v Yugoslavia*, CAT/C/29/D/161/2000 (2 December 2002); *Ayder and others v Turkey*, App no 23656/94, Judgment of 8 January 2004, paras 104–11.   [14] *The Greek Case* (1969) 12 YB 468, 504 (emphases added).

3) subjection to noise: pending their interrogations, holding the detainees in a room where there was a continuous loud and hissing noise;

4) deprivation of sleep: pending their interrogations, depriving the detainees of sleep;

5) deprivation of food and drink: subjecting the detainees to a reduced diet.[15]

The European Court of Human Rights, however, decided in 1978 that these techniques should be considered as inhuman treatment rather than torture. It invoked the definition of torture found in the recently adopted UN Declaration against Torture (UNDAT). Article 1(2) UNDAT had defined torture as an aggravated and deliberate form of cruel, inhuman, or degrading treatment or punishment. For the European Court, the five techniques did not meet this criterion 'as so understood', the techniques being undeserving of the 'special stigma' of torture.[16] This was a controversial decision. After all, the definition of torture in the UNDAT had made clear that the pain or suffering inflicted did not have to be physical. It could also be *mental* pain or suffering. Many found it hard to understand what kind of mental pain or suffering might be required if the mixed mental *and* physical pain and suffering caused by interrogation techniques did not constitute torture.

The year 1984, also the title of George Orwell's futuristic novel which has his hero, Winston Smith, tortured by being in a room full of rats to which he was known to be phobic, brought us the UNCAT and its authoritative definition of torture. According to Article 1:

For the purposes of this Convention, the term 'torture' means any act by which severe pain or suffering, whether physical or mental, is intentionally inflicted on a person for such purposes as obtaining from him or a third person information or a confession, punishing him for an act he or a third person has committed or is suspected of having committed, or intimidating or coercing him or a third person, or for any reason based on discrimination of any kind, when such pain or suffering is inflicted by or at the instigation of or with the consent or acquiescence of a public official or other person acting in an official capacity. It does not include pain or suffering arising only from, inherent in or incidental to lawful sanctions.

While the definition is formally only applicable to the states parties to the UNCAT and the Committee against Torture that monitors its implementation, it has proven to be the first port of call for most bodies seeking to identify practices of torture. The definition largely follows that of UNDAT, with one notable exception: it does not describe torture as an aggravated and deliberate form of inhuman treatment. The definition has three core elements:

1. pain or suffering that must be severe; it may be physical or mental;

2. it must be inflicted for a certain kind of purpose, that is, the sort of public purpose traditionally associated with torture; and

3. it must be inflicted by or under the aegis of public officialdom.

---

[15] See *Ireland v UK* (1978) 2 EHRR 25, para 96.   [16] Ibid, para 167.

Each of these elements will be considered briefly. The first element, *severity of pain or suffering*, is common to most understandings of the term torture[17] and is found in the Article 7 ICC Statute definition of torture as a crime against humanity and in the definition of torture as a war crime in the Elements of Crimes adopted under the ICC Statute.[18] As indicated, there is no requirement for aggravation of pain or suffering. However, it should be noted that Article 16 UNCAT does make provision for cruel, inhuman, or degrading treatment or punishment that 'does not amount to torture'. This can lend itself to an interpretation that would reintroduce the idea of aggravation, but the better view is that it does not.

It is unclear to what extent the practice of the European Court of Human Rights may have been influenced by this evolution. Certainly, it has seen fit at least to attenuate the application of its distinction between torture and inhuman treatment. In the 1999 *Selmouni* case, it decided that the kind of serious beatings that had occurred in a number of cases, including *Ireland v UK*, and would earlier have been classified as inhuman treatment, would now be considered as torture. It invoked its doctrine of the ECHR as 'a living instrument' and argued that the definition of torture had to evolve with democratic society's understanding of the term.[19] It is probable that the European Court was also signalling that it would have been prepared to treat practices such as the five interrogation techniques similarly. The Court continues to distinguish torture from inhuman treatment that 'does not reach the level of severity' to constitute torture. However, it gives little away as to what is the criterion for inhuman treatment. Earlier, inhuman treatment had to be severe, thus requiring torture to be more than severe. It is possible that it may now require a certain level of seriousness of pain or suffering, but without rising to the level of 'severe', for treatment to be considered 'inhuman'. What is clear is that, after *Selmouni*, the Court has brought down the threshold of pain or suffering required for a finding of torture.

The second element, *purpose*, was always part of European Commission and Court case law and it is found in all but one of the existing definitions of torture. Indeed, in the definition of torture as a war crime in the Elements of Crimes adopted under the ICC Statute, the only distinction between torture and inhuman (or cruel) treatment is the purposive element. However, there is one definition that omits the purposive element, namely that in Article 7 ICC Statute defining torture as a crime against humanity. This may be explained by the fact that crimes against humanity can be committed by unofficial groups, thus making the attribution of motivation more difficult than in respect of states or other officially constituted bodies. Also, unlike the other definitions, that of Article 7 is limited to persons in custody, thus implicitly assigning some public purposive context. The definition remains an unsatisfactory outlier. The approach taken by UNCAT and the ICC Elements of Crime, making purpose the key distinctive factor between torture and cruel or inhuman treatment, may be the most satisfactory one.

---

[17] Inter-American Convention to Prevent and Punish Torture, Art 2 refers to 'physical or mental pain' without qualification.   [18] Elements of Crimes, Arts 8(2)(a)(ii)-1 and 8(2)(c)(i)-4.

[19] (2000) 29 EHRR 403, para 101.

Finally, as a third element, the UNCAT definition requires public *official responsibility* for the pain or suffering. This is not found in the ICC-related definitions. This is perhaps inevitable as crimes against humanity and war crimes are not necessarily committed by public officials in the sense of state officials. A party to an armed conflict may well not be a state. However, it must have sufficient elements of organization such as to endow it with the status of party to an armed conflict within the meaning of international humanitarian law. Similarly, a crime against humanity must also be committed in the context of an attack against a civilian population. This institutional dimension should be seen as substituting for the public official requirement, as is the case in respect of war crimes.

2.3.2 Specific practices

While most findings of torture have involved an accumulation of cruel acts, some specific practices have been found to be torture. We have already seen this in respect of the *falanga* and sustained beatings with instruments. Others include water suffocation,[20] 'Palestinian hanging' (tying a person's hands behind their back and suspending them in the air),[21] and rape.[22]

Since the suffering involved in torture can be physical or mental, it is clear that psychological torment, such as that to which Orwell subjected his fictional hero Winston Smith, may fall within the legal definition of torture. The classic example is the Human Rights Committee finding that the threat of amputation of a concert pianist's hands constituted torture.[23] Explicit and implicit threats of torture and death in circumstances where the threats were credible were found by the Inter-American Court of Human Rights to be torture.[24]

As far as other ill-treatment is concerned, it includes, first, any treatment that would amount to torture, but was not inflicted for a public purpose. Even since *Selmouni*, the European Court of Human Rights has found some beatings to be inhuman or degrading rather than torture. The reluctance to find torture may be attributable to the fact that in these cases there seem to be circumstances in which the facts, including the behaviour of the affected individual, are in doubt.[25] The unnecessary use of handcuffs or other physical restraints may, under certain circumstances, amount to prohibited ill-treatment,[26] as can unnecessary or oppressive strip-searching,[27] and displaying an alleged terrorist in prison garb.[28]

---

[20] *José Vicente and Amado Villafañe Chaparro and others v Colombia*, CCPR/C/60/D/612/1995 (14 June 1994). The case is evidently consistent with the proposition that 'waterboarding'—briefly authorized for use by US personnel in the reaction to the atrocities of 11 September 2001—is torture.

[21] *Aksoy v Turkey* (1997) 23 EHRR 553, para 64.

[22] Case 10.970, *Mejía v Peru*, IACommHR Report No 5/96 (1 March 1996) Annual Report 1995, 157, 186–7; *Case of the Miguel Castro-Castro Prison v Peru*, IACtHR Series C No 160 (25 November 2006) para 311; *Aydin v Turkey* (1998) 25 EHRR 251, para 86.

[23] *Estrella v Uruguay*, CCPR/C/18/D/74/1980 (23 March 1983), para 8.3.

[24] *Maritza Urrutia v Guatemala*, IACtHR Series C No 103 (27 November 2003) paras 91–5.

[25] See eg *Egmez v Cyprus* (2002) 34 EHRR 29, paras 78–9.

[26] *Hénaf v France* (2005) 40 EHRR 44, paras 55–60.   [27] *Iwanczuk v Poland* (2004) 38 EHRR 8.

[28] *Loayza-Tamayo v Peru*, IACtHR Series C No 33 (17 September 1997), paras 46(d) and 58.

As far as persons in detention are concerned, they are at particular risk of ill-treatment during the *investigative phase* of detention, when the police or other detaining authority is seeking information of concern or a confession. This is because during this phase normal safeguards are not always respected. Thus, instead of detainees having prompt access to a lawyer and others from outside the place of detention, such as family members, or a medical practitioner, the detaining authority holds them at its sole mercy. This is generally called 'incommunicado detention'. Rules concerning the right to liberty aim at restricting this period of detention.[29] However, there is strong treaty body authority for the proposition that prolonged incommunicado detention in itself can violate the right of detainees to be treated with humanity and respect for their human dignity and the prohibition of torture and other ill-treatment.[30] Moreover, the UN Human Rights Council has clearly stated that prolonged incommunicado detention can amount to torture or other ill-treatment.[31] The Human Rights Committee has found that the US practice of capturing and detaining terrorist suspects in various parts of the world, as well as transferring them from place to place, violated the prohibition on torture and ill-treatment.[32]

The second phase of detention is the *remand phase*, the phase in which, typically, a judicial authority will order continued detention on criminal charges. As in this phase the detaining authority will usually be different from the investigating authority (the prison authorities rather than the police or security services), detainees are generally better protected from ill-treatment. However, even after being formally remanded in custody, people may remain in the hands of the police or other investigating authority. Therefore, human rights bodies tend to recommend that the period of pre-remand detention not exceed a very few days (typically not more than two or three)[33] and that places of remand be under an authority administratively separate from that responsible for the police or similar security agency.

The *post-conviction phase* raises two kinds of issue. The first is the conditions of detention, the second is the nature of the punishment.

As to the first, the fact that someone has been sentenced to a term of imprisonment does not mean that there are no limits to how the prisoner may then be treated. On the contrary, the basic principle is that conditions should be no more oppressive than those necessary to maintain the deprivation of liberty which is the object of the punishment.[34] Accordingly, standards have been developed to assist in this, notably the UN Standard Minimum Rules for the Treatment of Prisoners.[35] These cover such matters as avoidance of overcrowding, recreation, education and work, limits to time

---

[29] See Chapter 14, below.

[30] *Aber v Algeria*, CCPR/C/90/D/1439/2005 (16 August 2007), para 7.3; *Suárez-Rosero v Ecuador*, IACtHR Series C No 35 (12 November 1997), paras 90–1.

[31] Human Rights Council Res 8/8 (18 June 2008), para 7(c).

[32] Concluding observations: US, CCPR/C/USA/CO/3/Rev.1 (18 December 2006) paras 12 and 16.

[33] See eg Report of the Special Rapporteur on torture, E/CN.4/2003/68 (17 December 2002) para 26(g); ECPT Standards, CPT/Inf/E (2002) I-Rev 2006, paras 40–6.

[34] See eg the UN Basic Principles for the Treatment of Prisoners, GA Res 45/111 (14 December 1990) para 5.   [35] At the European level, the Council of Europe has adopted the European Prison Rules.

spent confined in cells, fair administration of discipline, and the limits to disciplinary punishment (including solitary confinement or segregation). Not every breach
of every rule will necessarily involve a violation of the prohibition of torture or ill-
treatment or the right to treatment with respect for humanity and human dignity.
However, the more serious or widespread the breach of the Rules, the more likely will
be a finding of a violation of one of these human rights. Treaty bodies now routinely
invoke the Standard Minimum Rules in finding prison conditions to violate these
rights.[36]

With regard to the second issue, the nature of the punishment, it will be recalled
that the UNCAT definition of torture excludes 'lawful sanctions'. Does that mean
that the prohibition of cruel, inhuman, and degrading *punishment* can only apply
either to oppressive prison conditions or punishment inflicted extrajudically, for
example by the police? The answer has to be negative. There is extensive treaty body
authority finding various forms of corporal punishment to violate the prohibition.
The first was the 1978 *Tyrer* case in which the European Court of Human Rights
found the infliction of a judicially ordered three strokes of the birch on a young person to be a degrading punishment violating Article 3 ECHR.[37] More recently, the
Inter-American Court of Human Rights found the lashing of a naked adult strapped
to a metal contraption, until he fainted, to be torture in violation of Article 5 ACHR.[38]
The Human Rights Committee has long been clear in its rejection of corporal punishment as a violation of Article 7 ICCPR.[39] Similarly, the Human Rights Council has
reminded governments that 'corporal punishment can amount to cruel, inhuman or
degrading punishment or even to torture'.[40] This begs the question of the exclusion
of lawful sanctions from the definition of torture. The proper understanding is that
the exclusion refers to those sanctions that are lawful under both national *and* international law. Since it is widely accepted that corporal punishment at least amounts to
cruel, inhuman, or degrading punishment, it does not qualify as a 'lawful sanction'
and, accordingly, is not immunized against being categorized as torture.

2.4 TYPES OF OBLIGATION

The prohibition of torture is in formal terms primarily a negative obligation. The
state is required to refrain from engaging in the practices concerned, either directly
through its agents' acts or indirectly by its agents' omissions when there is a duty to act.
However, the latter dimension already can be understood as an embryonic positive
obligation. It arises to avoid the circumvention of the rule by simply blaming the acts
on others (paramilitary groups, 'death squads', vigilantes, and so on), in circumstances

---

[36] eg *Mukong v Cameroon*, CCPR/C/51/D/458/1991 (10 August 1994); *Greek Case*, n 14; *Dickson v UK*,
App no 44362/04, Judgment of 4 July 2007, para 30 (note the Court relied more heavily, as it generally does,
on the European Prison Rules; see paras 31–6); *Raxcacó-Reyes v Guatemala*, IACtHR Series C No 133 (15
September 2005) paras 99–102.   [37] *Tyrer v UK* (1978) 2 EHRR 1.
[38] *Caesar*, n 9, paras 49(27) and (28).   [39] General Comment 20, n 1.
[40] Human Rights Council Res 8/8 (18 June 2008) para 7(a).

in which the acts may well have been committed with 'a nod and a wink' from state authorities. Because such collusion is hard to prove, other positive obligations have been developed.

Thus, it is generally accepted that where there are grounds for believing that torture has taken place, there is an obligation on the state to initiate an effective investigation into the situation, typical elements of which are reflected in the Istanbul Principles. Moreover, not only should such an investigation be capable of sustaining a prosecution of those found to be responsible, there seems to be an obligation to initiate such prosecutions when the facts permit. Indeed, it is this very obligation that is increasingly seen as the basis for the impermissibility of granting amnesties to persons responsible for torture (and probably other ill-treatment).[41] The obligation to prosecute is reinforced by Article 7 UNCAT, which requires states parties to submit for prosecution the case of anyone in their jurisdiction against whom there is sufficient evidence of having committed torture, regardless of the jurisdiction in which the torture was committed and the nationality of the perpetrator (a form of universal jurisdiction). This applies unless the person is extradited to another state wishing to exercise jurisdiction. It was on this basis that in 1999 the UK House of Lords upheld the detention order made by a magistrate against former Chilean President Augusto Pinochet Ugarte, pending processing of an extradition request from Spain.[42]

A further arguably positive obligation is to refrain from exposing a person to torture or ill-treatment by sending that person to a country where he or she faces a real risk of treatment in violation of the prohibition. Interestingly, the case law began in cases involving the death penalty.[43] It was consolidated in the 1996 *Chahal v UK* case in which a Sikh former torture victim from India could not, according to the European Court of Human Rights, be returned to India even on national security grounds.[44] Requested by the UK to revisit the issue, especially in relation to terrorism cases, the Court in the 2008 case of *Saadi v Italy* resoundingly and unanimously reaffirmed its position.[45] This dimension of the prohibition is codified for states parties to UNCAT in its Article 3. It is to be noted that this provision applies to torture, but not expressly to other cruel, inhuman, or degrading treatment or punishment.

What the limits of positive obligations are is unclear. In principle, the question to be asked is: how far are the acts in question attributable to the state? But, once acts of omission rather than commission are in question and once we envisage an obligation to prevent torture and ill-treatment, the harder it becomes to identify the borderlines of responsibility. As is reflected in the practice of the Human Rights Committee, the obligations may extend to action to prevent such phenomena as human trafficking

[41] See eg HRC, General Comment 31, HRI/GEN/1/Rev.9 (Vol I) 243, para 18.
[42] *Pinochet (No 3)*, n 9. See UNCAT, Arts 5–8.
[43] *Amekrane v UK* (1973) 16 YB 356; *Soering v UK* (1989) 11 EHRR 439; *Ng v Canada*, CCPR/C/49/D/469/1991 (7 January 1994). See also HRC, General Comment 31, n 41, para 12. [44] n 7.
[45] n 7.

and domestic violence.[46] It is not controversial that such obligations are ones of means, not of result, often known as 'due diligence'.[47] What means may be appropriate in any given situation, or what diligence is due, may well be far from evident. One factor that may be relevant in making any assessment is the extent to which the state may be said to have an interest in the perpetration or continuation of the harm suffered by the victims. The less the interest, the higher may be the threshold to attribute responsibility to the state.

2.5 RELATIONSHIP WITH OTHER HUMAN RIGHTS

There are various connections between the prohibition of torture and ill-treatment and other human rights. For example, one of the rules for a fair trial is that one may not be compelled to testify against oneself. Clearly, testimony coerced by prohibited ill-treatment would fall foul of that prohibition. As already seen, rules relating to the right to liberty provide an essential guarantee against prohibited ill-treatment. Moreover, some forms of arbitrary detention such as prolonged detention may amount to a violation of the prohibition of ill-treatment. This will be especially true in respect of the most extreme form of detention, namely enforced disappearance. In that case, among other rights, the right to life may also be engaged, as it evidently is when death occurs under torture.

3   THE RIGHT TO LIFE

The right to life is dealt with very early and summarily in the UDHR. According to Article 3, '[e]veryone has the right to life, liberty and security of person'. There is no further reference to the right to life in the UDHR. This nevertheless leaves it as the first substantive right, after the Article 2 affirmation of the principle of non-discrimination. It was not further developed partly because of a lack of consensus as to what issues it covers, notably the death penalty.

The right to life has been considered the 'supreme human right'[48] and 'the fountain from which all human rights spring'.[49] On the other hand, treaty provisions giving effect to it are not couched in the same absolute language as those prohibiting torture. Typically, they will insist that 'no-one shall be arbitrarily deprived' of life. Indeed, it is not hard to think of circumstances in which states may be expected to sanction the taking of life. Warfare is the most obvious example and killings committed lawfully under international humanitarian law will not in principle be considered as violating

[46] See eg HRC, General Comment 28, HRI/GEN/1/Rev.9 (Vol I) 228, paras 11–12.
[47] See eg *Velásquez-Rodriguez v Honduras*, IACtHR Series C No 4 (29 July 1988) para 172. See also Chapter 6, above.   [48] HRC, General Comment 6, HRI/GEN/1/Rev.9 (Vol I) 176, para 1.
[49] Report of the UN Special Rapporteur on summary and arbitrary executions, E/CN.4/1983/16 (31 January 1983) para 22.

the right to life. The forces of law may also sometimes be required to take life, notably to protect the lives of others. And, of course, for centuries the death penalty, though now on the retreat, figured in most national legislation.

These considerations make the right to life a more complex concept than the prohibition of torture and ill-treatment. This in turn may help to explain why the right as a whole has not been the object of the same sustained campaigning and attention as that prohibition. Rather, work has focused on particular aspects, with the major emphasis being on the death penalty, as reflected in abolitionist protocols to general human rights treaties. Some 'soft law' instruments have still been adopted, notably in relation to deprivation of life in law enforcement situations. Moreover, the second earliest thematic mechanism created by the UN Commission on Human Rights in 1982 was the mandate of Special Rapporteur on extrajudicial, summary, and arbitrary executions.

In practice, most of the case law concerns the central issues of deprivation of life by state authorities, either by the maintenance of law and public order or by recourse to the death penalty. This will, accordingly, be the principal focus of what follows.

3.1 SOURCES

Article 6 ICCPR, Article 4 ACHR, and Article 4 ACHPR all guarantee the right not to be 'arbitrarily deprived of life'.[50] In contrast, Article 2 ECHR prohibits any intentional deprivation of life except for certain, listed purposes. In the practice of other treaty bodies, those purposes would take the killing out of the designation of 'arbitrary'. All these articles make, in various ways, provision for the death penalty. The ICCPR-OP2, the Sixth and Thirteenth Protocols to the ECHR, and the Second Protocol to the ACHR all contemplate abolition of the death penalty. The main 'soft law' sources protecting the right to life are the UN Basic Principles on the Use of Force and Firearms by Law Enforcement Officials (1990), the UN Principles on the Effective Prevention and Investigation of Extra-legal, Arbitrary and Summary Executions (1989), and the UN Economic and Social Council's Safeguards guaranteeing protection of the rights of those facing the death penalty (ECOSOC Safeguards) (1984).

3.2 LEGAL STATUS

There can be little doubt that the right to life is a rule of customary international law, even if it has not received the same legislative attention, for example by way of treaty-making, as the prohibition of torture. This is even suggested in the specific wording of the language of Article 6(1) ICCPR, which speaks of the 'inherent right to life'. Less certain is whether it is a rule of *jus cogens*. It has not had the same degree of case law so asserting as the prohibition of torture, but then the occasion has not arisen. It is

---

[50] ACHPR, Art 4 reads: 'Human beings are inviolable. Every human being is entitled to respect for his life and the integrity of his person. No one may be arbitrarily deprived of this right.'

true that the core content of the rule has not been defined with the same precision. Nevertheless, because of its importance, it is non-derogable in those treaties that contemplate derogations.[51] Murder, in the context of a widespread or systematic attack against a civilian population, is a crime against humanity and, together with wilful killing, a war crime. The prohibition of murder is treated as a *jus cogens* rule in the American Law Institute's Restatement of US Foreign Relations Law.[52] This core content of the right cannot seriously be contested as being *jus cogens*, as must the prohibition of the death penalty without basic fair trial standards; so, unnecessary and disproportionate killings deserve to fall into the same category.

3.3 SCOPE: BEGINNING AND END OF LIFE

When does life begin? If, as according to Article 4 ACHR, life is protected 'in general, from the moment of conception', then state-tolerated abortion could be held to violate the right. In practice, only one case is believed to have dealt with the merits of the issue so far, and no violation was found. This was despite the fact that the Inter-American Commission on Human Rights had recourse to, though was not applying, the ACHR.[53]

Euthanasia and assisted suicide, both illegal in many states, but permitted in some, also raise questions. On the one hand, a genuine right (to life) cannot comfortably be considered to be not only an entitlement but also an obligation imposed on the rightholder. However, this did not deter the European Court of Human Rights from insisting that Article 2 ECHR does not comprehend a right to die.[54] Moreover, there is an issue of human dignity and possibly degrading treatment if one is denied the option of a longed-for death just because one is no longer physically capable of killing oneself. It is troubling that the European Court has refused to accept that denial of the right to needed assistance to commit suicide infringes Article 3.[55] On the other hand, the vulnerability of many people to improper influence means that the law should be very careful to contemplate any intentional third-party involvement in a deprivation of life.

3.4 COMPONENTS

3.4.1 Protection against killings by security forces

Different bodies use different terms to describe unlawful killings by agents of public authority: 'extra-legal' or 'extrajudicial' 'killings' or 'executions'. Regardless of terminology, wherever there is intentional resort to outright killings of those considered

---

[51] ICCPR, Art 4; ECHR, Art 15; ACHR, Art 27.   [52] n 10.

[53] Case 2141, *Baby Boy Case* (USA), IACommHR Res 23/81 (6 March 1981). See also *KL v Peru*, CCPR/ C/85/D/1153/2003 (22 November 2005) para 6.3 (distress caused by refusal of medical authorities to carry out an apparently legal therapeutic abortion violates Art 7 ICCPR).

[54] *Pretty v UK* (2002) 35 EHRR 1, paras 39–41.

[55] Ibid, paras 54–6. Compare the more nuanced approach in the HRC, Concluding Observations: the Netherlands, CCPR/CO/72/NET (27 August 2001) para 5; CCPR/C/NLD/CO/4 (11 August 2009) para 7.

undesirable, be they street children, political opponents, or suspected organized criminals, this is clearly murder by any definition and is at the core of the prohibition of arbitrary deprivation of life.

The central question is what other killings fall into this category. Here, guidance may be sought from the deprivations of life not regarded as contravening Article 2 ECHR, which include those resulting 'from the use of force which is no more than absolutely necessary: (a) in defence of any person from unlawful violence; (b) in order to effect a lawful arrest or to prevent the escape of a person lawfully detained; (c) in action lawfully taken for the purpose of quelling a riot or insurrection.'

It is generally accepted that law enforcement measures must conform to the principles of necessity and proportionality. The Article 2 ECHR limitation of the force to the minimum necessary clearly meets the *necessity* principle, requiring that the means used is no more than necessary to achieve the objective. Less reassuringly, the text of Article 2 does not guarantee the test of *proportionality*; it does not explicitly require the level of force to be no more than the harm to be avoided. Clearly, the use of lethal force could be the only way to stop a pub brawl, or to prevent the escape of someone imprisoned for contempt of court, but it would evidently be disproportionate.

The UN Basic Principles on the Use of Force and Firearms come to our assistance here. Principle 9 reads:

Law enforcement officials shall not use firearms against persons except in self-defence or defence of others against the imminent threat of death or serious injury, to prevent the perpetration of a particularly serious crime involving grave threat to life, to arrest a person presenting such a danger and resisting their authority, or to prevent his or her escape, and only when less extreme means are insufficient to achieve these objectives. In any event the intentional lethal use of firearms may only be made when strictly unavoidable in order to protect life.

It is clear from this text that the principle of proportionality is strictly drawn. Not only may *potentially* lethal force be used solely to protect life and limb from *imminent* threat, but *intentional* lethal force may only be used to protect life. Principles 14 and 16 reaffirm this standard in respect of dispersal of unlawful, violent assemblies, and avoidance of escape from custody, respectively.

The practice of treaty bodies is consistent with the Principles. An early example of the principle of necessity is found in the Human Rights Committee case of *Guerrero v Colombia*, where the state was found to have violated Article 6 ICCPR as the police had waited in a location inhabited by suspected terrorists and, on their arrival, shot them without making any attempt to arrest them.[56] An even more stringent application of the principle is found in the case of *McCann and others v UK* before the European Court of Human Rights. British security personnel summarily killed IRA members avowedly on 'mission' to detonate a bomb in a crowded place in Gibraltar. The security personnel

---

[56] CCPR/C/15/D/45/1979 (31 March 1982). For reckless lethal attacks on premises violating the right to life, see *Gül v Turkey* (2002) 34 EHRR 435, paras 79–83; *Zambrano Vélez and others v Ecuador*, IACtHR Series C No 166 (4 July 2007) para 108.

had been briefed to believe that the victims were armed, that there was a bomb in their car, and that they could detonate it from a remote control device on their person. In fact it turned out that they were not armed, there was no bomb in the car, nor did they have a detonator. The Court found that the UK had violated Article 2 ECHR by failing to take various planning measures that could have avoided the fatal outcome.[57]

The clearest example of the proportionality principle is found in the case of *Nachova and others v Bulgaria*. Invoking the UN Basic Principles, the European Court found that 'recourse to potentially deadly force cannot be considered as "absolutely necessary" where it is known that the person to be arrested poses no threat to life or limb and is not suspected of having committed a violent offence'.[58] Here the Court is evidently using the language of necessity in Article 2 to embrace proportionality. In the case of *Detention Centre of Catia* in which Venezuelan prison guards fired indiscriminately into prisoners they suspected of being involved in an escape, the Inter-American Court of Human Rights applied the principles of necessity and proportionality, finding that 'the actions of the security forces ... were neither proportionate to the existing threat of danger, nor strictly necessary to keep the peace and order in the Detention Centre of Catia'.[59]

3.4.2 Protection against the death penalty

Inconsistent as it may seem, while international law apparently rules out corporal punishment as a cruel, inhuman, or degrading punishment—or even torture—it has not yet done so in respect of the death penalty. While the framers of the UDHR may have contemplated that at some time international law would reach that point, it had not then and still has not. This is because international law is not a system that operates by majority rule. State practice is a key element and as long as a substantial minority of states maintain the death penalty—especially states as influential as China, India, and the USA—international law will have to reflect that reality.

All the human rights treaty norms guaranteeing the right to life, except Article 4 ACHPR, contemplate the possibility of the death penalty. Since any treaty provision has to be interpreted in the context of the treaty as a whole, this means that it is not possible to interpret the provisions on treatment of prisoners without reference to those on the right to life. The Human Rights Committee has indeed made the point that, but for the death penalty provisions of Article 6 ICCPR, it would find the death penalty to violate Article 7.[60]

Nevertheless, the last quarter of the twentieth century witnessed a trend towards abolition that is steady and sustained. The fact that the community of states was willing to adopt abolitionist protocols to human rights treaties makes it increasingly difficult for abolitionist states to deny that the death penalty is a human rights issue. Promoting ratification of the protocols has also become a focus of abolitionist campaigning

---

[57] (1996) 21 EHRR 97.   [58] (2006) 42 EHRR 43, paras 71–4, 96, 107.
[59] *Montero-Aranguren and others (Detention Centre of Catia) v Venezuela*, IACtHR Series C No 150 (5 July 2006) paras 69–74.   [60] *Ng v Canada*, n 43, para 16.2.

activities. Even before the adoption of the ICCPR-OP2, the Human Rights Committee had felt that the actual language of Article 6 preserving the death penalty permitted it to conclude that 'all measures of abolition should be considered as progress in the enjoyment of the right to life'.[61] Meanwhile, at the political level, the UN General Assembly long ago accepted that the objective should be 'progressive restriction' of the number of offences to which the punishment applies 'with a view to the desirability of abolishing this punishment in all countries'.[62] It has, more recently, called on states that retain the death penalty to adopt moratoria on its use.[63]

As to the abolitionist protocols themselves, all but one envisage commitments that permit states to carve out an exception for wartime situations (few have done so in fact). The exception is Protocol 13 to the ECHR, adopted precisely to fill this gap left by Protocol 6. It is worth noting that, insofar as a commitment to adherence at least to Protocol 6 is a condition of membership of the Council of Europe, the 47-country area of Europe, from the Atlantic to the Urals, is now effectively a death-penalty-free zone.[64]

If the death penalty as such remains a permissible exception to the right to life, it is clear that states do not have a free hand to resort to it at will. There is a range of far-reaching substantive, procedural, and personal limitations that have to be respected.

Substantive limitations

The most important substantive limitation is that of Article 6(2) ICCPR and Article 4(2) ACHR, requiring that imposition of the death penalty be limited to 'the most serious crimes'. The prohibition of arbitrary deprivation of the right to life of Article 4 ACHPR may be expected to be understood at least as strictly as the ICCPR and ACHR provisions. The first paragraph of the ECOSOC Safeguards endorses the notion of 'the most serious crimes'.

The treaty provisions offer no definition of what elements would place a crime among the most serious. The ECOSOC Safeguards are helpful here. For them, the scope of the term 'should not go beyond intentional crimes with lethal or other extremely grave consequences'.[65] The Human Rights Committee has found a mandatory death penalty for armed robbery where death did *not* result to contravene Article 6(2) ICCPR.[66] It has subsequently also found the mandatory death penalty, even in murder cases, to violate Article 6(1).[67] It is not clear whether it does so by virtue of its not being covered by Article 6(2) because of its non-serious nature. The latter is the position taken by the Inter-American Court of Human Rights.[68] This would mean that not even all murder

---

[61] HRC, General Comment 6, n 48, para 6.   [62] GA Res 2857 (XXVI) (20 December 1971).
[63] GA Res 62/149 (18 December 2007) and 63/168 (18 December 2008).
[64] The Russian Federation, despite its commitment, has not yet ratified Protocol 6 but has implemented a formal moratorium. On 2 March 2010, the European Court of Human Rights concluded that the death penalty is no longer permitted, even under Article 2 ECHR. *Al-Saadoon and Mufdhi v UK*, App no 61498/2008, Press Release, 2 March 2010.   [65] Para 1.
[66] *Lubuto v Zambia*, CCPR/C/55/D/390/1990/Rev.1 (30 June 1994) para 7.2.
[67] *Thompson v St Vincent and the Grenadines*, CCPR/C/70/D/806/1998 (18 October 2000) para 8.2.
[68] *Hilaire, Constantine and Benjamin et al. v Trinidad and Tobago*, IACtHR Series C No 94 (21 June 2002) paras 106–7.

would be sufficiently serious to fall within the category. It is worth noting that the same court also found the 'simple crime of kidnapping' to fall outside the notion of 'most serious' and so a death penalty imposed for it violated Article 4 ACHR.[69]

Further substantive limitations following from Articles 6(2) and 15 ICCPR are that both the crime and the prescribed punishment must be non-retroactive, that is, provided by law at the time of the commission of the acts in question. In addition, under Article 4(2) ACHR, the death penalty may not be extended to crimes to which it does not 'presently' apply, while Article 4(3) ACHR prohibits reintroduction in states that have abolished it. It is also possible to interpret Article 6(2) ICCPR in the same way. Since it refers to 'countries which have not abolished the death penalty', it may be logical to infer that the privilege is not available to countries that *have* abolished the penalty. Article 4(4) ACHR also prohibits the use of the death penalty for 'political offenses or related common crimes'.

Procedural limitations

The main procedural limitation is that the death penalty may only be imposed after a fair trial, as provided for under Article 14 ICCPR, including a right of appeal. While this is not stated in Article 6 ICCPR directly, Article 6(2) provides that the death penalty must not be contrary to the provisions of the Covenant. The General Assembly has called on all states to respect 'as a minimum' Articles 6, 14, and 15.[70] The Human Rights Committee has made clear its view that this means that, not only is Article 6 non-derogable, but so is Article 14 when it comes to the application of the death penalty.[71]

A few of the many examples of findings of a violation of Article 6 because of a violation of Article 14 in death penalty cases are: a trial in absentia ending in a death sentence in the absence of any effective attempt to notify the person accused;[72] a murder trial after the accused had pleaded guilty to manslaughter in a case involving the same incident;[73] and deficient or non-existent legal representation.[74] The right of a foreign national to consular assistance may also fall within Article 14. This was the opinion of the Inter-American Court of Human Rights applying the comparable Article 4 ACHR and also referring to Article 14 ICCPR.[75]

Remarkably, despite the absence of a verbal linkage in the ECHR and the ACHPR, the European Court of Human Rights and the African Commission on Human and Peoples' Rights have read the respective fair trial provisions together with the right to life provisions. So, in the case of Abdullah Öcalan, the leader of the Turkish PKK movement, the European Court held that implementation of the death penalty would

---

[69] *Raxcacó-Reyes*, n 36, paras 67–72.

[70] GA Res 35/172 (15 December 1980); this was the first of several resolutions to the same effect.

[71] HRC, General Comment 29, n 9, para 15.

[72] *Mbenge et al. v Zaire*, CCPR/C/18/D/16/1977 (25 March 1983) paras 14(1)–(2) and 17.

[73] *Richards v Jamaica*, CCPR/C/59/D/535/1993/Rev.1 (29 April 1997) paras 7.2, 7.5.

[74] eg *LaVende v Trinidad and Tobago*, CCPR/C/61/D/554/1993 (17 November 1997) para 5.8; *Aliev v Ukraine*, CCPR/C/78/D/781/1997 (7 August 2003) para 7.3; *Saidova v Tajikistan*, CCPR/C/81/D/964/2001 (8 July 2004) para 68; *Aliboeva v Tajikistan*, CCPR/C/85/D/985/2001 (18 October 2005) para 6.4.

[75] Advisory Opinion OC-16/99, *The Right to Information on Consular Assistance in the Framework of Guarantees of the Due Process of Law*, IACtHR Series A No 16 (1 October 1999) paras 68–87.

be impermissible under Article 2 ECHR as he had not received a fair trial according to Article 6: Öcalan had been held in incommunicado detention for ten days, then allowed only two one-hour supervised meetings per week with his lawyers before his trial that took place in a special security court that initially included a military judge.[76] Similarly, the African Commission found a violation of Article 4 ACHPR in respect of the execution of celebrated playwright Ken Saro-Wiwa after a summary trial for murder by a special court whose members were chosen by the executive and without right of appeal that involved multiple violations of the fair trial guarantee of Article 7.[77]

The right of appeal is explicitly guaranteed by Article 14(5) ICCPR, so its denial in death penalty cases is a violation not only of that provision but also of Article 6.[78] The ECOSOC Safeguards contain the same guarantee.[79] The right has to be effective, so both the trial court and an appeal court must provide a written judgment where that is a condition for further appeal.[80] In addition, Article 6(4) ICCPR and Article 4(6) ACHR require the possibility of submitting a clemency petition. The Human Rights Committee has found violations in cases where executions took place while appellate or clemency procedures were underway.[81]

A further procedural dimension is that the process in which the death penalty is carried out must cause the minimum possible suffering if it is not to violate the prohibition of ill-treatment. Thus, the Human Rights Committee held that execution by gas asphyxiation was incompatible with Article 7 ICCPR.[82] The method of execution is not the only relevant factor. The leading European Court of Human Rights case, *Soering v UK*, found that sending a young German man to face death row conditions in Virginia for six to eight years, when he could be tried in (abolitionist) Germany, would violate Article 3 ECHR.[83] Finally, where the death penalty is shrouded in secrecy, close family members of the executed person can be victims of inhuman treatment. This has been the case with the practice that was common in the former Soviet Union of treating the date of execution and place of burial as a state secret, thus causing an unacceptable 'state of uncertainty and mental distress' to family members.[84]

Personal limitations

The main personal limitation on the application of the death penalty is that, under Article 6(5) ICCPR, Article 4(5) ACHR, and Article 37 Convention on the Rights of the Child, it may not be imposed on persons under 18. The Human Rights Committee has found the very imposition of a death sentence on a person under 18 at the time of the offence to violate the ICCPR, despite later commutation of the sentence.[85]

---

[76] *Öcalan v Turkey* (2005) 41 EHRR 985, para 166.

[77] *International Pen et al. v Nigeria*, Communication nos 137/94, 154/96, and 161/97.

[78] *Mansaraj et al. v Sierra Leone*, CCPR/C/72/D/841/1998 (16 July 2001) paras 5.6 and 6.2.

[79] Para 6.   [80] *Pratt and Morgan v Jamaica*, CCPR/C/35/D/210/1986 (6 April 1989) paras 13.5, 14(b).

[81] *Ashby v Trinidad and Tobago*, CCPR/C/74/D/580/1994 (19 April 2002) para 10.8; *Chikunova v Uzbekistan*, CCPR/C/89/D/1043/2002 (16 March 2007) para 7.6.   [82] *Ng v Canada*, n 43, para 16.4.

[83] n 43, paras 106–11.   [84] *Lyashkevich v Belarus*, CCPR/C/77/D/887/1999 (24 April 2003) para 9.2.

[85] *Johnson, Clive v Jamaica*, CCPR/C/64/D/592/1994 (25 November 1998) para 10.3.

According to Article 6(5) ICCPR, Article 4(5) ACHR, and paragraph 3 ECOSOC Safeguards, the death penalty may also not be carried out on pregnant women and, according to the ECOSOC Safeguards, recent mothers. The ECOSOC Safeguards also immunize 'persons who have become insane', and the Human Rights Committee has decided that the reading of a death warrant for the execution of a mentally incompetent person was a violation of Article 7 ICCPR.[86] Under Article 4(5) ACHR, states parties may not execute persons over 70 at the time of the offence.

3.5 TYPES OF OBLIGATION

As with the prohibition of torture and ill-treatment, the right not to be arbitrarily deprived of life is primarily a negative obligation. To the extent that there is no treaty obligation prohibiting the use of the death penalty, states are simply obliged to refrain from having recourse to it when not respecting the legal limitations that apply to it. Other deprivations of life involving the intentional killing of people by public authorities are to be avoided, if they do not meet the criteria of necessity or proportionality considered above.

It is notable that three of the provisions guaranteeing the right to life (Article 6(1) ICCPR, Article 2(1) ECHR, and Article 4(1) ACHR) stipulate that the right 'shall be protected by law'. Such language has the connotation of positive obligation. It clearly lends itself to an interpretation, confirmed by practice, that states must investigate apparent unlawful killings. This is the thrust of the UN Principles on the Effective Prevention and Investigation of Extra-legal, Arbitrary and Summary Executions.

Thus, there have been numerous findings of state violations of the right to life because of the absence of an effective investigation, even when the killing could not be found on the evidence to be firmly attributable to the state. The European Court of Human Rights has found violations where the state was unable to show serious activity by investigating prosecutors,[87] or where the prosecutors confined themselves to interviewing the relevant security units involved without interviewing relevant non-official witnesses,[88] or where they made no effort to identify the unit responsible.[89] The UK coroners' inquest system was also found wanting in a series of Northern Ireland cases in which there was an alleged 'shoot-to-kill' policy by the security forces. This was because the inquiry could not compel the presence

---

[86] *RS v Trinidad and Tobago*, CCPR/C/74/D/684/1996 (2 April 2002) para 7.2.

[87] *Kaya v Turkey* (1999) 28 EHRR 1, paras 86–92.

[88] *Musayev and others v Russia*, App nos 57941/00, 58699/00, and 60403/00, Judgment of 26 July 2007, para 162.

[89] *Khashiyev and Akayeva v Russia*, App nos 57942/00 and 57945/00, Judgment of 24 February 2005, para 158.

of police and other security force witnesses, could not make a finding of 'unlawful killing', and was neither prompt nor expeditious.[90]

In the case of *Amirov v Russian Federation*, the Human Rights Committee found a failure of effective investigation and so a violation of Article 6 ICCPR, where prosecutors opened and closed the investigation into the rape and murder of a woman in the Chechen Republic, numerous times, but without securing the testimony of federal agents who had seen the body at the time it was found.[91] The UN Principles and statements by treaty bodies are clear in understanding that there is an obligation on states to prosecute when an investigation determines that individuals are responsible for an unlawful killing. For example, the failure to do this was part of the violation in *Amirov*.[92]

As with the prohibition of ill-treatment, exposing someone to the threat of a violation of the right to life is itself a violation of the prohibition or ill-treatment, as well as presumably of the right to life. The cases of *Soering* and *Ng* already discussed are the leading cases on the matter.[93]

There is also an evident obligation to protect people from death from third parties. But, as with the prohibition of torture, it is an obligation of means, not of result. The question will always be: did the state exercise 'due diligence' when apprised of circumstances that may have suggested that a person's life required protection? While finally not finding a violation, the European Court of Human Rights essentially followed this approach in respect of a schoolmaster who stalked a former student and then killed her. The Court held that the stalking itself did not suggest likely lethal consequences, but it was clear that if there had been evidence of impending harm, the state would have violated Article 2 ECHR.[94] Also, if it is difficult to justify rules permitting euthanasia and assisted suicide, it is because of the positive obligation on states to protect life and the need to avoid people being improperly influenced to seek or accept aid in terminating their lives.

3.6 RELATIONSHIP WITH OTHER HUMAN RIGHTS

The links with the prohibition of torture and ill-treatment have already been discussed. An additional dimension here is the need even for the death penalty to avoid unnecessary suffering. The connection with the right to a fair trial is of central importance as regards the lawfulness (or otherwise) of the death penalty.

There is also a connection with the notion of security of person, as suggested by Article 3 UDHR. Although the European Court of Human Rights has not been willing

---

[90] *Jordan v UK* (2003) 37 EHRR 2, para 142; *Kelly and others v UK*, App no 30054/96, Judgment of 4 May 2001, para 136; *McKerr v UK* (2002) 34 EHRR 20, para 157; *Shanagan v UK*, App no 37715/97, Judgment of 4 May 2001, para 122.   [91] CCPR/C/95/D/1447/2006 (2 April 2009) para 11.4.

[92] Ibid.

[93] n 43. See also *Judge v Canada*, CCPR/C/78/D/829/1998 (20 October 2003) para 6.1 (holding that an abolitionist state that sends someone to another country to face the death penalty cannot benefit from the exception of Art 6(2) ICCPR for states that have not abolished the death penalty and so violates Art 6(1)).

[94] *Osman v UK* (1998) 29 EHRR 245, paras 121–2.

to give content to the idea outside the context of deprivation of liberty, the Human Rights Committee has done so. For example, failure to give adequate protection to a person receiving death threats has been found to violate the Article 9 ICCPR guarantee of security of person.[95] To the uncertain extent that the right to life may be engaged in situations of economic and social deprivation, there is a connection with the corresponding economic and social rights.

4 CONCLUSION

The prohibition of torture and ill-treatment and the right to life are both situated by the language of the International Bill of Human Rights and other international instruments as directly based on the concept of human dignity, which inspires the whole corpus of human rights law, and as at the core of the right to personal integrity.

The understanding of the scope of the prohibition of torture and ill-treatment is capable of much elasticity and was indeed drafted in language intended to avoid rigid definitions of what might technically be called torture. Nevertheless, in the light of sustained attention to the problem of torture, notably of people deprived of liberty, there has been a focus on definitions of that concept, the UNCAT definition being the most influential. On the key issue of what the borderline may be between torture and other ill-treatment, this definition seems to avoid the approach of the European Court of Human Rights, according to which torture is seen as requiring even greater pain or suffering than that already required for the treatment to be considered inhuman. Rather, it is the purpose of the treatment (for example, obtaining information or confessions) that marks the treatment out as being torture or not. Also, the mental form of torture as exemplified by the Orwellian rats should not be downplayed. While a few states retain corporal punishment in their legislation and apply it in practice, the consistent view of human rights bodies has been to find such punishment to be cruel, inhuman, or degrading. Indeed, the Inter-American Court of Human Rights has found a manifestation of it to be torture.

As to the right to life, the aspects that have received most attention have been those relating to the limits on lethal force that can be used in the maintenance of law and public order and to the applicability of the death penalty. In the absence of authoritative definitions in treaties, international 'soft law' standards and the practice of human rights bodies have provided the principal guidance, especially in the area of recourse to lethal force. The crucial tests of whether a particular use of such force is lawful are those of necessity and proportionality. That is, the force must not only be the least harmful necessary to achieve a legitimate law enforcement objective, it

---

[95] Compare *Delgado Páez v Colombia*, CCPR/C/39/D/195/1985 (12 July 1990) paras 5.5, 5.6, 6 with *Bozano v France* (1987) 9 EHRR 297, para 53.

must furthermore not exceed the harm to be avoided by its use. The right to life does not as yet rule out recourse to the death penalty. However, many states are parties to protocols to human rights treaties that prohibit the death penalty. The other states are bound to respect a number of substantive limitations (notably, the death penalty must be used only for the most serious crimes), procedural limitations (notably, the rules concerning the rights to a fair trial, to appeal, and to seek clemency), and personal limitations (notably, the lower age limit of 18).

There is no serious doubting that the prohibition of torture is a rule of *jus cogens*. There is persuasive authority suggesting this also applies to other prohibited ill-treatment. While there is not as much explicit evidence in respect of the right to life (apart from with regard to outright official murder), the better view is that its status as 'the supreme human right' that, like the prohibition of torture and ill-treatment, is non-derogable must put it on a par with that prohibition.

FURTHER READING

EVANS and MORGAN, *Preventing Torture: A Study of the European Convention for the Prevention of Torture and Inhuman or Degrading Treatment or Punishment* (Oxford University Press, 1998).

GINBAR, *Why Not Torture Terrorists? Moral, Practical, and Legal Aspects of the 'Ticking Bomb' Justification for Torture* (Oxford University Press, 2008).

HOOD and HOYLE, *The Death Penalty: A Worldwide Perspective* (Oxford University Press, 2008).

INGELSE, *The UN Committee against Torture: An Assessment* (Kluwer Academic Publishers, 2001).

MELZER, *Targeted Killing in International Law* (Oxford University Press, 2008).

NOWAK and McARTHUR, *The United Nations Convention against Torture: A Commentary* (Oxford University Press, 2008).

RODLEY and POLLARD, *The Treatment of Prisoners under International Law* (Oxford University Press, 2009).

SCHABAS, *The Abolition of the Death Penalty in International Law* (Cambridge University Press, 2002).

USEFUL WEBSITES

Association for the Prevention of Torture: <http://www.apt.ch>

Amnesty International: <http://www.amnesty.org>

European Committee for the Prevention of Torture and Inhuman or Degrading Treatment or Punishment: <http://www.cpt.coe.int/en/>

Hands Off Cain: <http://www.handsoffcain.info>

Human Rights Watch: <http://www.hrw.org>

UN Special Rapporteur on Torture: <http:www2.ohchr.org/english/issues/torture/
rapporteur/index.htm>

UN Committee against Torture: <http://www2.ohchr.org/english/bodies/cat/index.htm>

UN Sub-Committee on Prevention of Torture: <http://www2.ohchr.org/english/bodies/
cat/opcat/index.htm>

11

ADEQUATE STANDARD OF LIVING

Asbjørn Eide

SUMMARY

This chapter considers the right to an adequate standard of living and its components, namely, the rights to food, housing, and health. These rights are, in whole or in part, contained in principal international and regional human rights instruments, which impose an obligation on states to take a range of measures to ensure everyone can enjoy them. A particular challenge is to ensure the right to an adequate standard of living to those groups of people who have special needs or are particularly vulnerable. The chapter explores the relationship between the right to an adequate standard of living and other human rights and highlights the need for international action in the progressive implementation of the right.

1 INTRODUCTION

The right to an adequate standard of living was first introduced into international human rights law through the Universal Declaration of Human Rights (UDHR), Article 25(1) of which provides:

Everyone has the right to a standard of living adequate for the health and well-being of himself and his family, including food, clothing, housing and medical care and necessary social services, and the right to security in the event of unemployment, sickness, disability, widowhood, old age or other lack of livelihood in circumstances beyond his control.

Among the main inspirations for this provision was US President Franklin D Roosevelt's 'Four Freedoms' address to Congress in 1941.[1] In that speech, Roosevelt referred to four fundamental human freedoms: freedom of speech, freedom of

[1] On the origin of Roosevelt's concern with freedom from want, see McGovern, *The Third Freedom: Ending Hunger in Our Time* (Simon & Schuster, 2001).

religion, *freedom from want*, and freedom from fear. The inspirational legacy of that speech is expressly recognized in the preamble to the UDHR:

Whereas disregard and contempt for human rights have resulted in barbarous acts which have outraged the conscience of mankind, *and the advent of a world in which human beings shall enjoy freedom of speech and belief and freedom from fear and want has been proclaimed as the highest aspiration of the common people.*[2]

Article 25 UDHR can also be seen as an elaboration of Article 1 UDHR, which states that 'All human beings are born free and equal in dignity and rights. They are endowed with reason and conscience and should act towards one another in a spirit of brotherhood.' A life in dignity requires an adequate standard of living. Human rights are based on the assumption that individuals are not only rational but also have a social conscience, and are therefore concerned with the dignity of their fellow human beings. Such concern has to be put into practice through appropriate state implementation of human rights as public goods of society as a whole. The right to an adequate standard of living is also closely linked to Article 22 UDHR, which states that everyone is entitled to the realization of economic, social, and cultural rights indispensable for their dignity and the free development of their personality, and guarantees a right to social security.

This chapter starts, in Section 2, with an analysis of the meaning and key features of the right to an adequate standard of living. Section 3 examines the normative content of this right and its components, namely, the rights to food, housing, and health. The right to water is a necessary component of each of these rights, and is briefly addressed under the right to food. Section 4 explores the difficulties and special obligations in ensuring the right to an adequate standard of living to particular groups of people. Section 5 addresses the relationship between the right to an adequate standard of living and other human rights. Section 6 examines the question of progressive implementation of this right. Section 7 addresses the justiciability of the right to an adequate standard of living and the need for international action in its implementation.

2 MEANING AND FEATURES

Article 25 UDHR has been supplemented with further guarantees of an adequate standard of living, including Article 11 of the International Covenant on Economic, Social and Cultural Rights (ICESCR) and Article 27 of the Convention on the Rights of the Child (CRC). None of these instruments precisely define the term 'adequate standard of living', but it can to some extent be understood from the context. Article 25 UDHR refers to 'a standard of living adequate for the health and well-being of himself and of his family, including food, clothing, housing and medical care and necessary social services'. According to Article 11 ICESCR, an adequate standard of

---

2 UDHR, second preambular para (emphasis added).

living includes 'adequate food, clothing and housing'. In addition, under Article 12 of the same covenant, states parties have recognized the right of everyone to the highest attainable standard of health. The standard of living guaranteed to every child by Article 27 CRC is one 'adequate for the child's physical, mental, spiritual, moral and social development'.

While the basic necessities referred to in these instruments include food, clothing, housing, and healthcare, an adequate standard of living requires more than simply these. Precisely how much more is required cannot be stated in general terms, but will depend on the conditions in the society concerned. The essential point is that everyone should be able, without shame and without unreasonable obstacles, to be a full participant in ordinary, everyday interaction with other people. In other words, everyone should be able to enjoy their basic needs under conditions of dignity. No one should have to live under conditions whereby the only way to satisfy their needs is by degrading or depriving themselves of their basic freedoms, such as through begging, prostitution, or bonded labour. In purely economic terms, an adequate standard of living implies a living above the poverty line of the society concerned, which according to the World Bank comprises two elements: 'The expenditure necessary to buy a minimum standard of nutrition and other basic necessities and a further amount that varies from country to country, reflecting the cost of participating in the everyday life of society'.[3]

2.1 THE SUBSIDIARITY PRINCIPLE

The enjoyment of the right to an adequate standard of living depends on a combination of efforts by adult individuals to take care of their own needs and those of their dependants, and measures taken by the state to facilitate everyone's enjoyment of the right. To some extent, the obligations of the state are subsidiary to the responsibility of the individual: state responsibility only comes into play when individuals cannot manage by themselves to secure their own or their dependants' standard of living. The responsibility of the international community is of an even more subsidiary nature, namely to encourage and assist states in implementing their obligations, to criticize them if they fail to do so, and to assist states whose resources are too limited to fulfil their obligations under international human rights law.

Thus individuals are expected, wherever possible through their own efforts and through the exploitation of their own resources, to find ways to ensure the satisfaction of their needs. Use of one's resources, however, presupposes that the person has resources that can be used—typically land, other capital, or labour. Access to food and housing, for example, depends, first, on the assets held by the individual (ownership of land or capital) or his or her rights to common resources (for example fishing grounds). Second, it depends on income from work (in the formal or informal sector, whether employed by others or self-employed). Third, it may depend on income in the form of social security. For most children, their standard of living depends on that of

---

[3] World Bank, *World Development Report 1990* (OUP, 1990) 26.

their parents. This has also often been the case for women, who may be dependent on their family or husband, though the situation is increasingly changing in favour of greater economic autonomy of women.

2.2 STATE OBLIGATIONS

The subsidiary nature of state obligations varies greatly, depending on the differences in the level of assistance needed by individuals, the resources at the disposal of the state, and the different components of the right. To illustrate: in most societies there is a considerable difference between the role played by the state regarding the realization of the right to food or to housing, on the one hand, and the realization of the right to health, on the other hand. In economic terms, food and housing are mainly considered to be private goods, whereas healthcare is primarily seen as a public good and therefore a duty of the state. In spite of these differences, states do have obligations under international human rights law in regard to all these rights, although the content of the obligations varies from one to the other.[4]

Under the right to an adequate standard of living, states must, first, *respect* the individual's freedom to take the necessary action and use the necessary resources, alone or in association with others. It is in regard to the latter that collective or group rights become important: resources belonging to a collective of persons, such as an indigenous population, must be respected if such a population is to satisfy its needs through their use. Similarly, the rights of peoples to exercise permanent sovereignty over their natural resources may be essential for them to be able, through their own collective efforts, to satisfy their needs.

Second, states have an obligation to *protect* individuals' freedom of action and use of resources necessary to secure their basic needs. For example, states may be required to provide protection against fraud, unethical behaviour in trade and contractual relations, the marketing of dangerous products, and the dumping of hazardous waste. This is probably the most important aspect of the rights to food, housing, and water, requiring the state to act not as provider but protector. This function is similar to the obligation of states to protect civil and political rights, such as the right to life or freedom from slavery, from violation by third parties.

Third, states have, as a last resort, the obligation to *fulfil* everyone's right to an adequate standard of living—that is, to function as the provider. This may take two forms. First, states may have to *facilitate* people's access to and utilization of resources and means to ensure their livelihood if they lack the opportunity to do so themselves. Second, states may have to directly *provide* means and resources for the satisfaction of basic needs (in the form of direct aid or social security) when no other possibility exists. The direct provision of resources can also be seen as a separate, fourth, level of state obligations. Direct provision may become necessary during periods of

---

[4] See Eide, 'State Obligations Revisited' in Barth Eide and Kracht (eds), *Food and Human Rights in Development, Vol I* (Intersentia, 2007) 137.

widespread unemployment (such as during a recession), sudden crises or disasters, or with regard to the disadvantaged, the elderly, or others who have been marginalized.

2.3 EQUALITY AND NON-DISCRIMINATION AS AN OVERARCHING PRINCIPLE

The duty of states to ensure equality and non-discrimination runs through all human rights instruments as a core principle and is essential to the enjoyment of economic, social, and cultural rights, including the right to an adequate standard of living. Article 2(2) ICESCR obliges states parties 'to guarantee that the rights enunciated in the present Covenant will be exercised without discrimination of any kind as to race, colour, sex, language, religion, political or other opinion, national or social origin, property, birth or other status'. More specifically, Article 3 requires states to ensure the equal right of men and women to enjoy all Covenant rights. The obligations arising from the principle of equality and non-discrimination have been elaborated by the Committee on Economic, Social and Cultural Rights in its General Comment 20, adopted in May 2009. The Committee has made it clear that states must eliminate formal and substantive, as well as direct and indirect, discrimination.[5] The Committee has also elaborated the meaning of equality and non-discrimination in the context of specific Covenant rights, including the rights to housing,[6] food,[7] health,[8] and water.[9]

3 NORMATIVE CONTENT

This section explains the different elements of the right to an adequate standard of living, namely the rights to food, housing, and health. The main legal sources and different components of each of these rights are considered and challenges to their realization set out.

3.1 THE RIGHT TO FOOD

At the core of the right to an adequate standard of living is the right to food. While human beings do not live by bread alone, without food there is no life, and with the wrong food, life is shorter and more prone to ill-health. Access to adequate food and to food security has been a dominant concern in the evolution of civilizations and in the formation of states. Neglect or violation of the right to food is probably the most serious global human rights issue in terms of the number of people whose rights are

---

[5] See Chapter 9, above, for an explanation of these concepts.

[6] CESCR, General Comment 4, HRI/GEN/1/Rev.9 (Vol I) 11; General Comment 7, HRI/GEN/1/Rev.9 (Vol I) 38.   [7] CESCR, General Comment 12, HRI/GEN/1/Rev.9 (Vol I) 55.

[8] CESCR, General Comment 14, HRI/GEN/1/Rev.9 (Vol I) 78.

[9] CESCR, General Comment 15, HRI/GEN/1/Rev.9 (Vol I) 97.

not ensured. Access to water is of crucial importance for the enjoyment of all the elements of the right to an adequate standard of living, including the right to food, and is therefore also briefly dealt with in this section.

3.1.1 Sources

The guarantee of the right to food of Article 25 UDHR is further elaborated in Article 11 ICESCR. While Article 11(1) recognizes everyone's right to adequate food, Article 11(2) obliges states parties to adopt more immediate and urgent steps to ensure 'the fundamental right of everyone to be free from hunger'. The right to food is also contained in other international human rights instruments, such as the CRC (Articles 24 and 27), and regional instruments such as the Additional Protocol to the American Convention on Human Rights in the Area of Economic, Social and Cultural Rights ('Protocol of San Salvador') (Article 12). While the African Charter on Human and Peoples' Rights (ACHPR) does not contain an express reference to the right to food, the African Commission on Human and Peoples' Rights, in its decision in *SERAC v Nigeria*, has suggested that the right is implicit in the ACHPR because it is inextricably linked to human dignity and is essential for the enjoyment of other rights.[10]

3.1.2 Components and obligations

In its General Comment 12, the Committee on Economic, Social and Cultural Rights defined the right to food as follows: 'The right to adequate food is realized when every man, woman and child, alone or in community with others, has physical and economic access at all times to adequate food or means for its procurement'.[11] According to the Committee, 'adequate food' implies, first, 'the *availability* of food in a quantity and quality sufficient to satisfy the dietary needs of individuals, free from adverse substances, and acceptable within a given culture'.[12] *Availability* means that either people must be able to feed themselves directly from natural resources or well-functioning distribution and processing systems must exist; *dietary needs* implies that the diet as a whole contains all the necessary nutrients for physical and mental growth, development, and maintenance; *free from adverse substances* sets requirements for food safety; and *cultural or consumer acceptability* implies the need also to take into account perceived non nutrient-based values attached to food.[13] Second, the right to food requires 'the *accessibility* of such food in ways that are sustainable and that do not interfere with the enjoyment of other human rights',[14] encompassing both physical and economic accessibility.[15]

The legal obligations of states parties to the ICESCR under the right to food have been interpreted by the Committee in paragraph 15 of the same General Comment:

The obligation to *respect* existing access to adequate food requires States parties not to take any measures that result in preventing such access. The obligation to *protect*

---

[10] Communication No 155/96 (27 May 2002).   [11] General Comment 12, n 7, para 6.
[12] Ibid, para 8 (emphasis added).   [13] Ibid, paras 9–12.   [14] Ibid, para 8 (emphasis added).
[15] Ibid, para 13.

requires measures by the State to ensure that enterprises or individuals do not deprive individuals of their access to adequate food. The obligation to *fulfil (facilitate)* means the State must pro-actively engage in activities intended to strengthen people's access to and utilization of resources and means to ensure their livelihood, including food security. Finally, whenever an individual or group is unable, for reasons beyond their control, to enjoy the right to adequate food by the means at their disposal, States have the obligation to *fulfil (provide)* that right directly. This obligation also applies for persons who are victims of natural or other disasters.[16]

The Committee has pointed out that some of the measures required from states are of a more immediate nature, while others are more long term in character.[17] The right to food is violated when a state fails to ensure the satisfaction of, at the very least, the minimum essential level required to be free from hunger. Resource constraints do not absolve the state from responsibility; it still has to show that every effort has been made to use all the resources at its disposal in an effort to satisfy, as a matter of priority, those minimum obligations.[18] Furthermore, any discrimination in access to food, as well as to means and entitlements for its procurement, constitutes a violation of Article 11 ICESCR.[19] The Committee has emphasized that violations can occur through the direct action of states or other entities insufficiently regulated by states. Non-state actors also have responsibilities in the realization of the right to food, and states should provide an environment that facilitates implementation of these responsibilities.[20]

3.1.3 The right to water

An adequate standard of living requires access to adequate water for personal and domestic use. While the right to water is not expressly mentioned in either Article 11 or 12 ICESCR, it is clearly implied. Water is required in producing, preparing, and consuming food. Water is necessary for personal hygiene and sanitation and therefore is also an integral part of the right to health.

As with the right to food, the Committee on Economic, Social and Cultural Rights has spelled out the different components of the right to adequate water in a General Comment. According to the Committee, adequacy implies that the water supply for each person must be sufficient and continuous (*availability*), that water must be safe (*quality*), and that water and water facilities have to be within physical reach and affordable for all, without discrimination (*accessibility*).[21] The Committee has emphasized that the right to water includes freedoms, for example the right to be free from interferences such as disconnections or contamination of water supplies, as well as entitlements, such as the right to a system of water supply and management that provides equality of opportunity for people to enjoy the right to water.[22]

---

[16] Original emphases.   [17] Ibid, para 16.   [18] Ibid, para 17.   [19] Ibid, para 18.
[20] Ibid, paras 19–20.   [21] General Comment 15, n 9, para 12.   [22] Ibid, para 10.

3.1.4 Realization

Extensive international attention has been paid to the right to food since the World Food Summit, held at the invitation of the Food and Agriculture Organization of the UN (FAO) in Rome in November 1996. At that summit, governments from all parts of the world declared it unacceptable that more than 800 million people throughout the world, particularly in developing countries, did not have enough food to meet their basic nutritional needs. They recognized that this was not the result of a lack of food supplies, which in fact had increased substantially, but due to a lack of physical or economic *access* to food. Governments at the summit committed themselves to achieving food security for all and to an ongoing effort to eradicate hunger in all countries, with an immediate view to reducing the number of undernourished people to half the 1996 level no later than the year 2015.

Conditions differ widely between states, and therefore the most appropriate ways in which to implement the right to adequate food also vary considerably. Nevertheless, all states parties to the ICESCR and the CRC are obliged to take the measures required to ensure that everyone is free from hunger, and thereupon move as quickly as possible to a situation where everyone can enjoy their right to adequate food. In so doing, the different levels of state obligations discussed above should be applied, using the particular combination of measures warranted by the national situation.

Therefore, every state should have, or should develop, a national strategy to implement the right to food. The first step in any such strategy should be to map the situation for different groups and regions within the country, taking into account the differences that might exist on the basis of gender, ethnicity, or race, and between rural and urban areas. Such mapping is necessary to identify those who are food-insecure and to develop appropriate responses to food insecurity. Having identified the groups that are food-insecure, the national strategy should recreate food security for those groups and the population as a whole. When resource constraints emerge, measures should be undertaken to ensure, as a minimum, that vulnerable population groups and individuals do not face hunger. This should be achieved through social programmes, safety nets, and international assistance.

In the elaboration and implementation of national strategies for the right to food, people's informed participation is essential. Thus, states must ensure that particular conditions in different regions of the country are taken into account. Furthermore, attention must be given to all aspects of the food chain, from production to consumption. This includes paying attention to the processing of food in order to ensure food safety and the physical distribution of food in order to enable access for all. Finally, any national strategy should give particular attention to the need to prevent discrimination in access to food or resources for food.

In November 2004 the FAO Council adopted the 'Voluntary guidelines to support the progressive realization of the right to adequate food in the context of national food security'.[23] The objective of these guidelines, elaborated by an

---

[23] Available at <http://www.fao.org/docrep/meeting/009/y9825e/y9825e00.htm>.

The right to health requires states to adopt and implement measures ensuring the right of access to health facilities, goods, and services to all on a non-discriminatory basis, including to vulnerable or marginalized groups that otherwise might not have such access. This also requires the equitable distribution of all health facilities, which are often concentrated in the main urban areas, leaving rural and less important urban areas unattended.

As the Committee has pointed out, a state is in violation of its obligation to protect people's health if it fails to take all necessary measures to safeguard persons within its jurisdiction from infringements of the right to health by third parties. This may include omissions such as the failure to discourage production, marketing, and consumption of tobacco, narcotics, and other harmful substances; the failure to discourage the continued observance of harmful traditional medical or cultural practices; or the failure to enact or enforce laws to prevent the pollution of water, air, and soil by extractive and manufacturing industries.[33]

3.3.3 Realization

Realization of the right to health is closely linked to the realization of other economic and social rights. It is crucial that states ensure freedom from hunger and access for all to essential and sufficient food, which is nutritionally adequate and safe. The high level of child mortality, particularly in developing countries, is caused primarily by insufficient or inadequate food and unsafe and polluted water. Furthermore, realization of the right to health depends on access to basic shelter, housing and sanitation, and an adequate supply of safe and potable water.

The Committee on Economic, Social and Cultural Rights has urged all states parties to adopt and implement a national public health strategy and plan of action, on the basis of epidemiological evidence, addressing the health concerns of the entire population. It has pointed out that the strategy and plan of action should be devised, and periodically reviewed, on the basis of a participatory and transparent process. They should include methods, such as right-to-health indicators and benchmarks, by which progress can be monitored, and should give particular attention to all vulnerable or marginalized groups. In addition, everyone should be ensured access to essential drugs as defined under the WHO Action Programme on Essential Drugs.[34]

Of key importance is, finally, the task of ensuring reproductive, maternal (pre-natal as well as post-natal), and child healthcare. Maternal mortality is the leading cause of death among women and girls of reproductive age. It is estimated that half a million women and girls annually die from complications related to pregnancy and childbirth. If pregnancy-related injuries and disabilities are included, such as haemorrhage, infection, brain seizures, hypertension, anaemia, and obstetric fistulae, it is probable that tens of millions of women and girls are affected.

---

[33] Ibid, para 51.   [34] Ibid, para 43.

4 GROUPS OF PEOPLE

Human rights, including the right to an adequate standard of living, are equally applicable to everyone. In practice, however, it has proved necessary to give special attention to the situation of some groups of people, either because they are vulnerable, have been neglected, or have particular needs. It has been recognized that separate attention has to be given to the standard of living of different members of the family, including women and children. In addition, three particularly vulnerable groups of people will be discussed in this section: indigenous peoples, Dalits in South Asia, and the Roma in Europe.

4.1 WOMEN

International human rights bodies have recognized that women may face greater difficulties than men in reaching an adequate standard of living. The Committee on Economic, Social and Cultural Rights has therefore urged states to include in their national strategies to implement the right to food guarantees of women's full and equal access to economic resources, including the right to inheritance and owner-ship of land and other property, credit, natural resources, and appropriate technology. Such strategies should also contain measures to respect and protect self-employment and work which provides adequate remuneration to ensure a decent living for wage-earners and their families (as stipulated in Article 7(a)(ii) ICESCR).[35]

Healthcare is of particular importance for motherhood and childhood. Article 12 CEDAW requires states to 'take all appropriate measures to eliminate discrimination against women in the field of health care in order to ensure, on a basis of equality between men and women, access to health care services, including those related to family planning' and to ensure to women appropriate services in connection with preg-nancy, confinement, and the post-natal period. The Committee on Economic, Social and Cultural Rights has underlined the need to develop and implement a comprehen-sive national strategy for promoting women's right to health to meet these require-ments. It has pointed out that the realization of women's right to health requires the removal of all barriers interfering with access to health services, education, and infor-mation, including in the area of sexual and reproductive health. It has also emphasized the importance of preventive, promotive, and remedial action to shield women from the impact of harmful traditional cultural practices and norms that deny them their full reproductive rights.[36]

Article 14 CEDAW requires states to pay special attention to the particular prob-lems faced by rural women. In particular, states must ensure to such women the right to adequate living conditions, particularly in relation to housing, sanitation, electri-city and water supply, transport, and communications. Furthermore, they must be

---

[35] General Comment 12, n 7, para 26.   [36] General Comment 14, n 8, para 21.

given the right to participate in the elaboration and implementation of development planning at all levels and to have access to adequate healthcare facilities, including information, counselling, and services in family planning.

4.2 CHILDREN

Article 27 CRC guarantees 'the right of every child to a standard of living adequate for the child's physical, mental, spiritual, moral and social development'. This involves adequate food, housing, nursing, and care. Article 27(2) provides that the parent(s) or others responsible for the child have the primary responsibility to secure the conditions of living necessary for the child's development.

While ensuring the child's right to an adequate standard of living is the primary responsibility of the parents, it is not exclusive. According to Article 27(3) CRC, states must take appropriate measures to assist parents to implement this right. If necessary, they have to provide material assistance and support programmes, particularly with regard to nutrition, clothing, and housing. In addition, many children grow up in single-parent households, or are orphaned or have parents that have absconded or neglect their responsibility, and, in such situations, where other relatives do not take over the responsibility, the state has a primary duty to ensure for the child an adequate standard of living through appropriate institutions or placement with foster parents.

Under the right to health, states have a duty to diminish infant and child mortality. Article 12(2)(a) ICESCR expressly requires states to make 'provisions for the reduction of the still-birth rate and of infant mortality and for the healthy development of the child'. Similar obligations are contained in Article 24(2)(a) CRC and flow from Article 6 CRC, which provides that every child has the inherent right to life and that states 'shall ensure to the maximum extent possible the survival and development of the child'. This obligation may be understood as requiring measures to improve child and maternal health, sexual and reproductive health services, pre- and post-natal care, access to information, as well as to resources necessary to act on that information.

More generally, Article 24 CRC guarantees the right of the child to the enjoyment of the highest attainable standard of health and to facilities for the treatment of illness and rehabilitation of health. Thus, states must ensure that no child is deprived of his or her right of access to healthcare services. Furthermore, they have an obligation to ensure the provision of necessary medical assistance and healthcare to all children, combat disease and malnutrition, and develop preventive healthcare. The obligation of state parties to combat disease and malnutrition reflects the dominant problems facing children in many developing countries. A large number of children, particularly in the poorer sector of the population, die before the age of 5, due to a combination of malnutrition, unsafe water and sanitation, and communicable diseases. The risks can be substantially reduced through readily available technology such as oral rehydration therapy and immunization against the common childhood diseases, but this alone is not enough. It is also essential to ensure provision of adequate nutritious food and clean drinking water.

4.3 INDIGENOUS PEOPLES

The indigenous peoples of the world are generally among the most impoverished. Many of them are struggling to maintain and preserve their own culture, but much of their land has been taken away from them, and what little is left does not have the capacity to provide them with enough in terms of food and housing. While efforts to strengthen their rights have had some positive results in recent years, such as the adoption in 1989 of the ILO Convention on the Rights of Tribal and Indigenous Peoples (No 169) and the UN Declaration on the Rights of Indigenous Peoples,[37] they still suffer from severe deprivations. When they are displaced and live on 'welfare', their culture is undermined and the alien lifestyle leads to high degrees of alcoholism, suicide, and sometimes criminal behaviour. In line with the UN Declaration on the Rights of Indigenous Peoples, conditions must be established, including through recognition of their rights to land and natural resources, which make it possible for them to preserve their culture while sustaining a livelihood which ensures for them an adequate standard of living. This close link between rights to land and natural resources on the one hand and economic survival on the other hand has been highlighted by the Inter-American human rights bodies in a number of cases.[38] In the *Yakye Axa Indigenous Community* case, the Inter-American Court of Human Rights held that Paraguay had violated the rights of the members of that community to live a dignified existence, which follows from the right to life, by delaying the restitution of their ancestral lands and thus making it difficult for them to obtain food, clean water, adequate housing, and healthcare.[39]

The Committee on Economic, Social and Cultural Rights has repeatedly addressed the problems faced by indigenous peoples in its General Comments. It has drawn attention to the particular vulnerability of indigenous peoples whose ancestral land may be threatened. In several places corporations involved in oil or other mineral extraction have aggravated the situation of indigenous peoples, degraded their land, and caused their displacement.[40] The Committee has also emphasized that as part of their obligations to protect people's resource base for food, states parties should take appropriate steps to ensure that activities of the private business sector are in conformity with the right to food.[41] With regard to the right to housing, it has pointed out that indigenous peoples are among those vulnerable groups who suffer most from evictions.[42] Finally, the Committee has called on states to take particular care that indigenous peoples and ethnic and linguistic minorities are not excluded from social security systems through direct or indirect discrimination, particularly through

---

[37] See Chapter 17, below.
[38] See Case 11.140, *Mary and Carrie Dann v United States*, IACommHR Report No 75/02 (27 December 2002); *Mayagna (Sumo) Awas Tingni Community v Nicaragua*, IACtHR Series C No 79 (31 August 2001); *Yakye Axa Indigenous Community v Paraguay*, IACtHR Series C No 125 (17 June 2005).
[39] *Yakye Axa Indigenous Community*, ibid, paras 164–8 and 176.
[40] General Comment 12, n 7, para 13.   [41] Ibid, para 27.
[42] General Comment 7, n 6, para 10.

the imposition of unreasonable eligibility conditions or lack of adequate access to information.[43]

Indigenous peoples often live in remote areas with the lowest level of access to modern healthcare, and when they can reach healthcare stations, there is often a poor understanding of, and respect for, their cultural requirements. The Committee has argued that indigenous peoples have the right to specific measures to improve their access to health services and care. Health services should be culturally appropriate and thus take into account traditional preventive care, healing practices, and medicines. States should provide resources for indigenous peoples to design, deliver, and control such services. The Committee has noted that, in indigenous communities, the health of the individual is often linked to the health of the society as a whole and has a collective dimension. Therefore, development-related activities that lead to the displacement of indigenous peoples, denying them their sources of nutrition and breaking their symbiotic relationship with their lands, have a deleterious effect on their health.[44]

4.4 DALITS IN SOUTH ASIA AND ROMA IN EUROPE

Many other minorities are subject to discrimination, undermining their standard of living. These include the low-castes or Dalits in South Asia—particularly in India—which as a result of social practices are often marginalized, deprived of access to the means of adequate food and housing, and given access only to the lowest, most menial work. While such practices are generally prohibited under the respective national laws, enforcement of the law is often weak and segments of the police and other law enforcement agencies are themselves socialized in the same discriminatory attitudes which keep such practices alive. In its General Comment 20 of 2009, the Committee on Economic, Social and Cultural Rights pointed out that the prohibited ground of discrimination of 'birth' listed in Article 2(2) ICESCR also includes *descent*, especially on the basis of caste and analogous systems of inherited status. Therefore, states parties should take steps to prevent, prohibit, and eliminate discriminatory practices directed against members of descent-based communities and act against dissemination of ideas of superiority and inferiority on the basis of descent.[45] A somewhat comparable situation exists in parts of Europe, where the Roma and the Sinti are subject to widespread social discrimination, and where governments are unable fully to eradicate these practices. For example, the UN Committee on the Elimination of Racial Discrimination held that the authorities of a town in the Slovak Republic had violated the prohibition of racial discrimination when, upon pressure from parts of the population, they cancelled a resolution to build adequate housing for local Roma.[46]

---

[43] General Comment 19, HRI/GEN/1/Rev.9 (Vol I) 152, para 35.
[44] General Comment 14, n 8, para 27.   [45] E/C.12/GC/20, para 26.
[46] *LR et al. v Slovak Republic*, CERD/C/66/D/31/2003 (7 March 2005).

5 RELATIONSHIP WITH OTHER
HUMAN RIGHTS

The right to an adequate standard of living is closely linked to other human rights. Most obviously, it is heavily dependent on the realization of other economic and social rights, such as the right to social security, dealt with below. Other economic rights of importance to an adequate standard of living are the right to property and the right to work. Economic rights have a dual function, most clearly demonstrated in regard to the right to property. On the one hand, this right serves as a basis for entitlements which can ensure an adequate standard of living, while on the other hand it is a basis of independence and, therefore, freedom. Similarly, the right to work is also a basis of both independence (provided the work is freely chosen by the person concerned) and an adequate standard of living (provided that sufficient income is obtained from work).

The right to an adequate standard of living is also linked to cultural rights, which, according to Article 27 UDHR and Article 15 ICESCR, contain the following elements: the right to take part in cultural life, the right to enjoy the benefits of scientific progress and its applications, the right to benefit from the protection of the moral and material interests resulting from any scientific, literary, or artistic production of which the beneficiary is the author, and the freedom indispensable for scientific research and creative activity. These rights intersect in several ways with the right to an adequate standard of living. To mention one example: the right to benefit from advances in scientific progress can be a basis for claiming a right of access to affordable new medicine, which may be crucial in treating diseases such as HIV/AIDS.

Finally, as explained below, the right to an adequate standard of living may also coincide or, on the other hand, clash with civil and political rights.

5.1 THE RIGHT TO SOCIAL SECURITY AND
SOCIAL ASSISTANCE

The right to social security is essential when people are not able to secure an adequate standard of living themselves, particularly when they do not have the necessary property or are not able to work due to unemployment, old age, or disability. The drafters of the UDHR considered social security to be one of the core guarantees for the right of everyone to an adequate standard of living.

The general guarantee of an adequate standard of living set out in Article 25 UDHR includes 'the right to security in the event of unemployment, sickness, disability, widowhood, old age or other lack of livelihood in circumstances beyond his control'. But the UDHR also contains a separate guarantee of the right to social security that uses stronger terms. Article 22 states that '[e]veryone, as a member of society, has the right to social security'. Article 9 ICESCR guarantees 'the right of everyone to social security, including social insurance', while Article 10 of the same covenant refers to social security within the context of the protection of the family, mothers, and children. CEDAW contains a range of social security guarantees relevant to women, including the right of women to social security, particularly in cases of retirement, unemployment, sickness, invalidity and old age, and other incapacity to work, as well as the right to paid leave (Article 11(1)(e)), the right to family benefits (Article 13(a)), and the right of rural women to benefit directly from social security programmes (Article 14(2)(c)). The CRC provides for the right of the child to benefit from social security, including social insurance (Article 26). The right to social security is also explicitly mentioned in regional human rights instruments, including the American Declaration of the Rights and Duties of Man (Article XVI), the Protocol of San Salvador (Article 9), and the European Social Charter (Articles 12, 13, and 14).

Social security must be distinguished from social assistance and charity. Charity is irrelevant in the present context, because it involves neither a right of the individual nor a duty imposed on the state. It is, therefore, not a human rights issue. Social assistance is often discretionary and therefore neither a right nor a duty, but in some states it is sufficiently well regulated in law and practice to make it conform to requirements of human rights law.

Measures to implement the right to social security as set out in Article 9 ICESCR can include contributory or non-contributory schemes, or a combination of the two. The Committee on Economic, Social and Cultural Rights, in its General Comment 19, has defined these two types of provision of social security benefits as follows. *Contributory* (or insurance-based) schemes, such as social insurance, which is expressly mentioned in Article 9, generally involve compulsory contributions from beneficiaries, employers, and, sometimes, the state, in conjunction with the payment of benefits and administrative expenses from a common fund. *Non-contributory* schemes include universal schemes, which provide the relevant benefit to everyone who experiences a particular risk or contingency, and targeted social assistance schemes, where benefits are received by those in a situation of need.

In recent years, an embryonic form of social security under the name of 'cash transfer progammes' has emerged in some developing countries where the social security system has had a very limited reach. These programmes, which provide payments in cash to individuals or households, are normally targeted at the poorest and most vulnerable sections of the population. The transfers may be in the form of non-contributory old-age pensions, disability grants, child support grants, widow's allowances, or household transfers to persons in extreme poverty. Some of these programmes are conditional, for example requiring that the supported children attend school. The UN Independent Expert on the Question of Extreme Poverty has recognized that these cash transfer programmes can assist states in fulfilling their human rights obligations. However, she has also pointed out that this requires that the programmes are fully integrated within broader social protection systems. Their legal and institutional frameworks must take into account the international and national standards regarding the right to social security.[47]

The Committee on Economic, Social and Cultural Rights has expressed its concern over the very low levels of access to social security. About 80 per cent of the global population currently lack access to formal social security, with 20 per cent of them living in extreme poverty. The Committee has emphasized that this denial of or lack of access to adequate social security has undermined the realization of many Covenant rights.[48]

5.2 CIVIL AND POLITICAL RIGHTS

Torture and ill-treatment is not only a violation of core civil rights but also a violation of the right to health. Severe violations of the right to health or the right to be free from hunger may lead, in turn, to violations of the right to life, which is a civil right. On the other hand, there can also be conflicts between these different categories of rights. To give just one example, while the state has an obligation under international human rights law to take measures to protect the right to health, such measures must comply with the rights of people who carry infectious diseases such as their rights to physical integrity, privacy, and liberty. In each specific case, the need to protect the health of the public at large has to be balanced against individual interests. Thus, the European Court of Human Rights has held that an individual can only be compulsorily isolated to prevent him from spreading the HIV virus *as a last resort*, that is, where less severe measures are insufficient to safeguard the public interest.[49]

6 PROGRESSIVE IMPLEMENTATION

It is obvious that, today, the right of everyone to an adequate standard of living is far from realized. Nearly one billion people suffer from hunger and malnutrition and the number is growing. Possibly two billion, out of the total of 6.7 billion now living on earth, have substandard housing or no housing at all. There are enormous gaps between the standards set by international human rights law and the reality that many people face. This is also the case for many civil and political rights. Some may consider that human rights that are not applied in practice do not deserve the name 'rights'. In many quarters, there is scepticism towards economic and social rights such as the right to an adequate standard of living.

---

[47] Report of the independent expert on the question of human rights and extreme poverty, A/HRC/11/9 (27 March 2009).   [48] General Comment 19, n 43, paras 7 and 8.
[49] *Enhorn v Sweden* (2005) 41 EHRR 633.

It has to be borne in mind that economic and social rights were adopted as 'standards of achievement', to be achieved through progressive measures both at the national and international level. Article 2 ICESCR envisages a progressive realization of the Covenant rights and acknowledges the constraints due to the limited available resources. However, it also imposes obligations which are of immediate effect. In particular, states parties must guarantee that the rights will be exercised without discrimination of any kind and must take immediate and progressive steps towards full realization of the relevant rights by all appropriate means, including particularly the adoption of legislative measures. The Committee on Economic, Social and Cultural Rights has pointed out that such steps should be deliberate, concrete, and targeted as clearly as possible towards meeting the obligations recognized in the Covenant.[50]

Full realization would require that human rights are given priority in development processes. Regrettably, this has often not been the case. Both at the national and international level, there are serious mal-developments. The most pressing problem is the unregulated and misdirected process of globalization culminating with the recent financial crisis, which has led to a tremendous increase in inequality worldwide, particularly within states. Development can produce not only wealth but also poverty, unless development projects themselves are human rights-based.[51]

As explained above, violations imputable to the state can occur either by direct action by the state and its agencies or by its failure to ensure economic and social rights. The Committee on Economic, Social and Cultural Rights has pointed out that in determining which actions or omissions amount to a violation, it is important to distinguish the inability of a state party to comply from its unwillingness to do so. Should, for instance, a state party argue that resource constraints make it impossible to provide access to food for those who are unable by themselves to secure such access, then it has to demonstrate that every effort has been made to use all the resources at its disposal in an effort to satisfy, as a matter of priority, its minimum obligations. A state claiming that it is unable to carry out its obligation for reasons beyond its control has the burden of proving that this is the case and that it has unsuccessfully sought to obtain international support to ensure the availability and accessibility of the necessary food. Furthermore, any discrimination in access to food, as well as to means and entitlements for its procurement, constitutes a violation of the ICESCR.[52]

---

[50] General Comment 3, HRI/GEN/1/Rev.9 (Vol I) 7, para 2.

[51] See further Eide, 'Human Rights-Based Development in the Age of Economic Globalization: Background and Prospects' in Andreassen and Marks (eds), *Development as a Human Right: Legal, Political, and Economic Dimensions* (Harvard University Press, 2007) 220, and Salomon, *Global Responsibility for Human Rights: World Poverty and the Development of International Law* (OUP, 2007). See also Chapter 27, below.   [52] CESCR, General Comment 12, n 7, paras 17 and 18.

7 THE IMPORTANCE OF INTERNATIONAL ACTION

Most states have some legislation relating to food, housing, and health. However, such legislation is often fragmented, does not guarantee rights for all, and is weakly enforced or not enforced at all. International economic, social, and cultural rights therefore serve as a comprehensive normative framework that not only guides the content of national legislation in this area, but may also serve as a substitute for it. In the absence of sufficient national legislation or its enforcement, the economic, social, and cultural rights contained in international instruments can thus play an important role for the individual. But are these rights justiciable?[53] Behind this widely discussed question is a more fundamental one: what is the nature of international economic, social, and cultural rights?

The answer is not as difficult as is often thought. International human rights law serves two functions: first, it provides directive principles. Second, under some conditions, it provides subjective rights that are amenable to adjudication by courts. How national courts have enforced international guarantees of economic, social, and cultural rights is discussed in Chapter 22, below, so the discussion here will focus on the first issue.

The notion of directive principles is well known from constitutional law. In India, for example, directive principles of state policy are contained in the constitution as guidelines to the central and state governments, to be considered when framing laws and policies. These provisions are not directly enforceable by any court, but they are considered to be fundamental principles of governance that must be applied by state authorities.[54] Similar principles are also found in other constitutions such as that of Ireland, which focus on social justice and economic welfare. Such directive principles play an important role in the political process, but there are normally no national monitoring authorities supervising their implementation. In addition, they are often general and vague in their wording and therefore leave a wide margin for political disagreement concerning their implementation.

This is where international human rights law, and in particular guarantees of economic, social, and cultural rights, have an important additional value. International monitoring bodies can pursue a dialogue with each state on the optimal implementation of the directive principles and can elaborate and clarify the content of state obligations under international human rights standards. This is what the Committee on Economic, Social and Cultural Rights has done by issuing its General Comments, several of which concern the right to an adequate standard of living.

---

[53] Developments in international and comparative law show that economic and social rights are increasingly relied upon in the practice of courts and comparable institutions. For a recent overview, see Langford (ed), *Social Rights Jurisprudence: Emerging Trends in International and Comparative Law* (CUP, 2008).
[54] See further Chapter 22, below.

This monitoring through state reports will soon be supplemented by a new proced-ure created by the Optional Protocol to the ICESCR, which was adopted in December 2008 and will come into force upon the tenth ratification. Under the Optional Protocol, individuals who claim that their economic, social, and cultural rights have been vio-lated can bring a complaint to the Committee after having exhausted available domes-tic remedies. This new procedure will undoubtedly add to the impact of economic, social, and cultural rights. However, it will not reduce the importance of the monitor-ing process, which in some respects can produce more comprehensive effects than complaint procedures.[55]

In addition, the UN Human Rights Council and its predecessor, the Commission on Human Rights, have developed important thematic mechanisms to report on and promote the implementation of the right to an adequate standard of living. The reports by these Special Rapporteurs or Independent Experts play a very important role in advancing the enjoyment of the right to an adequate standard of living. There are Special Rapporteurs on the right to food, the right to housing, and the right to health and Independent Experts on the right to water and on extreme poverty.

8 CONCLUSION

Intended to promote and ensure freedom from want, the right to an adequate standard of living was given a central place in the proclamation of universal human rights from the very beginning in 1948. It has since been elaborated in international standards and clarified in detailed General Comments and practice. Several guidelines have been adopted for the implementation of the different components of an adequate standard of living, namely, the rights to food, water, housing, and health. The relevant inter-national human rights standards serve both as directive principles and as subjective rights. While their main function has been as directive principles pursued through international monitoring and reporting, there is an emerging trend also to use them as subjective rights in adjudicative bodies.

Enormous gaps remain, however, in the implementation of the right to an adequate standard of living. Regrettably, this right is not given the priority it should have in development processes. The creation of wealth for some is often associated with the creation of poverty for others, at least in the relative sense and sometimes even in the absolute sense.

---

[55] See (2009) 27 *Nordic JHR* 1.

FURTHER READING

CRAVEN, *The International Covenant on Economic, Social and Cultural Rights* (Oxford University Press, 2002).

BARTH EIDE and KRACHT (eds), *Food and Human Rights in Development: Volume I: Legal and Institutional Dimensions* (Intersentia, 2005).

——, —— and —— (eds), *Food and Human Rights in Development: Volume II: Evolving Issues and Emerging Applications* (Intersentia, 2007).

EIDE, KRAUSE, and ROSAS (eds), *Economic, Social and Cultural Rights* (Martinus Nijhoff, 2001).

HEALTH AND HUMAN RIGHTS: *AN INTERNATIONAL JOURNAL* (Francois-Xavier Bagnaud Centre for Health and Human Rights).

KENT (ed), *Global Obligations for the Right to Food* (Rowman & Littlefield, 2008).

LANGFORD (ed), *Social Rights Jurisprudence* (Cambridge University Press, 2008).

LECKIE (ed), *Housing, Land, and Property Restitution Rights of Refugees and Displaced Persons: Laws, Cases, and Materials* (Cambridge University Press, 2007).

TOEBES, *The Right to Health as a Human Right in International Law* (Intersentia, 1999).

UNESCO ETXEA, *The Human Right to Water: Current Situation and Future Challenges* (Icaria Editorial, 2008).

USEFUL WEBSITES

UN Committee on Economic, Social and Cultural Rights: <**http://www2.ohchr.org/english/bodies/cescr/index.htm**>

UN Special Rapporteur on the right to food: <**http://www2.ohchr.org/english/issues/food/index.htm**>

UN Special Rapporteur on adequate housing as a component of the right to an adequate standard of living: <**http://www2.ohchr.org/english/issues/housing/index.htm**>

UN Special Rapporteur on the right of everyone to the enjoyment of the highest attainable standard of physical and mental health: <**http://www2.ohchr.org/english/issues/health/right/index.htm**>

UN Independent Expert on the issue of human rights obligations related to access to safe drinking water and sanitation: <**http://www2.ohchr.org/english/issues/water/iexpert/index.htm**>

UN Independent Expert on human rights and extreme poverty: <**http://www2.ohchr.org/english/issues/poverty/expert/index.htm**>

European Committee of Social Rights: <**http://www.coe.int/t/dghl/monitoring/socialcharter/ecsr/ecsrdefault_EN.asp**>

12

THOUGHT, EXPRESSION, ASSOCIATION, AND ASSEMBLY

Kevin Boyle

SUMMARY

The four freedoms introduced in this chapter—thought, expression, association, and assembly—are interrelated and fundamental freedoms of the individual. They are essential for the exercise of all other rights. None are absolute in the sense that their exercise may never be restricted. International law provides the grounds on which each freedom may be required to be balanced against the rights of others or broader community interests. It also offers principles to safeguard against abuse of restrictions by the state. Freedom of thought includes freedom of conscience, religion, or belief. Freedom of expression includes freedom of opinion and freedom of information. Media freedom is also protected in international human rights law as essential for the enjoyment of freedom of expression. Freedom of association concerns the right to establish autonomous organizations through which individuals pursue common interests together. The right of assembly protects non-violent, organized, temporary gatherings in public and private, both indoors and outdoors.

1 INTRODUCTION

1.1 FOUR FREEDOMS AND THEIR RELATIONSHIPS

The freedoms of thought, expression, association, and assembly, often described as fundamental freedoms, are closely related civil and political rights. The guarantee of each is necessary for the enjoyment of the other and indeed for the exercise of all human rights. Thus freedom of expression is necessary if freedom of thought is to be exercised. In turn freedom of expression has little meaning without the individual having freedom to think. The right to practise or to teach a religion includes the freedom to publish religious literature or broadcast religious programmes. If religious communities or denominations are to exist, their freedom of association is essential, as is their right to assemble for religious purposes. Freedom of expression is essential when people come together to pursue their interests through other associations, such as trade unions, political parties, or community groups. The European Court of Human Rights (European Court) has defined one of the objectives of the freedom of association as the protection of opinions and the freedom to express them.[1] Freedom of expression is essential also to the freedom to assemble and the right to demonstrate over grievances. Thus, while each freedom is distinct in theory, in practice they are interrelated and interdependent.

The consecutive location of the freedoms in all international human rights texts, beginning with the Universal Declaration of Human Rights (UDHR), reflects their complementary nature. Article 18 UDHR proclaims freedom of thought, conscience, religion, or belief, Article 19 freedom of opinion and expression, and Article 20 the freedoms of association and assembly. Each of the freedoms is pivotal for the individual's right to democratic participation, a right proclaimed in Article 21 UDHR. Each freedom needs also to be understood as integrating the right to equality and non-discrimination in Article 2 UDHR. Denials of the freedoms often occur in the context of discriminatory policies directed at particular groups or minorities, for example religious or ethnic minorities.

Each freedom, as defined in international law, is expressed as a freedom of the individual but also has a collective dimension. Thus Article 18 UDHR provides that freedom of thought, religion, or belief is to be enjoyed 'alone or in communion with others'. Freedom of expression includes not only the right of a speaker to communicate with others but the right of others to hear what the speaker has to say. By definition the freedom of association or assembly concerns the collective activities of individuals.

1.2 LIMITATIONS

A common feature of these freedoms is that none is unconditional in the sense that its exercise by the individual or group cannot be limited by the state. International human rights standards set out the grounds of permitted limitation or restriction. Two categories of restriction are envisaged. First, the freedoms may legitimately be regulated by law to protect the rights and freedoms of others. Second, restriction may be justified for different public interest reasons, namely, public order, health, morality, or national security. The constant challenge arising in practice is how to strike a balance, which is acceptable in a democratic society, between the right to exercise the freedom, on the one hand, and the need to protect the rights of others and the public interest, on the other hand.

---

[1] *Ouranio Toxo and Others v Greece*, App no 74989/01, Judgment of 20 October 2005, para 35.

Most violations of these freedoms arise over patently unjustified restrictions by governments. The killing of journalists, censorship of the Internet, or the arbitrary banning of political movements or religious denominations occur with depressing frequency. But even where these freedoms are broadly respected, difficult questions can arise over how to respond to direct conflict between the freedoms themselves or with other rights. In the case of the news media, for example, conflict arises on a daily basis between freedom of the press and the right to privacy. The tensions and misunderstandings which can arise between freedom of religion and freedom of expression were vividly demonstrated in the worldwide controversy over the publication of cartoons of the Prophet Mohammad in a Danish newspaper in 2005.[2] Another contemporary example, which is discussed below, concerns the wearing in public places of religious symbols or dress. In several countries the wearing of the Islamic headscarf (*Hijab*) has been prohibited in schools or universities. This interference with freedom of religion, as it is, has been held to be justified on various grounds including the maintenance of a state's secular principles. In other countries such as the UK, the balance has been drawn differently. Religious symbols and dress are accommodated within school policy on uniforms.[3] In summary, a society which enjoys the freedoms under discussion is not one in which there are no restrictions on their exercise. It is rather one in which the boundaries of freedom are openly debated and democratically resolved under the rule of law.

Limitations are discussed further below as regards each freedom but some general principles applicable to all can be set out here.[4]

- *Legality*: any limitation on a freedom must be set down or prescribed in law. A restriction cannot be legitimate where it is the arbitrary whim of an official. National law must set out the ground of restriction in clear and precise terms.

- *Legitimate aim*: the interference or restriction must follow a legitimate purpose, that is, be based on one of the exhaustive grounds of limitation listed in the international standards which define the freedom.

- *Proportionality*: the restriction must be 'necessary' in the sense that there is 'a pressing social need' for it and that any measure taken is the minimum required to achieve the purpose of the limitation in a democratic society.

- *Presumption of freedom*: freedom is the rule, its limitation the exception. In the *Sunday Times Case*, which involved a claim of justified judicial restriction on the publication of information by a newspaper, the European Court noted that freedom of expression is not a right that is to be balanced equally with the permissible restrictions. It is rather a right that is subject to a limited number of restrictions that must be narrowly construed and convincingly justified,

---

[2] Cram, 'The Danish Cartoons, Offensive Expression, and Democratic Legitimacy' in Hare and Weinstein (eds), *Extreme Speech and Democracy* (OUP, 2009) 311.

[3] Bacquet, 'Manifestation of Belief and Religious Symbols at Schools: Setting Boundaries in English Courts' (2009) 4 *Religion and HR* 121.

[4] See also Chapter 6, above.

ultimately to a court.[5] Thus one should start with a strong presumption in favour of the freedom in question. The onus is on the authorities in the particular case to show that it is legitimate to restrict it.

The following sections consider, in turn, the right to freedom of thought (Section 2), freedom of expression (Section 3), freedom of association (Section 4), and freedom of assembly (Section 5). Each section explains the sources of the respective right, its scope, and the limitations that can be imposed on it.

2 FREEDOM OF THOUGHT, CONSCIENCE, AND RELIGION

2.1 SOURCES

This freedom is enshrined in Article 18 UDHR and in Article 18 of the International Covenant on Civil and Political Rights (ICCPR) as well as its Article 27 concerning the rights of minorities. It is also to be found in all regional human rights instruments.[6] The equality and non-discrimination provisions of the ICCPR (Articles 2, 3, and 26) and their equivalents in the regional instruments are vital for the enjoyment of the freedom. The Human Rights Committee has adopted a General Comment on the scope and meaning of Article 18 of the Covenant.[7] No international human rights treaty specifically devoted to freedom of thought, conscience, and religion has ever been adopted. However, an important Declaration was agreed by the UN General Assembly in 1981,[8] which provides the mandate of the Special Rapporteur on freedom of religion or belief, appointed by the UN Human Rights Council.[9]

2.2 SCOPE

Article 18 UDHR proclaims:

Everyone has the right to freedom of thought, conscience and religion; this right includes freedom to change his religion or belief, and freedom, either alone or in community with

---

[5] *Sunday Times v UK* (1979) 2 EHRR 245, para 65.

[6] European Convention on Human Rights (ECHR), Art 9; Protocol 1 to the ECHR, Art 2; Charter of Fundamental Rights of the European Union, Art 10; American Convention on Human Rights (ACHR), Art 12; African Charter on Human and Peoples' Rights (ACHPR), Art 8; Arab Charter on Human Rights, Art 30.

[7] HRC, General Comment 22, HRI/GEN/1/Rev.9 (Vol I) 204.

[8] Declaration on the Elimination of All Forms of Intolerance and Discrimination Based on Religion or Belief, GA Res 36/55 (25 November 1981).

[9] Wiener, 'The Mandate of the Special Rapporteur on Freedom of Religion or Belief—Institutional, Procedural and Substantive Legal Issues' (2007) 2 *Religion and HR* 3.

others and in public or private, to manifest his religion or belief in teaching, practice, worship and observance.

The UDHR by its nature could not specify fully the substance of this freedom in international law. That came with the drafting of Article 18 ICCPR. The predominant focus of both texts is on freedom of religion. However, the scope of the right is wider. It protects freedom of thought, that is, the right of the individual to have independent thoughts, ideas, and beliefs. This includes, for instance, an individual's right not to have to accept a political ideology or a religion with which he or she disagrees. Freedom of conscience, the individual's moral sense of right and wrong, is also explicitly recognized and protected. One common instance in which this freedom is invoked, considered below, arises where a citizen refuses on grounds of conscience to undertake compulsory military service. Finally, Article 18(4) ICCPR offers specific safeguards against the indoctrination of children. It establishes a duty on the state to respect the liberty of parents or guardians to determine the religious and moral education of their children in conformity with their own convictions. The child's right to freedom of thought, conscience, and religion is provided for in the Convention on the Rights of the Child (CRC).[10]

2.3 FREEDOM OF RELIGION OR BELIEF

While freedom of religion is the central concern of Article 18 ICCPR, that provision speaks of 'religion or belief', thus underlining the intention of the drafters that all beliefs, including beliefs other than religious, are protected. The Human Rights Committee has confirmed this understanding in its General Comment: 'Article 18 protects theistic, non-theistic and atheistic beliefs, as well as the right not to profess any religion or belief.'[11]

There is no definition of religion offered in any international human rights instrument. It is probably impossible to agree a definition given the sheer diversity of religious ideas in the world. However, the significance of religion as one of the 'fundamental elements in [the] conception of life' for believers is recognized in international human rights law.[12] Freedom of religion is an individual right but has a collective aspect also. It means the right to hold spiritual beliefs and *to live by them*, whether in private or in public, alone or in community with others. The Human Rights Committee has stated that the term religion or belief is to be broadly construed. It is not limited to traditional religions.[13] New religions are as entitled to protection as old ones. But there are limits. A Canadian group, the 'Assembly of the Church of the Universe', whose beliefs required the cultivation and worship of marijuana which they termed 'God's tree of life' had a complaint of a violation of their freedom of religion dismissed. The

---

[10] Art 14. [11] General Comment 22, n 7, para 2. [12] 1981 Declaration, n 8, preamble.
[13] General Comment 22, n 7, para 2.

Committee thought it inconceivable that the cultivation and worship of a narcotic drug could be a protected religion or belief under Article 18 of the Covenant.[14]

2.3.1 Manifestation of religion

Article 18 ICCPR speaks of the right to manifest religion through 'worship, observance, practice and teaching'. The Human Rights Committee has offered guidance as to the wide range of activities encompassed by these words:

The concept of *worship* extends to ritual and ceremonial acts giving direct expression to belief, as well as various practices integral to such acts, including the building of places of worship, the use of ritual formulae and objects, the display of symbols, and the observance of holidays and days of rest. The *observance and practice* of religion or belief may include not only ceremonial acts but also such customs as the observance of dietary regulations, the wearing of distinctive clothing or head coverings, participation in rituals associated with certain stages of life, and the use of a particular language customarily spoken by a group. In addition, the *practice and teaching* of religion or belief includes acts integral to the conduct by religious groups of their basic affairs, such as the freedom to choose their religious leaders, priests and teachers, the freedom to establish seminaries or religious schools and the freedom to prepare and distribute religious texts or publications.[15]

2.3.2 Freedom to change religion or belief

It follows from the freedom of thought and conscience that one may decide to change one's beliefs. The individual's right to change or choose religious belief is contested particularly by the Islamic faith. In some Muslim majority countries conversion to another religion constitutes the offence of apostasy, punishable by death. While the freedom to change a religion or belief is stated explicitly in Article 18 UDHR, it is formulated differently in the ICCPR, reflecting Muslim sensitivities over the issue.[16] Article 18 ICCPR speaks of 'freedom to have or to adopt a religion or belief of his choice'. But despite this difference of language, the Human Rights Committee has confirmed that Article 18 guarantees that anyone may replace a current religion with another religion or become an atheist.[17]

2.3.3 Proselytism

Article 18(2) ICCPR stipulates that there must be no coercion of the individual in the decision to either retain or to change beliefs. Subject to this prohibition on forced conversion, the right to spread one's faith and to seek to persuade others to convert to it is protected as the manifestation of religion.[18] Proselytism or missionary activity by religious groups is, however, a controversial matter according to some religions. Conversion from Islam is prohibited for Muslims and in India several states have

---

[14] *MAB, WAT and JAYT v Canada*, CCPR/C/50/D570/1993 (25 April 1994).

[15] General Comment 22, n 7, para 4 (emphases added).

[16] Boyle, 'Freedom of Religion in International Law' in Rehman and Breau (eds), *Religion, Human Rights and International Law* (Brill, 2007) 37–40.   [17] General Comment 22, n 7, para 5.

[18] *Kokkinakis v Greece* (1994) 17 EHRR 397.

passed anti-conversion laws aimed primarily at inhibiting conversion from Hinduism to Christianity. The major Christian churches, Roman Catholic, Orthodox, Protestant, and Evangelical denominations, are engaged in a joint effort to create a code of conduct for religious conversions.

2.3.4 Religion and the state

International human rights law does not require a separation between religion and the state. Such separation is to be found in the constitutional arrangements of many states, following the long-established examples of France and the USA. But in other states the relationships range from fusion of state and religion to formal recognition in law of the majority faith. The sole principles on religion and the state that international human rights law insists upon are those of pluralism and non-discrimination. Thus the existence of a state church should not entail the suppression of, or discrimination against, minority faiths or new religions.[19] It is the duty of the state to defend religious diversity in a democratic society, and to insist on the values of pluralism and tolerance should tensions arise from the coexistence of different faiths or beliefs.[20] The European Court has ruled that for democracy to function properly, the state has to remain neutral and impartial in its relations with various religions, denominations, and beliefs.[21] In states that require the registration of religions to give legal status to a denomination, neither the law nor its application should discriminate between religions by refusing, for example, to register some faiths while recognizing others. All religions must have the freedom to establish communities or organizations and these should be autonomous in their activities, including in determining their own leadership without interference from the state.[22]

While there may be exceptional cases,[23] the state has no general authority to decide whether a religion is legitimate or not. In *Moscow Branch of the Salvation Army v Russia*, the branch was refused registration by the city authorities. The authorities claimed that it was a paramilitary organization because of the word 'army' in its name and because its members wore uniforms and had ranks similar to those used in the military.[24] The branch complained to the European Court which found a violation of its freedom of association in the context of the guarantee of freedom of religion. The Court emphasized that the guarantee of freedom of religion meant the state had no discretion to decide whether religious beliefs or the means used to manifest them were legitimate. It could not be credibly argued that the Salvation Army advocated the violent overthrow of the constitution or threatened the security of the state.

[19] General Comment 22, n 7, para 9.
[20] *Serif v Greece* (1999) 31 EHRR 561; *Metropolitan Church of Bessarabia and others v Moldova* (2002) 35 EHRR 306.   [21] *Hasan and Chaush v Bulgaria* (2002) 34 EHRR 1339.
[22] Ibid.   [23] *MAB, WAT and JAYT v Canada*, n 14.
[24] *Moscow Branch of the Salvation Army v Russia* (2006) 44 EHRR 912.

2.4 LIMITATIONS

2.4.1 *Forum internum* and *forum externum*

An important distinction is to be drawn between those dimensions of the freedom of religion or belief which may be subject to limitation and those which may never be limited. Under Article 18(3) ICCPR it is the manifestation of the freedom of religion or belief in 'worship, observance, practice and teaching' (the forum externum) which may be limited. The individual's freedom of thought, conscience, religion, or belief (forum internum), guaranteed in Article 18(1), must be respected by the state unconditionally, and that includes the freedom to have or adopt a religion or belief of one's choice. Thus no one may be compelled to reveal his or her thoughts or beliefs, for example by a requirement to swear a religious oath or to carry a religious affiliation in an identity card.[25] Equally, as Article 18(4) makes clear, there may be no restriction on the liberty of parents in regard to the moral and religious education of their children.

2.4.2 Grounds of limitation

Manifestation of religious belief may be limited on the grounds set out in Article 18(3) ICCPR: 'public safety, order, health, or morals or the fundamental rights and freedoms of others'. National security, however, is not included as a permissible ground in the case of freedom of religion, whereas it is a permissible ground with the other freedoms. As explained above, any restriction applied on one of the permitted grounds must be prescribed by law and be necessary in a democratic society.

The Islamic veil (Hijab)

A contemporary and complex issue regarding religious manifestation concerns state regulation of the wearing of religious dress or symbols in public spaces, which amounts to an interference with the believer's freedom to express their religious beliefs or identity. The injunction to women in the Koran of *Hijab* or modesty is the religious source of the headscarf or the *burka* worn by some Muslim women.[26] International human rights bodies have taken different positions as to whether the wearing of the veil in public may be restricted by the state. The Human Rights Committee found that the exclusion from a university in Uzbekistan of a practising Muslim university student for wearing a headscarf interfered with her rights under Article 18 ICCPR.[27] The Committee held in line with its General Comment[28] that the freedom to manifest her religion encompasses the right to wear clothes or attire in public which was in conformity with her religion. The Committee was also of the view that her exclusion from studies amounted to a violation of her right to be free from coercion in matters of religion under Article 18(2).

[25] General Comment 22, n 7, para 3; *Buscarini and Others v San Marino* (2000) 30 EHRR 208; *Alexandridis v Greece*, App no 19516/06, Judgment of 21 February 2008.
[26] McGoldrick, 'Extreme Religious Dress: Perspectives on Veiling Controversies' in Hare and Weinstein (eds) n 2, 400.   [27] *Hudoyberganova v Uzbekistan*, CCPR/C/82/D/931/2000 (5 November 2004).
[28] See n 7.

In contrast, in *Leyla Sahin v Turkey*, the European Court upheld a similar Turkish regulation which prevented the applicant from continuing her medical studies at Istanbul University because she refused to remove her headscarf on religious grounds.[29] The majority of the judges considered that the interference with her religious freedom was justified in the interests of the rights and freedoms of others, which it linked to the Turkish constitutional principles of equality and secularism. In 2004 a French law banned the wearing of conspicuous religious symbols in state schools invoking the constitutional principle of secularism. The law prohibited not only the Islamic veil but also Jewish skullcaps, Sikh turbans, and Christian crosses. The European Court rejected complaints over this law brought by several Muslim girl pupils and Sikh boys over their expulsion from school. The children had worn substitute headwear, kerchiefs in the case of the girls and under-turbans in the case of the boys, which they refused to remove.[30] Noting that the pupils could still continue their schooling by correspondence courses, the Court found that the interference with their freedom to manifest their religion was justified and proportionate to the aims pursued, namely the rights and freedoms of others and public order. In some Muslim majority countries it is compulsory for women to wear a veil, a requirement which may also violate the freedom of religion. A human rights approach would argue that it should be for the individual to decide whether to wear religious dress or not. States should respect and seek to accommodate that choice.

Conscientious objection to military service

In a number of states conscription laws require that male adult citizens (in the case of Israel females also) have a legal duty to undertake a period of military training or service. For some individuals such a duty conflicts with their conscience due to their religious or philosophical beliefs, and they assert the right to refuse to undertake military service. International human rights standards are evolving in the direction of accepting that such refusal is a manifestation of the individual's conscience and should be protected under the guarantee of freedom of thought, conscience, and religion. The right to conscientious objection to military service has been recognized by the Human Rights Committee and other UN bodies.[31] Similarly, the European Union (EU) Charter of Fundamental Rights and Freedoms recognizes a right to conscientious objection to military service.[32] The European Court of Human Rights, however, has recently ruled that there is no duty under

---

[29] App no 44774/98, Judgment of 10 November 2005.

[30] *Aktas v France, Bayrak v France, Gamaleddyn v France, Ghazal v France, J Singh v France, R Singh v France,* App nos 43563/08, 14308/08, 18527/08, 29134/08, 25463/08, and 27561/08, Admissibility decisions of 17 July 2009.

[31] General Comment 22, n 7, para 11; *Mr Yeo-Bum Yoon and Mr Myung-Jin Choi v Republic of Korea,* CCPR/C/88/D/1321–1322/2004 (23 January 2007). See also CHR Res 1998/77 (22 April 1998); UN Working Group on Arbitrary Detention, Recommendation 2, E/CN.4/2001/14, paras 91–4; Analytical Report of the OHCHR on best practices in relation to conscientious objection to military service, E/CN.4/2006/51 (27 February 2006).

[32] EU Charter of Fundamental Rights, Art 10.

the European Convention on Human Rights (ECHR) to recognize conscientious objection to military service or to provide alternative public service for such objectors.[33] Nevertheless all member states of the Council of Europe with the exception of Turkey do recognize such a right. On the other hand, the Inter-American Commission on Human Rights has declined to accept that obligatory military service may conflict with freedom of conscience.[34]

3 FREEDOM OF OPINION AND EXPRESSION

3.1 SOURCES

This freedom is contained in Article 19 UDHR and in Articles 19 and 20 ICCPR. It is found in similar but not identical formulations in the regional human rights instruments.[35] There are also important provisions in the UN Convention on the Elimination of Racial Discrimination (ICERD), in particular Article 4 which concerns the prohibition of racist speech and organizations. The CRC recognizes the child's right to freedom of expression.[36] Since 1993 there exists the position of Special Rapporteur on the promotion and protection of the right to freedom of opinion and expression, who is now appointed by the Human Rights Council.[37]

3.2 SCOPE

Freedom of expression has been described as the touchstone of all rights. Not only is freedom of expression inseparable from freedom of thought, association, and assembly, it is essential for the enjoyment of all rights, including economic, social, and cultural rights. It is a vital freedom for development, the functioning of democracy, and modern economies.

Article 19 UDHR provides the foundation for the fuller definition of the freedom in the ICCPR:

Everyone has the right to freedom of opinion and expression; this right includes freedom to hold opinions without interference and to seek, receive and impart information and ideas through any media and regardless of frontiers.

Although this text was drafted over 60 years ago, it powerfully expresses the ideal of freedom of speech in today's era of the Internet and other digital communication

---

[33] *Vahan Batayan v Armenia*, App no 23459/03, Judgment of 27 October 2009. See also, *Thlimmenos v Greece* (2000) 31 EHRR 411; *Ülke v Turkey*, App no 39437/98, Judgment of 24 January 2006.

[34] Case 12.219, *Cristián Daniel Sahli Vera et al. v Chile*, IACommHR Report No 43/05 (10 March 2005).

[35] ECHR, Art 10; EU Charter of Fundamental Rights, Art 11; ACHR, Arts 13 and 14; ACHPR, Art 9; Arab Charter on Human Rights, Art 32.   [36] Arts 12 and 13.

[37] Report of the Special Rapporteur on the promotion and protection of the right to freedom of opinion and expression, A/HRC/11/4 (30 April 2009).

technologies. Freedom of expression is an individual right. It means the freedom, without interference or penalty, to speak one's mind. Freedom of expression has also its collective components. Human beings communicate with others, not with themselves. The freedom includes the right to hear other views and to exchange ideas and information with others. It also includes the right to inform oneself and to be informed. Hence, the crucial importance of all media as means of communication.

3.2.1 Freedom of opinion

Article 19 ICCPR guarantees freedom of opinion as well as expression. Human beings have diverse and differing opinions on all kinds of subjects, including political and social affairs. Article 19(1) provides that everyone is entitled to hold such views without interference. No one can be forced to think in a particular way. Nor should anyone suffer prejudice, discrimination, or repression because of their views or opinions. The freedom to hold opinions may not be restricted. In the words of the Human Rights Committee: 'it is a right to which the Covenant admits no restriction'.[38] In other words people may think what they like.

3.2.2 Freedom of expression

Article 19(2) ICCPR sets out the positive meaning of freedom of expression under international law. Its scope is extensive. The right is defined as including freedom to seek, receive, as well as impart information and ideas of all kinds. Freedom *to seek* includes active and investigative journalism in the public interest. Freedom *to receive* has been interpreted by the European Court as including the right of the public to be informed and the duty of the mass media to impart information to the public.[39] The freedom to *impart* extends to every kind of information and idea expressed through any media of choice, 'either orally, in writing or in print, [or] in the form of art'.[40] As the Court has noted, the freedom 'is applicable not only to "information" or "ideas" that are favourably received or regarded as inoffensive or as a matter of indifference, but also to those that offend, shock or disturb the State or any sector of the population.'[41]

Freedom of expression is to be enjoyed 'without regards to frontiers', in other words it does not stop at the borders of the state. This clause was intended to outlaw forms of censorship such as the Cold War practice of radio jamming of foreign broadcast signals and extends in today's digital age, for example, to the blocking of access to the Internet or mobile phones.

3.2.3 Media freedom

There is no explicit recognition or protection offered to the press and other media in the international human rights standards, although such is often to be found in national laws and constitutions. At the international level, the freedoms and responsibilities of the press have been developed from the guarantee of freedom of expression of

---

[38] General Comment 10, HRI/GEN/1/Rev.9 (Vol I) 181, para 1.
[39] *Thorgeir Thorgeirson v Iceland* (1992) 14 EHRR 843, para 63.   [40] ICCPR, Art 19(2).
[41] *Handyside v UK* (1976) 1 EHRR 737, para 49.

the individual. The protection afforded under human rights standards to all media—modern mass electronic and print media and the new information communication technologies—is justified because of their role in making people's freedom of expression meaningful and their contribution to democratic life. All such means of communication provide access to news and to opportunities to exchange information and ideas. International and national standards on freedom of expression have largely been shaped by the struggle for journalistic and artistic independence against government licensing and censorship of media. That struggle continues in different parts of the world. Media freedom is thus inseparable in practice from the enjoyment of freedom of expression in society. The media has a watchdog role on the exercise of power in society, and free media facilitates political debate. As the European Court has put it:

Freedom of the press affords the public one of the best means of discovering and forming an opinion of the ideas and attitudes of political leaders. In particular it gives politicians the opportunity to reflect and comment on the preoccupations of public opinion; it thus enables everyone to participate in the free political debate which is at the core of the concept of a democratic society.[42]

But media in all its forms is also a source of considerable power, including economic power. The international standards speak therefore of the media's duties and responsibilities. Media regulation is necessary to ensure democratic accountability and to guard against excessive concentration of ownership. Regulatory regimes, whether self-regulation or established by legislation, will differ according to different media. Thus public, private, or community broadcasting systems and the print media will often be subject to different regulatory codes. But all such regulatory systems should protect editorial freedom and operate independent of government.

3.2.4 Freedom of information laws

The most striking advance in the norms on freedom of expression over recent years has been the growth of laws implementing the right to access official information held by governments. Democracies, both new and old, have come to understand that transparency affords governments and public administration legitimacy in the eyes of the public. In all world regions, governments have established 'the right to know' through legislation. An 'access to information law' works on the principle of maximum disclosure: all official information should be made public as a matter of principle, unless there are legitimate reasons justifying non-disclosure.

In *Claude Reyes and others v Chile* the Inter-American Court of Human Rights became the first international tribunal to hold that there is a right to access information held by the government, derived from the guarantee of freedom of expression.[43] The case originated in a request for information made by three environmental activists about a controversial deforestation project which was ignored by the government.

---

[42] *Castells v Spain* (1992) 14 EHRR 445, para 43.
[43] IACtHR Series C No 151 (19 September 2006). See also *Társaság a Szabadságjogokért v Hungary*, App no 37374/05, Judgment of 14 April 2009.

The Council of Europe has recently adopted the first international treaty on access to official documents.[44]

3.3 LIMITATIONS

If people may think what they like, they may not always say or write what they like. As opposed to freedom of opinion, freedom of expression is not an absolute right. Under Article 19(3) ICCPR its exercise carries with it 'special duties and responsibilities'. Such language acknowledges the power of the media, but also the justification of restriction where it is necessary to respect the rights or reputations of others, and where it is necessary on grounds of national security, public order, public health, or morals. It is possible to examine only some of these grounds here. But as discussed above, it is crucial how restrictions are applied because if wrongly or excessively invoked, they can 'chill' the freedom or even eliminate it. Thus a ground such as national security in the context of counter-terrorism is often misapplied or abused to the detriment of freedom of expression.[45]

3.3.1 Privacy

One right which may clash with freedom of expression is privacy.[46] In *Von Hannover v Germany*, Princess Caroline of Monaco, who had campaigned for many years over paparazzi taking pictures for publication in European magazines of her and her children, complained to the European Court.[47] The Court found that her right to privacy was violated. There was no justification for the constant media intrusion in her private life. The public interest was not advanced since the photographs were published to satisfy public curiosity, not to contribute to public debate. The Court considered that the Princess, although a member of a royal family, exercised no official functions and was thus a private person. While public figures such as politicians and popular celebrities do have a right to private life, it is less extensive given that they are willingly in the public arena.[48]

3.3.2 Defamation

To publish a false statement about another which damages his or her reputation is a civil and often a criminal wrong. But the implementation of laws which impose liability for defamation can, and often do, undermine the freedom of the media to fulfil their function of informing the public and to comment critically on public affairs. Given the vital importance of free media in a democracy, international human rights standards have been directed at ensuring that national laws on defamation are applied

---

[44] Council of Europe Convention on Access to Official Documents (27 November 2008).

[45] Barendt, 'Incitement to, and Glorification of Terrorism' in Hare and Weinstein (eds) n 2, 446.

[46] ICCPR, Art 17.

[47] (2005) 40 EHRR 1. For discussion of the implications of this judgment for press freedom, see Fenwick and Phillipson, *Media Freedom under the Human Rights Act* (OUP, 2006) 668.

[48] *Krone Verlag GmbH and Co KG v Austria* (2003) 36 EHRR 57.

as narrowly as possible as regards 'political speech'. Robust criticism of the government or a politician should be tolerated in the interests of open debate on political issues. In *Lingens v Austria*, a journalist was convicted of criminal libel because he had accused a former Prime Minister of Austria of political opportunism and of using his influence to prevent an investigation of a political ally for Nazi crimes. The European Court found that Austrian law, which required Lingens to prove the truth of what were his opinions, operated as an excessive interference with press freedom.[49] There is an increasing trend towards the abolition of criminal penalties for defamatory statements based on the argument that civil remedies such as the payment of damages is a sufficient sanction and the threat of criminal prosecution has a chilling effect on freedom of expression.

3.3.3 Hate speech

Control of the advocacy of violence, hatred, and discrimination against individuals or groups on the basis of their race, colour, ethnicity, religious beliefs, sexual orientation, or other status presents a challenge to all states. The Internet has added a global dimension to the availability of propaganda advocating violence or hatred of others. Articles 19(3) and 20 ICCPR and Article 4 ICERD provide the legal framework for restriction on such speech. The use of speech to incite violence is a criminal offence in virtually all states. But to strike an acceptable balance between the right to freedom of expression and restraint on other forms of objectionable speech is in practice often difficult.

Islamophobia and Anti-Semitism

Incitement to ethnic, racial, or religious hostility, hatred, and discrimination is not protected speech. A current concern is the widespread expression, particularly in Europe, of prejudice and hostility towards Muslims, sometimes termed Islamophobia. In 2001–2, a member of the British National Party displayed a large poster in his flat window with a photograph of the Twin Towers in flames with the caption 'Islam out of Britain—Protect the British People' and a symbol of a crescent and star in a prohibition sign. He was convicted of displaying hostility to a racial or religious group. His complaint to the European Court that his freedom of expression was infringed was dismissed.[50] The poster, the Court held, represented a vehement attack against Muslims linking the group as a whole with a grave act of terrorism.

Like Islamophobia, Anti-Semitism is a widespread phenomenon, which frequently finds expression in Holocaust denial. Holocaust denial or negationism denies the Nazi genocide against Jews during the Second World War or seeks to minimize its true scale. Such speech is a criminal offence in several European states. A French historian, Robert Faurisson, in an interview with a magazine said it was his personal

---

[49] (1986) 8 EHRR 407.

[50] *Mark Anthony Norwood v UK*, Application no 23131/03, Admissibility Decision of 16 November 2004.

conviction that there were no homicidal gas chambers for the extermination of Jews in Nazi concentration camps. When convicted over these comments, he claimed before the Human Rights Committee that his freedom of expression had been violated. The Committee upheld the conviction as a justifiable interference with his freedom of expression under Article 19 ICCPR.[51] It was persuaded by the French government's argument that holocaust denial is the main vehicle of anti-Semitism in France.

Blasphemy

Criticism of religion, as distinct from incitement to hatred of people because of their religious beliefs, is currently a highly contested freedom of expression issue at the international level. The Human Rights Council, led by Muslim majority states, has passed resolutions calling for action to suppress 'defamation of religions'.[52] But others, mostly Western states, have rejected the need to protect religious institutions or doctrines from robust criticism, satire, or even ridicule. Nevertheless, a number of European states retain offences of blasphemy in their criminal codes although these are rarely invoked. The UK abolished the common law offences of blasphemy and blasphemous libel in 2008. This ongoing debate over the relationship between freedom of expression and freedom of religion was provoked by the publication of the Danish cartoons of the Prophet Mohammad in 2005.[53]

4 FREEDOM OF ASSOCIATION

4.1 SOURCES

Freedom of association is proclaimed as an individual right in Article 20 UDHR and is included in both international covenants as well as regional instruments.[54] Article 22 ICCPR provides a general guarantee of freedom of association. It also includes the right to form and join trade unions, a right independently recognized in Article 23(4) UDHR. Article 8 of the International Covenant on Economic, Social and Cultural Rights (ICESCR) provides for the association rights of trade unions. Trade union rights are more fully protected in the international agreements of the International Labour Organization (ILO).[55] The ILO Committee on Freedom of Association, comprising an equal number of representatives of governments, employers, and unions, oversees the protection of trade union freedoms.[56]

---

[51] *Robert Faurisson v France*, CCPR/C/58/D/550/1993 (8 November 1996).

[52] Parmar, 'The Challenge of "Defamation of Religions" to Freedom of Expression and the International Human Rights System' [2009] *EHRLR* 353.   [53] Cram, n 2.

[54] ECHR, Art 11; EU Charter of Fundamental Rights, Art 12; ACHR, Art 16; ACHPR, Art 10; Arab Charter on Human Rights, Art 24.

[55] Freedom of Association and Protection of the Right to Organize Convention 1948 (No 87), Right to Organize and Collective Bargaining Convention 1949 (No 98).   [56] See also Chapter 13, below.

4.2 SCOPE

Freedom of association is the freedom to pursue collective action. It protects the right of individuals to form associations for common purposes, free from government interference. It includes the right of the association independently to determine its membership, appoint officers, employ staff, and generally conduct its own affairs subject only to the law. While linked historically with trade unions, the freedom includes the freedom to establish and belong to political parties, which are vital for the functioning of democracy. But the right of the individual to establish and participate in all manner of civil society associations or voluntary organizations is equally part of this freedom. Article 16 of the American Convention on Human Rights (ACHR) speaks of the right to establish associations for 'ideological, religious, political, economic, labor, social, and cultural, sports, or other purposes'. This freedom is also of central importance to the activities of human rights defenders. The Declaration on Human Rights Defenders, passed by the UN General Assembly in 1999, affirms the right of human rights activists to form, join, and participate in NGOs for the purpose of, inter alia, seeking and imparting information about human rights, discussing and developing new ideas on human rights, and advocating on issues of human rights.[57]

4.2.1 The right not to associate

The right to associate includes the negative freedom to choose not to belong to an association and not to be compelled to join one. The negative formulation of the right is included in the UDHR (Article 20(2)) but not in the ICCPR. The explanation for its absence concerns the status of collective bargaining agreements between trade unions and employers over the employment of union members only (closed shop agreements). For the same reason the right to freedom of association under Article 11 ECHR is also silent on the right not to associate. The European Court has approached compulsory union membership on a case-by-case basis. In *Young, James and Webster v UK*, the Court found that the dismissal of individuals employed prior to a closed shop agreement violated the right to freedom of association of the dismissed employees.[58] In *Sigurjonsson v Iceland*, the same Court examined an Icelandic law that made taxi drivers' licences contingent upon membership of a union.[59] The applicant had been licensed before the regulation came into force, had principled reasons for objecting to union membership, and lost his licence as a result of his refusal to join. The Court found that the government interest in this rule—facilitating the regulation of public transport—was relevant but not sufficient to justify the extreme consequence of non-membership of the union.

In *Gustafsson v Sweden* the applicant owned a restaurant. He was not a member of the restaurant employers association and was not bound by any collective agreement which the union representing restaurant workers had agreed with the association. Because he refused to enter into a substitute agreement recognizing the rights of his

---

[57] GA Res 53/144 (8 March 1999).   [58] (1981) 4 EHRR 38.   [59] (1993) 16 EHRR 462.

workers to collective bargaining, his business was placed under a boycott by the union. The applicant complained that the union's actions violated his negative freedom of association, which the state should have protected. The European Court noted the special role in Sweden of collective agreements in labour relations and held that there had not been a violation of the negative right of association.[60] These cases illustrate the tension which can arise between the individual and collective dimensions of the freedom of association.

4.2.2 The right to strike

The Human Rights Committee has held that the right to association in the ICCPR does not include a right to strike. In *JB et al. v Canada*, the Committee noted that ILO Convention No 87 had been interpreted to provide such a right and that the ICESCR includes the right to strike along with its recognition of trade union rights.[61] The Committee pointed out that 'each international treaty, including the [ICCPR] has a life of its own and must be interpreted in a fair and just manner'.[62] The drafting history of the ICCPR and ICESCR proved persuasive to the Committee. Having been drafted in parallel discussions, the inclusion of the right to strike in the ICESCR without similar language in the ICCPR suggested that the right of association in that covenant was not intended to protect the right to strike.

4.3 LIMITATIONS

The Human Rights Committee addressed the type of activities that constitute an interference with the right of association in *Korneenko et al. v Belarus*. In that case, the authorities stripped a human rights organization, 'Civil Initiatives', of its recognition because it had violated domestic regulations governing associations. Its official documentation was said to suffer from 'deficiencies' and it was accused of using equipment purchased with foreign grants for propaganda purposes. A domestic court ordered the dissolution of the group. The key determination for the Committee was whether the dissolution of the organization amounted to an interference with the right of association. The Committee held that the ICCPR protected all activities of an association. Dissolution of a group amounts to a severe interference with the freedom and must be strictly justified by reference to the grounds of limitation in Article 22(2). The government had failed to do this. Even if the NGO's documentation had been defective the extreme step taken of dissolving it was a disproportionate response. The Committee found a violation.[63]

Where domestic law requires registration of civic associations in order to obtain legal personality, a refusal or delay by the authorities in registration may constitute an interference with the freedom of association.[64]

---

[60] (1996) 22 EHRR 409.   [61] CCPR/C/OP/1 (18 July 1986).   [62] Ibid, para 6.2.
[63] CCPR/C/88/D/1274/2004 (10 November 2006).
[64] *Ismayilov v Azerbaijan*, App no 4439/04, Judgment of 17 January 2008.

4.3.1 Banning political parties

Political parties are an essential form of association if democracy is to exist. Without an effective democracy, human rights cannot be guaranteed. Political parties thus must be guaranteed the fullest freedom of association and compelling reasons must be given for any interference with the freedom. That principle applies most particularly where political parties are banned or dissolved.

In *Refah Partisi (the Welfare Party) and Others v Turkey*, the European Court upheld the decision of the Turkish Constitutional Court to disband the largest political party in the state.[65] The judgment sparked considerable controversy as at the time the Refah party was serving in a coalition government. Certain of its leaders were accused of advocating the introduction of Islamic law (*Sharia*) in Turkey, and violating the secular principles of the Turkish Constitution. The Court recognized that closure constituted an extreme interference in the right of association, but concluded unanimously that it was justifiable. It noted that 'protection of public safety and the rights and freedoms of others and the prevention of crime might depend on safeguarding the principle of secularism'.[66] The Refah party was likely poised to be able to implement policies that could undermine the democratic and secular nature of Turkey and threaten the rights of others.

The decision in *Refah* can be contrasted with an earlier Turkish case, *United Communist Party of Turkey and Others v Turkey*.[67] The Turkish Constitutional Court dissolved this political party on the basis that the party advocated class domination and threatened the territorial integrity of the state. The European Court found that the dissolution of the party was disproportionate. The party had not undertaken activities or adopted stances that would threaten the territorial integrity or national security of the state and the use of terminology that the state found offensive or threatening was not enough to justify the extreme step of dissolution of a political party.

Thus unless a party threatens the democratic nature of a state, it cannot be suppressed, even if the party espouses offensive ideas. In *Ouranio Toxo and Others v Greece*, a political party representing the Macedonian minority adopted a name that was deemed offensive to the majority Greek population. The government removed a sign with the party's name on it, claiming that the name—written in Macedonian— was specifically intended to elicit memories of a violent battle between the Greek and Macedonian people and exacerbated tensions in the region. The party replaced the sign. In response, citizens, including political leaders, attacked the headquarters of the party and destroyed its equipment. The Court determined that the removal of the sign constituted an arbitrary interference. Concerns over regional tensions did not justify removing the sign. The use of a minority language, regardless of its ability to inflame the sentiments of others, could not be said to constitute a threat to democratic society. The Court again noted the essential role played by political parties in democratic systems and emphasized the importance of political pluralism for democracy. It

---

[65] (2003) 37 EHRR 1.   [66] Ibid, para 66.   [67] (1998) 26 EHRR 121.

found that Article 11 had been violated by both the government's acts and its failure to protect the party's premises.[68]

4.3.2 Additional limitations applicable to military and police

Article 22(2) ICCPR provides that members of the armed forces and of the police may be restricted by law in their exercise of the right of association. The provision, however, does not deny the right of military and police to freedom of association. It recognizes only that the state may regulate the exercise of that freedom. There are similar restrictions in the ECHR and the ACHR.

5 FREEDOM OF ASSEMBLY

5.1 SOURCES

The freedoms of assembly and association are contained in one article in the UDHR and the ECHR.[69] The ICCPR (Article 21) and other regional instruments separate the rights.[70] While the rights of assembly and association are closely connected, they are distinct. They are both vital democratic freedoms that enable individuals to act collectively to promote their interests. Freedom of assembly is qualified as a right of 'peaceful assembly' or in the ACHR a right to 'peaceful assembly, without arms'. Specific types of assemblies, such as religious assemblies, are additionally protected by Article 18 ICCPR, as are private assemblies in one's home by Article 17 ICCPR.

5.2 SCOPE

The right of assembly protects non-violent, organized gatherings in public and private, both indoors and outdoors. A broad range of assemblies is encompassed, including political, economic, artistic, and social gatherings. The right also extends to counter-protests, though states have an obligation to ensure counter-demonstrators do not interfere with the initial demonstration.[71] Thus states must not only abstain from interfering with the right, but are also required to take positive measures to protect peaceful assemblies. Although the right envisages temporary gatherings, it also protects mass political protests that may last for weeks or months.

The African Commission on Human and Peoples' Rights found that the convictions and executions of four indigenous Ogoni activists violated their right to life and also their right of assembly. The Nigerian government alleged that the activists were responsible for the deaths of four men following a rally for indigenous rights. The activists were not accused of perpetrating the deaths, but held responsible

---

[68] n 1.   [69] UDHR, Art 20; ECHR, Art 11.   [70] ACHR, Art 15; ACHPR, Art 11.
[71] *Plattform 'Ärzte Für Das Leben' v Austria* (1988) 13 EHRR 204.

because their peaceful assembly 'incited' the killings. The Commission held that the executions were part of a widespread attempt to intimidate protestors and limit demonstrations.[72]

5.3 LIMITATIONS

Restrictions on peaceful assembly may be imposed under Article 21(2) ICCPR, provided these are prescribed by law and necessary in a democratic society in the interests of national security or public safety, public order, the protection of public health or morals, or the protection of the rights and freedoms of others. Outright banning of a demonstration may prove necessary but clearly requires the strongest justification. In *Öllinger v Austria*, the European Court held that the state's duty to protect the right of assembly as far as possible should have included considering alternatives to a total ban on a small counter-protest at a cemetery on All Saints Day where a commemoration was to take place for former SS soldiers.[73]

5.3.1 Prior notifications and permits

Regulation of demonstrations or gatherings through prior notification or issuing of a permit by the authorities before a march or public meeting can take place is compatible with the freedom to assemble. In *Kivenmaa v Finland*, the Human Rights Committee accepted that a requirement to notify the police of an intended demonstration in a public place in Helsinki six hours before its commencement would be compatible with the permitted limitations laid down in Article 21 ICCPR.[74] Such administrative procedures enable other rights and interests to be balanced with the right to assemble, for example the freedom of movement of others, national security, public order, and the normal circulation of traffic. Undue delays or arbitrariness in the issuance of permits, however, can constitute a violation of the right. In *Baczkowski v Poland*, the European Court heard a complaint over the mayor of Warsaw's refusal to authorize a march and different other public gatherings to protest over discrimination, including against gay people. The mayor had said publicly before considering the applications for permits that he would ban any public propaganda for homosexuality. The Court found, inter alia, that the mayor's refusal to permit the demonstrations constituted a discriminatory interference with the right to freedom of assembly.[75]

The dispersal of a spontaneous peaceful demonstration, one that occurs, for example, in response to an unexpected political event, solely because of the absence of prior notice may amount to a disproportionate restriction on freedom of peaceful

---

[72] *International Pen, Constitutional Rights Project, Interights on behalf of Ken Saro-Wiwa Jr and Civil Liberties Organisation v Nigeria*, Communication nos 137/94, 139/94, 154/96, and 161/97 (31 October 1998) paras 1–2, 106.   [73] App no 76900/01, Judgment of 29 June 2006.
[74] CCPR/C/50/D/412/1990 (9 June 1994).   [75] App no 1543/06, Judgment of 3 May 2007.

assembly.[76] However, the police can disperse a demonstration where there was ample time to file notice of a public demonstration in advance but this was not done.[77]

5.3.2 Repressive restrictions

Any restriction on assembly must be shown to be necessary in a democratic society. In *Oscar Elías Biscet et al. v Cuba*, the Inter-American Commission on Human Rights held that restrictions on the right of assembly are illegal if used solely to suppress the opposition.[78] The petitioners claimed they were arrested, detained, and intimidated because they discussed dissident publications at their weekly meetings. The Commission concluded that the convictions were an arbitrary restraint on freedom of assembly since their primary purpose was to constrain political opposition.

6 CONCLUSION

In this chapter four freedoms—freedom of thought, expression, association, and assembly—were introduced. The freedoms were discussed along with the body of international human rights norms and jurisprudence which have helped to define their scope since each was proclaimed in the UDHR in 1948. Each freedom was examined as a discrete freedom of the individual. But it was also noted that each has a collective component. All are interrelated and mutually reinforcing. The freedoms share the common feature that they are not unconditional entitlements. In practice their exercise needs balancing against the rights and freedoms of others and against certain public interest considerations, which are carefully and exhaustively set out in the international standards governing each freedom. A challenge common to all the freedoms is how to ensure that, where such restrictions are in principle necessary, they are implemented by the state in a proportionate manner. That requires a democratic society and one built on the rule of law. The freedoms are, in turn, part of the foundations of a democratic society.

The right to dissent and to speak out, the freedom to come together with others in independent associations to promote common interests, and the freedom to demonstrate are all essential if a democratic society based on the participation of its members is to function successfully. The guarantee of freedom for all media and media workers is also crucial in a democracy to ensure the free flow of information and the accountability of those who exercise political, economic, or other sources of power over others. However, the media, whether in their traditional forms of print and broadcasting or operating through new global communication technologies such

---

[76] *Bukta and Others v Hungary*, App no 25691/04, Judgment of 17 September 2007.

[77] *Éva Molnár v Hungary*, App no 10346/05, Judgment of 7 October 2008.

[78] Cases 771/03 and 841/03, IACommHR Report No 57/04 (14 October 2004).

as the Internet, also exercise considerable power. The media therefore have 'duties and responsibilities' and are subject to regulation by law which seeks to ensure democratic accountability for the exercise of that power without undermining their independence.

The fundamental character of these freedoms does not prevent their systematic denial in many parts of the world. Many human rights organizations, intergovernmental and non-governmental, work to defend them. The role of the independent experts or thematic Special Rapporteurs whose mandates concern the promotion and protection of the different freedoms was noted. Their interventions on behalf of victims and annual reports to the Human Rights Council provide an important source of information on the scale of the challenge facing the enjoyment of these freedoms as universal rights.

FURTHER READING

BARENDT, *Freedom of Speech* (Oxford University Press, 2007).

EVANS, C., *Freedom of Religion under the European Convention on Human Rights* (Oxford University Press, 2001).

EVANS, M.D., *Religious Liberty and International Law in Europe* (Cambridge University Press, 1997).

—— *Manual on the Wearing of Religious Symbols in Public Areas* (Council of Europe, 2009).

FENWICK and PHILLIPSON, *Media Freedom under the Human Rights Act* (Oxford University Press, 2006).

HARE and WEINSTEIN (eds), *Extreme Speech and Democracy* (Oxford University Press, 2009).

INTERNATIONAL LABOUR ORGANIZATION, *Law on Freedom of Association: Standards and Procedures* (Geneva, 1995).

LEADER, *Freedom of Association: A Study in Labor Law and Political Theory* (Yale University Press, 1992).

OSCE, *Guidelines on Freedom of Peaceful Assembly*, available at: <http://www.osce.org/item/23835.html>.

—— *Venice Commission Guidelines for Review of Legislation Pertaining to Religion or Belief*, available at: <http://www.osce.org/publications.odihr/2004/>.

REHMAN and BREAU (eds), *Religion, Human Rights and International Law: A Critical Examination of Islamic State Practices* (Brill, 2007).

USEFUL WEBSITES

International Labour Organization: <**http://www.ilo.org**>

On freedom of religion or belief:

Human Rights Without Frontiers: <**http://www.hrwf.net/**>

Forum 18: <**http://www.forum18.org/**>

On freedom of expression:

Article 19: Global Campaign for Freedom of Expression: < **http://www.article19.org/**>

Amnesty International, Learn about Human Rights: Freedom of Expression: <**http://www.amnesty.org/en/freedom-of-expression**>

On freedom of information:

Access Info Europe: < **http://www.access-info.org/**>

Freedom Info.org: <**http://www.freedominfo.org/countries/index.htm**>

13

EDUCATION AND WORK

Fons Coomans

SUMMARY

This chapter focuses on the normative content of the right to education and the right to work. It discusses the sources of these rights under international human rights law and their main features and components. Both rights should be understood in terms of different entitlements and freedoms. Next, the obligations resulting from each right are set out, demonstrating that states have both negative and positive obligations. Finally, the relationship of each right with other human rights is highlighted, thus illustrating that all human rights are interrelated and interdependent.

1 INTRODUCTION

This chapter discusses two human rights that belong to the category of economic, social, and cultural rights, namely the right to education and the right to work. It was long argued that this category of human rights is different from civil and political rights. The latter were said to be capable of immediate implementation, cost-free, and only entailing negative obligations (obligations not to interfere) for states. Economic, social, and cultural rights, on the other hand, were seen as subject to progressive realization, requiring financial resources, and entailing positive obligations (obligations to actively take measures). These differences were also said to imply that civil and political rights could be enforced by courts, whereas economic, social, and cultural rights were seen as non-justiciable, that is, not suitable for review by courts. This traditional view, which emphasized the inherent differences between the two categories of rights, dominated until the late 1980s. Gradually, however, this approach has given way to a view that stresses the unity, equality, and interdependence of all human rights.[1]

Section 2 of the chapter deals with the right to education and Section 3 with the right to work and work-related rights. The chapter explains how the modern view of the nature of economic, social, and cultural rights can be applied to these rights. Each

---

[1] See Chapter 8, above.

section first discusses the sources of the right under international human rights law, its main features, and components. Next, the obligations resulting from each right are discussed. Finally, the relationship of each right with other human rights is highlighted. Both rights are crucial for one's ability to live a life in dignity and develop one's personality.[2]

2 THE RIGHT TO EDUCATION

The right to education has been included in many constitutions and international treaties. States have agreed that illiteracy must be eliminated and that all children must attend school. However, there is a big gap between theory and reality. Worldwide there are still 100 million children of primary school age who do not have access to education. The right to education is crucial for a person's self-fulfilment and the development of society as a whole. This section explains what the right to education is and what states should do to make this key right a reality for those who lack access to education.

2.1 SOURCES

2.1.1 Universal instruments

Article 26 of the Universal Declaration of Human Rights (UDHR) has been the basis for further guarantees of the right to education in later human rights instruments. It provides for the three basic characteristics of the right to education, namely, recognition of the right to receive an education, a guarantee for the exercise of parental rights in matters of education, and a reference to the aims of education.

Article 26 UDHR was transformed into legally binding form through two provisions of the International Covenant on Economic, Social and Cultural Rights (ICESCR), which in comparison to other Covenant rights are rather detailed: Articles 13 and 14. The right to education laid down in Article 13 ICESCR is a universal right, granted to every person, regardless of age, language, social or ethnic origin, or other status. Article 13(1) lists the aims that education should achieve in society. Article 13(2) enumerates the different steps that states must take to achieve the full realization of the right to education, in particular the specific obligation to make education available and accessible in a non-discriminatory way. In performing this duty, states have a degree of discretion within the limits of the standards of Article 13 and the key provision of Article 2(1), which states:

Each State Party to the present Covenant undertakes to take steps, individually and through international assistance and co-operation, especially economic and technical, to the maximum of its available resources, with a view to achieving progressively the full realization of

---

[2] See UDHR, Art 22.

the rights recognised in the present Covenant by all appropriate means, including particularly the adoption of legislative measures.

Article 14 deals with the implementation of primary education in states that have not yet realized this goal. It requires states to adopt a plan of action for the introduction of free and compulsory primary education. Article 13(3) and (4) guarantees the rights of parents in matters of education and the freedom to establish schools outside the public school system.

Other relevant universal instruments include the UN Educational, Scientific and Cultural Organization (UNESCO) Convention against Discrimination in Education, adopted in 1960, which aims to eliminate discrimination in education and promote equality of opportunity and treatment. The historical background of this convention is the discrimination and segregation in education under the *apartheid* regime in South Africa. It remains relevant today as an important interpretation of the phenomenon of discrimination and exclusion in education. Article 10 of the Convention on the Elimination of All Forms of Discrimination against Women (CEDAW) requires states to ensure to women equal rights with men in the field of education. It lists a number of particular measures and goals, such as access to the same curricula and reduction in female student drop-out rates. The Convention on the Rights of the Child (CRC) also contains a number of provisions relating to the right to education. Article 28 lists the measures that states must take progressively to realize this right. It includes one new element that is lacking in previous instruments, namely the obligation to ensure that school discipline is administered in a manner consistent with the child's dignity. This may be understood as a ban on applying corporal punishment in schools. Article 29(1) deals with the aims of education, while Article 29(2) guarantees the freedom of individuals and bodies to establish schools. Finally, Article 32(1) calls for protective measures against economic exploitation of children (child labour) which may interfere with the child's education.

2.1.2 Regional instruments

The right to education is also guaranteed by regional human rights instruments. In Europe, the relevant provision is Article 2 of the First Protocol to the European Convention on Human Rights (ECHR). This norm guarantees access to public educational institutions without discrimination and requires states to abstain from interference in the free exercise and free choice of education by pupils and parents. The European Commission and the European Court of Human Rights have interpreted this provision as requiring states only to maintain the level of educational services existing at a given time, without imposing an obligation to expand educational facilities or to increase funding for education.[3] Access to education within the context of

---

[3] The European Court of Human Rights has interpreted the meaning and scope of Art 2 in three leading judgments: *Case relating to certain aspects of the laws on the use of languages in education in Belgium* (*Belgian Linguistics Case No 2*) (1968) 1 EHRR 252; *Kjeldsen, Busk Madsen and Pedersen v Denmark* (1976) 1 EHRR 711; and *Campbell and Cosans v UK* (1982) 4 EHRR 293.

labour and other professional activities is covered by the right to vocational training laid down in Article 10 of the European Social Charter (1961). Educational rights of national minorities are guaranteed by Articles 12 to 14 of the Council of Europe Framework Convention for the Protection of National Minorities (1995). For example, Article 13 recognizes the right of persons belonging to a national minority to set up and manage their own (private) educational institutions, without entailing any financial obligations for state parties. Finally, the EU Charter of Fundamental Rights guarantees the right to education in Article 14. This provision contains the key elements of the ECHR and the European Social Charter relating to education, but it adds that the right to education includes the possibility of receiving free compulsory education (Article 14(2)). The latter element is also a key part of Article 13 ICESCR.

Article 17(1) of the African Charter on Human and Peoples' Rights (ACHPR) provides that '[e]very individual shall have the right to education'. The Charter does not elaborate on this brief and generally worded provision. However, the African Charter on the Rights and Welfare of the Child contains a detailed provision on the right to education in Article 11. It is modelled on other human rights instruments, in particular the ICESCR and the CRC. It also contains some elements that are relevant from an African perspective. These include a clause that education shall be directed to the preservation and strengthening of positive African morals, traditional values, and cultures, and to the promotion and achievements of African unity and solidarity (Article 11(2)(c) and (f)). Furthermore, Article 11(6) stipulates that states parties shall take all appropriate measures to ensure that children who become pregnant before completing their education shall have an opportunity to continue their education on the basis of their individual ability. This means that they should not be banned from attending school.

The Additional Protocol to the American Convention on Human Rights in the Area of Economic, Social and Cultural Rights (Protocol of San Salvador) deals with the right to education in Article 13. This provision is very similar to Article 13 ICESCR. It includes the rights to receive an education and to choose an education. What is special about this Protocol is that the complaints procedure of the American Convention on Human Rights (ACHR) applies to two of its provisions, namely certain trade union rights (Article 8a) and the right to education (Article 13). That means that there is a mechanism open to individuals to enforce these rights in case they 'are violated by action directly attributable to a State Party to this Protocol'.[4]

Finally, Article 41 of the Arab Charter on Human Rights, adopted in 2004, provides for the right to education and requires states to eradicate illiteracy. It contains references to free primary and fundamental education and the aims of education. However, it lacks a provision guaranteeing parental rights and the freedom to establish schools.

From this overview, it becomes clear that Article 26 UDHR has been, and still is, a major source of inspiration for the drafting of universal and regional provisions on the

---

[4] Protocol of San Salvador, Art 19(6).

right to education. However, subsequent developments, changing views, and regional particularities have been taken into account in more recent instruments.

2.2 FEATURES

Two aspects of the right to education as laid down in international documents can be identified. On the one hand, realization of the right to education demands an effort on the part of the state to make education available and accessible. It implies a positive state obligation. This may be defined as the *right to receive an education* or the *social dimension* of the right to education. On the other hand, there is the personal freedom of individuals to choose between state-organized and non-public education, which can be translated, for example, in parents' freedom to ensure their children's moral and religious education according to their own beliefs. From this stems the freedom of natural persons or legal entities to establish their own educational institutions. This is the *right to choose an education* or the *freedom dimension* of the right to education. It requires the state to follow a policy of non-interference in private matters. It implies a negative state obligation. Both aspects can be found in Articles 13 and 14 ICESCR. Article 13(2) and Article 14 cover the social dimension, while Article 13(3) and (4) embodies the freedom dimension.

In addition, the right to education has been explained by the Committee on Economic, Social and Cultural Rights and the UN Special Rapporteur on the right to education to include four interrelated features.

- *Availability*: functioning educational institutions and programmes have to be available in sufficient numbers, through a public educational system and allowing private parties to establish non-public schools.
- *Accessibility*: educational institutions and programmes have to be accessible to everyone, without discrimination on any ground, also implying physical and economic accessibility.
- *Acceptability*: the form and substance of education, including curricula and teaching methods, have to be relevant, culturally appropriate, of good quality, and in accordance with the best interests of the child; this includes a safe and healthy school environment.
- *Adaptability*: education has to be flexible, so that it can adapt to the needs of changing societies and communities and respond to the needs of students within their specific social and cultural context, including the evolving capacities of the child.[5]

This '4-A' scheme is a useful device to analyse the content of the right to receive an education and the obligations of states parties resulting from it as well as to measure the level of its realization.

---

[5] CESCR, General Comment 13, HRI/GEN/1/Rev.9 (Vol I) 63. Preliminary Report of the Special Rapporteur on the Right to Education, E/CN.4/1999/49 (13 January 1999) part II.

2.3 THE AIMS OF EDUCATION

Education can be used or abused to prepare children well or badly for life.[6] Education in Nazi Germany was an example of brainwashing children. Indeed, the formulation of the aims of education as contained in international human rights instruments reflects the aftermath of the Second World War. This is clear from Article 26 UDHR, which provides that education should contribute to avoiding conflicts between nations, groups, and people by promoting understanding, tolerance, and friendship and the maintenance of peace. In addition, education must be directed to the full development of the human personality and to strengthening respect for human rights. By emphasizing the individual's sense of dignity and ability to participate in a free society, Article 13(1) ICESCR makes it clear that the interests of the individual should be central to education.

It is noteworthy that some instruments emphasize specific aims, such as the elimination of stereotyped concepts of the role of men and women at all levels and in all forms of education (Article 10(c) CEDAW) or the development of a child's personality, talents, and mental and physical abilities through education (Article 29(1)(a) CRC). The CRC also adds further goals for education, such as the development of respect for the natural environment and for people of indigenous origin. These common aims, laid down in a number of international instruments, reflect a 'broad universal consensus on the major aims and objectives of the right to education'.[7] They also constitute the foundation for education about human rights in schools worldwide.[8]

2.4 COMPONENTS

On the basis of treaty law, general comments of the Committee on Economic, Social and Cultural Rights, and case law, the following four key components of the right to education can be identified.

2.4.1 Access to education on a non-discriminatory basis

The essence of the right to education is the right to access available educational facilities. In more concrete terms, this means the right of access to existing public educational institutions on a non-discriminatory basis.[9] This right is violated, for example, if people belonging to a specific ethnic, linguistic, or religious group have restricted access to existing public educational institutions, as is the case for Roma children in some European countries.[10] In addition, education provided by the state should be of the same quality for all groups. Girls, for example, should not be given

---

[6] Tomasevski, *Education Denied* (Zed Books, 2003) 60.

[7] Nowak, 'The Right to Education' in Eide, Krause, and Rosas (eds), *Economic, Social and Cultural Rights* (Martinus Nijhoff, 2001) 251.

[8] See eg UNESCO/OHCHR, Plan of Action: World Programme for Human Rights Education (2006).

[9] ICESCR, Arts 2(2) and 3; ICCPR, Art 26; CRC, Art 2.

[10] See *DH and Others v Czech Republic*, App no 57325/00, Judgment of 13 November 2007. Coomans, 'Discrimination and Stigmatisation Regarding Education: The Case of the Romani Children in the Czech

education of an inferior quality compared to boys.[11] Another, extreme, example was the situation in Afghanistan where the Taliban regime banned girls and women from all types of educational institutions.[12] In some African countries, female students are forced to disclose a pregnancy and leave school once the pregnancy has been discovered. This practice was found to be discriminatory by the Botswana Court of Appeal.[13]

2.4.2 The right to enjoy free and compulsory primary education

A second key component of the right to education is the right to enjoy primary education in one form or another, not necessarily in the form of traditional classroom teaching. Primary education is so fundamental for the development of a person's abilities that it can be rightfully defined as a minimum claim. Accordingly, the Supreme Court of India has held the right to (primary) education to be implicit in the right to life.[14] International human rights law does not define the term 'primary education', but guidelines have been developed by international organizations such as UNESCO.[15] Primary education relates to the first layer of a formal school system and usually begins between the ages of 5 and 7 and lasts approximately six years, but in any case no fewer than four years.[16] Primary education includes the teaching of basic learning needs or basic education.

The term 'basic education' is frequently used, for example in outcome documents of international conferences such as the World Declaration on Education for All, but it is not part of international human rights law.[17] Basic education relates to the content of education rather than the form it takes (formal or non-formal schooling). Apart from a school and classroom system, basic education may be given in less traditional forms, such as village- or community-based, or in the open air. Usually, basic education is aimed at children within the framework of primary schooling. However, basic education is also relevant for other persons who lack the basic knowledge and skills. This dimension is referred to as 'fundamental education' in Article 13(2)(d) ICESCR. The enjoyment of this right is not limited by age or gender; it extends to children, youth, and adults, including older persons; it is an integral component of adult education and life-long learning.[18]

Republic' in Willems (ed), *Developmental and Autonomy Rights of Children: Empowering Children, Caregivers and Communities* (Intersentia, 2002).

[11] See UNESCO Convention Against Discrimination in Education, Art 1(1) and CEDAW, Art 10.

[12] See Human Rights Watch, *1999 World Report*. See also Report of the UN Secretary-General on the situation of women and girls in Afghanistan, E/CN.4/Sub.2/2000/18 (21 July 2000).

[13] Quansah, 'Is the Right to Get Pregnant a Fundamental Right in Botswana?' (1995) 39 *J Afr L* 97.

[14] *Unni Krishnan and Others v State of AP and Others*, 1 SCC 645 (4 February 1993).

[15] See eg UNESCO, Statistical Yearbook and Revised Recommendation concerning the Standardization of Educational Statistics (1978).

[16] See Preliminary Report of the Special Rapporteur on the Right to Education, n 5, paras 75–9; Melchiorre, 'At what age?...' (2004) available at: <http://www.right-to-education.org>.

[17] Millennium Development Goal No 2 aims at achieving 'universal primary education'. See <http://www.un.org/millenniumgoals>.   [18] CESCR, General Comment 13, n 5.

The right to free and compulsory primary education also implies that no one, for example parents or employers, can withhold a child from attending primary education.[19] It is the only provision in the UDHR and the ICESCR in which the exercise of a right is linked to meeting an obligation, namely to attend primary education. States have an obligation to protect this right from encroachments by third persons. According to Article 13(2)(a) ICESCR primary education shall be compulsory. There is a worldwide trend to extend compulsory schooling beyond primary schooling. The rationale for a minimum length of compulsory schooling beyond 11 years of age is that it should last at least to the minimum age of employment.[20] Obviously it is not sufficient that primary education is compulsory by law. What is also necessary is an official state inspection service to supervise and enforce this duty with respect to parents, schools, employers, and pupils themselves.

There are a number of factors which may influence actual attendance of children at school. These include inadequacy of school services, such as the distance between a student's home and the school, lack of transportation facilities, lack of running water and sanitation facilities at school, teaching in a language other than the child's mother tongue, and teaching materials and methods that do not fit in with the cultural background of children and their parents (adaptability of education). Other factors relate to the socio-economic and cultural status of parents, including their inability to pay for school attendance of their children, traditional attitudes regarding the education of girls, and loss of family income that a child attending classes would otherwise earn.

Article 13(2)(a) ICESCR also stipulates that primary education shall be free. The rationale behind this entitlement is 'that children would not have to pay for their schooling or remain deprived of it when they cannot afford the cost. Children cannot wait to grow, hence their prioritized right to education in international human rights law. The damage of denied education while they are growing up cannot be retroactively remedied.'[21] The degree to which primary education is really free is determined by a number of direct and indirect costs, such as school fees, expenses for textbooks, extra lessons, meals at school canteens, school transport, school uniforms, medical expenses, and boarding fees. In some countries it is the practice that the village community or parents provide labour for constructing, running, or maintaining the school, which may be seen as a form of indirect cost. Another form of indirect cost for parents is taxation. Its effects upon the accessibility of education will depend upon the progressiveness of the tax system: do low income groups pay less, in absolute and relative terms, compared to high income groups?[22]

---

[19] See CESCR, General Comment 11, HRI/GEN/1/Rev.9 (Vol I) 52.

[20] See Progress report of the Special Rapporteur on the Right to Education, E/CN.4/2000/6 (1 February 2000) para 46 and Table 3. See also Melchiorre, n 16.

[21] Report of the Special Rapporteur on the Right to Education, E/CN.4/2004/45 (15 January 2004) para 8.

[22] See background paper prepared by the Special Rapporteur on the Right to Education, E/C.12/1998/18 (30 November 1998) para 12.

Primary education must be a priority when allocating resources, because it deals with the fundamental basis for a person's development and the development of society as a whole.[23] It is the responsibility of states to provide for primary education and maintain educational services. They cannot waive that responsibility by giving more room to the private sector or by stimulating public–private partnerships for the financing of the educational infrastructure. With respect to the right to education in the ECHR, the European Court of Human Rights has held that a state cannot absolve itself of responsibility by delegating its obligations to private school bodies.[24] UNICEF has emphasized that 'only the State...can pull together all the components into a coherent but flexible education system'.[25] The Committee on Economic, Social and Cultural Rights has stressed that 'Article 13 [ICESCR] regards States as having principal responsibility for the direct provision of education in most circumstances'[26] and that states have an immediate duty to provide primary education for all.[27] For those states that have not yet realized compulsory and free primary education, there is an 'unequivocal obligation' to adopt and implement a detailed plan of action as provided for in Article 14 ICESCR.[28]

2.4.3 Free choice of education

Yet another key component of the right to education is free choice of education without interference by the state or a third person, in particular, but not exclusively, with regard to religious or philosophical convictions. This component is violated when a state fails to respect the free choice of parents with regard to religious instruction of their children. Public education entails the danger of political goals, that is, the danger that the state will promote the most influential 'philosophy of life'.[29] Thus, a state must ensure an objective and pluralist curriculum and avoid indoctrination in this dominant philosophy.[30] However, in many states there is only limited, or no, opportunity to attend education of one's own choice: there may only be state-controlled education or, where available, private education is too expensive for parents. There is no obligation under international human rights law for states to provide financial support to private educational institutions. If they do, however, they must do so in a non-discriminatory way.[31]

2.4.4 The right to be educated in the language of one's own choice

A more controversial question is whether the right to be educated in the language of one's own choice is a key component of the right to education. In the *Belgian Linguistics*

---

[23] See CESCR, General Comment 13, n 5, para 51: 'States parties are obliged to prioritise the introduction of compulsory, free education'.   [24] *Costello-Roberts v UK* (1993) 19 EHRR 112.
[25] UNICEF, *The State of the World's Children 1999*, 63.
[26] CESCR, General Comment 13, n 5, para 48.   [27] Ibid, para 51.
[28] CESCR, General Comment 11, n 19, para 9.
[29] See ACHPR, Art 17(3): 'The promotion and protection of morals and traditional values recognized by the community shall be the duty of the State.'
[30] *Kjeldsen, Busk Madsen and Pedersen*, n 3. The Court emphasized that Art 2 of the First Protocol should be interpreted in light of Art 8 (right to privacy), Art 9 (freedom of conscience and religion), and Art 10 (freedom to receive information) ECHR.
[31] See *Waldman v Canada*, CCPR/C/67/D/1996 (5 November 1999).

Case, the European Court of Human Rights stated that 'the right to education would be meaningless if it did not imply, in favour of its beneficiaries, the right to be educated in the national language or in one of the national languages, as the case may be'.[32] This means that it is the state that determines whether a specific language is to be a national or official language as a medium of instruction in education. In addition, the European Court stressed that individuals cannot claim a right to state-funded education in the language of their own choice, thus rejecting claims of a positive state obligation in that regard.

On the other hand, a state must respect the freedom of individuals to teach, for instance, a minority language in schools established and directed by members of that minority. This does not imply, however, that a state must allow the use of this language as the only medium of instruction; this would be dependent on the educational policy of the state. As a minimum, states must not frustrate the right of members of national, ethnic, or linguistic minorities to be taught in their mother tongue at institutions outside the official system of public education, albeit they are not obliged to fund these institutions. This right of minorities is solidly established in international law.[33] It was a cornerstone of the minority protection system established under the auspices of the League of Nations after the First World War. Moreover, the right of minorities to establish educational institutions in which they are entitled to use their own language was characterized by the Permanent Court of International Justice in 1935 as 'indispensable to enable the minority to enjoy the same treatment as the majority, not only in law but also in fact'. The Court considered these institutions as 'suitable means for the preservation of their racial peculiarities, their traditions and their national characteristics'.[34] It is in this sense that the right to be educated in the language of one's own choice belongs to the key components of the right to education.

2.5 TYPES OF OBLIGATIONS

Obligations of states resulting from Articles 13 and 14 ICESCR may be derived from these treaty provisions themselves, Article 2(1) ICESCR, and General Comments 3, 11, and 13 of the Committee on Economic, Social and Cultural Rights. They may be divided into general obligations and specific obligations. *General obligations* include immediate obligations to prohibit discrimination in law and in fact, in the area of education, and to take steps to make primary education compulsory and free. Moreover, states are obliged not to take retrogressive measures, such as the introduction of school fees where previously education was free, and to protect the most vulnerable groups in society through special programmes, such as schooling for street children. *Specific obligations* include obligations to draft, adopt, and implement a comprehensive

[32] n 3, para 3.

[33] See eg ICCPR, Art 27; Document of the Copenhagen Meeting of the Conference on the Human Dimension of the CSCE (1990) sections 32–4; Declaration on the Rights of Persons Belonging to National or Ethnic, Religious and Linguistic Minorities, Art 4; European Charter for Regional or Minority Languages, Art 8; Framework Convention for the Protection of National Minorities, Arts 12–14.

[34] *Minority Schools in Albania*, PCIJ, Advisory Opinion, Series A/B No 64 (1935) 17.

national education strategy, to establish minimum standards for private educational institutions, to develop curricula that conform to the purposes of education, and to set up a school inspection system.

The typology of obligations introduced by the Committee on Economic, Social and Cultural Rights (obligations to respect, to protect, and to fulfil)[35] can be used to further define and refine the nature of states' obligations.

The obligation to *respect* the right to education requires states to abstain from interference. They must not prevent children from attending education, for example by closing educational institutions in times of political tension without complying with the limitations clause of Article 4 ICESCR.[36] In addition, states must not discriminate on the basis of sex or ethnic origin with respect to admission to public schools. Detailed standards of non-discrimination and equal treatment of individuals in education are laid down in the UNESCO Convention against Discrimination in Education, particularly in its Articles 1 and 3. The obligation to respect can be characterized as an obligation of conduct: it requires the state to follow the specific course of action specified in the treaty provision.

The obligation to *protect* requires states to guarantee the exercise of the right to education in horizontal relations (between private groups or individuals). For example, they must protect against discrimination of students in obtaining access to non-public schools. Other examples of the obligation to protect are the adoption and enforcement of legislation to combat child or bonded labour in private labour relations, or arrangements for monitoring and enforcing compulsory primary education.

The nature of the right to education is such that positive state action is needed to achieve the full realization of this right. In the view of the Committee on Economic, Social and Cultural Rights, 'it is clear that article 13 regards States as having principal responsibility for the direct provision of education in most circumstances'.[37] This statement can be seen as a confirmation of the obligation to *fulfil*. The obligation to fulfil requires states to make the various types of education available and accessible for all and to maintain that level of realization, which may involve a variety of measures. While it may be necessary to adopt legislation to provide a legal framework, the primary means of realizing the right to education are policy measures as well as financial and material support. The obligation to fulfil implies that states have a substantial degree of latitude, depending also on the specific level of education and the wording of the respective treaty obligation. Compare, for example, the following clauses: 'primary education shall be compulsory and available free to all' (Article 13(2)(a) ICESCR); 'secondary education... shall be made generally available and accessible to all by every appropriate means, and in particular by the progressive introduction of free education' (Article 13(2)(b) ICESCR). Implementation of the latter clause gives more latitude to states than the former. Therefore, the obligation to fulfil should be characterized as an obligation of result, leaving the choice of means to the state, providing the result achieved conforms to international standards.

---

[35] See Chapter 6, above.   [36] CESCR, General Comment 13, n 5, para 59.   [37] Ibid, para 48.

Particular elements of the right to education give rise to *minimum core obligations* as defined by the Committee on Economic, Social and Cultural Rights in its General Comment on the nature of states parties' obligations.[38] Such obligations are not limited to cost-free (negative) obligations to respect but also include positive obligations to protect and to fulfil. Minimum core obligations emanating from the right to education apply irrespective of the availability of resources.[39] According to the Committee, the minimum core obligations with respect to the right to education include obligations:

to ensure the right of access to public educational institutions and programmes on a non-discriminatory basis; to ensure that education conforms to the objectives set out in article 13(1) [ICESCR]; to provide primary education for all in accordance with article 13(2)(a); to adopt and implement a national educational strategy which includes provision for secondary higher and fundamental education; and to ensure free choice of education without interference from the State or third parties, subject to conformity with 'minimum educational standards' (article 13(3) and (4)).[40]

It is obvious that for many states meeting these core obligations is a challenge from legal, policy, and financial points of view.

2.6 RELATIONSHIP WITH OTHER HUMAN RIGHTS

Education is a social good in that it creates opportunities and provides choices to people. In this sense, education is an end in itself. However, it is also a means to an end, because it helps to achieve economic growth, health, poverty reduction, personal development, and democracy. Therefore, the right to education should be characterized as an 'empowerment right'. Such a right 'provides the individual with control over the course of his or her life, and in particular, control over...the state'.[41] In other words, exercising an empowerment right enables a person to experience the benefit of other rights: 'the key to social action in defense of rights...is an educated citizenry, able to spread its ideas and to organize in defense of rights'.[42] Education enables people to make a contribution to society as independent and emancipated citizens. Civil and political rights, such as freedom of expression, freedom of association, or the right to political participation only obtain substance and meaning when a person is educated. Galbraith has emphasized that 'education not only makes democracy possible; it also makes it essential. Education not only brings into existence a population with an understanding of the public tasks; it also creates their demand to be heard.'[43] In this sense, education is a threat to autocratic rule. Governments have used the education system for building nations, for instance through the introduction of a national language. Often this happened to the detriment of the languages and cultures of ethnic

---

[38] CESCR, General Comment 3, HRI/GEN/1/Rev.9 (Vol I) 7.

[39] 'Maastricht Guidelines on Violations of Economic, Social and Cultural Rights' (1998) 20 *HRQ* 691.

[40] CESCR, General Comment 13, n 5, para 57.

[41] Donnelly and Howard, 'Assessing National Human Rights Performance: A Theoretical Framework' (1988) 10 *HRQ* 214, 215.   [42] Ibid, 234–5.

[43] Galbraith, *The Good Society: The Humane Agenda* (Houghton Mifflin, 1996).

minorities and indigenous groups. For such groups, the right to education is an essential means to preserve and strengthen their cultural identity.

Education enhances social mobility: it helps people to escape from discrimination based on social status and to move up the social ladder. Moreover, education promotes the realization of other social, economic, and cultural rights, such as the right to work, the right to food, or the right to health: an educated person will have a greater chance of finding a job, will be better equipped to secure his or her own food supply, and is more aware of public health dangers. In general, education promotes the fulfilment of the right to an adequate standard of living; it provides people with access to the skills and knowledge for full membership of society. From the perspective of the rights of the child, education contributes to socializing children into understanding and accepting views different from their own. In other words, education unlocks the enjoyment of other human rights and contributes in an important way to the promotion of the essence of human rights, namely living in human dignity.

Finally, the right to education has a clear overlap with civil rights, such as freedom of religion and the right to privacy: the freedom of parents to determine the (religious) education of their children is not only part of the right to education but also of the freedom of religion[44] and is an issue belonging to people's private lives. Similarly, the right to education is linked to the freedom of association through the freedom to establish private educational institutions.

The right to education, through its links with other rights, accentuates the unity, indivisibility, and interdependence of all human rights. It is related to civil and political rights by its freedom dimension and the obligation of states to abstain from interference with that freedom. It is also linked to other economic, social, and cultural rights through its social dimension which calls for state action to make the right to receive an education effective.

3   THE RIGHT TO WORK AND WORK-RELATED RIGHTS

In the age of economic globalization, millions of workers in many parts of the world experience the flexibility of the world labour market on a daily basis. They may benefit from new jobs created as a result of foreign direct investment, or they may lose their job, because their employer fires them and moves the company to a country where labour is cheaper. As jobs move from one part of the world to another, so too do workers. Many migrant workers from developing countries try to find a living in rich countries by taking on work that is badly paid and often of an inferior status and quality. It is particularly in this type of situation that workers' rights come to the fore. These rights are meant to counter the negative consequences of economic globalization for

---

[44] See ICESCR, Art 13(3) and ICCPR, Art 18(4).

labour, such as extreme forms of income inequality, exploitation of workers (including women, children, and migrant workers), and high levels of unemployment. The reaction of the international community to these consequences has been the call for social justice and decent work.[45] Workers' rights are crucial in this respect. They aim at protecting and promoting working conditions by laying down international minimum standards. The International Labour Organization (ILO) has played, and continues to play, a key role in setting, implementing, and monitoring these standards. This section of the chapter discusses the right to work and so-called work-related rights, including, among others, the right to the enjoyment of just and favourable working conditions, the right to strike, and trade union rights.

3.1 SOURCES

3.1.1 Universal instruments

A discussion of the right to work and work-related rights should start with the origins of the ILO, which was established in 1919 after the First World War. From the preamble to its constitution it is clear that the achievement of social justice was considered to be crucial for the establishment of lasting peace between states. In addition, it was deemed important to improve labour conditions of workers in order to prevent social unrest, which could possibly result in social and political revolutions such as the one that took place in Russia in 1917.[46] Thus, governments at that time had a self-interest in improving labour conditions, although sentiments of justice and humanity were also mentioned as guiding concerns in the preamble. In this respect, it is interesting to note that in 1944 the ILO stated explicitly that 'labour is not a commodity'.[47] Hundreds of binding conventions and non-binding recommendations have been adopted within the framework of the ILO over the years. The tripartite structure of the organization provides a framework for representatives of governments, workers, and employers to agree on new rules. These are usually called international labour standards.

The early establishment of the ILO meant that it was far ahead in laying down work-related rights when the UN started its normative human rights activities after the Second World War. The ILO contributed actively to the drafting of both the UDHR and the ICESCR. Article 23 UDHR and Articles 6 to 8 ICESCR contain a number of elements that relate to the protection of the right to work, such as the free choice of work, equal pay for equal work, and trade union rights. Trade union rights are also part of the International Covenant on Civil and Political Rights (ICCPR), Article 22 of which recognizes the right to form and join trade unions. The ICCPR also provides for the prohibition of forced labour in Article 8(3). There are a number of further universal human rights instruments that deal with work-related rights. Pursuant to

---

[45] See ILO Declaration on Social Justice for a Fair Globalization (2008).

[46] The text of the Constitution is available at: <http://www.ilo.org>.

[47] Declaration Concerning the Aims and Purposes of the International Labour Organization (Declaration of Philadelphia) (1944).

Article 5(e)(i) and (ii) ICERD, states have an obligation to prohibit and eliminate racial discrimination in the enjoyment of the right to work and the right to form and join trade unions. Article 11 CEDAW lays down detailed obligations for states aimed at eliminating discrimination in the field of employment. Article 32 CRC recognizes the right of children to be protected from economic exploitation and hazardous work. There is a clear link here with the elimination of child labour. Article 10(3) ICESCR serves a similar purpose, adding that states 'should set age limits below which the paid employment of child labour should be prohibited and punishable by law'. Note the use of the permissive 'should' instead of the more mandatory 'shall'.

The work-related rights of migrant workers are of particular importance. The International Convention on the Protection of the Rights of All Migrant Workers and Members of their Families lays down a number of relevant rights. Its main feature is the principle of non-discrimination with respect to rights granted to migrant workers and members of their families (Article 7). This principle has been elaborated for matters of employment and labour conditions in Article 25. However, Article 52 allows for restrictions that states of employment may impose on migrant workers' free choice of remunerated activities. Furthermore, the Convention contains a number of provisions that are applicable to particular categories of migrant workers, such as frontier workers and seasonal workers.[48] Some aspects of the Convention do not apply to migrant workers and members of their families who are non-documented or in an irregular situation.[49]

The Convention on the Rights of Persons with Disabilities is based on the principles of, among others, non-discrimination, full and effective participation and inclusion of disabled people in society, and equality of opportunity (Article 3). As is made clear by Article 27, these principles also apply to matters of work and employment. This means, for example, that states have to prohibit discrimination on the basis of disability with respect to conditions of recruitment for jobs and to promote employment opportunities and career advancement for persons with disabilities in the labour market. Among numerous other positive obligations, states must also ensure that reasonable accommodation is provided to persons with disabilities in the workplace.

3.1.2 Regional instruments

The European Social Charter (1961), the Additional Protocol to the European Social Charter (1988), and the Revised European Social Charter (1996) all aim at protecting the rights of workers. They extensively regulate various aspects of the right to work, employment conditions, vocational training, participation of workers in the determination of labour issues, and access to social security, social assistance, and welfare services. The Charter also identifies specific groups that need special protection, such as women, children, elderly persons, and migrant workers. The Charter does not recognize individual rights that are directly enforceable against the state. Although rights language is used, its provisions are framed as state obligations rather than individual

[48] Arts 57–63.   [49] See Art 5.

rights. For example, Article 1 of the Revised European Social Charter, dealing with the right to work, reads: 'With a view to ensuring the effective exercise of the right to work, the Contracting Parties undertake...to accept as one of their primary aims and responsibilities the achievement and maintenance of as high and stable a level of employment as possible, with a view to the attainment of full employment.' The Charter of Fundamental Rights of the European Union stipulates in Article 5 that no one shall be required to perform forced or compulsory labour. In addition, it contains a number of workers' rights, including protection in the event of unjustified dismissal (Article 30) and the right of workers to information and consultation (Article 27).

Article 15 of the ACHPR provides that every individual shall have the right to work under equitable and satisfactory conditions and receive equal pay for equal work. Interestingly, the Charter also contains duties that are imposed on the individual, one of them being 'to work to the best of his abilities and competence' (Article 29(6)). Article 15 of the African Charter on the Rights and Welfare of the Child provides protection against child labour in similar terms to those of Article 32 CRC. Measures to protect children cover both the formal and informal sectors of employment.

In the Americas, the Protocol of San Salvador provides for the right to work in Article 6. Its wording is quite modern in that it refers to the notions of dignity and decency that have been essential features of recent debates about the right to work.[50] Article 7 lists a range of labour conditions that should be just, equitable, and satisfactory. Like Article 24 UDHR, it recognizes that workers have a right to rest, leisure, and paid holidays, and remuneration for national holidays (Article 7(h)).

In the Arab Charter on Human Rights, one comprehensive article deals with a number of aspects of the right to work. Article 34 provides that the right to work is a natural right of every citizen. It also requires states to provide, to the extent possible, a job for the largest number of those willing to work. The reference to 'those willing to work' is unique in the texts of human rights instruments. Article 34 also prescribes non-discriminatory treatment of men and women in matters of training, employment, job protection, and remuneration.

3.1.3 ILO conventions

Conventions adopted within the framework of the ILO are special conventions, because they deal with one or more particular labour issue(s). As the ILO has always stated, labour standards included in its conventions and recommendations are universal in nature. They are deliberately set low in order to achieve a worldwide reach, although more favourable national working conditions remain applicable.[51] The ILO conventions recognize that there are economic disparities between states and that these differences may have an impact on the way states implement their obligations.[52] What is decisive in the end is whether a state has complied with its treaty obligations.

---

[50] Art 6(1) reads: 'Everyone has the right to work, which includes the opportunity to secure the means for living a dignified and decent existence by performing a freely elected or accepted lawful activity.'
[51] ILO Constitution, Art 19(8).   [52] See also ibid, Art 19(3).

The conventions address diverse issues relating to the right to work and work-related rights, and many of them have a long history. The first ILO convention, adopted in 1919, dealt with the regulation of hours of work in industrial plants,[53] while another early convention was designed to counter unemployment.[54] More recent conventions deal with the elimination of the worst forms of child labour and the safety and health of workers in mines.[55]

3.2 FEATURES

The right to work has a number of special features. First of all, it is an aggregate right, that is, it includes a number of components, such as claims to employment, free choice of work, improvement of working conditions, and trade union rights. Furthermore, the nature of the right to work, understood as a claim to employment, is such that it is not possible to enforce it directly against the state. It is not a subjective right enforceable by courts. Most people are employed by private employers rather than the state. This means that the state must regulate, monitor, and enforce labour rules by laying down mechanisms that workers can use to enforce their rights against employers. Many labour standards thus apply in horizontal relationships between employers and employees. To implement the ILO conventions, states have to bring their domestic law and practice in conformity with the international standards and employers have to comply with the domestic law. The advantage of ILO standards is that they are specific and detailed, thus giving clear guidance to states as to how to implement them. Consequently, compared to other economic, social, and cultural rights, the right to work and work-related rights are well developed in terms of their normative content.

The detailed nature of ILO standards has helped to clarify the meaning of relevant provisions in human rights instruments. For example, Article 7(b) ICESCR mentions safe and healthy working conditions as a component of just and favourable conditions of work, without further explanation. ILO conventions and recommendations have been helpful in defining what this means for specific types of activity or categories of workers. For example, there is a convention on safety and health in the agricultural sector,[56] and a convention on the labour conditions of seafarers.[57] These detailed rules may be used by human rights supervisory bodies to explain the nature and scope of human rights obligations.

Traditionally, there was little cooperation and coordination between international labour circles, on the one hand, and the human rights movement, on the other hand. The ILO and trade unions paid little attention to the use of human rights language to promote their cause and human rights activists largely ignored labour rights issues

---

[53] Hours of Work (Industry) Convention 1919 (No 1).
[54] Unemployment Convention 1919 (No 2).
[55] Convention No 182 (1999) and Convention No 176 (1995) respectively.
[56] Convention No 184 (2001).   [57] Maritime Labour Convention (2006).

in their campaigns.[58] This situation has changed gradually over time. The ILO has been devoting special attention to the role of human rights in achieving social justice. For example, in 2009 it proposed an international labour standard in the form of a Recommendation on HIV/AIDS and the World of Work, which is meant to give impetus to anti-discrimination policies at the workplace level. On the other hand, the human rights community is focused increasingly on violations of workers' rights which often result as a negative consequence of the globalization of production and trade. For example, Amnesty International has broadened its mandate to include economic, social, and cultural rights and has drawn attention to the discrimination and abuse of internal migrant workers in China as a side-effect of uncontrolled business practices and economic growth.[59]

3.3 COMPONENTS

The right to work is composed of several key components. One of the most fundamental rights is the *freedom from slavery*, guaranteed by Article 8(1) ICCPR. Slavery is 'the status or condition of a person over whom any or all of the powers attaching to the right of ownership are exercised'.[60] Thus, a slave is unable to exercise the right of individual self-determination. Although slavery has been eradicated in many countries, it still exists in parts of Asia and Africa. For example, caste and ethnic status underpin the use of slavery in Niger, Mauritania, and Mali, where tens of thousands of people are ascribed slave status at birth and are then considered to be the property of their 'masters' who force them to work without pay.[61] In India many children work long hours in the cotton industry to pay off the debts of their parents. This is not freely chosen work, but bonded labour.

Forced or compulsory labour has also been banned under international human rights law. 'Forced or compulsory labour' is 'all work or service which is exacted from any person under the menace of any penalty and for which the said person has not offered himself voluntarily'.[62] In 1957, ILO member states agreed on new standards concerning the abolition of forced labour, committing themselves not to make use of forced labour as a means of political coercion or education or as a punishment for holding or expressing certain views; as a method of mobilizing and using labour for purposes of economic development; as a means of labour discipline; as a punishment for having participated in strikes; or as a means of racial, social, national, or religious discrimination.[63] The convention was directed against communist states that imposed forced labour in so-called labour camps for political opponents and states such as Rhodesia

[58] Leary, 'The Paradox of Workers' Rights as Human Rights' in Compa and Diamond (eds), *Human Rights, Labor Rights, and International Trade* (University of Pennsylvania Press, 1996) 22.

[59] Amnesty International, *China: Internal Migrants: Discrimination and Abuse* (1 March 2007).

[60] Slavery Convention (1926), Art 1(1).

[61] See <http://www.antislavery.org> for more information on current forms of slavery.

[62] See ILO Forced Labour Convention (No 29) (1930), Art 2(1).

[63] See ILO Convention Concerning the Abolition of Forced Labour (No 105) (1957), Art 1.

and South Africa that applied forced labour of black workers as part of their discriminatory laws and practice. Not all forms of 'compulsory' labour qualify as prohibited labour under international labour law and human rights law. Both the 1930 Forced Labour Convention and the ICCPR provide for exceptions, including compulsory military service and work required of persons in detention.[64]

The counterpart of the prohibition of slavery and forced labour is the *freedom to work*, which means the right to free choice of work or occupation. Workers have a right, not a duty, to work. This right is codified in several human rights instruments, such as Article 6(1) ICESCR and Article 1(2) Revised European Social Charter. An example of a restriction of the free choice of work is the prohibition of night work for women, as originally required by ILO standards.[65] This was meant to protect women from the adverse consequences night work would have on their health. Today, the prohibition of night work for women has been increasingly relaxed with a reference to the equality of treatment and opportunity between men and women. Recent standards provide for the regulation and protection of night work of both women and men.[66]

Another key component of the right to work and work-related rights is the principle of *non-discrimination and equal treatment*, which is part of every human rights treaty. For example, Article 7(a)(i) ICESCR provides for 'equal remuneration for work of equal value without distinction of any kind, in particular women being guaranteed conditions of work not inferior to those enjoyed by men, with equal pay for equal work'. ILO standards lay down more specific rules and other grounds of discrimination that are prohibited.[67] Examples include trade union membership and action, marital status, pregnancy, and family responsibilities.

The right to work also includes the *right to seek work*, which implies that states must design, adopt, and implement active employment policies aimed at creating jobs and reducing unemployment. States are under a duty to act, not to succeed in providing everyone with a job. In some communist states, the right to work was constitutionally guaranteed and the authorities claimed that there was full employment, when in reality there was hidden unemployment. Today, the internationalization of economic processes has limited the role of governments to influence employment through national measures, but raising employment figures remain one of the major concerns.[68]

The right to work implies a right to, not just any kind of work but, *decent work*. Although there is no conclusive definition of 'decent work', this concept, which is at the heart of current ILO policies and programmes, implies that work has to be of an acceptable quality in terms of conditions of work, feelings of value and satisfaction, relations between employer and employee, and remuneration. The right to a fair

---

[64] See Forced Labour Convention (No 29), Art 2(2) and ICCPR, Art 8(3).

[65] ILO Night Work (Women) Convention (No 4) (1919).

[66] ILO Night Work Convention (No 171) (1990). For a discussion, see Servais, *International Labour Law* (Kluwer Law International, 2005) 188–91.

[67] See ILO Discrimination (Employment and Occupation) Convention (No 111) (1958).

[68] See also ILO Employment Policy Convention (No 122) (1964) and Revised European Social Charter, Art 1(1).

remuneration is part of several human rights instruments.[69] It includes, inter alia, the right to equal pay for work of equal value. Fair remuneration is meant to guarantee to workers and their families a decent standard of living. The wage level is subject to a number of factors, such as the standard of living in a country, the type of work, and the situation on the labour market. For the European region, the European Committee on Social Rights has determined that the net minimum wage should amount to at least 60 per cent on the net national average wage.[70] Decency also implies that a certain minimum level of protection has to be met. For example, there is agreement that certain forms of child labour do not meet that standard, as is evidenced by the ILO Convention on the Worst Forms of Child Labour.[71] According to this convention, the worst forms of child labour include work which, by its nature or the circumstances in which it is carried out, is likely to harm the health, safety, or morals of children (Article 3(d)).

Other components of the right to work include the right to have access to free employment services in order to find a job as guaranteed by Article 1(3) Revised European Social Charter, and protection of employment security, that is, protection against unjustified dismissal. ILO Convention No 158 (1982) sets out reasons that cannot be invoked to justify a dismissal, such as union membership or the exercise of a right by a worker, such as maternity leave.

Finally, there are some instrumental rights, such as the freedom of association, the right to bargain collectively, and the right to strike that serve the purpose of promoting and protecting the right to work and work-related rights.

The critical importance of some fundamental work-related rights has been proclaimed and confirmed in a key Declaration adopted by all member states of the ILO in 1998. The Declaration on Fundamental Principles and Rights at Work establishes an obligation of member states, arising from the very fact of membership of the ILO, to respect, promote, and realize a number of *core principles and rights* laid down in ILO conventions. These include:

- freedom of association and effective recognition of the right to collective bargaining;
- elimination of all forms of forced or compulsory labour;
- effective abolition of child labour; and
- elimination of discrimination in respect of employment and occupation.

The significance of this Declaration lies in the fact that states agreed that they have these obligations even if they have not ratified the relevant conventions.[72] Furthermore, the principles referred to above have universal reach and application, applying to all

---

[69] See ICESCR, Art 7(a)(i); Revised European Social Charter, Art 4; Protocol of San Salvador, Art 7(a); ACHPR, Art 15.
[70] See Digest of the Case Law of the European Committee on Social Rights (2008) 43.
[71] ILO Convention No 182 (1999).
[72] ILO Declaration on Fundamental Principles and Rights at Work and Its Follow-Up (1998).

member states of the ILO with respect to both their domestic and international policies and practice. As a consequence, for example, importing and exporting states may
not benefit from commodities produced through the use of forced labour or the worst
forms of child labour.

3.4 OBLIGATIONS

Obligations resulting from the right to work and work-related rights can be derived
from the treaty provisions themselves as well as the explanations given by the
Committee on Economic, Social and Cultural Rights, for example in its General
Comment 18. However, these obligations have been formulated in general terms, often
making it difficult to monitor implementation.

As explained above, pursuant to Article 2(1) ICESCR, states must progressively
realize the rights included in the ICESCR by taking appropriate measures, such as
the adoption of legislation. Article 6(2) ICESCR lists a number of steps that states parties must take to achieve the full realization of the right to work, such as setting up
vocational guidance and training programmes. Some obligations are not subject to
progressive realization, but have an immediate effect. One example is the obligation to
guarantee that the right to work can be exercised 'without discrimination of any kind',
as provided for in Article 2(2) ICESCR.

The Committee on Economic, Social and Cultural Rights has identified further
obligations resulting from the right to work by using the typology of obligations 'to
respect, to protect and to fulfil'.[73] These entail both negative obligations to abstain from
interference and positive obligations to act. Under the obligation to *respect* the state
must not, for example, apply forced or compulsory labour and must allow the establishment and functioning of trade unions. The obligation to *protect* requires states to
lay down in domestic law standards for labour relations between private employers
and employees (for example minimum wages, working hours, and safety rules), to
monitor compliance with the law, and to enforce it in case of infringement. The obligation to *fulfil* requires states, for instance, to develop an active employment policy to
counter unemployment.

The Committee on Economic, Social and Cultural Rights has characterized some
obligations as *minimum core obligations* which must be realized under all circumstances. These include, for example, the obligation to ensure non-discrimination and
equal opportunity in matters of employment, for instance with respect to the right of
access to employment for women, migrants, and disabled people.[74] Another core obligation is the obligation to abolish the worst forms of child labour pursuant to applicable ILO standards.

As far as the obligations arising from ILO conventions are concerned, two broad
categories can be distinguished. First, some of the conventions entail immediate

---

[73] CESCR, General Comment 18, HRI/GEN/1/Rev.9 (Vol I) 139, paras 22-8.
[74] Ibid, para 31.

obligations for states. An example is the Equal Remuneration Convention (No 90) (1951), which stipulates in Article 2 that states shall ensure the application to all workers of the principle of equal remuneration for men and women workers for work of equal value. States may use different methods to implement this principle, including national laws or regulations, legally established or recognized machinery for wage determination, or collective agreements between employers and workers. Other conventions, in contrast, contain obligations that are programmatic in nature, that is, they provide for programmes of action that set general objectives for domestic policy. These conventions allow for policy freedom and discretion for authorities regarding how best to implement the standards. An example is the Human Resources Development Convention (No 142) (1975) which requires states to adopt and develop policies and programmes of vocational guidance and vocational training.

3.5 RELATIONSHIP WITH OTHER HUMAN RIGHTS

The right to work and work-related rights are linked to the enjoyment of other human rights. They play a key role in facilitating the right to an adequate standard of living laid down in Article 25 UDHR and Article 11 ICESCR. When people earn money through work, they are in a much better position to get access to food, medical care, housing, and education. Income generated through work is instrumental in acquiring property, such as a house or land. In addition, decent work, not any kind of work, and just and favourable working conditions contribute to living in dignity. There are also links with the right to social security, that is, the right to access and maintain benefits in order to secure protection from a lack of work-related income, caused by illness, disability, maternity, employment injury, unemployment, old age, or death of a family member.[75] This right is thus complementary to the right to work and work-related rights. The right of children not to be subject to child labour is closely linked to the need to make the right to education a reality.[76]

There are also relationships with civil and political rights, such as the right to information concerning work-related issues, freedom of expression to speak out about abuses at the workplace, and freedom of association with regard to trade unions. Finally, the enjoyment of other rights has an impact on the enjoyment of the right to work. Workers who are well trained and of good health will probably find it easier to find a suitable job and will perform better. This relationship has been acknowledged in international human rights law, including in the ILO Conventions[77] and the Revised European Social Charter.[78]

Due to its different dimensions and its links to other work-related rights, the right to work is a composite and complex right. In practice, it is particularly relevant to the horizontal relationships between employers and employees. Similar to the right to

[75] See CESCR, General Comment 19, HRI/GEN/1/Rev.9 (Vol I) 152, para 2. (This General Comment deals with the right to social security laid down in Article 9 ICESCR.) See Chapter 11, above.
[76] See Worst Forms of Child Labour Convention (No 182) (1999), Art 7(2).
[77] See Servais, n 66, 201–8.   [78] Arts 10–13.

education, it becomes clear with the right to work that all human rights are interrelated and interdependent. International human rights law is less developed with regard to the right to work than the international standards established within the framework of the ILO. The implementation of the right to work at the domestic level can benefit from the detailed rights and obligations laid down in ILO conventions. Similarly, it can be argued that ILO standards should be seen and applied as human rights norms, because they touch upon the protection of human dignity.

4 CONCLUSION

This chapter has demonstrated that both the right to education and the right to work are important for living a life in dignity. Both rights are critical for the development of society as a whole, but also for achieving self-fulfilment and 'moving up the social ladder'. Their content, but also their realization, reflects the idea that all human rights are indivisible, interdependent, and interrelated. The modern approach to economic, social, and cultural rights emphasizes the importance of clarifying the normative content of each right by identifying its different dimensions, framed as entitlements and freedoms. These give rise to positive and negative obligations for states. It is a challenge for states to phrase, implement, and monitor their domestic policies in accordance with international standards. This is particularly so when implementation requires allocation of scarce (financial) resources in a period of economic recession. Human rights monitoring bodies, international organizations, and NGOs should be aware of these different dimensions when monitoring implementation of these rights by states.

FURTHER READING

CHAPMAN and RUSSELL (eds), *Core Obligations: Building a Framework for Economic, Social and Cultural Rights* (Intersentia, 2002).

COOMANS (ed), *Justiciability of Economic and Social Rights—Experiences from Domestic Systems* (Intersentia, 2006).

——'Justiciability of the Right to Education' (2009) 2 *Erasmus LR* 427.

DONDERS and VOLODIN (eds), *Human Rights in Education, Science and Culture* (UNESCO/Ashgate, 2007).

EIDE, KRAUSE, and ROSAS (eds), *Economic, Social and Cultural Rights* (Martinus Nijhoff, 2001).

HOWARD-HASSMANN and WELCH, JR (eds), *Economic Rights in Canada and the United States* (University of Pennsylvania Press, 2006).

MUNDLAK, 'The Right to Work: Linking Human Rights and Employment Policy' (2007) 146 *Intl Lab Rev* 189.

RODGERS, LEE, SWEPSTON, and VAN DALE, *The ILO and the Quest for Social Justice, 1919–2009* (International Labour Office, 2009).

SERVAIS, *International Labour Law* (Kluwer Law International, 2005).

TOMASEVSKI, *Education Denied* (Zed Books, 2003).

USEFUL WEBSITES

ILO: <**http://www.ilo.org**>
UNESCO: <**http://www.unesco.org**>
International Network for Economic, Social & Cultural Rights: <**http://www.escr-net.org**>
Anti-Slavery: <**http://www.antislavery.org**>

14

ADMINISTRATION OF JUSTICE

Sangeeta Shah

SUMMARY

The fair and proper administration of justice is essential for the enjoyment of all human rights. A number of human rights seek to achieve this goal. The right to liberty regulates state powers of detention and provides safeguards against ill-treatment of detainees. The right to a fair trial sets out how court proceedings should be conducted and court systems organized. Although both these rights set out extensive guarantees for individuals who are suspected of having committed a criminal offence, they also provide general protections for all individuals subject to national justice systems. These rights seek to prevent the arbitrary use of executive power and create a climate conducive to the realization of human rights.

1 INTRODUCTION

How justice is dispensed has a profound effect on the realization of human rights. Without fair and proper administration of justice, human rights are almost meaningless. Actions that violate human rights cannot be effectively challenged and stopped. Therefore, there is a need to regulate how individuals should be treated under national justice systems. This was recognized as early as 1215 in the Magna Carta, which gave certain individuals what can now be considered to be the origins of the rights to liberty and fair trial.[1] These rights set out safeguards to ensure that notions of 'due process' are adhered to in the operation of regimes of detention, the investigation and prosecution of criminal charges, and the conduct of court proceedings. This chapter considers the content of both the right to liberty, including freedom from arbitrary detention (Section 2), freedom from enforced disappearance (Section 3), and security of the

---

[1] The rights were only accorded to noblemen. See Chapter 1, above.

person (Section 4), as well as the right to a fair trial (Section 5), all of which contribute to the fair and efficient administration of justice.

2 FREEDOM FROM ARBITRARY DETENTION

The ideal is that no one should be deprived of their liberty. However, there may be valid reasons for assuming custody of an individual. For example, it may be necessary to detain convicted criminals who pose a threat to the community. As such, traditionally, the main concern of human rights activists has been the capricious use of detention powers by oppressive governments in order to subdue their opponents. Beyond this, it was recognized that restrictions on liberty are permitted and may even be required.

However, even where the grounds for detention may be justified, individuals in detention are susceptible to violations of their human rights. They are regularly 'forgotten', left to languish in prisons or mental health facilities, or may be subjected to torture or ill-treatment, either at the hands of their captors or by virtue of the conditions in which they are held.[2] The right to liberty recognizes these concerns. It is an umbrella of protections, which seeks to prevent the arbitrary use of detention powers and provide safeguards to eradicate ill-treatment or 'disappearance' from instances of permitted detention. This section of the chapter first surveys the sources of the right to freedom from arbitrary detention and then considers how these twin aims are realized.

2.1 SOURCES

Article 9 UDHR provides that: 'No one shall be subjected to arbitrary arrest, detention or exile'. This pithy, yet powerful, provision was extended and its protections elaborated in Article 9 International Covenant on Civil and Political Rights (ICCPR). The Human Rights Committee has since articulated a general comment on the right to liberty[3] and the right has been guaranteed in other UN human rights treaties and declarations, including the Convention on the Protection of the Rights of Migrant Workers (Article 16), the Convention on the Rights of Persons with Disabilities (Article 14), and the Declaration on the Rights of Indigenous Peoples (Article 7). All regional human rights instruments also guarantee the right to liberty.[4] Freedom from arbitrary detention is a rule of customary international law and the Human Rights Committee has

---

[2] See Chapter 10, above.   [3] HRC, General Comment 8, HRI/GEN/1/Rev.9 (Vol I) 179.
[4] ECHR, Art 5; European Charter of Fundamental Rights, Art 6; ADHR, Art I; ACHR, Art 7; ACHPR, Art 6; Arab Charter on Human Rights, Art 14.

gone as far as claiming that this rule is peremptory in nature, that is, it may be a *jus cogens* norm.[5]

There are a number of non-binding instruments that serve to elaborate upon the implications of the right, including the UN Standard Minimum Rules for the Treatment of Prisoners,[6] UN Body of Principles for the Protection of All Persons under Any Form of Detention or Imprisonment,[7] UN Basic Rules for the Treatment of Prisoners,[8] UN Rules for the Protection of Juveniles Deprived of their Liberty,[9] the Council of Europe Minimum Rules for the Treatment of Prisoners,[10] and the Inter-American Commission of Human Rights' Principles and Best Practices on the Protection of Persons Deprived of Liberty in the Americas.[11]

Given the importance of the concerns regarding arbitrary detention, in 1991 the then UN Commission on Human Rights created a Working Group on Arbitrary Detention,[12] whose mandate has been renewed by the UN Human Rights Council.[13] The Working Group receives and investigates communications regarding possible cases of arbitrary detention, and also issues its own form of general comment: 'deliberations', on issues concerning arbitrary detention, which are an invaluable source of information.[14]

2.2 SCOPE

2.2.1 What constitutes a deprivation of liberty?

Although most issues concerning the right to liberty involve the arrest and detention of an individual in the context of criminal proceedings, the protections afforded by the right to liberty are not restricted to such situations. Rather, the Human Rights Committee has stressed in its general comment on Article 9 ICCPR that the provision is applicable to 'all deprivations of liberty, whether in criminal cases or in other cases such as, for example, mental illness, vagrancy, drug addiction, educational purposes, immigration control etc'.[15] This is not an exhaustive list and there may be other situations where a deprivation of liberty may occur.

It is important to note the limits of the scope of right to liberty provisions. For example, house arrest has been considered to be a deprivation of liberty,[16] while restrictions upon movement which confined an individual to his home during non-working hours was not a deprivation of liberty but a restriction upon the right to freedom of movement.[17] Similarly, restrictions upon movement within a state, a city, or even parts

---

[5] HRC, General Comment 29, HRI/GEN/1/Rev.9 (Vol I) 234, para 11.
[6] ECOSOC Res 663C(XXIV) (31 July 1957).   [7] GA Res 43/173 (9 December 1988).
[8] GA Res 45/111 (14 December 1990).   [9] GA Res 45/113 (14 December 1990).
[10] Committee of Ministers Res (73)5 (19 January 1973).
[11] OEA/Ser/L/V/II.131 doc.26 (March 2008).   [12] CHR Res 1991/42 (5 March 1991).
[13] HR Council Res 6/4 (28 September 2007).   [14] See Chapter 18, below.
[15] General Comment 8, n 3, para 1.
[16] *Madani v Algeria*, CCPR/C/89/D/1172/2003 (21 June 2007).
[17] *Trijonis v Lithuania*, Application no 2333/02 (17 March 2005).

of a city have been held to be restrictions on freedom of movement and not deprivations of liberty.[18] Right to liberty provisions are concerned with narrow notions of detention involving the imposition of severe restrictions upon a person's physical being. However, this does not mean that short periods of detention are excluded. Detention for a period of 55 minutes has been held to engage Article 5, the arbitrary detention provision, of the European Convention on Human Rights (ECHR).[19]

2.2.2 Permissible deprivations of liberty

Not all deprivations of liberty will constitute a violation of a state's obligations. Article 9(1) ICCPR provides that: 'No one shall be subjected to arbitrary arrest or detention. No one shall be deprived of his liberty except on such grounds and in accordance with such procedures as are established by law.' Therefore, only where a deprivation of liberty is unlawful and/or arbitrary, will it constitute a violation of Article 9(1). Other international treaties have similar provisions on arbitrary detention.[20]

The ECHR sets out a more restrictive approach to detention. Rather than simply protecting individuals against illegal and/or arbitrary detention, Article 5(1) ECHR provides an exhaustive list of grounds upon which detention is justified. These are:

1. execution of a sentence after conviction by a competent court;
2. non-compliance with a lawful court order or legal obligation;
3. reasonable suspicion of having committed an offence, to prevent flight having done so, or to prevent the commission of an offence where the ultimate aim is to bring the person before a competent court;
4. educational supervision in the case of minors;
5. prevention of the spread of infectious diseases;
6. where persons are of unsound mind, alcoholics, drug addicts, or vagrants; and
7. prevention of unauthorized entry into the state or where action is being taken with a view to deportation or extradition.

Detention on grounds other than those listed is not permissible under the ECHR.

If the detention does not meet the specific Article 5(1) ground upon which it was justified it will not be permitted. For example, in the wake of the attacks of 11 September 2001, a law was passed in the UK which authorized the detention of non-UK nationals who were suspected terrorists and could not be deported for fear that they may suffer torture abroad. The UK government justified these measures on the basis that they were immigration measures and as such were permitted under Article 5(1)(c) ECHR. However, the European Court of Human Rights disagreed, holding that the detention measures were not measures taken with a view to deportation as there was no prospect

---

[18] *Celepli v Sweden*, CCPR/C/51/D/456/91 (18 July 1994); *Karker v France*, CCPR/C/70/D/833/98 (26 October 2000).   [19] *Novotka v Slovakia*, Application no 47244/99 (4 November 2003).
[20] eg ACHR, Art 7; ACHPR, Art 6.

that the detained individuals could be removed from the UK. Therefore the powers of detention were considered to be a violation of Article 5(1) ECHR.[21]

None of the grounds set out in Article 5(1)(c) ECHR by itself is enough to justify detention. As with the other treaties, the detention must also be lawful and not arbitrary.

Legality

Any deprivation of liberty must be pursuant to domestic law. It must be both sanctioned by and in conformity with any procedural requirements set out in national legislation. For example, the detention of psychiatric patients in secure hospitals should only take place where there is a legal basis to do so. Similarly, where arrest warrants are mandatory and arrest takes place without one, a violation of the right to liberty will be found.[22] For example, in an attempt to arrest former President Garcia, the Peruvian army arrested his wife and children. As the army lacked constitutional authority to arrest individuals and the arrests were not based upon a court order, the Inter-American Commission of Human Rights held that the arrests were unlawful and thus in violation of the arbitrary detention provisions of the American Convention on Human Rights (ACHR).[23]

Arbitrariness

Whether detention is arbitrary will depend upon considerations of 'inappropriateness, injustice and lack of predictability' as well as 'unreasonableness'.[24] Thus, detention is arbitrary where 'it is not necessary in all the circumstances of the case' and so some form of proportionality assessment must take place.[25] The administrative detention of Cuban citizens seeking refuge in the USA in 1980 was criticized by the Inter-American Commission of Human Rights as being arbitrary for a number of reasons.[26] First, the level of discretion given to immigration officers meant that it was not clear when a refugee would be detained—thus there was an unacceptable level of unpredictability. Second, each refugee was required to justify why they should not be detained, an increasingly difficult task as the time spent in detention increased, and this was considered to be unjust. The US government advanced an argument that it was necessary to detain the Cubans as otherwise all states would be allowed 'to exile their unwanted-but-not-dangerous nationals knowing that they would have to be released into the communities of other states'.[27] However, the Commission was not convinced that this argument could 'justify the petitioners' treatment as reasonable'.[28] The Australian policy of compulsory detention of asylum-seekers until

---

[21] *A and others v UK* (2009) 49 EHRR 29.
[22] *Gangaram Panday v Suriname*, IACtHR Series C No 16 (21 January 1994).
[23] Case 11.006, IACommHR Report No 1/95.
[24] *Van Alphen v Netherlands*, CCPR/C/39/D/305/1988 (23 July 1990).
[25] *A v Australia*, CCPR/C/59/D/560/93 (3 April 1997) para 9.2. See also *Garcia v Peru*, n 23, para 47.
[26] Case 9903, *Rafael Ferrer-Mazorra et al. v United States*, IACommHR Report No 51/01.
[27] Ibid, para 133.   [28] Ibid, para 241.

their status has been determined has similarly been held to be disproportionate and thus arbitrary.[29]

Where the detention of an individual would lead to a violation of another human right or is the result of a violation of another human right, such as the right to a fair trial, it will be considered arbitrary. As such violations of Article 9(1) ICCPR have been found when individuals were arrested for their political views in contravention of Article 19 ICCPR.[30] Similarly, detention on the basis of ethnic origin alone will be arbitrary.[31] Therefore, arrests on the basis of racial profiling, without further evidence, are prohibited.[32]

2.3 GUARANTEES TO THOSE DEPRIVED OF THEIR LIBERTY

Even if a state is justified in depriving someone of their liberty, the state's obligations regarding that individual do not end. Although states may legitimately restrict the enjoyment of some rights, such as freedom of expression, when necessary, the general position is that individuals do not lose their human rights as a consequence of detention. In addition to these general protections, there are a number of specific guarantees of treatment that must be accorded to detainees. Most of these are entitlements for those individuals who have been arrested or detained pursuant to a criminal charge, although some are safeguards of general application to all detainees.

2.3.1 Rights of all detainees

Right to be informed of reasons for detention

Article 9(2) ICCPR provides that '[a]nyone who is arrested shall be informed, at the time of arrest, of the reasons for his arrest'. Similar guarantees can be found in Article 5(2) ECHR and Article 7(4) ACHR. This elementary safeguard exists to ensure that individuals know why they are being detained, which serves both to reduce the distress of being incarcerated, as well as allowing detainees to challenge the reasons for their detention. Thus it applies to anyone who is in detention, not just those who are arrested pursuant to a criminal charge. The reasons for arrest must contain sufficiently detailed information to indicate why the individual is being incarcerated. So when individuals were told that they had breached state security, but no further details were given, the Human Rights Committee held that a violation of Article 9(2) ICCPR had occurred.[33] The reasons for arrest must be communicated to the detainee promptly, though not necessarily at the moment of arrest. So, while a delay of seven days has

---

[29] *A v Australia*, n 25; *C v Australia*, CCPR/C/76/D/900/1999 (28 October 2002); *Baban v Australia*, CCPR/C/78/D/1014/2001 (6 August 2003).

[30] *Mukong v Cameroon*, CCPR/C/51/D/458/1991 (21 July 1994); *Kanana v Zaire*, CCPR/C/49/D/366/1989 (2 November 1993).

[31] 27/89, 46/91, 49/91, and 99/93, *Organisation Mondiale Contre La Torture v Rwanda*, 10th Annual Activity Report of the ACommHPR (1997).

[32] CERD Committee, General Recommendation XXXI, HRI/GEN/1/Rev.9 (Vol II) 306, para 20.

[33] *Ilombe and Shandwe v Democratic Republic of Congo*, CCPR/C/86/D/1177/2003 (17 March 2006).

been considered too long,[34] a period of seven hours has been considered satisfactory.[35] Where overnight delays have occurred because of the need for an interpreter, this has been considered acceptable.[36]

Right to humane treatment

Article 10(1) ICCPR provides that all detainees, regardless of the reason for their detention, must be 'treated with humanity and with respect for [their] inherent dignity'.[37] This fundamental protection has implications for the treatment of the individual as well as the conditions of detention. While most cases of severe ill-treatment will be considered inhuman treatment or torture contrary to Article 7 ICCPR, Article 10(1) is triggered by attacks on dignity that do not reach the severity of suffering threshold required by Article 7 ICCPR.[38] States are obliged to protect all individuals from 'any hardship or constraint other than that resulting from the deprivation of liberty'.[39]

Fulfilment of a detainee's right to humane treatment is inextricably linked to the conditions of detention in which they are held. States must ensure that these conditions are adequate, and so must provide satisfactory light, ventilation, bedding, sanitary facilities, food, and clothing, as well as access to appropriate medical care where necessary. Although ensuring such minimum conditions may be financially expensive, the Human Rights Committee has emphasized that the 'fundamental nature of the right means that the application of this rule…cannot be dependent on the material resources available in the State Party'.[40] The Committee found a violation of Article 10(1) ICCPR in *Wanza v Trinidad and Tobago* where the author was detained in a windowless cell, ventilated by an 18 x 18 inch opening, for between 22 and 23 hours a day, whilst on weekends or holidays, when the number of prison staff was too low, he was not permitted to leave the cell at all.[41] A number of the recommendations and declarations adopted by the UN and regional bodies listed above set out minimum standards of detention below which a violation would be found. There must be strict state regulation of *all* detention facilities, even where they are run by private organizations, to ensure that conditions of detention are appropriate.

Right to challenge legality of detention

A further element of the guarantees against arbitrary detention is the right to bring *habeas corpus* proceedings; that is, detainees should have the opportunity to challenge the *legality* of their detention, and be released should it be considered unlawful.[42] This right of challenge aims to provide redress where incarceration is not necessary. Review

---

[34] *Grant v Jamaica*, CCPR/C/56/D/597/1994 (22 March 1996) para 8.1.
[35] *Fox, Campbell and Hartley v UK* (1991) 13 EHRR 157, para 42.
[36] *Hill and Hill v Spain*, CCPR/C/59/D/526/1993 (2 April 1997) para 12.2.
[37] See also ACHR, Art 5(2).   [38] See Chapter 10, above.
[39] HRC, General Comment 21, HRI/GEN/1/Rev.9 (Vol I) 202, para 3.   [40] Ibid, para 4.
[41] CCPR/C/74/D/683/1996 (26 March 2002).
[42] ICCPR, Art 9(4); ECHR, Art 5(4); ACHR, Art 7(6).

of the legality of detention must be conducted by an independent court of law,[43] not by an administrative or executive body, and must take place without delay. In order for the right to be effective, detainees must have access to a lawyer, and individuals cannot be kept incommunicado.

This guarantee of review is particularly important where detention continues for a long period of time. In such situations, the rationale for detention may cease to be relevant. Therefore there is a right to *periodic* review of detention in certain circumstances. If the circumstances surrounding the detention have not changed, or the detention has only been for a short period of time, then there is no requirement of periodic review. Where a person is serving a sentence of detention as a punishment which has been imposed by a court of law, it is assumed that the court that imposed the sentence has reviewed the necessity of the detention. However, in cases of life imprisonment, or where there is a discretionary sentence of detention to be served after a mandatory 'tariff' period, human rights bodies have clearly stated that there should be periodic reviews of the necessity of detention.[44] The key question is: does the detainee remain such a danger to society as to warrant continued detention?

Remedies for unlawful detention

Articles 9(4) and 9(5) ICCPR provide for two specific remedies where detention is found to be unlawful: release and compensation. Similar rights are provided for in Article 10 ACHR and Article 5(5) ECHR. Thus, national courts must have the power to order release and award compensation. In the case of *A and others v UK*, mentioned earlier, the European Court of Human Rights found a violation of Article 5(5) ECHR. The individuals concerned had been released from detention as a result of a national court decision, but they had not been paid any compensation for the time they spent in unlawful detention.[45]

2.3.2 Rights of those detained on a criminal charge

In addition to those rights discussed above, human rights law provides specific protections to individuals who are detained pursuant to a criminal charge, or who have been arrested on the basis of a suspicion that they have committed a criminal offence. Prevention and punishment of crimes is one of the broadest bases upon which states may ground detention. The considerable powers of the state in these circumstances must be kept in check with mechanisms for accountability of law enforcement officers and safeguards for arrested persons.

All individuals who are arrested pursuant to a criminal charge must be brought 'promptly before a judge or other officer authorized to exercise judicial power'.[46] This should be an automatic process and not one which is dependent upon a request by the arrested individual. The idea behind such a procedure is to ensure independent

[43] On the meaning of 'independent court', see below.

[44] *Rameka v New Zealand*, CCPR/C/79/D/1090/2002 (6 November 2003); *Stafford v UK* (2002) 35 EHRR 32. [45] n 21.

[46] ICCPR, Art 9(3); ACHR, Art 7(5); ECHR, Art 5(3).

judicial supervision of the actions of law enforcement officers so that release can be ordered where detention is not appropriate. Thus, the judge or judicial officer should be empowered to order the release of detainees. If they cannot do so, the protections provided by this right will be illusory. Furthermore, the judge or other officer should be 'independent, objective and impartial in relation to the issues dealt with'.[47] A public prosecutor who is involved in the proceedings or receives instruction from the public prosecutor's office is not sufficiently independent to exercise this role of review. As regards the requirement of 'promptness', the Human Rights Committee has stated that a delay of a 'few days' from the moment of arrest may be permissible but has refrained from setting out a timeframe, preferring to take a case-by-case approach as different circumstances may require different time periods.[48] However, there is some guidance: five days has been considered too long by the Human Rights Committee,[49] while the European Court of Human Rights has considered four days and six hours to be too long.[50] It has been contended that 'the limit of promptness for the purposes of the article 9(3) [ICCPR] guarantee of judicial review lies somewhere around 3 days'.[51]

Protections afforded to those detained on a criminal charge continue beyond this first appearance before a judge. Article 9(3) ICCPR provides that such persons 'shall be entitled to trial within a reasonable time or to release' pending trial. Article 5(3) ECHR and Article 7 ACHR provide similar guarantees. The general rule is that individuals should not be kept in pre-trial detention unless it is really necessary to do so. Essentially these provisions provide a qualified right to release pending trial where exceptions are permitted 'to ensure the presence of the accused at the trial, to avert interference with witnesses and other evidence, or the commission of other offences'.[52] 'Public order', where the release of a suspected offender may give rise to a social disturbance,[53] and the 'personal safety of the suspect', where release of suspects may leave them vulnerable to attack, will also be relevant considerations.[54] International human rights bodies have advocated the use of financial guarantees or the removal of travel papers and passports, rather than pre-trial detention, to secure the attendance of a suspect at trial.

However, as part of the right to humane treatment and in order to maintain the presumption of innocence, individuals held in pre-trial detention should be kept segregated from convicted criminals (Article 10(2)(a) ICCPR). They are to be treated as innocent individuals until proven guilty of an offence. Article 10(2)(b) ICCPR also provides that '[a]ccused juveniles shall be separated from adults and brought as speedily as possible for adjudication'.

---

[47] *Kulomin v Hungary*, CCPR/C/50/D/521/1992 (22 March 1996).
[48] General Comment 8, n 3, para 2.
[49] *Nazarov v Uzbekistan*, CCPR/C/81/D/911/2000 (6 July 2004).
[50] *Brogan and others v UK* (1989) 11 EHRR 117.
[51] Joseph, Schultz, and Castan, *The International Covenant on Civil and Political Rights* (OUP, 2004) 325.   [52] *WBE v Netherlands*, CCPR/C/46/D/432/1990 (23 October 1992), para 6.3.
[53] *Letellier v France* (1992) 14 EHRR 83.
[54] *IA v France*, Application No 28213/95 (23 September 1998).

Furthermore, where release is not possible, the trial of the accused must take place within a reasonable period of time. What is considered *reasonable* is, once again, a matter to be determined on a case-by-case basis, but factors that will be taken into account include: the complexity of the case, the conduct of the accused (have they delayed the proceedings with challenges or by subverting investigations), and the efficiency of national authorities (a 'lack of budgetary appropriations for the administration of criminal justice... [will] not justify unreasonable delays').[55] Of primary concern is 'whether the time that has elapsed, for whatever reason, before judgment is passed on the accused has at some stage exceeded a reasonable limit whereby imprisonment without conviction imposes a greater sacrifice than could, in the circumstances of the case, reasonably be expected of a person presumed innocent'.[56]

Finally, Article 10(3) ICCPR obliges states to ensure that detention following a conviction for a criminal offence is aimed at the reformation and social rehabilitation of offenders, not simply punishment. So, in *Kang v Republic of Korea*, the Human Rights Committee found a violation of this provision where the author had been held in solitary confinement for 13 years for failing to abandon his political views.[57]

2.4 EMERGENCY DETENTION POWERS

The right to liberty has been the subject of many derogations by states from their human rights obligations.[58] Detention, particularly indefinite detention without charge, is often seen as an important tool by states to deal with emergencies, particularly in the fight against terrorism.[59] Although the right to liberty is a right that can be derogated from, the essential protections that it affords serve to prevent violations of rights which are not derogable, such as freedom from torture and ill-treatment. Recognizing these further positive effects of the right to liberty, human rights bodies have stated that the procedural safeguards discussed above, including judicial oversight of arrests and the right to bring *habeas corpus* proceedings, must remain in place during times of emergency. For example, the Human Rights Committee has confirmed that '[i]t is inherent in the protection of rights explicitly recognized as non-derogable... that they must be secured by procedural guarantees, including, often, judicial guarantees' and so 'the right to take proceedings before a court to decide without delay on the lawfulness of detention must not be diminished by a State party's decision to derogate from the

---

[55] *Fillastre and Bizouarn v Bolivia*, CCPR/C/43/D/336/1988 (5 November 1991) para 6.5.

[56] *Wemhoff v Germany* (1979–80) 1 EHRR 55; Case 11.245, *Giménez v Argentina*, IACommHR Report No 12.96 (1 March 1996) para 83.   [57] CCPR/C/78/D/878/1999 (15 July 2003).

[58] See Chapter 6, above.

[59] See eg the UK's derogations from ICCPR and ECHR communicated to the relevant authorities on 18 December 2001. The text of the derogation from the ECHR can be found at: <http://conventions. coe.int/Treaty/EN/v3MenuDecl.asp>; and, the text of the derogation from the ICCPR can be found at: <http://treaties.un.org/Pages/ViewDetails.aspx?src=TREATY&mtdsg_no=IV-4&chapter=4&lang=en>. Both derogations were withdrawn on 16 March 2005.

[ICCPR]'.[60] The Inter-American Court[61] and the European Court of Human Rights have made similar statements.[62]

3 ENFORCED DISAPPEARANCE

The most egregious violation of the right to liberty is an 'enforced disappearance', which comprises the secret deprivation of a person's liberty by state agents who refuse to inform anyone of the arrest.[63] In such a situation, the victim is removed from the protection of the law and cannot make use of the judicial safeguards described above. Such abductions often result in the death of the victim. This practice of enforced disappearance was used systematically in Latin America in the 1960s and 1970s, and its usage has spread across the globe. Although not specifically prohibited in general international human rights instruments, each of the international human rights bodies has confirmed that enforced disappearance will constitute a violation of the right to liberty, the right to humane conditions of detention, and possibly the right to life.[64] Enforced disappearance may also result in violations of the prohibition of torture and ill-treatment both in respect of the victim and family members who are left worrying about the fate of abducted individuals.[65] There are two conventions specifically directed at the eradication of the practice of enforced disappearance: the Inter-American Convention on Forced Disappearance of Persons (1994) and the UN Convention for the Protection of All Persons against Enforced Disappearance (2006). These treaties oblige state parties to criminalize the practice of enforced disappearance and adopt further administrative and legal measures, in addition to those which exist to prevent arbitrary detention, to bring to an end the practice of 'secret detention'.

4 SECURITY OF THE PERSON

Treaty provisions on the right to liberty invariably contain a reference to protection of the 'security of the person', which places a positive obligation on states to investigate threats to the person from both state and non-state actors and provide protection for

---

[60] General Comment 29, n 5, paras 15–16.

[61] OC-8/87, *Habeas Corpus in Emergency Situations*, IACtHR Series A No 8 (30 January 1987); OC-9/87, *Judicial Guarantees in States of Emergency*, IACtHR Series A No 9 (6 October 1987).

[62] *Brannigan and McBride v UK* (1994) 17 EHRR 539, para 62.

[63] See Convention for the Protection of All Persons against Enforced Disappearance, Art 2; Inter-American Convention on Forced Disappearance of Persons, Art II; Rome Statute of the International Criminal Court, Art 7(2)(i).

[64] See *Sarma v Sri Lanka*, CCPR/C/78/D/950/2000 (16 July 2003); *Coronel v Columbia*, CCPR/C/76/D/778/1997 (24 October 2002); *Velásquez-Rodriguez v Honduras*, IACtHR Series C No 4 (29 July 1988); 24/97, *Mouvement Burkinabé des Droits de l'Homme et des Peuples v Burkina Faso*, 14th Activity Report (2001); *Kurt v Turkey* (1999) 27 EHRR 373; *Timurtas v Turkey* (2001) 33 EHRR 6.

[65] See eg *Mojica v Dominican Republic*, CCPR/C/51/D/449/1991 (25 July 1994).

individuals where such threats are credible. Some human rights bodies have restricted the right to security of the person to those individuals who are threatened with arbitrary detention. In the *Garcia* case discussed above, the Inter-American Commission decided that there had been a violation of the right to personal security because Garcia was 'threatened with arbitrary and unlawful arrest'.[66] The Human Rights Committee, extending the protections beyond the detention context, has stated that '[i]t cannot be the case that, as a matter of law, States can ignore known threats to the life of persons under their jurisdiction, just because he or she is not arrested or otherwise detained'.[67] Therefore it has found violations of the right to security where there was a failure to investigate credible death threats.[68]

5 THE RIGHT TO A FAIR TRIAL

The right to a fair trial is 'aimed at the proper administration of justice'.[69] Human rights treaty provisions on fair trial establish a complex set of rules that cover two aspects of how the right is to be secured. First, there are rules which specify how court proceedings should be conducted. In general, fair trial guarantees are not primarily concerned with the *outcome* of judicial proceedings, but rather the *process* by which the outcome is achieved. Fairness of outcome is not guaranteed. Second, there are structural rules regarding the organization of domestic court systems. Securing the right to a fair trial can require a high level of investment in the court system. It should be noted that human rights law does not seek to impose a particular type of court system on states but rather implements the principle that there should be a separation of powers between the executive and the judiciary.

5.1 SOURCES

Article 10 UDHR provides that '[e]veryone is entitled in full equality to a fair and public hearing by an independent and impartial tribunal, in the determination of his rights and obligations and of any criminal charge against him'. The UDHR also provides further, more specific protections applicable when determining a criminal charge, in Article 11. The general and specific criminal protections are merged into one, extremely detailed, provision of the ICCPR: Article 14. Due to their importance, aspects of fair trial guarantees can be found in most of the UN human rights treaties, including: Article 40 of the Convention on the Rights of the Child (CRC), Article 18 of the Migrant Workers Convention, Article 5(a) of the Convention on the Elimination of Racial Discrimination (ICERD), Article 15 of the Convention against Torture (UNCAT), and Article 13 of the Convention on

---

[66] n 23 above, 100.   [67] *Delgado Páez v Columbia*, CCPR/C/39/D/195/1985 (12 July 1990) para 5.5.
[68] *Jayawardena v Sri Lanka*, CCPR/C/75/D/916/2000 (22 July 2002).
[69] HRC, General Comment 13, HRI/GEN/Rev.9 (Vol I) 184, para 1.

the Rights of Persons with Disabilities. All regional treaties guarantee the right to a fair trial.[70]

Despite the sophisticated treaty provisions on the right to a fair trial, this is an area that has evolved by means of considerable elaboration by international human rights bodies. The 'fundamental principles of fair trials' form part of customary international law and the Human Rights Committee considers them to be peremptory norms of international law.[71]

Particular aspects of the right to a fair trial are also elaborated upon in numerous declarations and guiding principles, including the Basic Principles on the Independence of the Judiciary,[72] the Basic Principles on the Role of Lawyers,[73] and the UN Standard Minimum Rules for the Administration of Juvenile Justice.[74]

Not all prosecutions will take place nationally. International law imposes liability on individuals for certain international crimes,[75] and these crimes are sometimes tried at the international level. International criminal tribunals must also ensure a fair trial of the accused and fair trial guarantees are provided in the relevant statutes and rules of procedure.[76] These rules are based upon the protections found in Article 14 ICCPR and customary international law.

5.2 SCOPE

Though concerns regarding the conduct of judicial proceedings have traditionally focused on how *criminal* trials should be conducted, the right to a fair trial extends beyond the criminal trial to civil and certain administrative proceedings. Article 14(1) ICCPR provides that guarantees should apply to the determination of both rights and obligations in a 'suit at law' as well as criminal charges, while Article 6(1) ECHR refers to the determination of both criminal charges and 'civil rights and obligations'. What is meant by the terms 'suit at law' and 'civil rights and obligations' has been a difficult question to answer.

The Human Rights Committee has interpreted the term 'suit at law' widely:

[T]he concept... is based on the nature of the right in question rather than on the status of one of the parties or the particular forum provided by domestic legal systems for the determination of particular rights. The concept encompasses (a) judicial procedures aimed at determining rights and obligations pertaining to the areas of contract, property and torts in the area of private law, as well as (b) equivalent notions in the area of administrative law such as the termination of employment of civil servants for other than disciplinary reasons, the determination of social security benefits or the pension rights of soldiers, or procedures

---

[70] ECHR, Arts 6 and 7; ACHR, Arts 8 and 9; ACHPR, Art 7; Arab Charter, Arts 12, 13, 16, and 17.
[71] General Comment 29, n 5, para 11.   [72] GA Res 40/32 (29 November 1985) Annex.
[73] A/CONF.144/28/Rev.1, 118 (1990).   [74] GA Res 45/100 (14 December 1990) Annex.
[75] See Chapter 24, below.
[76] eg ICTY Statute, Art 21 and ICTR Statute, Art 20. See Cassese, *International Criminal Law* (OUP, 2008) ch 18; Zappalà, *International Criminal Trials and Respect for Human Rights in International Criminal Proceedings* (OUP, 2003).

regarding the use of public land or the taking of private property. In addition it may (c) cover other procedures which, however, must be assessed on a case by case basis in the light of the nature of the right in question.[77]

Similarly, Article 8(1) ACHR specifies that fair trial guarantees are to be accorded in all proceedings which involve 'the determination of ... rights and obligations of a civil, labour, fiscal, or any other nature'. The case law of the European Court of Human Rights suggests that the reference to 'civil rights and obligations' means that 'most substantive rights that an individual may arguably claim under national law fall within Article 6 [ECHR] unless they quintessentially concern the exercise of the public power of the state'.[78] Most importantly, for all the international bodies, the application of fair trial rights to a 'suit at law' or the determination of 'civil rights and obligations' does not depend on whether national law has provided that the issue should be determined by a court or another body.

Similarly, what constitutes a criminal charge is not restricted to what national law considers 'criminal' and thus punishable under the law. If this were the case, then states could avoid some of their human rights obligations by simply designating certain charges as something other than criminal. Rather, the idea of 'criminal charge' extends to those offences which are criminal in nature, because they apply to the population at large, and are accompanied by sanctions that 'must be regarded as penal because of their purpose, character or severity'.[79] The expulsion of aliens or disciplinary measures against soldiers, however, will not be considered 'criminal'. In the criminal context, the right to a fair trial is triggered at the moment official notification of a charge is given. Therefore, there may be some overlap with the protections granted by the right to liberty.

5.3 GENERALLY APPLICABLE FAIR TRIAL GUARANTEES

What does the right to a fair trial entail? Article 14 ICCPR provides fair trial guarantees of general application that apply to all types of judicial proceedings (considered in this section) as well as detailed guarantees specific to criminal trials (considered in Section 5.4, below). The generally applicable guarantees are set out in Article 14(1) ICCPR, which provides, inter alia, that '[a]ll persons shall be equal before the courts and tribunals. ... everyone shall be entitled to a fair and public hearing by a competent, independent and impartial tribunal established by law'.[80] It should be noted that procedural aspects of a number of human rights obligations include recourse to judicial procedures and the general rights of due process will apply in these contexts. To take an example referred to above, Article 9(4) ICCPR provides that detainees have the right to have the legality of their detention determined by a court. Such review proceedings must be conducted according to the fundamental principles relating to a fair trial. Failure to do so will constitute violations of both Articles 9(4) and 14(1) ICCPR.

---

[77] General Comment 32, HRI/GEN/1/Rev.9 (Vol I) 248, para 16 (footnotes omitted).

[78] Harris *et al.*, *Harris, O'Boyle and Warbrick: The Law of the European Convention on Human Rights* (OUP, 2009) 212.   [79] General Comment 32, n 77, para 15.

[80] See also ECHR, Art 6(1); ACHR, Art 8(1).

5.3.1 Equality before the courts

The right to equality before courts and tribunals is a specific application of the right to non-discrimination, contained in Article 26 ICCPR, to judicial proceedings.[81] It incorporates the right of equal access to courts and the rights of all parties to proceedings to equality of arms and to be treated without discrimination.

Equal access

Although not explicitly provided for in fair trial provisions, all human rights bodies have confirmed that there is a right to access courts of first instance to determine a criminal charge or rights and obligations in a suit at law. All individuals must have an equal chance to pursue their legal rights. As the Human Rights Committee has stated, 'access to administration of justice must be effectively guaranteed in all such cases to ensure that no individual is deprived, in procedural terms, of his/her right to claim justice'.[82]

Ensuring equal access to courts and tribunals involves substantial activity on the part of states. They must ensure that judicial systems are organized so that 'all individuals...who may find themselves in the territory or subject to [their] jurisdiction' can access the courts.[83] This involves ensuring that there are no legal impediments to accessing justice. For example, statutory provisions that only allow for husbands (and not wives) to bring proceedings regarding matrimonial property in the courts have been found to violate Article 14(1) ICCPR.[84] But it is not just legal impediments that the state must remove. Access to courts and tribunals can be severely hampered if no legal assistance is available or only available at a prohibitively high cost. Article 14(3)(d) ICCPR obliges states to provide free legal aid in criminal cases where the interests of justice so demand and the individual concerned cannot afford to pay. Although there is no corresponding provision for civil proceedings, the Human Rights Committee has encouraged states 'to provide free legal aid...for individuals who do not have sufficient means to pay for it'.[85]

However, states may restrict access to courts where such restrictions are based on law, can be justified on objective and reasonable grounds, and are not discriminatory.[86] One area where the issue of restricting access to justice has been extremely contentious is where claims of state immunity have barred judicial proceedings. *Al Adsani v UK* concerned a claim in tort that had been initiated before the courts in the UK regarding torture alleged to have been committed by the government of Kuwait.[87] The Kuwaiti government relied upon the customary international law rule of state immunity, which provides that a state is immune from proceedings in foreign courts regarding certain official acts. This claim of immunity was upheld by the UK courts. The European Court of Human Rights held, by nine votes to eight, that restricting

---

[81] See Chapter 9, above.
[82] General Comment 32, n 77, para 9.   [83] Ibid.
[84] *Ato del Avellanal v Peru*, A/44/40 (1988) 196.
[85] General Comment 32, n 77, para 10. See also *Airey v Ireland* (1979–80) 2 EHRR 305; OC-11/90, *Exceptions to the Exhaustion of Domestic Remedies*, IACtHR Series A No 11, para 28.
[86] General Comment 32, n 77, para 9.   [87] *Al Adsani v UK* (2002) 34 EHRR 11.

access to the courts by virtue of the rule of state immunity was permissible because it pursued the legitimate aim of 'complying with international law to promote comity and good relations between states through the respect of another's state sovereignty'.[88] Thus applying the customary rule of state immunity to civil proceedings for torture did not violate the right to a fair trial.

Equality of arms and treatment without discrimination

The right to equality before the courts also includes protections of equality of arms and treatment without discrimination. Equality of arms means that all parties should be provided with the same procedural rights unless there is an objective and reasonable justification not to do so and there is no significant disadvantage to either party. Thus, if only the prosecutor, but not the defendant, is allowed to appeal a decision to a higher court, this will constitute a failure to guarantee equality of arms.[89] The essence of the guarantee is that each side should be given the opportunity to challenge all the arguments put forward by the other side.[90] Where courtroom conditions are not conducive to securing equality of arms there will be a violation. For example, in *Gridin v Russian Federation* the author of the communication was the defendant of multiple rape allegations and his trial had attracted much media publicity. The courtroom was filled with people who shouted that the author should be sentenced to death. The Human Rights Committee held that 'the failure of the trial court to control the hostile atmosphere and pressure created by the public in the courtroom, which made it impossible for defence counsel to properly cross-examine the witnesses and present his defence... violated the author's right to a fair trial'.[91]

There should be no differential treatment of persons during court proceedings. Like cases should be treated alike unless there are objective and justifiable reasons not to do so. On this basis, the Human Rights Committee held in *Kavanagh v Ireland* that a situation where the Director of Public Prosecutions decided, with unfettered discretion, whether or not individuals accused of certain crimes would face a jury trial raised issues of equality before the law.[92] The treaties aimed at eradicating specific forms of discrimination, such as the ICERD and the Convention on the Elimination of All Forms of Discrimination against Women (CEDAW), explicitly emphasize that there should not be distinction as to race, colour, national origin, heritage, or sex during court proceedings.[93] Distinction on these grounds will never be justifiable.

5.3.2 Hearing by a competent, independent, and impartial tribunal

The courts and tribunals before which claims are heard and criminal charges are determined must be 'competent, independent and impartial' and established pursuant to national law. The requirement that tribunals be *established by law* means that the basic

[88] Ibid, para 54. [89] *Weiss v Austria*, CCPR/C/77/D/1086/2002 (3 April 2003).
[90] General Comment 32, n 77, para 13. [91] CCPR/C/69/D/770/1997 (20 July 2000) para 8.2.
[92] CCPR/C/71/D/819/1998 (4 April 2001). Although note that the majority found a violation of ICCPR, Art 26 and decided not to go on and examine whether there had been a breach of Art 14(1).
[93] See ICERD Art 5(a); CEDAW Art 15(2). See also General Recommendation XXXI, n 32.

rules on jurisdiction, organization, and membership of the court should be contained in legislation. This acts as a safeguard against executive abuse of court procedures.

Courts and tribunals are those institutions which are empowered to make legally binding decisions on the basis of the rules of law applicable within a state. Therefore a panel which can make recommendations as to a particular course of action but not binding decisions, such as a parole board, will not be considered a *competent* court or tribunal for the purposes of fair trial provisions.

The requirement of independence refers to the institutional setup of the courts. States are obliged to establish courts so that any form of interference with the activities of judges is thwarted. There are essentially two aspects to this. First, the courts should be fully independent of the executive and the parties to a dispute. Thus, courts should not take direction from government ministers or departments on how to decide a case.[94] Second, states must ensure that there are safeguards in place to preserve the independence of the judiciary, including 'clear procedures and objective criteria for the appointment, remuneration, tenure, promotion, suspension and dismissal of the judiciary and disciplinary sanctions taken against them'.[95] Providing such procedures and guarantees aims to remove the threat that justice may be subverted by appointing 'sympathetic' judges, corruption, or the removal of judges from their post.

Related to the consideration of independence is the idea of *impartiality* of the courts. There are two aspects to this. First, judges of the court must be *subjectively* impartial. That is, they must act without any personal bias towards either party in a case. Similarly, they must not harbour preconceptions about the action before them and must remain uninfluenced by the media and public perception. In general, there will be a presumption that judges are impartial unless there is evidence to the contrary. The court should also be *objectively* impartial, so that the court and its judges must *appear* to the impartial observer to be free from bias. Justice must be seen to be done. For example, in *Piersack v Belgium* the presiding judge in the applicant's case had been the head of the public prosecutor's department during the investigation of the case. Although there was no evidence that the judge had knowledge of the investigation, the European Court of Human Rights held that he was not objectively impartial.[96]

Concerns have been expressed by international human rights bodies regarding the use of military courts to try civilians. There are two grounds for such concerns. First, it is argued that military courts violate the principle of equality before the law because military trials deviate from the normal criminal trial procedures in a state, creating a distinction in the manner in which individuals are tried. As such there need to be justifications for their use which are based on objective and reasonable grounds. The Human Rights Committee has stated that '[t]rials of civilians by military or special courts should be exceptional, i.e. limited to cases where the State party can show that

---

[94] See *Bahamonde v Equatorial Guinea*, CCPR/C/49/D/468/1991 (20 October 1993).

[95] General Comment 32, n 77, para 19. See also the UN Basic Principles on the Independence of the Judiciary and the reports of the UN Special Rapporteur on independence of the judiciary, available at: <http://www2.ohchr.org/english/issues/judiciary/index.htm>.

[96] (1983) 5 EHRR 169.

resorting to such trials is necessary and justified by objective and serious reasons, and where with regard to the specific class of individuals and offences at issue the regular civilian courts are unable to undertake the trials'.[97]

The second concern is that military courts are not sufficiently impartial to fulfil the requirements of fair trial provisions. In the words of the African Commission of Human Rights:

Withdrawing criminal procedure from the competence of the courts established within the judicial order and conferring [it] onto an extension of the executive necessarily compromises the impartiality of the courts. Independent of the qualities of the persons sitting in such jurisdictions, their very existence constitutes a violation of the principles of impartiality and independence of the judiciary.[98]

Thus, some have argued that military trials of civilians are, of themselves, a violation of the right to be tried by an independent and impartial court. There may even be concerns regarding impartiality where only one member of the court is a serving military officer while the others are civilians.[99]

The Human Rights Committee has held that a state must demonstrate that there is both a need for the military trial, and, if this is demonstrated, that the military courts have afforded the full protection of the rights of the accused according to Article 14 ICCPR.[100] Thus, according to the Committee, if it can be shown that the military trial is necessary, has maintained impartiality, and afforded the civilian a fair trial in procedural terms, then the military trial will not result in a violation of Article 14(1) ICCPR. The procedural requirements of a fair trial are considered next.

5.3.3 Fair and public hearing

'Fair'

Fair trial guarantees explicitly provide for a right to a fair hearing in both civil and criminal proceedings.[101] The content of this right is ever-evolving as new situations are considered by international human rights bodies, though there is a core minimum for criminal trials. The principle of fairness includes 'the absence of any direct or indirect influence, pressure or intimidation or intrusion from whatever side and for whatever motive'.[102] All judicial proceedings must adhere to this principle. Other aspects of a fair hearing include, inter alia, the right to equality of arms discussed above, the right to attend hearings, and the expeditious disposal of proceedings.[103]

The right to attend hearings is based on the idea that individuals will wish to monitor proceedings concerning their interests. However, it is not an absolute guarantee.

---

[97] General Comment 32, n 77, para 22 (footnotes omitted).

[98] 54/91, *Malawi African Association v Mauritania*, 13th Annual Activity Report of the ACommHPR (2000) para 98. See also Case 11.084, *Salinas v Peru*, IACommHR Report No 27/94 (1994); *Durand and Ugarte v Peru*, IACtHR Series C No 68, para 125.   [99] *Incal v Turkey* (2000) 29 EHRR 449, paras 71–2.

[100] See *Madani v Algeria*, n 16, para 8.7.

[101] ICCPR, Art 14(1); ECHR, Art 6(1); ACHR, Art 8(1).   [102] General Comment 32, n 77, para 25.

[103] See further Harris *et al.*, n 78, 246–71.

In criminal trials, a hearing in the absence of the defendant (*in absentia*) is generally not compatible with the idea of a fair hearing.[104] However, there are three exceptions to this general position. First, an individual may waive his right to be at the trial. Second, where the authorities have tried diligently but failed to inform the individual of the trial date because, for example, she has moved away from her stated address, then there will be no violation of fair trial guarantees. Finally, if an individual aims to evade justice by not attending the trial, there will be no violation. As regards civil proceedings, the right to be present at proceedings has been interpreted flexibly in accordance with different national legal systems. The presence of legal representatives may suffice. However, the European Commission of Human Rights has stated that where 'the personal character and manner of life of the party concerned is directly relevant to the formation of the court's opinion', for example in child custody hearings, then there is a right to be present.[105]

A further aspect of the right to a fair trial is that there should be no excessive procedural delays in the resolution of a dispute. Delays serve to call the effectiveness of the judicial system into question. Furthermore, it is clear that a delay in determining a criminal charge will leave the defendant unsure of his/her fate and, although the guilt or innocence of the defendant is yet to be determined, public perceptions of guilt are often encouraged by long delays. Thus, there is a specific provision in the ICCPR (Article 14(3)(c)) that provides that everyone charged with a criminal offence should 'be tried without delay'. Although there is no comparable explicit protection in Article 14(1), the Human Rights Committee has interpreted the notion of 'fair hearing' to include the expeditious disposal of proceedings and so it is applicable to civil proceedings also.[106] The entire duration of proceedings from the moment an individual is informed of a criminal charge or civil proceedings are initiated until a final appeal decision is made is taken into account when deciding whether there has been undue delay. There is no absolute time limit within which judicial proceedings should take place. Instead, there are a number of considerations that need to be taken into account when assessing the reasonableness of a delay. These include: the length of each stage of the proceedings, the complexity of the legal issues at stake, the detrimental effects on the individual concerned caused by the delay, the availability of remedies to accelerate proceedings, and the outcome of any appeal proceedings.[107] The organization of a state's judicial system is implicated in the enjoyment of this right. Where delays to the administration of justice are caused by budgetary constraints, states must ensure that more resources are allocated to the judicial system. States are obliged to take appropriate measures to deal with temporary backlogs of cases.[108]

---

[104] *Maleki v Italy*, CCPR/C/66/D/699/1996 (15 June 1999).   [105] *X v Sweden* (1959) 2 YB 354, 370.

[106] *Fei v Columbia*, CCPR/C/53/D/514/1992 (4 April 1995). ACHR, Art 8(1) and ECHR, Art 6(1) explicitly provide this protection for both the determination of civil claims and criminal charges.

[107] *Deisl v Austria*, CCPR/C/81/D/1060/2002 (23 August 2004).

[108] *Zimmermann v Switzerland* (1994) 6 EHRR 17.

'Public'

Article 14(1) ICCPR also provides all individuals with a right to a public trial. Trials that are shrouded in secrecy are more likely to involve manipulation of the justice system; such trials have been used to suppress 'dissident' groups in some states. There are two elements to this right. First, the trial itself should be conducted publicly and orally. Therefore, information regarding upcoming court proceedings should be made readily available in good time and sufficient facilities should be provided in courtrooms to allow the press and other members of the public to observe the proceedings.[109] However, this aspect of the right is qualified and Article 14(1) contains an exhaustive list of situations where hearings can be conducted without public scrutiny: 'for reasons of public morals, public order (ordre public) or national security in a democratic society, or when the interest of the private lives of the parties so requires, or to the extent strictly necessary in the opinion of the court in special circumstances where publicity would prejudice the interests of justice'. The language of these restrictions implies that a condition of holding a trial without public scrutiny is that the principles of a democratic society must be upheld, so that questions of proportionality will come into play. Furthermore, for pre-trial proceedings or appellate proceedings based on purely written submissions, there is no need for public access.[110]

The second element to the right to a public trial provides that judgments should be made available to the public. Article 14(1) ICCPR provides that there may be exceptions to this rule where 'the interest of juvenile persons otherwise requires or the proceedings concern matrimonial disputes or the guardianship of children'.[111] In all other circumstances no restrictions to access to judgments are permitted. Therefore, even where the trial has been conducted without public scrutiny, the Human Rights Committee has stated that 'the judgment, including the essential findings, evidence and legal reasoning must be made public'.[112]

5.4 FAIR TRIAL GUARANTEES IN CRIMINAL PROCEEDINGS

A detailed account of what constitutes a fair criminal trial is to be found in most human rights treaty provisions on the right to a fair trial. In addition to the generally applicable principles discussed above, Article 14 ICCPR, for example, contains a further six paragraphs regarding the rights of defendants in criminal trials. Similar detailed guidance can be found in Article 6 ECHR and Article 8 ACHR.

---

[109] *Van Meurs v The Netherlands*, CCPR/C/39/D/215/1986 (13 July 1990).

[110] *Axen v Germany* (1984) 6 EHRR 195; *Helmers v Sweden* (1993) 15 EHRR 285.

[111] ECHR, Art 6(1) does not allow for any exceptions to this right, while the ACHR only provides this guarantee in the criminal context: see Art 8(5). No equivalent protections are set out in the ACHPR.

[112] General Comment 32, n 77, para 29.

5.4.1 Presumption of innocence

All treaty provisions on the right to a fair trial contain a guarantee of the right to be presumed innocent until proven guilty.[113] The Human Rights Committee has stated that this guarantee is one of the 'fundamental principles of fair trial' and consti- tutes a rule of *jus cogens*.[114] This right applies from the moment that an individual is accused, even before a formal criminal charge is issued, until a determination of the charge by the final appeal court. State authorities, including judges, must refrain from any conduct that would influence the outcome of a trial to the defend- ant's disadvantage. Therefore declarations of the guilt of an individual before trial would constitute a violation of this right.[115] Similarly, judges should not begin a trial with a preconceived idea. Investigatory actions, such as fingerprinting, taking DNA samples, and searches of property, however, do not violate the presumption. As the presumption of innocence must be maintained at all times during the trial, the burden of proof rests upon the prosecution to prove guilt beyond a reasonable doubt. Where such reasonable doubt exists, the court must decide in favour of the accused.

5.4.2 Freedom from self-incrimination

Closely related to the presumption of innocence is the right not to be compelled to incriminate oneself. This right is provided for in Article 14(3)(g) ICCPR as well as Articles 8(2)(g) and 8(3) ACHR, and has been read into what constitutes a fair trial for the purposes of Article 6(1) ECHR.[116] This right is 'to be understood in terms of the absence of any direct or indirect physical or undue psychological pressure from the investigating authorities on the accused, with a view to obtaining a confession of guilt'.[117] Article 15 UNCAT prohibits the use of evidence obtained by torture 'in any proceedings, except against a person accused of torture as evidence that the state- ment was made', while the Human Rights Committee has gone further to state that any evidence arising from treatment contrary to Article 7 ICCPR, that is torture *or* inhuman or degrading treatment or punishment, should be excluded from evidence. In fact, the UK House of Lords has held that even evidence obtained by a third party, who is not involved in the proceedings, by means of torture should not be admissible in court.[118] Other instances of improper pressure will be decided on a case-by-case basis, examining whether the 'very essence of the right' not to incriminate oneself has been destroyed.[119] So where adverse inferences are drawn in court from a suspect's silence during questioning, whether a violation has occurred will depend on whether there was other evidence pointing to guilt.[120]

---

[113] ICCPR, Art 14(2); ACHR, Art 8(2); ACHPR, Art 7(1)(b); ECHR, Art 6(2). See also ICTY Statute, Art 21(3); ICTR Statute, Art 20(3); ICC Statute, Art 66(1).   [114] General Comment 29, n 5, para 11.
[115] See *Gridin v Russian Federation*, n 91; *Allenet de Ribemont v France* (1995) 20 EHRR 557.
[116] See eg *Saunders v UK* (1996) 23 EHRR 313.   [117] General Comment 32, n 77, para 41.
[118] *A v Secretary of State for Home Affairs* [2005] UKHL 71.
[119] *John Murray v UK* (1996) 22 EHRR 29.   [120] Ibid.

5.4.3 Right to be informed of the charge

Individuals accused of a criminal offence have the right to be informed of the charge that they are facing. This is in addition to the right of those detained to know the reason for their detention (see above), and applies from the moment the individual is formally charged or publicly named as an accused person.[121] This right, provided for in Article 14(3)(a) ICCPR, Article 7(4) ACHR, and Article 6(3)(a) ECHR, must be fulfilled promptly, without inexcusable delay. At the stage of being formally charged, suspects are entitled to be informed of the full details of the charge against them, including the type of offence and the elements upon which the accusation has been founded, in a language that they understand, so that they may begin to formulate a defence.

5.4.4 Right to an adequate defence

Beyond these protections are those that elaborate on the principle of equality of arms. So, for example, Article 14(3)(b) ICCPR provides that everyone is entitled 'to have adequate time and facilities for the preparation of his defence and to communicate with counsel of his own choosing'. Article 8(2)(c) ACHR and Article 6(3)(b) ECHR contain similar provisions. What is considered adequate time will depend upon the nature and complexity of the case. There are certain minimum levels of facilities, however, that must be accorded to all defendants for their defence to be effective. Explicitly provided for is the guarantee that defendants must be able to communicate with their counsel. They must also be provided with all the materials that the prosecution is to use in court as well as any other material that may be exculpatory. Exculpatory evidence does not only include evidence that suggests innocence, but also material regarding the gathering of evidence which may show some impropriety. For example, where there is information that the evidence against the defendant has been obtained by torture, this should be transmitted to the defence. The materials must be presented so that the defendant or his counsel is able to understand them. Therefore, where the defendant requires translation of documents but his counsel does not, there is no obligation on the state to provide such translations.[122]

There are other rights associated with aspects of an adequate defence that are guaranteed by international human rights law. Defendants have the right to choose whether to defend themselves personally or to have counsel represent them during a trial.[123] Although the key principle is that individuals must be allowed to defend themselves, this right is not unlimited. If the interests of justice require a lawyer to represent the accused, then a lawyer may be assigned against the wishes of the accused. Such interests apply when an individual is charged with a serious offence but unable to act in her own interests, when the defendant is obstructing justice, or in order to prevent intimidation of witnesses if they are examined by the accused during the trial.[124] Any

---

[121] General Comment 32, n 77, para 31.
[122] *Harward v Norway*, CCPR/C/51/D/451/1991 (16 August 1994).
[123] ICCPR, Art 14(3)(d); ACHR, Art 8(2)(d); ACHPR, Art 7(1)(c); ECHR, Art 6(3)(c).
[124] General Comment 32, n 77, para 37.

restriction on the choice of representation must be strictly proportionate to the serious purpose articulated.

Should the defendant require legal representation in order to exercise his defence but does not have the means to pay, states are obliged to provide legal aid where the interests of justice so require.[125] The seriousness of the offence and the possible punishment will be relevant to this consideration. So, where 'deprivation of liberty is at stake, the interests of justice...call for legal representation'.[126] Similarly, free legal assistance should be given if the proceedings may result in the death penalty.[127] The interests of justice may also require legal aid where the personal circumstances of the defendant require it. For example, the case of *Quaranta v Switzerland* concerned a young adult with a drug addiction from an underprivileged background who was convicted for drugs offences. The European Court of Human Rights held that he was not capable of presenting his case in an adequate manner and that the Swiss authorities should have provided him with legal aid.[128] The legal assistance provided must be effective. If the counsel provided is negligent in their duties, then the state will have breached its obligation. Furthermore, where the court proceedings are conducted in a language which the defendant cannot understand, interpreter assistance should be offered free of charge.[129]

The right to an effective defence also includes the right of the defendant 'to examine, or have examined, the witnesses against him and to obtain the attendance and examination of witnesses on his behalf under the same conditions as witnesses against him'.[130] Essentially this secures the same powers for the defendant to compel witnesses to appear and cross-examine them as are granted to the prosecution. What is key is that the principle of fairness is upheld at all times. For example, in *Peart v Jamaica* the principal witness for the prosecution had made a written statement that indicated a person other than the defendant had committed the relevant crime.[131] However, the statement was not made available to the defence until after an appeal to the conviction had been rejected. The Human Rights Committee held that this was a serious obstruction of the defence in its cross-examination of the lead witness and thus precluded a fair trial of the defendant. Where cross-examination may lead to serious concerns for the safety of the witness, then restrictions upon the right to examine may be implemented. The interests of the defence must be balanced against those of witness called to testify and so, in extreme cases, witnesses may remain anonymous. However, even where the witness remains anonymous to the public and the defendant, an effective examination of their testimony must still be facilitated.

5.4.5 Right to review

Everyone convicted of a crime is entitled to have the judgment reviewed by a higher court in accordance with procedures set out in national law. This right is aimed at

---

[125] ICCPR, Art 14(3)(d); ECHR, Art 6(3)(d). ACHR, Art 8(2)(e) leaves it to states to decide whether to provide legal aid.   [126] *Benham v UK* (1996) 22 EHRR 293, para 61.
[127] General Comment 32, n 77, para 38.   [128] A 205 (1991).
[129] ICCPR, Art 14(3)(f); ACHR, Art 8(1)(a); ECHR, Art 6(3)(e).
[130] ICCPR, Art 14(3)(e). See also ACHR, Art 8(2)(f); ECHR, Art 6(3)(d).
[131] CCPR/C/54/D/464/1991 (24 July 1995).

correcting miscarriages of justice, so higher courts are required to conduct an evaluation of the evidence presented at the trial and the conduct of the trial. This right is set out in Article 14(5) ICCPR and Article 8(2)(h) ACHR, while a more restrictive version of the right is to be found in Article 2 Protocol 7 ECHR. The African Commission on Human Rights confirmed in *Constitutional Rights Project v Nigeria* that this right is also protected by the ACHPR. The Commission criticized certain provisions of Nigerian law that precluded any judicial appeal of convictions for which the death penalty was imposed. It held that 'to foreclose any avenue of appeal to "competent national organs" in criminal cases bearing such penalties clearly violates Article 7(1)(a) of the African Charter, and increases the risk that severe violations may go unaddressed'.[132] Obviously all review proceedings must adhere to the principles of a fair trial discussed above.

Where a newly discovered fact shows conclusively that there has been a miscarriage of justice and so a conviction is overturned or a pardon given, all affected individuals are entitled to compensation for the punishment already endured.[133] In *WJH v Netherlands* the author had been convicted of a number of offences but served no time in detention. Following a challenge to the conviction, the Dutch Supreme Court set aside the verdict and remitted the case back for consideration by a lower court, which acquitted him on procedural grounds. The Human Rights Committee rejected a claim that the Netherlands had violated its obligation to grant compensation for the initial conviction as 'the final decision in this case ... acquitted the author, and since he did not suffer any punishment as a result of his earlier conviction'.[134] Therefore, miscarriages of justice must be distinguished from acquittals on appeal. It is only for miscarriages of justice that compensation is due.

5.4.6 *Ne bis in idem*

All major human rights treaties provide that the principle of *ne bis in idem* is applicable to all individuals who are charged with a criminal offence.[135] The principle essentially maintains that no person shall be tried twice for the same offence in the same jurisdiction, often known as 'double jeopardy'. There are certain exceptions to this general rule. If there is evidence of newly discovered facts or there were serious defects in the earlier proceedings that affected the outcome of the case, the interests of justice may demand that cases should be reopened. Furthermore, individuals may be tried for the same offence in different jurisdictions. In the case of *AP v Italy* the author of the communication was convicted by a Swiss court of being involved in a kidnapping conspiracy which had taken place in Italy. Four years later, after the author had served his sentence, an Italian court convicted him of the same offence. The Human Rights Committee held that Article 14(7) ICCPR was not engaged in this case because it 'does

---

[132] 60/91, 8th Annual Activity Report of the ACommHPR (1994–1995) 13.
[133] ICCPR, Art 14(6); ACHR, Art 10; ECHR Protocol No 7, Art 3.
[134] CCPR/C/45/D/408/1990 (22 July 1992).
[135] ICCPR, Art 14(7); ECHR Protocol No 7, Art 4; ACHR, Art 8(4); ACHPR, Art 7(2).

not guarantee *ne bis in idem* with regard to the national jurisdiction of two or more States'.[136]

5.5 PROTECTION OF JUVENILES

Juveniles require special protection in criminal procedures. Recognition of this fact is set out in Article 40 CRC and Article 14(4) ICCPR. Underpinning both these provisions is the idea that children should be spared the stigma of being labelled criminals as far as possible and where offences are made out they should be met with educational rehabilitation rather than punitive measures. Thus states should establish 'an appropriate criminal justice system, in order to ensure that juveniles are treated in a manner commensurate with their age' where measures such as mediation between the perpetrator and the victim are contemplated as an alternative to criminal trials.[137] Where criminal trials are held, juveniles should

be informed directly of the charges against them and, if appropriate, through their parents or legal guardians, be provided with appropriate assistance in the preparation and presentation of their defence; be tried as soon as possible in a fair hearing in the presence of legal counsel, other appropriate assistance and their parents or legal guardians, unless it is considered not to be in the best interest of the child, in particular taking into account their age or situation.[138]

5.6 NO PUNISHMENT WITHOUT LAW

The fundamental right of 'no punishment without law' is protected by all human rights treaties that address the administration of justice. States may not derogate from this obligation in times of emergency.[139] To mete out punishment for actions where there is no law prohibiting the conduct is an obvious abuse of state power. Therefore, laws that are so vague that individuals cannot know how to regulate their actions so that they act in accordance with the law will constitute a violation of the right.

The right also includes the prohibition of retroactive legislation. This encompasses, first, a guarantee not to be punished for acts or omissions that 'did not constitute a criminal offence under national or international law' at the time of the offence (*nullum crimen sine lege*). Second, where harsher penalties are introduced after the commission of an offence, they may not be applied (*nulla poena sine lege*). There are two restrictions upon this aspect of the right. First, retroactive legislation will be permitted where the new law is more lenient than the old one. Second, legislation that is enacted to introduce criminal sanctions for international crimes, such as war crimes, can be applied retrospectively as long as the conduct was a crime under international law at the time of commission.[140]

---

[136] CCPR/C/OP/2 at 67 (1990).   [137] General Comment 32, n 77, paras 43 and 44.
[138] Ibid, para 42.   [139] ICCPR, Art 15; ACHR, Art 9; ACHPR, Art 7; ECHR, Art 7.
[140] See ICCPR, Art 15(2); ECHR, Art 7(2).

The question of the application of retrospective legislation has arisen before both the European Court of Human Rights and the Human Rights Committee in cases concerning convictions for the killings of individuals who had attempted to flee the former German Democratic Republic (GDR) in the period from the early 1960s to 1989. In *Streletz, Kessler and Krenz v Germany* the applicants, senior party officials and members of the GDR National Council, argued that their conduct was not one that had attracted criminal prosecution at the time.[141] However, the German courts that had convicted the applicants had applied the GDR criminal code of 1968 which explicitly stated that anyone who committed crimes against human rights would be punished. The European Court noted that the reason that prosecutions had not been forthcoming at the time of the killings was because the individuals concerned, by virtue of their high status within the state apparatus, had maintained a situation of impunity. It was quite clear to the Court that the killings had been disproportionate and a violation of the right to life and therefore attracted criminal punishment under the GDR criminal code. The Human Rights Committee arrived at a similar conclusion in *Baumgarten v Germany*.[142] However, this is not to say that violations of human rights always give rise to retrospective criminal responsibility—these findings are restricted to the application of the GDR criminal code.

6 CONCLUSION

Rights regarding the administration of justice are some of the oldest protections granted by law to individuals. Today, it is recognized that securing the rights to liberty and a fair trial is a necessary pre-requisite for the enjoyment of all other human rights. Since the drafting of the Magna Carta, a substantial body of norms, guidelines, and jurisprudence regarding these rights has developed to give more specific protections to all individuals. As criminal justice systems are often manipulated to the detriment of the enjoyment of human rights, a significant proportion of the human rights framework for the administration of justice is devoted to this area. However, rights regarding the administration of justice are also concerned with issues such as the judicial resolution of civil disputes and the use of detention powers beyond the criminal justice context. Any failure to regulate these concerns is bound to raise questions about the credibility of a justice system.

FURTHER READING

DÖRR, 'Detention, Arbitrary' in Wolfrum (ed), *Max Planck Encyclopaedia of International Law* (Oxford University Press, 2007).

DOSWALD-BECK and KOLB (eds), *Judicial Process and Human Rights: UN, European, American and African Systems: Texts and Summaries of International Case-Law* (Engel, 2004).

---

[141] (2001) 33 EHRR 751. [142] CCPR/C/78/D/960/2000 (19 September 2003).

RODLEY and POLLARD, *The Treatment of Prisoners under International Law* (Oxford University Press, 2009) chs 8, 9, 11.

SCOVAZZI and CITRONI, *The Struggle Against Enforced Disappearance and the 2007 United Nations Convention* (Martinus Nijhoff, 2007).

TRECHSEL, 'Why Must Trials be Fair?' (1997) 31 *Israel LR* 94.

—— *Human Rights in Criminal Proceedings* (Oxford University Press, 2005).

WEISSBRODT, *The Right to a Fair Trial: Articles 8, 10 and 11 of the Universal Declaration of Human Rights* (Martinus Nijhoff, 2001).

—— and WOLFRUM (eds), *The Right to a Fair Trial* (Springer, 1997).

USEFUL WEBSITES

UN Working Group on arbitrary detention: <**http://www2.ohchr.org/english/issues/detention/index.htm**>

UN Special Representative on independence of the judiciary: <**http://www2.ohchr.org/english/issues/judiciary/index.htm**>

15

SEXUAL ORIENTATION AND GENDER IDENTITY

Michael O'Flaherty

SUMMARY

Worldwide, people are subject to persistent human rights violations because of their actual or perceived sexual orientation and gender identity. The range of violations demonstrates that the members of sexual minorities are highly vulnerable to human rights abuse. This chapter assesses the forms of their vulnerability and identifies the applicable international human rights law. It will be seen that the jurisprudence focuses on issues of non-discrimination and privacy and that important human rights protections can also be derived from the range of other civil, political, economic, social, and cultural human rights of general application. The chapter concludes with an examination of a recent exercise in the clarification of the application of human rights law concerning issues of sexual orientation and gender identity, the Yogyakarta Principles.

1 INTRODUCTION

Typically, to be different to the majority in any society is to be vulnerable to prejudice, discrimination, and even attack. The greater the difference, the greater the risk. The story of the human rights movement is replete with moments defined by the identification of such vulnerable minorities and efforts to protect them. Thus, today, treaties address the situation of ethnic, racial, indigenous, religious, and other communities. However, the protection afforded by international law is by no means confined to groups that have been explicitly recognized in the treaties. International human rights treaty law has proved itself to be flexible in addressing the plight of groups whose vulnerability may not have been in the minds of the treaty drafters. One of the most vibrant contemporary human rights debates concerns the extent to which international law offers protection to members of what are sometimes termed 'sexual minorities'—about whom there is no explicit reference whatsoever in the treaty law.

A wide range of terms are used to describe the diverse members of sexual minorities, such as homosexuals, bisexuals, gays, lesbians, transsexuals, transgender, and inter-sex. Other terms, such as 'queer', can be considered pejorative in some contexts and acceptable in others. The variety of designations and usages, as well as the manner in which some of them have changed over time, can give rise to confusion on the part of the lawyer seeking to identify applicable provisions of human rights law. With this in mind, recent discourse on the application of human rights law has tended to cluster issues around two categorizations: 'sexual orientation' and 'gender identity'. An authoritative document that we will consider below, the Yogyakarta Principles,[1] describes 'sexual orientation' as, 'each person's capacity for profound emotional, affectional and sexual attraction to, and intimate sexual relations with, individuals of a different gender or the same gender or more than one gender'.[2] 'Gender identity' is described as 'each person's deeply felt internal and individual experience of gender, which may or may not correspond with the sex assigned at birth, including the personal sense of the body (which may involve, if freely chosen, modification of bodily appearance or function by medical, surgical or other means) and other expressions of gender, including dress, speech and mannerisms'.[3] Of course, these definitions are no more than intellectual constructs and, as such, can be subject to criticism. However, they have some force in that they tend to reflect the contexts in which affected people experience discrimination, exclusion, and attack in many societies. They also—and this is especially the case with regard to 'sexual orientation'—are grounded in the jurisprudence of human rights courts and treaty-monitoring bodies. To the extent possible, this chapter will employ these terms.

2 FORMS OF VULNERABILITY TO HUMAN RIGHTS ATTACK

Before we examine the extent of applicable human rights law, it is important to take account of the situation in which people of diverse sexual orientations and gender identities find themselves. Even the briefest of global surveys demonstrates a remarkable degree of vulnerability and abuse.[4] Seven states maintain the death penalty for consensual same-sex practices and reports are commonplace of persons who are killed because of their sexual orientation or gender identity. Perpetrators often go unpunished. Persons with diverse gender identities are particularly likely to be targeted for violence. They are 'often subjected to violence...in order to "punish" them for

---

[1] The Yogyakarta Principles on the Application of International Human Rights Law in Relation to Sexual Orientation and Gender Identity (2007), available at: <http://www.yogyakartaprinciples.org>.

[2] Ibid, preamble.   [3] Ibid.

[4] For an extensive review of the forms of vulnerability, see O'Flaherty and Fisher, 'Sexual Orientation, Gender Identity and International Human Rights Law: Contextualising the Yogyakarta Principles' (2008) 8 *HRLR* 207.

transgressing gender barriers or for challenging predominant conceptions of gender roles',[5] and transgender youth have been described as 'among the most vulnerable and marginalized young people in society'.[6] Violations directed against lesbians because of their sex are often inseparable from violations directed against them because of their sexual orientation. For example, the recent multiple rape of a lesbian was arranged by her family in an attempt to 'cure' her of her homosexuality.[7] Same-sex sexual relations between consenting adults constitute a criminal offence in some 80 states. Some states apply laws against 'public scandals', 'immorality', or 'indecent behaviour' to punish people for looking, dressing, or behaving differently from what are considered to be the social norms.

Serious problems have also been identified regarding the enjoyment of economic, social, and cultural rights. For example, people have been denied employment or employment-related benefits or have faced dismissal because of their sexual orientation or gender identity. In the context of the right to adequate housing, lesbian and transgender women are reported to be at a high risk of homelessness; discrimination based on sexual orientation or gender identity when renting accommodation has been experienced both by individuals and same-sex couples; and children have been thrown out of the family home by their families upon learning of their sexual orientation or gender identity. Transgender persons often face obstacles in seeking access to gender-appropriate services at homeless shelters. Materials referencing issues of sexual orientation and gender identity have been banned from school curricula; student groups addressing sexual orientation and gender identity issues have been prohibited; students have faced high levels of bullying and harassment because of their actual or perceived sexual orientation or gender identity; and, in some cases, young persons who express same-sex affection have been expelled from school. In some countries, laws have prohibited the 'promotion of homosexuality' in schools. Numerous health-related human rights violations based on sexual orientation and gender identity have been documented. People have been forcibly confined in medical institutions, subjected to 'aversion therapy', including electroshock treatment, and inter-sex people have been subjected to involuntary surgeries in an attempt to 'correct' their genitals.

The plight in which people of diverse sexual orientations and gender identities find themselves is well summed up in a comment by an Indonesian human rights expert, Siti Musdah Mulia: 'I realise that compared to other minority groups, LGBT [Lesbian, Gay, Bisexual and Transgender] people suffer more stigmas, stereotypes and discriminatory treatment, and even ruthless exploitation. The majority community (in Indonesia) still considers homosexuality as illicit, often as unmentionable.'[8]

---

[5] Report of the Special Rapporteur on the question of torture and other cruel, inhuman or degrading treatment or punishment, A/56/156 (3 July 2001) para 17.

[6] Report of the Special Rapporteur on the sale of children, child prostitution and child pornography, E/CN.4/2004/9 (5 January 2004) para 123.

[7] Report of the Special Rapporteur on violence against women, its causes and consequences, E/CN.4/2002/83 (31 January 2002) para 102.

[8] Musdah Mulia, 'Promoting LGBT Rights through Islamic Humanism' (1–6 June 2008).

3 REVIEW OF LAW AND JURISPRUDENCE

As we have already observed, there are no specific references to issues related to sexual orientation or gender identity in the regional and global human rights treaties. However, the UN human rights treaty-monitoring bodies and the European Court of Human Rights have developed a significant body of jurisprudence on the topics. Their findings tend to be clustered in three groups: protection of privacy rights, combat of discrimination, and ensuring other general human rights protection to all, regardless of sexual orientation or gender identity. We will look at each of these in turn.

3.1 PROTECTION OF PRIVACY RIGHTS

Both the European Convention on Human Rights (ECHR), in Article 8, and the International Covenant on Civil and Political Rights (ICCPR), in Article 17, contain provisions for the protection of an individual's privacy. These reflect a perception of the drafters that there is an autonomous zone within which a person may live a personal life and make choices without interference. While the scope and the limits of that private space are impossible to chart outside the context of specific cases, it is acknowledged that 'respect for private life must also comprise to a certain degree the right to establish and develop relationships with other human beings'.[9]

The first successful international human rights cases on issues of sexual orientation were brought under the ECHR and invoked the privacy argument with regard to same-sex sexual activity. In *Dudgeon v UK*[10] and *Norris v Ireland*,[11] the criminalization of such practices was deemed a violation of Article 8 ECHR. In *Modinos v Cyprus*, the European Court, taking account that many of the prohibitions were not actually enforced in practice, held that even a 'consistent policy' of not bringing prosecutions under the law was no substitute for full repeal.[12] Privacy arguments were also successful regarding a ban on recruitment to the military of homosexuals: *Smith and Grady v UK*[13] and *Lustig-Prean and Beckett v UK*.[14]

The European Court of Human Rights has also been willing to recognize privacy protection with regard to issues of gender identity. The approach of the Court reflects a perception that privacy protection may extend to the choices one makes regarding one's own choice of gender identity or expression. Interestingly, the cases are not about any effort of states to prohibit forms of gender identity choices. Instead, they address the positive obligation on the state to take the administrative actions, such as amendment of identity documents, that are necessary for the affected individuals to live in their changed gender identity. In *Goodwin v UK*[15] and *I v UK*,[16] the European Court reversed a long line of previous case law and held that the UK's refusal to change the

---

[9] *Niemietz v Germany* (1993) 16 EHRR 97, para 29.   [10] (1982) 4 EHRR 149.
[11] (1988) 13 EHRR 186.   [12] (1993) 16 EHRR 485.   [13] (1999) 29 EHRR 493.
[14] (1999) 29 EHRR 548.   [15] (2002) 35 EHRR 447.   [16] (2002) 35 EHRR 18.

legal identities of two transsexual women constituted a violation of Article 8 ECHR. In *Van Kuck v Germany*, the Court considered the case of a transsexual woman whose health-insurance company had denied her reimbursement for costs associated with sex-reassignment surgery. It found a violation of Article 8, holding that the German courts had failed to respect 'the applicant's freedom to define herself as a female person, one of the most basic essentials of self-determination'.[17] In *L v Lithuania*, the Court considered that the state was required to legislate for the provision of full gender-reassignment surgery whereby a person in the 'limbo' of partial reassignment could complete the process and be registered with the new gender identity.[18]

The Human Rights Committee, in the communication *Toonen v Australia*, adopted the approach of the European Court of Human Rights and considered that a criminal prohibition on same-sex sexual activity, even if unenforced, constituted an unreasonable interference with Mr Toonen's privacy under Article 17 ICCPR.[19] The Human Rights Committee has not had the occasion since, in its consideration of individual cases, to consider other applications of the right to privacy in the context of sexual orientation or gender identity. This, in itself, tells us nothing regarding the position of the Committee since it can only develop case-specific jurisprudence on the basis of the complaints that are submitted to it. More tellingly, the Human Rights Committee has never taken the opportunity to explore the range of applications of a privacy approach in the context of its review of periodic reports submitted by states parties to the ICCPR. Here it has addressed privacy rights exclusively in the context of the criminalization of same-sex sexual activity. Taking account of the relatively vigorous and wide-ranging engagement with privacy issues in the European context, including with regard to the duties that fall to states regarding issues of gender identity, this dearth of practice is notable and may reflect unease with the issues on the part of the membership of the Human Rights Committee.

3.2 DISCRIMINATION

As we have seen, people of diverse sexual orientations and gender identities are subject to multiple forms of discrimination. It is not surprising, then, that a considerable body of practice has developed in the work of the international human rights treaty-monitoring bodies. Again, though, as in the case of privacy, and probably for the same reasons as noted above, the focus has been on sexual orientation rather than gender identity. The Committee on Economic, Social and Cultural Rights has addressed sexual orientation-related discrimination in its general comments. In General Comments 18, on the right to work,[20] 15, on the right to water,[21] and 14, on the right to the highest attainable standard of health,[22] it has indicated that the International Covenant on

---

[17] (2003) 37 EHRR 51, para 73.   [18] (2008) 46 EHRR 22.
[19] CCPR/C/50/D/488/1992 (4 April 1994).
[20] CESCR, General Comment 18, HRI/GEN/1/Rev.9 (Vol I) 139.
[21] CESCR, General Comment 15, HRI/GEN/1/Rev.9 (Vol I) 97.
[22] CESCR, General Comment 14, HRI/GEN/1/Rev.9 (Vol I) 78.

Economic, Social and Cultural Rights (ICESCR) proscribes any discrimination on the basis of, inter alia, sex and sexual orientation, 'that has the intention or effect of nullifying or impairing the equal enjoyment or exercise of [the right at issue]'. The Committee has consistently based this prohibition on the terms of the anti-discrimination provision, Article 2(2) ICESCR, which prohibits discrimination on a variety of specified grounds as well as one termed 'other status'. In 2009, the Committee adopted a General Comment on non-discrimination specifying that, ' "other status" as recognised in article 2(2) includes sexual orientation. States parties should ensure that a person's sexual orientation is not a barrier to realising Covenant rights.'[23] The Committee, in its general comments, also invokes the provision addressing the equal rights of men and women, Article 3 ICESCR, as a basis for its prohibition of sexual orientation-related discrimination.[24]

The Committee on the Rights of the Child has also addressed sexual orientation-related discrimination in a general comment. In General Comment 4, it stated that, '[s]tate parties have the obligation to ensure that all human beings below 18 enjoy all the rights set forth in the Convention [on the Rights of the Child] without discrimination (art. 2), including with regard to "race, colour, sex, language, religion, political or other opinion, national, ethnic or social origin, property, disability, birth or other status." These grounds also cover [inter alia] sexual orientation.'[25] The Committee on the Rights of the Child thus adopts the same approach as the Committee on Economic, Social and Cultural Rights by placing sexual orientation in the 'other status' category.

Both the Committee on Economic, Social and Cultural Rights and the Committee on the Rights of the Child have occasionally raised issues of sexual orientation-related discrimination when considering periodic reports of states parties. The Committee on Economic, Social and Cultural Rights did so regarding eight of the 70 states considered between 2000 and 2006, and the Committee on the Rights of the Child regarding five of the 186 states considered in the same period. In each case, the Committees expressed concern in their 'concluding observations'. Given the non-binding and flexible nature of these treaty body outputs, they are not always a useful indicator of formal obligations under the treaty. However, where the treaty body expresses concern about a specific practice, we can surmise that serious issues arise under the treaty. Examples include the Committee on Economic, Social and Cultural Rights' regret, in 2005, that Hong Kong's anti-discrimination legislation failed to cover sexual orientation-related discrimination,[26] and its concern, in 2000, that Kyrgyzstan classified lesbianism as a sexual offence in its penal code.[27] While the Committee on the Elimination of Discrimination Against Women has not addressed the issues in a general comment,

---

[23] CESCR, General Comment 20, E/C.12/GC/20 (10 June 2009) para 32.
[24] See eg General Comment 18, n 20, para 12(b)(i).
[25] CRC, General Comment 4, HRI/GEN/1/Rev.9 (Vol II) 410, para 6.
[26] CESCR, Concluding Observations: People's Republic of China (including Hong Kong and Macau), E/C.12/1/Add.107 (13 May 2005) para 78.
[27] CESCR, Concluding Observations: Kyrgyzstan, E/C.12/1/Add.49 (1 September 2000) para 17.

on a number of occasions, it has criticized states for discrimination on the basis of sexual orientation. For example, it too addressed the situation in Kyrgyzstan and recommended that 'lesbianism be reconceptualised as a sexual orientation and that penalties for its practice be abolished'.[28]

Issues of sexual orientation have received extensive attention in the work of the Human Rights Committee. In *Toonen*, the Committee said that 'the reference to "sex" in articles 2, paragraph 1, and 26 is to be taken as including sexual orientation'. The Committee accordingly considered that sexual orientation-related discrimination is a suspect category in terms of the enjoyment of ICCPR rights (Article 2) and, more generally, for equality before and equal protection of the law (Article 26). A small number of individual cases have illustrated the Human Rights Committee's approach. In *Young v Australia*[29] and *X v Colombia*,[30] the Committee was of the view that distinctions made in law between same-sex partners who were excluded from pension benefits, and unmarried heterosexual partners who were granted such benefits, constituted violations of the ICCPR. However, not every case has been successful. In *Joslin v New Zealand*, the differential treatment under taxation regulations of same-sex unmarried couples (for whom marriage was not available in law) and heterosexual married couples was considered not to constitute a violation of Article 26 ICCPR. And yet, an individual concurring opinion of two members observed that 'the Committee's jurisprudence supports the position that such differentiation may very well, depending on the circumstances of a concrete case, amount to prohibited discrimination'.[31]

The Human Rights Committee frequently raises the issue of discrimination on the basis of sexual orientation in its consideration of periodic reports. During the period 2000–6, it did so regarding 13 of the 84 states under review and, for example, criticized many states for the criminalization of homosexual sexual relations and the failure to incorporate sexual orientation into anti-discrimination legal frameworks. It also expressed concern regarding unequal ages of consent for sexual activity, failure to prohibit employment-related discrimination, and lack of education programmes to combat discriminatory attitudes.

The European Court of Human Rights has generated a substantial body of jurisprudence concerning discrimination both on the grounds of sexual orientation and gender identity. In *Salgueiro da Silva Mouta v Portugal*, it held that a judge's denial of child custody to a homosexual father on the ground of his sexual orientation was discriminatory.[32] In *Karner v Austria*, the Court considered that the failure of Austria to permit a homosexual man to continue occupying his deceased partner's flat was discriminatory, since this entitlement, available to family members under Austrian law, did not apply to same-sex partners. Austria claimed that excluding homosexuals aimed to protect 'the family in the traditional sense', but the Court considered that it had not demonstrated how the exclusion was necessary to that aim.[33] In *L and*

---

[28] CEDAW, Concluding Observations: Kyrgyzstan, A/54/38 (5 February 1999) para 128.
[29] CCPR/C/78/D/941/2000 (6 August 2003).   [30] CCPR/C/89/D/1361/2005 (14 May 2007).
[31] CCPR/C/75/D/902/1999 (30 July 2002).   [32] (1999) 31 EHRR 1055.
[33] (2003) 38 EHRR 24.

V v Austria[34] and *SL v Austria*,[35] the Court considered that Austria's differing age of consent for heterosexual and homosexual relations was discriminatory. As the Court put it, the differing age 'embodied a predisposed bias on the part of a heterosexual majority against a homosexual minority', which could not 'amount to sufficient justification for the differential treatment any more than similar negative attitudes towards those of a different race, origin or colour'.

One area of discrimination in which the European Court has been slow to find a violation of the Convention has been that of the adoption of children. In the case of *Frette v France*, a homosexual man complained regarding a refusal to allow him to adopt a child for reasons of his sexual orientation.[36] The Court found against him, referring to the fast-evolving and very diverse practice across Europe, as well as the conflicting views of experts as to what would be in the best interests of the child. The decision in *Frette* is unsatisfactory. It posits false dilemmas such as a supposed tension between the rights of the man and the child. There is no such tension. The tension is between the rights of homosexual and heterosexual prospective adoptive parents, with the best interests of the child as the overarching consideration. Issues such as these were handled in a better manner in *EB v France*. In that case, the Court, while maintaining the paramount principle of the best interests of the child, held that, 'in rejecting the applicant's application for authorisation to adopt, the domestic authorities made a distinction based on considerations regarding her sexual orientation, a distinction which is not acceptable under the Convention'.[37]

Overall, we can consider that the European Court of Human Rights and the treaty bodies have mapped out an extensive range of areas and contexts in which sexual orientation-related discrimination is prohibited. The European Court has extended this consideration also to discrimination on the grounds of gender identity. Furthermore, as we will see later, it can also be assumed that the protections extend very much further than is specifically indicated in the jurisprudence and the review of periodic reports: they apply for the non-discriminatory enjoyment of all human rights.

3.3 GENERAL HUMAN RIGHTS PROTECTION

The Human Rights Committee and the other treaty bodies, in the review of periodic reports, frequently insist on the entitlement of people of diverse sexual orientations and gender identities to benefit from the protection of other human rights of general application. In other words, and for instance, if torture is always prohibited then it cannot be countenanced when perpetrated against members of sexual minorities. On this basis the Human Rights Committee has expressed concern to specific states regarding violent crimes perpetrated against persons of minority sexual orientation, including by law enforcement officials; the failure to address such crime

---

[34] (2003) 36 EHRR 55.   [35] (2003) 37 EHRR 39.   [36] (2003) 38 EHRR 21.
[37] (2008) 47 EHRR 21, para 96.

in legislation on hate crime; the frequent failure of states to investigate such acts; and the need for training of law enforcement and judicial officials in order to sensitize them to the rights of sexual minorities. The Committee on the Rights of the Child has expressed concern that homosexual and transsexual young people often do not have access to the appropriate information, support, and necessary protection to enable them to live their sexual orientation. On a number of occasions, the Committee against Torture has expressed concern about the torture of homosexuals and regarding complaints of threats and attacks against sexual minorities and transgender activists.

The reports of the 'special procedures' of the Human Rights Council constitute a particularly valuable repository of examples of the application for people of diverse sexual orientations and gender identities of general human rights protections, as well as of the principle of non-discrimination. The Council's Working Group on Arbitrary Detention has frequently invoked *Toonen* as a basis for its finding of arbitrary detention of homosexuals. A former Independent Expert on the situation of human rights defenders was assiduous in condemning attacks on members of sexual minorities.[38] She drew attention to such human rights violations as summary execution; torture; arbitrary detention; unreasonable impediments to freedom of expression, movement, and association; and participation in public life.

A number of the 'special procedures' have drawn attention to the intersectional nature of many human rights violations, where already vulnerable people face heightened risk when promoting the rights of people of diverse sexual orientations and gender identities. For example, the Independent Expert on minority issues has referred to the multiple forms of exclusion of members of minority communities, based on aspects of their identities and personal realities such as sexual orientation or gender expression that challenge social or cultural norms.[39]

Some of the 'special procedures' that address economic, social, and cultural rights have drawn attention to the extent to which violations of these rights are at issue for people of diverse sexual orientations and gender identities. The work of a former Special Rapporteur on the right to health is particularly notable. In 2004, he observed that 'fundamental human rights principles, as well as existing human rights norms, lead ineluctably to the recognition of sexual rights as human rights. Sexual rights include the right of all persons to express their sexual orientation, with due regard for the well-being and rights of others, without fear of persecution, denial of liberty or social interference.'[40] There are also examples of contributions of this kind at the regional level. Country reports and follow-up reports of the Inter-American Commission on Human Rights refer to such violations as 'social-cleansing' (killing) of homosexuals

---

[38] Report of the Special Representative of the Secretary-General on human rights defenders, E/CN.4/2006/95/Add.1 (22 March 2006).

[39] Report of the Independent Expert on minority issues, E/CN.4/2006/74 (6 January 2006).

[40] Report of the Special Rapporteur on the right of everyone to the enjoyment of the highest attainable standard of physical and mental health, E/CN.4/2004/49 (16 February 2004) para 54.

and the treatment of lesbian prisoners.[41] The Council of Europe Commissioner for Human Rights often draws attention to violations at the country level.[42]

The UN and regional level examples clearly reinforce the assertion that human rights of general application may not be constrained on the basis of sexual orientation or gender identity. But how does one distinguish rights of general application from those that are intended only to benefit a certain category of people? The answer to this question will usually be straightforward. For instance, the ICCPR limits the right to participate in political life to citizens. The question arises though of when a generally stated human right is limited in terms of who may benefit. For our purposes, the issue concerns when a right exclusively addresses the situation and choices of what we might term sexual majorities. This is the context for one of the most charged of contemporary debates concerning the rights of sexual minorities: whether international human rights law recognizes a right of same-sex marriage or of same-sex family life. The Human Rights Committee, in *Joslin*, has been unequivocal on the matter of same-sex marriage. It contends that the right to marriage (Article 24(2) ICCPR) refers to a right of a man and a woman and that same-sex marriage is thereby excluded from the protection of the Covenant. The European Court of Human Rights has taken a similar position to the Human Rights Committee on the issue of same-sex marriage,[43] though, in *Goodwin*, it indicated that the determination of sex cannot be undertaken using solely biological criteria.

It is less clear whether international human rights law recognizes the rights of same-sex unmarried families. Article 23(1) ICCPR states the fundamental importance of the family and its entitlement to protection by the state, without reference to the form of family under consideration. Only in Article 23(2) do we find reference to the right of men and women to marry and found families. It is not necessarily the case that Article 23(2) restricts the meaning of the word 'family' in Article 23(1). And interestingly, the Human Rights Committee, in *Young* and in *X*,[44] has criticized state practices that impede same-sex couples from benefiting from family-related benefits, such as transfer of pension entitlements. These cases, however, only addressed issues of inequality before the law (Article 26 ICCPR) and, in *X*, in a dissenting opinion of two members, it was observed that 'a couple of the same sex does not constitute a family within the meaning of the Covenant and cannot claim benefits that are based on a conception of the family as comprising individuals of different sexes'.[45] The European Court of Human Rights, for its part, has indicated that homosexual stable relationships are not equivalent in rights to heterosexual relationships.[46] However, in the *Salguiero da Silva Mouta* case, the Court found a violation of the right to family life of a man in a homosexual relationship, albeit the family unit under consideration was that of the man and

footnotes:

---

[41] Annual Report of the Inter-American Commission on Human Rights 2006, ch IIIC(1).

[42] Memorandum to the Polish Government, CommDH(2007)13 (20 June 2007).

[43] See eg *Sheffield and Horsham v UK* (1999) 27 EHRR 163.   [44] n 29 and n 30.

[45] n 30, separate opinion of Mr Abdelfattah Amor and Mr Ahmed Tawfik Khalil.

[46] See the citations and discussion in Walker, 'Moving Gaily Forward? Lesbian, Gay and Transgender Human Rights in Europe' (2001) 2 *Melbourne JIL* 122.

his daughter rather than that of him and his partner.[47] And, in *Goodwin*, the Court was willing to interpret the terms in Article 8 ECHR 'the right of a man and a woman to marry' in a flexible manner taking account of changes in society. The flexibility displayed in *Goodwin* may well lead the European Court at some point to elaborate the rights of same-sex families. Ultimately, the Court, the Human Rights Committee, and the other treaty bodies, at some future date, may take due account of the various commentaries, many of which lean towards a flexible understanding of the term 'family',[48] as well as the increasing recognition by states of diversity of family forms, as reflected in the Declaration on the International Year of the Family.[49]

One final uncertainty may be observed concerning the reach of human rights law to address abuses related to sexual orientation or gender identity. It remains unclear how far a human rights approach can go in terms of the regulation of practices of non-state actors.[50] This issue is of obvious importance since so many of the forms of abusive behaviour are to be found outside the state sector, such as in the workplace, privately owned housing, religious communities, and so forth.

4 LEGAL INITIATIVES TO BRIDGE THE GAP BETWEEN LAW AND PRACTICE

This chapter's review of the law has shown the long reach of international human rights standards as regards the particular situation of people of diverse sexual orientations and gender identities. Fundamental principles, such as those of non-discrimination and of the universal application of general human rights standards, have been strongly affirmed. However, as has also been demonstrated, the courts, the treaty bodies, and the independent experts, limited as they are by the facts before them or their various mandates, have only indicated the actual application of these principles to a limited number of circumstances.

As a result, a certain degree of legal uncertainty persists. That uncertainty is compounded by the terminological confusion, referred to above, which is to be found throughout the case law, comments of treaty bodies, and reports of special procedures. In particular, issues of gender identity have been little understood, with, for instance, some special procedures and states referencing transsexuality as a 'sexual orientation', and others frankly acknowledging that they do not understand the term.

There has been a significant recent initiative to address the uncertainty regarding the reach of the law (and the terminological confusion). In 2007, a group of experts produced a text known as the Yogyakarta Principles on the application of international

---

[47] n 32.

[48] See eg CRC, 'Day of General Discussion on Children Without Parental Care', CRC/C/153 (17 March 2006) para 644.

[49] Celebration of the Tenth Anniversary of the International Year of the Family and Beyond, GA Res 59/147, A/RES/59/147 (25 January 2005).   [50] See Chapter 25, below.

human rights law in relation to sexual orientation and gender identity.[51] This document was authored by 29 international human rights specialists and has a tripartite function.[52] In the first place, it constitutes a 'mapping' of the experiences of human rights violations experienced by people of diverse sexual orientations and gender identities. Second, the application of international human rights law to such experiences is articulated. Finally, the Principles spell out the nature of the obligation on states for implementation of each of the human rights.

The Principles have no binding force. They are neither a treaty nor the finding of a judicial or quasi-judicial body. Nevertheless, they carry the authority of their expert authors and have been considered by many states and experts to constitute a careful articulation of the state of existing law. Accordingly, they bear examination in some detail. Each principle comprises a statement of the law, its application to a given situation, and an indication of the nature of the state's duty to implement the legal obligation. Principles 1 to 3 address the principles of the universality of human rights and their application to all persons without discrimination, as well as the right of all people to recognition before the law. The experts placed these elements at the beginning of the text in order to recall the fundamental significance of the universality of human rights and the scale and extent of discrimination against people because of their actual or perceived sexual orientation or gender identity, as well as the manner in which they are often rendered invisible within society and its legal structures. Principles 4 to 11 deal with the fundamental rights to life, freedom from violence and torture, privacy, access to justice, and freedom from arbitrary detention. Principles 12 to 18 address non-discriminatory enjoyment of economic, social, and cultural rights, including accommodation, employment, social security, health, and education. Principles 19 to 21 concern the importance of the freedom to express oneself, one's identity, and one's sexuality, without state interference, based on sexual orientation or gender identity, including the rights to participate peaceably in public assemblies and events and otherwise associate in community with others. Principles 22 and 23 address the right to seek asylum from persecution based on sexual orientation or gender identity. Principles 24 to 26 deal with the rights to participate in family life, public affairs, and the cultural life of the community, without discrimination based on sexual orientation or gender identity. Principle 27 recognizes the right to defend and promote human rights without discrimination based on sexual orientation and gender identity, and the obligation of states to ensure the protection of human rights defenders. Principles 28 and 29 affirm the importance of holding rights violators accountable, and of ensuring redress for those whose rights are violated.

A notable feature of the principles is the manner in which they spell out in some detail the legal obligations of the state with regard to each of the rights that are affirmed. A general typology for the obligations can be observed. States must: (1) take all necessary legislative, administrative, and other measures to eradicate impugned practices;

[51] n 1.   [52] Address of the Rapporteur, launch event of the Principles (March 2007).

(2) take protection measures for those at risk; (3) ensure accountability of perpetrators and redress for victims; and (4) promote a human rights culture by means of education, training, and public awareness-raising. Also, in the document's preamble, as we have already observed, the experts proposed the definition of the terms 'sexual orientation' and 'gender identity'. These formulations, drawing on their wide usage within academic writing and advocacy communities, establish a personal scope of application for the Principles. The preface also includes references that acknowledge the imperfections of the text and the need to keep its contents under review with a view to future reformulations that would take account of legal changes as well as developing understandings of the situation of people of diverse sexual orientations and gender identities.

5 CONCLUSION

This chapter has assessed the actual human rights situation of people of diverse sexual orientations and gender identities worldwide as well as the extent of the application to them of international human rights law. The gap between law and practice has been highlighted and a major initiative to address that gap, the Yogyakarta Principles, has been discussed. These Principles are presented as a form of *aide-mémoire* that indicates the contemporary state of the law and presents it in an integrated and coherent manner. The constraints of discussion within a textbook are such that our reflection may go no further. Readers are, however, encouraged also to examine the relevant national and international politics. It is of particular utility to study the practice in such international diplomatic fora as the Human Rights Council and the General Assembly. For instance, it will be of interest to examine and assess the impact of an 18 December 2008 statement in support of full protection of human rights for persons of diverse sexual orientations and gender identities that was proclaimed at the General Assembly on behalf of 66 states (the authors of which acknowledged the extent to which its contents were informed by the Yogyakarta Principles),[53] as well as of what is sometimes described as the 'counter-statement' that was delivered to the General Assembly on the same day on behalf of 57 other states.[54] The publication of such competing statements recalls the extent to which the subject area is highly controversial and in a state of political flux. We are thus precluded from drawing any firm conclusions as to prospects for better enforcement of the law or its further development. We can no more than observe that with regard to the plight of many members of sexual minorities, the universal enjoyment of human rights remains an elusive and distant goal.

---

[53] Statement of Argentina (18 December 2008) video-archived (at 2 hours, 25 mins) at: <http://www.un.org/webcast/ga.html>.

[54] Statement of Syria (18 December 2008), video-archived (at 2 hours, 32 mins) at: <http://www.un.org/webcast/ga.html>.

FURTHER READING

CORREA, PETCHESKY, and PARKER, *Sexuality, Health and Human Rights* (Routledge, 2008).

MARKS and CLAPHAM, *International Human Rights Lexicon* (Oxford University Press, 2005) 327–44.

O'FLAHERTY and FISHER, 'Sexual Orientation, Gender Identity and International Human Rights Law: Contextualising the Yogyakarta Principles' (2008) 8 *HRLR* 207.

SANDERS, 'Human Rights and Sexual Orientation in International Law', available at: <http://www.ilga.org>.

WINTEMUTE and ANDENAES (eds), *Legal Recognition of Same-Sex Partnerships: A Study of National, European and International Law* (Hart Publishing, 2001).

USEFUL WEBSITES

International Commission of Jurists: <**http://www.icj.org**>

Human Rights Watch: < **http://www.hrw.org/en/category/topic/lgbt-rights**>

International Lesbian, Gay, Bisexual, Trans and Intersex Association: <**http://www.ilga.org**>

ARC International: <**http://www.arc-international.net**>

16

WOMEN'S RIGHTS

Dianne Otto

SUMMARY

International human rights law prohibits discrimination against women in their enjoyment of all human rights and fundamental freedoms. While non-discrimination is an essential component to the realization of women's rights, its comparative approach measures women's equality against men's enjoyment of rights, reinforcing the masculinity of the universal subject of human rights law, whose rights are fully promoted and explicitly protected. To the extent that violations experienced exclusively or primarily by women are expressly recognized in the founding human rights instruments, they are treated as a sub-category of the universal and formulated as 'protective' measures rather than as human rights. There have been many efforts to address the resulting marginalization of women's rights, including the adoption of the Convention on the Elimination of All Forms of Discrimination Against Women and the mainstreaming of women's human rights. While these efforts have been successful in many respects, there are continuing conceptual and practical problems, including, not only the limitations of anti-discrimination law, but the danger that specific recognition of women's rights violations may simply reproduce women's secondary status.

1 INTRODUCTION

In 1945, the UN Charter recognized the principle that human rights and fundamental freedoms should be enjoyed by everyone 'without distinction as to ... sex'.[1] Since then, international human rights instruments have repeatedly affirmed that women and men must equally enjoy the human rights they enumerate, without discrimination on the ground of sex.[2] The new era of universal human rights promised women, for the

---

[1] Art 1(4).
[2] See eg Universal Declaration of Human Rights (UDHR), Art 2; International Covenant on Civil and Political Rights (ICCPR), Arts 2(2) and 3; International Covenant on Economic, Social and Cultural Rights (ICESCR), Arts 2(1) and 3.

first time in international law, the full recognition of their humanity, marking a decisive break with the longstanding legal representation of women as lacking full legal and civil capacity. Significantly, the promise of equality also extended to the private realm of the family.[3] Women were no longer to be treated as the dependants of men, or as the property of their fathers or husbands.

Yet there has been widespread resistance to taking these obligations seriously, as evidenced by the many sweeping reservations to the Convention on the Elimination of All Forms of Discrimination Against Women (CEDAW). The CEDAW was adopted in 1979 to draw specific attention to the entrenched nature of women's inequality and the need for significant affirmative measures to address it. Unashamedly, some of the reservations to the CEDAW challenge the very idea of women's equality with men.[4] As former UN High Commissioner for Human Rights, Louise Arbour, said in a statement to the Human Rights Council in 2008, 'women and girls continue to be regarded as lesser beings in many corners of the world', despite the adoption of the Universal Declaration of Human Rights (UDHR) 60 years earlier.[5] Restrictions on women's freedom of movement, discriminatory property and inheritance laws, and practices such as male guardianship continue to 'put women at the risk of being subjected to abuse, violence and oppression, both inside and outside their homes'.[6] In some countries, historic hard-won advances towards the recognition of women's rights are now under threat, or have been wound back, in the face of cultural or religious 'fundamentalisms',[7] or in the name of thwarting international terrorism.[8]

The grim reality is that women fare considerably worse than men on almost every indicator of social well-being, despite the assumption by all states of at least some international legal obligations to promote their equal enjoyment of human rights, and despite many good intentions. Violence against women continues to be pervasive around the world, endangering women's lives in both public and private spheres.[9] The World Health Organization estimates that every day 1,500 women and girls die of preventable complications related to pregnancy and childbirth.[10] As an international group of eminent global leaders, brought together by Nelson Mandela, recently observed, religious teachings and customary practices 'have been [mis]used throughout the centuries to justify and entrench inequality and discrimination against women and girls', denying them 'fair access to education, health, employment, property and

---

[3] UDHR, Art 16(1). See further ICCPR, Art 23(4).

[4] Clark, 'The Vienna Convention Reservations Regime and the Convention on Discrimination Against Women' (1991) 85 *AJIL* 281; Cook, 'Reservations to the Convention on the Elimination of All Forms of Discrimination Against Women' (1990) 30 *Virginia JIL* 643. On reservations to human rights treaties generally, see Chapter 6, above.

[5] 'Statement by Louise Arbour, UN High Commissioner for Human Rights, on the occasion of the 8th Session of the Human Rights Council', Meeting on Human Rights of Women, Geneva, 5 June 2008.

[6] Ibid.

[7] Report of the Secretary-General, In-depth study on all forms of violence against women, A/61/122/Add.1 (6 July 2006) para 58.

[8] Faludi, *The Terror Dream: Fear and Fantasy in Post-9/11 America* (Scribe, 2008).

[9] Report of the Secretary-General, n 7, paras 363–4.

[10] Human Rights Council Res 11/8 (17 June 2008) paras 1 and 2.

influence within their own communities'.[11] Women's inequality is still widely regarded as 'natural' and as prescribed by religious teachings and cultural traditions.

Although the lack of political will presents an extremely significant barrier to the realization of women's rights and equality, it is not the only problem. International human rights law itself presents some obstacles. As Douzinas has observed, human rights 'construct humans', rather than the reverse, and therefore '[a] human being is someone who can successfully claim rights'.[12] This presents a conundrum for women's human rights advocates because, in crafting laws that respond to the gendered realities of women's lives, there is the risk of reconstituting gender stereotypes through reproducing those realities, rather than challenging them. At the same time, 'special' measures designed to address women's specific injuries and disadvantage continue to affirm the maleness of the universal subject of human rights law, as men need no special enumeration of their gender-specific injuries.[13] Charlesworth has called this the 'paradox of feminism'; whether women's rights are best protected through general norms that treat women as the same as men, or through specific norms applicable only to women.[14] Ultimately, the paradox forces us to ask hard questions about how women's inclusion as full subjects of the universal regime of human rights law might be achieved.

This chapter examines the many efforts to promote women's equality and rights through international human rights law, and discusses some of the ongoing dilemmas about how best to achieve the full inclusion of women. Section 2 describes the treatment of women in international law prior to the adoption of the UN Charter, in order to emphasize the significance of the subsequent shift to the promotion of women's equality. It examines the non-discrimination approach favoured by the drafters of the founding human rights instruments, highlighting the importance of the approach as well as some of its limitations. Section 3 examines the innovative approach taken in the CEDAW, the drafters of which aimed to address the problems attending the concept of non-discrimination by promoting a strong version of women's substantive equality. Yet while the CEDAW fostered a better understanding of the measures that may be necessary to achieve women's equal enjoyment of human rights, it also reinforced the marginalization of women's rights practically and conceptually. The human rights treaty bodies tacitly used the existence of the CEDAW Committee as an excuse to continue their neglect of women's rights, and different administrative arrangements helped to 'ghettoise' both the CEDAW Committee and its work. To tackle this marginalization, a new strategy of 'gender mainstreaming' was adopted during the 1990s, which sought to reinterpret mainstream human rights to be inclusive of women's experiences. This is examined in Section 4. The chapter

---

[11] The Elders, 'Equality for Women and Girls', available at: <http://www.theelders.org/womens-initiatives>.   [12] Douzinas, 'The End(s) of Human Rights' (2002) 26 *Melbourne ULR* 445, 457.

[13] Otto, 'Lost in translation: re-scripting the sexed subject of international human rights law', in Orford (ed), *International Law and Its Others* (CUP, 2006) 318–56.

[14] Charlesworth, 'Not Waving but Drowning: Gender Mainstreaming and Human Rights in the United Nations' (2005) 18 *HHRJ* 1.

concludes, in Section 5, by drawing attention to some continuing obstacles presented by the law itself, which prevent women from successfully claiming and enjoying human rights.

2 A NEW ERA OF NON-DISCRIMINATION ON THE GROUND OF SEX AND EQUALITY WITH MEN

While the UN Charter was the first international treaty to promote women's equality with men, it was not the first time that women were constituted as a category in international law. This section will briefly describe how women appeared in earlier international legal texts before examining how women's rights were recognized by the foundational human rights instruments. While the idea of women's equality with men was a radical and visionary development, of great importance to women (and men), this approach failed to acknowledge the specificity of many human rights violations suffered exclusively or predominantly by women and therefore failed to construct them as fully human.

2.1 THE POSITION PRIOR TO 1945

Before 1945, international law had taken a paternalistic or 'protective' approach to women, treating them as the property, extension, or dependants of men, as primarily mothers and wives, and as incapable of full autonomy and agency.[15] Women were valued for their pre-marital chastity, their prioritization of motherhood and domesticity, and their acceptance of the heterosexual family hierarchy and the paternal protection of the state and its laws. The laws of war, for example, required an occupying power to respect 'family honour and rights', treating women as part of (male) family property and reputation, to be protected by the law.[16] Early international labour conventions prohibited women from certain types of work, such as night work and mining, on the basis that this interfered with their domestic and reproductive responsibilities.[17] Anti-trafficking conventions made women's consent to working in the sex industry irrelevant, thereby treating all sex workers as victims, needing rescue and rehabilitation.[18] None of these conventions constructed women as rights-bearers. Instead,

[15] Hevener, 'International Law and the Status of Women: An Analysis of International Legal Instruments Related to the Treatment of Women' (1978) 1 *Harvard Women's LJ* 131, 133–40.

[16] See Convention Respecting the Laws and Customs of War on Land (Hague Convention II) Art 46; and Convention Respecting the Laws and Customs of War on Land (Hague Convention IV), Art 46.

[17] See eg International Labour Organization, Maternity Protection Convention 1919 (Convention 3); International Labour Organization, Convention Concerning Night Work of Women Employed in Industry 1919 (Convention 4); International Labour Organization, Convention Concerning the Employment of Women on Underground Work in Mines of All Kinds 1935 (Convention 45).

[18] International Agreement for the Suppression of the White Slave Traffic 1904; International Convention for the Suppression of White Slave Traffic 1910; International Convention for the Suppression of the Traffic in Women and Children 1921; Convention for the Suppression of the Traffic in Women of Full Age 1933. See

women were granted 'protections', sometimes in the form of 'privileged' treatment, because of their socially ascribed secondary status.

2.2 THE UDHR AND THE INTERNATIONAL COVENANTS

Following the Second World War, the shift from protectionism to universal human rights promised to recognize women as fully human, for the first time, by granting them the same human rights as men. The primary means for achieving women's equality, adopted by the drafters of the UDHR, was to prohibit discrimination based on sex in the enjoyment of universal rights and freedoms.[19] This approach was chosen instead of recognizing rights that were specific to women's experience, fearing the latter would compromise the idea of 'universality' of rights and wrongly emphasize women's difference from men rather than their common humanity.[20]

In transforming the UDHR into legally binding instruments, the International Covenant on Economic, Social and Cultural Rights (ICESCR) and the International Covenant on Civil and Political Rights (ICCPR) followed suit, relying largely on the prohibition of sex discrimination in the enjoyment of the rights they enumerated to achieve women's equality.[21] As the Covenants did not define 'discrimination' or 'equality', many states parties interpreted their obligations narrowly, as requiring formal, rather than substantive, equality.[22] However, an additional provision was included as Article 3 common to the two Covenants, which required states parties to ensure 'the equal right of men and women to the enjoyment of all...[rights] set forth in the present Covenant', indicating that special attention must be paid to achieving women's equality and, by the use of the term 'enjoyment', suggesting that equality in outcome (substantive equality) was the goal, although states parties were slow to acknowledge this.

The obligation to ensure that women enjoy the same rights as men was a very significant step forward for women. States parties were required to treat women and men alike when they are in a comparable situation. Think, for example, of the importance to women of the universal franchise, the freedom to move and to express their opinions to the same extent as men, of equal pay, and education on the same basis as men. In addition, the unprecedented acknowledgement that women and men 'are entitled to equal rights as to marriage, during marriage and at its dissolution',[23] broke through the tradition in liberal legal thinking that exempted the private sphere from

---

further, Doezema, 'Loose Women or Lost Women? The Re-Emergence of the Myth of White Slavery in the Contemporary Discourses of Trafficking in Women' [2000] *Gender Issues* 23, 24.

[19] UDHR, Art 2. This type of non-discrimination provision is described as a 'subordinate norm' because it prohibits discrimination only with respect to the rights and freedoms set out in the instrument.

[20] Morsink, 'Women's Rights in the Universal Declaration' (1991) 13 *HRQ* 229. For a critical analysis see Bequaert Holmes, 'A Feminist Analysis of the Universal Declaration of Human Rights' in Gould (ed), *Beyond Dominance: New Perspectives on Women and Philosophy* (Rowman & Allanheld, 1983) 250.

[21] ICESCR, Art 2(2); ICCPR, Art 2(1).   [22] See Chapter 9, above.

[23] UDHR, Art 16(1); ICCPR, Art 23(4).

legal scrutiny.[24] This provision dispensed with the public–private dichotomy that has served to shield many of the human rights violations experienced by women in the 'private' realm of the family from public scrutiny and deliver impunity to perpetrators. However, as would soon become apparent, this development was in tension with states' responsibilities to protect the institution of the family and enshrine the right to privacy within families as also set out in the UDHR and ICCPR.[25] For many Third World women, the issue of private actors violating their rights is not only a concern within their communitarian and extended-family networks, but also an issue of the unregulated activities of global private actors, such as transnational corporations and banks.[26] The policies and practices of global economic actors exploit local resources and labour, with highly gendered effects, compounding the difficulties that poor states have in complying with their human rights obligations. Yet the 'private' conduct of the marketplace is not directly regulated by human rights law.

Despite these shortcomings, the prohibition of discrimination against women left little doubt that the differences between women and men, which had previously been treated as immutable and used to justify women's inequality, were to be understood as socially constructed and therefore changeable. International human rights law had the potential to challenge the 'naturalness' of many discriminatory beliefs and practices, and assist in the task of changing oppressive stereotypes about 'women' and, simultaneously, challenging dominating stereotypes about 'men'. While ground-breaking, the preferred method of realizing women's full humanity by promoting their equal and non-discriminatory enjoyment of human rights soon proved to be problematic, both conceptually and in practice.

Conceptually, non-discrimination was interpreted as a formal (*de jure*) rather than substantive (*de facto*) obligation, which required women to be granted the same rights as men, regardless of whether this achieved equality of outcome. Treating women in the same way as men works well when women's and men's experience of human rights violations are directly comparable, as in the first communication concerning sex discrimination considered by the Human Rights Committee. The communication was brought by a group of Mauritian women, complaining that legislation discriminated against women because it granted automatic residency to the foreign wives of Mauritian men while it denied automatic residency to the foreign husbands of Mauritian women.[27] On these facts, the Human Rights Committee easily found that the legislation made an 'adverse distinction based on sex' because it adversely affected married women's enjoyment of ICCPR rights related to privacy and family life, as compared to married men.[28]

---

[24] Romany, 'State Responsibility Goes Private: A Feminist Critique of the Public/Private Distinction in International Human Rights Law' in Cook (ed), *Human Rights of Women: National and International Perspectives* (University of Pennsylvania Press, 1994) 85.

[25] UDHR, Arts 12 and 16(3); ICCPR, Arts 17(1) and 23(1).

[26] Oloka-Onyango and Tamale, '"The Personal is Political" or Why Women's Rights Are Indeed Human Rights: An African Perspective on International Feminism' (1995) 17 *HRQ* 691, 702.

[27] *Aumeeruddy-Cziffra et al. v Mauritius*, CCPR/C/12/D/35/1978 (9 April 1981).

[28] Ibid, paras 9.2(b)2(i)8 and 9.2(b)2(ii)4.

However, a comparison with the rights that men enjoy does not help in situations where women's experiences are substantially different from men's, as in the case of the right to work. Rights recognized by the ICESCR that protect the right to work assume a male model of employment, which makes women's unremunerated work in the family and their poorly remunerated work in the informal sector invisible.[29] This approach also fails to take account of women's often interrupted patterns of paid work, the problem of gender segregation in the workforce, and the need for maternity leave and childcare provision. A further problem with the comparative approach of equality and non-discrimination is that, when the Covenants depart from it by explicitly referring to women's different experience, international law's discursive heritage of treating women protectively tends to re-emerge, as in the requirement that states parties ensure 'special protection' (rather than rights) for mothers for a period before and after childbirth.[30] The result is that women are included in the Covenants by reference to the gendered specificities of their lives, which need 'special' treatment to be addressed. This approach constructs women's experience as non-universal and has the effect of buttressing the masculinity of the universal subject. The ICESCR also describes the right of everyone to an adequate standard of living 'for himself [sic] and his family',[31] breathing life into the erroneous stereotype that all women are dependent on male household breadwinners, although the Committee on Economic, Social and Cultural Rights has since strongly repudiated this interpretation.[32]

In practice, drawing formal comparisons between women and men proved to be a blunt means of promoting women's substantive equality. The narrow focus of a comparison does not take account of the need to redress the institutionalized history of discrimination and disadvantage that often affects women's ability to exercise their rights in the same way as men, for example by ensuring they have the information, autonomy, and mobility to exercise their right to vote. A formal comparison also ignores the need to create enabling circumstances that will make women's equal enjoyment of rights possible, which may involve changing deeply embedded social and cultural attitudes that stigmatize or punish women for exercising their rights.

The limitations of relying on the prohibition of sex discrimination to do all the work of ensuring that women fully enjoy universal human rights and fundamental freedoms was soon apparent.[33] In addition to interpreting equality as a formal rather than substantive obligation, women's human rights violations were rarely addressed by human rights treaty bodies in the early years of their operation because the comparative standard of non-discrimination did not force them to rethink their own gendered

---

[29] ICESCR, Arts 6, 7, and 8. See further, Promoting Women's Enjoyment of their Economic and Social Rights: Expert Group Meeting, EGM/WESR/1997/Report (1–4 December 1997) paras 46–8.

[30] ICESCR, Art 10(2).   [31] Ibid, Art 11(1).

[32] CESCR, General Comment 4, HRI/GEN/1/Rev.9 (Vol I) 11, para 6.

[33] Petersen, 'Whose Rights? A Critique of the "Givens" in Human Rights Discourse' (1990) 15 *Alternatives* 303.

frameworks, and human rights NGOs were preoccupied with addressing Cold War violations experienced by men in the public sphere, such as the freedom of political expression and the release of political prisoners.

3 THE SUBSTANTIVE EQUALITY APPROACH OF CEDAW

In an attempt to counter the marginalization of women within the general framework and application of international human rights law, the CEDAW was adopted by the UN General Assembly and opened for ratification in 1979. Although the CEDAW takes the same general approach as the Covenants by promoting non-discrimination on the ground of sex and women's equality with men, it highlights the specificity of women's experience of discrimination and advances a strong form of women's substantive equality as the international norm. This section discusses the positive features of the approach to women's rights taken by the CEDAW and then examines some of its limitations. It begins with a discussion of three strategies adopted by the CEDAW to promote a robust understanding of women's equality: the adoption of a comprehensive definition of discrimination against women; the promotion of the use of temporary and permanent 'special measures' to address the institutionalized effects of women's historical disadvantage and to counter disadvantage that might otherwise be associated with women's reproductive functions; and the requirement that states parties tackle the causes of women's inequality by promoting social change in all spheres of life, including in families.

3.1 TOWARDS A ROBUST UNDERSTANDING OF EQUALITY

The first step towards advancing women's substantive equality is the provision of a comprehensive definition of 'discrimination against women' in Article 1:

[it] shall mean any distinction, exclusion or restriction made on the basis of sex which has the effect or purpose of impairing or nullifying the recognition, enjoyment or exercise by women, irrespective of their marital status, on a basis of equality of men and women, of human rights and fundamental freedoms in the political, economic, social, cultural, civil or any other field.

This definition covers a wide range of conduct and, importantly, prohibits discriminatory treatment (direct discrimination) as well as discriminatory outcome (indirect discrimination), and intended (purposive) discrimination as well as unintended discrimination (discrimination in effect). Both 'sex' and 'marital status' are specified as prohibited grounds of discrimination against women, and it should further be noted that other provisions in the CEDAW (for example Article 11(2) in the field of employment) also prohibit discrimination on the grounds of 'pregnancy' and 'maternity'.

The definition specifically promotes substantive equality by requiring that women must be able to 'enjoy' or 'exercise' their human rights and fundamental freedoms, and makes it clear that the prohibition of discrimination against women applies to all fields of life, not only the public sphere. Indeed, the application of the CEDAW to private actors, including individuals and organizations, is made explicit in many instances in the text.[34] The CEDAW Committee, which monitors its implementation, has made it clear that states parties have the obligation to act with 'due diligence' to ensure that private actors do not violate the Convention.[35] The Committee has also reinforced a substantive approach to women's equality in its interpretations of the CEDAW, constituting a more gender-inclusive subject of human rights law. For example, the Committee has urged states parties to adopt criteria in the determination of equal pay that facilitate the comparison of the *value* of the work usually done by women with the *value* of those more highly paid jobs usually done by men,[36] and to implement health measures that address 'the distinctive features and factors that differ for women in comparison with men'.[37]

The second way that the CEDAW reinforces the norm of women's substantive equality is by making it clear that non-identical treatment aimed at addressing women's specific experiences of disadvantage may be necessary to hasten the achievement of women's equality. The CEDAW distinguishes between temporary and permanent measures. Article 4(1) promotes the use of 'special temporary measures' (also known as 'affirmative action', 'positive action', or 'reverse discrimination'), which are directed towards 'accelerating de facto equality between women and men' by remedying the effects of past or present discrimination against women and promoting the structural, social, and cultural changes necessary to support the realization of women's substantive equality.[38] Such discriminatory measures are not prohibited, as long as they do not entail 'the maintenance of unequal or separate standards' for women and men and are discontinued when their objectives have been achieved. Thus 'temporary' may result in the application of the measures for a sustained period of time, until their objectives have been realized.[39] Some specific references to temporary special measures can be found in the text of the CEDAW, such as measures in the field of education that increase women's functional literacy (Article 10(c)) and reduce the drop-out rates of female students (Article 10(f)). On many occasions the CEDAW Committee has advocated special temporary measures, such as the adoption of quotas to achieve gender balance in political bodies.[40]

The CEDAW supports permanent 'special measures' to ensure that non-identical treatment of women due to their biological differences from men is not considered

---

[34] See eg Arts 2(e), 2(f), 3, 5, and 6.

[35] CEDAW Committee, General Recommendation 19, HRI/GEN/1/Rev.9 (Vol II) 331, para 9.

[36] CEDAW Committee, General Recommendation 13, HRI/GEN/1/Rev.9 (Vol II) 325, para 2.

[37] CEDAW Committee, 'General Recommendation 24, HRI/GEN/1/Rev.9 (Vol II) 358, para 12.

[38] See further CEDAW Committee, General Recommendation 25, HRI/GEN/1/Rev.9 (Vol II) 365.

[39] Ibid, para 20.

[40] CEDAW Committee, General Recommendation 23, HRI/GEN/1/Rev.9 (Vol II) 347, para 29.

discriminatory and does not work to their disadvantage. Article 4(2) makes it clear that measures 'aimed at protecting maternity' are not discriminatory, and this point is reinforced by other more specific provisions including measures safeguarding women's reproductive capacities in the field of employment (Article 11(1)(f)) and measures that provide women with appropriate reproductive health services (Article 12(2)). Recognizing that these provisions have a 'protective' orientation, the CEDAW Committee has emphasized that the term 'special', when used in the context of the CEDAW, breaks with the past paternalistic usage of the term to indicate that a group suffering discrimination is weak or vulnerable, and refers instead to measures designed to serve a specific human rights goal.[41]

The third way that the CEDAW promotes women's substantive equality is by requiring that states parties address the underlying causes of women's inequality. As acknowledged above, religious teachings and cultural practices have often been (mis) used to reinforce dominant beliefs about women's secondary status, generating systemic discrimination against women, which may be so prevalent that it is perceived as 'natural'. To tackle systemic discrimination, Article 5(a) requires states parties to work towards 'the elimination of prejudices and customary and all other practices which are based on the idea of the inferiority or the superiority of either of the sexes or on stereotyped roles for men and women'. This obligation is echoed in other provisions, such as the requirement that gender stereotypes be removed from school programmes and textbooks (Article 10(c)) and the deeming of legal instruments to be null and void if they restrict the legal capacity of women (Article 15(3)). Article 5(b) builds further on states parties' social change obligations by requiring that they promote change in sex-stereotyped attitudes and practices in families, including by 'recognition of the common responsibility in the upbringing and development of their children'. Some specific aspects of this obligation are also spelled out in other provisions, such as the requirement to establish a network of childcare services 'to enable parents to combine family obligations with work responsibilities and participation in public life' (Article 11(2)(c)), and access to 'information and advice on family planning' that will help to ensure the health and well-being of families (Article 10(h)). Although there are good grounds for the CEDAW's negative view of social, religious, and cultural traditions, it must be remembered that they can also lend valuable support to women's equality.[42]

3.2 LIMITATIONS OF THE CEDAW APPROACH

The approach taken by the CEDAW also has some limitations, four of which will be highlighted: its continuing reliance on a comparison with men; the lack of reference to violence against women; the assumption of normative married heterosexuality; and

---

[41] General Recommendation 25, n 38, para 21.

[42] Nyamu-Musembi, 'Are Local Norms and Practices Fences or Pathways? The Example of Women's Property Rights' in An-Na'im (ed), *Cultural Transformation and Human Rights in Africa* (Zed Books, 2002) 126; Obiora, 'Feminism, Globalization, and Culture: After Beijing' (1997) 4 *Glob Legal Stud J* 355.

the very limited acknowledgement of multiple and intersectional forms of discrimination. The CEDAW Committee has ameliorated many of these problems by treating the CEDAW as a dynamic instrument that must be read in light of changing circumstances, and progressively interpreting its provisions in Concluding Observations to states parties' periodic reports and in General Recommendations. However, it is difficult for these efforts to completely overcome the limitations in the CEDAW text and approach without supporting interpretations from other human rights bodies and good faith implementation by states parties.

The first limitation is that the CEDAW approach still relies fundamentally on a comparison between women and men, like the Covenants. This is problematic for two reasons. First, it does not allow women to claim rights that men do not enjoy, except as 'special measures'. Consider the example of women's reproductive rights, such as access to information, advice, and services related to family planning (Articles 10(h) and 12(1)) and the right to 'decide freely and responsibly [sic] on the number and spacing of their children' (Article 16(1)(e)), which are all to be enjoyed 'on a basis of equality of men and women'. This leaves little room, if any, for the recognition of women's specific, standalone reproductive rights, such as contraception and abortion, unless they qualify as 'measures protecting maternity' (Article 4(2)). By contrast, the Protocol on the Rights of Women in Africa (PRWA) recognizes women's autonomous right to sexual and reproductive health, including the right to control their own fertility, to decide on the number and spacing of children, to choose any method of contraception, and to have family planning education.[43]

The CEDAW's reliance on comparing women with similarly situated men is also problematic because it does not address discrimination between different groups of women. For example, denying unmarried women access to reproductive technologies is prohibited by the CEDAW only if unmarried men (the relevant comparator) are able to access the technology. The comparison does not do justice to women's interests because men have very different needs for reproductive assistance than women. Another example is the cultural practice of evicting a widow from her deceased husband's family home, which is clearly adverse treatment due to sex and marital status, but is not discrimination prohibited by the CEDAW because there is no relevant male comparator. It is generally not the practice that husbands live in the family home of their wives, let alone face eviction if they are widowed.

A second limitation of the CEDAW is its lack of reference to violence against women, which is a silence that may be explained by the reliance on a comparative model, because gendered violence does not affect men in the same way as women. The failure in CEDAW to make specific reference to rights associated with security of the person suggests that at the time of drafting, such abuses were thought of as primarily affecting men. Much has changed since then. The General Assembly adopted the Declaration on the Elimination of Violence Against Women in 1993, recognizing that gendered violence is 'one of the crucial social mechanisms by which women are forced into a

---

[43] Art 14(1).

subordinate position compared with men'. A year earlier, the CEDAW Committee adopted General Recommendation 19, which interpreted gender-based violence as a form of 'discrimination against women' that is prohibited by the CEDAW. Thus, violence 'directed against a woman because she is a woman or that affects women disproportionately' breaches specific CEDAW provisions, even though they do not expressly make reference to violence.[44] This approach has been applied in the jurisprudence of the CEDAW Committee under its Optional Protocol procedure, which has found violations of states obligations to eliminate discrimination against women in family relations (Article 16) where states parties have not acted positively, with due diligence, to protect complainants from domestic violence.[45] Treating violence against women as a form of discrimination is an effective way to ensure that the CEDAW obligations encompass the issue. However, the anti-discrimination framework prevents the CEDAW Committee from condemning gendered violence as a direct human rights violation, such as a violation of the right to life or the right to be free from torture or cruel, inhuman, and degrading treatment, without the complication of a comparison with men.

Addressing violence against women as a human rights violation has been much more comprehensively taken up by two regional human rights instruments. The first, the Inter-American Convention on the Prevention, Punishment and Eradication of Violence Against Women (CPPEVAW), recognizes that such violence 'prevents and nullifies' a woman's 'full and free exercise of her civil, political, economic, social and cultural rights'.[46] CPPEVAW defines violence against women broadly as 'any act or conduct, based on gender, which causes death or physical, sexual or psychological harm or suffering to women, whether in the public or the private sphere'.[47] This definition does not confine violence against women to a form of sex discrimination, but recognizes that it may constitute a human rights violation in itself, without the need for a male comparator. States parties must adopt a wide range of positive measures to eliminate such violence, including by applying 'due diligence' to 'prevent, investigate and impose penalties'.[48] The second regional human rights instrument explicitly to prohibit violence against women is the PRWA, which extends the definition even further by including acts which 'cause *or could cause* [women] physical, sexual, psychological, and *economic harm*', threats, and all such acts during armed conflict.[49] Violence against women is recognized as a violation of the right to dignity,[50] the rights to life, integrity, and security of the person,[51] and the right to be protected from harmful practices.[52] The particular vulnerability of asylum-seeking and internally displaced women, and elderly and disabled women, is also recognized.[53] These regional developments build on and complement efforts at the international level.

---

[44] General Recommendation 19, n 35, paras 1 and 6.

[45] *AT v Hungary*, A/60/38, Annex III (26 January 2005); *Goekce v Austria*, CEDAW/C/39/D/5/2005 (6 August 2007); *Yildrim v Austria*, CEDAW/C/39/D/6/2005 (1 October 2007).   [46] Art 5.

[47] Ibid, Art 1.   [48] Ibid, Art 7(b).   [49] PRWA, Art 1(j) (emphasis added).

[50] Ibid, Art 3(4).   [51] Ibid, Art 4.   [52] Ibid, Art 5(d).

[53] Ibid, Arts 11(3), 22(b), and 23(b).

A third limitation of the CEDAW is that, like the Covenants, women's experience of 'family life' is assumed to be married and heterosexual (Article 16(1)), except in their rights as a parent which are to be enjoyed regardless of marital status (Article 16(1)(d)). One result of the emphasis on 'marriage' and the equal rights of 'spouses' is that the diversity of family forms within which women live, including customary and de facto heterosexual and lesbian partnerships, is rendered invisible. Consequently, the text ignores human rights violations that take place within different family formations, like the unequal sharing of income and assets in a customary marriage or violence in a lesbian relationship, and fails to protect women's equal rights when a non-marital relationship breaks down. The CEDAW Committee has gone some way towards rectifying this problem by acknowledging that various forms of the family exist, using the terminology of 'spouse or partner',[54] and insisting that women and men are treated equally in families, whatever form they take.[55] However, it has not yet dealt explicitly with the issue of same-sex partnerships. A second result of the CEDAW's normative focus on heterosexual marriage is that women's sexuality is reduced to procreative concerns, such as family planning and the spacing of children. This means that the CEDAW also fails to address the discrimination that many women face for expressing their sexuality outside marriage, whether in committed relationships, in pursuit of sexual pleasure, as lovers of other women, or as sex workers.

The fourth limitation is that the CEDAW largely treats 'women' as a homogeneous group who share the same experience of discrimination. Yet sex discrimination can intersect with other forms of discrimination and create experiences of discrimination that are not fully comprehended by the concept of sex discrimination. This has been called 'compound' or 'intersectional' discrimination,[56] and its most extreme forms are experienced by the most disadvantaged groups of women. While the CEDAW makes some limited distinctions between women, on the basis of maternity, and age in respect of child marriage, there is only one significant exception to the general pattern. Article 14 requires that states parties 'take into account the specific problems faced by rural women and the significant roles which rural women play in the economic survival of their families',[57] and many of the rights it enumerates do not rely on a comparison with men. This usefully enables the CEDAW Committee to draw comparisons between rural and urban women, and the Committee has interpreted 'rural' very broadly in many of its Concluding Observations in order to discuss intersectional forms of discrimination faced by rural women, such as age, ethnic, caste, and indigenous discrimination.[58] While only occasionally using terms such as 'multiple' or 'double' discrimination, the CEDAW Committee has also drawn attention to discrimination faced by specific groups in the context of Article 5(a), which requires

---

[54] See eg CEDAW Committee, General Recommendation 21, HRI/GEN/1/Rev.9 (Vol II) 337, para 22.

[55] Ibid, paras 13, 18, 29, 33, and 39.

[56] Crenshaw, 'Demarginalizing the Intersection of Race and Sex: A Black Feminist Critique of Anti-Discrimination Doctrine, Feminist Theory and Antiracist Politics' (1989) *U Chi LF* 139.

[57] There is also a reference to 'rural women' in CEDAW, Art 10(a) about vocational guidance and access to studies.   [58] See eg India, A/54/38 (01/02/2000) paras 51–3; China, A/54/38 (03/02/99) para 294.

modification of social and cultural attitudes and practices that are inconsistent with
women's equality.[59] A number of General Recommendations have been adopted that
focus on the CEDAW's application to specific groups of women,[60] and others have
stressed that special attention must be paid to the needs of women belonging to vulnerable and disadvantaged groups.[61] Despite this, the CEDAW Committee has not yet
drawn attention to the intersectionality of the discrimination experienced by complainants under the Optional Protocol, despite four of its first five decisions on the
merits involving immigrant or minority women.[62]

As with violence against women, the more recent regional women's rights instruments fill some of the gaps in CEDAW. CPPEVAW requires states parties to adopt
measures that take 'special account' of women whose vulnerability to violence is
compounded by such factors as their 'race or ethnic background', their 'status as
migrants, refugees or displaced persons...while pregnant or...disabled, of minor age,
elderly, socio-economically disadvantaged, affected by armed conflict or deprived of
their freedom'.[63] The PRWA has provisions that address the rights of asylum-seeking
and internally displaced women, elderly women, and women with disabilities. The
Protocol also recognizes specific rights that must be enjoyed by widows,[64] and 'women
in distress', which includes poor women, women heads of families, pregnant or nursing women, and women in detention.[65] Both instruments recognize women's diversity
more fully than the CEDAW, and draw attention to the need to address the compound
effects of other forms of discrimination.

There is little doubt that the almost universal ratification of the CEDAW, the work
of the CEDAW Committee, and the efforts of many women's rights and human rights
NGOs,[66] has advanced the project of making international human rights law more
gender inclusive. However, the adoption of a specialist women's rights treaty has also,
in many respects, reinforced women's marginalization. The high number of reservations to the CEDAW, particularly those that defeat its object and purpose, tends
to undermine the idea that women's equality and rights are as universal as 'men's'
rights. Rather than prompting the other human rights treaty committees to take
women's rights more seriously, the CEDAW has had the opposite effect of reinforcing the marginalization of women's rights.[67] Exacerbating its separation from the

[59] See eg Sweden, A/56/38 (31/07/2001) para 356.
[60] CEDAW Committee, General Recommendation 18, HRI/GEN/1/Rev.9 (Vol II) 330 (disabled women); General Recommendation 26, CEDAW/C/2009/WP.1/R (women migrant workers). A General Recommendation on older women is forthcoming.
[61] CEDAW Committee, General Recommendation 24, HRI/GEN/1/Rev.9 (Vol II) 358, para 6.
[62] See *Nguyen v The Netherlands*, A/61/38, Annex VIII (14 August 2006); *Szijjarto v Hungary*, A/61/36, Annex VIII (14 August 2006); *Goekce v Austria*, n 45; *Yildrim v Austria*, n 45.   [63] CPPEVAW, Art 9.
[64] PRWA, Art 20.   [65] Ibid, Art 24.
[66] Dairiam, 'From Global to Local: The Involvement of NGOs' in Schopp-Schilling (ed), *The Circle of Empowerment: Twenty-Five Years of the UN Committee on the Elimination of Discrimination Against Women* (Feminist Press, 2007) 313.
[67] Brynes, 'The "Other" Human Rights Treaty Body: The Work of the Committee on the Elimination of Discrimination Against Women' (1989) 14 *YJIL* 1; Reanda, 'Human Rights and Women's Wrongs: the United Nations Approach' (1981) 3 *HRQ* 11.

mainstream, the CEDAW Committee until recently met in New York, rather than in Geneva where all other treaty committees meet,[68] making it difficult to integrate the CEDAW Committee's interpretative work and coordinate approaches to women's equality and rights across the treaty regime. While a specific convention focusing on women's equality was necessary to address women's marginalization in international human rights law, it was not sufficient.

4 MAINSTREAMING WOMEN'S HUMAN RIGHTS

As a result of the CEDAW's limited impact, another major effort to advance the prospects of women successfully claiming their human rights emerged, which refocused attention on the general human rights instruments and promoted the 'mainstreaming' of women's human rights.[69] 'Gender mainstreaming' was adopted as a system-wide strategy by the 1993 Vienna World Conference on Human Rights and reaffirmed by the 1995 Beijing World Conference on Women. These developments prompted the chairpersons of the human rights treaty committees to commit fully to integrating gender perspectives into their working methods.[70] This led eventually to the adoption of General Comments by four treaty committees, which aim to comprehensively incorporate women's experience of human rights violations into the coverage of their respective treaty texts. This section examines each of these General Comments, noting the diversity of thinking about how to achieve gender mainstreaming that emerges. It also highlights the tenacity of protective representations of women, especially in the context of addressing gendered violence, and concludes that women are not yet constructed as fully human by international human rights law.

4.1 RE-IMAGINING THE UNIVERSAL SUBJECT: THE APPROACH OF THE HUMAN RIGHTS COMMITTEE

The Human Rights Committee led the way in 2000 with the adoption of General Comment 28 on equality between men and women.[71] The General Comment works through each of the ICCPR rights, bringing gender-specific violations into the mainstream by re-imagining the subject of the ICCPR as a woman. For example, it is recognized that the right to life (Article 6) may be violated if women have no option but

---

[68] This practice was changed from 1 January 2008, when responsibility for servicing the CEDAW Committee was transferred from the Division for the Advancement of Women in New York to the Office of the High Commissioner for Human Rights in Geneva, which also services the other human rights treaty bodies.

[69] Bunch, 'Women's Rights as Human Rights: Towards a Re-Vision of Human Rights' (1990) 12 *HRQ* 486; Kouvo, *Making Just Rights? Mainstreaming Women's Human Rights and a Gender Perspective* (Iustus Forlag, 2004).

[70] Report of the Sixth Meeting of Persons Chairing the Human Rights Treaty Bodies, A/50/505 (4 October 1995) para 34(a)–(f).   [71] HRC, General Comment 28, HRI/GEN/1/Rev.9 (Vol I) 228.

to resort to backyard abortions or if they are living in extreme poverty,[72] and the right
to be free from torture and other cruel, inhuman, and degrading treatment (Article 7)
may be violated if a state party fails to protect women from domestic violence.[73] The
General Comment clearly promotes women's equality as a substantive concept and
accepts that different treatment of women and men may be necessary to achieve equality. The result is an ambitious and creative 'feminization' of ICCPR rights.[74]

However, some of the problems associated with seeking to include women by reference to their 'difference' are also evident. The extensive cataloguing of women's
specific injuries and disadvantages, particularly the emphasis on violence, threatens
to reproduce women's marginalization by inviting protective responses. Indeed, the
frequent use of the language of 'protection' is disquieting.[75] It recalls the historically
conditioned tendency to slide into protective responses when thinking about women
as 'victims' of gendered and sexual violence, working against legal responses that
empower women as full subjects of human rights law.

4.2 ANALYSING THE RELATIONSHIP BETWEEN GENDER AND RACIAL DISCRIMINATION: THE APPROACH OF THE COMMITTEE ON THE ELIMINATION OF RACIAL DISCRIMINATION

The Committee on the Elimination of Racial Discrimination, which monitors implementation of the International Convention on the Elimination of All Forms of Racial
Discrimination (ICERD), was initially resistant to the idea of gender mainstreaming.[76]
However, it eventually adopted General Recommendation XXV on the 'gender-related
dimensions of racial discrimination'.[77] Rather than identifying the gender issues associated with each of the substantive rights recognized by the ICERD, as in General
Comment 28 of the Human Rights Committee, it elaborates a methodology for ana-
lysing the relationship between gender and racial discrimination, which will enable
the Committee to develop 'a more systematic and consistent approach', in conjunction
with states parties.[78] The method requires particular consideration of gender in: (1)
the form and manifestation of racial discrimination; (2) the circumstances in which it
occurs; (3) its consequences; and (4) the availability and accessibility of remedies.[79]

This approach opens the way to a deeper understanding of the structural dimensions of the intersection of race and gender discrimination and how they work together
to intensify women's inequality. The methodology is very flexible, allowing for diverse
and shifting conceptions of race, which, like gender, is socially constructed. However,

---

[72] Ibid, para 10.   [73] Ibid, para 11.

[74] See further, Otto, '"Gender Comment": Why Does the UN Committee on Economic, Social and
Cultural Rights Need a General Comment on Women?' (2002) 14 *Can J Women & L* 1.

[75] General Comment 28, n 71, paras 8, 10, 11, 12, 16, and 22.

[76] Crooms, 'Indivisible Rights and Intersectional Identities or, "What Do Women's Human Rights Have
to Do with the Race Convention?"' (1997) 40 *Howard LJ* 619; Gallagher, 'Ending Marginalisation: Strategies
for Incorporating Women into the UN Human Rights System' (1997) 19 *HRQ* 283.

[77] CERD, General Recommendation XXV, HRI/GEN/1/Rev.9 (Vol II) 287.   [78] Ibid, para 3.

[79] Ibid, para 5.

like General Comment 28, the few examples of the intersectional discrimination provided are dominated by a concern with addressing violence against women,[80] also
running the risk of eliciting protective responses. General Recommendation XXV is
notable for its use of the language of 'gender'. The discourse of gender has the advantage of acknowledging the relational quality of the gender stereotypes that privilege
men and disadvantage women, and thus points to the necessity of changing the stereotypes that benefit men as well as those that normalize women's disadvantage. On the
other hand, the language of gender has its dangers, foremost among them being the
tendency for men's interests again to dominate.[81]

4.3 ADDRESSING THE INEQUALITY OF BOTH WOMEN AND MEN: THE APPROACH OF THE COMMITTEE ON ECONOMIC, SOCIAL AND CULTURAL RIGHTS

The risk that 'gender' mainstreaming will refocus attention away from women's disadvantage and back to men is evident in General Comment 16, adopted in 2005 by the
Committee on Economic, Social and Cultural Rights.[82] In many respects, the approach
taken is similar to General Comment 28 of the Human Rights Committee, especially
in the attention given to identifying the gender dimensions of each of the rights enumerated in the ICESCR and the emphasis on addressing gendered violence. Its distinc-
tiveness lies in its identification of men, as well as women, as potentially suffering sex
discrimination and inequality in the enjoyment of ICESCR rights. General Comment 16
even suggests that men may be victims of domestic violence perpetrated against them by
women.[83] This position is controversial because it appears to deny the persistent reality
of women's inequality vis-à-vis men by approaching sex inequality as a problem without a hierarchy. Ultimately, it is hard to decide whether this is a deeply conservative
denial of the systemic nature of women's inequality, or a radical attempt to recognize the
social construction of the male/female gender dichotomy and the importance of changing the way 'men' are imagined in the process of re-imagining 'women' as equal.

4.4 RECOGNIZING GENDER AS A KEY FACTOR: THE APPROACH OF THE COMMITTEE AGAINST TORTURE

In 2008, the Committee against Torture adopted a General Comment on implementation obligations which makes some important observations about the gender dimensions of the Convention Against Torture (UNCAT).[84] It is emphasized that special
attention must be given to protecting marginalized groups or individuals who are
'especially at risk of torture', including those who may be at risk because of 'gender,

---

[80] Ibid, para 2.
[81] Baden and Goetz, 'Who Needs [Sex] When You Can Have [Gender]? Conflicting discourses on gender at Beijing' in Jackson and Pearson (eds), *Feminist Visions of Development: Gender Analysis and Policy*
(Routledge, 1998) 19.   [82] HRI/GEN/1/Rev.9 (Vol I) 113.
[83] Ibid, para 27.   [84] CAT, General Comment 2, HRI/GEN/1/Rev.9 (Vol II) 376.

sexual orientation, transgender identity... or any other status or adverse distinction'.[85] States parties are requested to provide additional information in their periodic reports about the implementation of UNCAT with respect to women, keeping in mind that 'gender is a key factor' that can intersect with other characteristics of a person to make them more vulnerable to torture or ill-treatment.[86] The Committee notes that women are particularly at risk in contexts that include 'deprivation of liberty, medical treatment, particularly involving reproductive decisions, and violence by private actors in communities and homes'.[87] Notably, the Committee uses the terminology of 'gender' and takes a similar approach to the Committee on Economic, Social and Cultural Rights by observing that men too may be subject to gendered violations of UNCAT, 'such as rape or sexual violence and abuse', and that men and boys, as well as women and girls, may be subject to violations 'on the basis of their actual or perceived non-conformity with socially determined gender roles'.[88] Unlike General Comment 16 of the Committee on Economic, Social and Cultural Rights, which seems to collapse the difference between women's and men's gendered experience, this approach makes an effort to identify the specificity of human rights violations that are experienced solely or primarily by men, and is therefore preferable.

While all the General Comments aimed at gender mainstreaming promote non-discrimination on the ground of sex and women's equal enjoyment of human rights in a substantive sense, taking their lead from the CEDAW, they also reinterpret mainstream human rights to be more inclusive of women's experience. These reinterpretations alleviate the need to compare women's experience with that of men's by reconstructing the universal standard itself, so that it is more gender-inclusive. Positive as these developments are, the real test is whether the Committees are able to integrate their new interpretations into all aspects of their work, and hold states parties accountable for their implementation. Although it is early days, the record so far has been patchy,[89] and the old urge to protect women rather than to recognize their rights continues to be seductive,[90] especially when it comes to women from the Third World.[91] The cost of women's 'inclusion' may yet prove to be their continuing marginalization.

5 CONCLUSION

The history of women's rights in international human rights law reveals a conundrum: how to insist on the recognition of women's specific human rights abuses without reproducing their secondary status and encouraging protective responses. While every

---

[85] Ibid, para 21.   [86] Ibid, para 22.   [87] Ibid.   [88] Ibid.

[89] Charlesworth, n 14; Kouvo, n 69.

[90] Otto, 'The Exile of Inclusion: Reflections on Gender Issues in International Law over the Last Decade' (2009) 10 *MJIL* 11.

[91] Kapur, 'The Tragedy of Victimisation Rhetoric: Resurrecting the "Native" Subject in International/Postcolonial Feminist Legal Politics' (2001) 10 *Colum J Gender & L* 333.

effort to more fully recognize women's rights in the development, interpretation, and implementation of international human rights law has met with some success, these efforts have also highlighted new challenges. While anti-discrimination law can be a very powerful means of promoting women's enjoyment of human rights, the comparative standard that it relies upon presents quandaries about how best to frame, measure, and realize women's substantive equality, which have yet to be resolved. While recognizing gendered violence as a violation of women's human rights has been a massive achievement, the historical pull towards embracing protective responses highlights the challenge of promoting, instead, a rights-based response that takes women's sexual injuries seriously while also respecting women's sexual agency. While the need to take account of other forms of discrimination which intersect with or compound discrimination against women is increasingly acknowledged, there remain many conceptual and practical problems about how to make such discrimination legally cognizable and hold states parties accountable for addressing it. Finally, while gender mainstreaming has led to radical reinterpretations of mainstream human rights instruments, emphasizing the interdependence of ideas about 'men' and 'women' and the realization that women's equality depends on challenging accepted wisdom about dominant masculinities, it has also highlighted the dilemma of how fully to embrace 'gender' as a socially constructed category. While there is still a long way to go before the present day realities of human rights abuses suffered by women become fully legally cognizable, we also need new thinking about legal representations that will challenge the gender stereotypes that underpin gendered human rights abuses.

FURTHER READING

ASKIN and KOENIG (eds), *Women and International Human Rights Law*, vols I–III (Transnational, 1999–2001).

BANDA, *Women, Law and Human Rights: An African Perspective* (Hart Publishing, 2005).

BUSS and MANJI (eds), *International Law: Modern Feminist Approaches* (Hart Publishing, 2005).

COOK, *Human Rights of Women: National and International Perspectives* (University of Pennsylvania Press, 1994).

—— and CUSACK, *Gender Stereotyping: Transnational Legal Perspectives* (University of Pennsylvania Press, 2009).

KNOP (ed), *Gender and Human Rights* (Oxford University Press, 2004).

MACKINNON, *Are Women Human? And Other International Dialogues* (Harvard University Press, 2006).

MERRY ENGLE, *Human Rights and Gender Violence: Translating International Law into Local Justice* (University of Chicago Press, 2006).

PETERS and WOLPER (eds), *Women's Rights/ Human Rights: International Feminist Perspectives* (Routledge, 1995).

SCHOPP-SCHILLING (ed), *The Circle of Empowerment: Twenty-Five Years of the UN Committee on the Elimination of Discrimination Against Women* (Feminist Press, 2007).

WING (ed), *Global Critical Race Feminism: An International Reader* (NYU Press, 2000).

USEFUL WEBSITES

Women's Human Rights Resources: **<http://www.law-lib.utoronto.ca/diana/mainpage.htm>**

CEDAW materials (DAW to 31 December 2007): **<http://www.un.org/womenwatch/daw/cedaw/>**

CEDAW materials (OHCHR): **<http://www2.ohchr.org/english/bodies/cedaw/index.htm>**

Division for the Advancement of Women (DAW): **<http://www.un.org/womenwatch/daw/daw/index.html>**

Office of the Special Adviser on Gender Issues and Advancement of Women: **<http://www.un.org/womenwatch/osagi/>**

United Nations Development Fund for Women (UNIFEM): **<http://www.unifem.org/>**

Women Watch (UN Inter-Agency Network on Women and Gender Equality): **<http://www.un.org/womenwatch/>**

International Women's Rights Action Watch (IWRAW): **<http://www1.umn.edu/humanrts/iwraw/>**

IWRAW Asia-Pacific (IWRAW-AP): **<http://www.iwraw-ap.org/index.htm>**

17

RIGHTS OF PEOPLES AND MINORITIES

Robert McCorquodale

SUMMARY

This chapter concerns the human rights of two particular groups: those of peoples and minorities. The right of self-determination is a right that protects a group as a group entity in regard to their political participation, as well as their control over their economic, social, and cultural activity as a group. It is a right that applies to 'peoples' in all states and can be exercised in many ways, with most exercises of the right today being within the boundaries of a state. The right cannot be limited by the rights of others and by the general interests of the international community except in restricted circumstances. Rights of minorities can be seen as both individual and group rights, and have been the subject of increasing international human rights protection in recent years.

1 INTRODUCTION

1.1 GROUP RIGHTS

Most of the discussion in this book, and the focus of many of its chapters, is about the human rights of individual human beings. This is not surprising, as the historical and conceptual bases of human rights generally developed from considerations concerning the needs and oppression of individuals, and almost all national constitutional and legislative protections of human rights have been drafted to protect the rights of individuals. Similarly, the vast majority of human rights protected in international and regional treaties, such as the right to life, the right to an adequate standard of living, the right to education, and the right to freedom of thought, protect the rights of individual human beings.

However, human rights do not need to be limited to those of individual human beings. Conceptually, human rights can be understood in terms of the need to protect the dignity of a group (or a 'people'), and a group's physical integrity, as well as its civil, cultural, economic, political, and social engagement. As human rights should reflect lived realities, it is necessary to see them as more than about individuals. After all, most societies accord an importance to communities, collectives, and families, and humans possess a general communal quality. International human rights law is conceived and exercised within the context of communities, with rights being limited (in all except a few instances) by the rights of others and the general interests of the relevant community.[1] Each individual is a part of one or many groups and an individual's identities, histories, and engagements are affected by belonging to groups and by the communities within which they live.

In a number of situations it is a group of individuals who are oppressed because of the fact that they belong to a group or they have a group identity and sense of human dignity that is dependent on them belonging to a group. For example, the prohibition on genocide is a human right premised on the need to protect a group as a group from actions against the group's physical integrity and not only to protect the individual's right to life. Similarly, many indigenous groups have an identity that is dependent on them being a group rather than being a selection of individuals. Therefore, group rights (sometimes called 'collective rights') are intended to protect a group (for example, a people) from oppression *as a group*.

1.2 GROUP RIGHTS v RIGHTS OF INDIVIDUALS

Many individual human rights do have the effect of protecting a group. For example, the right of freedom of assembly, the right to join a trade union, and the right of freedom of religion, all enable groups to gather, have protection, and express their thoughts. Yet each of these rights is an individual right under international human rights law. It is an individual right exercised in concert with other individual human rights but it can only be held and claimed by an individual human being. While there is now some case law that enables legal entities, such as religious institutions and corporations, to bring claims on behalf of individuals (and perhaps even in their own right),[2] these remain individual rights that may lead indirectly to the protection of a group. They are not rights that directly protect a group as a group.

The UN Human Rights Committee considered the difference between group rights and individual rights when considering the right of self-determination (which is a group right), when they stated:

The right of self-determination is of particular importance because its realization is *an essential condition* for the effective guarantee and observance of individual human rights and for the promotion and strengthening of those rights. It is for that reason that States set forth the right of self-determination in a provision of positive law in both Covenants [the

---

[1] The limitations on human rights are discussed in Chapter 6, above.
[2] See eg *Autronic AG v Switzerland* (1990) 12 EHRR 485; *Singer v Canada*, CCPR/C/51/D/455/1991 (8 April 1993); and 155/96, *Social and Economic Rights Action Center and the Center for Economic and Social Rights (SERAC) v Nigeria*, 15th Activity Report of the ACommHPR (2001).

International Covenant on Civil and Political Rights and the International Covenant on Economic, Social and Cultural Rights] and placed this provision as article 1 apart from and before all of the other rights in the two Covenants.[3]

In making this statement, the Human Rights Committee both recognizes the difference between group rights and individual rights, and acknowledges that when groups are subject to oppression as a group and their rights are not able to be exercised, then the individuals within those groups are also not able to exercise their individual rights. The Committee made the difference even clearer when they took the view that a group who brought a complaint under the Optional Protocol to the International Covenant on Civil and Political Rights (ICCPR-OP1) alleging a breach of the right of self-determination could not do so because the specific terms of the ICCPR-OP1 only enabled complaints by 'individuals'.[4] While there is some criticism of the Committee taking this stance, other international human rights treaties do not tend to contain the restriction that only individuals are able to bring a complaint.

1.3 RELEVANCE OF THE RIGHT OF SELF-DETERMINATION AND THE RIGHTS OF MINORITIES

While there are a range of group rights, such as the prohibition on genocide, the right to development, and the right to a clean environment, the specific focus of this chapter is on the right of self-determination (sometimes called the right to self-determination). This is because the right of self-determination is protected under the International Covenant on Civil and Political Rights (ICCPR) and the International Covenant on Economic, Social and Cultural Rights (ICESCR), it has been considered in case law and other jurisprudence, and it has wide and significant impacts across the international community, as will be shown.

The rights of minorities have similar wide and significant impacts, as there are minorities in every state. While these rights have often been seen as within the compass of individual rights, it will be shown that they are also now considered as group rights. One type of collective that has been especially affected by the development of peoples and minorities rights is indigenous peoples, and so they are considered at various points in this chapter.

The acknowledgment that peoples, minorities, and indigenous groups have human rights, and that their rights should be protected in international law, has taken a long time. There is still some way to go for them to be fully understood and respected. However, they are important human rights that affect the whole of the international community. With the reality that almost every state in the world has some current or potential issue connected with group rights, it is important that these rights are understood, respected, and applied appropriately.

---

[3] HRC, General Comment 12, HRI/GEN/1/Rev.9 (Vol I) 183, para 1 (emphasis added).
[4] *Ominayak and the Lubicon Lake Band v Canada*, A/45/40 (Vol II) Annex IX, 1, para 32.1.

2 THE RIGHT OF SELF-DETERMINATION

2.1 CONCEPT

Claims have been made for centuries about matters that could now be seen in terms of self-determination, with some writers tracing it as far back as the early stages of the institution of government. However, the use of self-determination in an international legal context primarily developed during the immediate post-First World War period, with US President Wilson stating that, '[P]eoples may now be dominated and governed only by their own consent. "Self-determination" is not a mere phrase. It is an imperative principle of action, which statesmen will henceforth ignore at their peril.'[5]

At about the same time Marxist thought on national liberation took root in the USSR. The combined effect of these ideas (and others) was that self-determination, despite its vague content and the sense to which it could be applied to a range of situations, became an accepted term of use in international relations. Then in 1945 the UN Charter proclaimed that one of the purposes of the UN was 'respect for the principle of equal rights and self-determination of peoples'.[6]

Since that time, through resolutions of the Security Council and the General Assembly, in decisions and opinions of the International Court of Justice (ICJ), in treaties, and in state practice—some of which will be referred to below—the idea of self-determination of peoples has been restated, reinforced, and reinvigorated. It has also been used in diverse contexts and become a part of international law, not least because 'couching political goals in the language of legal entitlement has an undisputed rhetorical appeal'.[7]

2.2 DEFINITIONS

Despite the general acceptance that self-determination is part of international law, it was not until the conclusion of the two international human rights covenants that it was accepted that self-determination was a human right and that some form of legal definition was provided. Article 1 ICCPR and ICESCR (being the only human right protected in both the Covenants) provides:

1. All peoples have the right of self-determination. By virtue of that right they freely determine their political status and freely pursue their economic, social and cultural development.

---

[5] Wilson, *War Aims of Germany and Austria* (1918), reproduced in Baker, Dodd, and Leach (eds), *The Public Papers of Woodrow Wilson: War and Peace* (Harper and Brothers, 1927) 177 at 182. Wilson was supported by the British Prime Minister, Lloyd George, who declared that one reason for the UK entering the First World War had been the 'principle of self-determination' and that future territorial questions should be resolved by respecting 'the consent of the governed': address to the Trade Union Conference, 5 January 1918, reported in *The New York Times Current History* (New York) 270.   [6] UN Charter, Art 1(2).

[7] Drew, 'Self-Determination, Population Transfer and the Middle-East Peace Accords' in Bowen (ed), *Human Rights, Self-Determination and Political Change in the Occupied Palestinian Territories* (Martinus Nijhoff, 1997) 127.

2. All peoples may, for their own ends, freely dispose of their natural wealth and resources without prejudice to any obligations arising out of international economic co-operation, based upon the principle of mutual benefit, and international law. In no case may a people be deprived of its means of subsistence.

3. The States Parties to the present Covenant, including those having responsibility for the administration of Non-Self-Governing and Trust Territories, shall promote the realization of the right of self-determination, and shall respect that right, in conformity with the provisions of the Charter of the United Nations.

The definition in Article 1(1) is largely repeated in all the subsequent international and regional human rights treaties and documents that contain a right to self-determination, although the African Charter on Human and Peoples' Rights (ACHPR) elaborates on it slightly.[8]

Yet this definition does not clarify all aspects of the right. While it is evident that it is a right that is applicable in economic, social, and cultural contexts (with Article 1(2) of the Covenants dealing with a particular economic manifestation of the right and Article 55 UN Charter referring to economic and social aspects of the right), as well as in political contexts, and that it is a right of peoples as distinct from individuals, there is not much other elaboration. Indeed, the lack of clarification as to who are the 'peoples' who have the right has been a major stumbling block for many diplomats and writers.

There have been many attempts to establish a definition of 'peoples'.[9] The definition often referred to is that of an influential group of UNESCO experts:

A people for the [purposes of the] rights of people in international law, including the right to self-determination, has the following characteristics:
(a) A group of individual human beings who enjoy some or all of the following common features:
   (i)   A common historical tradition;
   (ii)   Racial or ethnic identity;
   (iii) Cultural homogeneity;
   (iv)   Linguistic unity;
   (v)   Religious or ideological affinity;
   (vi)   Territorial connection;
   (vii) Common economic life.

---

[8] ACHPR, Art 20 provides:
   1. All peoples shall have the right to existence. They shall have the unquestionable and inalienable right to self-determination. They shall freely determine their political status and shall pursue their economic and social development according to the policy they have freely chosen.
   2. Colonized or oppressed peoples shall have the right to free themselves from the bonds of domination by resorting to any means recognized by the international community.
   3. All peoples shall have the right to the assistance of the States parties to the present Charter in their liberation struggle against foreign domination, be it political, economic or cultural.
This has been considered by the African Commission in, eg, 147/95 and 149/96, *Dawda Jawara v The Gambia*, 13th Activity Report of the ACommHPR (2000); 75/92, *Katangese Peoples' Congress v Zaire*, 8th Activity Report of the ACommHPR (1995).

[9] See eg Kiwanuka, 'The Meaning of "People" in the African Charter of Human and Peoples' Rights' (1988) 82 *AJIL* 80.

(b)   The group must be of a certain number who need not be large (e.g. the people of micro States) but must be more than a mere association of individuals within a State.

(c)   The group as a whole must have the will to be identified as a people or the conscious-ness of being a people—allowing that groups or some members of such groups, though sharing the foregoing characteristics, may not have the will or consciousness.

(d)   Possibly the group must have institutions or other means of expressing its common characteristics and will for identity.[10]

This definition appears to be an 'objective' one that can be applied to all relevant groups around the world, by providing some criteria that should be met for a 'people' to be established. However, an objective definition is impossible—and is likely to reinforce a developed-world, colonial, male construct of a 'people'[11]—and there would be few groups who have been universally accepted as peoples having the right of self-determination (including some of those who are in former colonies) who would meet all these crite-ria. This impossibility is acknowledged in paragraph (c) of the above definition, where a 'subjective' criterion is included. This is because a key aspect of 'self' is self-identification, where the group identifies themselves consciously as a 'people'. This is an essential part of the definition of a 'people', not least because 'nations and peoples, like genetic popula-tions, are recent, contingent and have been formed and reformed constantly throughout history',[12] often due to the oppression that they have received or to attain certain ends.[13]

In fact, in many situations, it is evident who are the 'peoples' with the right of self-determination. This can be because the relevant national constitution, legislation, or practice indicates this. For example, the Scots in the UK, the Basques in Spain, and the Aceh people in Indonesia, are all accepted as peoples with the right of self-determination. There is also, as will be shown below, universal acceptance that the right of self-determination applies to all peoples in colonial territories, as well as sig-nificant state practice that applies it beyond the colonial context. Consistent oppres-sive action by those in power over another group may also indicate an acceptance of the group as a 'people', not least because it may be a catalyst for the self-identification of the group as a people with the right of self-determination. External recognition by a state or group of states can be very useful for the group (such as the recognition by many states of the Palestinian people) but it is not conclusive of the group being a people for the purposes of the right of self-determination.

---

[10] Final Report and Recommendations of an International Meeting of Experts on the Further Study of the Concept of the Right of People for UNESCO, SNS–89/CONF.602/7 (22 February 1990). For a similar definition, see International Commission of Jurists, *Events in East Pakistan* (ICJ, 1972) 49.

[11] See Charlesworth, Chinkin, and Wright, 'Feminist Approaches to International Law' (1991) 85 *AJIL* 613; Gaete, 'Postmodernism and Human Rights: Some Insidious Questions' [1991] *Law and Critique* 149.

[12] Kamenka, 'Human Rights, Peoples' Rights' in Crawford (ed), *The Rights of Peoples* (Clarendon Press, 1988) 127 at 133. See also Allott, 'The Nation as Mind Politic' (1992) 24 *NYUJILP* 1361.

[13] Chinkin and Wright, 'Hunger Trap: Women, Food and Self-Determination' (1993) 14 *Michigan JIL* 262, 306, propose that 'food, shelter, clean water, a healthy environment, peace and a stable existence must be the first priorities in how we define or "determine" the "self" of both individuals and groups, instead of the present definitions, which are based on masculinist goals of political and economic aggrandizement and aggressive territoriality'.

Indeed, if such external state recognition was conclusive it would allow the possibility of the existence of a human right (as distinct from the ability of a human right to be exercised) being dependent on the whims of governments. Above all, dependence on the government for the existence of a right would undermine the concept of a human right as being, for example, inherent in human dignity.[14]

Therefore, it is necessary to adopt a very flexible definition as to who are a 'people'. A definition is required that is broad and inclusive, not decided by states alone or imposed on a group, and is adaptable to the many circumstances that exist worldwide. The definition must respect the self-identification of a group as a people. There would need to be some territorial nexus for a 'people' with a right of self-determination. Yet a 'people' can include just a part of a population in a state and it can include groups that live across state territorial boundaries (which reflect the fact that in reality there is no 'nation-state'). It would include those who are subject to 'alien subjugation, domination and exploitation'.[15] If a broad and adaptable definition is adopted, then the focus on the right of self-determination under international human rights law is in relation to how and when the right can be exercised. As with all human rights, the concept of the right itself (being to protect the human dignity of the group as a group) cannot be dependent on governments determining the right. Further, a broad definition of the possessors of this human right is consistent with the need to protect as many people as possible from violations of human rights by a state, considering both the inequality of power between a state and its inhabitants and the non-reciprocal nature of human rights treaties. Such a broad definition would then be consistent with the approach to other human rights in this book.

3 THE APPLICATION OF THE RIGHT OF SELF-DETERMINATION

3.1 COLONIAL CONTEXT

From the earliest time that the UN focused on self-determination as part of international law, it applied it to colonial territories. In 1960 self-determination was considered in the context of 'the necessity of bringing to a speedy and unconditional end colonialism in all its forms and manifestations'.[16] Article 1(3) ICCPR and ICESCR makes express reference to the special responsibility of colonial powers in regard to the right of self-determination:

The States Parties to the present Covenant, including those having responsibility for the administration of Non-Self-Governing and Trust Territories, shall promote the realization

---

[14] See Chapter 2, above.

[15] Declaration on Independence for Colonial Countries and Peoples, GA Res 1514 (XV), 14 December 1960.   [16] Ibid, preamble.

of the right of self-determination, and shall respect that right, in conformity with the provisions of the Charter of the United Nations.[17]

The term 'Non-Self-Governing Territories' refers to the list of territories held by the UN that was meant to designate which were colonial territories. While this list was never comprehensive (especially as it was possible for states unilaterally to remove territories from the list), the term was a recognized UN abbreviation for colonial territories or colonies.

The ICJ has consistently held that the right of self-determination applies to all peoples in all colonial territories. In its *Namibia Opinion* concerning the illegal presence of South Africa in Namibia, the Court's view was:

[T]he subsequent development of international law in regard to non-self-governing territories, as enshrined in the Charter of the United Nations, made the principle of self-determination applicable to all of them.... The ultimate objective of the sacred trust was the self-determination and independence of the peoples concerned.[18]

This position was confirmed by the ICJ in the *Western Sahara Case*, with Judge Dillard stating that '[t]he pronouncements of the Court thus indicate, in my view, that a norm of international law has emerged applicable to the decolonisation of those non-self-governing territories which are under the aegis of the United Nations'.[19]

State practice confirms that the right of self-determination applies to all peoples in colonial territories. This is evident not only from the vast number of colonial territories that have exercised their right of self-determination to become members of the UN, but also because of the acceptance by the colonial powers that they have a legal obligation to allow this exercise. For example, the British government stated in 1982:

It is true that [the UK] took the position in the 1960s that self-determination was a principle and not a right.... Not only has my country [now] endorsed the right to self-determination in the sense of the [UN] Charter, the [International Human Rights] Covenants and the Friendly Relations Declaration [1970], but we have gone a great deal further to disprove the allegation that we are the colonial Power *par excellence*. Since General Assembly Resolution 1514 (XV) was adopted at the end of 1960, we have brought to sovereign independence and membership of [the UN] no less than 28 States. We are proud of our record, and I think we have every right to be.[20]

Some writers have concluded from this consistent state practice, *opinio juris*, and lack of any denial by states, that the right of self-determination of colonial peoples is now a matter of *jus cogens*.[21]

---

[17] The special responsibility of colonial powers in regard to self-government of Non-Self-Governing Territories is also stated in UN Charter, Art 73.   [18] *Namibia Opinion* [1971] ICJ Rep 16, para 52.

[19] *Western Sahara Case* [1975] ICJ Rep 12, per Judge Dillard at 121, and see Majority Opinion at paras 54–5.

[20] Statement by the UK's representative in the Security Council on 25 May 1982 (1983) 54 *BYBIL* 371–2.

[21] See eg Cassese, *Self-Determination of Peoples: A Legal Appraisal* (CUP, 1995) 140; Crawford, *The International Law Commission's Articles on State Responsibility: Introduction, Text and Commentaries* (CUP, 2002) in relation to Art 41. See Chapter 5, above, for an explanation of *jus cogens*.

3.2 OUTSIDE THE COLONIAL CONTEXT

While it is clear that the right of self-determination applies to all colonial peoples as a part of customary international law (and perhaps as a matter of *jus cogens*), there remains the question as to whether it also applies outside the colonial context. State practice shows that it has definitely been applied outside the colonial context. For example, when East and West Germany were united into one state in 1990, it was expressly stated in a treaty signed by four of the five permanent members of the UN that this was done as part of the exercise of the right of self-determination by the German people.[22] The right of self-determination was also referred to in the context of the dissolution of the USSR and Yugoslavia,[23] internally within states and the ICJ confirmed that the right of self-determination applies to the Palestinian people in its *Advisory Opinion on the Wall*.[24]

The ICJ has gone further and has declared that the right of self-determination is 'one of the essential principles of contemporary international law' and has 'an *erga omnes* character'.[25] By having an *erga omnes* character it means that there is an obligation on *all states* to protect the right of self-determination. This makes clear that it is not only an obligation on colonial powers and so the right applies to peoples beyond the colonial context.

Indeed, since 1960 the right of self-determination has not been expressed in any international or regional instruments solely in the context of colonial territories but as a right of 'all peoples'. This is seen in the Declaration on Principles of International Law 1970 (which is often considered as being internationally agreed clarifications of the principles of the UN Charter) which provides:

[All States should bear] in mind that subjection of peoples to alien subjugation, domination and exploitation constitutes a violation of the principle [of equal rights and self-determination of peoples], as well as a denial of fundamental human rights, and is contrary to the Charter of the United Nations.[26]

In fact, even the 1960 Declaration on Independence of Colonial Countries and Peoples dealt with colonialism 'in all its forms and manifestations'. The forms and manifestations of colonialism relevant to the application of the right of self-determination are about the oppressive *nature* of the administrative power over a people and not simply about the physical distance of the administering colonial power from the colonial territory. Hence, where a group or groups in a state administer power in such

---

[22] Treaty on the Final Settlement With Respect to Germany (1990) 29 *ILM* 1186.

[23] See eg the terms of the European Community's Declaration on Yugoslavia and its Declaration on the Guidelines on Recognition of New States in Eastern Europe and the Soviet Union (16 December 1991) (1992) 31 *ILM* 1486.

[24] *Legal Consequences of the Construction of a Wall in the Occupied Palestinian Territory* (Advisory Opinion) [2004] ICJ Rep 136, paras 118 and 122.

[25] *East Timor Case* [1995] ICJ Rep 90, para 29. The HRC also requires all states party to the ICCPR to report on their protection of the right of self-determination: HRC General Comment 12, n 3, para 3.

[26] GA Res 2625(XXV) (24 October 1970) Annex.

a way that there is 'subjugation, domination and exploitation' of another group that oppresses, demeans, and undermines the dignity of that group, then the right of self-determination may apply to the latter group. Therefore, the right of self-determination applies to any peoples in any territory (including non-colonial territories) who are subjected to 'alien subjugation, domination and exploitation'. Indeed, it would be contrary to the concept of a human right if the right of self-determination could only be exercised once (such as by a colonial territory) and then not again. So, all peoples in all states have the right of self-determination.

3.3 INDIGENOUS PEOPLES

Indigenous peoples are essentially 'those living descendants of pre-invasion inhabitants of lands now dominated by others'.[27] The protection of the rights of indigenous peoples was addressed specifically (although without a definition of indigenous peoples) in the Declaration of the Rights of Indigenous Peoples.[28] Importantly for the purposes of this chapter, the Declaration proclaims:

Article 1

Indigenous peoples have the right to the full enjoyment, as a collective or as individuals, of all human rights and fundamental freedoms as recognized in the Charter of the United Nations, the Universal Declaration of Human Rights and international human rights law.

Article 3

Indigenous peoples have the right to self-determination. By virtue of that right they freely determine their political status and freely pursue their economic, social and cultural development.

Article 4

Indigenous peoples, in exercising their right to self-determination, have the right to autonomy or self-government in matters relating to their internal and local affairs, as well as ways and means for financing their autonomous functions.

The Declaration confirms that indigenous people can have group (or 'collective') rights and they do have the right of self-determination, which they can exercise 'in conformity with international law'[29] (see further in the next section, below). Whilst the Declaration is not binding in international law, there is a general consensus, based on the near uniformity in acceptance of this Declaration and other state practice, that indigenous peoples have the right of self-determination.[30] Further, now that the right of self-determination is accepted as applying outside the colonial context to all peoples

---

[27] Anaya, *Indigenous Peoples in International Law* (OUP, 2005) 3.
[28] A/RES/61/295 (13 September 2007).   [29] Ibid, preamble.
[30] Lâm, *At the Edge of the State: Indigenous Peoples and Self-Determination* (Transnational Publishers, 2000). The Declaration was adopted by 143 votes in favour, four against (Australia, Canada, New Zealand, and the USA—though changes in government in some of these states has had important impacts), and 11 abstentions.

subject to alien subjugation, domination, and exploitation, then it must be able to be applied to indigenous groups.

Besides the Declaration, there are a wide range of rights that have been considered by international human rights bodies to be essential to protect indigenous peoples. These include rights to be consulted about decisions affecting their land and, in considering issues of discrimination, that their particular economic and social characteristics, including their vulnerable situation, should be taken into account.[31]

4 THE EXERCISE OF THE RIGHT OF SELF-DETERMINATION

4.1 EXTERNAL AND INTERNAL SELF-DETERMINATION

Under international human rights law, there is a concentrated focus on the *exercise* of a human right. This is usually because a particular issue has arisen due to an alleged restriction on the exercise of a right by a state. Similarly, the exercise of the right of self-determination is a crucial aspect in understanding the right.

The Declaration on Principles of International Law set out the principal methods as to how the right of self-determination can be exercised. It provided that:

The establishment of a sovereign and independent State, the free association or integration with an independent State or the emergence into any other political status freely determined by a people constitute modes of implementing the right of self-determination by that people.

While the vast majority of peoples in colonial territories exercised their right of self-determination by independence, this was not the only method of exercise that was either available or used. For example, the British and the Italian Somaliland colonies joined into one state of Somalia, part of the British colony of Cameroon merged with the French colony of Cameroun to form the new state of Cameroon and the remaining part joined with the existing state of Nigeria, and Palau and a number of other Pacific Ocean islands formed a free association with the USA (that is, they had general self-government but their foreign affairs and defence were controlled by the USA).

In non-colonial situations, a range of exercises of the right of self-determination have occurred. While many have been by independence, such as Bangladesh from Pakistan and Montenegro from its union with Serbia, others have been by merger (for example the two Yemens), or by free association (for example Bougainville with Papua New Guinea). Some have occurred after a period of international territorial administration, such as the declaration of independence by Kosovo in 2008, or after prolonged armed conflict, such as Eritrea from Ethiopia.

---

[31] See eg *Mayagna (Sumo) Awas Tingni Community v Nicaragua*, IACtHR Series C No 79 (31 August 2001); and *Yakye Axa Indigenous Community v Paraguay*, IACtHR Series C No 125 (17 June 2005).

In these situations, there has been a change in the international relationships between the peoples exercising their right of self-determination and the original state/colonial power, as well as with other states and international actors. These are considered exercises of *external* self-determination.

Yet, self-determination can also be exercised by *internal* means, where there is a change in the internal relationships and administrations within a state but no change in the external relationships. The Organization of Security and Co-operation in Europe (OSCE), which comprises all West and East European states, the then USSR, USA, and Canada, accepted that self-determination could be exercised by external and internal methods, when it declared:

> By virtue of the principle of equal rights and self-determination of peoples, all peoples have the right, in full freedom, to determine, when and as they wish, their internal and external political status, without external interference, and to pursue as they wish their political, economic, social and cultural development.[32]

The Declaration on Principles of International Law expresses internal self-determination as being where 'a government [is] representing the whole people belonging to the territory without distinction as to race, creed or colour'. The Canadian Supreme Court considered that internal self-determination in relation to the peoples of the province of Québec enabled the 'residents of the province freely [to] make political choices and pursue economic, social and cultural development within Québec, across Canada, and throughout the world. The population of Québec is equitably represented in legislative, executive and judicial institutions.'[33]

Accordingly, there are a range of internal exercises of the right of self-determination. After all, 'customary and treaty law on internal self-determination [do not] provide guidelines on the possible distribution of power among institutionalized units or regions'.[34] For example, outside the colonial context there has been devolution of some legislative powers to Scotland and Wales in the UK, control over cultural and linguistic matters within the Swiss cantons, and a form of federalism in Bosnia-Herzegovina, Iraq, and Sudan. These methods are often called forms of autonomy or governance. In many instances, the method of exercise has been by agreement with the government for significant autonomy within a state, such as Crimea in Ukraine, Mindanao in the Philippines, and the northern regions of Mali.[35]

What is shown by all these examples is that there are many possible exercises by peoples of their right of self-determination. While independence—called 'secession' when it is from an existing independent state—is often seen as the only option in non-colonial contexts, it is but *one option* of very many forms of exercise, and not normally the first option lawfully able to be exercised under international law. The Supreme

---

[32] Helsinki Final Act 1975, Principle VIII.

[33] *Reference Re Secession of Québec* [1998] 2 SCR 217, (1998) 37 ILM 1342, para 136.

[34] Cassese, n 21, 332.

[35] For details of these and other exercises, see Weller, 'Settling Self-Determination Conflicts: Recent Developments' (2009) 20 *EJIL* 111.

Court of Canada made this clear when it was considering the position of its federal province of Québec's request for independence:

International law contains neither a right of unilateral secession nor the explicit denial of such a right, although such a denial is, to some extent, implicit in the exceptional circumstances required for secession to be permitted under the right of a people to self-determination, e.g., the right of secession that arises in the exceptional situation of an oppressed or colonial people.... The recognized sources of international law establish that the right to self-determination of a people is normally fulfilled through internal self-determination—a people's pursuit of its political, economic, social and cultural development within a framework of an existing state. A right to external self-determination (which in this case potentially takes the form of the assertion of a right to unilateral secession) arises in only the most extreme of cases and, even then, under carefully defined circumstances.[36]

What the court is indicating—which is consistent with the generally accepted position—is that, in most instances outside the colonial context, independence will not be considered to be the legitimate first step in the exercise of the right of self-determination. However, should other methods of exercise, such as internal self-determination, be made impossible due to the actions of the state, and if there is increased oppression of the group as a group, then it may be argued that, in those limited circumstances, the people could exercise their right of self-determination by seeking independence as a last resort.[37]

In any event, there must be flexibility in the forms of exercise of the right of self-determination. In many instances, the exercise will be dependent on the particular context and the resolution of a dispute. For example, the Badinter Committee, which was established by the European Community (EC, now European Union) to clarify the legal position during the dissolution of Yugoslavia, held that:

In the Committee's view one possible consequence of [the right of self-determination] might be for the members of the Serbian population in Bosnia-Herzegovina and Croatia to be recognized under agreements between the Republics as having the nationality of their choice, with all the rights and obligations which that entails with respect to the states concerned.[38]

This suggestion of different nationalities and sovereign powers within one state is a possibility that should be explored. It could also operate across states, as has happened to some extent with the peace agreements concerning Northern Ireland, where both the British and Irish governments were involved in the key negotiations and both signed the various peace agreements, even though Northern Ireland is entirely within the UK. While such solutions challenge traditional notions of sovereignty, they acknowledge the breadth of impact of the right of self-determination and seek to provide effective means to exercise the right as fully as possible.

---

[36] *Reference Re Secession of Québec*, n 33, paras 112, 126.

[37] See *Aaland Islands Opinion*, International Committee of Jurists (1920) LNOJ Spec Supp 3, and *Loizidou v Turkey* (1997) 23 EHRR 513, per Judges Wildhaber and Ryssdal.

[38] Badinter Commission, Opinion 2, (1992) 31 ILM 1495, para 3.

4.2 PROCEDURES FOR EXERCISING THE RIGHT OF SELF-DETERMINATION

The exercise of the right of self-determination must be by the people themselves. The ICJ confirmed this when it emphasized 'that the application of the right of self-determination requires a free and genuine expression of the will of the peoples concerned'.[39] In most instances the will of the people can be determined by a popular consultation, such as by referendum or elections. For example, the Badinter Committee decided that the will of the peoples in Bosnia-Herzegovina had to be ascertained, possibly by a referendum carried out under international supervision.[40]

However, there may be exceptional circumstances where there is no consultation, such as where the position is clear in all the circumstances. For example, during the dissolution of the USSR few referenda were held. Yet this can be manipulated. When Indonesia sought to integrate West Papua, which had been under a separate Dutch colonial administration from the rest of Indonesia just a few indigenous leaders were asked their views as to whether they would accept Indonesian control and, probably under military threats, agreed to accept this control. Similarly, the people of Hong Kong were not fully consulted about the transfer of sovereignty of that separate, distinctive region to China. Even if the geopolitical situation is one where the choices of the people may be limited, they must be able to make a free and genuine decision on a clear question, which is their own decision and is not imposed by governments or others. In ensuring that the genuine will of the people is clear, it is important that the views of all within the group, including those of women and minorities, are heard and listened to equally.

As regards to the majority needed at a popular consultation, it must be at least 50 per cent plus one. It is not clear if this should be the majority of all people eligible to vote, the majority of people who do vote, or if it should be both or some other majority. The decision on the necessary majority and form of public consultation is important, especially as the numbers voting can be affected by a boycott (for example by smaller groups who may seek a different exercise of their right of self-determination) or other circumstances. The practice during the dissolution of Yugoslavia varied considerably. In Bosnia-Herzegovina, it was assumed that 50 per cent plus one was sufficient and a boycott by the Serbian population (who comprised over 30 per cent of the population) did not affect the result with over 60 per cent of all those eligible to vote voting in favour of independence. In Montenegro the EU stated that there had to be a majority of 55 per cent of votes cast and there had to be a participation of at least 50 per cent plus one of those eligible to vote. This required majority was probably based on the opinion polls suggesting that approximately half of the population supported independence while a relatively large share of the population strongly opposed it.[41]

---

[39] *Western Sahara*, n 19, para 55.
[40] Badinter Commission, Opinion 4, (1992) 31 ILM 1495, para 4.
[41] See, 'Crnogorsko javno mnjenje uoči referenduma' (23 December 2000), available at: <http://www.aimpress.ch/dyn/pubs/archive/data/200012/01223–005-pubs-pod.htm>. My thanks to Jure Vidmar for this reference.

The actual voters in the referendum may not always be easy to decide. This is seen in the debate over which people to include in a referendum on Western Sahara, being primarily whether those who could vote was limited to those who were living in Western Sahara at the time of the ICJ opinion or if it could include those (mainly Moroccans) who have moved there since.[42] Further, even if a majority of the people choose to exercise their right of self-determination by seeking secession from a state, this will not automatically lead to that result (though it may give a strong mandate to a people in their consultations with the relevant government), as there can be limitations on the exercise of the right of self-determination.

5 LIMITATIONS ON THE EXERCISE OF THE RIGHT OF SELF-DETERMINATION

5.1 RIGHTS OF OTHERS

Almost all human rights (with the exception of absolute rights such as the prohibition on torture) have limitations on their exercise. These limitations are to protect the rights of others or the general interests of the society (such as public order and public health). The right of self-determination is a human right and, because it is not an absolute right, it has limitations on its exercise. These are limitations on the ability of the peoples with the right to exercise that right fully and legitimately under international law.

In relation to the limitation in regard to the rights of others, each of the two international human rights Covenants provides:

Nothing in the present Covenant may be interpreted as implying for any State, group or person any right to engage in any activity or perform any act aimed at the destruction of any of the rights and freedoms recognized herein or at their limitation to a greater extent than is provided for in the present Covenant.[43]

This limitation applies to the right of self-determination. Therefore, where there is another people with the right of self-determination within the state or region (for example with the Israelis and Palestinians) or a smaller people with the right of self-determination within a broader people (as with most colonial territories), then the right is limited in its exercise in order to take into account the right of the other people. As shown in earlier chapters, this right is limited only to the extent to which it enables all rights to be exercised as fully as possible in the circumstances.

An example of the operation of this limitation is found in the decision of the Canadian Supreme Court concerning the potential secession (through the exercise of the right of self-determination) of the people of the province of Québec. The court

---

[42] *Western Sahara*, n 19.   [43] ICESCR and ICCPR, Art 5(1).

noted that the rights of the indigenous ('aboriginal') peoples in the province were also affected:

> We...acknowledg[e] the importance of the submissions made to us respecting the rights and concerns of aboriginal peoples in the event of a unilateral secession, as well as the appropriate means of defining the boundaries of a seceding Québec with particular regard to the northern lands occupied largely by aboriginal peoples. However, the concern of aboriginal peoples is precipitated by the asserted right of Québec to unilateral secession. In light of our finding that there is no such right applicable to the population of Québec, either under the Constitution of Canada or at international law, but that on the contrary a clear democratic expression of support for secession would lead under the Constitution to negotiations in which aboriginal interests would be taken into account, it becomes unnecessary to explore further the concerns of the aboriginal peoples in this Reference.[44]

The court not only acknowledged the rights of the indigenous people in this passage but also the human rights and constitutional rights of other parts of Canada. It determined that, even if there had been a clear majority of the people of Québec who wished to secede, they could not do so without negotiations with the other parts of Canada. However, this does not necessarily give a permanent veto power to the other parts of Canada, as the internal right of self-determination of the people of Québec must not be restricted.

5.2 TERRITORIAL INTEGRITY

The limitation on the exercise of the external right of self-determination that is most often asserted by governments is 'territorial integrity'. This is a claim that asserts that the state itself should not be divided up and is broadly based on the general interests of international peace and security. This limitation on the right of self-determination was expressed in the Declaration on Principles of International Law:

> Nothing in the foregoing paragraph [recognizing the right of self-determination] shall be construed as authorizing or encouraging any action which would dismember or impair, totally or in part, the territorial integrity or political unity of sovereign and independent States conducting themselves in compliance with the principle of equal rights and self-determination of peoples as described above and thus possessed of a government representing the whole people belonging to the territory without distinction as to race, creed or colour.

This is an important potential limitation on the exercise of the right. However, it is only a justifiable limitation in certain situations, namely when an exercise of external self-determination (such as independence) is being sought and when a state is 'possessed of a government representing the whole people belonging to the territory without distinction as to race, creed or colour'. In other words, it can only be a legally justifiable limitation on the exercise of the right of external self-determination when a state is *already* enabling full internal self-determination for those people.

---

[44] *Reference Re Secession of Québec*, n 33, para 139.

A particular aspect of this limitation on the exercise of the right of self-determination is the international legal principle of *uti possidetis juris*. This principle provides that states emerging from colonial administrative control must accept the pre-existing colonial boundaries. Its purpose is to achieve stability of territorial boundaries and to maintain international peace and security. This was made clear by a Chamber of the ICJ:

The maintenance of the territorial *status quo* in Africa is often seen as the wisest course, to preserve what has been achieved by peoples who have struggled for their independence, and to avoid a disruption which would deprive the continent of the gains achieved by much sacrifice. The essential requirement of stability in order to survive, to develop and gradually to consolidate their independence in all fields, induced African states judiciously to consent to the respecting of colonial frontiers.[45]

While this has been uniformly accepted as a principle applicable solely to colonial territories, it was surprisingly applied by the Badinter Committee to the former Yugoslavia.[46] This latter application was probably incorrect, as it confused historically established boundaries with colonial boundaries (as the former will not have resulted from colonial determinations). There is some scope for considering that historically established boundaries (as was the case in much of the former Yugoslavia and the USSR) may be accepted as prima facie the appropriate territorial boundaries on independence even in non-colonial contexts, unless there are agreements to the contrary.

The principle of *uti possidetis juris* may appear to be a sound one in terms of preserving international peace and security at the time of independence. However, it has not prevented many boundary disputes (which still are the most numerous cases before the ICJ).[47] This is mainly because many of these boundaries were created to preserve the interests of the colonial states and were not related to natural or cultural boundaries understood by the peoples on the ground. As one of the architects of these decisions said at the time:

We have been engaged...in drawing lines upon maps where no white man's feet have ever trod; we have been giving away mountains and rivers and lakes to each other, but we have only been hindered by the small impediment that we never knew exactly where those mountains and rivers and lakes were.[48]

One example of this ignorance is the Caprivi Strip in Namibia, which is a finger of land only 20 miles wide stretching to Zambia and Zimbabwe. This was included in the 1890s as part of then German South West Africa 'due to poor geographical knowledge, since the intention had been to secure access to the Zambezi for the German colony, in the [mistaken] belief that an important communications route was involved'.[49] The

---

[45] *Frontier Dispute Case (Burkina Faso v Mali)* [1986] ICJ Rep 554 (Chamber of the ICJ), para 25.

[46] Badinter Committee Opinion 2, n 38, para 1.

[47] See Craven, *The Decolonization of International Law* (OUP, 2007).

[48] Lord Salisbury, speaking in 1890, as quoted in the Separate Opinion of Judge Ajibola, in *Territorial Dispute (Libya v Chad)* [1994] ICJ Rep 6, 53.

[49] Shaw, *Title to Territory in Africa* (Clarendon Press, 1986) 51.

ICJ recognized these problems when they stated that 'uti possidetis juris is essentially a retrospective principle, investing as international boundaries administrative limits intended originally for quite other purposes'.[50] It could be argued that the principle gives legitimacy to political or diplomatic actions purely on the basis that those actions occurred during the colonial era.

Therefore, the principle of uti possidetis juris is of questionable legitimacy as a limitation on the right of self-determination. It should only apply, if at all, in (the now very few) situations of decolonization.

5.3 OTHER LIMITATIONS

There are two other potential limitations on the exercise of the right of self-determination that are often raised: competing claims over the relevant territory by states; and the use of force. It is not uncommon for there to be a situation where more than one state asserts sovereignty over a territory where there are people with a right of self-determination. The ICJ recognized this situation in the *East Timor Case*, where they accepted that Portugal, as the colonial power, and Indonesia, as the occupying power, had forms of sovereignty over the same territory, as did the people of East Timor, who had the right of self-determination.[51] In many instances, a state will assert that an early treaty enables them to gain sovereignty (as did China in relation to Hong Kong and as Spain does in relation to Gibraltar), notwithstanding the wishes of the people of that territory. This situation was considered in the *Western Sahara Case*:

[T]he consultation of the people of a territory awaiting decolonization is an inescapable imperative.... Thus even if integration of territory was demanded by an interested State, as in this case, it could not be had without ascertaining the freely expressed will of the people—the very *sine qua non* of all decolonization.[52]

Therefore, even where there may be a lawful competing claim by another state over a particular territory, the peoples on that territory still have a right of self-determination that they must be able to exercise.

In relation to the use of force, it is not uncommon that the peoples seeking to exercise their right of self-determination use force and have force used against them. The general position appears to be that set out in the Declaration on Principles of International Law:

Every State has the duty to refrain from any forcible action which deprives peoples referred to above in the elaboration of the present principle of their right to self-determination and freedom and independence. In their actions against and resistance to such forcible action in pursuit of the exercise of their right to self-determination, such peoples are entitled to seek and to receive support in accordance with the purposes and principles of the Charter of the United Nations.

---

[50] *Land, Island and Maritime Dispute (El Salvador v Honduras)* [1992] ICJ Rep 355, 388.
[51] *East Timor (Portugal v Australia)* [1995] ICJ Rep 90, para 32.
[52] *Western Sahara Case*, n 19, per Judge Nagendra Singh, 81.

This makes clear that a state cannot use disproportionate force to prevent the exercise of the right of self-determination (which was one basis of criticism about Serbia's actions during the dissolution of Yugoslavia). The people themselves are entitled to support from other states when forcible action occurs against them as a people. That support must be in accordance with the purpose and principles of the UN Charter, so occupation by one state to 'support' a people's right of self-determination in another state (such as seemed to occur by Russia in Georgia in relation to South Ossetia in 2008) would not be lawful. Significantly, when the Protocols to the Geneva Conventions 1949 were agreed in 1977, its protection extended to wars of national liberation, being 'armed conflicts which peoples are fighting against colonial domination and alien occupation and against racist regimes in the exercise of their right of self-determination'.[53] The restrictions on the use of force against peoples seeking to exercise the right of self-determination do not seem to restrict the peoples themselves using force to assert their right of self-determination, such as the people of Eritrea, though other human rights issues may then arise as their force cannot infringe the human rights of others, such as minorities.

6 MINORITIES

6.1 RIGHTS OF MINORITIES

At the same time that self-determination was being developed as part of international law, rights relating to minorities were being set out in treaties. At the Paris Peace Conference in 1919 after the First World War a number of treaties were drafted to protect minorities in the new states being created. The obligations to protect minorities under these treaties largely related to giving minorities some autonomy. They were imposed solely on new states in Europe as a condition for settlement of territorial boundaries.[54]

However, significant development of minority rights did not occur until the adoption of the Article 27 ICCPR, which provides:

In those States in which ethnic, religious or linguistic minorities exist, persons belonging to such minorities shall not be denied the right, in community with the other members of their group, to enjoy their own culture, to profess and practice their own religion, or to use their own language.

Subsequently, the Declaration on the Rights of Persons Belonging to National or Ethnic, Religious and Linguistic Minorities (Declaration on Minority Rights) was

---

[53] Protocol Additional to the Geneva Conventions of 12 August 1949, and Relating to the Protection of Victims of International Armed Conflicts (Protocol I) 1977, Art 1(4).

[54] See Macklem, 'Minority Rights in International Law' (2008) 6 *IJConL* 531; Berman, 'But the Alternative is Despair: European Nationalism and the Modernist Renewal of International Law' (1992–1993) 106 *Harvard LR* 1792.

adopted by the General Assembly in 1992.[55] The Declaration provides guidance about the development of law in this area, though now there may be a customary international law obligation on all states to protect the rights of minorities.[56]

Within Europe there are two specific treaties dealing with rights of minorities[57] and the OSCE has devised a range of documents on minority rights, including the Document of the Copenhagen Meeting of the Conference on the Human Dimension 1990, which states:

The participating States will respect the right of persons belonging to national minorities to effect participation in public affairs, including participation in the affairs relating to the protection and promotion of the identity of such minorities. The participating States note the efforts undertaken to protect and create conditions for the promotion of the ethnic, cultural, linguistic, and religious identity of certain national minorities by establishing, as one of the possible means to achieve these aims, appropriate local or autonomous administrations corresponding to the specific historical and territorial circumstances of such minorities and in accordance with the policies of the State concerned.[58]

The OSCE has also created a High Commissioner on National Minorities, whose mandate is to investigate tensions arising from large-scale minority situations rather than complaints from individuals concerning violations of the rights of minorities, and the High Commissioner may gather and receive information from any source and undertake consultations with high-level government officials and minority representatives alike.[59] In addition, protections of the rights of minorities were contained in the EC documents regarding the dissolution of the former Yugoslavia and the former USSR, and were applied by the Badinter Committee.[60]

6.2 DEFINING 'MINORITIES'

Article 27 ICCPR and the Declaration on Minority Rights provide protections for those who are 'ethnic, religious or linguistic' minorities. Similarly, a UN Special Rapporteur has determined that:

[Minorities are groups who are] numerically inferior to the rest of the population of a State, in a nondominant position, whose members—being nationals of the State—possess ethnic, religious, or linguistic characteristics differing from those of the rest of the population and show, if only implicitly, a sense of solidarity, directed towards preserving their culture, traditions, religion or language.[61]

---

[55] A/RES/47/135/Annex (18 December 1993).   [56] Badinter Committee Opinion 2, n 38, para 2.
[57] European Charter for Regional and Minority Languages 1992, Framework Convention for the Protection of National Minorities 1995.
[58] Document of the Copenhagen Meeting of the Conference on the Human Dimension of the Conference (now Organization) for Security and Co-operation in Europe 1990, para 35.
[59] Establishment of the OSCE High Commissioner on National Minorities, Helsinki Summit of Heads of State, (9–10 July 1992), available at: <http://www.osce.org/documents/mcs/1992/07/21998_en.pdf>.
[60] EC's Declaration on Yugoslavia and its Declaration on the Guidelines on Recognition of New States in Eastern Europe and the Soviet Union (16 December 1991).
[61] Capotorti, UN Special Rapporteur, Study on the Rights of Persons Belonging to Ethnic, Religious and Linguistic Minorities, E/CN.4/Sub.2/384/Rev.1 (1979), para 242.

However, there is a concern that there are other minorities who are excluded from these definitions, such as the Roma and Turkish migrant workers in Germany, where processes of integration and assimilation may have meant a loss of linguistic or ethnic identity.[62]

It is also not clear how minorities are determined. Are they the minority within the territorial boundaries of a state or are they minorities in a region within a state if that region has some of its own governance (or autonomy)? What if the minority has been created by immigration or if there is no majority as such because it is a multi-ethnic state? It would appear that the state-focused nature of the international human rights legal system means that it is largely minorities within a state as a whole who are protected by this law. Thus, the Human Rights Committee determined that English-speaking citizens in Québec could not be protected under Article 27.[63]

6.3 EXERCISE OF MINORITY RIGHTS

The types of rights for which minorities have protection are, as Article 27 ICCPR provides: 'to enjoy their own culture, to profess and practice their own religion, or to use their own language'. The Declaration on Minority Rights adds to these the rights to participate in cultural, religious, social, economic, and public life, to participate in decisions on the national and, where appropriate, regional level, and to associate with other members of their group and with persons belonging to other minorities.

In some instances the exercise of minority rights does raise issues of conflict between the individual and the group. In the case of *Lovelace*,[64] the claim by a divorced indigenous Canadian to return to the indigenous land was upheld despite Canadian law (intending to protect the indigenous minority) precluding her from so doing. However, a Swedish law that protected the identity of the Sami minority as a whole by revoking the reindeer husbandry rights of those who pursued more lucrative work was held to be valid despite the consequent restriction imposed on the individual Sami.[65] The Human Rights Committee's view was that 'a restriction upon the right of an individual member of a minority must be shown to have a reasonable and objective justification and to be necessary for the continued viability and welfare of the minority as a whole'.[66] Therefore, there are times when the minority rights protection of an individual will be limited by the broader interest of the group as a whole. These examples also show that indigenous peoples may be able to assert their human rights through the use of minority rights protections.[67]

6.4 INDIVIDUAL v GROUP RIGHTS

The concept of human rights of minorities embodies both the protection of the rights of individuals who are part of a minority group, as well as that of protecting the minority

---

[62] See Pogany, 'Minority Rights and the Roma of Central and Eastern Europe' (2006) 6 *HRLR* 1.

[63] *Ballantyne, Davidson, McIntyre v Canada*, CCPR/C/47/D/359/1989 and 385/1989/Rev.1 (5 May 1993).

[64] *Sandra Lovelace v Canada*, A/36/40 at 166 (1981).

[65] *Ivan Kitok v Sweden*, CCPR/C/33/D/197/1985 (27 July 1988).   [66] Ibid, para 15.

[67] It has been argued that the UN approach has been to accommodate the rights of indigenous peoples but to seek assimilation of minorities more generally: Kymlicka, 'The Internationalization of Minority Rights' (2008) 6 *IJConL* 5.

group as a group, according minorities a collective right to enjoy the common traits of their group. There are two views as to how these rights should be approached. The individual rights approach to minority rights argues that such rights must be vested in, and be exercised by, the individual members claiming affiliation with the minority group rather than the minority group itself. In contrast, the group rights approach recognizes that the collective qualities that the minority possess, such as their group culture and their group language (being an inherent part of their human dignity), distinguishes them from the majority and so requires them to be protected as a group. However, it should be noted that, under both approaches, who is a minority may change over time and location, and this makes the right somewhat contingent on historical circumstances, which is unusual for a human right.[68]

It is clear that Article 27 ICCPR is solely an individual right for those who are part of a minority. For example, the HRC has rejected group claims based on Article 1 (right of self-determination), as discussed earlier, but accepted that same claim under Article 27 as long as it was argued as an individual right.[69] However, there is a strong argument that where 'national' minorities are concerned then treating the right as a group right is the appropriate approach.[70] Indeed, it is strongly argued that minorities can form a 'people' for the purposes of the right of self-determination,[71] especially as the definitions for each group are very similar, that the right of self-determination is now more commonly exercised by internal means and as many minorities use the language of self-determination.[72] For example, the Badinter Committee considered that the shared ethnic, religious, and linguistic background of Serbians from Bosnia-Herzegovina and Croatia with Serbians in Serbia did not prevent them from being a 'people' for the purposes of the right of self-determination even though they had specific minority rights protection as well.[73] While the exercise by a minority of their right of self-determination may be limited to internal self-determination, in that minority groups would usually seek to exercise their right by enabling some degree of autonomy over matters of relevance to their culture, language, religion, or ethnic identity, it does not mean that they do not possess a right of self-determination.

7 CONCLUSION

Human rights are not only in relation to rights of individual human beings; they can also protect a group as a group. One of these group rights is the right of self-determination. This right applies to a wide range of people, not just those in colonial

---

[68] See Macklem, n 54.   [69] *Ominayak and the Lubicon Lake Band*, n 4, 27.

[70] eg the OSCE High Commissioner for National Minorities has given advice to minorities and governments as if they were applying a group right: see Thio, 'Developing a "Peace and Security" Approach towards Minorities' Problems' (2003) 52 *ICLQ* 11.

[71] Wright, 'Minority Groups, Autonomy, and Self-Determination' (1999) 19 *OJLS* 605.

[72] Thornberry, *International Law and the Rights of Minorities* (OUP, 1991).

[73] Badinter Committee, Opinion 2, n 38.

territories and not just those recognized by some states as having the right. It is a right of all peoples in all territories. This right can be limited in its exercise due to others' rights (such as others' right of self-determination) and where the general interests of the relevant society is legitimately applied. In the exercise of this right, there are many alternatives, such as internal control over the people's own cultural affairs, with independence now being difficult to justify legally in the first instance in most contexts. Both indigenous groups and minorities can assert a right of self-determination. There are also individual minority rights protected under international human rights law, which encompass cultural, ethnic, linguistic, religious, and national minorities. In exercising these individual rights, the collective rights of the group as a group will need to be taken into account.

With both the right of self-determination and minority rights, the intention is to enable the rights-holders to determine their political, economic, social, and cultural destiny as they wish, while not overriding the legitimate interests of others affected. Both sets of rights developed once it was generally accepted that the traditional approach to international law and to the determination of boundaries had a severe consequence on some groups. These rights are, therefore, a reflection of the changing of values in the international community away from a state-based and solely state-interested system towards a more flexible system. Indeed, the reason behind many of the claims relating to the right of self-determination, and those in relation to minority and indigenous rights, is because the unjust, state-based international legal order has failed to respond appropriately to the legitimate aspirations of peoples.

FURTHER READING

ALSTON (ed), *Peoples' Rights* (Oxford University Press, 2001).

ANAYA, *Indigenous Peoples in International Law* (Oxford University Press, 2005).

CASSESE, *Self-Determination of Peoples: A Legal Reappraisal* (Cambridge University Press, 1995).

CHINKIN and WRIGHT, 'Hunger Trap: Women, Food and Self-Determination' (1993) 14 *Michigan JIL* 262.

CRAWFORD (ed), *The Rights of Peoples* (Oxford University Press, 1988).

GHANEA and XANTHAKI (eds), *Minorities, Peoples and Self-Determination: Essays in*

Honour of Patrick Thornberry (Martinus Nijhoff, 2005).

KLABBERS, 'The Right to Be Taken Seriously: Self-Determination in International Law' (2006) 28 *HRQ* 186.

KYMLICKA, 'The Internationalization of Minority Rights' (2008) 6 *IJConL* 1.

MCCORQUODALE, *Self-Determination in International Law* (Ashgate, 2000).

THORNBERRY, *International Law and the Rights of Minorities* (Oxford University Press, 1991).

PART IV

PROTECTION

18

UNITED NATIONS

Markus Schmidt

SUMMARY

According to its Charter, the promotion and protection of human rights is one of the principal purposes of the UN. This chapter considers the work of the UN in the field of human rights. Particular attention is given to the Human Rights Council, the treaty bodies that monitor state compliance with the core UN human rights treaties, and the Office of the High Commissioner for Human Rights. The work of other UN organs should not be overlooked and so the role of the General Assembly, Security Council, Secretary-General, and International Court of Justice are also considered.

1 INTRODUCTION

Human rights have pervaded much of the political discourse since 1945. The massive affront to human dignity committed during the Second World War and the need to prevent the horrors of another world war prompted the codification, at the international level, of human rights and fundamental freedoms. Thus, Article 1 UN Charter identifies 'promoting and encouraging respect for human rights and for fundamental freedoms for all without distinction as to race, sex, language or religion' as one of the principal purposes of the UN.

The Universal Declaration of Human Rights (UDHR), adopted on 10 December 1948, was the first step taken by the UN towards achieving that objective. In 1948 most governments recognized the UDHR but they insisted that its provisions were not legally binding on them. Since that date, human rights and fundamental freedoms have been codified in hundreds of universal and regional, binding and non-binding, instruments. At the level of the UN, the codification process remains in progress, but the main challenge today is implementation at the national level of these international standards. A further challenge is to enhance both the effectiveness and the visibility of the existing UN monitoring mechanisms in the field of human rights, be they Charter- or treaty-based.

This chapter examines the work of the UN in the field of human rights, and analyses the operation of its principal human rights organs and the mandate of the Office of the High Commissioner for Human Rights (OHCHR). It provides insight on both the promise of the UN systems for the promotion and protection of human rights, and the difficulties these systems face in realizing this promise.

2 THE HUMAN RIGHTS COUNCIL

A number of bodies have been created on the basis of provisions in the UN Charter which emphasize the importance of human rights to the work of the organization. The preamble to the Charter reaffirms the 'faith in fundamental human rights, in the dignity and worth of the human person, [and] in the equal rights of men and women'. While Article 1 lists respect for human rights as one of the purposes of the organization, Articles 55 and 56 oblige member states to take both joint and separate action to ensure respect for and observance of human rights and fundamental freedoms for all. Bodies that are established according to these provisions are known as Charter-based bodies and include the now defunct Commission on Human Rights and its replacement—the Human Rights Council.

2.1 1946–2006: FROM THE COMMISSION ON HUMAN RIGHTS TO THE HUMAN RIGHTS COUNCIL

In 1946 the UN Economic and Social Council (ECOSOC), one of the principal organs of the UN, created the Commission on Human Rights. For 60 years thereafter, the Commission, composed of 53 delegates from UN member states, performed countless activities for the protection and promotion of human rights. It made numerous important contributions to international standard-setting in the field of human rights, including drafting the UDHR, the International Covenant on Civil and Political Rights (ICCPR), the International Covenant on Economic, Social and Cultural Rights (ICESCR), and many other instruments. The Commission also developed UN institutional capacity to promote and protect human rights. Over the years it constantly refined its working methods and procedures, creating a Sub-Commission on the Promotion and Protection of Human Rights to prepare thematic studies and allowing civil society to participate in its activities to an extent not known in other parts of the UN system. Through the establishment and operation of a special procedures system, consisting of experts mandated to investigate particular human rights issues or human rights violations in particular countries, and a confidential mechanism for individuals to report consistent patterns of gross and systematic violations of human rights in a country, established on the basis of ECOSOC Resolution 1503, the Commission on Human Rights helped improve the human rights situation in many countries.

Inevitably, the Commission on Human Rights had its detractors and it became increasingly subject to criticism. In particular, attention was focused on the high level of politicization that bedevilled much of its work. In 2005, in a report on UN reform, former Secretary-General Kofi Annan identified the shortcomings of the Commission as follows:

The Commission's capacity to perform its tasks has been increasingly undermined by its declining credibility and professionalism...States have sought membership of the Commission not to strengthen human rights but to protect themselves against criticism or to criticize others. As a result, a credibility deficit has developed, which casts a shadow on the reputation of the United Nations system as a whole.[1]

These observations, uncharacteristically blunt for a serving Secretary-General, set the stage for the replacement of the Commission by a new mechanism—the Human Rights Council.

The Secretary-General's report had important implications for the direction and future of the UN human rights programme. The assumption underlying his call for reform was that the system should go from 'standard-setting', that is, the negotiation of new instruments, to implementation on the ground in order to address human rights emergencies and crises. This call for reform echoed the findings of a High-Level Panel of Experts mandated to formulate recommendations on systemic UN reform.[2] In December 2004, the High-Level Panel made several recommendations for change to the UN human rights programme, which included overhaul of the Commission on Human Rights, universal membership of the Commission, an Annual Report of the UN High Commissioner for Human Rights to the General Assembly, and increased interaction between the High Commissioner and the Security Council. The Secretary-General set aside the recommendation for a Commission on Human Rights based on universal membership and instead proposed the creation of a smaller Human Rights Council, which would meet as a standing body and be a subsidiary body of the General Assembly. He suggested that the Human Rights Council should function as a 'chamber of peer review' and that its principal task would be the evaluation of the fulfilment by *all* states of *all* their human rights obligations. Every member state would periodically come up for a comprehensive review of its human rights situation.[3]

It comes as no surprise that the initial reaction of most states to the Secretary-General's proposal was predominantly negative. However, the momentum for change was sufficient for substantive negotiations on the establishment of a Human Rights Council to begin in the summer of 2005. Several draft resolutions were prepared, which made it clear that various issues stood in the way of consensus. These included: the composition of the Council, including the number of members and their eligibility to serve; whether election of members by the General Assembly would take place by

[1] In Larger Freedom: Towards Development, Security and Human Rights for All, Report of the Secretary-General, A/59/2005 (21 March 2005) para 182.

[2] A More Secure World: Our Shared Responsibility, Report of the High-Level Panel on Threats, Challenges and Change, A/59/565 (2 December 2004).   [3] In Larger Freedom, n 1, Addendum 1.

simple majority or two-thirds majority; the functions and mandates of the Council, including the creation of a peer review mechanism for monitoring state compliance with human rights obligations; whether the Council would operate as a standing body, with several regular annual sessions and special sessions for urgent situations, or a body that would meet as required; and transitional measures and arrangements. Having resolved most of these concerns, on 15 March 2006, the General Assembly adopted Resolution 60/251 establishing a Human Rights Council.[4]

2.2 COMPOSITION, WORKING METHODS, AND MANDATE

The Human Rights Council is composed of 47 members. All UN member states are eligible for Council membership, not only those with a good human rights track record or those which have ratified the majority of international human rights instruments and cooperate with the respective monitoring mechanisms. Members are elected by a simple majority vote of the members of the General Assembly. Candidates for election to the Council are expected to make a number of pledges and commitments regarding their performance on human rights issues. Many of the first declared candidates did indeed file such pledges with the OHCHR.[5] These pledges included promises of better cooperation under the UN treaty-based reporting procedures, standing invitations to the special procedures mandate holders, and ratification of international instruments to which the state concerned is not yet a party.

Council membership is broken down into regional groupings. The African and Asian groups are allocated 13 seats each. Eight seats are reserved for the Latin American and Caribbean group, six for the Eastern European group, and seven for the West European and others group. This gives the African and Asian groups an automatic majority in Council decision making and, as will be seen below, this has had important implications for the work of the Council.

The Human Rights Council meets regularly throughout the year, with at least three regular annual sessions. There must be at least ten weeks of scheduled sessions to allow the Council to adopt a comprehensive approach to human rights and respond effectively to human rights situations as they develop. In addition, special ad hoc sessions, lasting one or two days at a time, may be scheduled at the request of a Council member that has garnered the support of at least one-third of the Council's membership.

The principal duties of the Human Rights Council are spelled out in paragraph 5 of General Assembly Resolution 60/251. These include: to promote human rights education and learning, to serve as a forum for dialogue on thematic issues, to make recommendations to the General Assembly on developing new human rights standards, to help prevent human rights violations through dialogue and cooperation, and to respond promptly to human rights emergencies. Paragraph 5(e) stipulates that the

---

[4] A/RES/60/251 (15 March 2006).
[5] The pledges made by each member are available at: <http://www2.ohchr.org/english/bodies/hrcouncil/elections.htm>.

Council shall undertake a 'universal periodic review' (UPR), based on objective and reliable information, of the fulfilment by each state of its human rights obligations and commitments in a way that ensures universality of coverage and equal treatment. The review is to be based on a constructive dialogue and should complement, not duplicate, the work of the bodies mandated to oversee state compliance with the principal human rights treaties. In addition to these primary duties, the Council was also mandated to take on, review, and consolidate all the roles undertaken by the Commission on Human Rights. It has been emphasized that when fulfilling this mandate, the Council's work should be based on the principles of *transparency*, *non-selectivity*, *inclusiveness*, and *de-politicization*. However, this has been no easy task.

2.3 UNIVERSAL PERIODIC REVIEW

The UPR mechanism was conceived as a form of 'peer review' of UN member states' action to fulfil their human rights obligations as well as a means of identifying areas in which help and advice are required to help states meet these obligations. The performance of states is measured against the relevant standards found in the UN Charter, the UDHR, the UN human rights treaties to which the state is a party, as well as those voluntary commitments and pledges that the state has made in the field of human rights.

General Assembly Resolution 60/251 left the modalities of the UPR procedure for the Council to work out. Between June 2006 and June 2007, frequently referred to as the 'institution-building period', comprehensive consultations took place among Council members regarding how the UPR was to be conducted.[6] They culminated in the adoption of Human Rights Council Resolution 5/1 on 18 June 2007.[7] Set out in detail in this resolution as well as in subsequent general guidelines for the preparation of information in anticipation of the review,[8] the UPR procedure represents a hard-fought compromise between the divisive views of member states.

The UPR mechanism operates as follows. Each UN member state is reviewed once every four years. Thus, the Human Rights Council will review 48 states per year. Reviews are to take place during three two-week sessions held each year, with 16 states being reviewed in each session. The review is conducted by a UPR Working Group, which consists of all members of the Council, and is chaired by the President of the Human Rights Council. Each review is facilitated by a group of three Council members, each from a different regional group, who are drawn by lot. This group is referred to as the 'troika'. Reviews are based on three reports:

(1) *The national report*: this report is prepared by the state under review and is not to exceed 20 pages. It should include details of human rights achievements, best practices, challenges and constraints, and key priorities for the state. In preparing

---

[6] See Loulichki, 'The Universal Periodic Review or the Promise of a New Mechanism for the Protection of Human Rights' in Müller (ed), *The first 365 days of the United Nations Human Rights Council* (Swiss Government, 2007) 80.   [7] A/HRC/RES/5/1 (18 June 2007).

[8] HR Council Res 6/102, A/HRC/RES/6/102 (27 September 2007).

their reports, states are encouraged to adopt a broad consultative process with relevant stakeholders, such as local NGOs and national human rights institutions.

(2) *Compilation of UN information*: this report gathers together relevant recommendations, observations, and comments on the state under review made by the UN treaty bodies, special procedures mandate holders, and summaries of other relevant UN documents. The report is produced by the OHCHR and is not to exceed ten pages.

(3) *Summary of stakeholders' information*: this report is also prepared by the OHCHR and it too should be no more than ten pages. It compiles additional 'credible and reliable' country information from relevant stakeholders such as NGOs, national human rights institutions, academic sources, and regional organizations. The OHCHR has established a complex in-house mechanism for the compilation of both this report and the compilation of UN information.

The review itself is a three-hour long interactive dialogue between the state under review and the UPR Working Group. All Council members and observers can participate in the dialogue. After the review, the troika submits an 'outcome report' (which summarizes the dialogue, recommendations made by the Working Group on how to improve human rights protection within the state, and the state's responses to these recommendations) for adoption by the UPR Working Group. A final outcome report is then submitted to the next ordinary session of the Human Rights Council. One hour is allowed for discussion of the report in which all member states, observers, NGOs, and other stakeholders may participate. At the end of this discussion, the final outcome report is adopted. This report serves as the basis for the next review the state undergoes.

The Secretary-General has characterized the UPR as a mechanism which has 'great potential to promote and protect human rights in the darkest corners of the world'.[9] Country reviews under the UPR formally began in April 2008, and by the end of May 2009, 80 states had been reviewed under the procedure. It is too early to give an authoritative evaluation of the effectiveness of the process, but some preliminary observations are possible.

First, it can be said that the vast majority of states reviewed under UPR have engaged in a constructive and open dialogue with the Council. Only a few have attempted to manipulate the dialogue by seeking to steer the discussion to marginal human rights issues. Second, the outcome reports adopted by the Human Rights Council contain numerous recommendations addressed to the state concerned which cover a broad range of human rights issues. However, many recommendations remain extremely vague, some to the point of not being implementable. Since the first UPR review session, the number of recommendations addressed to each state has grown steadily, and for some the number of recommendations is unreasonably large. Many states, such as Algeria, China, Pakistan, the UK, Ukraine, and the United Arab Emirates, have explicitly rejected one or several recommendations addressed to them.

---

[9] Secretary-General's video message to the opening of the fourth Council session, 12 March 2007, available at: <http://www.un.org/webcast/unhrc/archive.asp?go=004>.

Experience of the UPR mechanism so far has shown that it is complementary to, and not in competition with, the procedures of the UN treaty bodies (see Section 3, below). Fears of a UPR mechanism resulting in conciliatory and accommodating reviews of the human rights situation in most states, which would undermine or reduce the effectiveness of the reporting procedures before the treaty bodies, have been unjustified. Instead, during UPR sessions, Council members frequently quiz states about their follow-up to treaty body recommendations, and the final outcome documents often contain concrete recommendations to this effect. Conversely, the treaty bodies have started to engage with the commitments made by states parties under the UPR process.

Overall, there is reason to be cautiously optimistic. The UPR procedure is complex, but it encapsulates the principles of transparency and inclusiveness. It has the potential, provided the state under review displays the necessary political will, to generate a genuine national platform for the improvement of human rights protection. Follow-up to UPR recommendations is under discussion, both within the Council and the OHCHR. The modalities of the review will have to be fine-tuned by the time the first review cycle of all UN member states ends in late 2011. By that time, it will be possible to determine whether the UPR truly represents the 'value added' that distinguishes the work of the Human Rights Council from that of the former Commission on Human Rights.

2.4 RESPONSES TO COUNTRY SITUATIONS

When it comes to responding to serious human rights situations that arise in countries, the Human Rights Council has operated in ways that are in many respects reminiscent of the working methods of the former Commission. Since June 2006, the Council has held a number of special sessions. Roughly half (six out of 13) of the special sessions convened so far have focused on the human rights situation in the Israeli Occupied Territories. Other special sessions have focused on the human rights situation in Darfur (Sudan), the Democratic Republic of Congo, Myanmar, Sri Lanka, and Haiti while two special sessions had a thematic focus (the effects of the global economic crisis and the world food crisis). In May 2009, Council members from EU states experienced serious difficulties when trying to collect the 16 endorsements from other Council members required to convene a special session on Sri Lanka. When it was finally held, the outcome was disappointing for many and considered too mild by Western observers. This would suggest that Council members, especially those from the Western group, must not only be able to assemble the necessary votes for the convening of a special session but must also have a suitable strategy in place to secure the acceptance of their proposed draft resolution.

Thus, it has been argued that the politicization which bedevilled much of the work of the former Commission has crept into the Human Rights Council's examination of country situations. Even discussions of country situations during regular sessions have given rise to robust and often politically charged exchanges. The debates about the human rights situation in Sri Lanka and the Democratic Republic of the Congo during the tenth Council session in March 2009 are illustrative.

The operation of regional groups and alliances in the Human Rights Council assumes particular importance in this context. Since 2006, the Organization of the Islamic Conference, an alliance of Council members belonging both to the African and Asia and Pacific groups, has played an important role in the discussion of country situations, and occasionally has proved the decisive group in determining whether a country resolution is adopted or defeated. It is arguably responsible for the fact that nearly half the Council's special sessions have focused on the human rights situation in the Israeli Occupied Territories. This has led to charges that the Human Rights Council is selective and politically biased and among the 'most notorious quagmires in international politics'.[10] Conversely, a number of country situations, such as Zimbabwe, regarding which many Western Council members have sought to convene a special session, have largely escaped such scrutiny. Arguably, this is because the African and Asian groups, which command an automatic majority in the Council, rarely support such special sessions. It must, however, also be noted that no special session has been requested regarding states which are, or were, strategically or politically important for Western states. Proposals to examine a particular country situation can easily be sabotaged if regional alliances are sufficiently strong and Council members from the region make clear that they would vote against a country resolution.

2.5 SPECIAL PROCEDURES

The development of the special procedures mechanisms was undoubtedly one of the major achievements of the former Commission on Human Rights. From the creation of the first special procedure mandate in 1980, that of the Working Group on Enforced and Involuntary Disappearances, to the end of the Commission's final session, the special procedures system evolved remarkably. These mechanisms, which consist of Independent Experts who work individually or as working groups, were developed to address either country-specific situations or thematic issues that concern all states. General Assembly Resolution 60/251 mandated the Human Rights Council to review and, where necessary, rationalize and improve all mandates and mechanisms of the former Commission 'in order to maintain a system of special procedures'.

The review, rationalization, and improvement of special procedures mandates is a continuing task for the Human Rights Council, and any decision to discontinue, merge, or streamline mandates must be guided by the need to enhance human rights protection and promotion. Four country-specific mandates have been discontinued since 2006, and two thematic mandates have been added.[11] In general, one may discern a slow but probably irrevocable trend towards the abolition of country mandates.

---

[10] Farrow, 'Beware of the UN Human Rights Council' *Wall Street Journal* (6 April 2009).

[11] The country-specific mandates on Belarus, Cuba, the Democratic Republic of the Congo, and Liberia were eliminated. Thematic mandates on access to water and sanitation, and cultural rights have been added.

By the end of 2008, there were a total of 38 special procedures mandates: eight country-specific mandates;[12] ten thematic mandates focusing on civil and political rights;[13] eight thematic mandates in the area of economic, social, and cultural rights;[14] nine mandates focusing on specific groups;[15] and three separate mandates dealing with transnational corporations and business, international solidarity, and the Working Group on African Descent.

Special procedures mandate holders are selected from a list of prominent human rights experts that is maintained on the basis of technical criteria developed by the Human Rights Council. A consultative group proposes names of experts for vacant mandates, and the Council President makes an appointment after consulting Council members. Each mandate holder is to act in his or her personal capacity and independently. The maximum tenure is six years. While the denomination of experts varies from mandate to mandate—'Special Rapporteur', 'Independent Expert', 'special representative of the Secretary-General', 'member of working group'—the status of all mandate holders is equal. They benefit from such diplomatic privileges and immunities as are required for the discharge of their duties. The Human Rights Council adopted a Code of Conduct for Special Procedures mandate holders in June 2007 which imposes certain standards of behaviour on rapporteurs,[16] though it has been criticized by some mandate holders for overly restricting their activities.

Since 1993, mandate holders have met annually for one week to discuss themes of common interest and examine the possibility of harmonization of their working methods. They also interact with the High Commissioner for Human Rights, the Bureau of the Human Rights Council, the chairpersons of the human rights treaty bodies, and representatives of national human rights institutions and NGOs. A Coordination Committee of mandate holders was established in 2005 which regularly discusses issues of relevance for the special procedures system.

Mandate holders engage in a number of activities. All mandate holders conduct *country visits* and *fact-finding missions*. Currently, 66 states have extended 'standing invitations' to mandate holders and so any special procedure may visit these states. For a mandate holder to visit any other state, a specific invitation must be extended. Before the start of a country visit, the terms of reference for the fact-finding mission will have to be negotiated with the government concerned. During their visits, mandate holders meet with all relevant stakeholders and visit places of detention or shelters, as appropriate. Before they leave, they will debrief the authorities and the media on

[12] Burundi, Cambodia, Democratic Peoples' Republic of Korea, Haiti, Myanmar, Occupied Palestinian Territories, Somalia, and Sudan.

[13] Torture, summary executions, freedom of expression and opinion, freedom of religion, independence of judges and lawyers, racism, counter-terrorism, human rights defenders, Working Group on Arbitrary Detention, and the Working Group on Enforced and Involuntary Disappearances.

[14] Food, education, housing, health, extreme poverty, toxic waste, access to water, economic reform, and debt.

[15] Migrants, internally displaced persons, violence against women, sale of children, minorities, indigenous peoples, trafficking, slavery, and the Working Group on Mercenaries.

[16] HR Council Res 5/2, HRC/RES/5/2 (18 June 2007).

their (preliminary) findings and conclusions. A comprehensive report on the mission, including specific conclusions and recommendations, is subsequently transmitted to the Human Rights Council.

Most mandate holders examine *complaints* from individuals, groups (including minority or indigenous groups), human rights defenders, or other interested persons regarding human rights violations which fall within the area(s) covered by their respective mandate. A 'quick response desk' in the OHCHR screens complaints and channels them to the relevant mandate holders for appropriate action. 'Letters of allegations' are addressed to governments and non-state actors to request clarification regarding allegations of human rights violations. Where the alleged violations are yet to occur or time-sensitive (imminent loss of life, life-threatening situations, ongoing or imminent damage of a severe nature) 'urgent appeals' are dispatched. Joint urgent appeals signed by several mandate holders are now common.

The Working Group on Arbitrary Detention has developed the most sophisticated complaints procedure among the special procedures mandates, and it adopts elaborate and reasoned opinions in response to complaints regarding arbitrary arrest and detention. As a result of decisions or urgent appeals of the Working Group, individuals have been released from detention or afforded another remedy.

Some mandate holders *develop authoritative opinions and standards* for their work. Thus, for example, the Working Group on Arbitrary Detention has issued a legal opinion on the status of detainees in Guantánamo Bay,[17] and the Special Representative of the Secretary-General on internally displaced persons has developed the Guiding Principles on Internal Displacement.[18] Research is often undertaken on a specific theme related to mandates, either at the request of the Human Rights Council or at the mandate holder's initiative, and annual thematic reports are presented to the Council. Such research often includes questionnaires to governments, NGOs, and other relevant stakeholders, in order to obtain comprehensive and up-to-date information. At the end of their tenure, mandate holders often present a special report which analyses the global human rights situation as regards their mandate. Finally, mandate holders frequently organize, in conjunction with the OHCHR, governments, and NGOs, seminars or consultations which contribute to the analysis of emerging human rights issues.

Mandate holders contribute to *raising awareness of the special procedures* by issuing joint or individual press statements and engaging in regular contact with the media, especially during country visits and Human Rights Council or General Assembly sessions. Attendance at activities and meetings organized by governments, NGOs, or academic institutions is used as a platform to raise awareness about their mandates, to create and develop partnerships, and learn about new developments. Some mandate holders, for example the Special Rapporteur on violence against women, convene regional meetings with NGOs.

[17] E/CN.4/2003/8 (16 December 2002) paras 61–4 and 74. See also Opinion 5/2003, E/CN.4/2004/3/Add.1 (26 November 2003) 33.   [18] E/CN.4/1998/53/Add.2 (11 February 1998).

2.6 COMPLAINT PROCEDURE

Paragraph 6 of General Assembly Resolution 60/251 enjoins the Human Rights Council to maintain a 'complaint procedure', while leaving the Council free to keep, revise, or replace existing mechanisms. The Council complaint procedure is mostly based on the '1503 procedure' created by ECOSOC in May 1970 and executed by the Commission on Human Rights.[19] This confidential procedure, the oldest human rights complaint mechanism in the UN system, was concerned with patterns of gross violations rather than dealing with individual cases. The new Council complaint procedure is similarly concerned with identifying 'consistent patterns of gross and reliably attested violations of all human rights and all fundamental freedoms occurring in any part of the world and under any circumstance'.[20] Despite criticism that the 1503 procedure was overly confidential and inefficient because of delays in deciding on complaints, it became clear during the Council's institution-building period that most Council members favoured retention of the 1503 procedure as a basis for work. They preferred introducing targeted but real improvements to the existing system.[21]

The admissibility criteria of the 1503 procedure are retained. Complaints will be considered inadmissible if they have manifestly political motivations or are inconsistent with the purposes of the UN. Thus, complaints should originate from victims or representatives of victims, including NGOs. Complaints must be accompanied by a factual description of the alleged violation as well as an indication of what rights have been violated. They should not be based solely on media reports. Domestic remedies should be exhausted before a complaint is submitted and situations being dealt with by a special procedure or other UN or regional complaints mechanism will not be considered.

Complaints cannot go directly to the Human Rights Council. Rather, a substantial level of pre-screening is exercised by the OHCHR Secretariat as well as two Council working groups: the Working Group on Communications (WGC) and the Working Group on Situations (WGS). Both working groups are composed of five members, each representing one of the five regional groups active in the Council. Complaints are registered and summarized in a monthly confidential list of communications and transmitted to the respondent government for observations. Complaints and government replies are first examined by the WGC, which transmits cases it considers admissible to the WGS. The WGS prepares a report for the Human Rights Council plenary and makes recommendations for action. Proceedings in the working groups are confidential. They are conducted on the basis of written materials alone, such that neither governments nor complainants appear before them. A novel feature of the procedure, compared to the former 1503 procedure, is that where the WGS recommends that the Council consider a complaint or situation in a public meeting, the Council must do so at its next session as a matter of priority.

---

[19] ECOSOC Res 1503 (XLVII) (27 May 1970).   [20] HR Council Res 5/1, n 7, para 85.
[21] See Godet, 'Complaint Procedure' in Müller, n 6, 107.

It is questionable whether the Council's complaint procedure is an improvement on the former 1503 procedure. At the fourth session of the WGC in March/April 2009, the working group had before it 40 files of communications relating to 23 states. National governments had presented replies to 33 out of the 40 files: a reply rate of 87.5 per cent. However, only two communications were transmitted to the WGS for further action. The remaining communications were either kept pending, postponed, or expressly discontinued. The Council itself has taken action on very few communications. Therefore, whether there needs to be further review or outright termination of the complaint procedure should be candidly assessed.

2.7 HUMAN RIGHTS COUNCIL ADVISORY COMMITTEE

Under Human Rights Council Resolution 5/1, the Human Rights Council Advisory Committee was set up to operate as a 'think-tank' for the Council. The Advisory Committee acts under the direction of the Council and generally conducts studies and provides research-based advice. Consisting of 18 independent and impartial experts, the Advisory Committee replaces the larger Sub-Commission on the Promotion and Protection of Human Rights, which was composed of 26 experts. The nomination procedure for Advisory Committee members is designed to ensure that the best possible expertise is made available to the Council.[22] Candidates for membership should be of high moral standing and have recognized competence and expertise in the field of human rights. The Advisory Committee convenes for two annual sessions, for a maximum of ten days per year.

The work of the Advisory Committee is implementation-oriented and the scope of its advice is limited to thematic issues linked to the mandate of the Human Rights Council: protection and promotion of all human rights. Unlike the former Sub-Commission, it is not within the remit of the Advisory Committee to adopt resolutions or decisions, nor can it examine and decide on specific country situations. Instead the Advisory Committee may make proposals to the Council for the incremental enhancement of procedural efficiency, as well as further research proposals within the scope of the work directed by the Human Rights Council. In the discharge of its mandate, the Advisory Committee is actively to engage with states, national human rights institutions, NGOs, and other civil society stakeholders. Council members and observers, UN specialized agencies and other intergovernmental institutions, and NGOs may participate in the work of the Advisory Committee.

As the Advisory Committee has met only a few times since its inception, it is too early to assess its effectiveness. It may be argued that Human Rights Council members were keen to create a successor to the former Sub-Commission that would focus exclusively on research and expert advice, and refrain from examining or pronouncing itself on politically sensitive country situations. During its second session in January 2009, the Advisory Committee adopted, and transmitted to the Council, recommendations

---

[22] HR Council Dec 6/102, HRC/DEC/6/102 (27 September 2007).

on: human rights education and training; missing persons; gender mainstreaming; subsidiary bodies of the Human Rights Council; the elimination of discrimination against persons affected by leprosy; the protection of civilians in armed conflicts; and the right to food.[23] However, these issues are disparate and beg the question whether the Advisory Committee will be able to make a worthwhile impact.

2.8 CONCLUSION

The establishment of the Human Rights Council in 2006 was heralded as the dawn of a new era. Whether the Council indeed fulfils the high hopes that have been placed in it, remains to be seen. The Council itself must review its work and functioning in 2011 and report its recommendations to the General Assembly. Several observers and NGOs have criticized, or even dismissed outright, the activities of the Council as being directed by 'an alliance of repressive regimes that seek to spoil needed reforms and undermine the few meaningful mechanisms that already exist'.[24] They point to the fact that numerous states with questionable human rights records have been elected to the Council. Furthermore, around half of the special sessions convened so far have unfairly 'targeted' Israel, whereas other serious country situations have not been scrutinized, let alone criticized. In short, they accuse the Human Rights Council of perpetuating the double standards that prompted the demise of the former Commission. Such criticism is understandable and, even if it comes from NGOs and governments which are historically wary of UN human rights bodies, should not be brushed aside. However, this critique overlooks the fact that it is normal for the activities of an intergovernmental body to be influenced to a significant extent by political considerations. It would be naive to assume that the politicization of the former Commission would simply disappear with a differently constituted Council.

The Council's inability or unwillingness to examine a number of critical country situations *is* a matter of concern and should be addressed. There is now a growing awareness among members that if the Council is to fulfil its mandate in a credible manner, it would be desirable to achieve a more balanced geographic spread in the convening of special sessions. Also of concern are attempts to restrict or circumscribe existing mandates which cover forms of expression deemed offensive to a particular religion. The quasi-automatic majority that two regional groups command in the Council, often supported by the Organisation of the Islamic Conference, should not be used or abused to prevent the examination of country situations or to limit mandates in the interest of a particular group or faith. Finally, regular Council resolutions that condemn 'defamation of religions' as the equivalent of manifestations of racism remain a major concern, not only because they deeply divide Council members, but

---

[23] Report of the Advisory Committee, A/HRC/AC/2/L.8 (3 February 2009).

[24] Neuer, 'Human Rights at UN Council a Sham', 29 December 2008, available at: <http://jta.org/news/article/2008/12/29/1001866/sixty-years-on-the-un-remains-in-the-dark-on-human-rights>.

also because they seek to place impermissible limitations on the right to freedom of expression.[25]

On the other hand, the Council has been swift and decisive in adopting new human rights instruments, such as the International Convention for the Protection of all Persons from Enforced Disappearance and the Optional Protocol to the ICESCR. The experience with the UPR mechanism, while recent, has on balance been positive, and most states reviewed under the mechanism have found the exercise positive and constructive. While some country-specific special procedures mandates have been eliminated, the future of the special procedures system as a whole appears secure, and the interactive dialogue of Council members with mandate holders has been substantive if at times robust. Finally, attempts to revisit established practices for the participation of NGOs in the work of the Council have so far been resisted.

3 THE TREATY-BASED BODIES

When the UDHR was adopted in December 1948, there was broad agreement that the rights enshrined therein should be further spelled out in treaties which would bind those states which ratified or acceded to them. 1966 saw the adoption of the International Convention on the Elimination of Racial Discrimination (ICERD), the ICCPR, and the ICESCR. Since then, a further six 'core' UN human rights instruments have been negotiated and adopted, initially under the auspices of the former Commission on Human Rights and more recently by the Human Rights Council. These are set out in Table 18.1. By mid-June 2009, all UN member states had ratified at least one of the core UN human rights instruments, and 137 states were parties to at least six of the core instruments. While it is often argued today that no further human rights standard-setting activities are required and that new instruments would largely duplicate rather than complement the content of existing ones, new instruments have been proposed or are under active consideration, such as an Optional Protocol to the Convention on the Rights of the Child to introduce an individual complaints mechanism for violations of the convention.[26]

For each of the existing core human rights treaties, an expert body composed of between ten and 23 independent experts—a 'treaty body'—monitors the implementation of the treaty guarantees by states parties. Treaty body experts are elected at biannual meetings of states parties to the instruments, on the basis of their moral authority and expertise in the field of human rights. They are fully independent and not subject to any instruction from their respective governments. The treaty bodies hold two or

---

[25] See HR Council Res 4/9, HRC/RES/4/9 (30 March 2009), sponsored by Pakistan.
[26] See HR Council Res 11/1, HRC/RES/11/1 (17 June 2009).

Table 18.1 Overview of the UN treaty bodies

Instrument	Monitoring body	Number of states parties
International Convention on the Elimination of Racial Discrimination (ICERD)	Committee on the Elimination of Racial Discrimination (18 members)	173
International Covenant on Civil and Political Rights (ICCPR)	Human Rights Committee (18 members)	165
First Optional Protocol to the ICCPR (ICCPR-OP1)	Human Rights Committee	113
Second Optional Protocol to the ICCPR on the Abolition of the Death Penalty (ICCPR-OP2)	Human Rights Committee	72
International Covenant on Economic, Social and Cultural Rights (ICESCR)	Committee on Economic, Social and Cultural Rights (18 members)	160
Optional Protocol to the ICESCR (ICESCR-OP)	Committee on Economic, Social and Cultural Rights	0 (not yet in force)
Convention against Torture and Other Forms of Cruel, Inhuman and Degrading Treatment (UNCAT)	Committee against Torture (10 members)	146
Optional Protocol to UNCAT (UNCAT-OP)	Subcommittee on Prevention of Torture (10 members)	50
Convention of the Elimination of All Forms of Discrimination against Women (CEDAW)	Committee on the Elimination of Discrimination against Women (23 members)	186
Optional Protocol to CEDAW (CEDAW-OP)	Committee on the Elimination of Discrimination against Women	99
Convention on the Rights of the Child (CRC)	Committee on the Rights of the Child (18 members)	193
Optional Protocol on Sale of Children, Child Prostitution and Child Pornography	Committee on the Rights of the Child	136
Optional Protocol on Children in Armed Conflict	Committee on the Rights of the Child	130
International Convention on the Rights of Migrant Workers and their Families (ICRMW)	Committee on the Rights of Migrant Workers (10 members)	42
Convention on the Rights of Persons with Disabilities (CRPD)	Committee on the Rights of Persons with Disabilities (18 members)	83
Optional Protocol to the CRPD (CRPD-OP)	Committee on the Rights of Persons with Disabilities	52
International Convention for the Protection of all Persons from Enforced Disappearances	Committee on Enforced Disappearances (10 members)	18 (not yet in force)

three regular sessions of two to four weeks' duration per year, mostly in Geneva, but also in New York.

Each treaty body has developed different tools to monitor state compliance with treaty norms, including state reporting, the issuance of general comments, inquiries, and individual communication procedures.

3.1 STATE REPORTING

States parties to the core UN human rights treaties undertake to report regularly on how they implement the treaty protections at the national level. Initial reports must generally be submitted to the relevant treaty body within one year of ratification. Thereafter, periodic reports are due in accordance with the provisions of the treaty or the established practice of the treaty body concerned; the periodicity varies from two to five years.

All treaty bodies have issued detailed reporting guidelines on the form and content of initial and periodic reports, which are designed to help states parties discharge their reporting obligations in a timely and efficient manner.[27] Thus, state reports should set out the legal, administrative, and judicial measures taken to give effect to the treaty provisions and should mention any difficulties encountered in implementing the rights. In addition, states are to submit a 'Core Document' to be used by all treaty bodies, which sets out the general domestic legal and constitutional framework for the protection of human rights.

State reports are prepared at the national level, either under the direction of a lead ministry or an inter-ministerial committee. The preparation of the report offers states parties the opportunity to undertake a comprehensive review of measures they have taken to harmonize national laws and policies with provisions of the relevant international human rights instrument; monitor the progress made in the enjoyment of the rights set out in the treaties; identify shortcomings and problems with the domestic implementation of treaty rights; and evaluate future needs and the potential for more effective treaty implementation. Treaty body reporting guidelines urge states to provide concrete examples of treaty implementation, and not to focus exclusively on the relevant constitutional and legal framework.

Once a report has been submitted to a treaty body it is translated into the working languages of the committee concerned by the Secretariat of the treaty bodies, provided by the OHCHR. Once processed, the report is scheduled for examination by the treaty body at one of its sessions. There may be a delay in the consideration of the report, as some treaty bodies face a backlog of up to two years worth of reports awaiting examination. Prior to the session at which it will formally examine the state's report, normally one or two sessions in advance, the relevant treaty body will designate a country rapporteur who, in cooperation with the Secretariat and sometimes other experts,

---

[27] Compilation of Guidelines on the form and content of reports to be submitted by States Parties to the International Human Rights Treaties, HRI/GEN/2/Rev.5 (29 May 2008).

prepares a 'list of issues' which is sent to the state party. In its replies to this list of questions, the state party is given an opportunity to update the information contained in its report, or provide additional information omitted earlier or which the treaty body deems relevant for its assessment. Since 2008, the Committee against Torture has prepared lists of issues prior to the submission of the state report. These lists are based on all available information, including information provided by entities other than the state. The reply to this list of issues is considered to be the state party's periodic report. Other treaty bodies are considering adopting this example.

The examination of state reports takes place in public session, in the presence of a delegation of the state party concerned. Treaty body members aim to engage the delegation in a constructive dialogue on how the guarantees enshrined in the relevant instrument can be better respected. Experience shows that the dialogue is most effective and constructive if the state sends a high-level delegation of experts drawn from various ministries. A dialogue with UN-based diplomatic representatives is often unsatisfactory, especially if they are unfamiliar with all the legal issues raised in the report.

After this public examination, treaty bodies adopt 'concluding observations' or 'concluding comments'. These identify issues on which the state party has made progress in terms of treaty implementation since the last report, as well as remaining problems and concerns. Each concern is matched by a specific recommendation or practical advice designed to give the state suggestions on further steps to improve its implementation of treaty rights. There is a clear correlation between the substance of the treaty body–state dialogue and the substance and specificity of the recommendations in concluding observations. Treaty body observations and recommendations should therefore be as targeted, specific, pragmatic, and implementable as possible, so that the state party may reasonably act and follow-up on them.

Since 2001, all the treaty bodies have developed procedures for following-up on their concluding observations.[28] They generally invite states to report back within one year on what follow-up action has been taken. Most treaty bodies have appointed a Special Rapporteur for follow-up to concluding observations who is in regular contact with states parties. Where follow-up information is deficient or not forthcoming in spite of reminders, the follow-up rapporteur can organize meetings with government representatives to survey possible follow-up action and urge the state party to implement the committee's recommendations. Most treaty bodies report on the status of follow-up to their concluding observations in a specific chapter of their annual report to the General Assembly.[29]

An important feature of the reporting process is the contribution that NGOs make. All treaty bodies emphasize the importance of cooperation with NGOs, whether national or international, and the positive role NGOs can play at the domestic level in relation to follow-up to their recommendations. And so, despite a lack of explicit legal

---

[28] Report on the current working methods of the treaty bodies, HRI/MC/2009/4 (24 June 2009) paras 75–82. [29] eg Report of the HRC, A/62/40 Vol I (2007) ch VII.

authorization to do so, most treaty bodies have instituted formal mechanisms for con-sultations with NGOs.[30] NGOs regularly submit 'alternative', 'parallel', or 'shadow' reports to treaty bodies, which analyse and often challenge the content of the state party's report. Many treaty body members do rely on NGO information when prepar-ing their dialogue with the state party, or during the questioning of state delegations. Some treaty bodies have their own NGO constituency. For example, the Committee on the Rights of the Child works with a coalition of NGOs specializing in the promo-tion of children's rights. However, experience has shown that too many alternative reports may overwhelm a treaty body. Furthermore, there is a danger that conflicting information on the same issue will result in no discussion of that issue at all. However, if local NGOs coordinate themselves and submit alternative reports as a collaborative output, the impact can be considerable.

Reporting to the treaty bodies represents a significant burden for most states parties, particularly those that have ratified most or all of the core human rights instruments. It is not surprising, therefore, that many states face a serious reporting backlog. The reports of some states are more than a decade overdue. The difficulties with the report-ing procedure have prompted the treaty bodies to coordinate and streamline their procedures incrementally, and to discuss options for reform. States that experience difficulties with the reporting procedures may solicit technical assistance from the OHCHR. The OHCHR has conducted many reporting workshops for governments, often in partnership with other organizations and/or NGOs.

Where states have failed to submit reports despite repeated reminders from a treaty body, the relevant committee may initiate a process for consideration of the country situation in the absence of a report. This option, sometimes referred to as a 'review procedure', is reserved for those states the reports of which are excessively delayed. The state's performance in the fulfilment of its treaty obligations is examined by the treaty body in closed session on the basis of the existing information from relevant stakeholders. 'Provisional' concluding observations are drafted and transmitted to the state concerned for comments. Where the state does not respond, the treaty body will publish the concluding observations. The threat of such a review has resulted in most recalcitrant states agreeing to present the overdue report within a short deadline.[31]

3.2 GENERAL COMMENTS

Almost all treaty bodies, with the exception of the Sub-Committee for the Prevention of Torture and the Committee on the Rights of Persons with Disabilities, issue 'general comments'. In the case of the Committee on the Elimination of Racial Discrimination and the Committee on the Elimination of Discrimination against Women, these are termed 'general recommendations'. These comments and recommendations are

[30] See *Working with OHCHR: A Handbook for NGOs* (2007), available at: <http://www.ohchr.org/Documents/Publications/NGOHandbooken.pdf>.

[31] eg HRC, General Comment 30, HRI/GEN/1/Rev.9 (Vol I) 242. The process was used by the Human Rights Committee to examine the human rights situation in the Gambia in 2002.

adopted by consensus and provide authoritative guidance on the general treaty obligations of states parties or set out how the treaty bodies interpret the scope of application of the substantive provisions of the instruments they monitor. Many treaty provisions are couched in vague or ambiguous terms, and their scope is accordingly open to interpretation. Accordingly, general comments and recommendations offer extremely helpful interpretative guidance to states and other stakeholders. General comments also frequently deal with wider thematic or cross-cutting issues, such as the role of national human rights institutions, the obligations of states during states of emergency, violence against women, or gender-related dimensions of racial discrimination. One of the most widely commented upon and controversial general comments is General Comment 24 of the Human Rights Committee on the acceptability of reservations to the ICCPR and the ICCPR-OP1.[32] While not legally binding, general comments and recommendations are frequently invoked by states and complainants in the context of reporting and complaints procedures, and sometimes by national courts in their judgments.[33] They have been called 'a new species of soft law'.[34]

3.3 INQUIRIES

The Committee against Torture and the Committee on the Elimination of Discrimination against Women may initiate inquiry procedures upon receipt of reliable, well-founded indications of serious, grave, or systematic violations of the respective conventions by a state party. Inquiries may only be conducted in relation to states that have recognized the competence of the relevant Committee to conduct them. This has been done by 137 states parties regarding the procedure provided for in Article 20 UNCAT, and 94 states regarding the procedure set out in Articles 8, 9, and 10 CEDAW-OP.

The inquiry procedures under UNCAT and CEDAW-OP are confidential and the cooperation of the state party is required throughout the proceedings. Once a state has consented in principle to an inquiry, the relevant committee may urgently dispatch one or several members to undertake a confidential inquiry and report back. The findings of the members are then examined by the whole committee and subsequently transmitted to the state party with appropriate comments and recommendations. A report on the inquiry can only be published, or summarized in the committee's annual report, with the state party's consent. The Committee against Torture has conducted inquiries in Brazil, Mexico, Peru, Sri Lanka, Turkey, and the former Yugoslavia; the Committee on the Elimination of Discrimination against Women has conducted one inquiry which took place in Mexico.[35]

The UNCAT-OP has introduced a novel and essentially preventative inquiry mechanism. It establishes a system of complementary regular visits to places of detention

---

[32] HRC, General Comment 24, HRI/GEN/1/Rev.9 (Vol 1) 210. See Chapter 4, above.

[33] eg *Secretary of Security v Sakthevel Prabakar* [2005] 1 HKLRD 289.

[34] Tyagi, *The Work of the Human Rights Committee under the ICCPR* (CUP, 2010). See Chapter 5, above.

[35] CEDAW/C/2005/OP.8/MEXICO (27 January 2005).

conducted by both independent international and national bodies. UNCAT-OP's two-pillar approach relies on an international body, the Subcommittee on Prevention of Torture, as well as 'national preventive mechanisms' (NPMs), national bodies which must be established by each state party within one year after ratification of the UNCAT-OP. NPMs should have unrestricted access to all places of detention and all relevant information about the treatment and conditions of detention of individuals deprived of liberty. In order to discharge its mandate to advise states on national mechanisms and supervise their work, the Subcommittee should have the same level of unrestricted access as the NPMs. Since the beginning of its activities in 2007, the Subcommittee has conducted inquiries in Benin, Cambodia, Honduras, the Maldives, Mauritius, Mexico, Paraguay, and Sweden.

3.4 COMPLAINTS PROCEDURES

The ability to claim that human rights have been violated is an important part of the protection mechanisms under the UN human rights treaties. The ICCPR-OP1, ICESCR-OP, UNCAT, and ICERD provide for a state party to complain that another state party has breached their human rights obligations under the relevant treaty.[36] These are known as inter-state complaints mechanisms. However, to date there have been no inter-state complaints under any of the UN treaties. Instead, attention has been focused on mechanisms for individuals to complain that their rights under a particular treaty have been violated by a state party.

Five treaty bodies, the Human Rights Committee, the Committee against Torture, the Committee for the Elimination of Racial Discrimination, the Committee for the Elimination of Discrimination against Women, and the Committee on the Rights of Persons with Disabilities, currently implement optional individual complaints procedures. These procedures allow individuals to complain to one of the treaty bodies that a state party has violated their Convention rights. As these are optional complaints mechanisms, states must accept the competence of the relevant committee to receive individual complaints. To date, the take-up has been variable with 113 states authorizing the Human Rights Committee to receive complaints, while only 53 states parties have accepted the competence of the Committee on the Elimination of Racial Discrimination to consider individual complaints. The ICRMW and the ICESCR-OP also provide for optional individual complaints procedures. However, these are not yet functioning as the requisite number of ratifications has not been achieved.

The procedure for the examination of individual complaints is generally characterized as 'quasi-judicial'. It is written and confidential; no oral hearings take place. Complaints are initially pre-screened by the Petitions Unit of the OHCHR, as to their compatibility with the provisions of the relevant treaty and fulfilment of certain basic procedural and admissibility requirements. While complainants do not need to be legally represented, it is advisable for them to secure legal representation. However,

---

[36] ICCPR, Art 41; ICESCR-OP, Art 10; UNCAT, Art 21; ICERD, Arts 12–13.

there is no system of legal aid to help with this. Complaints can also be brought by third parties on behalf of individuals provided they have given their written consent or are unable to do so.

A treaty body member designated as Special Rapporteur for New Communications (Human Rights Committee, Committee against Torture) or a Working Group (Committee on the Elimination of Discrimination against Women) decides on the registration of complaints and issues instructions on how to proceed with new cases. Once formally registered, the complaint is normally transmitted to the respondent state party for comments. Deadlines for comments vary, but states generally have six months to submit comments on both the admissibility and merits of a communication. As the treaty bodies are careful to apply the principle of equality of arms, each party must be able to comment on the other's submissions and allegations. Therefore, the state party's observations are sent to the complainant for comments. If a state party fails to respond to a complaint, the relevant treaty body usually bases its assessment of the situation on the facts as submitted by the complainant, provided they are credible and are properly substantiated.

Treaty bodies may issue interim measures of protection in situations of particular urgency which require immediate action to prevent irreparable harm to the complainant. These are often issued in death penalty and deportation or extradition cases.[37] The vast majority of states parties comply with such requests. Despite this, requests for interim measures should remain confined to the most urgent and exceptional situations—too liberal a practice may jeopardize the state party's compliance with the request. The Human Rights Committee and the Committee against Torture have been criticized by a number of states for being over-generous with their requests for interim measures and so have begun to issue requests for 'provisional measures of protection'. These provisional measures may be lifted upon receipt of plausible information from the state party that the request is not or no longer justified. Treaty bodies regard compliance with interim measures requests as inherent in a state party's treaty obligations, and any failure to comply with them is a serious breach thereof.[38]

Decisions on admissibility are adopted either at the level of the Committee plenary (Committee on the Elimination of Racial Discrimination, Committee against Torture, Committee on the Elimination of Discrimination against Women) or at the level of a working group (Human Rights Committee). The Committees examine a number of admissibility criteria.[39] First, the complainant must show that she/he is a 'victim' of a violation of provisions of the instrument she/he invokes. The complainant must personally be affected by the impugned state action. Therefore, general claims by groups or an individual not affected by the alleged violation ('*actio popularis*') are

---

[37] Rules of Procedure of the Human Rights Committee, Rule 92; Rules of Procedure of the Committee against Torture, Rule 108(1); Rules of Procedure of the Committee on the Elimination of Discrimination against Women, Rule 63.

[38] eg *Piandiong v The Philippines*, CCPR/C/70/D/869/1999 (19 October 2000) para 5.2.

[39] These admissibility criteria are set out in the ICCPR-OP1; CERD, Art 14; UNCAT, Art 22; CEDAW-OP; CPRD-OP.

not permissible. Second, the complaint must relate to events which occurred *after* the entry into force of the complaint mechanism for the state party concerned (admissibility *ratione temporis*). The Human Rights Committee has examined complaints where events occurred prior to the entry into force of the ICCPR-OP but produced effects after the entry into force which of themselves may constitute a violation of the ICCPR. Third, the complaint must relate to rights that are actually protected by the instrument invoked by the complainant (admissibility *ratione materiae*).

Fourth, the same matter must not be under examination by another international investigation or settlement procedure, such as the European Court of Human Rights, the Inter-American Court of Human Rights, or the African Commission on Human and Peoples' Rights. Most European states parties have entered a reservation to the ICCPR-OP1 to the effect that once the European Court has disposed of a complaint, it cannot subsequently be considered by the Human Rights Committee.[40]

Fifth, the complainant must have exhausted all available domestic remedies. This means that, in principle, the highest court of the state party concerned must have considered and dismissed the case before a treaty body may consider it. The rule does not apply if the pursuit of domestic remedies has been 'unreasonably prolonged'. This is an assessment that must be made on a case-by-case basis. Most treaty bodies also interpret the rule to the effect that remedies must not only be available but also *effective*, and as such offer a reasonable prospect of effective redress.[41]

Since 2006, the Working Group on Communications of the Human Rights Committee may declare complaints inadmissible and its decision becomes final if no other Committee member objects before the end of the session at which the admissibility decision was adopted. Complaints declared admissible are referred back to the state party for observations on the merits, if such observations have not already been given. Once provided and the complainant has been given a reasonable opportunity to respond to these observations, or the deadline for submission has expired, the treaty body will examine the merits of the case.

Treaty bodies generally adopt decisions on complaints—called 'views' or 'opinions'—by consensus. Consensual decision making is arguably ill-suited for such quasi-judicial procedures, as the elusive quest for consensus is not only extremely time-consuming but also tends to weaken the outcome of decisions or the cogency of the legal argumentation. One way to avoid such pitfalls is for those experts who do not share the opinion of the majority to append individual (dissenting or concurring) opinions to the final decisions. This does not in any way undermine the authority of the decision and is done in many cases. The participant judges of three judicial colloquia on the domestic application of international human rights norms and jurisprudence held in Nairobi (2006), Panama (2008), and Bangkok (2009) have all underlined

---

[40] See Phuong, 'The Relationship Between the European Court of Human Rights and the Human Rights Committee: Has the "Same Matter" Already Been "Examined"?' (2007) 7 *HRLR* 385.

[41] For an interpretation of admissibility criteria, see Möller and de Zayas, *The Case-Law of the Human Rights Committee, 1977–2008* (Engel Verlag, 2009).

that treaty body decisions must be thoroughly and cogently argued for them to be useful as a potential judicial precedent for the national judge.[42]

One, if not *the* principal, weakness of the treaty body complaints procedures is that the final merits decisions are not strictly speaking legally binding and thus cannot be enforced. However, in General Comment 33, the Human Rights Committee stated that although its views are non-binding they 'exhibit some important characteristics of a judicial decision'.[43] Furthermore the Committee stated that its views are an authoritative interpretation of the ICCPR by a body entrusted by states parties to give such interpretations, and, as such, the principle of good faith to treaty obligations requires that states cooperate with the Committee and inform it of action taken to implement its views. In order to strengthen the legal value of their decisions, the Human Rights Committee, Committee against Torture, and Committee on the Elimination of Discrimination against Women have created the mandate of Special Rapporteur(s) for follow-up on views. These rapporteurs monitor how states parties respond to the recommendations for a remedy following the finding of a violation. It is normally expected that states will submit follow-up information within a few months of a decision. The Special Rapporteurs are in regular contact with states parties and can, in certain circumstances, conduct on-site, follow-up missions. The annual reports of the treaty bodies to the General Assembly include a chapter in which state party follow-up to views is detailed. All follow-up information provided by the parties to a case is, in principle, public.

It is difficult to neatly categorize state party follow-up. Many states parties pay compensation to victims, even though some observe that they do so not as a matter of legal obligation but merely ex gratia. Others have released individuals detained or imprisoned arbitrarily, or commuted death sentences. Still others either do not provide follow-up information or will challenge the findings of the treaty body concerned. 'Enabling legislation', that is legislation that elevates decisions of treaty bodies to the level of enforceable title at the national level, remains a rarity. Only Colombia has such legislation. But the fact that all treaty bodies deciding on complaints have instituted and largely synchronized follow-up mechanisms has slowly, but undeniably, improved the level of compliance with their recommendations.

For many years, the treaty bodies developed their jurisprudence under the complaints procedures in what could be called 'splendid isolation' from the jurisprudential developments of regional human rights mechanisms or national tribunals. This raised the spectre of conflicting interpretations of substantively very similar if not identical provisions of international or regional human rights instruments. One such example is the different treatment of the 'death row phenomenon' and the prohibition of torture and cruel, inhuman, and degrading treatment under the ICCPR and the European Convention on Human Rights by the Human Rights Committee

---

[42] Judicial Colloquium on the Domestic Application of International Human Rights Norms, Outcome Document (23–5 March 2009) para 4(a).

[43] HRC, General Comment 33, CCPR/C/GC/33 (5 November 2008) para 11.

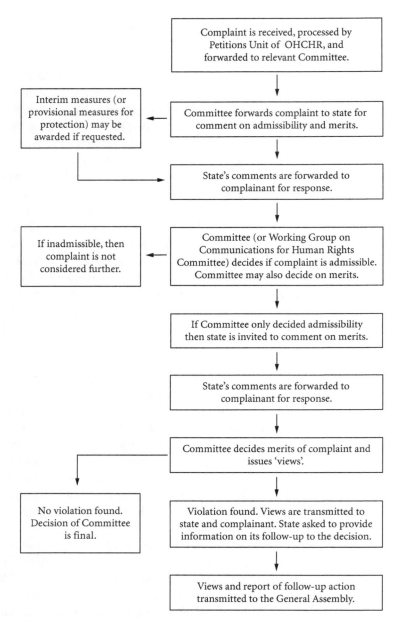

Figure 18.1 Individual complaints procedures

and the European Court of Human Rights.[44] More recently, comparative analyses of jurisprudence prepared by the OHCHR have helped treaty bodies to keep abreast of relevant developments in regional and national tribunals. This has led to a wel-

[44] Compare *Soering v UK* (1989) 11 EHRR 439 and *Barrett and Sutcliffe v Jamaica*, CCPR/C/44/D/270 and 271/1998 (30 March 1992).

come 'cross-fertilization' of human rights jurisprudence. The treaty bodies now take into account the relevant jurisprudence of regional courts and national tribunals when seized of complex or novel legal issues. Conversely, the regional mechanisms (for example the European Court of Human Rights and the Inter-American Court of Human Rights) and many national tribunals (for example the High Court of Australia and the Hong Kong Court of Final Appeal) now regularly rely on, or cite, treaty body jurisprudence. This is a felicitous development, which favours the emergence of substantively consistent and truly universal human rights jurisprudence.[45] The more thoroughly and cogently argued treaty body decisions are, the more likely it becomes that national courts, especially those with a common law tradition, will use and rely on such decisions as precedent.

3.5 TREATY BODY COORDINATION, HARMONIZATION, AND REFORM

Aware of the burden that the reporting and complaints procedures place on states parties, the treaty bodies have for many years sought to improve their effectiveness by streamlining and harmonizing their working methods and practices. Even so, numerous differences in their working methods remain in areas such as the treatment of NGO information, the preparation of lists of issues, or the procedure for the examination of reports. Many states parties complain that such procedural differences place an additional burden on them, and so they urge further mainstreaming of treaty body procedures.

Since 1984, the treaty body chairpersons have assembled, first on an ad hoc basis and then annually, to discuss issues of common concern, working methods, common approaches to thematic issues, and so on. Since 2002, this has been formalized as an 'Inter-Committee Meeting', which has become the principal forum for discussion of treaty body reform.

In a 2002 report, the UN Secretary-General identified modernization of the UN treaty system as a crucial element in the UN goal to promote and protect human rights. He called on the treaty bodies to craft a more coordinated approach to their activities by standardizing their reporting requirements and allowing states parties to produce a *single report* summarizing their compliance with the full range of treaties to which they are a party.[46] In reply to the first recommendation, the treaty bodies have prepared harmonized reporting guidelines under all core instruments.[47] In relation to the second recommendation, the treaty bodies have organized extensive consultations with all stakeholders and concluded that the production of a single report would

---

[45] See eg Schmidt, 'Vers une jurisprudence internationale en matière des droits de l'homme: l'expérience du Comité des droits de l'homme de l'ONU' in Delas, Côté, Crépeau, and Leuprecht (eds), *Les juridictions internationales: complémentarité ou concurrence?* (Bruylant, 2005) 163–8.

[46] Strengthening of the United Nations: An Agenda for Further Change, A/57/387 (9 September 2002) paras 52–4.

[47] Effective implementation of international instruments on human rights, including reporting obligations under international instruments on human rights, A/63/280 (13 August 2008) Annex, para 42(d).

present an enormous substantive and logistical challenge for states parties and would not necessarily meet the Secretary-General's objectives. The idea of a single report was therefore rejected. Instead, the treaty bodies opted for expansion of the Core Document to include a comprehensive presentation of the state party's legal framework for human rights protection, coupled with information on the implementation of substantive human rights provisions common to more than one instrument. This 'Common Core Document' (or 'Expanded Core Document') should be submitted to *all* treaty bodies, together with a targeted, treaty-specific report for each treaty body.

Most treaty bodies have completed their guidelines for the treaty-specific reports. Training has been provided to some states parties on the preparation of the Common Core Document, and a number of states, including Angola, Australia, Cyprus, the Czech Republic, Ethiopia, Israel, Kyrgyzstan, Monaco, Nicaragua, Poland, Timor Leste, and Turkmenistan, have submitted them. The acceptance of the concept of the Common Core Document complemented by treaty-specific reports is growing amongst states parties. As a result, it is expected that states will better comply with their reporting obligations and that treaty body documentation will be rationalized.

In 2005, the High Commissioner for Human Rights made another, more far-reaching, proposal for treaty body reform. She called for discussions on proposals for a unified treaty system, and the replacement of the existing treaty bodies by a single, unified, standing treaty body.[48] Under the auspices of the OHCHR, a detailed concept paper was prepared.[49] The paper expressed a strong preference for the unification of the treaty body system but, regrettably, did not contain any substantive discussions of other, less radical, reform options. The concept paper was discussed during a meeting with all stakeholders convened in Liechtenstein in July 2006. It quickly transpired that a majority of stakeholders—many states parties, most treaty bodies and experts, and numerous NGOs—were wary of the proposal to create a single standing body. They pointed out that the establishment of such a body would jeopardize and eventually undermine the specificity of the core human rights instruments and their respective monitoring bodies. Others noted that the concept paper 'merges two logically distinct issues, unification (a question of institutional design) and mainstreaming (an implementation methodology, capable of deployment by a unified body *or* separate body)'.[50] Others considered that the creation of a single body merging all treaty body activities was premature and politically unrealistic, but that some form of unification, such as a single body for examination of complaints, would be feasible.

---

[48] Plan of Action submitted by the High Commissioner for Human Rights. Annex to 'In Larger Freedom: Towards Development, Security and Human Rights for All', Report of the Secretary-General, A/59/2005/Add.3 (26 May 2006).

[49] Concept Paper on the High Commissioner's Proposal for a Unified Standing Treaty Body, HRI/MC/2006/CRP.1 (14 March 2006).

[50] O'Flaherty and O'Brien, 'Reform of the UN Human Rights Treaty Monitoring Bodies: A Critique of the Concept Paper on the High Commissioner's Proposal for a Unified Standing Treaty Body' (2007) 7 *HRLR* 141, 167.

Given the less than enthusiastic reception of the unified single standing body proposal, it is not being pursued it in any significant way.[51] The concept of a single unified body has, however, provided a much-needed impetus for further harmonization
of treaty body procedures and working methods. The Inter-Committee Meeting has
set up a number of working groups that have been entrusted with the formulation of
proposals for further mainstreaming, for example treatment of reservations to human
rights treaties, or identification of best practice in follow-up. Most states parties have
welcomed these harmonization activities.

3.6 CONCLUSION

The activities of the human rights treaty bodies have developed greatly in terms of
scope and sophistication in the last two decades. The state reporting procedures have
developed significantly and are being increasingly harmonized to allow states parties
to shoulder an ever-increasing reporting burden. The quality, specificity, and employ-
ability of concluding observations and recommendations has gradually improved,
thereby making it possible for states parties to follow-up on recommendations in a
meaningful way. Follow-up procedures have helped to keep domestically engaged
those states parties which display little or no political will to implement treaty body
recommendations.

The treaty bodies' jurisprudence under the individual complaints procedures has
broadened and improved substantively and qualitatively over the years. The most
positive development of the last decade has been the increasing 'cross fertilization'
of human rights jurisprudence. UN treaty bodies now take into account the relevant jurisprudence of regional human rights mechanisms and national courts when
examining particular legal issues, and the regional mechanisms and national courts
increasingly rely on the decisions of the treaty bodies. Follow-up to decisions of the
treaty bodies has also improved, with increasing numbers of states granting appropriate remedies following a finding of a violation of rights at their hands.

Despite these unquestionably positive achievements, the treaty bodies continue to
face challenges. First, the state reporting procedures must be further harmonized and
simplified to prompt *all* states parties to meet their reporting obligations and reduce
the large number of overdue reports. Further efforts are necessary to expedite the
acceptance of the Common Core Document and targeted treaty-specific reports by
all states parties. Second, some of the treaty-based complaints procedures face a backlog of pending cases that must be reduced as a matter of priority. While the quality of decisions has improved, consensual decision making is slow and cumbersome
and should be reviewed and gradually abandoned. The non-binding nature of treaty
body decisions remains a concern. Although it is currently politically unrealistic to
call for treaty amendments that would make all final decisions under the treaty-based

---

[51] The current High Commissioner for Human Rights confirmed in her address to the Ninth Inter-
Committee Meeting on 29 June 2009 that the pursuit of a unified treaty body is no longer on her agenda.

complaints procedures legally binding and executable,[52] follow-up procedures that strengthen the domestic implementation of decisions should be further developed. Finally, further reform endeavours with the ultimate objective of holistic and harmonious functioning of the treaty body system should continue. This is all the more necessary with the entry into force of new instruments and the likely establishment of new monitoring mechanisms and bodies.

4 THE OFFICE OF THE UN HIGH COMMISSIONER FOR HUMAN RIGHTS

Since the adoption of the UDHR the international community has sought to establish a body within the UN that could effectively deal with human rights violations. Proposals for the creation of a UN High Commissioner for Human Rights were advanced as early as the mid-1950s when Costa Rica made such a proposal. For political reasons of the time and against the backdrop of the Cold War, the proposal was politely noted and filed away by the former Commission on Human Rights and the Third Committee of the General Assembly.

The 1993 World Conference on Human Rights and its final outcome document, the Vienna Declaration and Programme of Action, reactivated discussions about the institution and mandate of a High Commissioner for Human Rights. Paragraph 18 of the Vienna Declaration called on the General Assembly to 'begin, as a matter of priority, consideration of the question of the establishment of a High Commissioner for Human Rights'. The General Assembly reacted swiftly and set up a special working group on the issue, and, on 20 December 1993, General Assembly Resolution 48/141 was adopted by an overwhelming majority. The first UN High Commissioner for Human Rights, José Ayala Lasso from Ecuador, took office in April 1994. Since then there have been four other High Commissioners.[53]

The High Commissioner has the responsibility of promoting and protecting the effective enjoyment by all of all human rights. In order to carry out this mandate, the High Commissioner is to liaise with competent UN bodies and issue recommendations on how to improve promotion and protection of human rights, as well as rationalize and strengthen the UN human rights machinery. The High Commissioner should also coordinate UN education and public human rights information programmes. States should be helped to realize their human rights obligations by providing advisory, technical, and financial services, and engaging governments in dialogue aimed at improving human rights protection. As well as enhancing international cooperation

---

[52] Such a proposal was made by the Human Rights Committee in a contribution to the preparatory process for the 1993 World Conference for Human Rights—it was not taken up by the Conference plenary.

[53] Mary Robinson (Ireland); Sergio Vieira de Mello (Brazil); Louise Arbour (Canada); Navanethem Pillay (South Africa). Bertrand G. Ramcharan (Guyana) was Acting High Commissioner from August 2003 to June 2004.

for the promotion of human rights, the High Commissioner should play an active role in removing current obstacles to the full realization of all human rights, and in preventing the continuation of human rights violations throughout the world. Finally, the High Commissioner is to promote the realization of the right to development. The mandate of the High Commissioner is widely perceived to be one of the most politically sensitive and difficult positions in the UN system.

The High Commissioner fulfils this extensive mandate mostly through the OHCHR. The OHCHR has greatly developed in terms of the scope of its activities, the mandates it supports and services, and the human and financial resources made available to it.[54] Yet the OHCHR's activities are mostly funded by voluntary contributions. For example, in 2008, regular funding from the UN regular budget constituted less than 30 per cent of total expenditure, with the remainder being made up of voluntary funding. The dependence on voluntary contributions is problematic as the OHCHR consistently relies on the contributions of major donors to implement what really are its *core* activities. Furthermore, major donor countries may be tempted to peg sizeable voluntary contributions to achieve some political leverage over the content of programmes, or influence staffing policy. At the end of 2008, the OHCHR had 990 full-time staff members, of which almost 500 were based in field offices throughout the world. The key activities of the OHCHR are discussed below.

4.1 TECHNICAL COOPERATION ACTIVITIES

One of the High Commissioner's most important priorities is to strengthen the UN programme of advisory services and technical assistance in the field of human rights. The programme itself has existed since the 1950s, but it was not until the establishment by the General Assembly in the mid-1980s of a Voluntary Fund for Technical Cooperation that it experienced remarkable growth. Under the programme, a variety of activities can be supported and financed. Most importantly, technical assistance can be given to any state requesting it, ranging from the reorganization of the penitentiary system to country-specific training courses for law enforcement officers or judges. In 2008, for example, the OHCHR trained approximately 11,000 police and other law enforcement personnel in human rights principles and standards, and 16 states enacted or initiated human rights-related legislation based on advice and technical assistance received from the OHCHR.[55] Regional workshops are also facilitated, at which officials from the same region can discuss region-specific human rights issues.

Technical cooperation is something to which states readily agree. Such assistance is not forced upon states and can only be initiated and implemented with their express consent. In other words, it is a politically cheap way for states to cooperate with the overall UN human rights programme. Furthermore, the provision of technical assistance does not carry any judgment on the recipient state's human rights record, though

---

[54] See OHCHR, *2008 Report: Activities and Results* (2009), available at: <http://www.ohchr.org/Documents/Press/OHCHR_Report_2008.pdf>. [55] Ibid, 9.

a link between investigative and monitoring mechanisms and the provision of technical assistance is often easy to find.

A particular element of technical cooperation is what could be termed 'constitutional framework assistance'. For those states in transition to a democratically elected regime, or those which have manifested their desire to recast their political system by reference to democratic precepts, the OHCHR may provide expert assistance in drafting those parts of a new constitution that deal with fundamental human rights, the allocation and separation of powers, the regulation of states of emergency in constitutional law, and nationality, citizenship, and asylum issues. Following the end of the Cold War and during the 1990s, such assistance was provided to some former Soviet Republics (Georgia and Tajikistan) and former socialist states (Mongolia and Romania).

The UN and the OHCHR also devote considerable efforts to electoral assistance missions or, in more general terms, missions designed to help restore a state's democratic institutions. The UN Electoral Assistance Division in the Department of Political Affairs has provided assistance to many states. During the 1990s, the UN monitored elections and popular consultations in Cambodia, El Salvador, Mozambique, South Africa, and Timor Leste. The importance of the human rights components of electoral assistance programmes has developed gradually since the mid-1990s. Human rights issues have been fully integrated in recent electoral assistance programmes, such as the monitoring of the 2006 elections in the Democratic Republic of Congo and recent presidential elections in Gabon. Demand for UN electoral assistance has grown steadily, as has the duration and complexity of these operations and increased responsibility has been placed on the OHCHR.

Arguably, over the years, the advisory services and technical cooperation programme has become a victim of its own success. There are significantly more requests from states for assistance than the OHCHR can handle. Technical cooperation programmes tend to be complex and generally involve several overlapping conceptualization, formalization, and implementation stages. The OHCHR does not have the capacity or resources to mount comprehensive country programmes in every corner of the globe. Furthermore, the OHCHR does not always have the requisite expertise for all the states benefiting from technical assistance. It may lack knowledge of the constitutional and legal framework of the states concerned. Finally, the level of follow-up to, or evaluation of, completed technical cooperation programmes frequently is inadequate. Therefore, the impact of the programme at the domestic or regional level is often difficult to measure.

4.2 HUMAN RIGHTS EDUCATION AND INFORMATION

It is obvious that human rights can only be invoked and exercised by individuals who know about their rights. In many developing countries with high illiteracy rates, this is often not the case. Even in many developed countries, citizens are frequently unaware of UN human rights standards. The UN human rights education programme is designed to help alleviate this problem. In December 1994, the General Assembly adopted a resolution proclaiming the following decade as the UN Decade for Human Rights Education.[56] As a result, human rights education activities were significantly stepped up.

Under the OHCHR publication programme, numerous brochures, pamphlets, training manuals, background papers, and compilations of instruments are issued each year, in print and/or electronically. Publications are also issued jointly with other intergovernmental organizations, such as the World Health Organization or Inter-Parliamentary Union. Field presences, that is, country or regional offices of the OHCHR, also regularly issue publications suited to the needs of the countries they cover, in local languages. The impact of human rights education campaigns is difficult to assess. The OHCHR can point to reasonably successful human rights education activities, for example in Cambodia or Haiti. However, as the latter case shows, there are limits to such education activities if they are confronted with an uncooperative government or an obstructive or manipulative military regime.

4.3 HUMAN RIGHTS COMPONENTS OF PEACEKEEPING OPERATIONS

The UN has been engaged in peacekeeping operations for over 60 years, but with the end of the Cold War, the strategic context of such operations has changed significantly. It has shifted from 'traditional' missions involving purely military tasks to 'multidimensional' missions designed to ensure the implementation of comprehensive peace agreements. Today's peacekeepers not only help build sustainable institutions of governments, but also engage in human rights monitoring and security sector reform.

Most of the UN's peacekeeping operations include specific human rights components, for example in Iraq (UNAMI), Afghanistan (UNAMA), the Democratic Republic of Congo (MONUC), Sudan (UNMIS), and Haiti (MINUSTAH). The UN Department of Peace-keeping Operations (DPKO) has established a Criminal Law and Judicial Advisory Section, and cooperates closely with the OHCHR in the planning and staffing of the human rights components of peacekeeping operations. Such human rights components focus on observing, documenting, investigating, and reporting on the human rights situation in the relevant country or region; ensuring that the peace process promotes justice and equity; preventing and redressing human rights violations; building human rights capacities and institutions; and mainstreaming human rights into all UN programmes and activities. The OHCHR also assists in the planning and implementation of activities of diverse peacekeeping operations. It has created a Rapid Response Unit, allowing for the expeditious deployment of staff to peace missions. In 2008, for example, the OHCHR developed a training-of-trainers course for the Chadian police, in cooperation with the UN Mission in the Central African Republic and Chad (MINURCAT), which was recognized as a best practice to be followed. In cooperation with DPKO, the OHCHR has developed training

---

[56] A/RES/49/184 (23 December 1994).

modules on arrest, detention, and use of force and firearms for UN Police and Formed Police Units.[57] It has also provided regular human rights input into policy directives for peacekeeping missions and helped to define better the Office's role in relation to security sector reform.

4.4 HUMAN RIGHTS FIELD PRESENCES

Perhaps the most effective tool for preventing human rights abuses, including systematic and widespread violations, is the establishment of human rights field presences. If endowed with a sufficiently broad mandate and operating effectively they can serve as a reliable early warning mechanism. The genocide in Rwanda in 1994, which had been predicted by NGOs and development agencies on the ground, highlighted the need for the establishment of preventive mechanisms, of which human rights field presences were seen as part and parcel.

The first High Commissioner made the creation of field presences a priority, and a field office in Rwanda was set up in early summer 1994. Since then the OHCHR has taken numerous policy decisions designed to 'operationalize' its activities and create and strengthen field presences—whether country-specific, regional, or part of peacekeeping missions—throughout the world. By the end of 2008, the OHCHR ran or supported a total of 52 field presences.[58] Table 18.2 provides a survey, broken down geographically, of these presences.

The decision to create a field presence is taken in consultation with the relevant government, taking into consideration the domestic human rights situation, security and political considerations, human and financial resources, administrative arrangements, and the scope of activities to be undertaken (whether monitoring and/or technical cooperation activities). To establish a field presence, the OHCHR must negotiate a Memorandum of Understanding with the host government that delineates the activities of the presence: generally, human rights observation, technical cooperation activities, and public reporting. However, some field presences are restricted to technical cooperation only. To a large extent, country office mandates are standardized, while the specific focus of the presence's activities is determined in cooperation with the governments concerned and based on an assessment of national human rights concerns, the work of other actors already present, and the most effective means available to the OHCHR to address gaps in human rights protection. Reports on the work of field presences are regularly presented to the Human Rights Council for consideration and possible action.

The variety and complexity of field presences has grown beyond expectation since 1994. While some standalone field presences are tiny and closely associated with the local UN country team, other field offices, for example in Cambodia, Colombia, and Nepal, are staffed by numerous human rights officers recruited both internationally and locally. Where larger country offices or regional presences are actively engaged in

---

[57] OHCHR 2008 Report, n 54, 54.   [58] Ibid, 68–153.

Table 18.2 OHCHR field presences

Africa	Middle East and Northern Africa	Asia Pacific	Europe, North America, and Central Asia	Latin America and the Caribbean
REGIONAL OFFICES/CENTRES				
Central Africa (Yaoundé)	Middle East (Beirut)	South-East Asia (Bangkok)	Central Asia (Bishtek)	Latin America (Panama City)
East Africa (Addis Ababa)	Training and documentation centre for Southwest Asia and Middle East (Doha)	Pacific (Suva)	Europe (Brussels)	
Southern Africa (Pretoria)				
West Africa (Dakar)				
COUNTRY OFFICES				
Togo	Palestinian Occupied Territories	Cambodia	Kosovo	Bolivia
Uganda	Mauritania	Nepal		Columbia
				Guatemala
				Mexico
HUMAN RIGHTS COMPONENTS OF PEACE MISSIONS				
Burundi	Iraq	Afghanistan	Georgia	Haiti
Central African Republic		Timor Leste	Kosovo	
Chad				
Côte D'Ivoire				
Darfur (Sudan)				
Democratic Republic of Congo				
Guinea-Bissau				
Liberia				
Sierra Leone				
Somalia				
Sudan				
HUMAN RIGHTS ADVISORS				
Guinea		Indonesia	South Caucasus (Armenia, Azerbaijan, Georgia)	Ecuador
Kenya		Sri Lanka	Kyrgyzstan	
Niger		Papua New Guinea	Moldova	Nicaragua
Rwanda			Russian Federation	
			Serbia	
			Former Yugoslav Republic of Macedonia	

monitoring human rights violations and regular reporting thereon, relations with the host state's authorities can become strained. Sometimes the re-negotiation with the relevant government of the agreement for the field presence may become a politically difficult exercise that requires the personal involvement of the High Commissioner.

4.5 RELATIONSHIP WITH NATIONAL HUMAN RIGHTS INSTITUTIONS

The role of national human rights institutions is examined in Chapter 21, below. Here, it should be emphasized that the establishment and strengthening of such institutions in accordance with the Principles relating to the Status and Functions of National Institutions for the Promotion and Protection of Human Rights (Paris Principles)[59] is a priority objective of the OHCHR. Paris Principles-compliant national institutions are considered an essential element of a strong national human rights protection system, and a dedicated unit of the OHCHR assists national institutions in various ways. The OHCHR regularly provides advice on draft or existing laws relating to national human rights institutions, and in 2008 did so with regard to Bahrain, Bangladesh, Cambodia, Iraq, Lesotho, Liberia, Lithuania, Pakistan, Palau, and Tajikistan. It provides technical assistance designed to strengthen national institutions, for example in 2008 in Ethiopia, Kyrgyzstan, Malaysia, Mauritania, Mauritius, Sri Lanka, Timor Leste, and Uganda.[60] The OHCHR provides the Secretariat for the International Coordinating Committee of national institutions and supports the work of the Sub-Committee on Accreditation. It helps to organize regular international conferences of national human rights institutions, and supports an enhanced role for national institutions during sessions of the Human Rights Council. Finally, it prepares a number of educational tools and operational guides for national institutions, such as the 2008 operational guide on preventing torture.

4.6 VOLUNTARY FUNDS

Besides the UN Voluntary Fund for Technical Cooperation, the OHCHR supports and services several other voluntary funds established to assist vulnerable groups or fight particularly serious human rights violations. The Voluntary Fund for Indigenous Populations assists members of indigenous groups and provides fellowships for selected indigenous persons, allowing them to spend time in the OHCHR and acquaint themselves with the UN human rights machinery. The Voluntary Fund for Slavery was established to support programmes and activities designed to fight and eradicate slavery and slavery-like practices throughout the world, including the scourge of trafficking in human beings.

[59] GA Res 48/134, A/RES/48/134 (20 December 1993) Annex.
[60] OHCHR 2008 Report, n 54, 154–5.

The largest and wealthiest fund is the Voluntary Fund for Victims of Torture, which benefits from contributions totalling approximately US$12 million per year. It funds numerous projects throughout the world which are designed to help prevent torture, educate torture victims about their rights and possible remedies, and help rehabilitate victims of torture. All of the Torture Fund's projects and activities have to be approved, and their implementation monitored, by a Board of Trustees that meets twice annually in Geneva. The Fund's secretariat regularly visits funded projects and audits their activities.

4.7 RIGHT TO DEVELOPMENT AND THE MILLENNIUM DEVELOPMENT GOALS

The UN Declaration on the Right to Development, adopted in 1986,[61] and the Millennium Development Goals (MDGs), set out in the Millennium Declaration of September 2000,[62] have manifold implications for the work of the OHCHR. The Vienna Declaration and Programme of Action dealt extensively with the right to development and recognized that democracy, development, and respect for human rights are interdependent and mutually reinforcing. Today, development issues cut across much of the work of the OHCHR, and in the 2005 Plan of Action the High Commissioner committed the OHCHR to work more actively on the links between human rights and development activities, notably the MDGs. A dedicated unit of the OHCHR currently provides methodological expertise and field support in the areas of the right to development, poverty and aid policy issues, human rights indicators, human trafficking, anti-corruption policies, globalization, and trade. The work programme of the OHCHR in this area is largely defined by reference to decisions of the General Assembly and the Human Rights Council, and the work and recommendations of the latter's Open-Ended Working Group on the Right to Development. Another unit of the OHCHR focusing on implementation of the MDGs provides methodological support to UN country teams and human rights field presences. It also works on development policy and programming issues under the auspices of the UN Development Group, with particular expertise in the MDGs, poverty and aid policies, and policies to fight HIV/AIDS.

4.8 CONCLUSION

The growth of the UN human rights machinery in the course of the last 60 years has been truly remarkable. From a tiny Human Rights Division in 1947 with few staff members, it has now grown into the OHCHR with worldwide country presences and roughly 1,000 staff members. The role of the OHCHR has also developed considerably since 1994. The level of substantive servicing of both the Human Rights Council

---

[61] GA Res 41/128, A/RES/41/128 (4 December 1986).
[62] GA Res 55/2, A/RES/55/2 (8 September 2000).

and the treaty bodies has grown in sophistication, and the number of programmes implemented and activities conducted by the OHCHR has increased and diversified significantly.

Perhaps the most noteworthy development has been the gradual 'operationalization' of the OHCHR's activities. The rapid growth of OHCHR field presences in recent years has been driven by the conviction that if the work of the OHCHR and the various human rights bodies and mechanisms in Geneva and New York is to make a real difference, it must reach the rights-holders on the ground, at the country level. This in turn means engaging intensively with national governments, national human rights commissions, and a wide range of other stakeholders. At the same time, the OHCHR should be strategic in its decisions to open, expand, and maintain country or regional offices. To open new field presences without a strategic evaluation of the value added that a new presence is likely to yield and the resources its establishment requires, risks over-committing the OHCHR and spreading its finite resources too thin. Where host governments attempt to restrict or otherwise influence the activities of a field presence, the OHCHR should remain firm and be prepared to discontinue the field presence as a final resort.

5 HUMAN RIGHTS ACTIVITIES IN OTHER PARTS OF THE UN

Recently, there has been a general push to ensure that human rights are considered in all the activities of all UN programmes and activities—an endeavour pioneered by former Secretary-General Kofi Annan. In his first report on the renewal of the UN system published in 1997, he not only called for a strengthening of the UN human rights programme but also urged the integration of human rights into the activities of other UN Departments and specialized agencies.[63] This process is known as 'mainstreaming' human rights.

Since 1997, much progress has been made. For example, in her 2005 Plan of Action, the High Commissioner committed her office to work more closely with other parts of the UN system and national partners to integrate human rights into the full range of development activities, including in the area of the MDGs, poverty reduction strategies, and programmes to fight HIV/AIDS.

Human rights considerations have been integrated into a number of UN programmes, notably into Poverty Reduction Strategy Plans and UN Development Assistance Frameworks. A memorandum of understanding between the OHCHR and the UN Development Programme (UNDP) was concluded in 1998. Under its terms, the UNDP aims to develop a human rights approach to sustainable human development and strengthen its capacity in the human rights area. The OHCHR has actively

---

[63] Renewing the United Nations: A Programme for Reform, A/51/950 (14 July 1997) paras 78 and 79.

supported the UNDP. For example, in 2008, the OHCHR focused on strengthening support to the role of UN Resident Coordinators, who are funded and managed by UNDP and lead UN country teams in over 130 countries, in promoting human rights as a common value of the UN. Also during 2008, human rights were integrated into Poverty Reduction Strategy Plans in Liberia and Sierra Leone, and UN Development Assistance Frameworks reviews in nine countries.[64] However, it is arguable that the memorandum of understanding with the UNDP is not applied evenly, and that its terms should be reviewed and brought up to date.

The Action 2 Global Programme, launched in 2004, was designed as a multi-agency initiative with the objective of reinforcing the capacity of UN country teams to integrate human rights-based approaches into their work and support governments and civil society to strengthen national human rights protection systems. Under the Action 2 Programme, over 60 governments have received direct support in the form of advisory services, seed funding for capacity building, learning tools, training, and deployment of human rights advisers.

This drive towards mainstreaming human rights into the work of the UN accompanies the activity of the main UN organs in the area of human rights. The work of the General Assembly, Security Council, and International Court of Justice will be examined in the following sections.

5.1 GENERAL ASSEMBLY

The General Assembly, the UN's principal deliberative organ composed of all member states, is regularly seized of human rights issues. In fact, Article 13 UN Charter provides that the Assembly 'shall initiate studies and make recommendations for the purpose of . . . assisting in the realization of human rights and fundamental freedoms for all without distinction as to race, sex, language, or religion'. It is generally the Third Committee of the General Assembly, responsible for social, humanitarian, and cultural issues, which reviews human rights issues. The Third Committee examines and adopts the annual reports of the human rights treaty bodies, and regularly conducts thematic discussions in which Special Rapporteurs of the Human Rights Council participate.

The plenary General Assembly regularly adopts human rights-related declarations, such as on the right to development,[65] or on the rights of indigenous peoples.[66] At the beginning of each session of the General Assembly, a treaty ratification event is organized, at which member states are urged to ratify or accede to one or several of the core human rights instruments to which they are not yet parties. The General Assembly also formally adopts new instruments in the field of human rights which have been adopted by the Council.[67] The General Assembly also discusses and endorses the results

---

[64] OHCHR 2008 Report, n 54, 45–7.   [65] n 61.
[66] GA Res 61/295, A/RES/61/295 (13 September 2007).
[67] eg GA Res 61/106, A/RES/61/106 (13 December 2006) which adopted the CRPD.

and outcome documents of international or world conferences dealing with human rights, such as the 2001 World Conference against Racism, Racial Discrimination, Xenophobia and Related Intolerance, held in Durban, South Africa in 2001, and the Durban Review Conference, held in Geneva in 2009.

5.2 SECURITY COUNCIL

The Security Council, the UN body with primary responsibility for the maintenance of international peace and security, can adopt resolutions that are binding on all member states of the UN.[68] Since the end of the Cold War, the Council has often characterized massive human rights violations as threats to international peace. Thus, the Security Council is regularly seized of human rights issues and frequently conducts emergency meetings which touch upon the human rights situation in particular countries or regions, such as the situations in the Great Lakes region (Democratic Republic of Congo, Uganda, Rwanda), Darfur, Myanmar, or the Occupied Palestinian Territories. Under the 'Arias formula',[69] which allows the Security Council to meet with non-members of the Council, special procedures of the Human Rights Council may, and regularly do, brief members of the Security Council about the human rights situation in particular countries. Furthermore, the Security Council has often authorized the deployment of peacekeeping operations to monitor and maintain peace; the OHCHR's contribution to such operations has already been discussed.

Under Article 41 UN Charter, the Security Council may impose economic sanctions to quell a threat to peace. Sanctions are imposed to persuade states to change their military, economic, or human rights policies. Examples of sanctions imposed on states because they violated human rights or international humanitarian law on a massive scale and by doing so posed a threat to regional or international security include those against Iraq during the regime of Saddam Hussein,[70] Angola during the civil war,[71] and Sudan for its policy in the Darfur region.[72] Although these sanctions were not adopted solely in order to stop human rights violations, the violations were taken into account. The effectiveness of such sanctions is difficult to assess and measure. Potentially they are a very important tool but, all too often, they are undermined by the workings of regional political alliances or a lack of political will of Security Council members to enforce them. Sanctions have been noted to harm innocent civilians rather than the political regime against which they are directed, as the devastating humanitarian results of 13 years of sanctions against Iraq demonstrate.[73]

---

[68] UN Charter, Art 25.

[69] Named after Nobel Peace laureate and Costa Rican President Oscar Arias.

[70] SC Res 661, S/RES/661 (6 August 1990).   [71] SC Res 864, S/RES/864 (15 September 1993).

[72] SC Res 1591, S/RES/1591 (29 March 2005).

[73] See The adverse consequences of economic sanctions, E/CN.4/Sub.22000/33 (21 June 2000); CESCR, General Comment 8, HRI/GEN/1/Rev.9 (Vol I) 43, para 3.

Since then, 'targeted' or 'smart' sanctions have been adopted, such as targeted restrictions on trade in arms, which are directed at those responsible for the violation of international law.

In 2001 the Security Council adopted Resolution 1373 which requests that states take certain measures to enhance the international campaign against terrorism. States are to report to the Security Council on what they have done, and these reports are examined by the Counter-Terrorism Committee of the Security Council. Members may comment on the human rights compatibility of the measures detailed in the report. Under the periodic state reporting procedures, the treaty bodies also quiz states parties about the human rights compatibility of counter-terrorism policies and measures set out in reports to the Counter-Terrorism Committee.[74]

5.3 SECRETARY-GENERAL

Under the tenure of former Secretary-General Kofi Annan, human rights have assumed a central role in UN programmes and activities. Annan arguably gave an impetus to the human rights programme that previous mandate holders were either unable or unwilling to give to it. The current Secretary-General, Ban Ki Moon, has reaffirmed the central role of human rights in the work of the UN, even if in somewhat softer language.

The Secretary-General chairs the UN system Chief Executives Board for Coordination, which is composed of the Executive Heads of all UN specialized agencies, funds, and programmes as well as of the World Bank, International Monetary Fund, International Atomic Energy Agency, and the World Trade Organization. Today, the Chief Executives Board regularly discusses human rights issues and launches important initiatives of relevance to the work of the OHCHR. In October 2007, for example, the Board endorsed a proposal from the Secretary-General and the High Commissioner for Human Rights to launch a year-long UN system-wide advocacy campaign to prepare for the commemoration of the sixtieth anniversary of the UDHR on 10 December 2008.[75]

Finally, the 'good offices' of the Secretary-General may, in particular cases, help address and resolve human rights violations affecting particular individuals or groups. Such 'good offices' tend to be reserved for politically sensitive and high visibility cases. The Secretary-General may also appoint special envoys or representatives for such cases, and direct them to broker a solution or compromise.[76]

---

[74] See Chapter 26, below.   [75] CEB/2007/2 (28 October 2007) paras 53–7.
[76] The case of Aung San Suu Kyi in Myanmar would be a case in point. See Franck and Nolte, 'The Good Offices Functions of the UN Secretary-General' in Roberts and Kingsbury (eds), *United Nations, Divided World: The UN's Roles in International Relations* (Clarendon Press, 1993) 143.

5.4 INTERNATIONAL COURT OF JUSTICE

The role of the International Court of Justice (ICJ), the principal judicial organ of the UN, is to settle legal disputes submitted to it by states and to hand down advisory opinions on legal questions referred to it by authorized UN organs and specialized agencies. Individuals cannot bring cases to the Court. Recent judgments and advisory opinions of the Court have drawn extensively on the provisions of the principal UN human rights instruments and the relevant pronouncements of the UN human rights treaty bodies. Judgments or advisory opinions may help clarify the interpretation of provisions of international human rights instruments, or spell out the legal obligations of states under these instruments.[77] In the more recent past, the ICJ has developed an increasingly human rights sensitive jurisprudence. This may be attributable, in part, to the fact that several of the ICJ's judges, past or present, had accumulated previous experience as members of the human rights treaty bodies or as special procedures of the former Commission on Human Rights.[78]

6 CONCLUSION

The UN human rights protection system has grown in ways that could hardly have been predicted at the time of the adoption of the UDHR. From timid beginnings, it has developed into a multi-tiered and sophisticated system with a multitude of international human rights instruments and their respective monitoring mechanisms, supported by a sizeable and increasingly operational OHCHR.

However, the growing politicization of the activities of the former Commission, precipitous or uncoordinated development of new mandates, the creation of new monitoring mechanisms which cannot be supported or serviced appropriately by the OHCHR, and the over-extension in the establishment of field presences have all bedevilled the work of the UN. On balance, though, the growth of the UN human rights protection system has contributed to an improvement of the human rights situation in many countries and in many thematic areas. So has the gradual and continuing mainstreaming of human rights into other UN programmes, notably into UN development activities. Today, the activities of the UN in the field of human rights are among the most visible of the organization, and the overwhelmingly public nature of these activities helps to disseminate knowledge of existing international

---

[77] See eg *Legal Consequences of the Construction of a Wall in the Occupied Palestinian Territory* [2004] ICJ Rep 136; *Application of the International Convention on the Elimination of All Forms of Racial Discrimination (Georgia v Russian Federation)* (pending).

[78] eg Judge Rosalyn Higgins, Judge Thomas Buergenthal, Judge Bruno Simma, or Judge Peter Kooijmans.

human rights standards.[79] National-level implementation of recommendations and decisions of treaty bodies, special procedures mandate holders, and the Human Rights Council improves slowly but steadily, even though there remains considerable room for the improvement of existing follow-up mechanisms.

After a decade of unprecedented growth, the UN human rights programme is now likely to enter a period of consolidation. The considerable budgetary and human resources increases of the last five years are unlikely to be repeated in the future. Major forthcoming challenges will be: the review of the procedures of the Human Rights Council, scheduled for 2011; coming to grips with, and possibly reducing, the level of politicization of Human Rights Council resolutions and decisions; further harmonization of the procedures of the treaty bodies and treaty body reform; and the consolidation of the field presences of the OHCHR, especially through the establishment of regional and sub-regional offices in those parts of the world with currently limited or no OHCHR presence. If all these challenges are addressed and resolved, the UN human rights programme is well positioned to help improve the protection of human rights where it matters most: at the national and grassroots levels.

FURTHER READING

ALSTON (ed), *The United Nations and Human Rights: A Critical Appraisal* (Clarendon Press, 1992).

—— 'Neither Fish nor Fowl: The Quest to Define the Role of the UN High Commissioner for Human Rights' (1997) 8 *EJIL* 321.

—— and CRAWFORD (eds), *The Future of Human Rights Treaty Monitoring* (Cambridge University Press, 2000).

CLAPHAM, 'Creating the High Commissioner for Human Rights: The Outside Story' (1994) 5 *EJIL* 556.

HANNUM, 'Human Rights in Conflict Resolution: The Role of the Office of the High Commissioner for Human Rights in UN Peacemaking and Peacebuilding' (2006) 28 *HRQ* 1.

HUMAN RIGHTS LAW REVIEW, Special Issue, 'Reform of the UN Human Rights Machinery' (2007) 7 *HRLR*.

LAUREN, '"To preserve and build on its achievements and to redress its shortcomings": The Journey from the Commission on Human Rights to the Human Rights Council' (2007) 29 *HRQ* 307.

O'FLAHERTY, 'The Concluding Observations of the United Nations Human Rights Treaty Bodies' (2006) 6 *HRLR* 27.

RODLEY, 'The United Nations Human Rights Council, its Special Procedures, and its Relationship with the Treaty Bodies: Complementarity or Competition?' in Boyle (ed), *New Institutions for Human Rights Protection* (Oxford University Press, 2009).

---

[79] In 2008, there were some 2.85 million visits to the OHCHR website: OHCHR 2008 Report, n 54, 61.

USEFUL WEBSITES

United Nations: <http://www.un.org>
Office of the High Commissioner for Human Rights: <http://www.ohchr.org>
Universal Human Rights Index: <http://www.universalhumanrightsindex.org>
International Court of Justice: <http://www.icj-cij.org>

19

THE AMERICAS

Jo Pasqualucci

SUMMARY

The Inter-American human rights system was created by the Organization of American States (OAS), an international organization comprised of all independent states in the Western hemisphere. The OAS has drafted and promulgated several human rights documents and treaties, primary of which are the American Declaration of the Rights and Duties of Man and the American Convention on Human Rights. The enforcement organs in the Inter-American system are the Inter-American Commission on Human Rights (the Commission) and the Inter-American Court of Human Rights (the Court). The Commission and the Court may consider individual complaints of human rights abuse. In addition, the Commission may conduct country studies or thematic studies, and the Court has advisory jurisdiction to assist the American states in complying with their global human rights obligations. Together, the Commission and the Court have made a major contribution to the recognition and protection of human rights in the Americas.

1 INTRODUCTION

The governance of many American states has evolved from the brutal dictatorships of the 1970s and 1980s to the democracies of today. Even in democracies, however, domestic judicial systems can be incapable of rectifying and putting an end to human rights abuses. Individuals can be powerless in the face of entrenched state errors or injustices. In some states there may not be laws that protect certain human rights. In most states, however, laws protect most human rights, but there may be insufficient political will to enforce them. Therefore, it is essential that the victims of human rights abuse have the opportunity to resort to regional systems, such as the Inter-American human rights system, to ensure and protect their rights when their domestic legal systems fail them.

Human rights protection in the Americas is governed by the OAS, an international organization comprised of the independent states of the Western hemisphere. Cuba had been excluded from participating in the OAS because it adopted a Marxist-Leninist form of government. On 3 June 2009, however, the OAS General Assembly voted by acclamation to revoke the 1962 resolution that suspended Cuba, thereby allowing Cuba to again participate in the OAS, after negotiations, if it so chooses.

The OAS has promulgated several human rights treaties and documents. The most influential of these are the American Declaration of the Rights and Duties of Man and the American Convention on Human Rights (ACHR). The two enforcement bodies, the Commission and the Court, have different but complementary functions and powers in promoting state observance and ensuring human rights in the Americas. A primary role for both organs is the processing of individual complaints which allege that an American state is liable for the violation of protected human rights. All individual petitions must first be filed with the Commission. Once proceedings have been completed by the Commission, under certain circumstances, the case may be submitted to the Court.

The cases initially submitted to the Inter-American Court involved gross and systematic human rights violations including disappearances, torture, and extra-judicial executions. The Court has issued precedent-setting jurisprudence, especially in the area of state responsibility for forced disappearances.[1] In more recent years the Court's jurisprudence has expanded to encompass many of the rights protected by the American Convention. In particular, the Court has rendered landmark decisions on amnesty laws, the rights of children and women, communal property rights of indigenous peoples, and freedom of expression, especially in the area of criminal defamation against public officials. The Inter-American human rights system has made substantial progress in protecting civil and political rights and promoting their observance in the Americas.

The effectiveness of the Inter-American human rights system was under study for many years culminating in major procedural changes in November 2009. Under the auspices of the OAS Committee on Juridical and Political Affairs, OAS member states, members of the Commission, judges on the Inter-American Court, NGOs, and other groups from civil society participated in a broad-based participatory and transparent reappraisal of the system. As a result, the Commission and the Court again modified their rules of procedure to enhance the role of victims, expedite the processing of cases, and provide for transparency.

2 HISTORICAL OVERVIEW

The OAS was formally created in 1948, when the sovereign states of the Americas adopted the Charter of the Organization of American States (OAS Charter). The OAS Charter is the constituent treaty which sets out the legal framework of the OAS. It

---

1 *Velásquez Rodríguez v Honduras* (Merits), IACtHR Series C No 4 (29 July 1988).

is binding on all OAS member states. The purposes of the OAS include strengthening peace and security, promoting and consolidating representative democracy, and eradicating extreme poverty. One of the basic principles of the OAS Charter affirms the ideal that fundamental rights are due to every human being without distinction as to race, nationality, creed, or sex.[2]

The 1948 conference which approved the OAS Charter also adopted the American Declaration. The American Declaration, which was adopted six months before the adoption of the Universal Declaration of Human Rights, was the first international statement of human rights. The Inter-American Court and Commission have both held that, although the Declaration was not initially adopted as a legally binding treaty, the Declaration is now a source of legal obligations for OAS member states.[3] Not all American states, including the USA, agree with that conclusion. The Declaration sets forth civil and political rights as well as economic, social, and cultural rights. In addition, it specifies corresponding duties owed by individuals to society and the state, such as the duties to vote, pay taxes, work, obey the law, and care for minor children and parents.

The Protocol of Buenos Aires, adopted in 1967, amended the OAS Charter to include the Inter-American Commission as a principal organ of the OAS. Under the Charter, the primary function of the Commission is to 'promote the observance and protection of human rights and to serve as a consultative organ of the Organization in these matters'.[4] At that time, no binding OAS human rights treaty was in effect in the Americas. In 1969 the American Convention on Human Rights was adopted. This Convention sets forth 23 civil and political rights that ratifying states (referred to as 'states parties') pledge to respect and ensure. Only one provision provides for the progressive development of economic, social, and cultural rights.

The OAS has adopted two Protocols to the American Convention: the Additional Protocol in the area of Economic, Social and Cultural Rights, also referred to as the 'Protocol of San Salvador', which entered into force in 1999; and the Protocol to Abolish the Death Penalty, which entered into force in 1991. Additional treaties adopted by the OAS are the Inter-American Convention on Forced Disappearance of Persons, which entered into force in 1996; the Inter-American Convention to Prevent and Punish Torture, which entered into force in 1987; the Inter-American Convention on the Prevention, Punishment and Eradication of Violence against Women, also known as the Convention of Belém Do Pará for the city in Brazil where it was adopted, which entered into force in 1995; and the Inter-American Convention on the Elimination of All Forms of Discrimination against Persons with Disabilities which entered into

---

[2] OAS Charter, Art 3(l).

[3] OC-10/89, *Interpretation of the American Declaration of the Rights and Duties of Man within the Framework of Article 64 of the American Convention on Human Rights*, IACtHR Series A No 4 (14 July 1989) paras 35–45; and Case 9647, *Roach and Pinkerton v US*, IACommHR Res 3/87 (22 September 1987) paras 46–9.

[4] OAS Charter, Art 106. The Commission was created by a resolution of the Fifth Meeting of Consultation of Ministers of Foreign Affairs in Santiago, Chile in 1959.

force in 2001. The OAS has also promulgated non-binding human rights declarations and resolutions. The most significant of these are the Inter-American Declaration of Principles on Freedom of Expression; the Principles and Best Practices on the Protection of Persons Deprived of Liberty in the Americas; the proposed American Declaration on the Rights of Indigenous Peoples; and the draft Inter-American Convention against Racism and All Forms of Discrimination.

The OAS, like the Council of Europe, has affirmed its commitment to democracy as the only acceptable type of political governance for a member state. The OAS adopted the Inter-American Democratic Charter in 2001 to guarantee democracy in the region. The OAS Charter recognizes that representative democracy is essential for stability, peace, development, and the protection of human rights. The OAS General Assembly relied on the Inter-American Democratic Charter in 2009 when it suspended Honduras from OAS participation as a result of a coup d'état that deposed the constitutionally elected president.[5] The Inter-American Court has affirmed in an advisory opinion the fundamental principle that a democratic form of government is essential to the protection of human rights.[6]

3 AMERICAN CONVENTION ON HUMAN RIGHTS

Twenty-four of the 35 OAS member states are states parties to the American Convention. The treaty has not been ratified by Belize, Canada, Suriname, the USA, and some Caribbean nations. Trinidad and Tobago, which had been a state party to the American Convention, denounced the treaty in 1998.

Under the ACHR, states parties undertake to respect and ensure the human rights specified in the Convention to all persons who are subject to their jurisdiction.[7] Jurisdiction, within the context of a human rights treaty, is not limited to the physical territory of the state; rather, it is generally regarded that a state's jurisdiction includes all areas over which it has effective control.[8] As explained by the Inter-American Commission, although the prisoners held by the USA in Guantanamo Bay, Cuba, were outside the physical territory of the USA, they were 'wholly within the authority and control of the United States government'.[9] Therefore, the USA could be held responsible for human rights abuses taking place there. States parties also agree to give legal effect to the rights and freedoms set forth in the ACHR at the domestic level. In accordance with that provision, some American states have incorporated international human

---

[5] OAS Press Release, 'OAS Suspends Membership of Honduras', 5 July 2009.

[6] OC-6/86, *The Word 'Laws' in Article 30 of the American Convention on Human Rights*, IACtHR Series A No 6 (9 May 1986), para 35.   [7] ACHR, Art 1(1).

[8] See Chapter 6, above.

[9] Guantanamo Bay Precautionary Measures Communication of March 12, 2002 from IACHR President Juan E Méndez to US Secretary of State Colin Powell (2002) 96 *AJIL* 730. See Tittemore, 'Guantanamo Bay and The Precautionary Measures Of The Inter-American Commission On Human Rights: A Case For International Oversight In The Struggle Against Terrorism' (2006) 6 *HRLR* 378.

rights standards in their laws and constitutions and have provided for the execution of the judgments of the Inter-American Court at the domestic level.

The rights and freedoms protected by the ACHR include the right to life, humane treatment, personal liberty, a fair trial, privacy, conscience and religion, property, equal protection, assembly, and to participate in government. The Convention also ensures the freedoms of thought and expression, conscious and religion, association, movement and residence, and freedom from slavery and *ex post facto* laws. Rights of the family and of the child are likewise recognized.

The ACHR establishes two organs to protect and enforce the rights set forth in the Convention: the Inter-American Commission and the Inter-American Court. Although the Commission and the Court are empowered to enforce international human rights law in the Americas, the first and foremost authorities to deal with claims of human rights abuse are national authorities. Only when there are defects in the domestic system and its efforts are not effective can the case be referred to the Inter-American Commission and the Inter-American Court.

States parties to the ACHR automatically agree to the right of an individual to file a petition with the Inter-American Commission alleging state violations of individual human rights.[10] Even the right of individual petition, however, may not be sufficient to allow all persons to avail themselves of the protection of the ACHR. Many victims of human rights abuse in the Americas have a limited education and live in poverty. Although they are authorized to file a complaint, they do not have the knowledge or means to do so. Also, in some states, victims and their families are intimidated and justifiably fear retaliation if they file a complaint with the Inter-American Commission. Therefore, the ACHR permits parties that are unrelated to the victim to file human rights petitions. Any person or non-government entity legally recognized in an OAS member state may file a petition with the Commission denouncing human rights violations. Thus, NGOs such as Americas Watch (now Human Rights Watch), the Center for Justice and International Law (CEJIL), or the World Council of Journalists—organizations with experience litigating before the organs of the Inter-American system—are often the formal petitioners in cases. These organizations have more resources than most individuals, are less susceptible to intimidation, and can generate local and international publicity.

4 INTER-AMERICAN COMMISSION ON HUMAN RIGHTS

The Inter-American Commission plays a dual role in the Inter-American human rights system. The Commission was created as a principal organ of the OAS under the OAS Charter, and it was also established as an organ for the protection of human rights

---

[10] ACHR, Art 4.

under the ACHR. Under the Charter, the Commission has authority to oversee the human rights obligations of all member states of the OAS. Thus, every American state has accepted the competence of the Commission to consider individual complaints concerning alleged human rights violations that occur in its jurisdiction, simply by virtue of the ratification of the OAS Charter.

If a complaint is filed against a state that has not ratified the ACHR, the Commission will determine whether the state violated the protections set forth in the American Declaration of the Rights and Duties of Man. For those 24 states that have ratified or acceded to the ACHR, however, the Commission determines whether there has been a violation of the Convention. The most complex aspect of the Inter-American system of individual petitions is that states have somewhat different human rights obligations depending on whether they have ratified the ACHR.

4.1 STRUCTURE AND COMPOSITION

The Inter-American Commission is composed of seven commissioners who are elected by secret ballot of all OAS member states at the OAS General Assembly. They are elected to four-year terms and may be re-elected once. Commissioners do not serve as representatives of states. They must be nationals of OAS member states, and no two commissioners may be nationals of the same state. Members of the Commission must be 'persons of high moral character and recognized competence in human rights'.[11]

The Commission is located at the OAS headquarters in Washington, DC. It is in session only on a part-time basis, but the Commission's Secretariat, composed of lawyers and human rights specialists, functions on a full-time basis. The Secretariat immediately consults the Commission in serious or urgent cases.

4.2 INDIVIDUAL COMPLAINT PROCEDURES

The primary function of the Commission is the examination of individual petitions denouncing human rights violations. Complaints to the Inter-American system alleging that an American state has violated individual human rights must first be filed and processed by the Inter-American Commission. Except for requests for provisional measures, the Commission must complete its proceedings before a case may be referred to the Inter-American Court. In 2008, the Commission received 1,323 individual petitions alleging human rights abuse against 26 OAS member states.[12] The average time for the processing of a complaint from submission to the Commission to referral to the Inter-American Court has been over eight years.[13]

---

[11] ACHR, Arts 34–7.

[12] Annual Report of the Inter-American Commission on Human Rights 2008, ch III, Section 1(a).

[13] CEJIL, Contributions to the Process of Reflection on Possible Reforms to the Procedures of the Inter-American Commission on Human Rights and the Inter-American Court of Human Rights (October 2008), available at: <http://www.civil-society.oas.org>.

Human rights petitions to the Commission must meet criteria of admissibility. A petition must state facts that tend to establish a violation of a guaranteed right. Also, to be admissible a petition must show that the petitioner has pursued and exhausted all remedies under domestic law when that is possible; that the petition was lodged within six months of the notification of a final judgment in the domestic court; that the subject of the petition is not pending in another international proceeding; and that the petition contains basic information such as the name, nationality, domicile, profession, and signature of the person who lodged the petition.[14] If the petition lacks the required content, the Commission may ask the petitioner to complete it. It is important that the Commission be flexible in this regard, as those who complain that their rights have been violated often do so without the assistance of attorneys. When the complaint is determined to be prima facie admissible, in that it satisfies the formal requirements of admissibility, the Commission will forward the pertinent portions of it to the state. The Commission then forwards the relevant parts of the government's response to the petitioner, along with a request for observations. If there is no governmental response, the Commission may treat the petitioner's allegations as presumptively true. States today generally do respond to the petitions presented.

After the Commission has made a formal decision that a case is admissible, it will consider the merits of the case. It may hold hearings for the purpose of receiving evidence. With the prior permission of the respondent state, and if the commissioners consider it to be necessary, the Commission may also carry out an on-site investigation in the state where the violations allegedly occurred.

At the request of either party or on its own initiative, the Commission will attempt to bring about a friendly settlement between the petitioner and the state. Friendly settlements may be beneficial to both states and victims, and the Commission has been encouraged to promote settlements more actively. Victims are more likely to receive the determined reparations when the state's express agreement is garnered through friendly settlement procedures. Friendly settlements also shorten the usually time-consuming nature of proceedings before the Commission. In the event that the parties reach a friendly settlement, the Commission will adopt a report, transmit it to the parties, and publish it.

In most cases, the petitioner and state do not reach a friendly settlement. In such instances, after consideration of the merits, if the Commission finds that the state has violated a right protected by the ACHR, it will recommend measures that the state should take to remedy the violation. If the state does not follow these recommendations, and it has accepted the jurisdiction of the Inter-American Court, the Commission's Rules of Procedure provide for the automatic referral of a case to the Court 'unless there is a reasoned decision by an absolute majority of the members of the Commission to the contrary'.[15] One of the Commission's primary concerns is whether the petitioner wishes the case to be referred to the Court. As a result, the Commission submits

---

[14] ACHR, Art 46(1). *Velásquez Rodríguez*, n 1, para 61.
[15] Inter-American Commission Rules of Procedure, Art 44(1).

almost all such cases to the Court. Consequently, the Court's caseload has increased substantially. The workload of the Commission had also increased as, at that time, the Commission played an active role in all cases before the Court.

In addition to authorizing individuals to file complaints of human rights abuses, the ACHR also authorizes inter-state complaints. State parties to the Convention may accept the competence of the Inter-American Commission to receive and examine communications in which one state alleges that another state party has violated individual human rights.[16] Inter-state complaints require reciprocity; both states must have made declarations accepting the competence of the Commission to examine state-to-state complaints. To date, only two inter-state complaints have been filed. The *Nicaragua v Costa Rica* complaint was declared inadmissible,[17] while a complaint by Ecuador was filed against Colombia in 2009. States are often hesitant to file a complaint against another state for fear of jeopardizing trade or other relations. Consequently, the inter-state complaint process, which historically had been the only avenue available in international law to deal with disputes, has not proven to be an effective curb to human rights violations in the Americas.

4.3 OTHER ROLES OF THE COMMISSION

Although the primary function of the Commission is the examination of individual complaints of human rights abuse, the Commission also studies and reports on human rights in a broader context. The Commission may prepare a country study when there are alarming reports about the human rights situation in a member state. Country reports and the adverse publicity they generate have contributed significantly to the downfall of military dictatorships and the eventual democratization of several states in the Americas. For instance, during the 'dirty war' in Argentina, when thousands of people were forcibly disappeared by the government, the Inter-American Commission made an official visit to Argentina. The Commission met with government officials and also heard testimony from victims and their families. Thousands of people waited in the streets to give testimony before the Commission or to support those who did. Some commentators credit the Commission's visit as one factor in the downfall of the ruling junta.[18]

The Commission also conducts thematic studies concerning violations of certain types of rights throughout the hemisphere, and it monitors the situation of particularly vulnerable groups. Commissioners may serve as thematic rapporteurs who analyse and report on the rights of migrant workers, persons of African descent, prisoners, indigenous peoples, women, and children. The Commission also has a rapporteur on freedom of expression, and a special unit on human rights defenders.

---

16 ACHR, Art 45(1).

17 Inter-State Case 01/06, *Nicaragua v Costa Rica*, IACommHR Report No 11/07 (8 March 2007).

18 Weissbrodt and Bartolomei, 'The Effectiveness of International Human Rights Pressures: The Case of Argentina, 1976–1983' (1991) 75 *Minn LR* 1009.

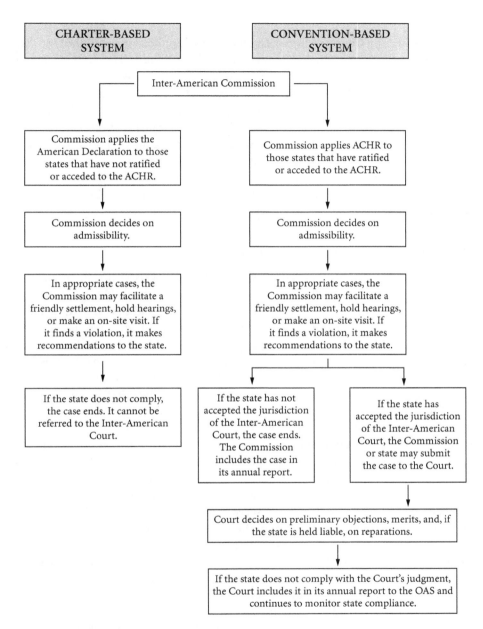

Figure 19.1 Individual petitions procedure

5 INTER-AMERICAN COURT OF HUMAN RIGHTS

The Inter-American Court of Human Rights is the sole judicial organ of the OAS. The Court was created in 1979 following the entry into force of the ACHR. The Convention authorizes the Court to adjudicate contentious cases, issue advisory opinions, and order states to take provisional measures to protect persons who are in grave and imminent danger. A state is subject to the jurisdiction of the Court if it has ratified the ACHR and explicitly accepted the Court's contentious jurisdiction. This jurisdiction empowers the Court to adjudicate cases of alleged violations of individual human rights protected by the ACHR for which a state government is responsible. As of 1 December 2009, 21 of the 24 states parties to the ACHR had filed declarations accepting the Court's contentious jurisdiction. Other states parties to the ACHR may accept the Court's jurisdiction by special agreement for a specific case.

5.1 STRUCTURE AND COMPOSITION

The Court is composed of seven judges who are elected to a six-year term by a vote of the states parties to the ACHR. Judges may be re-elected for one additional term, and they continue to hear cases that they have begun to hear and that are still pending when their terms expire. The judges are elected by secret ballot by an absolute majority of the states parties to the ACHR. A state party may nominate an individual who is a national from any OAS member state, not only from those states that have ratified the ACHR and accepted the jurisdiction of the Court. Thus, Judge Thomas Buergenthal, a US national, who was nominated by Costa Rica, was one of the initial judges elected to the Court, even though the USA has not ratified the ACHR.

No two judges may be nationals of the same state. Judges are to be chosen from 'jurists of the highest moral authority' who are recognized for their competence in human rights law and who possess the qualifications to be a judge in the nominating state or the state of the nominee's nationality. There is no vetting procedure similar to that of the Council of Europe to ensure that judges and commissioners are well qualified for their positions. The judges serve in their individual capacities and do not represent the states that nominate them. Judges may not hold other positions which are incompatible with their responsibilities on the Court, such as serving as officers of international organizations or as high-ranking government officials who are under the control of the executive branch. Although the Court previously allowed the respondent state to appoint an ad hoc judge to the Court when the contentious case originated from an individual petition, this practice has changed. The Court issued an advisory opinion interpreting the ACHR to permit ad hoc judges only in inter-state cases.[19] Even sitting judges, who are nationals of the respondent state shall not be permitted to participate in individual cases.[20]

---

[19] OC-20/09, *Article 55 of the American Convention on Human Rights*, Series A No 20 (29 September 2009).   [20] IACtHR, Rules of Procedure approved by the Court, 24 November 2009, Art 19.

The Inter-American Court sits on a part-time basis and decides cases in plenary session. In addition to its four regular sessions, the Court held five special sessions in 2008. In that year, it rendered 18 judgments and by the end of the year it was processing 110 contentious cases.

The Court is located in San José, Costa Rica where it holds most regular sessions. At the invitation of a state and with the agreement of the majority of the judges, the Court may convene in any OAS member state. In recent years, for example, it has held sessions in several countries including Argentina, Brazil, Chile, Colombia, El Salvador, Mexico, and Paraguay. When holding sessions away from the seat of the Court, the judges will often meet with government officials and civil society as well as hold seminars on the Inter-American system. In this way, the Court brings the system and its work in protecting human rights to the attention of the public.

The Court has a full-time Secretariat of attorneys and other staff. The official languages of the Court are English, French, Portuguese, and Spanish. Each year the judges decide on the working languages. Persons appearing before the Court may use their own languages, which will be interpreted into one of the working languages.

5.2 CONTENTIOUS CASES

Under the ACHR only the Commission and states have authority to refer cases to the Inter-American Court. This referral may take place only after the Commission has completed its proceedings. The individual victim or petitioner does not have standing to bring a case before the Court. The Commission now refers almost all cases to the Court when the state involved has accepted the Court's jurisdiction and the state has not complied with the Commission's recommendations. The state may make preliminary objections to the admissibility of an application or to the Court's jurisdiction to hear a case. If a state does not submit preliminary objections, or the case is not dismissed at the preliminary objections stage, the Court will address the merits of the case.

At the merits stage of the proceedings, the Court considers written briefs, affidavits from witnesses, other documentary evidence, and often holds public hearings to take oral testimony from witnesses and experts. Oral proceedings are not mandated in the Inter-American system. As a result of the increase in its caseload and for purposes of procedural economy, the Inter-American Court has attempted to limit the number of days scheduled for public hearings and the number of witnesses testifying at the hearings. Thus, the Court often accepts sworn declarations or affidavits in place of live testimony. Public hearings may not be necessary at the preliminary objections stage when the issues presented are questions of law, which can be adequately briefed by the parties. Conversely, public hearings on the merits of the case, especially when the facts are disputed, are essential to provide a full factual record, allow the victims the opportunity to tell their stories, and increase public understanding of the plight of victims and the overall situation in the state by attracting media attention.[21]

---

[21] See generally Cavallaro and Brewer, 'Reevaluating Regional Human Rights Litigation in the Twenty-First Century: The Case of the Inter-American Court' (2008) 102 *AJIL* 768.

The alleged victim's role before the Court has been steadily enhanced, and the Commission's role has been minimized. Although the ACHR specifies that the Commission must appear before the Court in all cases, the Commission no longer represents the alleged victim, who has standing before the Court once the case has been submitted. At all stages of the proceedings, the victims are represented by their own attorneys. If the alleged victims do not have legal representation, the Inter-American Court may, on its own motion, appoint Inter-American public defenders to represent them during the processing of the case.[22] The November 2009 changes in the Court's Rules of Procedure provide that generally only the alleged victim and the state will participate in hearings by conducting interrogations of witnesses. At the opening of the public hearing, the Commission presents the grounds for the case and any other matter that it considers relevant for its resolution. The Commission may present its written observations in response to any preliminary objections made by the state or question any expert witnesses proposed by the Commission. At the conclusion of the oral arguments, the Commission presents its final observations. Judges may question any witness or party.

At the conclusion of the proceedings the judges hold private deliberations, which remain confidential. The Court's judgments are binding on the parties to the case and cannot be appealed. The Court can interpret a judgment at the request of one of the parties to the case if there is disagreement as to the meaning or scope of the judgment. Even when the state has accepted partial or full responsibility for the violations, the Court's judgment should fully recount the proven facts to set forth an authoritative record of the events. This record provides support to human rights advocates when generating public opinion. The average duration of proceedings before the Inter-American Court, from the presentation of the application to the final judgment, has been 19 months.[23]

5.3 COURT-ORDERED REPARATIONS AND STATE COMPLIANCE

When the Inter-American Court determines that the state is liable for a violation of the victim's human rights, or the state voluntarily accepts responsibility for a violation, the Court orders the state to make reparations to the victim. One of the greatest contributions made by the Inter-American Court to international human rights law is the enhancement of the concept of reparations. The Court has ordered victim-centred reparations as well as reparations that will benefit specific communities or society as a whole.

Financial compensation was the traditional type of reparation when the state was held liable for a human rights violation, and it remains one aspect of reparations in the

[22] IACtHR, Rules of Procedure approved by the Court 24 November 2009, Art 37. The Inter-American Court and the Inter-American Association of Public Defenders signed an Agreement of Understanding on 25 September 2009 to provide free legal assistance to alleged victims who lack economic resources or legal representation before the Court. See IACtHR Press Release 15–09, 29 September 2009.
[23] Annual Report of the Inter-American Court 2008, n 12, 65.

Inter-American system. The ACHR specifies that 'fair compensation be paid to the injured party'.[24] Financial compensation includes, but is not limited to, loss of earnings, restitution of material property taken or destroyed, and payment for moral damages for emotional harm to the victim. Overall, states have complied with approximately 81 per cent of Court-ordered financial compensation awards, although payments are sometimes delayed beyond the period specified by the Court.[25] The state also must reimburse successful applicants for their costs and expenses. Financial compensation alone is not sufficient, however, for those who have suffered human rights abuses. As stated by the mother of a victim who had been executed by the Venezuelan military in El Amparo, '[m]y son was not a cow. I don't want money. What I want is justice.'[26]

The ACHR provision on reparations authorizes the Court 'to rule that the injured party be ensured the enjoyment of his right or freedom that was violated'. The Court drew on this aspect of its authority to order reparations when it ordered Peru to release Maria Elena Loayza Tamayo, a university professor who had been wrongfully imprisoned in Peru for several years.[27] Peru complied with the Court's order and released the prisoner.[28] Needless to say, not all states comply with all Court reparations orders. In 2009, Paraguayan lawmakers voted against the return of ancestral lands to the Yakye Axa indigenous community, despite a 2005 judgment by the Inter-American Court ordering the state to return the land to the people.[29]

Another, and very important, aspect of reparations under the ACHR is that the 'consequences of the measure or situation that constituted the breach of such right or freedom be remedied'.[30] Pursuant to this authority, the Inter-American Court has held that a state law is without legal effect, that the state amend or repeal domestic legislation, and even that the state undertake constitutional reform of provisions that do not comply with the state's freely assumed human rights obligations under the ACHR. For instance, the Court ordered Chile to implement domestic legal measures to guarantee the right to access information and to adapt its laws to comply with the ACHR. Chile fully complied with the Court-ordered reparations when the Chilean President signed the Law on Transparency of Public Functions and Access to Information of the State Administration.[31] The legislation was enacted in response to the Inter-American Court's judgment in *Claude Reyes v Chile* in which an environmental organization successfully challenged the Chilean government to release information regarding a deforestation project.[32] Chile's transparency law will limit governmental corruption by allowing the public access to information. Likewise, the Argentine Supreme Court struck down Argentina's amnesty laws, citing the Inter-American Court's

---

[24] ACHR, Art 63(1).   [25] Inter-American Court Annual Report 2008, n 11, 73.

[26] See Krsticevic, 'Conference on Reparations in the Inter-American System: A Comparative Approach' (2007) 56 *AmUniv LR* 1418, 1420–1.

[27] *Loayza Tamayo v Peru*, IACtHR Series C No 33 (17 September 1997).

[28] *Chicago Tribune* (17 October 1997) 28.

[29] See Amnesty International, 'Paraguayan Congress Risks Lives of 90 Indigenous Families' (28 June 2009), available at: <http://www.amnesty.org/en/news-and-updates/news>.   [30] ACHR, Art 63(1).

[31] Inter-American Court Annual Report 2008, n 11, 26.

[32] IACtHR Series C No 151 (19 September 2006).

earlier decision in the *Barrios Altos* case.[33] In *Barrios Altos*, the Court declared that two amnesty laws promulgated by the government of then Peruvian President Alberto Fujimori in 1995 were incompatible with the ACHR and hence without legal effect.[34] Reparations that require modification to domestic laws that violate the state's international obligations have a broader impact than individual financial reparations. All of society benefits from the changes, and human rights are advanced because new violations are prevented.

The Inter-American Court may also find that a domestic court ruling was not made in accordance with the due process guarantees of the ACHR. Following the *Raxcacó Reyes* case, Guatemala complied with the Court order to annul the death sentence imposed on the victim.[35] Guatemala also complied with the Court ordered reparations and held a new trial in the *Fermín Ramírez* case.[36] When appropriate, the Court may order the state to undertake various remedies such as providing human rights training to the state's armed forces and police, giving free medical and psychological treatment to victims of violence or imprisonment, awarding grants for higher education, and creating funds for the collective interest of a community. The Inter-American Court has been creative in its reparations orders. In the *Kawas Fernández v Honduras* case, in which an environmental activist was murdered in Honduras, the Court ordered, as one form of reparations, that the state implement a national campaign to educate the public about the work of environmental activists and their contributions to the defence of human rights.[37]

In the interest of general deterrence, and in an attempt to clear the names of victims who have often been maligned by the state, the Court generally orders the state to publish pertinent parts of its judgment. The Court may order the state to undertake a symbolic public act, such as participating in a public ceremony, so that society will learn the truth about the facts underlying the case. After the Court's judgment in the *Myrna Mack* case, Guatemala implemented one aspect of the Court's reparations order by holding a public function to acknowledge responsibility for the murder of the anthropologist and social activist. The President of Guatemala spoke at the meeting and hundreds of military personnel including high-ranking officers of the armed forces, the police, and members of the community attended.[38] Symbolic actions taken by states in compliance with Court-ordered reparations include naming streets or schools after victims or creating memorials. In addition, high-level state officials have apologized to victims in response to the Court's reparations decisions, and many are pre-empting such orders by apologizing to the victims during the Court's public hearings.

In an attempt to combat impunity, the Court regularly mandates that the state investigate human rights violations and identify, prosecute, and punish those responsible. The state's obligation persists until it has fully complied with this duty. However, states in

[33] Corte Suprema de Justicia [CSJN], 14/6/2005, 'Case of Julio Hector Simon/recurso de hecho', No 17.768 (Arg). [34] IACtHR Series C No 75 (14 March 2001).
[35] Inter-American Court Annual Report 2008, n 12, 18. [36] Ibid, 17.
[37] (Merits, Reparations and Costs), IACtHR Series C No 196 (3 April 2009), operative para 14.
[38] See Krsticevic, n 26, 1420–1.

many cases have not appeared to make good-faith efforts to fulfill such orders. The most likely reasons for this chronic failure are that either government or military personnel who are implicated in the human rights offences still wield power within the state, or that current officials do not want to set a precedent that could affect them in the future.

The Inter-American system lacks an effective formal institutional mechanism to enforce state compliance with its orders and judgments. It does not have an equivalent of the Committee of Ministers of the Council of Europe.[39] The ACHR provides that if a state has not complied with judgments of the Inter-American Court, the Court should inform the OAS General Assembly of the failure in its Annual Report and make pertinent recommendations regarding the state. Unfortunately, the OAS political bodies, in general, and its General Assembly, in particular, do not have the political will to impose any sanctions on states that fail to comply with their human rights obligations. The Court has attempted to address this shortcoming by maintaining cases on its docket and overseeing state compliance with its judgments, a function which is overburdening the Court.[40] At the end of 2008, the Court was monitoring state compliance in 94 cases. The Court holds private hearings to monitor compliance with its judgments and raises public awareness of state compliance by including a 'compliance with judgments' section on its website.

5.4 INTERIM MEASURES

International proceedings may be too slow to prevent the victim's injury or death in urgent situations. The ACHR affords the Commission and the Court the authority to act more expeditiously when warranted. '[I]n cases of extreme gravity and urgency, and when necessary to avoid irreparable damage to persons', the Convention authorizes the Court to 'adopt such provisional measures as it deems pertinent.'[41] The Commission may request that the Court take such measures even when the case is not yet on the Court's docket, such as when the person or persons to be protected are petitioners or witnesses before the Commission. The Commission is also authorized under its Rules of Procedure to request that the state take precautionary measures.

Pursuant to the ACHR, the Court can order a state to take immediate action or to refrain from some action if an individual's life or physical integrity is threatened. Provisional measures ordered by the Inter-American Court are binding on states parties to the ACHR. The most common circumstance warranting provisional measures for those cases already on the Court's docket involves threats to past and future witnesses. The Inter-American Commission and Court are often called upon to issue precautionary or provisional measures to protect human rights activists, journalists, and news organizations. These persons and organizations who report on human rights

[39] See Chapter 20, below.
[40] Remarks by Antônio Augusto Cançado Trindade, American Society of International Law Proceedings, 'The Future of International Law' (2007) 101 *ASIL Proc* 238, 240.
[41] ACHR, Art 63(2). Interim measures are referred to as 'precautionary measures' when ordered by the Commission and as 'provisional measures' when ordered by the Court.

abuses or official corruption may be considered by state agents to be traitors who have sullied the international reputation of the state. They may be subject to reprisals and, therefore, need special protection.[42]

Initially, the Inter-American Court restricted provisional measures to individually-named persons. This requirement proved problematic as naming of individuals could have the opposite effect from that desired; rather than protecting them, it could subject them to reprisals. The Court subsequently changed its criteria, stating that potential victims must be identifiable but not necessarily named individually.[43] In this way, entire communities threatened by authorities and paramilitary groups have been granted protection. For example, the 1,200 members of a peace community in Colombia, which was attempting to maintain its neutrality in the midst of civil conflict, were identifiable as those living in the community. Forty-seven members of the community had been murdered in the nine-month period before provisional measures were ordered.[44]

The Court has also ordered provisional measures to protect the populations of prisons and children's detention centres where overcrowding, inadequate living conditions, and untrained or abusive personnel resulted in violent outbreaks and the murder and injury of inmates. Provisional measures in such cases commonly consist of orders to the state to reduce overcrowding, confiscate weapons from prisoners, adapt the detention facilities to international standards, provide adequate medical care, and separate those convicted from those awaiting trial.[45]

At the end of 2008, the Court was monitoring compliance with 41 orders of provisional measures. In most cases, the Court orders the state to consult with the future beneficiaries of the measures to determine what protective measures would be most effective in the circumstances. Provisional measures have been unexpectedly effective in the Inter-American human rights system, although they can never serve as a solution for most human rights problems in the Western hemisphere.

5.5 ADVISORY JURISDICTION

A member state or organ of the OAS may request that the Inter-American Court issue an advisory opinion. An advisory opinion is an authoritative but non-binding explanation of a human rights provision or issue which can assist American states in understanding and complying with their international human rights obligations. Requests to the Court may concern interpretations of certain rights or procedures set

---

[42] See *Case of Gloria Giralt de García Prieto et al.* (Provisional Measures), IACtHR (26 September 2006); *Matter of Mery Naranjo et al.* (Provisional Measures), IACtHR (31 January 2008); *Matter of the Forensic Anthropology Foundation regarding Guatemala* (Provisional Measures), IACtHR (21 April 2006).

[43] *'Juvenile Reeducation Institute' v Paraguay*, IACtHR Series C No 112 (2 September 2004) para 108.

[44] *Peace Community de San José de Apartadó (Colombia)* (Provisional Measures), IACtHR (24 November 2000).

[45] See *The Matter of the Monagas Detention Center ('La Pica')* (Venezuela) (Provisional Measures), IACtHR (3 July 2007); *The Matter of the Children and Adolescents Deprived of Liberty in the 'Tatuapé Complex' of the CASA Foundation (Brazil)* (Provisional Measures), IACtHR (3 July 2007).

forth in the ACHR or in human rights provisions in other treaties. For example, in its request in the *Right to Information on Consular Assistance within the Framework of the Guarantees of Legal Due Process*, Mexico asked the Court's advice on whether the Vienna Convention on Consular Relations requires that an arresting state inform detained foreigners that they have the right to contact their national consulates.[46] The question arose because Mexican nationals, who had not had the opportunity to confer with the Mexican consulate, had been sentenced to death in the USA. The Inter-American Court interpreted the Vienna Convention to confer the right to receive consular assistance on detained foreign nationals.[47] Subsequent to the Court's advisory opinion, the US State Department issued and distributed a handbook to US law enforcement authorities informing them that foreign nationals have the mandatory right to assistance from their consulates.

At the request of a member state, the Court may also issue an advisory opinion regarding the compatibility of the state's domestic laws with international human rights instruments. For example, the Costa Rican government requested an advisory opinion pursuant to this clause when it asked the Court whether a proposed naturalization amendment to its constitution was in accordance with the ACHR and with Costa Rica's other international human rights obligations. The amendment in question would have allowed foreign women who married Costa Rican nationals to become naturalized Costa Rican citizens, but would not have provided the same opportunity for foreign males. The Inter-American Court relied on both the ACHR and natural law to determine that although states have the right to confer and regulate nationality, they may not do so by violating superior norms such as the right to non-discrimination.[48] After the Inter-American Court's advisory opinion in *Proposed Amendments to the Naturalization Provisions of the Costa Rican Constitution*, the Constitutional Chamber of the Supreme Court of Justice of Costa Rica declared, in accordance with the Court's opinion, that a state law on the naturalization of spouses could not discriminate on the basis of gender.[49]

The Inter-American Court draws on the medium of an advisory opinion to make important contributions to the development and evolution of principles of international law. In the *Proposed Amendments* opinion, the Court went beyond the question asked and specified that not all differences in treatment per se violate non discrimination provisions but only those that have 'no objective and reasonable justification'.[50] According to the Inter-American Court, some preferential and, thus, unequal treatment may be essential to obtain justice for those persons in a 'weak legal position'.[51]

---

[46] OC-16/99, *The Right to Information on Consular Assistance in the Framework of the Guarantees of Due Process of Law*, IACtHR Series A No 16 (1 October 1999). [47] Ibid, para 82.

[48] OC-4/84, *Proposed Amendments to the Naturalization Provisions of the Constitution of Costa Rica*, IACtHR Series A No 4 (19 January 1984).

[49] Exp 2965-S-91, Voto 3435–92, *Ricardo Fliman Wargraft v Director y el Jefe de la Sección de Opciones a Naturalizaciones*, Constitutional Chamber of the Supreme Court of Justice of Costa Rica (11 November 1992). [50] *Proposed Amendments*, n 48, para 56.

[51] Ibid.

Although an advisory opinion does not create legal obligations for states, it often exerts moral authority over them. It encourages, rather than compels, a course of action.

6 CHALLENGES TO THE INTER-AMERICAN SYSTEM

One of the biggest challenges to the Inter-American human rights system is chronic underfunding which imposes constraints on the functioning of the Inter-American Commission and the Inter-American Court. The increase in the number of contentious cases and requests for provisional measures, as well as the mounting number of judgments the Court is monitoring, stretch the Commission and Court's limited resources. Underfunding translates into fewer staff attorneys and an inadequate number of Commission or Court sessions. The work level warrants permanent sitting bodies to handle complaints expeditiously. The OAS General Assembly has resolved to examine the possibility that the Inter-American Commission and Court operate on a permanent basis, but funding is one of the major drawbacks to this consideration.[52]

For some years, the Commission and the Court have had to rely on voluntary contributions to supplement their allocation under the OAS budget. A percentage of these voluntary contributions come from OAS member states, some of which are subject to the jurisdiction of the Court.[53] Voluntary contributions, particularly those from states that are accused of human rights violations, can compromise the integrity of the Inter-American protection organs. Even the appearance of impropriety should be avoided. Also, commitments to make voluntary contributions can be withdrawn leaving the organs without the necessary funding to carry out scheduled work.

In the past, inadequate financial resources also negatively affected victim access to the Inter-American system. This problem may have been resolved in 2009 when the Permanent Council of the OAS created the Legal Assistance Fund of the Inter-American System of Human Rights to assist alleged victims of human rights abuse finance the cost of legal proceedings before the Inter-American Commission and Court.

Another basic challenge to the optimal functioning of the Inter-American human rights system is the lack of universality. All states should undertake to uphold the same criteria and principles of human rights protection. Belize, Canada, the USA, and some Caribbean Island nations have not ratified the ACHR or accepted the contentious jurisdiction of the Inter-American Court. Another three states have ratified the

---

[52] OAS General Assembly, Strengthening of human rights systems pursuant to the mandates arising from the Summit of the Americas, thirty-ninth Regular Session, OEA/Ser.P, AG/doc 5006/09 (4 June 2009).

[53] Contributors include: Canada, Chile, Colombia, Costa Rica, Denmark, Finland, France, Ireland, Italy, Mexico, Norway, the Republic of Korea, Spain, Sweden, USA, the European Union, the Inter-American Development Bank, the Office of the United Nations High Commissioner for Refugees, the Save the Children Foundation, and the University of Notre Dame. Draft Resolution, OEA/Ser.P, AG/doc. 4839/08 (22 May 2008).

ACHR but have not accepted the Court's jurisdiction. The lack of universality compli-
cates the functioning of the Inter-American human rights system. The Inter-American
Commission must apply different criteria when determining whether a state has violated
individual rights depending on whether the state is a party to the ACHR. Moreover, the
Commission cannot refer cases to the Inter-American Court if the respondent state has
not accepted the jurisdiction of the Court. The lack of universal ratification provides
an excuse to those states that have ratified human rights treaties that their treatment of
human rights should not be judged to a greater extent than states that do not ratify. The
Inter-American system for the protection of human rights will be more effective when
all states in the Western hemisphere have ratified all Inter-American and universal
human rights treaties and have accepted the jurisdiction of the Court.

States must do more, however, than merely ratify the ACHR and accept the jurisdiction of the Inter-American Court. States must also incorporate the substantive
rights of the ACHR and the judgments of the Inter-American Court into their legal
systems, and take the necessary legal measures to ensure that the judgments of the
Inter-American Court are self-executing in domestic courts. States must also follow
Commission recommendations. When states fulfill their duty to ensure and protect
rights on the domestic plane there will be fewer cases wherein one state repeatedly
engages in conduct that violates the same right of multiple victims. There will be fewer
human rights abuses, and the burden on international enforcement organs, such as
the Inter-American Court and Commission, will be eased.

7 CONCLUSION

The Inter-American human rights system has made significant progress in improving
the human rights situation in the Americas, although there are many improvements
still to be made. Initially it was feared that states would withdraw from the ACHR and
the jurisdiction of the Inter-American Court if they were held liable for human rights
violations and ordered to make reparations to victims. This problem did not materialize in a noteworthy respect. Trinidad and Tobago did denounce the ACHR and the
jurisdiction of the Inter-American Court in 1998 in a dispute over limitations on its
death penalty and the length of proceedings before the Inter-American Commission.
Peru also attempted to withdraw from the jurisdiction of the Court without denouncing the Convention. Although Trinidad and Tobago remains outside the Convention
system, Peru, after the fall of President Fujimori, announced by means of a legislative
resolution that the subsequent government considered itself subject to the contentious
jurisdiction of the Court.

Even before a Court judgment, states now acquiesce or acknowledge partial or total
international responsibility in approximately 42 per cent of contentious cases referred
to the Inter-American Court.[54] In response to Court-ordered reparations, states have

---

[54] Inter-American Court Annual Report 2008, n 12, 71.

paid financial compensation to the victims in 81 per cent of the cases, amended or repealed national laws, and held that self-amnesty laws are without legal effect. In these aspects, at least, the Inter-American human rights system is proving effective. The problem of impunity for human rights violations is still to be conquered. States, in general, have not complied with Court orders to investigate the violations and prosecute and punish the offenders.

The jurisprudence and reforms to the Inter-American human rights system are proving to be relevant to other human rights systems. The Inter-American system was the first human rights system to function in an underdeveloped region of the world where human rights abuses such as extra-judicial killings, torture, and disappearances were prevalent. The European human rights system initially dealt with states that had a history of democracy, and its cases primarily involved violations of the individual's due process rights. Since the Council of Europe admitted member states from the former Soviet Union, however, the European system is confronting the type of endemic abuses that have been common in the Inter-American system. Also, the African human rights system is likely to confront similar gross and systematic abuses. Consequently, the jurisprudence established by the Inter-American system should serve as a model for other regional human rights systems around the world.

FURTHER READING

ANTKOWIAK, 'Remedial Approaches to Human Rights Violations: the Inter-American Court of Human Rights and Beyond' (2008) 46 *Colum J Transnatl L* 351.

BUERGENTHAL, 'Remembering the Early Years of the Inter-American Court of Human Rights' (2005) 2 *NYU J Intl Law and Politics* 37.

—— and SHELTON, *Protecting Human Rights in the Americas: Cases and Materials* (NP Engel, 1995).

CAVALLARO and BREWER, 'Reevaluating Regional Human Rights Litigation in the Twenty-First Century: The Case of the Inter-American Court' (2008) 102 *AJIL* 768.

CERNA, 'Are We Headed in the Right Direction? Reflections on the New (2001) Rules of Procedure of the Inter-American Commission on Human Rights in Light of the Experience of the European System' in Bayefsky (ed), *Human Rights and Refugees, Internally Displaced Persons, and Migrant Workers: Essays in Memory of Joan Fitzpatrick and Arthur Helton* (Martinus Nijhoff, 2006) 387.

HARRIS and LIVINGSTONE (eds), *The Inter-American System of Human Rights* (Oxford University Press, 1998).

PASQUALUCCI, *The Practice and Procedure of the Inter-American Court of Human Rights* (Cambridge University Press, 2003).

—— 'Criminal Defamation and the Evolution of the Doctrine of Freedom of Expression in International Law: Comparative Jurisprudence of the Inter-American Court of Human Rights' (2006) 39 *Vand J Trans L* 379.

—— 'The Evolution of International Indigenous Rights in the Inter-American Human Rights System' (2006) 6 *HRLR* 281.

USEFUL WEBSITES

Inter-American Commission on Human Rights: <http://www.cidh.org>
Inter-American Court of Human Rights: <http://www.corteidh.or.cr>

20

EUROPE

Steven Greer

SUMMARY

This chapter considers the origins, historical development, and key characteristics of Europe's two pre-eminent transnational institutions for the legal protection of human rights—the Council of Europe and the European Union—and the challenges they face. The European Court of Human Rights, the Council of Europe's most significant achievement, is universally celebrated by human rights scholars and activists as the world's most successful international human rights tribunal. The relatively recent but rapidly developing interest in human rights shown by the European Union has also been widely welcomed. However, the European Court of Human Rights is in crisis, the most visible manifestation being the rising tide of individual applications which threatens to swamp it unless something dramatic is done soon, and the European Union's approach to human rights lacks coherence and consistency. There can be little doubt that both institutions face an increasingly interdependent future. But the form this should and is likely to take is only beginning to be debated.

1 INTRODUCTION

For two conflicting reasons Europe occupies a central and unique place in the history of international human rights law. First, it is, together with the USA, the birthplace of the now global processes of political, social, legal, and economic modernization which embody, amongst other things, liberalization, democratization, marketization, and internationalization. Second, and paradoxically, it was also the site of the Holocaust and a crucial theatre for the twentieth century's two world wars, events which together constituted or precipitated the most systematic and serious violations of human rights the world has ever seen.

In the second half of the twentieth century, this positive and negative heritage not only inspired and laid the foundations for international human rights law itself, it also led to increasing convergence in European political, constitutional, legal, and economic systems around a common institutional model formally defined by the values of democracy, human rights, the rule of law, and the democratically regulated market. These processes now operate on three principal and overlapping dimensions: European states, the Council of Europe, and the European Union (EU). While this chapter is devoted to the last two of these, it should be recognized that other international institutions with a human rights brief, including the UN and the Organization for Security and Cooperation in Europe, are also active across the continent. However, only the Council of Europe and the EU have legislative and/or judicial functions, without which the dynamic development of a distinctive European human rights law is not possible.

2 THE ORGANIZATION FOR SECURITY AND COOPERATION IN EUROPE

In addition to the Council of Europe and the EU, the most prominent pan-European intergovernmental organization with a human rights brief is the 56-member Organization for Security and Co-operation in Europe (OSCE), the largest regional security organization in the world.[1] Participating states from Europe, Central Asia, and North America have equal status and take politically, but not legally, binding decisions on a consensual basis. The OSCE was established in December 1994 as a more permanent post-Cold War version of the Conference on Security and Cooperation in Europe (CSCE). The CSCE was created in the early 1970s as an ad hoc multilateral forum for dialogue and negotiation between East and West in the phase of the Cold War known as détente. Its main achievements were the Helsinki Final Act, signed on 1 August 1975—which contained a number of key commitments on political, military, economic, environmental, and human rights issues central to the so-called 'Helsinki process'—and the Decalogue, ten fundamental principles governing the behaviour of states towards each other and towards their own citizens.

At its inception the OSCE was intended to assist in the management of the post-Cold War transition in Europe. Today, its main functions include crisis management, warning of and seeking to prevent impending conflict, and post-conflict rehabilitation. Among its wide-ranging security-related concerns, which include arms control and environmental issues, the OSCE monitors, reports on, and provides training and education in human rights, particularly in the fields of freedom of assembly and association, the right to liberty and fair trial, and the death penalty. Its four specialist human rights-related agencies are: the Office for Democratic Institutions and Human Rights (ODIHR), active in election observation, democratic development, and the promotion of human rights, tolerance, non-discrimination, and the rule of law; the Office of the Special Representative and Coordinator for Combating Trafficking in Human

---

[1] Galbreath, *The Organization for Security and Co-operation in Europe* (Routledge, 2007).

Beings, which supports the development and implementation of anti-trafficking policies; the OSCE Representative on Freedom of the Media who provides early warning
on violations of freedom of expression and promotes full compliance with OSCE press
freedom commitments; and the High Commissioner on National Minorities who
seeks to identify and to resolve ethnic tensions which might endanger peace, stability,
or friendly relations between participating states.

3 THE COUNCIL OF EUROPE

The Council of Europe was founded in Strasbourg in 1949 by ten West European
liberal democracies as one of a number of Cold War initiatives to promote their
interdependence, common identity, and collective security. Its main achievements,
and the principal focus of this chapter, were and remain, the European Convention
on Human Rights (ECHR) which, amongst other things, established the European
Court of Human Rights. The Council of Europe has also been responsible for over
200 other treaties on a wide range of issues. Three of the most important of these—
the European Social Charter, the European Convention for the Prevention of
Torture and Inhuman or Degrading Treatment or Punishment, and the European
Framework Convention for the Protection of National Minorities—are considered
further below. But first, the origins of the Council of Europe and its key institutions
will be reviewed.

3.1 ORIGINS

At the core of the political history of Europe in the nineteenth and twentieth centuries
is the story of the formation of nation-states and their struggles between competing
conceptions of their own identity—liberal or authoritarian—and their battles with
each other. By the end of the twentieth century three main lessons, both for human
rights and for international peace, had been learned. First, competitive European
nationalism, unrestrained by effective international institutions, is likely to result in
massively destructive international armed conflict. Second, the attempt after the First
World War to protect national minorities and to secure European peace by establishing a collective complaints procedure to the League of Nations had failed.[2] Third,
liberal democracies with regulated capitalist economies committed to the rule of law
and constitutional rights are essential not only for national prosperity and justice but
also for international peace.

Therefore, as the Second World War drew to a close, proposals for increased European
collaboration were debated by the Western allies including the USA. Towards the end
of 1948 the governments of Belgium, France, and the UK agreed to establish a Council

---

[2] See Chapter 1, above.

of Europe and invited Denmark, Ireland, Italy, Norway, and Sweden to participate in the negotiations. Luxembourg and the Netherlands joined later. At its foundation, the Council had four main objectives: to contribute to the prevention of another war between West European states; to provide a statement of common values contrasting sharply with Soviet-style communism, hence the almost exclusive emphasis on civil and political rights in the ECHR; to re-enforce a sense of common identity and purpose should the Cold War become an active armed conflict; and to establish an early-warning device by which a drift towards authoritarianism in any member state could be detected and dealt with by complaints from other states to an independent transnational judicial tribunal. This early-warning function was also itself inextricably linked to the prevention of war, since the slide towards the Second World War suggested the rise of authoritarian regimes in Europe made the peace and security of the continent more precarious. The Council of Europe's founding statute contains several core principles. Certain unspecified 'spiritual and moral values'—'the cumulative influence of Greek philosophy, Roman law, the Western Christian Church, the humanism of the Renaissance and the French Revolution'[3]—are said to constitute the 'common heritage' of the signatory states, to be the 'true source of individual freedom, political liberty and the rule of law', and to form the 'basis of all genuine democracy'. 'Closer unity' between like-minded European states is also deemed to be required in order to implement these principles and to promote 'economic and social progress'.[4]

3.2 KEY INSTITUTIONS

In addition to the European Court of Human Rights, considered in Section 4, below, the Council of Europe's key institutions are the Committee of Ministers, the Parliamentary Assembly, the Secretariat, the European Commissioner for Human Rights, the Congress of Regional and Local Authorities, and the Conference of International Non-governmental Organizations.

The Committee of Ministers, the executive and formal policy-making body, consists of the foreign ministers of member states who usually meet twice a year at ministerial level, and for several days a month at the level of Deputies, their Permanent Representatives in Strasbourg. In addition to having promulgated the Council of Europe's 200-plus treaties, the Committee of Ministers also supervises execution of judgments of the European Court of Human Rights.

The Parliamentary Assembly of the Council of Europe (PACE) has 318 members (plus a further 318 substitutes) elected on a proportional basis by, and from, national parliaments. It meets four times a year in Strasbourg's Palais de l'Europe which it shares with the European Parliament, the parliamentary body of the EU. PACE's chief functions are to make recommendations, to pass resolutions and express opinions about Council of Europe policy, to monitor state compliance with it, and to elect

---

[3] Robertson, *The Council of Europe: Its Structure, Functions and Achievements* (Stevens & Sons, 1961) 2.
[4] Statute of the Council of Europe, preamble.

the European Commissioner for Human Rights, the Secretary General and Deputy Secretary General of the Council of Europe, as well as judges to the European Court of Human Rights from the lists of three candidates presented by member states. It has no legislative powers.

The Secretary General presides over the Secretariat, the Council of Europe's bureaucracy, and also has some monitoring responsibilities with respect to the ECHR. The post of European Commissioner for Human Rights—not to be confused with the now defunct European Commission of Human Rights—was created in 2000 to promote education and awareness of human rights in member states including collaborating with national and international human rights institutions and ombudsmen, identifying human rights shortcomings in the law and practice of member states, and promoting effective observance of all Council of Europe human rights instruments. As part of his general monitoring responsibility the Commissioner can also receive individual complaints but can neither adjudicate them nor present them before any national or international court. However, when Protocol No 14 comes into effect (see below) the Commissioner will be able to submit written comments to the European Court of Human Rights, and to take part in Chamber and Grand Chamber hearings, although not to initiate litigation. The Congress of Local and Regional Authorities—with 318 members plus 318 substitutes drawn from local and regional representatives—advises the Committee of Ministers, PACE, and member states on a wide range of local and regional issues. The 400 or so NGOs with participatory status at the Council of Europe meet three or four times a year at the Conference of International Non-Governmental Organizations, constituting civil society's contribution to the Council of Europe's 'quadrilogue' with the Committee of Ministers, the Parliamentary Assembly, and the Congress of Local and Regional Authorities.

It is unclear whether the Council of Europe could be said to have an overall human rights policy beyond the very general one of drafting treaties and other documents and promoting state compliance with them. Nor is it clear which institution is most influential in policy formation. Some insiders claim specific policies are advocated by specific states, others claim that they originate in the various committees of the Secretariat, while others believe the goals and agendas of particular individuals are central. However, it is widely acknowledged that integration and coordination between the activities of the Council's many different agencies and institutions could be improved. While some insiders consider that PACE has the greatest legitimacy regarding human rights policy formation—particularly as it consists of members of national legislatures—others believe the European Commissioner for Human Rights has the most credibility when it comes to identifying priorities.[5]

3.3 KEY INSTRUMENTS

As already indicated, while the ECHR, considered in the following section, is the Council of Europe's principal achievement, three of its many other treaties—the

---

[5] Information for this paragraph was collected in July 2007 from interviews with some key Council of Europe officials in Strasbourg, generously funded by a Nuffield Foundation Social Sciences Small Grant.

European Social Charter, the European Convention for the Prevention of Torture and Inhuman or Degrading Treatment or Punishment, and the European Framework Convention for the Protection of National Minorities—also warrant brief discussion.

There are five significant differences between the European Social Charter 1961 (revised in 1996) and the ECHR. First, the ECHR contains mostly civil and political rights whereas the Charter contains a catalogue of social and economic rights, mainly those relating to housing, health, education, and work. Second, accession to the Charter, unlike the Convention, is not a condition of Council of Europe membership, and, to date, 39 of the Council's 47 states have signed and ratified the original, the revised Charter, or both. Third, the Charter has no judicial complaints process, nor, fourth, a right of individual complaint. Compliance is instead, fifth, monitored in two ways by the 15 independent and impartial members of the European Committee of Social Rights (ECSR). Under an optional protocol, the Committee can make reports on complaints received from employers' organizations, trade unions, and NGOs, which in turn may provide the basis for recommendations by the Committee of Ministers. The ECSR also publishes its 'conclusions' every year based on annual state self-assessment reports. If the Committee decides that states have not responded to its conclusions on previous reports appropriately, the Committee of Ministers, guided by a Governmental Committee—comprising representatives of states parties to the Charter and observers from European employers' organizations and trade unions— can also make appropriate resolutions and recommendations.[6]

The European Convention for the Prevention of Torture and Inhuman or Degrading Treatment or Punishment 1987 (ECPT)—amended as from March 2002—aims to 'strengthen by non-judicial means of a preventive nature',[7] the right of everyone detained by a public authority in a member state not to be subjected to torture or to inhuman or degrading treatment or punishment. It seeks to fulfil this objective by providing an enforcement regime based on unannounced visits to places of detention by the European Committee for the Prevention of Torture and Inhuman or Degrading Treatment or Punishment. The Committee is obliged to inform states of its intention to conduct a visit but not of the precise locations chosen for inspection. While all states are subject to periodic visits, in principle once every four years, ad hoc visits are at the Committee's discretion and are prompted by concerns expressed by individuals, groups, or other state parties that ill-treatment is occurring in a particular jurisdiction or at a particular place. The purpose of visits is to open up dialogue with the state concerned. Missions end with a meeting at which members of the delegation convey initial impressions to officials in the expectation of a response to the subsequent report. Although formally confidential, publication of reports has become the rule rather than the exception. The Committee is empowered to 'make a public statement' if a state fails to cooperate or to improve defects in its compliance with the ECPT to which its attention has been drawn. Confidential reports are also submitted to the Committee of Ministers and follow-up visits can be made to assess progress in implementing recommendations. Now a condition of Council of Europe membership, the

---

[6] Harris and Darcy, *The European Social Charter* (Transnational, 2000).   [7] ECPT, preamble.

ECPT has been signed and ratified by every member state. However, it is not clear if it has made any difference to preventing the torture or ill-treatment of detainees.[8]

The Framework Convention for the Protection of National Minorities 1995 marks a departure from the Council of Europe's commitment to individual rather than collective rights, prompted, in the 1990s, by the 'shock of interethnic violence that afflicted Eastern Europe with the unfreezing of the Cold War'.[9] The word 'Framework' indicates that the principles this instrument contains are not directly applicable in the domestic legal systems of member states but require implementation through national legislation and public policy. The Framework Convention aims to ensure that states respect the rights of national minorities and develop their culture and identity. States are also required to combat discrimination, promote equality, guarantee certain freedoms in relation to access to the media, minority languages, and education, and encourage participation of national minorities in public life. The Committee of Ministers monitors national compliance with the assistance of an appointed Advisory Committee of independent and impartial experts. The Advisory Committee examines the reports states are required to submit at five-yearly intervals or when the Committee of Ministers so requests. Meetings may also be held with officials and country visits may be conducted. Although the Advisory Committee does not deal with individual complaints, it may, nevertheless, receive information from individuals and other sources such as NGOs. In the light of the opinion of the Advisory Committee, the Committee of Ministers makes its final decision ('conclusion') concerning the adequacy of measures taken by any state party to implement the Framework Convention and may also, where appropriate, make recommendations. Conclusions, recommendations, the Advisory Committee's opinions, and any comments by the state concerned are made public. To date the Framework Convention has been signed and ratified by 39 of the Council of Europe's 47 member states.

4 THE EUROPEAN CONVENTION ON HUMAN RIGHTS

The Convention for the Protection of Human Rights and Fundamental Freedoms (more commonly known as the 'European Convention on Human Rights' or 'ECHR') was drafted by the Council of Europe in 1950 and entered into force in 1953. Its ratification has been a condition of membership of the Council of Europe since the beginning. The central objective of the ECHR is to provide an independent judicial process at Strasbourg which can authoritatively determine whether a Convention right has been violated by a given member state. This section considers the substantive rights

---

[8] Evans and Morgan, *Preventing Torture: A Study of the European Convention for the Prevention of Torture and Inhuman or Degrading Treatment or Punishment* (Clarendon Press, 1998) 159.

[9] Weller (ed), *The Rights of Minorities: A Commentary on the European Framework Convention for the Protection of National Minorities* (OUP, 2005) vii.

the Convention contains, reviews the establishment and development of its key institutions and processes, describes the current inter-state complaints process and the two
(under Protocols No 11 and 14) for individual applications, discusses the resolution of
complaints by friendly settlement and adjudication of the merits, and finally outlines
how the Committee of Ministers supervises the execution of the Court's judgments.

4.1 SUBSTANTIVE RIGHTS

The ECHR is similar in content to other international and national instruments which
deal with civil and political rights, particularly the International Covenant on Civil
and Political Rights. Article 1 requires member states 'to secure to everyone within
their jurisdiction' the rights and freedoms the Convention contains. Articles 2 to 13
provide the rights: to life; not to be subjected to torture or to inhuman or degrading
treatment or punishment; not to be held in slavery or servitude or to be required to
perform forced or compulsory labour; to freedom from arbitrary arrest and detention; to a fair trial; not to be punished without law; to respect for private and family
life, home, and correspondence; to freedom of thought, conscience, and religion; to
freedom of expression; to freedom of assembly and association; to marry; and to an
effective national remedy for the violation of a Convention right. Article 14 states that
the enjoyment of any Convention right shall be secured without discrimination on
any ground such as sex, race, colour, language, religion, political or other opinion,
national or social origin, association with a national minority, property, birth, or other
status. Article 15 provides for the suspension of all but a handful of rights 'in time of
war or other public emergency threatening the life of the nation', provided such 'derogations' are 'strictly required by the exigencies of the situation' and not incompatible
with other international legal obligations. Article 16 states that nothing in Articles
10, 11, and 14 shall be regarded as preventing restrictions on the political activities
of aliens. Article 17 prohibits anything in the Convention from being interpreted
as implying the right to engage in any activity, or to perform any act, aimed at the
destruction of any Convention right or freedom, or its limitation to a greater extent
than the Convention itself permits. Article 18 limits restrictions upon rights to those
purposes expressly provided.

   Fourteen subsequent protocols have either added further rights or instigated procedural reforms. The former are optional and usually come into effect when a specified
number of states have completed the formalities. Protocol No 1, for example, contains
rights to education, the peaceful enjoyment of possessions, and free elections, while
Protocol No 4 provides the right not to be imprisoned for debt, the right to freedom
of movement, the right of nationals not to be expelled from the state to which they
belong, and the right of aliens not to be collectively expelled. Protocol No 6 abolishes
the death penalty except in time of war. Protocol No 7 contains procedural safeguards
regarding the expulsion of aliens, the right of appeal in criminal proceedings, the right
to compensation for wrongful conviction, the right not to be tried or punished twice
in the same state for the same offence, as well as the equal right of spouses under the

law. Protocol No 12 outlaws discrimination in relation to any right 'set forth by law', in contrast with Article 14 ECHR which prohibits discrimination only with respect to Convention rights. Protocol No 13 outlaws the death penalty even in time of war. Protocol No 14bis (see Section 4.2, below), which will be in force for only a year, is the only procedural protocol so far to be introduced without universal assent. Once a universal procedural protocol comes into effect, its provisions are seamlessly incorporated into the revised text of the Convention and it no longer has a separate identity.

4.2 INSTITUTIONAL AND PROCEDURAL BACKGROUND

At its inception it was agreed that the Convention's main *modus operandi* should be complaints by states against each other (the 'inter-state process'). Some states also chose to permit individual applications before this became compulsory in 1998. The ECHR was at first, therefore, much more about protecting the democratic identity of member states through the medium of human rights, and about promoting international cooperation between them, than it was about providing individuals with redress for human rights violations by national public authorities.

When it was first established, the Convention system had three institutions. The European Commission of Human Rights was the first port of call for applications both from states and individuals. It ascertained the facts, determined if the admissibility criteria were satisfied, and explored the possibility of friendly settlement. If no settlement could be found the Commission expressed a non-binding opinion on whether the Convention had been violated. Then, providing the jurisdiction of the European Court of Human Rights—the second institution which began operating in 1959—had been accepted by the state or states concerned, the case could be referred by the Commission, the respondent state, or the state of which the applicant was a national—but not by individual applicants themselves—to the Court for a legally binding decision. The Committee of Ministers—the third institution—also decided cases over which the European Court did not have jurisdiction and those which the Commission did not refer to the Court. Both the Commission and the Court were staffed by part-time judges.

For most of its first 30 years the ECHR was largely ignored by just about everyone, including victims of human rights abuses, lawyers, politicians, jurists, and other commentators. Only 800 or so individual complaints were received by the Strasbourg institutions a year. But from the mid-1980s onwards things began to change dramatically. First, it became clear that inter-state complaints—just under two dozen in the Convention's entire history[10]—were largely a dead letter, not least because litigation is a hostile act in most circumstances and, therefore, not an ideal vehicle for cultivating international interdependence. Second, in sharp contrast, the rate of individual

[10] Committee of Ministers, Protocol No 14 to the Convention for the Protection of Human Rights and Fundamental Freedoms, Amending the Control System of the Convention, Explanatory Report (12 May 2004) para 11.

applications has risen steeply. By the late 1990s it was already clear that this had reached crisis proportions and in 2008 there were almost 50,000 applications, more than the grand total for the first four decades.[11] This was due partly to the third significant change: the huge expansion in the number of states belonging to the Council of Europe, from a mere ten in 1950 to 46 by the end of the 1990s and 47, with a combined population of 800 million, by the end of the first decade of the twenty-first century. All the former communist states of Central and Eastern Europe, except Belarus, are now members. A fourth change, and one of the key factors in the rising application rate, is the fact that the ECHR is now much better known by lawyers and by the general public throughout Europe. On 1 January 2009, for example, over 97,000 applications were awaiting a decision about admissibility, more than half of which had been lodged against one of three states. Two—Russia and Romania—joined the Convention system in the 1990s, while the third, Turkey, was one of the original signatories but did not permit individual applications until 1987.[12]

In response to the rising application rate, the judicial process was reformed by Protocol No 11 with effect from 1 November 1998. The European Commission of Human Rights was abolished and the restructured Court became a professional full-time institution with responsibility for registering applications, ascertaining the facts, deciding if the admissibility criteria are satisfied, seeking friendly resolution, delivering legally binding judgments, and issuing advisory opinions[13] at the request of the Committee of Ministers. Protocol No 11 also stripped the Committee of Ministers of its power to settle cases on the merits, a responsibility deemed incompatible with the now enhanced judicial character of the complaints processes, and limited its role to supervising the execution of the Court's judgments. Both the right of individual petition and acceptance of the Court's jurisdiction also became compulsory, although by the 1990s each had already been voluntarily endorsed by all member states.

However, by 2000, Protocol No 11 was already officially recognized as inadequate, not least because the consequences of the post-communist enlargement had not been adequately anticipated. In May 2004, after further debate, another modest reform package, Protocol No 14, was unanimously endorsed by all states parties. The most significant changes are to the applications and enforcement of judgments processes, considered further below. By early 2005 it had already become clear that these changes would not make much difference to the rising tide of applications and that something more radical was required. So in May 2005 a Group of Wise Persons was appointed to make further proposals. But their report, made public in November 2006, contains nothing new of any substance, largely recycles ideas already rejected in the course of the Protocol No 14 debate, and assumes that Protocol No 14 will soon come into

---

[11] European Court of Human Rights, The European Court of Human Rights—Some Facts and Figures 1959–2009, 4, available at: <http://www.echr.coe.int/NR/rdonlyres/ACD46A0F-615A-48B9-89D6-8480AFCC29FD/0/FactsAndFiguresEN.pdf>. [12] Ibid.

[13] To date, the Court has only delivered one: *Advisory opinion on certain legal questions concerning the lists of candidates submitted with a view to the election of judges to the European Court of Human Rights* (12 February 2008).

effect.[14] However, in December 2006, to everyone's great surprise and in spite of the fact that the Russian government had already approved it, the Russian parliament refused to ratify Protocol No 14, ostensibly because of objections to single-judge formations. This caused great consternation in Strasbourg and, notwithstanding intense diplomatic pressure, by May 2009 the Russian parliament had still not been persuaded to change its mind. As a result, the Council of Europe provided an interim set of optional measures intended to apply to the other 46 member states. Derived from Protocol No 14, Protocol No 14bis enabled admissibility decisions to be taken by single judge formations and for cases to be judged on the merits by three-judge committees where the Convention had patently been violated. The European Court also sought to manage its mushrooming workload by prioritizing applications according to the seriousness and urgency of the complaint. However, again to everyone's surprise, in January 2010 both chambers of the Russian parliament voted in favour of ratifying Protocol No 14, now scheduled to come into effect on 1 June 2010.

4.3 COMPLAINTS PROCEDURES

Protocol No 14bis does not alter the inter-state applications process at all and, until Protocol No 14 comes into effect individual applications will be processed in one of two ways. Protocol No 14bis will govern those applications made against states which have already agreed to be bound by it, either by signature and ratification or by a declaration that the corresponding provisions of Protocol No 14 will apply provisionally, while Protocol No 11 will apply to Russia and to any other states which have, by then, not yet completed the Protocol No 14bis formalities.

4.3.1 Inter-state applications

The inter-state applications process is set out in Figure 20.1, below. Although not frequently used, and less than a resounding success in correcting alleged violations, it can nevertheless have considerable symbolic significance.[15] In 2009, an application made by Georgia concerning multiple alleged violations of the Convention rights of Georgians living in the Russian Federation was ruled admissible by the European Court of Human Rights.[16] However, the more successful the Council of Europe becomes in cultivating interdependence between member states, the less likely inter-state complaints will be.

Applicant states lodge complaints against respondent states with the Registry of the Court which, as a result of Protocol No 14, can initiated the friendly settlement procedure (see Section 4.4.1, below) at any stage of the proceedings and not just post-admissibility as under Protocol No 11. Having received an application the Registry informs the Court's President who notifies the respondent state and allocates the complaint to

---

[14] Report of the Group of Wise Persons to the Committee of Ministers, Cm(2006)203 (15 November 2006).

[15] Greer, *The European Court of Human Rights: Achievements, Problems and Prospects* (CUP, 2006) 24–8.   [16] *Georgia v Russia (No 1)*, App no 13255/07, 3 July 2009.

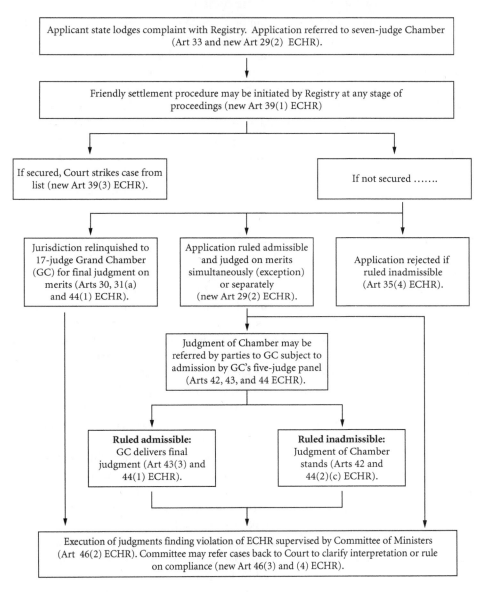

Figure 20.1 The inter-state applications process as amended by Protocol No 14

one of the Court's five Sections. A seven-judge Chamber, including the judges elected in respect of applicant and respondent states, is then constituted to consider admissibility, the requirements for which are much less exacting than those for individual applications. The ECHR must have been binding on the applicant and respondent states, and applicable to the persons concerned within the jurisdiction of the respondent state, at the material time and place. All domestic remedies must have been exhausted, except where the allegation concerns legislation or an ongoing administrative practice. The application must also be lodged with the Court within a period of six months from the date on which the final decision on the relevant subject matter was taken in the respondent state's legal system. While a prima facie case is not required in the formal sense, inter-state applications will be rejected as inadmissible if the allegations concerned are wholly unsubstantiated. Protocol No 14 permits the Committee of Ministers to refer cases decided against respondent states back to the Court for clarification about the original judgment or for a ruling about compliance, while the processes of friendly settlement, judgment of the merits, and the roles of the Court's Grand Chamber and the Committee of Ministers are substantially the same as under the individual applications process as amended by Protocol No 14 (see Sections 4.4 and 4.5, below).

4.3.2 Individual applications

Since Protocol No 11 will be redundant for individual applications when Protocol No 14 comes into effect on 1 June 2010, it is not necessary to discuss it in detail here. Under Protocol No 11 the management of formal applications was the responsibility of a Judge Rapporteur assisted by a case-processing lawyer from the Registry. The Judge Rapporteur examined and prepared the file, including requiring documents and further particulars from the parties, and channelled the complaint for an admissibility decision—together with proposals about its disposal—either to a three-judge committee, if it appeared to be clearly inadmissible, or to a Chamber of seven judges if its inadmissibility was not so clear. Under Article 28 ECHR a committee could, and still can, by unanimous and final decision, declare an application inadmissible, or strike it off the list, 'where such a decision can be taken without further examination',[17] a fate which befell between 80 and 90 per cent of applications rejected as inadmissible or struck off.[18] Cases which could not be settled unanimously were referred to a seven-judge Chamber for a decision on admissibility and merits together with a report from the Judge Rapporteur summarizing the facts, indicating the issues raised, and making a proposal as to what should happen next, for example a decision against admissibility or further correspondence with the parties. Currently, less than 5 per cent of formal individual applications cross the admissibility threshold.[19]

Protocol No 14 alters the individual applications process in several ways (see Figure 20.2, below). First, it will be possible for the friendly settlement procedure (see Section 4.4.1, below) to be initiated by the Registry at any stage of the proceedings and not just post-admissibility as before. Second, all formal applications will be channelled to 'formations' of a single judge and registry rapporteur rather than to three-judge committees. But the judge elected with respect to a particular state will not be permitted to sit on a single-judge formation hearing applications against that

---

[17] ECHR, Art 28.

[18] Report of the Evaluation Group to the Committee of Ministers on the European Court of Human Rights, EG Court 1 (2001) (27 September 2001) para 28.

[19] European Court of Human Rights, Annual Report 2008, 137, available at: <http://www.echr.coe.int/NR/rdonlyres/D5B2847D-640D-4A09-A70A-7A1BE66563BB/0/ANNUAL_REPORT_2008.pdf>.

Figure 20.2 The individual applications process as amended by Protocol No 14

state. While the rapporteur will manage the file containing all relevant documents, the judge can reject as inadmissible, or strike off the Court's list, the vast majority of applications (where such a decision can be taken without further examination), and direct the remainder to a committee or Chamber. Protocol No 14 preserves the existing admissibility tests and adds a new one. As before individual applications can be ruled inadmissible if the applicant (including legal persons and non-governmental organizations) was not a victim of a Convention violation, redress has not been sought through the national legal system as far as it could have been taken ('exhaustion of domestic remedies'), more than six months have elapsed between the last national decision on the matter and formal application to Strasbourg, the complaint is substantially the same as one already examined, it is incompatible with the Convention, it is an abuse of process, and/or it is 'manifestly ill-founded' (obviously has no hope of being settled in the applicant's favour). When it comes into effect Protocol No 14 will also enable the Court to reject as inadmissible complaints by applicants where no significant disadvantage has been suffered and the issue has been 'duly considered' by a domestic tribunal.[20] But, for the first two years the new applications procedure is in operation, this test may only be applied by Chambers and the Grand Chamber.

Under Protocol No 14, unanimous committees of three judges will also be able to decide simultaneously on admissibility and to judge the merits of applications which disclose clear-cut violations according to well-established Convention case law. Such 'manifestly well-founded' cases currently account for approximately 70 per cent of judgments, most of which concern 'repetitive' violations which the Court has already condemned in the respondent state concerned.[21] While states may contest recourse to this procedure, they cannot veto it. The judge elected with respect to the respondent state may be invited to participate as a member of a three-judge committee, particularly when the exhaustion of domestic remedies is at issue. It has been estimated that the combined effect of both single-judge formations and the new three-judge committee procedure will enhance the Court's case processing efficiency by 20–5 per cent.[22]

Protocol No 14 preserves the Court's power to strike an application off its list if the applicant does not intend to pursue it, the matter has been resolved (for example by friendly settlement between the parties), or where, for any other reason, further examination is no longer considered necessary. Legal aid will also continue to be available for individual applicants who lack sufficient means.

4.4 RESOLUTION OF COMPLAINTS

All admissible inter-state and individual applications—provided they have not been struck off or settled summarily in 'manifestly well-founded cases' by committees of three judges—are resolved either by friendly settlement or full adjudication of the merits.

---

[20] New Art 35(3)(b).
[21] The term 'manifestly well-founded', unlike 'manifestly ill-founded', is not an official term of art. Protocol No 14bis to the Convention for the Protection of Human Rights and Fundamental Freedoms, Explanatory Report (27 May 2009) para 16.   [22] Ibid, para 3.

4.4.1 Friendly settlement

Friendly settlement is open to the parties at any stage of the proceedings under Protocol No 14 as it was before. However when it comes into effect the European Court (in practice the Registry) will be able to place itself at the disposal of the parties at any stage of the proceedings, in both inter-state and individual applications, with a view to securing friendly settlement on the basis of respect for human rights. The Registry can also offer advice about the terms. In individual cases friendly settlements typically involve offers of money by the respondent state, some other benefit (for example a residence permit the applicant claims to have been deprived of by the alleged violation), and sometimes an undertaking to make legislative or policy changes. Nearly all friendly settlements are formally approved by the Court and recorded in the annual reports as 'judgments (friendly settlement only)'. Between 1 November 1998 and 31 December 2008 there were 898 judgments by friendly settlement, 9 per cent of the total number of judgments.[23]

4.4.2 Adjudication on the merits

Most admissible applications not resolved by friendly settlement or struck off for other reasons are judged on the merits by Chambers of seven judges. However, subject to the consent of the parties, a Chamber may relinquish jurisdiction to a Grand Chamber of 17 judges where the application raises a serious question affecting the interpretation of the ECHR or where there is a possibility of a departure from previous case law. Although this is not expressly limited to applications formally declared admissible, by definition, no inadmissible application could fulfil this test. But relinquishment to the Grand Chamber is extremely rare, occurring, for example, in an average of only five cases a year between 2002 and 2005, out of an annual average of around 850 judgments on the merits.[24] From 1959–2008 the Court delivered 10,573 judgments, half of which concerned four of the Council of Europe's 47 member states: Italy (1,953), Turkey (1,939), France (740), and Russia (643).[25] From 1959–98 the Court delivered a total of 837 judgments, only 8 per cent of the total from 1959 to 2008 and less than the annual average of around 970 from 1 November 1998 to 2008.[26] Between 1 November 1998 and 31 December 2008, judgments on the merits constituted 88 per cent of the Court's judgments, around 95 per cent of which resulted in a finding of at least one violation.[27] Over this period the provisions of the Convention most frequently found to have been violated were the right to fair trial under Article 6 (73 per cent of judgments finding at least one violation, 57 per cent of which concerned excessive length of proceedings), the right to peaceful enjoyment of possessions under Article 1 of Protocol No 1 (22 per cent), and the right to liberty and security under Article 5 (15 per cent).[28]

---

[23] Annual Report, n 19, 137, 139.

[24] Mowbray, 'An Examination of the Work of the Grand Chamber of the European Court of Human Rights' [2007] *PL* 507, 509; Annual Report, n 19, 139.

[25] Facts and Figures, n 11, 5. The first judgment on the merits was delivered in the case of *Lawless v Ireland* (1979–1980) 1 EHRR 15, on 1 July 1961.

[26] Facts and Figures, ibid, 5; Annual Report, n 19, 139.   [27] Annual Report, ibid, 137 and 139.

[28] Ibid, 139.

Judgments on the merits—which rely mostly on written submissions from the parties but in certain cases also oral public hearings—are drafted by a Judge Rapporteur, assisted by the judge elected in respect of the respondent state or in some cases by a drafting committee, and put to a vote of all judges sitting on the particular panel. Typically judgments contain summaries of the facts, the history of the dispute including a review of relevant domestic law, the arguments presented by both parties, relevant provisions of the ECHR, a concise statement of the substantive result, plus concurring and dissenting opinions if any.

In urgent cases, where serious consequences such as death or torture could ensue before the matter is resolved, a Chamber may 'indicate to the parties any interim measure which it considers should be adopted'.[29] The number of such requests has increased greatly in recent years, reaching over 3,000 in 2008,[30] mostly in cases involving imminent expulsion or extradition. As a result of the judgment of the Grand Chamber in *Mamatkulov and Askarov v Turkey*[31] the Court now regards interim measures as binding on respondent states with, in most cases, failure to comply constituting a violation of the obligation under Article 34 ECHR not to hinder the right of individual application. Breaches of interim measures are, however, uncommon.

In judging the merits, the primary issue the Court has to consider is whether, on the evidence presented, the respondent state has violated the ECHR. This involves interpreting the alleged misconduct in context and determining what the sparse and abstract statements of the relevant rights mean, guided by the fact that a handful of Convention rights are subject to no express exceptions and cannot be suspended under Article 15, while the remainder are subject to various express limitations and can also be suspended under Article 15. The Court also applies a dozen or so 'principles of interpretation' not found in the text of the Convention itself but identified and developed in the process of litigation.[32] These are rooted in the 'teleological principle', derived from Articles 31 to 33 of the Vienna Convention on the Law of Treaties 1969 which requires the text of international treaties to be interpreted in good faith according to the ordinary meaning of their terms in context—unless any special meaning was intended by the parties—and in the light of the overall object and purpose of the treaty in question. But, unlike most international treaties which are merely reciprocal agreements between states, the ECHR is a 'constitutional instrument of European public order in the field of human rights', which creates a 'network of mutual bilateral undertakings ... [and] ... objective obligations'.[33] The principle of effective protection of individual rights holds that, given the primary function of the ECHR, rights should be interpreted broadly and exceptions narrowly. This is linked to the principle of non-abuse of rights and limitations which prohibits states and others from undermining the protection of rights by abusing either the rights themselves or their limitations. However, the principles of implied rights and implied limitations allow some scope for extensions of rights, and also inherent but not extensive limitations, to be read into the

---

[29] Rules of Court, rule 39.   [30] Annual Report, n 19, 12.   [31] (2005) 41 EHRR 25.

[32] See Greer, n 15, ch 4.

[33] *Ireland v UK* (1980) 2 EHRR 25, para 239; *Austria v Italy* (1961) YB 116, 138.

text. The principle of positive obligations allows the Court to interpret the ECHR in a manner which imposes obligations upon states actively to protect Convention rights and not merely the negative obligation to avoid violating them.

Armed with the principle of autonomous interpretation the Court can define some of the Convention's key terms in order to prevent states conveniently re-defining their way around their obligations, for instance, by preventing crimes being re-designated as merely 'administrative infractions'. Similarly, the principle of evolutive, or dynamic, interpretation enables outmoded conceptions of how terms in the Convention were originally understood to be abandoned when significant, durable, and—according to the principle of commonality—pan-European changes in the climate of European public opinion have occurred, for example that homosexuality and transsexualism are aspects of private life requiring respect from public authorities. The twin principles of subsidiarity and review indicate that the role of the Court is subsidiary to that of member states and is limited to determining whether the Convention has been violated rather than acting as final court of appeal or fourth instance.

The principle of proportionality, closely allied with the margin of appreciation, limits interference with Convention rights to that which is least intrusive in pursuit of a legitimate objective, while the margin of appreciation, typically described as a 'doctrine' rather than a principle, refers to the room for manoeuvre the Strasbourg institutions are prepared to accord national authorities in fulfilling their Convention obligations. Pervasive in the ECHR are the closely related principles of legality, the rule of law, and procedural fairness—which seek to subject the exercise of public power to effective, formal legal constraints in order to avoid arbitrariness—and the principle of democracy, which assumes that human rights flourish best in the context of democratic political institutions and a tolerant social climate.

Even if a judgment declares the ECHR to have been violated, an award of compensation is not automatic and, although some general principles have been identified, the relevant case law is not consistent.[34] While the Court generally seeks to remain faithful to all its own previous decisions, these are not formally binding precedents, nor is there much doctrinal exposition as in the common law tradition. Most judgments on the merits, therefore, amount to little more than decisions on the facts where the precise circumstances of the dispute are held to constitute or not to constitute a violation of the ECHR, but which establish little of general application beyond. Moreover, judgments against respondent states typically declare only that the ECHR has been violated because the Court considers itself less well placed than national authorities to be more prescriptive about what precisely should be done to correct it.

However, recently, in a small number of so-called 'pilot judgments', the Court has shown greater willingness to indicate the type of remedial action required, primarily in order to stem floods of similar complaints. For example, in *Broniowski v Poland* the Grand Chamber held that the applicant's right to the peaceful enjoyment of possessions under Article 1 Protocol No 1 had been violated by the expropriation of his

---

[34] Harris *et al.*, *Harris, O'Boyle and Warbrick: Law of the European Convention on Human Rights* (OUP, 2009) 856.

property coupled with the payment of inadequate compensation. While in itself not an unprecedented outcome, the judgment added that, since this violation 'originated in a widespread problem which resulted from a malfunctioning of Polish legislation and administrative practice ... which has affected and remains capable of affecting a large number of persons',[35] appropriate measures were required to secure an adequate right of compensation or redress, not simply for the particular applicant, but for all similar claimants.[36] Subsequent applications complaining of violations stemming from the same state of affairs can, therefore, be directed back to the Polish authorities to settle according to the terms of the *Broniowski* judgment without the Court having to reconsider the merits afresh in each case.

A Chamber's verdict, whether unanimous or by majority, usually disposes of the matter. However, exceptional cases may be referred by one or more of the parties to a Grand Chamber of 17 judges within three months of the original judgment. Technically, such referrals are not 'appeals' but 're-hearings' and are conditional upon the approval of the Grand Chamber's five-judge 'admissibility' panel which is obliged to accede to them where the case in question raises, according to Article 43(2) ECHR, 'a serious question affecting the interpretation or application of the Convention or the protocols thereto, or a serious issue of general importance'. Judgments of Chambers become final under three circumstances: when the parties declare that they will not request a reference to the Grand Chamber, three months after the date of judgment if a reference to a Grand Chamber has not been made, or where a reference to a Grand Chamber has been made but the five-judge panel has rejected it. Between 2002 and 2005 an annual average of 116 cases were referred to the Grand Chamber but 91 per cent were rejected as inadmissible and, of the 23 judgments delivered, 13 confirmed the original verdict.[37]

4.5 SUPERVISION OF THE EXECUTION OF JUDGMENTS

Once a judgment finding a violation has been delivered, supervision of its execution passes to the Committee of Ministers which considers whether the obligation under Article 46(1) ECHR, to 'abide by the final judgment of the Court', has been discharged by the respondent state. Since this is a matter for negotiation, the respondent state effectively participates in supervising enforcement against itself. Judgments, including those involving friendly settlement, are referred to the Committee by the Directorate of Human Rights and Legal Affairs (one of five Directorates General of the Council of Europe's Secretariat) as soon as they are received, and are entered on the agendas of special human rights meetings of the Committee, which the Directorate also drafts and makes public. Not surprisingly, the Court's workload problems are also mirrored in the enforcement process with about 3,000 cases scheduled for each session, only 20–40 of which are actually debated.[38] At its human rights meetings the Committee

[35] (2005) 40 EHRR 495, para 189.   [36] Ibid, para 200.   [37] Mowbray, n 24, 512, 513, and 518.
[38] Harris *et al.*, n 34, 872.

first invites the respondent state to provide it with information about the remedial measures taken in response to the judgment. Applicants are not represented at these meetings, but are entitled to communicate with the Committee about the implementation of individual measures including the payment of compensation.

In the past what the Committee regarded as sufficient evidence of execution varied from case to case with little apparent rationale.[39] But it is now said to require more convincing evidence that the source of the violation has been effectively tackled.[40] Cases are listed for consideration at six-monthly intervals until the Committee is satisfied that the violation has been properly addressed. While awaiting final execution of judgments, interim resolutions can be passed which may simply note that execution has not yet occurred, report progress and encourage completion, or threaten the respondent state with more serious measures if full compliance is further delayed. When it is satisfied that any compensation has been paid, and that any other necessary measures have been introduced, the Committee of Ministers publicly certifies that its responsibilities under Article 46(2) ECHR have been exercised. This can take years, for example over eight-and-a-half in the notoriously protracted case of *Marcks v Belgium*, which involved discrimination between legitimate and illegitimate children in the law of affiliation.[41] States may find it difficult to correct the systemic source of the violation for various reasons, including: a lack of clarity in the Court's judgment, political problems, the daunting scale of the reforms required, managing complex legislative procedures, budgetary issues, adverse public opinion, the possible impact of compliance on obligations deriving from other institutions, and bureaucratic inertia.[42]

Protocol No 14 will involve the Court in the supervision of the execution of its own judgments in two ways, each activated by a two-thirds majority vote of the Committee of Ministers. First, where execution is hindered by problems in determining what the judgment means, the Court may be called upon to provide further clarification. Second, the Committee will be able to refer to the Grand Chamber the question of whether the respondent state has complied with the original judgment. Under these arrangements there will be no prospect of re-opening the original verdict nor of financial penalties.

At the end of the supervision of the execution of judgments process, there is, however, very little the Council of Europe can do with a state persistently in violation, short of suspending its voting rights on the Committee or expelling it from the Council of Europe altogether—each of which is likely to prove counterproductive in all but the most extreme circumstances.

---

[39] Tomkins, 'The Committee of Ministers: Its Roles under the European Convention on Human Rights' [1995] *EHRLR* 49, 59–60; Klerk, 'Supervision of the Execution of the Judgments of the European Court of Human Rights—The Committee of Ministers' Role under Article 54 of the European Convention on Human Rights' (1998) 45 *Netherlands ILR* 65, 77–8.

[40] Lambert-Abdelgawad, *The Execution of Judgments of the European Court of Human Rights* (Council of Europe Publishing, 2008) 37–8.   [41] Tomkins, n 39, 61.

[42] Steering Committee for Human Rights (CDDH), Guaranteeing the long-term effectiveness of the control system of the European Convention on Human Rights—Addendum to the final report containing CDDH proposals (long version) (9 April 2003) 34.

5 THE EUROPEAN UNION

For European integrationists, the Council of Europe was a missed opportunity and a bitter disappointment. Jean Monnet, the French Planning Commissioner, regarded it as 'entirely valueless' and President de Gaulle found it 'simply ridiculous'.[43] The French Foreign Minister, Robert Schuman, therefore, proposed a European Coal and Steel Community, founded in 1951 by six member states, the primary goal of which was the integration of the French and German coal and steel industries in order to prevent another Franco-German war. In 1957, the European Economic Community (EEC) developed this idea by establishing a common market among member states, and in 1965 the amalgamation of the EEC with the European Coal and Steel Community and the European Atomic Energy Community (also established in 1957) created the European Communities (EC). Further developments in 1992 transformed the European Communities into the 12-member European Union (EU). Retaining the distinctive identity of the European Communities as the 'First Pillar', the establishment of the EU added a 'Second Pillar' (a Common Foreign and Security Policy), and a 'Third Pillar' (Justice and Home Affairs) embracing such issues as asylum and immigration, drugs, judicial cooperation on civil and criminal justice, and police cooperation on terrorism and international crime. By the late 2000s, new members, mostly from the former communist bloc, brought the number of EU states to 27, over half that of the Council of Europe.

For much of its 40-year history the EEC/EC showed little overt interest in human rights. This was largely for three reasons. First, although the EEC/EC always regarded the ideals of democracy, human rights, and the rule of law as important and desirable, human rights were not initially seen as a priority for European economic integration. Second, it was, in any case, assumed that they were adequately covered by the Council of Europe and the ECHR to which all members of the EEC/EC, but not the EEC/EC itself, also belonged. Third, the European Court of Justice (ECJ) in Luxembourg, the principal judicial organ of the EEC/EC, generally interpreted Community law as it applied to member states—although not as it applied to the institutions of the Union itself—in accordance with the ECHR and the jurisprudence of the Strasbourg institutions. However, for several reasons, towards the end of the twentieth century the profile of human rights increased in the EC/EU. First, it became clear that the success of European integration hinged upon the supremacy of community law. But a rebellion threatened by national constitutional courts fearing the risks this posed to national constitutional rights compelled the ECJ increasingly to articulate its own fundamental rights jurisprudence. Second, the EU began to require respect for human rights as a condition of entering into formal trading and other relationships with non-EU states.

---

[43] Simpson, *Human Rights and the End of Empire—Britain and the Genesis of the European Convention* (OUP, 2001) 646.

It, therefore, became increasingly difficult for the EU not to have a developed human rights policy for its own internal affairs. Third, human rights are inextricably interwoven with Justice and Home Affairs issues. Fourth, in the late 1990s, the provision of a formal human rights document and more effective human rights monitoring arrangements were seen as offering a solution to the EU's 'legitimacy crisis' caused by the widening gap between the expanding vision of European integration, on the one hand, and the needs and aspirations of Europe's citizens, on the other hand. Fifth, Protocol No 14 to the ECHR enables the EU to become a party to the Convention.[44] Once this happens individuals will be able to complain to the European Court of Human Rights about alleged violations of the ECHR by the EU.

5.1 THE EUROPEAN COURT OF JUSTICE AND HUMAN RIGHTS

The ECJ operates on the basis that 'fundamental rights form an integral part of the general principles of law' of the EU, and that 'respect for human rights is ... a condition of the lawfulness of Community acts'.[45] In theory, therefore, violations of fundamental rights can be litigated before the ECJ by EU institutions against each other, by member states against each other, and/or by the Commission or individuals against member states or against EU institutions. However, in practice this rarely happens. Individuals can complain to the ECJ about a violation of their fundamental rights in one of two ways. Under Article 230 European Community Treaty, 'any natural or legal person' can initiate proceedings for review of the legality of acts of EU institutions against 'decisions addressed' to them or against those 'addressed to another person' which are, nevertheless, 'of direct and individual concern' to the applicant. But this is a very difficult test to satisfy since the ECJ has interpreted it to mean that the applicant has been affected 'by reason of certain attributes which are peculiar to them or by reason of circumstances in which they are differentiated from all other persons'.[46] The second route is more indirect. Under Article 234 European Community Treaty, a national court may ask the ECJ for a preliminary ruling on whether Community law, including that relating to fundamental rights, has been violated. But this is not available to litigants 'as a matter of right'.[47] Although neither of these two routes requires an 'exhaustion of domestic remedies' as under the ECHR, each is, nevertheless, an expensive and protracted process. It is hardly surprising, therefore, that the ECJ has heard few human rights complaints from individual applicants. Finally, the jurisdiction of the ECJ over actions of EU institutions and member states is limited. Although this includes activities under the Third Pillar, the ECJ has no jurisdiction at all in relation to the EU's Common Foreign and Security Policy which, by its very nature, raises many human rights issues.

[44] New Art 59 (2), ECHR.
[45] *Opinion 2/94 on Accession by the Community to the ECHR* [1996] ECR I-1759, paras 33 and 34.
[46] Case 25/62, *Plaumann & Co v Commission* [1963] ECR 95, 107.
[47] Case C-50/00 P, *Unión de Pequeños Agricultores v Council* [2002] ECR I-6677, para 42.

5.2 THE CHARTER OF FUNDAMENTAL RIGHTS

The Treaty of Nice 2001 both inaugurated the process of providing the EU with more formal constitutional foundations and provided it with its first formal statement of rights, the Charter of Fundamental Rights (EU Charter), which collects together, in a single document, rights which the EU has already recognized in various other disparate sources. However it was not until the Treaty of Lisbon 2009 that the EU Charter became legally binding on member states, subject to various exemptions granted to the UK, Poland, and the Czech Republic.

The EU Charter differs from the ECHR in five principal ways. First, it includes rights contained in the ECHR but not in precisely the same terms. For example, Article 6 EU Charter provides the right to liberty and security of the person in a single clause— 'everyone has the right to liberty and security of the person'—while Article 5 ECHR has no less than five clauses, one of which has six further sub-clauses (12 elements in total) for the same right. Article 52(3) EU Charter requires the meaning and scope of rights found in both the Charter and ECHR to be interpreted in the same way as those found in the latter. But, as the Council of Europe's Steering Committee for Human Rights put it, 'experience tends to show that it is difficult to avoid contradictions where two differently worded texts on the same subject-matter are interpreted by two different courts'.[48]

Second, the ECHR is largely confined to civil and political rights. The EU Charter, on the other hand, also includes a wide range of social, economic, cultural, and citizenship rights, similar in kind to those found in the European Social Charter discussed in Section 3.3, above.

Third, the ECHR provides different limitation clauses for each right. Article 52 EU Charter, on the other hand, sets out general limitations on all substantive Charter rights in the following terms. They must be provided for by law, respect the essence of the rights and freedoms in question, and be subject to the principle of proportionality. They must also be necessary and genuinely meet objectives of the general interest recognized by the EU or the need to protect the rights and freedoms of others. Those Charter rights which derive from Community Treaties, or the Treaty on European Union, must also be exercised under the conditions and within the limits defined by those treaties.

The fourth difference between the ECHR and the EU Charter is that the former generally binds member states in any and all of their activities, while Article 51(7) EU Charter indicates that it is addressed to the institutions of the EU, and to its member states, only as far as the formulation and implementation of EU law are concerned.

Finally, since the EU Charter does not provide any additional right of individual petition, the only recourse to the ECJ open to individual litigants for a breach of a Charter right remains the existing limited ones described in the previous section.

Before it acquired formal legal status the EU Charter was already being used as a point of reference by national courts and by EU institutions. The Commission, for example,

---

[48] Steering Committee for Human Rights (CDDH), Study of Technical and Legal Issues of a Possible EC/EU Accession to the European Convention on Human Rights, DG-II(2002)006 [CDDH(2002)010 Addendum 2] (25–8 June 2002) para 80.

regarded it as an essential vehicle for promoting an authentic EU rights culture, for strengthening citizens' rights, and for raising the level of protection across the Union. It also 'systematically and rigorously' checked EU legislative proposals for Charter compliance.[49] The ECJ also used the Charter to guide its interpretation of Community law.

5.3 THE FUNDAMENTAL RIGHTS AGENCY

Developing an idea first approved in 2003, the EU formally proposed, in June 2005, to expand the remit of its European Centre on Racism and Xenophobia to create a Fundamental Rights Agency (FRA) which came into operation on 1 January 2007. Using the Charter as its main point of reference, attempting to avoid overlap with the Council of Europe, and networking with national institutions, the FRA is intended to fulfil the following functions: to be an independent centre of expertise on fundamental rights issues through data collection, analysis, and networking; to provide relevant institutions and authorities of the EU and its member states with assistance and expertise when implementing Community law relating to fundamental rights; and to advise Union institutions and member states on how best to prepare or implement fundamental rights-related Union legislation. However, the FRA has no powers to examine individual complaints, to issue regulations, or to carry out 'normative monitoring' for the purposes of Article 7 EU Treaty.

6 CONCLUSION

As a result of lack of agreement, particularly between the UK and France, over the purpose and shape of pan-European institutions in the aftermath of the Second World War, Europe now has two overlapping transnational legal processes for protecting human rights. The better-known ECHR and the European Court of Human Rights—often mistakenly believed to be EU institutions—face a deepening crisis prompted by an exponentially increasing individual application rate which the Council of Europe has so far failed to tackle effectively. Protocol No 14 might alleviate this to some extent. But, even if it does, more radical reform is still likely to be required. An official review will be conducted between 2012 and 2015, and a decision about the need for more profound change by the end of 2019.

As the twenty-first century unfolds, the EU is also likely to expand and develop its human rights mission, bringing the rationales for both systems of international human rights law, how they should relate to each other, and why Europe should have two rather than one, under increasing scrutiny. There can, however, be little doubt that the European nation-state remains the most important arena for the legal protection of human rights. Assuming civil peace, a distribution of resources which is at least not gravely inequitable, and democratically regulated markets, human rights

---

[49] Goldberg, 'EU Charter—The Baby in the Bathwater?' [2005] *Justice Bulletin* 6.

are most effectively protected by genuinely democratic and rights-sensitive national legislative and executive institutions, independent, professional, and rights-aware national judiciaries, and by the provision of national justiciable constitutional rights. The main human rights-related functions of both the Council of Europe and the EU are, therefore, to attempt to encourage the development of all these elements where they have not yet firmly taken root in Europe, and to contribute to their preservation and protection where they have.

FURTHER READING

ALSTON and DE SCHUTTER (eds), *Monitoring Fundamental Rights in the EU: The Contribution of the Fundamental Rights Agency* (Hart Publishing, 2005).

—— with BUSTELO and HEENAN (eds), *The EU and Human Rights* (Oxford University Press, 1999).

BATES, *The Evolution of the European Convention on Human Rights: From Its Inception to the Creation of a Permanent Court of Human Rights* (Oxford University Press, 2010).

GREER, *The European Convention on Human Rights: Achievements, Problems and Prospects* (Cambridge University Press, 2006).

—— and WILLIAMS, 'Human Rights in the Council of Europe and the EU: Towards "Individual", "Constitutional", or "Institutional" Justice?' (2009) 15 *ELJ* 463.

HARRIS *et al.*, *Harris, O'Boyle and Warbrick: Law of the European Convention on Human Rights* (Oxford University Press, 2009).

JANIS, KAY, and BRADLEY, *European Human Rights Law: Text and Materials* (Oxford University Press, 2008).

TORRES PÉREZ, *Conflicts of Rights in the European Union: A Theory of Supranational Adjudication* (Oxford University Press, 2009).

WILLIAMS, *EU Human Rights Policies: A Study in Irony* (Oxford University Press, 2004).

—— 'Fundamental Rights in the New European Union' in Barnard (ed), *The Fundamentals of EU Law Revisited: Assessing the Impact of the Constitutional Debate* (Oxford University Press, 2007).

USEFUL WEBSITES

Council of Europe: <http://www.coe.int>

European Court of Human Rights: <http://www.echr.coe.int/echr>

European Commissioner for Human Rights: <http://www.coe.int/t/commissioner>

European Union: <http://europa.eu>

Charter of Fundamental Rights: <http://ec.europa.eu/justice_home/unit/charte/index_en.html>

European Union Agency for Fundamental Rights: <http://www.fra.europa.eu/fra>

European Court of Justice: <http://curia.europa.eu>

Organization for Security and Cooperation in Europe: <http://www.osce.org/>

21

AFRICA

Christof Heyns and Magnus Killander

SUMMARY

The national protection of human rights in Africa is monitored not only by the UN system but also through an extensive framework of regional instruments adopted by the African Union and its predecessor, the Organization of African Unity, as well as sub-regional organizations such as the Economic Community of West African States and the Southern African Development Community. However, the African Commission on Human and Peoples' Rights, established in 1987, remains the main human rights body of the continent. An African Human Rights Court has recently been established to complement the work of the Commission.

1 INTRODUCTION

The African continent of today is characterized, inter alia, by the coexistence of traditional and modern strands of society. As is the case in traditional societies across the world, recognition of values such as human dignity, a prohibition of harm to others, and the ideals of benevolent governance may be found in many African societies—the same norms that underlie much of the modern notion of human rights. However, the modern or full notion of human rights differs from the traditional notion in that the idea of enforcement of these norms is typically absent or not well developed in traditional societies. To the extent that people may be considered to be the bearers of human rights in such societies, these rights are rights in the weak sense of the word— the corresponding duty they impose is at best a moral or an aspirational one. Abusive governments, in the often used term, have to be endured 'like the weather'.

On the other hand, in terms of the modern notion of human rights, the duties imposed by these rights—which could be described as rights in the strong sense of the word—are regarded as enforceable. 'Enforcement' in this context primarily (and ideally) refers to enforcement through law, but behind legal enforcement there is the claim—either explicit or implicit—that if all other attempts to secure the rights fail, the point may be reached where self-help can be employed to ensure their realization. The concept of human rights does not operate in an anarchistic framework—it recognizes a general obligation to obey the law. But where the line is crossed and human rights violations are at stake, the duty to obey the law is at some point considered to have broken down.[1]

While there is an increasing recognition of human rights in Africa in the strong sense of the word, the continent is still facing a myriad of challenges to the realization of the human rights of its people. This is despite widespread formal commitment to human rights across the continent in the form of bills of rights, establishment of national human rights institutions, declarations by intergovernmental organizations, and the establishment of a regional human rights system.

Human rights violations in Africa, as elsewhere, take many forms. State repression was the hallmark of colonial rule in many parts of Africa. After independence, opposition politicians, journalists, and human rights defenders continue to be persecuted in many countries on the continent. However, human rights violations are not limited to the state. Many human rights violations, which in particular affect women and children, take place in private. These violations may take the form of domestic violence or be a result of harmful traditional practices such as female genital mutilation. While these violations take place in the private sphere, the state still has an important role in addressing the situation by legislation, education, and an institutional framework which supports the victims. Armed conflicts which may or may not involve the state also give rise to serious human rights violations.

In fact it could be argued that because the human rights ethos recognizes that at some point self-help or even resistance can be employed to validate rights claims, it can foster a climate in which people take the law into their own hands to pursue what they construe as legitimate human rights claims, even if these beliefs are not shared by others, who may in turn defend their own views. The mixture of traditional and modern societies in Africa provides an often unstable environment for the notion of human rights to take root.

Poverty and human rights violations go hand in hand in Africa, as is the case in other parts of the world.[2] However, the situation is particularly pronounced in Africa in view of the high levels of poverty. Most African countries have not made significant progress towards achievement of the Millennium Development Goals (MDGs) and in the realization of other socio-economic rights. While improvement in governance offers the best chance for the realization of socio-economic rights in Africa, a more equitable globalization process would also be beneficial. The global economic crisis also risks further diminishing resources available for the realization of human rights on the continent.

This chapter examines the role played by African regional intergovernmental organizations, in particular the African Union, in the realization of human rights. The focus is on the African Charter on Human and Peoples' Rights (ACHPR) and the

[1] Heyns, 'A "Struggle Approach" to Human Rights' in Heyns and Stefiszyn (eds), *Human Rights, Peace and Justice in Africa: A Reader* (Pretoria University Law Press, 2006) 15.   [2] See Chapter 27, below.

main organs, the Commission and the Court, which have been established to ensure its implementation.

2 HISTORICAL OVERVIEW

The Charter of the Organization of African Unity (OAU Charter), adopted in 1963, made few references to human rights. However, the Charter did set the task for the new organization of enforcing human rights norms by recognizing the goal of bringing an end to colonialism and apartheid in Africa. In the late 1970s, in the wake of the mass murders of the regimes of, for example, Idi Amin in Uganda, the OAU started to pay some attention to the human rights situation in its member states.

In 1978 President Jawara of The Gambia made the following statement before the UN General Assembly:

With the attainment of self-determination and independence, it would be ironic indeed if the freedom gained from the defeat of colonialism should...be denied our people by our own leaders. After centuries of a deliberate policy of dehumanisation, subjugation, and oppression, the minimum our people expect and must have is the full enjoyment of their political, economic, social, and cultural rights...It should be the duty of all of us to...ensure that...the people enjoy...their civil and political rights.[3]

Over the following years President Jawara, one of the few democratically elected leaders in Africa at the time, played a leading role in the development of the ACHPR, which is also known as the Banjul Charter, after the capital of The Gambia. The OAU Assembly adopted the ACHPR in 1981 and it entered into force in 1986. In 1987 the OAU Assembly elected the 11 members of the African Commission on Human and Peoples' Rights. The Commission recommended that, to guard its independence, the Secretariat of the Commission should not be located at the headquarters of the OAU in Addis Ababa, Ethiopia. A year later, the OAU Assembly decided that the Secretariat of the Commission should be located in Banjul.

With democratic elections in South Africa in April 1994, the OAU had finally succeeded in its main objective of the liberation of Africa from colonialism and apartheid. It was felt that the OAU was in need of transformation and in 2000 the OAU Assembly adopted the Constitutive Act of the African Union (AU). The AU was launched in Durban, South Africa, in 2002. The headquarters of the AU remain in Addis Ababa, Ethiopia.

The main principles of the OAU were sovereign equality and 'non-interference in the internal affairs of states'.[4] These principles have been retained in the AU Constitutive Act. However, it is noticeable that a number of new objectives have been added in the Act. These include the objective to 'promote and protect human and peoples' rights

---

[3] Alhaji Sir Dawda Kairaba Jawara, Statement at the 33rd session of the UN General Assembly, 22 September 1978, quoted in Touray, *The Gambia and the World—A History of the Foreign Policy of Africa's Smallest State 1965–1995* (Institut für Afrika-Kunde, 2000) 161.   [4] OAU Charter, Art 3.

in accordance with the ACHPR and other relevant human rights instruments'.[5] In addition to the commitments set out in the Constitutive Act, the AU established a new institutional framework with a mandate that includes the realization of human rights. The new institutions include the African Court on Human and Peoples' Rights, the Pan-African Parliament, the Peace and Security Council, the New Partnership for Africa's Development, and the African Peer Review Mechanism.

There are no entry requirements in terms of human rights practices for states to join the AU, and all the members of the OAU became members of the AU without scrutiny of their human rights records. However, there is at least a theoretical possibility that violations of human rights may lead to suspension from the AU and other sanctions.[6] AU inaction in the face of gross human rights violations in, for example, Darfur, Sudan, and Zimbabwe, however, illustrates that the principle of non-interference still dominates. In fact the AU has only used its power to sanction member states after military coups. For example, the AU Peace and Security Council in February 2009 imposed sanctions, including travel restrictions and freezing of assets, against the leaders of the Mauritanian military regime following the coup in August 2008.[7] In contrast, a sitting head of state runs little risk of being castigated by his peers in respect of how much he (to date, only one African head of state has been a woman) has manipulated an election to stay in power. Many current African presidents first came to power through military coups. Most of them have then tried to legitimize their rule through elections. For example, the democratically elected President Jawara of The Gambia, mentioned above, was deposed in a military coup in 1994 by the 29-year-old Yahya Jammeh who has remained in power ever since, and has turned The Gambia into an increasingly repressive state.

Concern over human rights in Africa by intergovernmental organizations is not limited to the AU. The UN plays a major role through treaty bodies, special procedures, field presences, and so on. Impunity is being addressed, among other matters, through the work of the International Criminal Court and the International Criminal Tribunal for Rwanda (ICTR). In addition, sub-regional African intergovernmental organizations have taken an increased interest in human rights. The AU has recognized eight Regional Economic Communities (RECs) as building blocks towards an African Economic Community.[8] The most active of these in the field of human rights is the Economic Community of West African States (ECOWAS).[9] The ECOWAS Community Court of Justice can hear complaints about human rights violations in member states without the requirement of exhaustion of local remedies. Among its case law can be mentioned cases dealing with arbitrary detention in The

---

[5] AU Constitutive Act, Art 3.   [6] AU Constitutive Act, Art 23.

[7] See communiqués of the 163rd and 168th meeting of the AU Peace and Security Council annexed to Letter dated 10 February 2009 from the Chargé d'affaires of the Permanent Mission of the Libyan Arab Jamahiriya to the UN addressed to the President of the Security Council, S/2009/85 (11 February 2009).

[8] Assembly/AU/Dec.112 (VII) (July 2006).

[9] On the human rights mandate of the RECs, see Viljoen, *International Human Rights Law in Africa* (OUP, 2007) 479.

Gambia and slavery in Niger.[10] The East African Court of Justice (EACJ) and the Tribunal of the Southern African Development Community (SADC) do not have explicit jurisdiction to deal with complaints of human rights violations, but have nevertheless dealt with human rights issues which were considered to constitute violations of their respective founding treaties.[11] Some RECs have also been active in human rights standard-setting. For example a SADC Protocol on Gender and Development was adopted in 2008.

At the domestic level, all 53 member states of the AU have written constitutions which recognize human rights.[12]

3 THE AFRICAN CHARTER AND OTHER RELEVANT TREATIES

The ACHPR has been ratified by all 53 member states of the AU.

3.1 NORMS RECOGNIZED IN THE AFRICAN CHARTER

The ACHPR goes further than the primary regional human rights conventions of Europe and the Americas in recognizing not only civil and political rights, but also economic, social, and cultural rights and not only individual rights but also peoples' rights. The Charter also provides for duties.

A number of shortcomings in respect of the provisions concerning civil and political rights in the ACHPR when compared to other international instruments can be noted. For example, the right to privacy and the right against forced labour are not explicitly mentioned in the Charter. Fair trial rights and the right of political participation are provided for in less detail than in other human rights treaties. However, the African Commission has, in resolutions and in its decisions on cases, interpreted the Charter in line with established international practice. Thus, the ACHPR has been interpreted to encompass some of the rights or aspects of rights not explicitly included. For example, the content of the fair trial rights in the ACHPR has been expounded by the African Commission in its detailed Principles and Guidelines on the Right to a Fair Trial and Legal Assistance in Africa which was adopted in 2003.

The inclusion in the ACHPR of socio-economic rights alongside civil and political rights emphasizes the indivisibility of human rights and the importance of developmental issues, which are obviously important matters in the African context. At

---

[10] *Manneh v The Gambia*, ECW/CCJ/JUD/03/08 (5 June 2008); *Koraou v Niger*, ECW/CCJ/JUD/06/08 (27 October 2008).

[11] *Katabazi* and *Others v Secretary General of the East African Community and Another* [2007] EACJ 3, (2007) *AHRLR* 119 (EAC 2007); *Campbell (Pvt) Ltd and others v Zimbabwe* [2007] SADCT 1 (28 November 2008).

[12] Heyns and Kaguongo, 'Constitutional Human Rights Law in Africa' (2006) 22 *S African JHR* 673.

the same time it should be noted that a modest number of socio-economic rights are explicitly included in the Charter. It only recognizes 'a right to work under equitable and satisfactory conditions' (Article 15), a right to health (Article 16), and a right to education (Article 17). Among rights not explicitly included are the rights to food, water, social security, and housing. The socio-economic rights in the ACHPR have generally received scant attention from the African Commission, but in its 2001 decision in *SERAC v Nigeria* the Commission dealt extensively with the issue.[13] In this case, which dealt with gross human rights violations in the oil-rich Ogoniland region of Nigeria, the African Commission deduced an implicit right to 'housing or shelter' in the ACHPR from the provisions on health, property, and family life in the Charter. Similarly, a right to food was read into the right to dignity.

In contrast to the individual rights in the Charter, peoples' rights are more fully developed in the ACHPR than in the UN covenants which set out only a right to self-determination. According to the Charter, all 'peoples' have a right to be equal (Article 19); to existence and self-determination (Article 20); to freely dispose of their wealth and natural resources (Article 21); to economic, social, and cultural development (Article 22); to peace and security (Article 23); and to a satisfactory environment (Article 24). Clearly, part of the motivation for the recognition of 'peoples' rights' lies in the fact that, historically, entire 'peoples' in Africa have been colonized and otherwise exploited. 'Peoples' can thus refer to the whole population of the country. For example, the African Commission has held that a military coup constituted not only a violation of the right to political participation in Article 13, but also violated the right to self-determination in Article 20.[14] Peoples' rights may also be exercised by a part of the population of a state 'bound together by their historical, traditional, racial, ethnic, cultural, linguistic, religious, ideological, geographical, economic identities and affinities, or other bonds'.[15]

In *Katangese Peoples' Congress v Zaire* the claimant requested that the African Commission recognize the independence of the Katanga province in the then Zaire (now Democratic Republic of the Congo). The Commission held:

In the absence of concrete evidence of violations of human rights to the point that the territorial integrity of Zaire should be called to question and in the absence of evidence that the people of Katanga are denied the right to participate in government as guaranteed by article 13(1) of the African Charter, the Commission holds the view that Katanga is obliged to exercise a variant of self-determination that is compatible with the sovereignty and territorial integrity of Zaire.[16]

The African Commission upheld this position in a recent case against Cameroon in which it held that grievances of the Anglophone part of Cameroon against the dominant Francophone part should not be 'resolved through secession but through a comprehensive national dialogue'.[17]

[13] 155/96, 15th Activity Report of the ACommHPR (2001–2002).
[14] 147/95 and 149/96, *Jawara v The Gambia*, 13th Activity Report of the ACommHPR (1999–2000) para 73.
[15] 266/03, *Gunme and Others v Cameroon*, 26th Activity Report of the ACommHPR (2009) para 171.
[16] 75/92, 8th Activity Report of the ACommHPR (1994–1995) para 6.   [17] *Gunme*, n 15, para 203.

In *SERAC v Nigeria*, discussed above, the African Commission found the Nigerian government guilty of violating Article 21 ACHPR by giving 'the green light to private actors, and the oil companies in particular, to devastatingly affect the well-being of the Ogonis'.[18] In this case, the Commission also found a violation of the right to a satisfactory environment in Article 24 ACHPR.

3.2 DUTIES AND LIMITATIONS

Articles 27, 28, and 29 ACHPR provide for individual duties towards the community. These range from duties towards the family, such as the maintenance of parents 'in case of need', to duties towards the state. The African Commission has not pronounced itself on the content of these duties except for its application of Article 27(2) ('the rights and freedoms of each individual shall be exercised with due regard to the rights of others, collective security, morality and common interest') as a general limitation clause.

Article 9(2) provides that '[e]very individual shall have the right to express and disseminate his opinions within the law'. The right seems to recognize the right in question only to the extent that it is not infringed upon by national law. Freedom of conscience and religion in Article 8, freedom of association in Article 10, freedom of assembly in Article 11, and freedom of movement in Article 12 are similarly restricted. This type of limitation is often referred to as a claw-back clause.[19] However, the African Commission has held that provisions in the ACHPR that allow rights to be limited 'in accordance with law', should be understood to require such limitations to be provided by domestic legal provisions that comply with the standards set by Article 27(2) and with international human rights law standards.

3.3 PROTECTION OF WOMEN, CHILDREN, AND VULNERABLE GROUPS

Article 18(2) ACHPR places a duty on the state to assist the family as 'the custodian of morals and traditional values recognized by the community'. However, such values may not discriminate as this would violate the general prohibition of discrimination in Article 2 and the specific prohibition of discrimination against women in Article 18(3), which also provides for the protection of the rights of women and children 'as stipulated in international declarations and conventions'. Article 18(4) provides for 'special measures of protection' for the aged and disabled.

The OAU Assembly in 1990 adopted the African Charter on the Rights and Welfare of the Child (Children's Charter). The Children's Charter can be seen as a regional response to the UN Convention on the Rights of the Child (CRC), adopted less than a year before the African treaty. The Children's Charter provides some increased protection compared to the CRC, including further protections for child soldiers, as well

---

[18] *SERAC*, n 13, para 58.   [19] See Chapter 6, above.

as protections against child marriages and for internally displaced children. Unlike the CRC, the Children's Charter also provides for duties for children.[20]

A separate Committee on the Rights and Welfare of the Child was established under the Children's Charter. The 11 members of the Committee were elected in July 2001 and the first meeting of the Committee was held in 2002. States have to report to the Committee within two years of the entry into force of the convention for the state party concerned and every three years thereafter. However, despite the fact that the Committee was established in 2001, it only began to consider the reports it had received in 2008.[21] Apart from state reporting, the Children's Charter, uniquely among international instruments for the protection of the rights of children, also provides for a communication procedure. The Committee does not have its own secretariat, and is serviced by the Department for Social Affairs at the AU Commission in Addis Ababa. The Committee has not functioned well and the question could be asked whether the Committee should be merged with the African Commission.

In 2003, the AU Assembly adopted the Protocol to the African Charter on Human and Peoples' Rights on the Rights of Women (Women's Protocol). Through its 24 substantive provisions the Women's Protocol provides much more comprehensive protection than the UN Convention on the Elimination of All Forms of Discrimination against Women (CEDAW). For example, the Women's Protocol includes provisions on domestic violence, trafficking, elimination of harmful practices, reproductive rights, HIV/AIDS, and inheritance and protection of elderly women. However, during the drafting of the Protocol, there were many controversial issues, including the question of polygamy which is recognized and practised in many African countries. For example, Kenyan President Kibaki has two wives, South African President Zuma has at least three wives, and King Mswati III of Swaziland, one of the world's last absolute monarchs, has 14 known wives. The CEDAW Committee has held that polygamy violates the right to equality in marriage.[22] In contrast, Article 6(c) Women's Protocol provides that 'monogamy is encouraged as the preferred form of marriage and that the rights of women in marriage and family, including in polygamous marital relationships are promoted and protected'. The African Commission and the African Court are responsible for monitoring the implementation of the Women's Protocol.

The OAU Convention Governing the Specific Aspects of Refugee Problems in Africa adopted in 1969 can be seen as the first African human rights treaty. The convention was a response to the 1967 Protocol which extended the application of the 1951 UN Refugee Convention to the whole world. The African Convention includes a broader definition of 'refugee' than the UN Convention, extending the protection to those seeking refuge because of 'external aggression, occupation, foreign domination

[20] Viljoen, n 9, 262–3.

[21] Mezmur and Sloth-Nielsen, 'An Ice-Breaker: State Party Reports and the 11th session of the African Committee of Experts on the Rights and Welfare of the Child' (2008) 8 *African HRLJ* 596.

[22] CEDAW Committee, General Recommendation 21, HRI/GEN/1/Rev.9 (Vol II) 337, para 14.

or events seriously disturbing public order'.[23] The AU adopted a Convention for the Protection and Assistance of Internally Displaced Persons in Africa in October 2009.

4 THE PROTECTIVE MECHANISMS

4.1 THE AFRICAN COMMISSION

4.1.1 Structure and composition

Article 30 ACHPR provides for the establishment of the African Commission on Human and Peoples' Rights. The African Commission was established in 1987 following the entry into force of the Charter in 1986. According to Article 45 ACHPR, the mandate of the Commission includes promoting human rights through research, dissemination of information, and cooperation with other human rights bodies. The Commission also has a mandate to interpret the provisions of the Charter and consider complaints against a state alleging that it has violated the ACHPR. The Commission has also been given the mandate to consider state reports on implementation of the Charter.

The African Commission consists of 11 Commissioners who serve in their individual capacities and are nominated by states parties to the Charter and elected by the AU Assembly. The independence of the Commission has sometimes been questioned as a number of civil servants and ambassadors have served on it. However, in a *note verbale* to the member states in April 2005 the AU Commission provided guidelines that excluded senior civil servants and diplomatic representatives from being elected.[24] These guidelines have been followed with regard to new appointments to the Commission. The Commission meets twice a year in regular sessions for a period of up to two weeks, alternating its meetings between its headquarters in Banjul and other African capitals.

4.1.2 The complaints procedure

Both states and individuals may bring complaints to the African Commission alleging violations of the ACHPR by states parties. The inter-state complaint procedure by which one state brings a complaint about an alleged human rights violation by another state is not often used. Only one such case has been decided by the Commission. In *Democratic Republic of the Congo v Burundi, Rwanda and Uganda*,[25] the Commission held that the three respondent states had violated a number of individual and peoples' rights during the presence of their armed forces on Congolese territory.

---

[23] OAU Convention Governing the Specific Aspects of the Refugee Problem in Africa, Art I(2).
[24] BC/OLC/66/VolXVIII (5 April 2005).
[25] 227/99, 20th Activity Report of the ACommHPR (2006).

Articles 55, 56, 57, and 58 ACHPR deal with 'other communications', that is, communications not submitted by a state. While the Charter is silent on who can bring such communications, the Commission has in its practice accepted complaints from individuals as well as from NGOs. From the case law of the Commission it is clear that the complainant does not need to be a victim or a family member of a victim.[26]

Article 56 ACHPR lists the admissibility criteria. These include that communications should indicate the author, be compatible with the Charter, not be written in disparaging or insulting language, not be based exclusively on media reports, be submitted within reasonable time, and not deal with a situation which has already been settled. In practice, the most important criterion for admissibility is the exhaustion of local remedies. The Commission has stated that for a case not to be admissible local remedies must be available, effective, sufficient, and not unduly prolonged.[27] In *Purohit and Another v The Gambia*, a case dealing with detention in a mental health institution, the Commission gave a potentially far-reaching decision on the exhaustion of local remedies when it held that:

[t]he category of people being represented in the present communication are likely to be people picked up from the streets or people from poor backgrounds and as such it cannot be said that the remedies available in terms of the Constitution are realistic remedies for them in the absence of legal aid services.[28]

When a complaint is lodged, the state in question is asked to respond in writing to the allegations against it. If it does not respond, and the admissibility criteria are met, the Commission proceeds on the basis of the facts as provided by the complainant. If a state has responded the Commission gives the complainant an opportunity to respond to the arguments by the state. The communication is then scheduled for a hearing at one of the sessions of the Commission. The complainant and respondent state are invited to make presentations at the hearing which is not public.

If the Commission finds a violation it may make recommendations. These may include that continuing violations should stop (for example, prisoners be released), or specific laws be amended or repealed. However, often the recommendations are rather vague, and the state party is merely urged to 'take all necessary steps to comply with its obligations under the Charter'.

The ACHPR does not contain a provision on interim or provisional measures. However, the Rules of Procedure of the Commission grant the Commission the power to grant provisional measures. The Commission has used provisional measures in a number of cases, for example when an execution has been imminent, often without success. It has held that the breaching of provisional measures constitutes a violation of Article 1 ACHPR.

The Commission has handed down approximately 150 decisions on communications since it was established in 1987. The individual complaints procedure is thus not used as

---

[26] *SERAC*, n 13, para 49.   [27] *Jawara*, n 14, paras 28–40.
[28] 241/01, *Purohit and Another v The Gambia*, 16th Activity Report of the ACommHPR (2002–2003) para 37.

frequently as would have been expected on a continent with the type of human rights problems that Africa experiences. This could, to some extent, be attributed to a lack of awareness about the system. Even where there is awareness, however, there is often not much faith that the system will make a difference. One reason for this may be that the Commission's recommendations are often vague and that the African Commission lacks a system of follow-up to its recommendations. It should be noted that while the Commission sometimes recommends compensation to the complainant it does not decide on the amount to award. It is also noticeable that, despite the relatively low number of cases, the Commission often takes more than five years to decide a case.

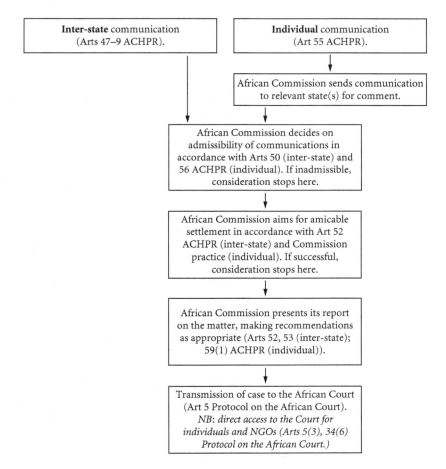

Figure 21.1 The African Charter communications procedure

4.1.3 Consideration of state reports

Each state party is required to submit a report every two years on its efforts to comply with the ACHPR. Reporting has been very tardy, and some states have never submitted a report. Reporting under the Charter allows the state to measure its legislation, policies, and practices against the norms of the ACHPR ('introspection'). This introspection is followed by 'inspection' by the African Commission in which it measures the performance of the state in question against the Charter. The objective is to facilitate a 'constructive dialogue' between the Commission and the states. The dialogue takes place at the public sessions of the African Commission.

NGOs are allowed to submit shadow or alternative reports, but the impact of this avenue is diminished by the lack of access of NGOs to the state reports to which they are supposed to respond. However, recently the Commission has begun to publish the state reports for the upcoming session on its website. Since 2001 the Commission has adopted concluding observations after considering the reports. However, the usefulness of the concluding observations is diminished by the fact that they are not widely disseminated by the Commission.

4.1.4 Special Rapporteurs and working groups

The Commission has appointed a number of Special Rapporteurs to deal with thematic human rights issues. The Special Rapporteurs are always members of the Commission. The Commission has also appointed working groups, some of which include members who are not Commissioners.

In the mid-1990s the Commission adopted the first Special Rapporteur mandates: the Special Rapporteur on extrajudicial, summary or arbitrary executions; the Special Rapporteur on prisons and conditions of detention; and the Special Rapporteur on the rights of women. The position of Special Rapporteur on extrajudicial, summary or arbitrary executions has been defunct since 2001. The Commission has more recently appointed Special Rapporteurs on freedom of expression and access to information; refugees and internally displaced persons; human rights defenders; and a focal point on the rights of older persons. The Commission has also established a committee to monitor the implementation of the Guidelines and Measures for the Prohibition and Prevention of Torture, Cruel, Inhuman or Degrading Treatment or Punishment in Africa (Robben Island Guidelines); and Working Groups on Indigenous People or Communities; Economic, Social and Cultural Rights; the Death Penalty; and the Rights of Older Persons and Persons with Disabilities in Africa.[29]

The Special Rapporteurs follow developments in the area covered by their mandate and engage with NGOs. They may issue press releases or write letters to governments when they receive reliable information about violations of the ACHPR. The Special Rapporteurs also undertake on-site visits and produce reports with recommendations to governments.

4.1.5 On-site visits

The Commission has conducted a number of on-site visits or missions. These can be divided into promotional and protective missions. Protective missions may be

[29] Final communiqué of the 45th ordinary session of the ACommHPR held in Banjul, The Gambia, 13–27 May 2009, para 31.

linked to a case under consideration by the Commission or to a situation of massive violations of human rights. Promotional missions help to give the Commission an understanding of the human rights situation in a country through meetings with governments and NGO representatives. They are often aimed at spreading knowledge about the Commission and its work. The missions are generally conducted by one or two members of the Commission, sometimes the Special Rapporteur on a specific issue, together with a legal officer from the Secretariat. Mission reports are adopted by the Commission as a whole at its sessions. Many reports have never been published, in print or on the internet, which diminishes their impact.

4.1.6 Resolutions

The African Commission has adopted resolutions on a number of human rights issues in Africa. In addition to country-specific and other more ad hoc resolutions, it has adopted resolutions on topics such as fair trial; freedom of association; human and peoples' rights education; humanitarian law; contemporary forms of slavery; anti-personnel mines; prisons in Africa; the independence of the judiciary; the electoral process and participatory governance; the International Criminal Court; the death penalty; torture; HIV/AIDS; maternal mortality; and freedom of expression. The Commission, in turn, has relied on these resolutions in its case law. Some of the resolutions, for example the Principles and Guidelines on the Right to a Fair Trial and Legal Assistance in Africa, are quite elaborate and can be seen as regional equivalents of the general comments adopted by the UN treaty bodies.

4.1.7 Relationship with NGOs

NGOs have often been instrumental in bringing cases to the African Commission. Sometimes they submit shadow reports, propose agenda items at the outset of Commission sessions, and provide logistical and other support to the Commission, for example by placing interns at the Commission and providing support to the Special Rapporteurs and missions of the Commission. NGO workshops are arranged prior to Commission sessions, and many NGOs participate actively in the public sessions of the Commission. NGOs also collaborate with the Commission in developing resolutions and new normative instruments. NGOs that wish actively to engage with the Commission need to apply for observer status, which to date has been granted to more than 400 African and international NGOs.[30]

4.1.8 Interaction with AU political bodies

The activity reports of the Commission, which reflect the decisions, resolutions, and other acts of the African Commission, are submitted to the AU summit, which is held twice a year. The activity report must be adopted by the AU Assembly before it can be published. Controversy arose in 2004 when Zimbabwe managed to delay the publication of a case against it due to lack of consultation by the Commission. At around

---

[30] Ibid, para 23.

the same time there was debate over the publication of country-specific resolutions.[31] However, since then the AU Assembly and Executive Council has reverted to its previous practice of serving as a rubber stamp for the Activity Report of the Commission. It could be argued that the principle that the very people in charge of the institutions whose human rights practices are at stake—the heads of state—should take the final decision on publicity, undermines the legitimacy of the system. On the other hand, it is clear that constructive engagement by the AU political organs could be used to put pressure on states to comply with the decisions of the Commission.

4.2 THE AFRICAN COURT ON HUMAN AND PEOPLES' RIGHTS

4.2.1 Background

The only monitoring mechanism included in the ACHPR is the African Commission. In 1994, the OAU Assembly adopted a resolution requesting the Secretary-General of the OAU to convene a Meeting of Experts to consider the establishment of an African Court on Human and Peoples' Rights. The decision to strengthen the regional human rights system with the establishment of a court should be seen in the context of the increased focus on human rights both in Africa and worldwide in the early 1990s. The Protocol on the African Court on Human and Peoples' Rights was adopted in Addis Ababa, Ethiopia, in 1998 (Protocol on the African Court). The Protocol entered into force in January 2004. Less than half the member states of the AU have ratified the Protocol. The seat of the court is in Arusha, Tanzania. In its first judgment, in December 2009, the Court declared it had no jurisdiction as Senegal did not allow direct access to the Court for individuals.

The AU Assembly decided at its summit in July 2004 that the African Human Rights Court should merge with the African Court of Justice. The reason behind the merger was seemingly a need to rationalize the AU structures to save money. The Court of Justice is one of the organs of the AU provided for in the Constitutive Act but it has not been established. It was meant to function as a court adjudicating disputes arising from the increasing integration of the member states of the AU. In July 2008 the AU Assembly adopted the Protocol on the Statute of the African Court of Justice and Human Rights. When this protocol enters into force, the new court will replace the current African Human Rights Court. Once established, the new court will have one human rights section and one general affairs section.

4.2.2 Composition

The African Court on Human and Peoples' Rights 'complements' the protective mandate of the African Commission under the Charter. The court consists of 11 judges nominated by states parties to the Protocol, and elected by the Assembly. Only the president holds a full-time appointment. The Protocol on the African Court provides that the judges are appointed in their individual capacities, and that their independence

---

[31] Killander, 'Confidentiality v Publicity: Interpreting Article 59 of the African Charter on Human and Peoples' Rights' (2006) 6 *African HRLJ* 572.

is guaranteed. Special provision is made in Article 18 Protocol on the African Court that '[t]he position of judge of the Court is incompatible with any activity that might interfere with the independence or impartiality of such a judge'. A judge will not be allowed to sit in a case if that judge is a national of a state which is a party to the case. The judges were elected by the Assembly in January 2006.

4.2.3 Procedure

In the majority of cases the Commission will take a case to the African Court if it has found a violation and established that the state has not complied with its recommendations. The exact procedure is not clear as the Commission and Court are still to finalize the harmonization of their rules of procedure. Individuals and those who act on their behalf will be able to take cases directly to the African Court only in respect of those states that have made an additional declaration specifically authorizing them to do so. Only two states, Burkina Faso and Mali, have made such a declaration. This opt-in process for direct access to the Court will remain the same under the merged court.

In respect of the Court's findings, the Protocol on the African Court determines that '[i]f the Court finds that there has been a violation of a human or peoples' right, it shall make appropriate orders to remedy the violation, including the payment of fair compensation or reparation'.[32] The Protocol provides that the Council of Ministers (now the AU Executive Council) shall monitor the execution of the judgments of the Court.[33] The Court may adopt provisional measures in cases of 'extreme gravity and urgency' when 'irreparable harm to persons' would otherwise ensue.[34]

In addition to its contentious jurisdiction, the African Court may also deliver advisory opinions at the request of the AU, any of its organs, or any 'African organisation recognised by the [AU]'.[35] It is unclear whether 'African organisations' include NGOs or is simply a reference to the Regional Economic Communities. The merged court will have advisory jurisdiction only at the request of AU organs.[36]

4.3 THE AU MAIN ORGANS AND HUMAN RIGHTS

4.3.1 Overview

The African human rights system is not limited to the African Commission, the African Court, and the Children's Committee. The AU also has the following main organs: the Assembly of Heads of State and Government, the Executive Council, the Permanent Representative Committee, the Pan-African Parliament, the African Court of Justice, the AU Commission (which replaced the OAU Secretariat), Specialised Technical Committees, the Economic, Social and Cultural Council, financial institutions, and the Peace and Security Council. A number of these organs have human rights mandates.

[32] Protocol on the African Court, Art 27(1).   [33] Ibid, Art 29(2).   [34] Ibid, Art 27(2).
[35] Ibid, Art 4(1).   [36] Statute of the African Court of Justice and Human Rights, Art 53(1).

4.3.2 Pan-African Parliament

The Pan-African Parliament (PAP) shall 'ensure the full participation of African peoples in the development and economic integration of the continent'. One of the Parliament's objectives is to '[p]romote the principles of human rights and democracy in Africa'. The PAP has held sessions twice a year since its inception in 2004. Each state party to the Protocol establishing the Parliament sends five national parliamentarians to the PAP, which is based in Midrand, South Africa. Currently the powers of the Parliament are purely consultative and advisory. In the implementation of its human rights mandate, the PAP has sent fact-finding missions to, for example, Darfur, and election observation missions to many AU member states. The PAP electoral observation mission to the Zimbabwe presidential election in 2008 concluded that the elections had not been free and fair. In contrast, the AU Assembly avoided criticizing the election. This episode is symptomatic of the general lack of impact of the PAP.

4.3.3 The Economic, Social and Cultural Council

The Economic, Social and Cultural Council (ECOSOCC) is an advisory organ made up of representatives nominated by civil society organizations of member states. One of ECOSOCC's objectives is to '[p]romote and defend a culture of good governance, democratic principles and institutions, popular participation, human rights and freedoms as well as social justice'. The statutes of ECOSOCC were adopted by the AU Assembly in July 2004. Since then ECOSOCC has been busy establishing its structures rather than establishing itself as a voice of civil society engaging with and putting issues such as human rights on the AU agenda.

4.3.4 Peace and Security Council

The attempts to develop mechanisms to deal with conflict in Africa are also of importance in trying to prevent massive human rights violations. The Protocol on the Peace and Security Council (PSC), adopted in 2002, entered into force in 2003. The PSC has a rotating membership of representatives of 15 AU member states. The criteria for membership include 'respect for constitutional governance...as well as the rule of law and human rights'. Article 4 PSC Protocol provides that the Council shall be guided by the AU Constitutive Act, the UN Charter, and the Universal Declaration of Human Rights. The Protocol further provides that one of the Council's objectives is to 'promote and encourage democratic practices, good governance and the rule of law, protect human rights and fundamental freedoms, respect for the sanctity of human life and international humanitarian law, as part of efforts for preventing conflicts'.

Article 19 PSC Protocol provides that the PSC 'shall seek close cooperation with the African Commission'. Nonetheless, from the activity reports of the Commission and the communiqués of the PSC, it appears that the two organs have not often collaborated, despite references to PSC resolutions in the Commission's country-specific resolutions.

4.4 THE AFRICAN PEER REVIEW MECHANISM

The Declaration on Democracy, Political, Economic and Corporate Governance (Governance Declaration) was adopted at the final OAU Assembly in Durban in 2002. The Governance Declaration provided for the establishment of an African Peer Review Mechanism (APRM) 'to promote adherence to and fulfilment of the commitments' in the Declaration.

The APRM grew out of the New Partnership for Africa's Development (NEPAD), adopted by the AU in 2001 as the development framework for the Union. The secretariats of the APRM and NEPAD are based in Midrand, South Africa. The highest decision-making body in the APRM is the APRM Forum consisting of the heads of state and government of the participating states. A panel of eminent persons with seven members oversees the review process and a member of this panel is chosen to lead the review team on its country mission.

Section 10 Governance Declaration provides as follows:

In the light of Africa's recent history, respect for human rights has to be accorded an importance and urgency all of its own. One of the tests by which the quality of a democracy is judged is the protection it provides for each individual citizen and for the vulnerable and disadvantaged groups. Ethnic minorities, women and children have borne the brunt of the conflicts raging on the continent today. We undertake to do more to advance the cause of human rights in Africa generally and, specifically, to end the moral shame exemplified by the plight of women, children, the disabled and ethnic minorities in conflict situations in Africa.

The APRM process consists of a self-evaluation by the state that has signed up to be reviewed and a review by an international review team. The outcome of the process is a national Programme of Action with time-bound action points to redress identified shortcomings.

The international review process consists of five stages. First, a background study is carried out by the secretariat assisted by consultants. This stage also includes a support mission to the country that will be reviewed. In the second stage, a review team led by one of the eminent persons visits the country for discussions with all stakeholders, after which the team prepares its report (third stage). A number of partner institutions and independent consultants participate in the review mission and assist in the preparation of the report. The fourth stage consists of the submission of the report to the APRM Forum and the discussion among peers. The fifth stage is the publication of the report and further discussion in other AU institutions such as the Pan-African Parliament. After concluding the reviews, participating states submit annual reports to the Forum on the implementation of the Programme of Action.

The APRM is voluntary and as of June 2009, 29 out of 53 AU member states had signed the Memorandum of Understanding which forms the legal basis for the review. Of these, only nine had reached the fourth stage of the process.

Many observers have emphasized the necessity for civil society to engage the APRM if the mechanism is to make any difference on the ground. The possibilities for such engagement vary greatly between participating states, as do the approaches to the independence of the national process from government interference.

The APRM integrates the political level of the AU in a way that other parts of the African human rights system have not done. As in other parts of the world, African leaders have not shown a great interest in criticizing their peers. Hence, there are reasons to be sceptical about whether 'peer pressure' will be employed in the process and whether the provisions on sanctions as a last resort against a recalcitrant state will ever be used. However, to focus solely on the pressure exercised at this level would be to underestimate the process as a whole.

There has not been much cooperation between the APRM and the African Commission on Human and Peoples' Rights, which is unfortunate. For example, despite the relevance of the APRM for the realization of human rights, no member of the African Commission has participated in a country review mission. The documents guiding the APRM process are cumbersome and repetitive and do not sufficiently address human rights.

5 CONCLUSION

Human rights protection in Africa clearly has a long way to go, and the mechanisms for their protection have been criticized by many commentators. All too often human rights violations are merely endured—like the weather—or it is left to those whose rights are infringed to seek their own redress, resulting in more violations. At the same time, the progress that has been made and the role of the official recognition of the concept of human rights on all levels on the continent—the regional, sub-regional, and the national—have to be recognized as steps in the right direction. By and large, the standards have been set and the foundations for the enforcement mechanisms have been laid.

The challenge remains primarily one of implementation—not only of the human rights standards and systems, but also of those policies aimed at addressing the root causes of human rights violations, such as poverty. But it remains a challenge to develop a more closely shared understanding of the nature and scope of what human rights claims legitimately entail on the continent, because ultimately people will take the law into their own hands to defend what they regard as their rights.

FURTHER READING

EBOBRAH, 'Litigating Human Rights before Sub-Regional Courts in Africa: Prospects and Challenges' (2009) 17 *African JCIL* 79.

EVANS and MURRAY (eds), *The African Charter on Human and Peoples' Rights: The System in Practice, 1986–2006* (Cambridge University Press, 2008).

HEYNS (ed), *Human Rights Law in Africa* (Martinus Nijhoff, 2004).

—— and KILLANDER (eds), *Compendium of Key Human Rights Documents of the African Union* (Pretoria University Law Press, 2007).

—— and —— 'The African Regional Human Rights System' in Gómez Isa and de Feyter (eds), *International Human Rights Law in a Global Context* (University of Deusto, 2009).

KILLANDER, 'The African Peer Review Mechanism and Human Rights: The First Reviews and the Way Forward' (2008) 30 *HRQ* 41.

—— 'African Human Rights Law in Theory and Practice' in Joseph and McBeth (eds), *Research Handbook on International Human Rights Law* (Edward Elgar, 2010).

OUGUERGOUZ, *The African Charter on Human and Peoples' Rights: A Comprehensive Agenda for Human Rights* (Kluwer Law International, 2003).

VILJOEN, *International Human Rights Law in Africa* (Oxford University Press, 2007).

—— and LOUW, 'State Compliance with the Recommendations of the African Commission on Human and Peoples' Rights, 1993–2004' (2007) 101 *AJIL* 1.

USEFUL WEBSITES

African Commission on Human and Peoples' Rights: <**http://www.achpr.org**>

African Union: <**http://www.africa-union.org**>

Centre for Human Rights, University of Pretoria: <**http://www.chr.up.ac.za**>

22

WITHIN THE STATE

Andrew Byrnes and Catherine Renshaw

SUMMARY

This chapter outlines the role and responsibility of the state for promoting and protecting human rights. The chapter first details the state's obligation to implement internationally guaranteed human rights and describes the different processes by which customary international law norms and international human rights treaties become part of domestic law. The chapter then discusses the principal domestic legal sources of protection of human rights: constitutional and legislative provisions as well as the common law. Finally, the discussion turns to some of the key institutions within the state that have a role in the protection and promotion of human rights: the courts, the executive, the legislature, ombudsmen, and national human rights institutions.

1 INTRODUCTION

The primacy of the state in the protection and fulfilment of internationally guaranteed human rights is the fundamental starting point of international human rights law. In the words of former UN High Commissioner for Human Rights, Louise Arbour: 'States remain the primary actors, the key conduits through which human rights must be realised. The obligation to respect and enforce human rights rests on states.'[1] As explained in Chapters 5 to 7, states are bound by human rights treaties and customary international law to ensure respect for, and the full enjoyment of, human rights of those persons subject to their jurisdiction. States carry out these obligations through a combination of legislative, institutional, judicial, administrative, financial, and other types of measures. Precisely which measures are used will depend on the specific treaty provision or customary international law obligation, and the political structure and practices of the state concerned. The touchstone for implementation of human

---

[1] Statement by Ms Louise Arbour, UN High Commissioner for Human Rights, on the opening of the 61st Session of the Commission on Human Rights (Geneva, 14 March 2005).

rights obligations is ultimately a substantive one—not merely whether necessary laws, institutions, and procedures are in place, but whether they ensure that persons within the state's jurisdiction in fact enjoy the rights guaranteed.

This chapter considers the various methods of protection of human rights at the national level, with a particular focus on legal protections and institutions with a specific rights mandate. Whether those individuals subject to the jurisdiction of the state enjoy human rights in reality depends on a range of factors, including the nature and content of substantive human rights protections applicable within the domestic system, the role of political and legal institutions in the implementation and enforcement of rights, the resources available to ensure the fulfilment of rights, the availability of remedies for violations of rights, the role of the media and other independent commentators, and the perception of the importance of rights among the members of the community and on the national political agenda.

Section 2 deals with *substantive* protections—the nature, status, and scope of human rights protections under national law. These include the incorporation or other use of international human rights norms in domestic law, constitutional guarantees of rights, human rights legislation, protection under the general law, including the concept of the rule of law, and the common law. Section 3 deals with *institutional* protections of human rights. It briefly outlines the types of institutions which commonly play a role in the implementation, monitoring, and protection of human rights, including the courts, the executive, the legislature, as well as mechanisms such as ombudsmen and national human rights institutions.

2 SUBSTANTIVE PROTECTIONS

A fundamental aspect of ensuring the fulfilment of human rights is their formal legal protection under national law. A state party to an international human rights treaty is in general not required directly to implement the provisions of the treaty into domestic law. What is required is that the protection and fulfilment of the rights guaranteed by the treaty are secured through domestic law and practice. While the level of domestic protection should not fall short of the international obligation, it can provide more generous protection.

There are a number of forms that legal protection of human rights may take in domestic legal systems, including:

1. the incorporation of treaty or customary international law protections into domestic law;

2. constitutional guarantees of human rights;

3. legislative protection of human rights, whether in the form of general human rights legislation or subject-specific legislation; and

4. protection of human rights through the common law.

In addition to human rights-specific protection, human rights can also be protected by laws which provide remedies for violations. Examples include defamation laws as protection of the right to privacy; landlord and tenant laws as protection of the right to property and the right to adequate housing; and criminal procedure laws as protection of the rights of the accused and victims of crimes. The positive obligation of the state to fulfil human rights may also be embodied in legislative frameworks which give effect to rights and which, in turn, may provide individual or group remedies for failure to ensure the enjoyment of these rights. Examples include legislation on education giving effect to the right to education; public housing legislation to ensure the right to adequate housing; and food safety and consumer protection laws as protection of the rights to life and to an adequate standard of living.

Underpinning all these is the protection afforded by concepts such as the rule of law, the *Rechtsstaatsprinzip*, or the principle of legality—essentially the principle that the exercise of the power of the state must be referable to a positive grant of constitutionally derived power and be subject to review and restraint by independent courts. Procedures such as the writ of habeas corpus in common law jurisdictions and the comparable *amparo* or *tutela* in some civil law jurisdictions are examples of remedies for violations of the principle of legality. The protection afforded by systems of administrative law also complements direct rights protection under domestic law (for example, the presumption that a statute does not authorize the making of regulations that infringe on fundamental rights and the resulting invalidity of infringing regulations).

2.1 INCORPORATION OF INTERNATIONAL HUMAN RIGHTS NORMS INTO DOMESTIC LAW

Human rights treaties—and to a lesser extent customary international law rules—can provide significant protection when they are incorporated into domestic law and are capable of being invoked before judicial, administrative, or other authorities. A person may be able to rely on each of these types of international law norms in a domestic legal system to challenge alleged violations of rights, though treaty-based norms are of greater practical importance. The extent of protection they afford depends in large part on their status in national law. Discussions of the place of international law in domestic legal systems often distinguish between *monist* systems, in which international law norms form part of domestic law without the need for legislative transformation, and *dualist* systems, according to which international and national law are two different systems, and rules of international law must be adopted or transformed by legislative enactment before they form part of the domestic legal order. In relation to customary international law rules, most legal systems have monist elements: these rules are automatically received into domestic law, though the effect of that reception varies considerably. When it comes to treaties, the variety of constitutional arrangements does not reflect a simplistic monist/dualist dichotomy.

2.1.1 Customary international law

In most dualist systems, in particular most common law jurisdictions, customary international law is accepted as 'part of the law of the land' or as 'a relevant source of law'. However, this is generally only to the extent that the applicable rule of customary international law is not inconsistent with binding judicial precedent or a legislative rule.

Under most monist systems, including most civil law systems, customary international law forms part of domestic law, its hierarchical status depending on the particular constitutional arrangements. In many civil law systems, constitutional provisions explicitly provide that customary international law rules form part of national law. In others, such as Argentina, no specific provision exists, but customary international law has been recognized by courts as part of the domestic legal order.[2] Customary international law rules may have a constitutional status, an enhanced statutory status (so that they prevail over all statutes, both prior and subsequent), or the same status as an ordinary statute. For example, Article 25 Basic Law of the Federal Republic of Germany provides: 'The general rules of public international law shall be an integral part of federal law. They shall take precedence over the laws and shall directly create rights and duties for the inhabitants of the federal territory.' This provision has the effect that rules of customary international law are part of federal law and prevail over federal statutes and the laws of the *Bundesländer* (the federal states).

2.1.2 Human rights treaties in monist jurisdictions

The extent to which persons can rely on human rights treaties as part of domestic law will depend on the place of those treaties in the national legal system and on whether the treaty or specific provisions of it, even when part of domestic law, are *directly applicable*. In this regard, it is common to contrast monist and dualist states. Yet this classification conceals a range of constitutional arrangements that defy such an easy categorization.

In some states, ratification of, or accession to, a treaty—the formal indication of a state's intention to be bound by that treaty as a matter of international law—triggers the incorporation of the treaty into the domestic legal system. This may simply follow ratification by the executive, as a result of an express or implied constitutional or statutory rule governing reception of treaties. In other cases, prior legislative approval of the ratification may be required before the treaty is received as part of domestic law. For example, under the US Constitution, in order to become 'the supreme law of the land', the President must receive the advice and consent of two-thirds of the Senate before the USA can ratify the treaty internationally. In other states, there are constitutional requirements that the legislature approve by ordinary law the international ratification of a treaty before it can become part of domestic law. In a sense, all these

---

[2] Vinuesa, 'Direct Applicability of Human Rights Conventions within the Internal Legal Order: The Situation in Argentina' in Conforti and Francioni (eds), *Enforcing International Human Rights in Domestic Courts* (Martinus Nijhoff, 1997) 149, 159–60.

models are 'monist', in that once the required steps are taken, the provisions of the treaty become part of domestic law.

Under other systems, the usual practice is to adopt a law 'ratifying' a specific treaty (rather than relying on a general rule of reception that applies to all treaties), as a result of which the treaty then becomes part of the domestic legal system. 'Ratifying' is used here in the sense of formal legislative approval at the national level and is different from the act of ratification which takes effect on the international plane, indicating the state's consent to be bound by the treaty.

Civil law jurisdictions with systems under which treaties become part of national law by one of the above routes include Brazil, Egypt, France, Japan, Mexico, Namibia, the Netherlands, the Russian Federation, and Switzerland. For example, Article 93 Netherlands Constitution provides: 'Provisions of treaties and of resolutions by international institutions which may be binding on all persons by virtue of their contents shall become binding after they have been published.' A number of common law states, such as Cyprus and Nepal, have also adopted such an approach.[3]

Another mechanism for reception of treaties as domestic law in a particular area— sometimes known as 'sector monism'—is a legislative provision providing that international treaties prevail over the provisions of existing legislation in that area should an inconsistency arise. For example, Section 15 Finnish Criminal Code provides:

If an international treaty binding on Finland or another statute or regulation that is internationally binding on Finland in some event restricts the scope of application of the criminal law of Finland, such a restriction applies as agreed. The provisions in this chapter notwithstanding, the restrictions on the scope of application of Finnish law based on generally recognised rules of international law also apply.[4]

In some states, ratified treaties generally, or a specific treaty, are given constitutional status. For example, in Austria, the European Convention on Human Rights (ECHR) has constitutional status, as do human rights treaties in a number of Latin American states (for example Argentina).[5] In other states treaties may be given supra-constitutional status. For example, in the Netherlands treaties that conflict with the Constitution may be approved by a two-thirds parliamentary majority and will then prevail over provisions of the Constitution.[6] In still other states the status may be less than constitutional but superior to other laws, whether pre-existing or subsequent. For example, Article 7(1) Constitution of Costa Rica provides: 'Public treaties, international agreements and concordats duly approved by the Legislative Assembly shall have a higher authority than the laws upon their enactment or from the day that they designate.'

In most other states, including the USA, the provisions of the treaty will be given effect as ordinary national laws, prevailing over existing inconsistent laws but subject to being overridden by subsequent national laws. In federal systems in which treaties

---

[3] See Constitution of Cyprus, Art 169(3) and Nepal Treaty Act 2047 [1990], Art 9(1).
[4] See also Norwegian Criminal Procedure Act, s 4.   [5] See Constitution of Argentina, Art 75(22).
[6] Constitution of the Netherlands, Art 91(3).

become part of the law of the land with the status of a federal legislative norm, they will prevail over both prior and subsequent state or provincial legislation and federal subordinate legislation. Germany and the USA are examples: directly applicable treaties prevail over inconsistent laws of the *Bundesländer* or of the constituent states of the USA, respectively.

Even if a treaty forms part of national law, there are additional requirements before it may be relied on directly as a source of rights by an individual. In particular, it must be 'directly applicable' or 'self-executing'.[7] Whether a treaty or a specific provision is directly applicable depends on a number of factors, including the intention of the drafters of the treaty (whether or not they intended that detailed implementing legislation would be required) and the nature of the treaty provision (in particular whether it is sufficiently precise to be applied directly or whether it is vague and general such that it requires further implementing legislation to give it content). It is possible for some provisions of a treaty to be considered directly applicable while others are not. For example, the Swiss Federal Supreme Court has held that Articles 7(1) and 12 Convention on the Rights of the Child (CRC) (rights of the child to registration on birth, a name, a nationality, and to know his or her parents; right of the child to be heard in proceedings) are directly applicable, while other provisions such as Articles 23 and 26 (right of disabled children to enjoy a full and decent life; right of the child to benefit from social security) are not.[8]

Treaties incorporated into domestic law can provide important protection of human rights, either on their own or as a complement to constitutional protections of rights. For example, in most member states of the Council of Europe the ECHR forms part of domestic law directly and can be invoked before the courts and other authorities. The courts of states parties to the ECHR regularly invoke its provisions as a direct source of rights or to inform their interpretation of constitutionally guaranteed rights. The same is true of the courts of many member states of the Organization of American States, for which the American Convention on Human Rights (ACHR) and other treaties are part of the domestic legal order, occasionally with constitutional status. UN and other regional human rights treaties as well as International Labour Organization (ILO) conventions may also provide protection not otherwise available under domestic law.

There are many examples of cases in which treaties have been successfully invoked before national courts. For example, in a case before the French Council of State, a resident of France who had brought her 4-year-old child to live with her without seeking official permission challenged an administrative decision to expel the child, on the ground that the expulsion would be contrary to the CRC. The court held that treaties could be directly relied on to challenge administrative action, found that the decision to separate the child from her mother would undermine the child's best interests con-

---

[7] See Kaiser, 'Treaties, Direct Applicability' in *Max Planck Encyclopedia of Public International Law*, available at: <http://www.mpepil.com>.

[8] *Bundesamt für Sozialversicherungen v K*, 8C_295/2008 (22 November 2008) para 4.2.

trary to Article 3 CRC, and annulled the decision.[9] Another example is the decision of the Supreme Court of Argentina in the *Campodónico de Beviacqua* case, in which a challenge had been brought against a governmental decision to stop providing medication to a child who suffered from a severe immunological condition and who was dependent on the drug. The court held that the right to health in the International Covenant on Economic, Social and Cultural Rights (ICESCR) and the Constitution of Argentina required the government to continue to provide the drug to the child.[10]

National courts have rarely had difficulty in finding most *civil and political rights* guarantees directly applicable. For example, the Dutch courts have held the right to be tried without undue delay (Article 14(3)(c) International Covenant on Civil and Political Rights (ICCPR)) to be directly applicable,[11] as have the Belgian courts in relation to the right to be informed of the nature of the charges for which one has been arrested (Article 14(3)(a) ICCPR)[12] and the right to free assistance of an interpreter (Article 14(3)(f) ICCPR).[13]

The courts of many states have also directly enforced a wide variety of treaty provisions relating to *economic and social rights*, be it in direct reliance on a treaty such as the ICESCR or an ILO convention as the primary norm, as a parallel source to a national law, or as an interpretive guide to national constitutional or legislative provisions. Other courts have not been so ready to find economic and social rights directly applicable, particularly where reliance is placed on the ICESCR. This reluctance has arisen not only from concern about the nature and justiciability of individual economic and social rights, but in particular from the terms of the ICESCR, under which states parties undertake to realize the rights guaranteed 'progressively'.[14] For example, in a case involving a challenge to an increase in university fees to be paid by students on the ground that it was inconsistent with Article 13(2)(c) ICESCR, the Swiss Federal Supreme Court held that in general the rights guaranteed by the ICESCR are not directly applicable. Rather than creating a justiciable right that could be invoked before the national courts, the treaty addressed not the individual but rather the legislator and did not provide a precise standard that could be applied by a national court.[15]

This approach seems to be based on an understanding of the obligations under the Covenant that does not reflect more recent analysis or international and national juris-

---

[9] Conseil d'État, Section, *Mlle Cinar* (22 September 1997), available at International Labour Organization, *Use of International Law by Domestic Courts: Compendium of Court Decisions* (December 2007) Case No 56: <http://training.itcilo.org/ils/CD_Use_Int_Law_web/Additional/English/default.htm>.

[10] Supreme Court of Argentina, *Campodónico de Beviacqua, Ana Carina c/ Ministerio de Salud y Acción Social Secretaría de Programas de Salud y Banco de Drogas Neoplásicas* (24 October 2000).

[11] See eg Court of Appeal of Arnhem, *Public Prosecutor v X* (1980) 11 *Netherlands YB of IL* 301.

[12] Cour de Cassation, *Pasikrisie belge*, 1984, I, 524 (17 January 1984) cited in Maresceau, 'Belgium' in Jacobs and Roberts (eds), *The Effect of Treaties in Domestic Law* (Sweet & Maxwell, 1987) 1, 18.

[13] Cour de Cassation, *Pasikrisie belge*, 1985, I, 239 (16 October 1984) cited in Maresceau, n 12, 18.

[14] See Chapter 8, above.

[15] *Verband Studierender an der Universität Zürich et al. v Regierungsrat des Kantons Zürich*, BGE 120 Ia 1, para 5c.

prudence. The work of the Committee on Economic, Social and Cultural Rights, in particular, has pointed out the directly applicable aspects of many of the rights in the ICESCR.[16] Other courts (in particular, but not only, in Latin America) have found that the 'progressive implementation' obligation under the ICESCR is no bar to finding that provisions of the ICESCR are directly applicable. For example, in *Mariela Viceconte v Estado Nacional (Ministerio de Salud y Ministerio de Economía de la Nación)*, a case involving a claim based on Article 12(2)(c) ICESCR in relation to the government's failure to arrange the production of a vaccine against Argentinean hemorrhagic fever, the Federal Administrative Court of Appeals of Argentina found a violation of the ICESCR and ordered the state to arrange for production of the vaccine.[17]

2.1.3 Human rights treaties in dualist jurisdictions

In systems which are dualist, the executive act of ratifying a treaty does not bring the treaty directly into domestic law. Rather, the treaty must be adopted by some authoritative legislative act (a statute, delegated or secondary legislation, or a decree) in order to be directly invoked before national courts. This reflects the principle that the law of the land should only be changed by acts of the legislature and not by executive acts alone. Most jurisdictions with a common law heritage follow this approach, including many members of the Commonwealth such as Australia, Canada, India, New Zealand, Nigeria, Tanzania, and the UK, as well as jurisdictions such as the Hong Kong Special Administrative Region of China and Ireland. A number of civil law states, such as Denmark, Norway, and Sweden, also have such systems.

In many such jurisdictions the legislative enactment of a human rights treaty as a whole into domestic law is relatively rare. Examples include the UK Human Rights Act 1998, the Irish European Convention on Human Rights Act 2003, the Nigerian African Charter on Human and Peoples' Rights (Ratification and Enforcement) Act 1983, and the Hong Kong Bill of Rights Ordinance 1991. The more common practice is either to fulfil the substantive treaty obligations by laws which are consistent with the treaty (sometimes drawing on its terms) or to enact specific parts of the treaty as directly enforceable national law. Thus, it is not the treaty provision itself that can be directly invoked as part of domestic law but the national legislative provisions that have transformed it into domestic law.

2.1.4 The relevance of unincorporated human rights treaties

Even in jurisdictions in which treaties do not form part of domestic law unless they have been specifically incorporated, or where an incorporated treaty provision is not directly applicable or self-executing, human rights treaty provisions may still have an impact on judicial and executive decision making and on the legislative process. In many states, courts have adopted approaches that allow unincorporated treaties to be taken into account. In the context of common law dualist systems, the Bangalore

---

[16] See Chapters 11 and 13, above.
[17] No 31.777/96, judgment of 2 June 1998, available at: <http://www.escr-net.org/caselaw/>.

Principles on the Domestic Application of International Human Rights Norms (1988) and subsequent reaffirmations of them by many judges have underlined the possibility, and responsibility, of courts to draw on international law standards when there is uncertainty or a gap in domestic law. Principle 7 Bangalore Principles states that:

it is within the proper nature of the judicial process and well-established judicial functions for national courts to have regard to international obligations which a country undertakes— whether or not they have been incorporated into domestic law—for the purpose of removing ambiguity or uncertainty from national constitutions, legislation or common law.

There are a number of ways in which unincorporated treaties (as well as customary international law standards) have been used in this indirect way. These include: presumptions that, where reasonably possible, legislation or constitutional provisions should be interpreted in a manner consistent with a state's obligations under international human rights law;[18] requirements for decision-makers to take into account a relevant unincorporated treaty in the exercise of administrative discretion;[19] creation of a legitimate expectation that decision-makers will apply the provisions of a treaty;[20] taking an unincorporated treaty into account in the development of the common law where the common law is unclear;[21] or drawing on such a treaty to identify the demands of public policy.

These possibilities are not confined to states with a common law system. Most legal systems adopt the principle of statutory interpretation that the legislature is presumed not to have legislated in a manner inconsistent with the state's international obligations. International norms may also be drawn on in determining the content of national conceptions of public policy or *ordre public*.

2.2 CONSTITUTIONAL GUARANTEES OF HUMAN RIGHTS

2.2.1 Development of constitutional rights

Constitutional guarantees of human rights can be found today in the overwhelming majority of national constitutions, though the scope and efficacy of these guarantees vary widely. Most constitutions set out to describe (and to limit) the power of those who govern and the way in which power is exercised, by protecting individual rights against the potentially intrusive power of the state and preventing the oppression of minorities or those without power through majoritarian political processes. As political documents often drafted in the wake of oppression, revolution, and the arrival of new political orders, national constitutions frequently embody the desire of their drafters to distinguish the new order from the old. The rights of those marginalized

---

[18] See *Vishaka v State of Rajasthan* [1997] INSC 665, (1997) 6 SCC 241 (Supreme Court of India).

[19] See eg *R v Director of Immigration, ex parte Simon Yin Xiang-jiang & Others* (1994) 4 HKPLR 264 (Hong Kong Court of Appeal).

[20] See eg *Minister for Immigration & Ethnic Affairs v Teoh* [1995] HCA 20, (1995) 183 CLR 273 (High Court of Australia).

[21] See *Mabo v Queensland (No 2)* (1992) 175 CLR 1, 42 (High Court of Australia).

under past systems of law, for example indigenous peoples or women, are often explicitly protected in new constitutions. At the same time, new constitutions are sometimes seen as a bulwark against the exercise of power by the incoming governments of states newly independent of their colonial masters. In some cases, constitutions may also provide protection against the violation of rights by non-state actors.

The different emphasis placed on rights in various national constitutions reflects, to a significant extent, the issues which preoccupied the nation at the period in history during which the constitution was drafted. The Spanish Constitution, for example, drafted after 36 years of Franco's dictatorship, grants rights of association but is careful to note that 'secret and paramilitary associations are prohibited' (Article 22). Fiji's Constitution, drafted in the wake of two racially motivated coups d'état, declares the right to freedom from discrimination, but is careful to preserve as lawful positive or affirmative measures to assist indigenous Fijians and Rotumans, perceived to have been disadvantaged under the former political order.

2.2.2 Content of constitutional rights

Typically, constitutionally protected rights address three principal concerns. First, they protect the right to choose political representatives. Second, they restrain the state from unduly interfering with individual liberties and property. Third, they place a duty on the state to assist the individual or group to realize their potential ('pursue happiness') through the opportunity to pursue economic, social, and cultural rights. Rights protected in modern constitutions have been influenced by international human rights instruments, above all the Universal Declaration of Human Rights (UDHR), the ICCPR, and the ICESCR. Many national courts draw on such instruments to interpret constitutional guarantees, sometimes as a matter of interpretive practice, in other cases in accordance with a constitutional stipulation such as that contained in Article 10(2) Constitution of Spain that '[p]rovisions relating to the fundamental rights and liberties recognized by the Constitution shall be construed in conformity with the Universal Declaration of Human Rights and international treaties and agreements thereon ratified by Spain'.

Most constitutions protect political rights (such as universal suffrage and the right to vote by secret ballot) and civil rights (such as freedom from torture, freedom from unreasonable searches and seizures, freedom of expression, and equality before the law). Economic, social, and cultural rights are less commonly found in constitutions and, where present, are often couched only in aspirational terms, as a duty on the part of the state to 'promote' certain rights rather than to 'guarantee' them.

For example, the Indian Constitution places economic, social, and cultural rights in a separate section to civil and political rights and describes them as 'Directive Principles of State Policy'.[22] The Constitution provides that these principles 'shall not be enforceable in any court' but are nevertheless 'fundamental in the governance of

---

[22] The model was the Constitution of Ireland, and the same approach has been adopted in the constitutions of Bangladesh, Nepal, Pakistan, and Sri Lanka.

the country and it shall be the duty of the state to apply these principles in making laws'. Despite the apparent separation of these principles from the enforceable rights sections of the Constitution, the Indian courts have effectively made them justiciable by interpreting the enforceable rights as including much of the content of the Directive Principles. A prominent example of this is the Supreme Court's interpretation of the right to life in Article 21 of the Constitution as including the rights to live with dignity, to livelihood, and to health.[23]

The South African Constitution provides a leading modern example of constitutional guarantees of wide-ranging economic and social rights that are subject to review by the courts. The rights guaranteed in the Bill of Rights include the right to adequate housing, the right to healthcare services, and rights to sufficient food, water, social security, and education. The obligation of the state is in general 'to take reasonable legislative and other measures, within its available resources, to achieve the progressive realisation' of the rights, but there are also unqualified guarantees against arbitrary eviction and refusal of emergency medical treatment. In a series of important cases, the South African courts have developed a standard for the reasonableness review of legislation and government policy in relation to a number of these constitutional guarantees.[24]

Many modern constitutions set out the permissible limitations that may be imposed on the exercise of protected rights, often drawing on the framework contained in international treaties. Generally, the state must demonstrate that any restriction is adopted in pursuit of a legitimate aim (for example 'to protect the rights and freedoms of others', to ensure 'national security', or to protect 'public order'), is provided for by law, and is a reasonable and proportionate restriction on the exercise of the right. Even where limitations are not expressly provided for in the text of a constitution, courts frequently imply similar limitations when adjudicating on the meaning and scope of a particular right.

2.3 LEGISLATIVE PROTECTION OF HUMAN RIGHTS

2.3.1 Legislative bills of rights

Fundamental rights protections are not always entrenched constitutionally. They can also be adopted by governments as ordinary pieces of legislation, with the same status as any other Act of Parliament. Important recent examples of such legislation include the New Zealand Bill of Rights Act 1990, the UK Human Rights Act 1998, and Israel's Basic Law: Human Dignity and Liberty 1992.[25] An earlier version of a statutory bill

---

[23] *Francis Coralie Mullin v The Administrator, Union of Territory Delhi* [1981] INSC 12, (1981) 2 SCR 516, 529. See generally Muralidhar, 'India: The Expectations and Challenges of Judical Enforcement of Social Rights' in Langford (ed), *Social Rights Jurisprudence: Emerging Trends in International and Comparative Law* (CUP, 2008) 102, 103.

[24] See Motala and Ramaphosa, *Constitutional Law: Analysis and Cases* (OUP, 2002) 389–413; Liebenberg, 'Adjudicating Social Rights under a Transformative Constitution' in Langford, n 23, 75.

[25] Ireland has also adopted a legislative bill of rights (the European Convention on Human Rights Act 2003), despite having a constitutional guarantee of rights. There are also a number of sub-national legislative

of rights was the Canadian Bill of Rights of 1960, which was largely ineffectual and was ultimately superseded by constitutional protection in the form of the Canadian Charter of Rights and Freedoms 1982. The decisions in these jurisdictions to adopt legislative bills of rights rather than constitutional ones reflect a variety of factors: the difficulty of achieving constitutional change due to complex amendment procedures; concerns about the impact that a constitutional bill of rights may have on the process of representative democracy (in particular perceptions that it involves the transfer to the judiciary of responsibility for decisions that are properly made by elected legislatures); concerns about freezing rights in constitutional form; and what is politically possible in a given context.

These legislative bills of rights commonly focus on the protection of civil and political rights, with limited inclusion of social, economic, and cultural rights (although the UK Human Rights Act includes protection of the right to property and the right to education). They usually provide that legislation is to be interpreted so far as possible to conform to the rights guaranteed. If this is not possible, the courts are not empowered to strike down the legislation, but may make a 'declaration of incompatibility', which invites parliament to reconsider the legislation. Recent examples of such bills of rights—sometimes described as 'parliamentary' or 'dialogue' bills of rights—have the goal of developing a 'culture of human rights' in government and the legislature. They aim to achieve this by requiring executive certification that bills are consistent (or not) with human rights, and in some cases by establishing parliamentary procedures for close scrutiny of bills and other aspects of government policy in light of human rights standards, combined with a procedure for the legislature to revisit its policy decisions following an adverse finding by a court in the form of a declaration of incompatibility. The Joint Committee on Human Rights of the UK parliament is a leading example of the possibilities for enhanced legislative scrutiny of human rights issues developed as a result of the new wave of 'parliamentary'/'dialogue' bills of rights.[26]

There are two obvious weaknesses to legislative protection of rights. The first is that legislation is capable of being repealed or amended by a later act of the legislature. The second is that parliament is able to pass legislation that is directly inconsistent with the legislative bill of rights and this later, inconsistent, legislation will prevail. However, in practice, courts, as well as legislators, have tended to view legislative bills of rights as having a status different from that of a normal piece of legislation—a quasi-constitutional or enhanced status. For example, the New Zealand courts have treated the New Zealand Bill of Rights Act as 'not entrenched but not an ordinary Statute either'.[27] In formal terms, however, these statutes still are subject to repeal or overriding just as any other ordinary statute.

bills of rights based on the ICCPR, eg the Human Rights Act 2004 of the Australian Capital Territory and the Victorian Charter of Human Rights and Responsibilities 2006.

[26] For the Joint Committee's work, see: <http://www.parliament.uk/parliamentary_committees/joint_committee_on_human_rights.cfm>. See also Klug, *Report on the Working Practices of the JCHR*, Appendix 1 to JCHR, *The Committee's Future Working Practices, Twenty-third Report of Session 2005–06* (July 2006).

[27] *Herewini v Ministry of Transport* (1992) 9 CRNZ 307, 326 (Fisher J).

2.3.2 Legislative protection of human rights through other means

Legislative protection of human rights is not confined to bills of rights or general human rights statutes. In many jurisdictions there exists extensive legislative protection of rights, particularly in fields such as discrimination, privacy, or labour rights. For example, many states have enacted legislation that prohibits discrimination on the grounds of race or ethnic origin, sex, pregnancy, marital status, sexual orientation, disability, and other grounds. Sometimes these laws take the form of a statute that covers one such ground or closely related grounds, as with the Australian federal Racial Discrimination Act 1975 and Sex Discrimination Act 1984, both of which give effect in part to relevant international treaties. Or they take the form of a general anti-discrimination statute that covers multiple grounds of discrimination. Other legislation of this sort may combine prohibitions of discrimination in certain areas with programmatic and institutional measures, as is the case with the Indian Persons with Disabilities (Equal Opportunities, Protection of Rights and Full Participation) Act 1995. In many cases such legislation is accompanied by the establishment of institutions that have an implementation or monitoring role which may have responsibility for resolving complaints of violations. Examples include the Dutch Equal Treatment Commission, the UK Equality and Human Rights Commission, and the various Scandinavian Equality Ombudsmen.

2.4 COMMON LAW PROTECTION OF HUMAN RIGHTS

For states with a common law heritage, the common law (judicial decisions determining the rights of persons in particular cases brought before the courts) contains principles that can provide significant protection against encroachment by the state. However, common law rules and presumptions must give way to a clear expression of legislative intent to displace or override them. The common law can operate to protect human rights in three key respects. First, it is a repository of rights developed in case law by judges. Second, the law-making function of judges enables them to apply principles of international human rights law when they interpret legislation or apply the common law in cases that come before them. A state's international obligations under treaties such as the ICCPR and the ICESCR are relevant to judicial approaches to statutory interpretation. Third, judges in some jurisdictions have found that the common law can operate to protect civil and political rights that exist in free and democratic societies, such as the right to freedom of communication.

The common law approach to interpreting legislation proceeds on the basis of the 'basic principle that Parliament did not intend to invade fundamental rights, freedoms and immunities'.[28] Thus, there are (rebuttable) presumptions that parliament did not intend to retrospectively change rights, infringe personal liberty, alter criminal law practices based on the principle of a fair trial, exclude the right to claim

---

[28] Spigelman, 'The Common Law Bill of Rights' in Spigelman, *Statutory Interpretation and Human Rights* (University of Queensland Press, 2008) 3, 24.

self-incrimination, authorize the commission of a tort, or interfere with the course of justice.[29] As common law rules or presumptions, these protections can be overridden by a legislature which is intent on doing so, and there are many examples of this occurring, in areas as diverse as counter-terrorism legislation and mental health legislation. Even long-established protections in the criminal process are not immune from being cut back, as is evidenced, for example, by recent efforts, some of which have been successful, to introduce limitations to the protection against 'double jeopardy' in criminal cases, the principle that an individual should not be in jeopardy of punishment by the state twice for the same offence.[30]

3 INSTITUTIONAL PROTECTIONS

All the organs of the state have a responsibility for observing and promoting human rights in their respective spheres of responsibility. Institutions that play an important role in the monitoring and enforcement of human rights include the courts, the legislature, and the executive as well as a range of further bodies which may or may not have a specific human rights mandate, including ombudsmen and national human rights institutions.

3.1 THE COURTS

As is apparent from the previous section, domestic courts may play an important role in protecting human rights through applying human rights guarantees contained in international or national law, interpreting legislation in a human rights-sensitive manner, and developing the common law. Courts with general jurisdiction will have the potential to protect human rights within the area of law they administer (for example administrative, criminal, or civil law). In some jurisdictions there may be specialized courts or administrative tribunals with a human rights jurisdiction—most frequently seen in the area of anti-discrimination law or industrial law.[31] In those states which guarantee human rights at the constitutional level, courts may protect human rights through constitutional review.

Under some legal systems, courts have the power to review the constitutionality of laws enacted by the legislature. The early and well-known example of the US Supreme Court in *Marbury v Madison* (1803), in which the Court held that it had the power to review the constitutionality of legislation, has influenced arrangements in many states. Constitutional review may take place before *any* court in some systems such as Australia, Canada, India, and the USA. In others, including Germany and Indonesia,

---

[29] Ibid, 26–9.

[30] See McNamara, 'Rolling Back an Established Right: "Reforming" the Rule against Double Jeopardy' in McNamara, *Human Rights Controversies: The Impact of Legal Form* (Taylor & Francis, 2007) 37–98.

[31] eg the Norwegian Equality Tribunal and the former New South Wales Equal Opportunity Tribunal.

the jurisdiction to review constitutionality may be vested in a constitutional court, the exclusive function of which is that of constitutional review. In yet others, such as South Africa, there may be a shared constitutional jurisdiction among the courts of general jurisdiction and a constitutional court, with the latter having the final say.

Some jurisdictions will permit a challenge to the constitutionality of a law to be launched only *after* a law has been enacted (Australia, Canada, Malaysia, and the USA), while others provide for constitutional review only *before* a law is enacted or commences operation (Sri Lanka and, until recently, France).[32] In these latter jurisdictions, the courts often also have the power to review the constitutionality or legality of executive acts, even if they cannot rule on the constitutionality of enacted laws. Some jurisdictions will limit constitutional challenges to cases in which an individual can show a particular interest in the case, while others also allow members of parliament, political parties, or state organs to seek rulings on constitutionality in the abstract (as with the *abstrakte Normenkontrolle* jurisdiction of the German Federal Constitutional Court).[33]

The scope and effectiveness of constitutional protection of rights by courts will depend on the courts' independence and their perception of their role as defenders of rights and place in the constitutional division of powers, as well as the extent of access to court in practice and the respect for court decisions shown by the government and the legislature.

Judicial interpretation of constitutional rights has often functioned to expand the substantive content of rights. The US Constitution, for example, does not explicitly mention a right to privacy, but the Supreme Court has derived such a right from other provisions of the Constitution, extending it into areas which include personal autonomy over reproductive decisions. In *Roe v Wade* it famously held that the right protected a woman's decision to terminate her pregnancy in certain circumstances.[34] The Indian courts, constrained from directly enforcing economic, social, and cultural rights included in the Constitution as mere 'Directive Principles of State Policy,' have by interpretation expanded the content of (justiciable) civil and political rights to encompass economic, social, and cultural rights. For example, the obligation on the state to provide free and compulsory education (a 'Directive Principle of State Policy' only), was held by the Supreme Court to be a 'fundamental right' guaranteed by the right to life and hence justiciable.[35] In a similar vein, the Supreme Court of Pakistan has held that the right to life in the Constitution of Pakistan includes the right to a healthy environment.[36]

---

[32] As the result of the passage of the *Constitutional Law on the Modernization of the Institutions of the Fifth Republic* of 23 July 2008, the Conseil Constitutionel has a limited role of review of constitutionality of laws, when matters are referred to it by other courts.

[33] Steinberger, *Models of Constitutional Jurisdiction* (Council of Europe Press, 1993).

[34] 410 US 113 (1973).

[35] *Unni Krishnan JP v State of Andhra Pradesh* [1993] INSC 60, (1993) 1 SCC 645.

[36] *Shehla Zia v WAPDA*, PLD 1994 SC 693.

3.2 THE EXECUTIVE

The role of the executive in protecting human rights is also critical. The executive should have procedures in place to ensure that it takes into account both its positive and negative obligations in relation to human rights when deciding on its policy priorities and in assessing the appropriateness of its approach to implementing them. Many states have detailed assessment procedures for ensuring that draft laws are consistent with human rights, both within the bureaucracy and also when proposals are put to cabinet for approval (for example, through requirements in cabinet procedures that the human rights implications of draft legislation be clearly identified).

3.3 THE LEGISLATURE

Legislatures also have an important role to play, both as guarantors of human rights through enactment of legislation but also as monitors of proposals put before them. The means by which legislatures carry out human rights monitoring vary widely.[37] Some legislatures have established a legislative committee with a specific human rights mandate to review legislative proposals (and sometimes other aspects of government policy and conduct) for human rights consistency. The UK Joint Committee on Human Rights is one such example. Other legislatures have established scrutiny of bills committees that have the responsibility to identify and draw to the attention of the legislature whether legislative proposals 'trespass unduly on personal rights and liberties' or violate a range of other standards.[38] Yet other legislatures may consider human rights issues in other substantive legislative committees, for example ones focusing on legal and constitutional affairs, foreign affairs and trade, or home affairs.

In some states, the role of ensuring that legislation conforms to the constitution may reside exclusively in the legislature instead of the courts. In China, for example, the Standing Committee of the National People's Congress has the power to issue formal, binding opinions on the interpretation of the Constitution. Furthermore, as noted above, in some of the systems with constitutional judicial review, members of parliament are authorized to seek rulings on the constitutionality of proposed legislation before its enactment or entry into force.

3.4 OTHER BODIES

There are many other types of national institutions that can contribute to the protection and enjoyment of human rights. Some of these may have an explicit human rights mandate, while others do not. Examples of institutions that do not necessarily have a specific human rights mandate but that may nonetheless protect human rights in fact

---

[37] See Inter-Parliamentary Union, PARLINE Database: Parliamentary Human Rights Bodies, available at: <http://www.ipu.org/parline-e/Instance-hr.asp>.

[38] eg the Australian Senate's Standing Committee on Scrutiny of Bills. See: <http://www.aph.gov.au/Senate/committee/scrutiny/cominfo.htm>.

include ombudsmen, parliamentary commissioners for administration (who may be entrusted with the task of monitoring public administration and responding to complaints of maladministration), public advocates, inspectors of prisons, data protection mechanisms, and telecommunications and broadcasting regulatory authorities. Institutions with a specific human rights mandate may include human rights commissions, equality bodies, ombudsmen with a specific human rights mandate, and public bodies or offices with responsibility for overseeing government.

3.4.1 Ombudsmen

The institution of the ombudsman has its roots in Scandinavia but has been taken up in many states.[39] While the original ombudsman institution developed in Sweden, its Norwegian and Danish variants have been particularly influential. The traditional model of an ombudsman has been an independent institution that is established by and answerable to parliament, with the power to consider complaints and conduct investigations on its own initiative, and to make recommendations to government rather than to adopt binding decisions. In terms of mandate, there are two main models of ombudsman (though some ombudsmen are hybrids of the two): the classical ombudsman and the human rights ombudsman.[40] It was estimated in 2003 that there were about 110 states in the world with classical or hybrid ombudsman institutions.[41]

Classical ombudsmen have jurisdiction to oversee government administration and to consider complaints of unfair, unjust, or poor administration. Such bodies are an important means of ensuring that citizens have an affordable and accessible avenue of complaining about administrative conduct. They do not generally have an explicit human rights mandate, but their actions may assist complainants in realizing their rights (for instance, a fair hearing by a government decision-maker or the granting of a social security benefit) and ensuring that constitutional and other legal guarantees of human rights are observed. In some cases, classical ombudsmen make explicit use of international and national human rights norms in their work. The institution of the classical ombudsman is to be found in all regions of the world.[42]

Human rights ombudsmen, on the other hand, have an explicit human rights mandate (and possibly a general maladministration mandate). This may be a specialized mandate focusing on specific human right issues. For example, the Norwegian Gender Equality Ombud had a specific role under the Gender Equality Act, while in Sweden there were until 2009 four Ombuds working in the area of equality and non-discrimination (the Ombudsman against Ethnic Discrimination, the Ombudsman

---

[39] See generally Reif, *The Ombudsman, Good Governance and the International Human Rights System* (Martinus Nijhoff, 2004); Gregory and Giddings (eds), *Righting Wrongs: The Ombudsman in Six Continents* (IOS Press, 2000); Hossain, Besselink, Selassie, and Völker (eds), *Human Rights Commissions and Ombudsman Offices: National Experiences Throughout the World* (Kluwer, 2000).   [40] Reif, n 39, 8–9.
[41] Ibid, 11.
[42] Examples include the Swedish Parliamentary Ombudsmen (Riksdagens ombudsmän), the UK's Parliamentary Commissioner for Administration (and similar institutions in many Commonwealth jurisdictions), the Australian Commonwealth Ombudsman, and the institution of the Defensor del Pueblo that is to be found in Spain and many Latin American states. See generally ibid, 187–92.

against Discrimination on grounds of Sexual Orientation, the Equal Opportunities Ombudsman, and the Children's Ombudsman)—these have now been replaced with one Equality Ombudsman with jurisdiction over all these issues. Similarly, a number of states have children's ombudsmen or commissioners. Alternatively, the mandate may be a more general human rights mandate, in which case the ombudsman institution may be very similar to a national human rights institution in its coverage.

Both classical and human rights ombudsmen can provide substantive protection for human rights, by explicitly applying and enforcing domestic and international human rights norms, or by applying standards of good administration without express reference to human rights norms.[43]

3.4.2 National human rights institutions

In the past 20 years, national human rights institutions (NHRIs) have become increasingly significant actors in promoting and protecting human rights within the state. These institutions, established by constitution or legislation, carry out dual functions in relation to the state. Their first role is to work with government in attempting to ensure that legislation complies with the state's international human rights obligations or constitutional guarantees, to educate government officials about human rights, and to advise government about the human rights implications of government action. Their second role is to critique government action that violates human rights and to provide remedies—be it through conciliation or adjudication—to individuals whose rights have been violated. The first role requires NHRIs to be able to work closely and effectively with government. The second role requires them to be staunchly independent of government. The experience of NHRIs over the past 20 years suggests that the balance between the two roles is sometimes a difficult one to achieve.

Nonetheless, NHRIs have been and continue to be established in all regions of the world, in very different political circumstances. One of the key factors driving their establishment is recognition that remedies for breaches of international human rights provided at the international level (for example, by the UN treaty-based bodies empowered to receive individual complaints) are inaccessible to most people. For reasons of access and affordability, remedies must be provided at the national level.

Recognizing that some states may attempt to establish NHRIs as mere human rights 'window-dressing', in 1993 the UN General Assembly adopted the Paris Principles, a set of standards aimed at ensuring the independence and effectiveness of NHRIs.[44] The Paris Principles provide guidelines as to the composition of NHRIs (requiring that they be representative of the pluralism in society) and the appointment of commission members (requiring that they have a clearly defined term of appointment and transparent procedures for appointment and dismissal). They further require NHRIs to be given competence to promote and protect human rights and as broad a mandate

---

[43] Reif, n 39, 103–12, provides an overview of the ways in which both classical ombudsmen and human rights ombudsmen can use domestic and international human rights norms in their work.

[44] Principles Relating to the Status and Functions of National Institutions for the Promotion and Protection of Human Rights, GA Res 48/134, Annex (1993).

as possible, which is to be clearly anchored in a constitutional or legislative text. In addition, they provide that NHRIs should be empowered to:

- make recommendations and report to government on matters concerning human rights (including in relation to legislative or administrative provisions and any situation of human rights violations they decide to take up);
- promote conformity of national laws and practices with international human rights standards;
- encourage ratification of international human rights treaties and implementation of international standards;
- contribute to reporting procedures under international instruments;
- assist in the formulation and execution of human rights teaching and research and increase public awareness through information and education; and
- cooperate with the UN, regional institutions, and national institutions of other states.

As well as these functions, many NHRIs have 'quasi-judicial' powers, such as the power to compel production of documents and giving of evidence, powers of investigation, and the power to conciliate complaints. Some NHRIs refer complaints to appropriate authorities for investigation or institution of legal proceedings. Where this is the case, NHRIs often possess the power to appear in courts and tribunals as *amicus curiae* in order to bring relevant principles of human rights law to the attention of the court. Many NHRIs also have the power to undertake public inquiries into human rights issues. Public inquiries have proved an effective way for NHRIs, with limited resources and subjected to multiple demands, to make a significant impact in certain areas. The publicity attached to these inquiries and the fact that they are undertaken by an organ within the state often make it politically difficult for governments to ignore findings and recommendations.

Despite their location within the state and their susceptibility to lack of independence from the government, NHRIs have the potential to be effective actors in strengthening human rights protection. Their ability to pursue issues and hold inquiries of their own accord sets them apart from the courts, which must wait for rights-relevant cases to be brought before them in order that they can make determinations that support the development of human rights law.

4 CONCLUSION

Securing the enjoyment of human rights within the state is a complex process, involving the interaction between substantive norms of human rights and their status in the domestic legal system, the availability and effectiveness of a range of institutions (including those with a specific human rights mandate), the legitimacy of human rights discourse among political leaders and the community, and the level of stability in a given society. All measures for the domestic protection of human rights rely for their efficacy on the allocation by the state of sufficient resources. The provision of legal aid and funding for public interest litigation, a judiciary, a legal profession, and a community educated in human rights are all essential to the realization of human rights.

FURTHER READING

ALSTON (ed), *Promoting Human Rights Through Bills of Right: Comparative Perspectives* (Clarendon Press, 1999).

CONFORTI and FRANCIONI (eds), *Enforcing International Human Rights in Domestic Courts* (Martinus Nijhoff, 1997).

FATIMA, *Using International Law in Domestic Courts* (Hart, 2005).

FENWICK, *Civil Liberties and Human Rights* (Routledge-Cavendish, 2007).

GARGARELLA, DOMINGO, and ROUX (eds), *Courts and Social Transformation in New Democracies: An Institutional Voice for the Poor?* (Ashgate, 2006).

HOSSAIN, BESSELINK, SELASSIE, and VÖLKER (eds), *Human Rights Commissions and*

Ombudsman Offices: National Experiences Throughout the World (Kluwer, 2000).

JAYAWICKRAMA, *The Judicial Application of Human Rights Law: National, Regional and International Jurisprudence* (Cambridge University Press, 2002).

LANGFORD (ed), *Social Rights Jurisprudence: Emerging Trends in International and Comparative Law* (Cambridge University Press, 2008).

SIMMONS, *Mobilizing for Human Rights: International Law in Domestic Politics* (Cambridge University Press, 2009).

USEFUL WEBSITES

Asia Pacific Forum of National Human Rights Institutions: <http://www.asiapacificforum.net/>

Interights, *Commonwealth and International Human Rights Case Law Databases*: <http://www.interights.org/database-search/index.htm>

International Labour Organization, *Use of International Law by Domestic Courts: Compendium of Court Decisions*: <http://training.itcilo.org/ils/CD_Use_Int_Law_web/Additional/English/default.htm>

Inter-Parliamentary Union, *PARLINE Database: Parliamentary Human Rights Bodies*: <http://www.ipu.org/parline-e/Instance-hr.asp>

National Human Rights Institutions Forum: <http://www.nhri.net>

Venice Commission of the Council of Europe, *CODICES, the Infobase on Constitutional Case-Law of the Venice Commission*: <http://www.codices.coe.int/>

World Legal Information Institute (database of national and international case law): <http://www.worldlii.org>

PART V

LINKAGES

23

INTERNATIONAL HUMANITARIAN LAW

Sandesh Sivakumaran

SUMMARY

International humanitarian law is concerned with the regulation of armed conflict. It is closely related to international human rights law. Although the two come from different historical backgrounds, they have common values, primarily those of respect for, and dignity of, the human person. International human rights law does not cease to apply in time of armed conflict. The continued applicability of international human rights law provides added value but also creates difficulties. Given the applicability of both international human rights law and international humanitarian law in time of armed conflict, it is important to discern the relationship between them.

1 INTRODUCTION

The principal body of international law that applies in time of armed conflict is international humanitarian law. International humanitarian law seeks to balance the violence inherent in an armed conflict with the dictates of humanity. It protects the civilian population from the ravages of conflict and establishes limitations on the means and methods of combat. International human rights law does not cease to apply in situations of armed conflict. Rather, it continues to apply alongside international humanitarian law. This continued applicability complements international humanitarian law and offers distinct advantages as far as the protection of the human person is concerned. It also poses some difficulties, not least identifying the exact relationship between the two bodies of law.

Section 2 considers the nature of international humanitarian law and identifies some of its cardinal principles and key rules. Section 3 explores the similarities and differences between international humanitarian law and international human rights law, comparing and contrasting their historical origins and conceptual approaches.

Given that international humanitarian law applies in situations of armed conflict, whether there is a need for international human rights law also to apply is the subject of Section 4. As these two bodies of law coexist, it is crucial to ascertain the relationship between them. Accordingly, this forms the subject of Section 5. Section 6 considers some of the difficulties with the application of international human rights law in time of armed conflict.

2 WHAT IS INTERNATIONAL HUMANITARIAN LAW?

The body of law that applies in time of armed conflict operates under numerous names: international humanitarian law, the law of war, or the law of armed conflict. It is the body of law which seeks to balance the violence inherent in armed conflict with the dictates of humanity. It belies the idea that 'when the guns go off the law becomes silent'. It is, quite simply, 'the last lifeline, when nothing else stands between mankind and a relapse into savagery'.[1]

International humanitarian law is comprised of treaties—principally, the Hague Regulations of 1899 and 1907, the Geneva Conventions of 1949, and the Protocols Additional to the Geneva Conventions of 1977—and customary international law.[2] Different rules govern international armed conflicts (traditionally fought between two or more states), situations of belligerent occupation (the placing of territory under the authority of a hostile army), and internal armed conflicts (fought between a state and an armed opposition group or two or more armed groups within the boundaries of a state). Treaty rules largely govern international armed conflicts and belligerent occupations, with only one provision of the four Geneva Conventions—Article 3, common to all four Conventions—and one principal treaty—Additional Protocol II—regulating the conduct of internal armed conflicts. Internal armed conflicts do benefit from detailed regulation at the level of customary international law but this is not to quite the same extent as international armed conflicts. This is because states viewed, and to some degree continue to view, internal armed conflicts as matters of domestic concern, jealously guarding their sovereignty.

The cardinal principles of international humanitarian law are those of distinction and unnecessary suffering. The principle of distinction provides that combatants (or fighters, in the language of internal armed conflict) should be distinguished from civilians and civilian objects should be distinguished from military objectives. The principle of unnecessary suffering prohibits the use of means (weapons) and

---

[1] Quentin-Baxter, 'Human Rights and Humanitarian Law—Confluence or Conflict?' (1985) 9 *Australian YIL* 94, 103.

[2] For a useful list of treaties, see <http://www.icrc.org/ihl.nsf/INTRO?OpenView>. For customary international law, see Henckaerts and Doswald-Beck, *Customary International Humanitarian Law* (CUP, 2005).

methods (tactics) of warfare that are of a nature to cause suffering or injury beyond that which is required for its military purpose. Underlying these principles are the fundamental tenets of humanity, military necessity, and chivalry.

The principal provisions of international humanitarian law seek to afford a measure of protection to civilians and other persons *hors de combat* (literally 'outside of combat'; primarily military personnel no longer fighting due to sickness, injury, or capture) and to place certain restrictions on the means and methods of warfare. Ideas of military necessity are imbued in the provisions and, as such, a state cannot justify violation of the rules by claiming that it was militarily necessary for it to do so. The rules of international humanitarian law are tailored for an exceptional situation—the state of war. Accordingly, there is no possibility of derogating from them on the basis of strategic expedience or necessity.

Let us consider some of the key rules.

Protections afforded to civilians and persons hors de combat: the guiding principle is one of humane treatment. This guarantee encompasses such prohibitions as violence to life and person, outrages upon personal dignity, the taking of hostages, collective punishments, slavery, and forcible displacement.[3] Special protections are in place for particular categories of persons including the wounded and sick, medical and religious personnel, women, and children.[4]

Targeting: the civilian population and civilian objects shall not be made the object of attack.[5] Indiscriminate attacks are similarly prohibited.[6] Equally forbidden are attacks that would violate the principle of proportionality, namely that the incidental loss of civilian life and damage to civilian property should not be excessive in relation to the concrete and direct military advantage anticipated.[7] In the event that an attack takes place, feasible precautions must be taken to avoid injury to the civilian population and damage to civilian objects.[8]

Means and methods of combat: the means of injuring the enemy are not unlimited. Some weapons are specifically prohibited, such as poison, biological and bacteriological weapons, gas, and other chemical weapons.[9] Weapons that are indiscriminate by nature or are of a nature to cause unnecessary suffering are similarly prohibited.[10] Equally, the methods of combat are not unlimited. For example, it is prohibited to order that there shall be no survivors, to kill those who have expressed a desire to surrender, and to make improper use of flags and uniforms.[11]

---

[3] See eg Additional Protocol I, Art 75; Additional Protocol II, Art 4.

[4] See eg Additional Protocol I, Arts 10, 15, 76, 77; Additional Protocol II, Arts 7–9.

[5] Additional Protocol I, Arts 51(2), 52(1).   [6] Ibid, Art 51(4).   [7] Ibid, Art 51(5)(b).

[8] Ibid, Art 57.

[9] See eg Geneva Protocol for the Prohibition of the Use in War of Asphyxiating, Poisonous or Other Gases, and of Bacteriological Methods of Warfare (1925); Convention on the Prohibition of the Development, Production and Stockpiling of Bacteriological (Biological) and Toxin Weapons and Their Destruction (1972); Convention on the Prohibition of the Development, Production, Stockpiling and Use of Chemical Weapons and on Their Destruction (1993).   [10] Additional Protocol I, Art 35(2).

[11] Ibid, Arts 40, 41, 39.

3 DIFFERENT HISTORIES; SHARED VALUES

International humanitarian law is sometimes described as the human rights law of armed conflict. Such a description has the potential to mislead, for, although the two bodies of law share some of the same purposes, they are historically different and indeed remain distinct.

International human rights law flourished in the immediate aftermath of the Second World War, with the adoption of the Universal Declaration of Human Rights (UDHR). It has since been followed by the International Covenant on Civil and Political Rights (ICCPR) and the International Covenant on Economic, Social and Cultural Rights as well as numerous treaties, declarations, and the like. International humanitarian law's first flourish took place in the 1860s with the conclusion of the Lieber Code (1863), the Geneva Convention on the Wounded (1864), and the St Petersburg Declaration on Explosive Projectiles (1868).

At a conceptual level, international humanitarian law applies between two or more competing factions (states and/or armed groups). International human rights law, however, regulates the relationship between the state and the individual. International humanitarian law operates on the basis of equality of parties; while the fundamental premise of international human rights law is the unequal relationship between the governor and the governed.

More markedly, the two sets of rules differ in their substance. Take the right to life. The right not to be arbitrarily deprived of one's life is fundamental to international human rights law, the supreme right on which all others are built. International humanitarian law accepts the killing of combatants and fighters as inherent in an armed conflict and tolerates the killing of civilians in certain circumstances. For example, a military objective may not be attacked if the attack 'may be expected to cause incidental loss of civilian life, injury to civilians, damage to civilian objects, or a combination thereof, which would be excessive in relation to the concrete and direct military advantage anticipated'.[12] Accordingly, incidental civilian casualties are tolerated provided they are not excessive in comparison with the anticipated military advantage. Thus, the rules of international humanitarian law, humanitarian though they may be, take as their starting point the combatant's privilege, namely the right to kill.

Given these differences, there was little interaction between the two bodies of law in the period immediately after 1945. Some of the great instruments of both areas were adopted at around the same time: the UDHR was adopted in 1948 and the four Geneva Conventions in 1949. Yet few persons participated in the drafting of both sets of instruments and the impact of the one on the other was minimal. Whilst international human rights law largely developed within the UN system, international humanitarian law developed outside, primarily through its guardian, the International

---

[12] Ibid, Art 51(5)(b).

Committee of the Red Cross (ICRC). Historically, the ICRC was wary of associating itself with the, politicized, UN; while the UN, having outlawed the threat or use of force in its Charter, was concerned about considering the law that applies during war lest it be thought that such outlawry was doomed from the outset.[13]

It took until 1968 and the International Conference on Human Rights in Tehran for the two bodies of law to come into close contact with one another. During that conference, convened by the UN in the International Year for Human Rights, a resolution was passed that called on all states to ratify the international humanitarian law treaties then in existence and requested the General Assembly to invite the Secretary-General to prepare a study on various aspects of international humanitarian law.[14]

Since the Tehran Conference, there has been greater interaction between international human rights and humanitarian law. International human rights law has influenced international humanitarian law and vice versa. The fundamental guarantees of the 1977 Additional Protocols, prohibiting murder, torture, and the like are a reflection of international human rights law and are inspired by that body of law.[15] The 1989 Convention on the Rights of the Child (CRC)—a human rights instrument—requires states parties to 'respect and to ensure respect for rules of international humanitarian law applicable to them in armed conflicts which are relevant to the child'.[16] The Optional Protocol thereto on the Involvement of Children in Armed Conflict, unusually for a human rights instrument, refers to armed groups, namely that they 'should not, under any circumstances, recruit or use in hostilities persons under the age of 18 years'.[17]

The mutual influence of the two sets of rules and the closer association between the bodies working with them is, in many respects, unsurprising given that they share similar goals, namely respect for, and dignity of, the human person. The idea of human dignity is at the very heart of international human rights law, human rights being derived from the 'inherent dignity of the human person'.[18] In international humanitarian law, the prohibition on 'outrages upon personal dignity' is based on this idea of human dignity.[19] It is also infused throughout that body of law. The Martens clause, for example, a residual clause contained in most humanitarian law instruments, provides that 'in cases not covered by the law in force, the human person remains under the protection of the principles of humanity and the dictates of the public conscience'.[20]

---

[13] Such was the concern that the International Law Commission—tasked by the UN with codifying and progressively developing international law—felt unable to place the revision of the law of armed conflict on its work agenda despite the urgent need for its revision as evidenced by the Second World War. See *1949 Yearbook of the International Law Commission* 281, para 18 (UN, 1956).

[14] 'Human Rights in Armed Conflicts', Res XXIII of the International Conference on Human Rights, Tehran (12 May 1968), reprinted in Schindler and Toman (eds), *The Laws of Armed Conflicts* (Martinus Nihoff, 2004) 347; GA Res 2444 (XXIII) (19 December 1968).

[15] Additional Protocol I, Art 75; Additional Protocol II, Art 4.   [16] CRC, Art 38(1).

[17] Optional Protocol to the Convention on the Rights of the Child on the Involvement of Children in Armed Conflict, Art 4(1).   [18] ICCPR, preamble; ICESCR, preamble.

[19] See eg Common Art 3(1)(c).   [20] See eg Additional Protocol II, preamble.

4 REASONS FOR THE APPLICATION OF HUMAN RIGHTS LAW IN ARMED CONFLICT

Given that a body of international law—international humanitarian law—is designed to regulate armed conflict, it is legitimate to ask whether there is need for another body of international law—international human rights law—to apply. Aside from the difference in substantive content, which is in itself an important reason, there are at least three other factors that suggest there is a role for international human rights law to play in time of armed conflict.

4.1 NON-APPLICABILITY OF INTERNATIONAL HUMANITARIAN LAW

It has been perceptively remarked that, 'the first line of defense against international humanitarian law is to deny that it applies at all'.[21] International humanitarian law presupposes the existence of an armed conflict; a declared war, which is nowadays rare; or occupation of territory, which usually, though not always, results from an armed conflict. An armed conflict, in turn, exists 'whenever there is a resort to armed force between States or protracted armed violence between governmental authorities and organized armed groups or between such groups within a State'.[22] In order to deny the applicability of international humanitarian law, states often contest the very existence of an armed conflict. This has been the approach, for example, of the Russian government in respect of the situation in Chechnya (1999–2009). Events may be characterized as internal tensions or disturbances ('troubles' or 'riots'), or the armed opposition group may be portrayed as criminals or terrorists (as was the case with the Kosovo Liberation Army (KLA) in Kosovo).

One of the key difficulties in this area is that no particular body is mandated to determine issues such as the existence of an armed conflict, the characterization of that conflict as international or internal, or whether territory can be described as occupied. These questions, and others, are left to the individual state and the armed group for their own determinations; yet such determinations will hardly be undertaken in a neutral manner. The views of third states and UN bodies may be influential, though, ultimately, they will not be determinative in the application of international humanitarian law by the parties. The pronouncements of international courts and tribunals may be authoritative but they are likely to be handed down some years after the

---

[21] Baxter, 'Some Existing Problems of Humanitarian Law' in *The Concept of International Armed Conflict: Further Outlook* (Proceedings of the International Symposium on Humanitarian Law, 1974) 2 cited in Meron, 'On the Inadequate Reach of Humanitarian and Human Rights Law and the Need for a New Instrument' (1983) 77 *AJIL* 589, 598.

[22] *Prosecutor v Tadić*, Decision on the Defence Motion for Interlocutory Appeal on Jurisdiction, IT-94-1-AR72, 2 October 1995, para 70.

conflict in question. The International Criminal Tribunals for the former Yugoslavia and for Rwanda, the work of which is still ongoing, are examples on point.

A further problem with the applicability of international humanitarian law to armed conflicts is that additional pre-requisites have to be satisfied before certain rules become applicable. For example, for the provisions of Additional Protocol II to apply, the armed conflict must take place:

[I]n the territory of a High Contracting Party between its armed forces and dissident armed forces or other organized armed groups which, under responsible command, exercise such control over a part of its territory as to enable them to carry out sustained and concerted military operations and to implement this Protocol.[23]

The requirement of territorial control on the part of the armed group constitutes a threshold difficult to surmount. As such, the treaty rules of Additional Protocol II will not be applicable to many an internal armed conflict, such as that involving the Sendero Luminoso (Shining Path) guerrillas in Peru, or the Kurdistan Workers' Party (PKK) in Turkey. The Protocol also requires the armed conflict to be waged between armed forces of the state and dissident armed forces, or armed forces of the state and an armed group. Thus, an internal armed conflict fought between two or more armed groups without the involvement of the state—such as the armed conflict in Somalia, which for many years did not have a central government—would not benefit from the protections afforded by the Protocol.

Given the uncertainty surrounding the existence of an armed conflict and the routine denial of the applicability of international humanitarian law, there is a very real need for a body of international law to be applicable at all times. International human rights law thus has an important role to play. It is true that a state may derogate from certain provisions of international human rights law, but a detailed regime governs the derogation procedure.[24] The difference in starting point between international human rights law and international humanitarian law reveals the potential importance of the former. The default presumption for international human rights law is that it applies; for international humanitarian law that it does not. International humanitarian law does not apply until the existence of an armed conflict is established. International human rights law does apply until the state derogates from it and continues to apply subject to the limited extent of the derogation.

Even with the applicability of international human rights law, there has been some concern over a potential lacuna in the international legal regulation of internal tensions and disturbances. International humanitarian law would not be applicable to such a situation given that the violence falls short of an armed conflict. Many provisions of international human rights law would not be applicable were the state to consider the tensions a grave public emergency and derogate from certain of its obligations. In light of such a potential lacuna, a group of experts has drafted a 'Declaration of Minimum Humanitarian Standards' outlining the fundamental standards of

[23] Additional Protocol II, Art 1(1).   [24] See Chapter 6, above.

humanity applicable regardless of the situation,[25] but this has not garnered the full support of states.

4.2 DUTY TO INVESTIGATE

Although a duty to investigate the loss of life does not appear in the text of the principal human rights treaties, it has been read into certain provisions of human rights law. The European Court of Human Rights, for example, has held that the obligation to protect the right to life, coupled with a state's general duty to secure convention rights pursuant to Article 1 European Convention on Human Rights (ECHR) implies that 'there should be some form of effective official investigation when individuals have been killed as a result of the use of force'.[26] The investigation is required to be prompt, thorough, and effective and should be undertaken by an independent and impartial body.[27] An investigation seeks to avoid the creation of a climate of impunity, which so often provides the setting for further violations. The obligation to investigate does not cease just because the loss of life occurred during a military operation: 'neither the prevalence of violent armed clashes nor the high incidence of fatalities can displace the obligation'.[28]

The general obligation to investigate the loss of life does not, as yet, form part of the corpus of international humanitarian law. In certain specified situations—such as in the case of deaths of prisoners of war[29]—a duty to investigate exists, but no general duty to investigate the loss of life can be identified. There are certainly cogent reasons as to why international humanitarian law *should* contain such a requirement, and of late, there is some authority for the existence of such a general duty. Notably, the Israeli Supreme Court has said that a 'thorough investigation' is to be performed in the event that a civilian suspected of taking an active part in hostilities is attacked.[30] It would seem, then, that international humanitarian law is moving in this direction but that it is not there just yet. Until such time, international human rights law fills the gap.

4.3 ENFORCEMENT

One of the principal means of enforcing international humanitarian law is the prosecution of individual offenders for breach of that law.[31] Prosecution may take place at

---

[25] Report of the Secretary-General prepared pursuant to Commission Resolution 1995/29, E/CN.4/1996/80 (28 November 1995), Annex.

[26] *Isayeva v Russia* (2005) 41 EHRR 38, para 209. See also *Myrna Mack Chang v Guatemala*, IACtHR Series C No 101 (25 November 2003) para 157; 74/92, *Commission Nationale des Droits de l'Homme et des Libertés v Chad*, 9th Activity Report of the ACommHPR (1995) para 22.

[27] See eg HRC, General Comment 31, HRI/GEN/I/Rev.9 (Vol I) 243, para 15; *Isayeva*, ibid, paras 209–14.

[28] *Kaya v Turkey* (1999) 28 EHRR 1, paras 87 and 91.

[29] Geneva Convention Relative to the Treatment of Prisoners of War of August 12, 1949, Art 121.

[30] *The Public Committee Against Torture in Israel v The Government of Israel*, HCJ 769/02 (2006) para 40.   [31] See Chapter 24, below.

the domestic level and, particularly with the advent of the permanent International Criminal Court, at the international level. Prosecution is not a remedy for all the world's ills: the International Criminal Court is of limited jurisdiction while domestic prosecutions are few and far between.

In addition to prosecutions, there are various non-judicial means by which to enforce international humanitarian law. An International Humanitarian Fact-Finding Commission is competent to inquire into any factual allegations of serious violations of the Geneva Conventions or Additional Protocols; however, in practice, this has never been used.[32] The ICRC is the pre-eminent organization working in the field of international humanitarian law and seeks to protect and assist those affected by armed conflict.[33] The ICRC operates on the basis of confidentiality, which allows it to gain access to situations when such access is denied to other organizations, but this also usually prevents it from publicizing violations. Belligerent reprisals—by which a serious violation of international humanitarian law by state A can be met with retaliatory action on the part of state B, subject to certain conditions, which would otherwise have constituted a breach of international humanitarian law—may be carried out so as to induce compliance with the rules on the part of state A. However, such retaliatory action could result in the loss of life or cause injury or suffering to innocent persons and so the legality of belligerent reprisals in the form of attacks on civilians has been questioned.[34]

There are many more enforcement mechanisms in the human rights field. Individuals may institute proceedings before a regional human rights court, a regional human rights commission, or a human rights treaty body mandated to hear their complaint. One state may file a complaint against another state before an empowered institution. Human rights treaty bodies scrutinize reports submitted by states parties to the principal human rights treaties on the measures they have taken to give effect to the treaty rights. The Human Rights Council reviews the human rights record of all member states of the UN every four years. Special Rapporteurs or Independent Experts of the Human Rights Council conduct fact-finding missions, prepare reports, and respond to individual complaints.[35] Numerous national and international NGOs monitor human rights violations and 'name and shame' governments.[36] The applicability of human rights law to situations of armed conflict is useful, then, for its enforcement mechanisms.

---

[32] Additional Protocol I, Art 90; Report of the International Fact-Finding Commission 1991–1996. See <http://www.ihffc.org>. [33] See <http://www.icrc.org>.

[34] For the view that customary international law prohibits such reprisals, see *Prosecutor v Kupreškić et al.*, Judgment, IT-95-16-T, 14 January 2000, paras 527–36. However, this position seems to have been rejected, implicitly, in *Prosecutor v Martić*, Judgment, IT-95-11-A, 8 October 2008, paras 263–7. Treaty law applicable to international armed conflicts does contain this proscription (Additional Protocol I, Art 51(6)) but a number of states have entered reservations to it. [35] See Chapter 18, above.

[36] See Chapter 4, above.

If human rights law is being applied with the primary aim of using its enforcement mechanisms, an alternative approach would be to bypass the applicable law and use the enforcement mechanisms to monitor not human rights law but humanitarian law. For a time, the Inter-American Commission on Human Rights did just this, applying international humanitarian law directly to several matters before it. In the *Abella* case, for example, the Inter-American Commission characterized violence at the *La Tablada* military base in Argentina as an armed conflict and proceeded to assess the events against the standards of international humanitarian law.[37] Various UN entities working in the area of human rights also apply and monitor international humanitarian law. However, such an approach raises issues of lack of expertise and overstepping of mandates. For the latter reason, the Inter-American Court of Human Rights held that neither it nor the Commission had the competence to apply directly international humanitarian law.[38] Rather, it could use international humanitarian law in its interpretation of the American Convention on Human Rights.[39] Despite some criticism on the part of states, UN entities—the Special Rapporteur on extrajudicial, summary or arbitrary executions and the Working Group on Arbitrary Detention, to name but two—continue to apply and enforce international humanitarian law.[40] The mandate of many of these entities, not being limited to international human rights law, makes that decision eminently sensible.[41]

5 THE RELATIONSHIP BETWEEN THE TWO BODIES OF LAW

That international human rights law applies in armed conflict is, today, beyond question. This is clear from the human rights treaties themselves. The ICCPR, for example, provides that a state party to the ICCPR may derogate from certain of its obligations '[i]n time of public emergency which threatens the life of the nation', a phrase that includes armed conflict.[42] Other, non-derogable, obligations continue to bind the state: armed conflict does not give a free pass to torture, enslave, and the like. A number of human rights treaties—the African Charter on Human and Peoples' Rights for one—do not contain derogation clauses. In respect of these treaties, no

[37] Case 11.137, *Abella v Argentina*, IACommHR Report No 55/97 (18 November 1997), paras 156, 176–89.   [38] *Las Palmeras v Colombia*, IACtHR Series C No 67 (4 February 2000) paras 32–4.
[39] *Bámaca-Velásquez v Guatemala*, IACtHR Series C No 70 (25 November 2000) para 209.
[40] See eg Report of the Special Rapporteur on extrajudicial, summary or arbitrary executions, E/CN.4/2005/7 (22 December 2004) paras 41–54; Report of the Working Group on Arbitrary Detention, E/CN.4/2003/8 (16 December 2002) paras 61–4.
[41] For an impassioned defence of the competence of UN human rights bodies over international humanitarian law, see Alston, Morgan-Foster, and Abresch, 'The Competence of the UN Human Rights Council and its Special Procedures in relation to Armed Conflicts: Extrajudicial Executions in the "War on Terror"' (2008) 19 *EJIL* 183.   [42] ICCPR, Art 4; ECHR, Art 15; and ACHR, Art 27 specifically mention 'war'.

derogation is permitted; the whole host of obligations remain applicable.[43] As the International Court of Justice (ICJ) put it:

[T]he protection offered by human rights conventions does not cease in case of armed conflict, save through the effect of provisions for derogation of the kind to be found in Article 4 of the International Covenant on Civil and Political Rights.[44]

The applicability of international human rights law to situations of armed conflict is also acknowledged by international humanitarian law treaties. The rules in Additional Protocol I relating to the treatment of persons in the power of a party to the conflict, for example, are described as being additional to 'other applicable rules of international law relating to the protection of fundamental human rights during international armed conflict'.[45] In the context of internal armed conflict, the preamble to Additional Protocol II recalls that 'international instruments relating to human rights offer a basic protection to the human person'.[46] Accordingly, major international law and human rights bodies such as the ICJ, the International Law Commission, and the Human Rights Committee have confirmed that international human rights law continues to apply in time of armed conflict.[47]

Far more difficult—and still unsettled—is the precise relationship between international human rights law and international humanitarian law. The most authoritative, though ultimately inconclusive, statement on point is the pronouncement of the ICJ in its *Wall* opinion. In that case, the ICJ was asked by the General Assembly to pronounce on the 'legal consequences arising from the construction of the wall being built by Israel, the occupying Power, in the Occupied Palestinian Territory... considering the rules and principles of international law'.[48] The rules and principles of international law in question included international human rights law and international humanitarian law. Accordingly, the ICJ had to consider the relationship between them. On this, the ICJ opined that:

As regards the relationship between international humanitarian and human rights law, there are... three possible situations: some rights may be exclusively matters of international humanitarian law; others may be exclusively matters of human rights law; yet others may be matters of both these branches of international law.[49]

It is worth exploring this statement in more detail.[50]

---

[43] *Commission Nationale des Droits de l'Homme et des Libertés*, n 26, para 21.

[44] *Legal Consequences of the Construction of a Wall in the Occupied Palestinian Territory* (Advisory Opinion) [2004] ICJ Rep 136, para 106. This was reiterated by the Court a few years later, in *Armed Activities on the Territory of the Congo (Democratic Republic of the Congo v Uganda)* [2005] ICJ Rep, para 216.

[45] Additional Protocol I, Art 72.   [46] Additional Protocol II, preamble.

[47] *Legality of the Threat or Use of Nuclear Weapons* (Advisory Opinion) [1996] ICJ Rep 226, para 25; Fragmentation of International Law: Difficulties arising from the Diversification and Expansion of International Law, Report of the Study Group of the International Law Commission, A/CN.4/L.682 (4 April 2006) para 104; General Comment 31, n 27, para 11.   [48] *Wall*, n 44, para 1.

[49] Ibid, para 106. This, too, was reiterated in *DRC v Uganda*, n 44, para 216.

[50] See Dinstein, 'Human Rights in Armed Conflict: International Humanitarian Law' in Meron (ed), *Human Rights in International Law* (Clarendon Press, 1985) 345.

5.1 RIGHTS EXCLUSIVELY MATTERS OF INTERNATIONAL HUMANITARIAN LAW

It is only natural that international humanitarian law, that body of law particularly designed to regulate the conduct of hostilities, contains rights that are not to be found in international human rights law. Take, for example, occupied territory. International humanitarian law contains a detailed body of rules relating to the law of occupation. The law of occupation strikes a delicate balance between the rights of the occupied, the occupying power, and the displaced sovereign. The rules relating to the requisitioning of property are a case in point. As regards 'public buildings, real estate, forests, and agricultural estates belonging to the hostile State, and situated in the occupied country', the occupying power is the usufruct, being able to use and enjoy but not damage or alter them. The occupying power can take into its possession certain property belonging to the sovereign 'which may be used for military operations' but requisitions from the general population are prohibited 'except for the needs of the army of occupation'.[51] These rules reflect the competing interests of the different actors—the occupied, the occupying power, and the displaced sovereign. This tripartite relationship does not map neatly onto classical international human rights law, which regulates the relationship between the state and the individual. Accordingly, many of the features of the law of occupation are not replicated in international human rights law.

5.2 RIGHTS EXCLUSIVELY MATTERS OF INTERNATIONAL HUMAN RIGHTS LAW

Equally, there are rights grounded in international human rights law that are nowhere to be found in international humanitarian law. The right not to be imprisoned on the ground of inability to fulfil a contractual obligation and the right to recognition as a person before the law are rights featured in the ICCPR from which there may be no derogation.[52] International humanitarian law contains no equivalent provisions. The American Convention on Human Rights lists as non-derogable the rights of the family and the right to a name.[53] Again, there are no equivalent rules in international humanitarian law.

5.3 RIGHTS MATTERS OF BOTH INTERNATIONAL HUMAN RIGHTS LAW AND INTERNATIONAL HUMANITARIAN LAW

In the majority of situations, a particular right will be grounded in both international human rights law and international humanitarian law. In such instances, the principle of *lex specialis* governs, such that the more specific rule will take precedence over the more general.[54] There are two variants of the *lex specialis* principle. The first

---

[51] Regulations respecting the Laws and Customs of War on Land, annexed to Convention (IV) respecting the Laws and Customs of War on Land, The Hague, 1907, Arts 55, 53, and 52 respectively.
[52] ICCPR, Arts 11 and 16.   [53] ACHR, Arts 17 and 18.
[54] See Fragmentation of International Law, n 47, paras 56–122.

applies in the event of a conflict between two norms. In this situation, the specific rule *modifies* the general rule to the extent of the inconsistency between them. The general rule does not fall away. It remains in the background and applicable to the extent that it does not conflict with the specific rule. The second variant applies when one norm is of greater specificity than the other norm, or is more tailored to the particular circumstances at hand, but there is no inconsistency between them. Here, the more specific rule is but an *application* of the more general rule. Although it may be useful to distinguish between these variants, a firm distinction between modification and application is hard to draw and somewhat artificial.

5.3.1 *Lex specialis* as modification

The first variant of the *lex specialis* principle is the modification of the general rule by the specific rule to the extent of any inconsistency between them. Recall our example of the right to life in international human rights law. The ICCPR protects against the arbitrary deprivation of life. This begs the question of when a deprivation of life is considered arbitrary. Does the use of nuclear weapons in armed conflict, for example, constitute an arbitrary deprivation of life? The ICJ has considered this issue:

In principle, the right not arbitrarily to be deprived of one's life applies also in hostilities. The test of what is an arbitrary deprivation of life, however, then falls to be determined by the applicable *lex specialis*, namely, the law applicable in armed conflict which is designed to regulate the conduct of hostilities. Thus, whether a particular loss of life, through the use of a certain weapon in warfare, is to be considered an arbitrary deprivation of life contrary to Article 6 of the Covenant [ICCPR], can only be decided by reference to the law applicable in armed conflict and not deduced from the terms of the Covenant itself.[55]

In this instance, the relevant rules of international humanitarian law constituted the *leges specialis* and so trumped, to the extent of the inconsistency, the equivalent rule found in international human rights law. Although this will be the usual case, it is important to note that the ICJ is not saying, as is sometimes thought, that the body of international humanitarian law always constitutes the *lex specialis*. The Court was considering one particular right—the right to life—and one particular aspect of that right—its compatibility with the use of nuclear weapons. It does not follow that the entire body of international human rights law is the *lex generalis* and the full corpus of international humanitarian law the *lex specialis*. Generalizations cannot be made at the level of the overarching body; it comes down to an analysis of the individual rule. Competing rules have to be identified and the specificity between them ascertained. Should the relevant rule of international human rights law—or, for that matter, international environmental law or international refugee law—contain the more specific rule, it would modify the general rule of international humanitarian law to the extent of the inconsistency between them.

---

[55] *Nuclear Weapons*, n 47, para 25.

5.3.2 *Lex specialis* as application

The second variation of the *lex specialis* principle is the application of the more specific rule as a detailed or tailored version of the general rule. Here, there is no conflict between the two rules. Rather, one provision is the more detailed version of the other or the more appropriate in the circumstances.

Consider the right to a fair trial in the context of internal armed conflict. The ICCPR provides for a lengthy list of fair trial guarantees.[56] For its part, Article 3, common to the four Geneva Conventions, requires the provision of 'judicial guarantees which are recognized as indispensable by civilized peoples'. No list of the required guarantees is provided. Additional Protocol II does contain such a list but that list is not self-contained. Rather, it refers to 'all necessary rights and means of defence'.[57] In order to interpret that clause, it is necessary to turn to the relevant rules of international human rights law, which form the *lex specialis* on point. The point here is that there is no conflict between the relevant rules of international human rights law and international humanitarian law. One contains a detailed body of regulation; the other, somewhat vague standards. In order to give content to the general rule, we need to apply its more specific counterpart.

Some care needs to be taken when importing ideas from one body of law into another, for they may be appropriate in one context but not in another. Some modification may be required in order to render the idea being transferred suitable to the body of law in which it now finds itself. As the International Criminal Tribunal for the former Yugoslavia has had occasion to observe, 'notions developed in the field of human rights can be transposed in international humanitarian law only if they take into consideration the specificities of the latter body of law'.[58]

For example, the use of torture is prohibited in both international human rights law and international humanitarian law. Torture is subject to a detailed definition in international human rights law; in international humanitarian law it is undefined. The international human rights law definition provides that torture is:

> any act by which severe pain or suffering, whether physical or mental, is intentionally inflicted on a person for such purposes as obtaining from him or a third person information or a confession, punishing him for an act he or a third person has committed or is suspected of having committed, or intimidating or coercing him or a third person, or for any reason based on discrimination of any kind, when such pain or suffering is inflicted by or at the instigation of or with the consent or acquiescence of a public official or other person acting in an official capacity. It does not include pain or suffering arising only from, inherent in or incidental to lawful sanctions.[59]

Given that the term 'torture' is undefined in international humanitarian law, at first sight, this ready-made definition looks useful. Closer inspection, however, reveals a problem. The definition requires 'a public official or other person acting in an official

---

[56] ICCPR, Arts 14–15. See Chapter 14, above.   [57] Additional Protocol II, Art 6(2)(a).

[58] *Prosecutor v Kunarac et al.*, Judgment, IT-96-23-T, 22 February 2001, para 471.

[59] UN Convention against Torture, Art 1(1).

capacity'. Armed groups fighting in internal armed conflicts are generally not going to be considered public officials or persons acting in an official capacity. Does this mean members of armed groups are not covered by the prohibition on torture? Clearly it could not be so. Thus, this particular aspect of the definition has been considered inapplicable for the purposes of the definition of torture under international humanitarian law.[60]

5.4 AN ALTERNATIVE APPROACH: REGULATION THROUGH APPLICATION OF INTERNATIONAL HUMAN RIGHTS LAW

In recent years, an alternative approach has been suggested, that of a human rights-based law of armed conflict. Although primarily a construct of scholars, the European Court of Human Rights has adopted what may be termed a human rights approach to internal armed conflict, regulating the conduct of hostilities through the application of not humanitarian law but human rights law.[61] The case of *Isayeva v Russia* concerned an aerial attack on a village just outside Grozny, Chechnya, as rebels were passing through it in retreat from the besieged Grozny. The applicant's son and other family members were killed by a bomb during the attack. In considering whether there was a violation of the right to life, the European Court held that '[a]ny use of force must be no more than "absolutely necessary" for the achievement of one or more of the purposes set out in' the ECHR and 'strictly proportionate to the achievement of the permitted aims'.[62] The European Court thus applied rules of human rights law to events arising out an internal armed conflict even though the relevant humanitarian law on point differs.

In international humanitarian law, civilians shall not be made the object of attacks; but combatants, fighters and persons taking a direct part in hostilities may be lawfully targeted. The ECHR, on the other hand, provides for the right to life but goes on to provide that deprivation of life shall not constitute a violation 'when it results from the use of force which is no more than absolutely necessary' in certain specified situations (in defence of a person, lawful arrest or detention, or to quell a riot).[63] This rule applies to combatants, fighters, and civilians alike, such that only force that is 'absolutely necessary' may be directed against a fighter. The exact consequences of this rule are yet to be seen but the implication is that lethal force may not be used against a fighter in situations in which it is feasible to arrest him.[64] Accordingly, to kill a fighter when it would have been possible to capture him may be a violation of human rights law. This is an important divergence from the position under international humanitarian law and it reflects the different starting points of the two bodies of law: for human rights law it is the right to life; for humanitarian law, the right to kill.

---

[60] *Kunarac* Trial Judgment, n 58, para 496.

[61] *Isayeva*, n 26. See Abresch, 'A Human Rights Law of Internal Armed Conflict: The European Court of Human Rights in Chechnya' (2005) 16 *EJIL* 741.   [62] *Isayeva v Russia*, ibid, para 173.

[63] ECHR, Art 2.

[64] See *de Guerrero v Colombia*, CCPR/C/15/D/45/1979 (31 March 1982), paras 13.2–13.3.

6 DIFFICULTIES WITH THE APPLICATION OF INTERNATIONAL HUMAN RIGHTS LAW TO ARMED CONFLICT

The application of human rights law to armed conflict gives rise to at least three distinct difficulties.

6.1 ASYMMETRICAL OBLIGATIONS BETWEEN THE PARTIES

Human rights are traditionally considered to govern the relationship between the state and the individual. The state is the holder of the obligation and the individual the beneficiary of the right. It should be recalled that, in internal armed conflicts—and the vast majority of conflicts in the world today are of such a character—the conflict is fought between a state and an armed group or between two or more armed groups. Injecting human rights standards into the equation may be, then, to impose additional obligations for one side (the state) but not the other (the armed opposition group). This inequality of obligation does not bode well for compliance: one party to the conflict is unlikely to abide by obligations that are not binding on the other. Once parties start to violate their obligations, there is the danger that, all too quickly, things will spiral out of control.

An alternative approach would be to impose human rights obligations on both parties to the conflict, that is to say, on armed groups as well as states. This has the advantage of parity of obligation, but it represents a shift in the conceptualization of human rights.[65] There is certainly evidence of some movement in this direction,[66] but it is too early to reach a definitive conclusion.

The imposition of human rights obligations on armed groups presupposes that those groups have the capacity to satisfy their obligations. This cannot be taken for granted, with certain human rights standards going beyond the reach of many armed groups. Human rights obligations may have to be limited to a subset of armed groups, such as those in control of a quantum of territory, for example the Revolutionary Armed Forces of Colombia (FARC) which controlled a sizeable tract of land in Colombia, or the Liberation Tigers of Tamil Eelam (LTTE), which used to have effective control over the north and east of Sri Lanka. However, even this shift is likely to face opposition

---

[65] See Chapter 25, below.

[66] See *Elmi v Australia*, CAT/C/22/D/120/1998 (14 May 1999); Institut de Droit International, 'The Application of International Humanitarian Law and Fundamental Human Rights in Armed Conflicts in which Non-State Entities are Parties' (Berlin, 1999); Report of the Special Rapporteur on extrajudicial, summary or arbitrary executions, Mission to Sri Lanka, E/CN.4/2006/53/Add.5 (27 March 2006), paras 25–7. See generally, Clapham, *Human Rights Obligations of Non-State Actors* (OUP, 2006), ch 7.

from states, unhappy with the state-like treatment being accorded to armed groups and any legitimacy this may afford them.

6.2 DIFFERENTIAL OBLIGATIONS WITHIN A COALITION

Large-scale international armed conflicts, such as the early years of the recent armed conflicts in Afghanistan and Iraq, often involve coalitions of states. They may also involve regional military alliances, such as the North Atlantic Treaty Organization (NATO) or the Economic Community of West African States Monitoring Group (ECOMOG). In such conflicts, individuals of several states fight alongside one another. Simplicity dictates that they would be bound by the same legal rules. Yet, states—even close allies—are not party to the same human rights treaties. Those that are may have entered reservations to particular provisions or have different understandings of the same rule. In addition, states outside a particular regional grouping would not be party to the regional human rights treaty to which other members of the coalition or organization are bound. These differing obligations pose difficult questions hitherto unresolved. For example, can troops from state A, which is party to the ECHR, lawfully transfer an individual in their custody to forces from state B if that individual may face the death penalty in state B?[67]

6.3 SPHERE OF APPLICABILITY: THE EXTRATERRITORIAL APPLICATION OF HUMAN RIGHTS TREATIES

States frequently fight outside their territorial boundaries. They do so as a matter of course in international armed conflicts; they also do so when they intervene on behalf of one side or another in an otherwise internal armed conflict. The question that this raises is whether, when a state acts outside its own territory, it continues to be bound by its human rights obligations.

Many human rights treaties do not contain a provision delimiting their territorial application. In respect of these treaties, the presumption is that they have extraterritorial effect.[68] Other treaties contain a clause to the effect that a state party is under an obligation 'to respect and to ensure to all individuals within its territory and subject to its jurisdiction the rights recognized' therein.[69] The 'and' is to be read disjunctively such that the obligation arises in respect of those individuals 'within its territory' and, in addition, those individuals 'subject to its jurisdiction'.[70] The question remains as to the meaning of the term 'jurisdiction'. On this, there is varied authority.[71]

---

[67] For one view, with additional complicating facts, see *R (Al-Saadoon and Mufdhi) v Secretary of State for Defence* [2008] EWHC 3098 (Admin).

[68] *Application of the International Convention on the Elimination of All Forms of Racial Discrimination (Georgia v Russian Federation)*, Provisional Measures Order [2008] ICJ Rep, para 109 (not yet reported; see <http://www.icj-cij.org>). [69] This is the language of ICCPR, Art 2.

[70] See *Wall*, n 44, para 111; *DRC v Uganda*, n 44, para 216. [71] See Chapter 7, above.

The Human Rights Committee has opined that 'a State party must respect and ensure the rights laid down in the [ICCPR] to anyone within the power or effective control of that State Party, even if not situated within the territory of the State Party'.[72] In the *Banković* case, the European Court of Human Rights held that jurisdiction is primarily territorial, such that member states of NATO were not bound by their obligations under the ECHR when engaged in airstrikes against the Federal Republic of Yugoslavia. The Court also held that certain extraterritorial acts of a state may constitute an exercise of its jurisdiction, namely when a state 'through the effective control of the relevant territory and its inhabitants abroad as a consequence of military occupation or through the consent, invitation or acquiescence of the Government of that territory, exercises all or some of the public powers normally to be exercised by that Government'.[73]

Regardless of the merits of these respective positions, the point here is that when a state engages in an armed conflict that takes place abroad, it is not always going to be bound by its human rights obligations. Thus, before we get to the stage of ascertaining the relationship between international human rights law and international humanitarian law, we first have to answer the question of whether international human rights law is even applicable.

7 CONCLUSION

International human rights law applies in time of armed conflict. This much is clear. Although existing alongside international humanitarian law, there is good reason for its application, not least the mechanisms for its enforcement. The exact relationship between international human rights law and international humanitarian law is still to be worked out. It is generally accepted that 'some rights may be exclusively matters of international humanitarian law; others may be exclusively matters of human rights law; yet others may be matters of both these branches of international law' but beyond this there is little agreement. Some difficulties with the application of international human rights law to situations of armed conflict remain. Despite this continued uncertainty, cognizance should be taken of the fundamental shift in the issue. The question is no longer *whether* international human rights law applies in time of armed conflict but *how* it applies. This movement from applicability to application is a significant one and is reflective of a more general trend towards what has been described as the 'humanization of international humanitarian law'.[74]

---

[72] General Comment 31, n 27, para 10.
[73] *Banković and others v Belgium* (2002) 44 EHRR SE5, para 71.
[74] See Meron, 'The Humanization of Humanitarian Law' (2000) 94 *AJIL* 239.

FURTHER READING

ABRESCH, 'A Human Rights Law of Internal Armed Conflict: The European Court of Human Rights in Chechnya' (2005) 16 *EJIL* 741.

ARNOLD and QUENIVET (eds), *International Humanitarian Law and Human Rights Law* (Martinus Nijhoff, 2008).

DINSTEIN, 'Human Rights in Armed Conflict: International Humanitarian Law' in Meron (ed), *Human Rights in International Law:* (Clarendon Press, 1985).

DOSWALD-BECK and VITÉ, 'International Humanitarian Law and Human Rights Law' (1993) 293 *IRRC* 94.

DRAPER, 'Humanitarian Law and Human Rights' in Meyer and McCoubrey (eds), *Reflections on Law and Armed Conflicts:* *Selected Works on the Law of War by the Late Professor GIAD Draper* (Kluwer, 1998).

FLECK (ed), *The Handbook of International Humanitarian Law* (Oxford University Press, 2008).

GREEN, *The Contemporary Law of Armed Conflict* (Manchester University Press, 2008).

KRIEGER, 'A Conflict of Norms: The Relationship between Humanitarian Law and Human Rights Law in the ICRC Customary Study' (2006) 11 *JCSL* 265.

MERON, 'The Humanization of Humanitarian Law' (2000) 90 *AJIL* 239.

PROVOST, *International Human Rights and Humanitarian Law* (Cambridge University Press, 2002).

USEFUL WEBSITES

Crimes of War <**http://www.crimesofwar.org**>

International Committee of the Red Cross <**http://www.icrc.org**>

International Humanitarian Fact-Finding Commission <**http://www.ihffc.org**>

24

INTERNATIONAL CRIMINAL LAW

Robert Cryer

SUMMARY

There are many links between human rights and international criminal law, and many human rights lawyers and activists are conversant with international criminal law. This chapter seeks to introduce the ideas behind international criminal law, the crimes themselves, and the interplay of those crimes with human rights law. It then looks to the main examples of prosecutions of international crimes and the non-prosecutorial options that have been adopted. It concludes with an analysis of the pros and cons of using international criminal law to protect human rights.

1 INTRODUCTION

International criminal law[1] has a great deal in common with international human rights law. Both are, at least in part, of post-Second World War vintage, as they were part of the response to, and attempted safeguard against, depredations of the type that characterized the Nazi era. Also both, unlike the bulk of international law, attempt to deal more or less directly with the actions of individuals rather than states. Broadly speaking, if international human rights law deals with the rights that are granted to individuals, international criminal law deals with their duties.[2]

The underlying idea of the parts of international criminal law that are of relevance to human rights is that certain conduct is seen as so unacceptable that it is not simply a matter of domestic jurisdiction, but something of concern to all. However, the level

---

[1] The term itself is a controversial one, with various different meanings. Here it will be used primarily to cover those crimes directly criminalized by international law. See Cryer, Friman, Robinson, and Wilmshurst, *An Introduction to International Criminal Law and Procedure* (CUP, 2010) ch 1.

[2] For a classic discussion of this see Lauterpacht, 'The Subjects of the Law of Nations Part I' (1947) 63 *LQR* 439; Lauterpacht, 'The Subjects of the Law of Nations Part II' (1948) 64 *LQR* 97.

of consensus on this differs amongst the various forms of conduct that are of interest to international criminal law, and as such, two different tracks have developed within international criminal law.

The first is direct international criminalization (international crimes in the narrow sense). These are crimes which are directly created by international law and are covered by the famous pronouncement of the Nuremberg International Military Tribunal (Nuremberg IMT) that:

Individuals have international duties which transcend the national obligations of obedience imposed by the individual State... [C]rimes against international law are committed by men, not by abstract entities, and only by punishing individuals who commit such crimes can the provisions of international law be enforced.[3]

Such international crimes may be prosecuted by international courts without reference to domestic law and, with the possible exception of the crime of aggression, by any state in the world on the basis of universal jurisdiction, as a matter of international law.[4] Only four crimes can currently claim this status: war crimes, crimes against humanity, genocide, and aggression. It is possible that individual acts of torture or terrorism that do not otherwise fall under the definitions of those four crimes may be added to this list as separate international crimes; some commentators are of the view that they are already directly criminalized by international law.[5] However, there is no agreement yet that this is the case, and the better view is that they are not.

The second track of involving international law in criminalization occurs when so-called 'transnational crimes' are created. Such crimes involve treaty-based regimes that require states to create crimes within their domestic legal order and often require states either to prosecute those who are found on their territory and who are suspected of such offences, or to extradite them to a state willing to prosecute them (a duty often called, if a little inaccurately, *aut dedere aut judicare*). Here therefore, the obligation is on states, to make such conduct criminal in their own domestic law, rather than on individuals directly.

There are a large number of treaties of this sort, which require states domestically to criminalize conduct. To the extent to which the conduct described in those treaties overlaps with human rights norms, they can be seen as part of human rights protection. The UN Convention against Torture and the UN Convention against Enforced Disappearance are two examples of such treaties. It ought to be noted though, that not all transnational crimes are relevant to human rights. The law relating, for example, to cutting undersea cables contained in the Convention for the Protection of Submarine Cables does not have any direct human rights implications. These treaties, whether relevant to human rights or not, do not create crimes in and of themselves. Rather,

---

[3] Nuremberg IMT, 'Judgment and Sentence' (1947) 41 *AJIL* 172, 221, 223.
[4] See Cryer, Friman, Robinson, and Wilmshurst, n 1, ch 8.
[5] Cassese, *International Criminal Law* (OUP, 2008) chs 7–8.

they require states parties to create crimes in their domestic legal orders.[6] The *locus* of the criminal liability for the individual is the domestic, rather than the international, legal order. As such, these treaties will not be covered in depth here.

2 HUMAN RIGHTS LAW AND INTERNATIONAL CRIMES

As stated above, there are four international crimes in the sense used here: genocide, crimes against humanity, war crimes, and aggression. Aggression, although described as the 'supreme international crime',[7] has not played an important role in the development of international criminal law, and its relationship to human rights law is, as things stand, somewhat nebulous. As this chapter will concentrate, for the most part, on the extent to which international crimes overlap with international human rights law, it will not deal with aggression further.

2.1 GENOCIDE

Genocide was created as a separate international crime in the 1940s. The term was first coined by Raphael Lemkin in his 1944 book *Axis Rule in Occupied Europe*.[8] Although the term was mentioned in the indictment at Nuremberg, it was not prosecuted separately to crimes against humanity. In 1946, however, the UN General Assembly, in Resolution 96(I) stated that:

Genocide is a denial of the right of existence of entire human groups, as homicide is the denial of the right to live of individual human beings; such denial of the right of existence shocks the conscience of mankind, results in great losses to humanity in the form of cultural and other contributions represented by these human groups, and is contrary to moral law and to the spirit and aims of the United Nations.... The General Assembly, therefore... affirms that genocide is a crime under international law.

As has been said elsewhere, genocide 'is a crime simultaneously directed against individual victims, the group to which they belong, and human diversity'.[9] In Resolution 96(I) the General Assembly directed the UN Economic and Social Council to begin the drafting of a convention against genocide. This (often convoluted) drafting process was brought to a close in 1948, when the Convention on the Prevention and Punishment of the Crime of Genocide (Genocide Convention) was completed. Article I Genocide Convention, echoing the language of General Assembly Resolution 96(I), provides that '[t]he Contracting Parties confirm that

---

[6] International Convention for the Protection of All Persons from Enforced Disappearance, Art 5 accepts that such conduct may amount to an international crime in the relevant context.

[7] Nuremberg Judgment, n 3, 186.　　[8] (Carnegie Endowment, 1944).

[9] Cryer, Friman, Robinson, and Wilmshurst, n 1, 203.

genocide, whether committed in time of peace or in time of war, is a crime under international law which they undertake to prevent and to punish'. As early as 1951, the year the Convention came into force, the International Court of Justice (ICJ) stated that owing to General Assembly Resolution 96(I) 'the principles underlying the Convention are principles which are recognized by civilized nations as binding on States, even without any conventional obligation'.[10] The ICJ has more recently declared that the prohibition of genocide is 'assuredly' an example of a norm having reached *jus cogens* status.[11]

2.1.1 Definition

Article II Genocide Convention contains the classic definition of genocide, which is:

[A]ny of the following acts committed with intent to destroy, in whole or in part, a national, ethnical, racial or religious group, as such:

    (a) Killing members of the group;

    (b) Causing serious bodily or mental harm to members of the group;

    (c) Deliberately inflicting on the group conditions of life calculated to bring about its physical destruction in whole or in part;

    (d) Imposing measures intended to prevent births within the group;

    (e) Forcibly transferring children of the group to another group.

This definition was repeated in the Statutes of the International Criminal Tribunal for the former Yugoslavia (ICTY) and the International Criminal Tribunal for Rwanda (ICTR),[12] and, despite some attempts to 'fix' the definition during the drafting of the Statute of the International Criminal Court (ICC), is essentially repeated in Article 6 of that Statute.[13] Like all crimes, genocide is made up of an external element (usually called the *actus reus*, or the conduct element in common law jurisdictions) and an internal element (also known as the *mens rea*, or the mental element).

2.1.2 External element

There is a common theme between all the underlying acts of genocide (killing, causing serious bodily harm, and so on), except, perhaps, the last (the forcible transfer of children). This is that the acts are related to physical, not cultural, destruction of the group. When the Genocide Convention was being drafted, there were those who suggested that 'cultural genocide' should be included: as a crime against diversity, genocide should be expanded to where a group is forcibly assimilated, so the group ceases to exist as a cultural, rather than physical, entity. This was rejected.

---

[10] *Reservations to the Convention on the Prevention and Punishment of the Crime of Genocide* (Advisory Opinion) [1951] ICJ Rep 15, 23.

[11] *Case Concerning Armed Activities on the Territory of the Congo* (New Application: 2002) (*DRC v Rwanda*) [2006] ICJ Rep 6, para 64.   [12] ICTY Statute, Art 4; ICTR Statute, Art 2.

[13] See von Hebel and Robinson, 'Crimes Within the Jurisdiction of the Court' in Lee (ed), *The International Criminal Court: The Making of the Rome Statute, Issues, Negotiations, Results* (Kluwer, 1999) 79, 89.

There have been some attempts to revive this notion. However, they were not accepted by the ICTY in the *Krstić* case. It was argued by the prosecution in that case that there was evidence that in customary, rather than treaty, law there was a crime of, essentially, cultural genocide. The Trial Chamber disagreed, and this was both upheld on appeal,[14] and agreed with by the ICJ when it dealt with the elements of genocide in the *Bosnian Genocide* case.[15]

The physical acts of genocide have clear overlaps with human rights law. Killing and inflicting serious bodily or mental harm (which can include sexual offences),[16] and deliberately inflicting conditions of life calculated to bring about a group's physical destruction raise fairly clear human rights issues. These types of acts can amount to a violation of civil and political rights, such as the right to life and the prohibition of torture or cruel, inhuman, and degrading treatment. In certain circumstances, they can, particularly inflicting conditions of life calculated to bring about the destruction of a group, also amount to a violation of economic, social, and cultural rights, such as the right to health and the right to food.[17] Imposing measures intended to prevent births within the group would certainly implicate issues of private, home, and family life, as well as likely being inhuman and degrading. The same is true of the transfer of children.

2.1.3 Protected groups

As can be seen, the Genocide Convention expressly limits itself to protecting 'national, ethnical, racial and religious' groups. In General Assembly Resolution 96(I), other groups, such as political and social groups, were included. However, their inclusion did not make it to the Convention's final draft. There are those who think that the definition of genocide should be expanded to cover political killings. There are understandable reasons for this, as often genocides are 'explained' by those who perpetrate them as political, rather than ethnic conflicts.[18] However, crimes against humanity do cover political killings, and it is questionable whether or not political groups are equivalent to the national, ethnic, racial, and religious groups to which they are

---

[14] *Prosecutor v Krstić*, Judgment, IT-98-33-T, 2 August 2001, para 580 and (on appeal) Judgment, IT-98-33-A, 19 April 2004, para 25.

[15] *Case Concerning Application of the Convention on the Prevention and Punishment of the Crime of Genocide (Bosnia and Herzegovina v Serbia and Montenegro)* [2007] ICJ Rep, para 344 (not yet reported; see <http://www.icj-cij.org>).

[16] See eg *Prosecutor v Akayesu*, Judgment, IT-96-4-T, 2 September 1998, para 731.

[17] The Elements of Crimes state that such conduct 'may include, but is not necessarily restricted to, deliberate deprivation of resources indispensable for survival, such as food or medical services, or systematic expulsion from homes'. This raises the difficult issue of whether or not 'ethnic cleansing' may be genocide. According to ICC Statute, Art 9, the 'Elements of Crimes'—a document which was drafted and agreed upon after the Rome Conference that created the ICC Statute—are to assist the ICC in interpreting the crimes subject to its jurisdiction. See Gadriov and Clark, 'Article 9' in Triffterer (ed), *Commentary on the Rome Statute of the International Criminal Court* (Hart, 2008) 505.

[18] Van Schaack, 'The Crime of Political Genocide: Repairing the Genocide Convention's Blind Spot' (1997) 106 *Yale LJ* 2259.

sometimes equated, as there is a permanence and immutability about those groups which does not apply to political groups.[19]

Even so, determining the existence and membership of groups is not as simple as the Genocide Convention might imply. This has caused interpretative problems, for example whether the terms 'national, ethnical, racial or religious' are to be interpreted separately or together. The ICTR, in its first major case, *Akayesu*, tried to define each of the terms separately. This led to problems. On such an interpretation, it was difficult to see the Hutus and Tutsis as different groups, yet they clearly saw themselves as being so.[20] More recently, and more authoritatively, the ICTY, after a detailed review of the relevant materials held that:

The preparatory work of the Convention shows that setting out such a list was designed more to describe a single phenomenon, roughly corresponding to what was recognised, before the second world war, as 'national minorities', rather than to refer to several distinct prototypes of human groups. To attempt to differentiate each of the named groups on the basis of scientifically objective criteria would thus be inconsistent with the object and purpose of the Convention.[21]

This is the preferable approach, given the difficulty of determining groups. The question of perceived difference (as, for example, in the 'Arab'/'African' divide in Darfur) has led to the adoption of a test which relies on the reality of the distinction in the eyes of the relevant population. If such a group is considered to exist in the relevant cultural context, then the perception of the perpetrator that the victim is a member of that group suffices for them to be considered a member for the purposes of genocide.[22]

2.1.4 The context of genocide

It is often thought that genocide, of necessity, involves collective action. After all, the Genocide Convention and its history show that it was intended to deal with situations such as the Holocaust, which involved large-scale collective perpetration. Some take the view that genocide, of its essence, requires a plan or policy.[23] The ICTY has taken the view that there could, in theory, be a 'lone *génocidaire*' acting outside any plan;[24] a finding that has been severely criticized by some.[25] The drafters of the ICC Statute took a middle path, creating guidance for the ICC to the effect that '[t]he conduct took place in the context of a manifest pattern of similar conduct directed against that group or was conduct that could itself effect such destruction'.[26] There are two aspects

---

[19] There was an attempt to read the convention as protecting all 'stable and permanent groups' in the *Akayesu* case, but this was a clear misreading of the Convention and its *travaux préparatoires*. See Cryer, Friman, Robinson, and Wilmshurst, n 1, 169–71.

[20] *Akayesu*, n 16, paras 511–15. It was this that led the Chamber to claim that the Convention protected all 'stable and permanent' groups.   [21] *Krstić* Trial Chamber, n 14, para 556.

[22] See eg *Prosecutor v Semanza*, Judgment, ICTR-97-20-T, 15 May 2003, para 317.

[23] Vest, 'A Structure-Based Concept of Genocidal Intent' (2007) 5 *JICJ* 781.

[24] *Prosecutor v Jelesić*, Judgment, IT-95-10-A, 5 July 2001, para 48.

[25] Schabas, 'The Jelesic Case and the *Mens Rea* of the Crime of Genocide' (2001) 14 *LJIL* 125.

[26] eg Elements of Crimes, Art 6(1)(a), Element 4, ICC/ASP/1/3.

to this and fulfilling either suffices for genocide. The first is that there are other people undertaking similar acts against the relevant group, although not necessarily with genocidal intent.[27] The second was designed to cover an example such as where one person obtained a nuclear weapon and used it against a protected group.[28] The ICC has upheld the applicability of this element of the crime,[29] but the ICTY has held that it does not reflect customary international law.[30]

2.1.5 Internal element

Genocide is distinguished from other crimes by its particular, high, *mens rea* require-ment. The perpetrator must act with the intent 'to destroy, in whole or in part, a national, ethnical, racial or religious group, as such'. This is not simply a discrimin-atory intent, it is an eliminationist one. The International Criminal Tribunals to date have taken a fairly strong line on this. It is the requirement of an eliminationist intent that has led to the charges relating to 'ethnic cleansing' in the former Yugoslavia to fail, as it was not proved that the policy was to destroy, rather than to discriminate and remove victims from certain areas.[31] There are difficulties involved in determining what amounts to a group, and how large the 'part' of the group has to be for this aspect of the crime, although the ICTY, ICJ, and ICC all agree that it must be 'substantial'.[32]

2.2 CRIMES AGAINST HUMANITY

The second major category of international crimes is crimes against humanity. These were first prosecuted before the Nuremberg IMT, where they were defined, in Article 6(c), as 'murder, extermination, enslavement, deportation, and other inhu-mane acts committed against any civilian population, before or during the war; or persecutions on political, racial or religious grounds in execution of or in connection with any crime within the jurisdiction of the Tribunal, whether or not in violation of the domestic law of the country where perpetrated.'

The most widely ratified definition of crimes against humanity is now that in Article 7 ICC Statute. This reads:

1. For the purpose of this Statute, 'crime against humanity' means any of the following acts when committed as part of a widespread or systematic attack directed against any civilian population, with knowledge of the attack:

   (a) Murder;

   (b) Extermination;

   (c) Enslavement;

---

[27] Oosterveld, 'Context of Genocide' in Lee *et al.* (eds), *The International Criminal Court: Elements of Crimes and Rules of Procedure and Evidence* (Transnational, 2001) 44, 47–8.   [28] Ibid, 46.

[29] *Prosecutor v al Bashir*, Decision on the Prosecution's Application for a Warrant of Arrest Against Omar al-Bashir, Pre-Trial Chamber 1, ICC-02/05-01/09, 4 March 2009, paras 126–8.

[30] *Prosecutor v Krstić*, Judgment, IT-98-33-A, 19 April 2004, para 224.

[31] See also *Bosnian Genocide*, n 15, para 190.

[32] *Bosnian Genocide*, ibid, para 198; *al Bashir*, n 29, para 146.

(d) Deportation or forcible transfer of population;

(e) Imprisonment or other severe deprivation of physical liberty in violation of fundamental rules of international law;

(f) Torture;

(g) Rape, sexual slavery, enforced prostitution, forced pregnancy, enforced sterilization, or any other form of sexual violence of comparable gravity;

(h) Persecution against any identifiable group or collectivity on political, racial, national, ethnic, cultural, religious, gender as defined in paragraph 3, or other grounds that are universally recognized as impermissible under international law, in connection with any act referred to in this paragraph or any crime within the jurisdiction of the Court;

(i) Enforced disappearance of persons;

(j) The crime of apartheid;

(k) Other inhumane acts of a similar character intentionally causing great suffering, or serious injury to body or to mental or physical health.[33]

Contrary to the Nuremberg definition, crimes against humanity do not need to be linked to an armed conflict and are therefore committable in peacetime.[34] There are, in essence, two types of crimes against humanity: 'murder-type' crimes against humanity and 'persecutive' crimes against humanity.[35] Broadly speaking, the latter consist of all crimes against humanity that are covered by Article 7(1)(h) while the former consist of all the other crimes set out in Article 7(1). Both have clear human rights implications.

2.2.1 Context: widespread or systematic attack

Although the relevant acts (murder, deportation, unlawful imprisonment, and so on) when undertaken by state actors are almost always violations of human rights, they must have an additional contextual element for them to amount to crimes against humanity. They must be committed against the backdrop of, and have a nexus to, a widespread or systematic attack against the civilian population. The terms have been most authoritatively defined by the ICTY: '[w]idespread refers to the large-scale nature of the attack and the number of victims, while the phrase "systematic" refers to the organized nature of the acts of violence and the improbability of their random occurrence'.[36] The ICC appears to agree with the ICTY on this.[37] It ought to be noted that the attack does not have to be a military attack.[38]

---

[33] Although it must be noted that this definition is not necessarily entirely reflective of customary international law on point. See Cassese, *International Criminal Law* (OUP, 2008) 123–6.

[34] Ratner, Abrams, and Bischoff, *Accountability for Human Rights Atrocities in International Law: Beyond the Nuremberg Legacy* (OUP, 2009) 52–9.

[35] Schwelb, 'Crimes Against Humanity' (1946) 23 *BYIL* 178, 190 (although Schwelb (rightly) rejects most of the legal differences between them, as will be seen, only the *mens rea* really differs).

[36] *Prosecutor v Kunarac, Kovać and Vuković*, Judgment, IT-96-23/1-A, 12 June 2002, para 94.

[37] *Al Bashir*, n 29, para 81.   [38] *Kunarac*, n 36, para 86.

2.2.2 Context: policy

It had been thought that the requirement that crimes against humanity be widespread or systematic also implied a separate requirement: that there was a policy to commit these acts. The idea that there was a separate requirement in customary international law was rejected by the ICTY in the *Kunarac* case.[39] However, the requirement is clearly present in the ICC Statute.[40] The debate in relation to the ICC has concentrated on what type of 'organization' can have such a policy. The relationship between this and the human rights obligations of non-state actors is an issue which has not yet been fully determined.[41]

2.2.3 External element

The physical acts that, when committed in context, amount to crimes against humanity all raise clear human rights issues. Torture and disappearances, for example, are both the subject of separate human rights/transnational criminal law treaties. Similarly, murder and deprivation of liberty (by state or other organizational action) in violation of fundamental standards of international law are clear violations of human rights.[42] The most detailed discussion of the interrelationship has occurred, however, with respect to 'persecutive' crimes against humanity. The Appeals Chamber of the ICTY has defined such crimes as:

[A]n act or omission which:

1. discriminates in fact and which denies or infringes upon a fundamental right laid down in international customary or treaty law (the *actus reus*); and

2. was carried out deliberately with the intention to discriminate on one of the listed grounds, specifically race, religion or politics (the *mens rea*).[43]

The *Kupreškić* Trial Chamber was careful, however, not to indicate a complete overlap between crimes against humanity and human rights law in this context, opining that cases from human rights and refugee law 'cannot provide a basis for individual criminal responsibility. It would be contrary to the principle of legality to convict someone of persecution based on a definition found in international refugee law or human rights law'[44] as they were created for different purposes. However,

---

[39] Ibid, para 98.

[40] ICC Statute, Art 7(2)(a) defines 'attack against any civilian population' as being 'a course of conduct involving the multiple commission of acts referred to in paragraph 1 against any civilian population, pursuant to or in furtherance of a State or organizational policy to commit such attack'.

[41] For a sceptical view see Schabas, 'Is Terrorism a Crime Against Humanity?' (2002) 8 *International Peacekeeping: The Yearbook of International Peace Operations* 255.

[42] On the overlap in relation to enslavement, see *Prosecutor v Kunarac, Kovač and Vuković*, Judgment, IT-96-23-T, 22 February 2001, paras 518 ff.

[43] *Prosecutor v Blaskić*, Judgment, IT-95-14-A, 29 July 2004, para 131.

[44] *Prosecutor v Kupreškić, Kupreškić, Kupreškić, Papić and Šntić*, Judgment, IT-95-16-T, 14 January 2000, para 589.

it used human rights instruments to assist with the task of defining 'persecution'.[45] As another Trial Chamber has said '[i]n practice, not every denial of a fundamental human right will be serious enough to constitute a crime against humanity. The underlying act committed on discriminatory grounds, considered in isolation or in conjunction with other acts, must be of the same gravity as other crimes... [against humanity].'[46]

The fact that words can, in some circumstances, be part of the *actus reus* of persecutive crimes against humanity has led to some discussion in the ICTR. In the *RTLM* Appeal the majority said that:

[H]ate speech targeting a population on the basis of ethnicity, or any other discriminatory ground, violates the right to respect for the dignity of the members of the targeted group as human beings, and therefore constitutes 'actual discrimination'.... However,... other persons need to intervene before such violations can occur; a speech cannot, in itself, directly kill members of a group, imprison or physically injure them.... [That said] ... it is not necessary that every individual act underlying the crime of persecution should be of a gravity corresponding to other crimes against humanity:... It is the cumulative effect of all the underlying acts of the crime of persecution which must reach a level of gravity equivalent to that for other crimes against humanity.[47]

Judge Meron, however, was sceptical about this, taking the view that the majority did not take sufficient account of the right of freedom of expression.[48]

Turning to the ICC, the drafters of the Elements of Crimes were concerned that crimes against humanity (in particular, but not only, persecutions and 'other inhumane acts') could be used to criminalize all human rights violations. Therefore, they included a statement in the introduction to those elements designed to limit that possibility:

Since article 7 pertains to international criminal law, its provisions... must be strictly construed, taking into account that crimes against humanity as defined in article 7 are among the most serious crimes of concern to the international community as a whole, warrant and entail individual criminal responsibility, and require conduct which is impermissible under generally applicable international law, as recognized by the principal legal systems of the world.[49]

This was included specifically at the behest of a small number of states that felt their practices might become crimes against humanity. It represents an unfortunate unwillingness to engage in self-reflection.

---

[45] Ibid, para 621. Although see *Prosecutor v Stakić*, Judgment, IT-97-24-T, 31 July 2003, para 721, which is more sceptical of the use of such instruments.

[46] *Prosecutor v Krajišnik*, Judgment, IT-00-39-T, 27 September 2006, para 735. This has been accepted by the ICTY Appeals Chamber. See eg *Prosecutor v Brđanin*, Judgment, IT-99-36-A, 3 April 2007, para 296.

[47] *Prosecutor v Nahimana, Barayagwiza and Ngeze*, Judgment, ICTR-99-52-A, 28 November 2007, paras 986–7.   [48] Ibid, Separate and Partially Dissenting Opinion of Judge Meron, paras 5–16.

[49] Elements of Crimes, n 26, Introduction to Elements for Art 7.

2.2.4 Internal element

The mental element of the crime is, first, that the person had the mental element required for the underlying crime (murder and so on). In addition, however, they have to have knowledge of the broader context in which their crimes are committed. In other words, the perpetrator must know that their actions took place in the context of a widespread or systematic attack on the civilian population. In the Appeal in *Tadić* it was said that:

The acts of the accused must comprise part of a pattern of widespread or systematic crimes directed against a civilian population and...the accused must have *known* that his acts fit into such a pattern. There is nothing in the Statute, however, which mandates the imposition of a *further* condition that the acts in question must not be committed for purely personal reasons, except to the extent that this condition is a consequence or a re-statement of the other two conditions mentioned.[50]

The Appeals Chamber of the ICTY supported its reasoning by citing a considerable amount of case law arising from the Second World War in which some people had denounced others to the Nazis, knowing what would happen to them, for personal reasons rather than because they were supporters of the Nazi policies. In stark contrast to the ICTY Statute, the ICTR Statute explicitly provides for the requirement of a discriminatory intent.[51] Although some thought this to be a part of the ICTY definition, it is now accepted that it is not, not least because the ICC Statute does not reflect such a condition. There is one exception: for those crimes against humanity which are persecutory it is also necessary for the perpetrator to have a discriminatory, although not persecutory, intention.[52]

2.3 WAR CRIMES

War crimes are the oldest of the international crimes. They are serious violations of international humanitarian law, for which there is individual criminal responsibility.[53] The relationship between humanitarian law and human rights law, and the main norms humanitarian law contains, are covered in Chapter 23, above. Suffice it to say here that war crimes can only be committed in times of armed conflict.

Humanitarian law (and thus war crimes law) is often split into 'Geneva' and 'Hague' law, the former dealing with the protection of those not taking part in a conflict and the latter dealing with targeting and weapon use. The two categories are not clear at the boundaries, but this still provides a useful way of dividing the area. The basic norms of 'Geneva' law can be found in Common Article 3 Geneva Conventions. This

---

[50] *Prosecutor v Tadić*, Judgment, IT-94-1-A, 15 July 1999, para 248.   [51] ICTR Statute, Art 3.

[52] *Blaškić* Appeal, n 43, paras 164–5.

[53] 'Grave breaches' of the Geneva Conventions, which are war crimes, are subject to a mandatory regime of universal jurisdiction.

is a distillation of the four Geneva Conventions of 1949, and is now considered applicable to all armed conflicts.[54] It reads (in part):

[E]ach Party to the conflict shall be bound to apply, as a minimum, the following provisions:

(1) Persons taking no active part in the hostilities, including members of armed forces who have laid down their arms and those placed *hors de combat* by sickness, wounds, detention, or any other cause, shall in all circumstances be treated humanely, without any adverse distinction founded on race, colour, religion or faith, sex, birth or wealth, or any other similar criteria. To this end, the following acts are and shall remain prohibited at any time and in any place whatsoever with respect to the above-mentioned persons:

(a) violence to life and person, in particular murder of all kinds, mutilation, cruel treatment and torture;

(b) taking of hostages;

(c) outrages upon personal dignity, in particular humiliating and degrading treatment;

(d) the passing of sentences and the carrying out of executions without previous judgment pronounced by a regularly constituted court, affording all the judicial guarantees which are recognized as indispensable by civilized peoples.

The human rights implications of much of this are clear. Torture and humiliating and degrading treatment are also prohibited by international human rights law, although the definition may not be quite the same. Murder, at least by state officials, and fair trial rights are also familiar to human rights law, and it is unsurprising that many human rights advocates refer to humanitarian law.

Many human rights lawyers are less comfortable with 'Hague' law. This law has some principles with which few would quarrel, such as that of unnecessary suffering, and the banning of poison, gas, and biological weapons. However, the law of war crimes (and humanitarian law), despite prohibiting direct attacks on civilians, permits proportionate incidental civilian deaths ('collateral damage') which are the result of an attack on a lawful military target. Many in the human rights community are uncomfortable with this, and the possibility of differing interpretations between human rights lawyers and military officials is something that the ICTY has accepted:

The answers to these questions [on proportionality] are not simple. It may be necessary to resolve them on a case by case basis, and the answers may differ depending on the background and values of the decision maker. It is unlikely that a human rights lawyer and an experienced combat commander would assign the same relative values to military advantage and to injury to non-combatants.[55]

---

[54] Different law applies in international and non-international armed conflicts, although there is increasing overlap between them.

[55] Final Report to the Prosecutor by the Committee Established to Review the NATO Bombing Campaign Against the Federal Republic of Yugoslavia, available at: <http://www.icty.org/sid/10052#IVA64d> para 50.

Of course, not all murders and the like that occur in wartime are war crimes. People still get involved in brawls when there are armed conflicts. Therefore, for such an activity to amount to a war crime, there has to be some nexus between the conflict and the violation. As the ICTY has said, 'what distinguishes a war crime from a purely domestic offence is that a war crime is shaped by and dependent upon the environment—the armed conflict—in which it was committed'.[56] It therefore stated that there had to be a nexus, which meant that:

The armed conflict need not have been causal to the commission of the crime, but the existence of an armed conflict must, at a minimum, have played a substantial part in the perpetrator's ability to commit it, his decision to commit it, the manner in which it was committed or the purpose for which it was committed. . . . In determining whether or not the act in question is sufficiently related to the armed conflict, the Trial Chamber may take into account, *inter alia*, the following factors: the fact that the perpetrator is a combatant; the fact that the victim is a non-combatant; the fact that the victim is a member of the opposing party; the fact that the act may be said to serve the ultimate goal of a military campaign; and the fact that the crime is committed as part of or in the context of the perpetrator's official duties.[57]

This aspect of war crimes law was parsed in the Elements of Crimes for the ICC as follows: '[t]he conduct took place in the context of and was associated with an . . . armed conflict . . . [and] . . . [t]he perpetrator was aware of factual circumstances that established the existence of an armed conflict'.[58] This was included to reflect a balance with the requirement that there be some mental element relating to the existence of an armed conflict. Thus, although the prosecutor needs to show knowledge of facts relating to the existence of the armed conflict, it is not necessary to prove that the alleged perpetrator made the, often complex, determinations about the existence of an armed conflict or its nature.[59]

3 PROSECUTIONS: INTERNATIONAL AND NATIONAL

Prosecutions are often, and not necessarily inaccurately, thought to be important from the point of view of human rights protection. For example, in the *Velasquez-Rodriguez* case, the Inter-American Court of Human Rights held that the failure to investigate the disappearance of the applicant's son and punish those responsible was part of the violation of his right to life.[60] In the European system, a failure to undertake a proper

---

[56] *Prosecutor v Kunarac, Kovać and Vuković*, Judgment, IT-96-23-A, 12 June 2002, para 58.
[57] Ibid, paras 58–9.
[58] Elements of Crimes, n 26, Introduction and eg Elements for Art 8(2)(a)(i), 4–5.
[59] See Dörmann, La Haye, and von Hebel, 'The Context of War Crimes' in Lee (ed), n 27, 120–3.
[60] *Velasquez-Rodriguez v Honduras*, IACtHR Series C No 4 (29 July 1988).

investigation can be part of a violation of the right to life.[61] It is increasingly, albeit controversially, thought that, in the circumstances of international crimes, the rights of the victims include a right to see those who have committed such crimes prosecuted. As will be seen, this is probably a little in advance of the current state of international law, but such views have gained considerable ground in the last decade, especially with respect to high-ranking offenders.[62]

There is a long, although not always illustrious, history of the prosecution of war crimes, both at the national and international level. There were initially plans to try German war criminals by the Allies after the First World War.[63] However, these floundered and only a small number of those defendants were tried in Leipzig, Germany, in proceedings considered strongly skewed towards the defence.[64]

Probably the most well-known prosecutions of the twentieth century occurred after the Second World War, when the Nuremberg and Tokyo International Military Tribunals were set up to try the major Axis war criminals in both spheres of that conflict. It is possible to trace the beginnings of modern international criminal law to the Nuremberg IMT, which tried Nazi leaders for war crimes, crimes against humanity, and aggression. The latter charge caused the most controversy, on the basis that the offence probably did not exist in international law at the time. However, it is questionable whether international law contained an absolute prohibition of retroactive criminal legislation at the time and later instruments such as the European Convention on Human Rights and the International Covenant on Civil and Political Rights (ICCPR) contain savings clauses that were in part designed to avoid the implication that the Nuremberg Charter violated human rights. For example, Article 15 ICCPR provides both that '[n]o one shall be held guilty of any criminal offence on account of any act or omission which did not constitute a criminal offence under national *or international* law at the time when it was committed' and that 'nothing in this article shall prejudice the trial and punishment of any person for any act or omission which, at the time when it was committed, was criminal according to the general principles of law recognized by the community of nations'.[65]

Overall, the general view of the Nuremberg IMT has been quite positive, in part because the President of the Tribunal, Sir Geoffrey Lawrence, exercised a firm but fair hand over the proceedings.[66] History has not been so kind to the Tokyo IMT, the fair trial standards of which have, in particular, been singled out for criticism.[67] There were also large numbers of other trials in countries occupied during the Second World War.

---

[61] *McCann v UK* (1995) 21 EHRR 67, para 161 (although in this case the investigation was considered sufficient).

[62] *Prosecutor v Kondewa*, Decision on Lack of Jurisdiction/Abuse of Process: Amnesty Provided by the Lomé Accord, SCSL-2004-14-AR72(E) 25 May 2004, separate opinion of Robertson J, para 48.

[63] Treaty of Versailles, Arts 227–9.

[64] See eg Bass, *Stay the Hand of Vengeance* (Princeton University Press, 2000) ch 3.

[65] Emphasis added. See Gallant, *The Principle of Legality in International and Comparative Law* (CUP, 2008) ch 4b.   [66] Tusa and Tusa, *The Nuremberg Trial* (BBC Books, 1995) 112.

[67] See generally Boister and Cryer, *The Tokyo International Military Tribunal: A Reappraisal* (OUP, 2008).

During the Cold War there was little movement on a permanent international criminal court, and national prosecutions for international crimes, such as that of Adolf
Eichmann in Jerusalem in 1960,[68] were the exception rather than the rule. A seminal
moment in international criminal justice came in 1993, however, when the Security
Council created the ICTY. It did so in Resolution 837, using an innovative interpretation of its powers under Chapter VII UN Charter.[69] It acted similarly in 1994 to create
the ICTR. Both had their difficulties in the beginning and had slow starts, particularly in the absence of cooperation from a number of states. However, the picture has
slowly brightened, and both tribunals, despite hiccups and high costs, have prosecuted
a number of high-ranking leaders (and sometimes those not so high ranking), and
catalysed the development of international criminal law more generally.

The most tangible evidence of this was the creation of the ICC. The ICC Statute
was drafted in Rome in 1998.[70] Despite opposition from some states (most notably,
but not limited to, the USA) the Statute entered into force in 2002, when there were
60 states parties. It currently has 110 states parties. The ICC, although permanent,
does not have jurisdiction over all international crimes. It can prosecute war crimes,
crimes against humanity, genocide, and may possibly in the future also be able to conduct proceedings related to aggression,[71] but only in relation to crimes committed by
nationals of states parties or on their territories.[72] The only exception to this is if the
Security Council refers a situation to the Court. The Security Council has done this
once, in Resolution 1593, which referred the situation in Darfur, Sudan to the ICC.

The jurisdiction of the ICC, unlike that of the ICTY and ICTR, is intended to be
'complementary' to that of states. In other words, the ICC can act only if states are
'unwilling or unable genuinely' to prosecute the offences themselves.[73] The precise
meaning of these terms is the subject of some controversy and some litigation before
the Court.[74] In addition to Darfur, the Court is currently dealing with the situations
in the Democratic Republic of Congo, the Central African Republic, and Uganda. The
fact that these are all African states has caused some to criticize the Court.[75] It ought
to be noted, on the other hand, that those three situations were all referred to the ICC
by the governments of those states. The indictment of President al Bashir of Sudan in
2009 has also led to criticism by some.

---

[68] *A-G of Israel v Eichmann* (1968) 36 ILR 18.

[69] See *Prosecutor v Tadić*, Decision on the Defence Interlocutory Appeal on Jurisdiction, IT-94-1-AR72,
2 October 1995, paras 34–5.

[70] There is also the significant development of 'internationalized' courts such as the Special Court for
Sierra Leone and the Extraordinary Chambers for Prosecuting the Khmer Rouge in Cambodia. See Cryer,
Friman, Robinson, and Wilmshurst, n 1, ch 9.

[71] ICC Statute, Art 5(1)(2). The crimes are defined in Arts 6–8. The ICC can only assert jurisdiction over
aggression if the Statute is amended to include a definition of that crime.   [72] ICC Statute, Art 12.

[73] ICC Statute, Art 17.

[74] See eg *Prosecutor v Katanga and Ngudjolo*, Judgment on the Appeal of Mr Germain Katanga against
the Oral Decision of Trial Chamber II of 12 June 2009 on the Admissibility of the Case, ICC-01/04-01/07-
1497, 25 September 2009.

[75] Oola, 'Bashir and the ICC: The Aura or Audition of International Justice in Africa?', Oxford Transitional
Justice Research Working Paper, available at: <http://www.csls.ox.ac.uk/documents/OolaFin.pdf>.

4 NON-PROSECUTORIAL OPTIONS

The Uganda situation has raised the possibility of using non-prosecutorial options to deal with the abuses that occurred there. The rebel group, the Lord's Resistance Army, has said that it will only disarm if its members are not prosecuted, but given amnesty, and undergo instead a form of local justice ceremony known as *mato oput*. This demonstrates that there are ways of dealing with international crimes other than by prosecution. The legality of some of them has come under fire in the last decade, from human rights groups in particular, but there is probably still room for them to play at least a complementary role for some offenders.

4.1 AMNESTIES

Amnesties are probably the most controversial option that does not involve prosecutions. Indeed, they prevent them. There are serious arguments about the lawfulness of amnesties under international law, both where there are treaties that create obligations to prosecute (for example the Geneva Conventions for grave breaches and the Genocide Convention for that crime) and under human rights law. In the former case, it is clear that a duty to prosecute is violated by a domestic law preventing prosecution.[76] With regard to human rights law, there are significant arguments that amnesties, certainly unconditional ones, are contrary to various human rights obligations such as the duty to investigate losses of life attributable to the state and the right of access to courts.[77] However, it is by no means clear that the case can yet be made that amnesties are always unlawful. It is true that the Inter-American Court of Human Rights has taken a strong line against amnesties, observing that:

This Court considers that all amnesty provisions, provisions on prescription and the establishment of measures designed to eliminate responsibility are inadmissible, because they are intended to prevent the investigation and punishment of those responsible for serious human rights violations such as torture, extrajudicial, summary or arbitrary execution and forced disappearance, all of them prohibited because they violate non-derogable rights recognized by international human rights law.[78]

Some take the view that this case has determined a more generally applicable norm against amnesties in international law,[79] but this may be stretching that court's jurisprudence a little too far. Other tribunals have not been as assertive.[80] The position

---

[76] Although on traditional principles of international law, an amnesty in one state would not prevent another state from prosecuting.

[77] Orentlicher, 'Settling Accounts: The Duty to Prosecute Human Rights Violations of a Former Regime' (1991) 100 *Yale LJ* 2537.

[78] *Barrios Altos Case* (*Chumbipuma Aguierre et al. v Peru*) IACtHR Series C No 75 (2001) para 41.

[79] Laplante, 'Outlawing Amnesty: The Return of Criminal Justice to Transitional Justice Schemes' (2008–2009) 48 *Virginia JIL* 915.

[80] See generally Seibert-Fohr, *Prosecuting Serious Human Rights Violations* (OUP, 2009).

on point was probably best summed up by the Special Court for Sierra Leone when it said that:

[T]hat there is a crystallising international norm that a government cannot grant amnesty for serious violations of crimes under international law is amply supported by materials placed before the Court [but the view] that it has crystallised may not be entirely correct... it is accepted that such a norm is developing under international law.[81]

The merits of amnesties are hotly contested, with some claiming that they foster reconciliation and others saying they allow powerful perpetrators, literally, to get away with murder, and create a culture of impunity that will only encourage future violations.

4.2 TRUTH AND RECONCILIATION COMMISSIONS

Amnesties can be accompanied by truth and reconciliation commissions, and where they are, there is often more sympathy for the amnesty. This was the case for the South African system which was set up in the aftermath of apartheid. In South Africa, a failure to fully inform the Truth and Reconciliation Commission of the crimes committed could lead to a refusal of amnesty and indeed did in some cases.[82] The merits and demerits of truth and reconciliation commissions are hotly contested. Some see them as providing the groundwork for later reconciliation; others do not feel that there can be a shared state-authorized truth. Much depends on the composition, mandate, and functioning of such bodies. It is sometimes suggested that lustration (the collective removal of people from their jobs) is an appropriate method of dealing with international crimes, but any collective measure is likely to be questionable on human rights grounds, especially the right to have rights and duties adjudicated at law.[83]

5 CONCLUSION

International criminal law and human rights have clear overlaps, both in substantive norms and in their underlying philosophies.[84] There is much to be said for using international criminal law to vindicate human rights. For example, as the Nuremberg IMT

---

[81] *Prosecutor v Kallon and Kamara*, Decision on Challenge to Jurisdiction: Lomé Amnesty Accord, SCSL-2004-15-AR72(E) and SCSL-2004-16-AR72(E), 13 March 2004, para 82.

[82] Prosecutions have not been notable by their successes though. See Bubenzer, *Post-TRC Prosecutions in South Africa* (Martinus Nijhoff, 2009).

[83] ICCPR, Art 14; *Casanovas v France*, CCPR/C/51/D/441/1990 (26 July 1994).

[84] Gasser, 'The Changing Relationship Between International Criminal Law, Human Rights Law and Humanitarian Law' in Doria *et al.* (eds), *The Legal Regime of the International Criminal Court: Essays in Honour of Professor Igor Blischenko* (Kluwer, 2009) 1111.

implied in its famous statement referenced above,[85] using criminal law actually brings home to high-level leaders that they personally, rather than only the impersonal state, will bear the consequences of their decisions. There is also the possibility that civil human rights claims will not provide for a sufficient sense of justice for the victims.[86] Another advantage that has been suggested is the possibility that victims will find testimony cathartic, although this is controversial.[87] Furthermore, it is at least arguable that subjecting facts to forensic scrutiny can later prevent denial of those atrocities.[88] However, whether prosecutions can have a significant deterrent effect on the commission of later human rights violations is a matter which is more the subject of, often sceptical, speculation rather than scientific proof.[89]

Perhaps the shadow side of this is that prosecutions for international crimes are, for a variety of reasons, selective, and so not all of those who commit such crimes can be prosecuted. Indeed, as has been noted above, not all human rights violations are also international crimes (although most, but, importantly, not all, international crimes would probably amount to human rights violations when committed by states). There are also those that question whether human rights and international criminal law are as coherent as many say. Robinson, for example, notes that:

Many of the prohibitions of ICL [international criminal law] are drawn from, and similar to, prohibitions in human rights and humanitarian law. Faced with familiar-looking provisions, ICL practitioners often assume that the ICL norms are coextensive with their human rights or humanitarian law counterparts, and uncritically transplant concepts and jurisprudence from other domains to flesh out their content. Such assumptions overlook the fact that these bodies of law have different purposes and consequences and thus entail different philosophical commitments.[90]

It is true that human rights law and international criminal law are not identical, but nor are they utterly separate, and a useful inter-judicial dialogue can only serve to improve both areas of law where human rights lawyers and international criminal lawyers are mindful of context.[91] For the most part, the interplay has been beneficial.

---

[85] Text at n 3.

[86] Although for the argument that this represents only one understanding of justice see Clarke, *Fictions of Justice: The International Criminal Court and the Challenge of Legal Pluralism in Sub-Saharan Africa* (CUP, 2009).   [87] Stover, *The Witnesses* (Penn State Press, 2007).

[88] Cohen, *States of Denial: Knowing About Atrocities and Suffering* (Polity, 2001).

[89] Harhoff, 'Sense and Sensibility in Sentencing: Taking Stock of International Criminal Punishment' in Engdahl and Wrange (eds), *Law at War: The Law as it Was and the Law as it Should Be: Liber Amicorum Ove Bring* (Martinus Nijhoff, 2008) 121, 127.

[90] Robinson, 'The Identity Crisis of International Criminal Law' (2008) 21 *LJIL* 925, 946.

[91] See Cryer, 'The Interplay of International Human Rights and International Humanitarian Law: The Approach of the ICTY' (2009) 14 *JCSL* 511.

FURTHER READING

BASSIOUNI (ed), *International Criminal Law Vols 1–III* (Martinus Nijhoff, 2008).

CASSESE, *International Criminal Law* (Oxford University Press, 2008).

—— et al. (eds), *The Oxford Companion to International Criminal Justice* (Oxford University Press, 2009).

CRYER, FRIMAN, ROBINSON, and WILMSHURST, *An Introduction to International Criminal Law and Procedure* (Cambridge University Press, 2010).

RATNER, ABRAMS, and BISCHOFF, *Accountability for Human Rights Atrocities in International Law: Beyond the Nuremberg Legacy* (Oxford University Press, 2009).

SCHABAS, *The UN International Criminal Tribunals* (Cambridge University Press, 2007).

—— *An Introduction to the International Criminal Court* (Cambridge University Press, 2008).

USEFUL WEBSITES

International Criminal Tribunal for the former Yugoslavia: <http://www.icty.org>

International Criminal Tribunal for Rwanda: <http://www.ictr.org>

International Criminal Court: <http://www.icc-cpi.int>

PART VI

CHALLENGES

25

NON-STATE ACTORS

Andrew Clapham

SUMMARY

It is increasingly recognized that human rights law has to address the challenge posed by non-state actors. This chapter starts with a reflection on how the term 'non-state actor' is used and why it is appropriate to look at the impact of non-state actors on the enjoyment of human rights. It then recalls the 'positive obligations' of states to protect those within their jurisdiction from abuses by non-state actors. Finally, it considers the human rights obligations of different non-state actors: international organizations, certain non-state actors under international criminal law, corporations, and armed non-state entities. The chapter argues that we should meet the following challenges: extending and translating certain norms so that they clearly denote the obligations of non-state actors; creating and adapting specific institutions to ensure jurisdiction over the activities of non-state actors; and adjusting our assumptions about who are the duty-bearers in the human rights regime.

1 INTRODUCTION

Even though the term 'non-state actor' can be defined quite simply as any entity that is not a state, it deserves some explanation. In some contexts the term is used to refer to benign civil society groups working for human rights—and it has become commonplace (even a cliché) to refer to the need to 'involve non-state actors in the conversation'. In other contexts, however, the term is understood to refer to some very 'uncivil' groups determined to acquire weapons of mass destruction and target them against a civilian population. The differing use of the term can be confusing not only in terms of understanding what is being alluded to, but also in comprehending the legal obligations involved.

Depending on the context, international law provides that states are either obliged to punish non-state actors or, alternatively, obliged to cooperate with them.[1] Although some commentators have sought to avoid ambiguity and focus the discussion by referring to those non-state actors that violate human rights as non-state perpetrators,[2] to follow this path so early in our discussion would obscure the fact that there are increasing expectations that non-state actors of all kinds should not only refrain from violations, but work to protect and promote human rights. Like states, non-state actors are seen as embodying the paradox that their capacity to violate contains within it the potential for protection. Recent scholarship has started to map the landscape so that actors are seen as both the source of human rights violations and motors for pressuring other actors to advance human rights. In this way, non-state actors can be the 'source and target of pressure at the same time' and such pressure can support or breach human rights.[3]

But even if we admit that the expression non-state actor means different things in different contexts, and that all such actors have the potential either to violate or to promote human rights, there is another problem we need to address. The problem is that the human rights regime has developed along state-centric lines. Human rights treaties were traditionally written by states as sets of obligations for states. The accompanying monitoring mechanisms provided for state accountability are based on traditional rules of state responsibility. To adjust this system, and to revise the assumptions that have grown up around it, tends to trigger considerable resistance.

Why would lawyers and governments want to exclude non-state actors from the state-centric regime of international law in general, and human rights law in particular? There are a number of reasons. First, with regard to armed opposition groups (also sometimes characterized as 'terrorists'), it is argued that suggesting such groups have human rights obligations under international law lends them a state-like status which renders them somehow 'legitimate'. This apparent enhanced legitimacy is considered by some governments to be undesirable. Second, in some circumstances, governments may be wary of allowing international organizations to assume state-like features by taking on international obligations, such as those relating to human rights. This has been the case, for example, with regard to the attitude of some governments towards the European Union playing a greater role as the bearer of human rights obligations. Third, corporations and international financial institutions such as the World Bank and the International Monetary Fund are usually not keen to take on a raft of responsibilities that they see as properly the responsibilities of states. In particular, in the imagined extension of all human rights obligations to corporations, there is a perceived

---

[1] See AU Convention for the Protection and Assistance of Internally Displaced Persons in Africa (2009), Art 1; SC Res 1540 (28 April 2004); and Cotonou Agreement between the Members of the African, Caribbean and Pacific Group of States and the European Community and its Member States (2000) Art 6.

[2] Spirer and Spirer, 'Accounting for Human Rights Violations by Non-State Actors' in Andreopoulos, Arat, and Juvilier (eds), *Non-State Actors in the Human Rights Universe* (Kumarian Press, 2006) 43.

[3] Arat, 'Looking beyond the State But Not Ignoring It', ibid, 8.

danger of undermining or diluting the responsibilities of states. For example, in 2006, John Ruggie, the UN Secretary-General's Special Representative on business and human rights, advised the UN Commission on Human Rights that: 'Corporations are not democratic public interest institutions and that making them, in effect, co-equal duty bearers for the broad spectrum of human rights...may undermine efforts to build indigenous social capacity and to make governments more responsible to their own citizenry.'[4]

We have, then, two perceived problems: a 'legitimacy' problem and a 'dilution' problem. These problems can be quite easily overcome. We can suggest that armed opposition groups and their members are increasingly accused of violations of international humanitarian law and even convicted of war crimes. Highlighting violations of these obligations ought to be seen as delegitimizing rather than anything else. The problem of legitimizing armed groups evaporates if we decouple human rights from the idea that human rights supposedly emerge from an essential link between governments and their citizens. When we see human rights as rights rather than self-imposed governmental duties, and when we envisage the rights project as founded on better protection for human dignity rather than privileges granted by states, we can start to see how we might imagine human rights obligations for non-state actors. Rather than concentrating on abstract questions of legitimacy we can take a more sentimental approach and imagine ourselves in the shoes of a victim. From the victim's perspective, the inhuman and degrading treatment is an assault on dignity whether it is suffered at the hands of a policeman, a rebel commander, or a private security company. With regards to dilution, we can suggest that corporations, international financial institutions, and development agencies have to respect human rights in ways that complement the responsibilities of states, rather than replacing state obligations.

We are already moving in this direction. It is worth considering the recent report on the 'Alliance of Civilizations', which fixes expectations on non-state actors without seeming to be worried about legitimacy. At the same time, the report cautions about demonizing non-state actors and leaving states out of the picture, thus addressing worries about dilution:

A full and consistent adherence to human rights standards forms the foundation for stable societies and peaceful international relations. These rights include the prohibition against physical and mental torture; the right to freedom of religion; and the right to freedom of expression and association.... The integrity of these rights rests on their universal and unconditional nature. These rights should therefore be considered inviolable and all states, international organisations, non-state actors, and individuals, under all circumstances, must abide by them....

Extremism and terrorism are not motivated solely by exclusivist interpretations of religion, nor are non-state actors alone in employing them.... a cursory look at the twentieth

[4] Interim Report of the Special Representative of the Secretary-General on the Issue of Human Rights and Transnational Corporations and Other Business Enterprises, E/CN.4/2006/97 (22 February 2006) para 17.

century indicates that no single group, culture, geographic region, or political orientation has a monopoly on extremism and terrorist acts.[5]

The most promising theoretical basis for human rights obligations for non-state actors is to remind ourselves that the foundational basis of human rights is best explained as rights which belong to the individual in recognition of each person's inherent dignity. The implication is that these natural rights should be respected by everyone and every entity. Moreover, we should recall that the Universal Declaration of Human Rights is written as a proclamation of rights; the obligations of states were not agreed upon at that time. The word 'state' hardly appears in the Declaration. Furthermore, if we leave aside the treaty regimes, with their state-centred monitoring mechanisms, and concentrate on general principles of international law or customary international law, it becomes apparent that even though the jurisdictional clauses of the treaty bodies preclude complaints against non-state actors, the substantive norms themselves may easily be adapted to apply to non-state actors. Before turning to the actual state of human rights law, let us look at four dynamics that challenge the traditional state-focused approach to human rights law.

2 THE CHALLENGE OF NON-STATE ACTORS

2.1 GLOBALIZATION

The globalization of the world economy and means of communication have highlighted the power of large corporations and their limited accountability in law for human rights abuses.[6] There exist today increased possibilities for enterprises to outsource different links in the manufacturing chain, by relying on supplies from subcontractors all over the world. In addition, competition between states to attract foreign direct investment has sometimes resulted in pressure on labour rights, in particular in the garment sector and in special export-processing zones with minimal regulation or control over employer practices. Moreover, foreign companies working in the extractive industry have had to resort to special security arrangements in the host state. This practice has led to serious questions about violence at the hands of public and private security guards in this context. The emerging framework for ensuring greater responsibility in these areas is international human rights law.[7]

In a first phase, emphasis was put on the state's duty to protect individuals from such non-state actors. However, this has proven inadequate. Imagine a corporation incorporated in one state with abusive security services operating in another state, the supplying of arms to abusive regimes, risks to health from the chemical or extractive

---

[5] Alliance of Civilizations: Report of the High Level Group (13 November 2006) paras 2.3 and 3.12.

[6] See eg Amnesty International, *Undermining Freedom of Expression in China: The Role of Yahoo!, Microsoft and Google* (2006); Flint, 'Don't be Evil?' (2006) 27 *Business LRev* 102–4.

[7] See eg Voluntary Principles on Security and Human Rights (2000).

industries operating in developing countries, or the complaints against US private military contractors for killings and allegations of torture in Iraq.[8] In each case to rely on the states concerned to protect people from such abuses is unworkable. Accordingly, a second approach has been suggested, namely that corporate activity should be simply dealt with by national legal tools such as tort or contract law. Transnational activity, with links to multiple jurisdictions, ought to make it easy to find an accountability mechanism; but the opposite is the case.[9] Globalization reminds us that corporate actors have the possibility to operate from multiple jurisdictions, which will not necessarily ensure that they are held accountable for human rights abuses. It also reminds us that governments competing for investment have shown little inclination to develop accountability for corporate abuses.

2.2 PRIVATIZATION

The privatization of sectors such as health, education, prisons, water, communications, security forces, and military training has forced us to think again about the applicability of human rights law to the private sector. Many assume that something which is privatized remains subject to human rights law as the concept of human rights is related to so-called 'public functions'. But this assumption is not borne out in practice. First, the whole point of privatization is to remove certain activity from the state-run sphere, increasing flexibility and usually diminishing accountability. The usual consequence is that the protections that have developed with regard to state activity no longer apply and, although in theory new private remedies should apply, such remedies tend not to include human rights protection in name. The same act therefore gets relabelled. What was once a human rights violation becomes a civil wrong, a tort, or a breach of contract. Second, the new entity which has taken on the former responsibilities of the state has something that the state did not have. The new non-state entity may have competing human rights which can be enforced or weighed against anyone claiming their rights against this non-state actor. So, for example, the owners and managers of a private shopping mall dominating a town centre will be able to claim respect for the enjoyment of their private property when protestors claim freedom of expression and assembly in that privatized space.[10]

2.3 FRAGMENTATION OF STATES

The increase in the number of internal armed conflicts involves a third phenomenon: the fragmentation of states as non-state actors take control of territory and populations. Such an exercise of power by armed opposition groups has led to greater expectations

---

[8] See International Commission of Jurists, *Report of the Expert Legal Panel on Corporate Complicity in International Crimes*, available at: <http://www.business-humanrights.org/Updates/Archive/ICJPaneloncomplicity>.

[9] See the Corporate Responsibility Coalition, *The reality of rights: Barriers to accessing remedies when business operates beyond borders* (London School of Economics and Political Science, 2009).

[10] *Appleby v UK* (2003) 37 EHRR 38.

of them. The demands go beyond international humanitarian law and international individual criminal responsibility. As we shall see below, the Special Rapporteurs of the UN Human Rights Council already report on human rights violations by all sides to an armed conflict, and the state/non-state actor boundary again seems less and less relevant. In this context we should also consider the assumption of state-like tasks carried out by the UN in situations such as those of Kosovo and East Timor. This has led to new developments with regard to the applicability of human rights law to the UN and other international organizations in the context of their protection work.

2.4 FEMINIZATION

The developments surrounding the international human rights of women have led to a complete reappraisal of the way in which the public/private divide has been constructed to delimit human rights law. Some treaties now specifically require the state to take action to protect women in the 'private sphere' or to guarantee women's rights in public and private life.[11] International obligations and commitments have been reconfigured through the prism of due diligence, to ensure that they cover daily harm to women and not only a narrow range of concerns of men. The feminization of human rights has shifted the emphasis to issues of violence against women, certain unfair labour practices, sexual exploitation, trafficking, and 'traditional practices' such as honour killings.

Let us now turn to the legal framework.

3 THE LEGAL FRAMEWORK

All human rights treaties contain positive obligations that oblige states to protect those within their jurisdiction from harms committed by non-state actors.[12] Different treaty bodies and international courts have addressed the extent of these obligations in different contexts. The Human Rights Committee has stated in relation to the International Covenant on Civil and Political Rights (ICCPR) that:

the positive obligations on States Parties to ensure Covenant rights will only be fully discharged if individuals are protected by the State, not just against violations of Covenant rights by its agents, but also against acts committed by private persons or entities that would impair the enjoyment of Covenant rights in so far as they are amenable to application between private persons or entities. There may be circumstances in which a failure to ensure Covenant rights as required by article 2 [ICCPR] would give rise to violations by States Parties of those rights, as a result of States Parties' permitting or failing to take appropriate measures or to exercise due diligence to prevent, punish, investigate or redress the harm caused by such acts by private persons or entities.[13]

---

[11] See Chapter 16, above.   [12] See Chapter 6, above.
[13] HRC, General Comment 31, HRI/GEN/1/Rev.9 (Vol 1) 243.

There is a rich vein of case law that allows us to determine the extent to which it is reasonable to expect states, not only to punish, but also to prevent, non-state actors from interfering with the enjoyment of human rights under human rights treaties.[14] There are a number of possibilities through which states may give effect to their positive obligation to protect individuals from harms committed by non-state actors.

First, some states may give effect to certain international human rights by simply incorporating treaty rights and obligations into their national legal orders. In some situations this may mean that the human rights obligation applies to certain non-state actors even in the absence of special legislation.[15]

A second possibility is that the jurisdiction in question allows for human rights claims against private entities in its constitution (such as South Africa) or has some legislation that is applied to facilitate human rights claims against non-state actors.

The growing number of cases being litigated under the US Alien Tort Statute (also known as the Alien Tort Claims Act) is significant in this context. The Alien Tort Statute confers upon US federal district courts original jurisdiction over 'any civil action by an alien for a tort only, committed in violation of the law of nations' wherever it may have taken place.[16] It has proven perfectly possible to bring a suit against a corporation for violating international law as the principal perpetrator. For example, cases have been brought against contractors providing interpretation and interrogation services to the USA at Abu Ghraib prison in Iraq in respect of torture and inhuman or degrading treatment[17] and against Blackwater (a private military contractor) alleging war crimes in connection with the killing of civilians.[18]

US courts have been gradually refining the list of violations of the 'law of nations'. Recent rulings have determined that genocide, slave trading, slavery, forced labour, and war crimes are actionable even in the absence of any connection to the state.[19] In addition, according to the *Kadic v Karadzic* judgment, where rape, torture, and summary execution are committed, these crimes 'are actionable under the Alien Tort Act, without regard to state action, to the extent they were committed in pursuit of genocide or war crimes'.[20] In fact, even though US courts, including the Supreme Court, have determined that violations of the 'law of nations' under this statute must be those that are 'specific, universal and obligatory' and have suggested that the drafters of the

[14] See eg *Case of X and Y v The Netherlands* (1985) 8 EHRR 235; *Velásquez Rodriguez v Honduras*, IACtHR Series C No 4 (29 July 1988); 204/97, *Mouvement Burkinabé des Droits de l'Homme et des Peuples v Burkina Faso*, ACommHPR; see generally Clapham, *Human Rights Obligations of Non-State Actors* (OUP, 2006) chs 8 and 9.

[15] See eg the situation in the Netherlands: Jägers and van der Heijden, 'Corporate Human Rights Violations: the Feasibility of Civil Recourse in the Netherlands' (2008) 33 *Brooklyn JIL* 834, 856. For more examples see Oliver and Fedtke (eds), *Human Rights and the Private Sphere* (Routledge-Cavendish, 2007).

[16] 28 USC § 1350.

[17] *Ibrahim et al. v Titan et al.*; *Saleh et al. v Titan et al.*, US District Court for the District of Columbia, Case 1:05-cv-01165-JR, Order of 6 November 2007.

[18] *Abtan et al. v Blackwater Worldwide et al.*, Case 1:07-cv-01831 (RBW) (filed 26 November 2007).

[19] *Wiwa v Royal Dutch Shell Petroleum (Shell)*, US District Court for the Southern District of New York (28 February 2002) 39. See also *Doe I v Unocal Corporation* (18 September 2002) paras 3 ff.

[20] *Kadic v Karadzic* 70 F3d 232, 243–4 (2d Cir 1995).

Alien Tort Statute probably had in mind a narrow set of violations such as piracy or an assault on an ambassador, the list is not exhaustive, as international law continues to evolve.[21] Claims concerning adult labour conditions have been held not to meet the requisite threshold. In 2007, in a case against the Bridgestone company concerning conditions at their plant in Liberia, a US court determined:

[T]here is a broad international consensus that at least some extreme practices called 'forced labor' violate universal and binding international norms. But the adult plaintiffs in this case allege labor practices that lie somewhere on a continuum that ranges from those clear violations of international law (slavery or labor forced at the point of soldiers' bayonets) to more ambiguous situations involving poor working conditions and meager or exploitative wages.[22]

A third possibility is that the incorporating legislation addresses the issue of non-state actors explicitly. This is the case for the Human Rights Act 1998 in the UK. Section 6, entitled 'Acts of public authorities', states in part:

(1) It is unlawful for a public authority to act in a way which is incompatible with a Convention [ECHR] right....

(3) In this section 'public authority' includes—

  (a) a court or tribunal, and

  (b) any person certain of whose functions are functions of a public nature,

  but does not include either House of Parliament or a person exercising functions in connection with proceedings in Parliament.

(4) In subsection (3) 'Parliament' does not include the House of Lords in its judicial capacity.

(5) In relation to a particular act, a person is not a public authority by virtue only of subsection (3)(b) if the nature of the act is private.

So a non-state actor with functions of a public nature carrying out acts which are not of a private nature has human rights obligations under the Act. Interpreting this conundrum has given rise to a rich stream of case law and has split the then Judicial Committee of the House of Lords in the context of a complaint against a residential care home,[23] and led to new legislation.[24]

Stepping back from the detailed interpretations in these cases, the question of whether to apply human rights to non-state actors has forced judges to reflect on the foundational rationale for human rights—to protect individual dignity—and admit that it does not matter from which side of the public/private divide the harm comes. At this point we find that opinions divide, not only on whether certain functions such as education, healthcare, restaurants, rented accommodation, social housing,[25]

---

[21] *Sosa v Alvarez-Machain et al.* 542 US 692 (2004), 732 and 734–7.

[22] *Roe et al. v Bridgestone Corporation et al.* 492 F Supp 2d 988 (26 June 2007), 21.

[23] *YL (by her litigation friend the Official Solicitor) (FC) (Appellant) v Birmingham City Council and others (Respondents)* [2007] UKHL 27.   [24] See Social Care Act 2009, s 145.

[25] See *R (Weaver) v London and Quadrant Housing Trust* [2009] EWCA Civ 587.

shopping malls, telephone services, residential care for the elderly, detention, and security are 'obviously' public functions, but also on the question of how much power should judges have to interpret such 'new' obligations for private actors? Our answer depends in part on our approach to human rights: must they be granted through the authoritative process of law-making? Or are they inherent in the individual generated from a basic obligation on us all to protect human dignity and autonomy?

In a case brought by Naomi Campbell against Mirror Group Newspapers for a breach of her privacy in respect of publication of a photograph of her leaving Narcotics Anonymous, the issue arose as to the weight (if any) to be given to her right to privacy as opposed to the freedom of expression and information claims made by the newspaper. In the past such a claim might have been seen as having nothing to do with human rights due to the absence of a state actor. Today, the expectations are different. Lord Hoffmann reflected this this in his speech:

What human rights law has done is to identify private information as something worth protecting as an aspect of human autonomy and dignity. And this recognition has raised inescapably the question of why it should be worth protecting against the state but not against a private person. There may of course be justifications for the publication of private information by private persons which would not be available to the state—I have particularly in mind the position of the media, to which I shall return in a moment—but I can see no logical ground for saying that a person should have less protection against a private individual than he would have against the state for the publication of personal information for which there is no justification. Nor, it appears, have any of the other judges who have considered the matter.[26]

Baroness Hale, in the same case, drew the logical conclusion that as the courts are public authorities, all their decisions should apply human rights law even in actions brought against non-state actors:

Neither party to this appeal has challenged the basic principles which have emerged from the Court of Appeal in the wake of the Human Rights Act 1998. The 1998 Act does not create any new cause of action between private persons. But if there is a relevant cause of action applicable, the court as a public authority must act compatibly with both parties' Convention rights.[27]

Lastly, in other situations, legislation has been *interpreted* to cover human rights claims brought against non-state actors. We can find a pervasive percolation of human rights values into judicial reasoning and constitutional interpretation, in ways that indirectly apply human rights obligations to non-state actors.[28]

---

[26] *Campbell v MGN Limited* [2004] UKHL 22, para 50.   [27] Ibid, para 132.

[28] See Gardbaum, 'The "Horizontal Effect" of Constitutional Rights' (2003) 102 *Michigan LRev* 387; Barak, 'Constitutional Human Rights and Private Law' in Friedmann and Barak-Erez (eds), *Human Rights in Private Law* (Hart Publishing, 2001) 13; Tushnet, 'The Issue of State Action/Horizontal Effect in Comparative Constitutional Law' (2003) 1 *Intl J Const L* 79.

4 THE OBLIGATIONS OF
INTERNATIONAL ORGANIZATIONS

A traditional starting point for the assertion that international organizations have international obligations is the International Court of Justice's statement that international organizations are subject to 'general rules of international law'.[29] As Christian Tomuschat points out:

Substantively, international organizations may be characterized as common agencies operated by States for the fulfilment of certain common tasks. Now, if States acting individually have been subjected to certain rules thought to be indispensable for maintaining orderly relations within the international community, there is no justification for exempting international organizations from the scope *ratione personae* of such rules.[30]

Many would agree with Tomuschat that, even if states can limit the powers of the organization they create, they 'cannot thereby shield their creation from becoming liable towards other subjects of international law on account of [their] activities'.[31] This reasoning has been reflected in the approach of the European Court of Human Rights:

The Court is of the opinion that where States establish international organisations in order to pursue or strengthen their cooperation in certain fields of activities, and where they attribute to these organisations certain competences and accord them immunities, there may be implications as to the protection of fundamental rights. It would be incompatible with the purpose and object of the Convention [ECHR], however, if the Contracting States were thereby absolved from their responsibility under the Convention in relation to the field of activity covered by such attribution. It should be recalled that the Convention is intended to guarantee not theoretical or illusory rights, but rights that are practical and effective.[32]

But this approach, developed in the context of employment relations, with regard to international entities such as the European Space Agency, has been revisited in complaints regarding peace operations in Kosovo. The issue arose in stark terms in the context of applications brought by Agim and Bekir Behrami against France, and Ruzhdi Saramati against France, Germany, and Norway in the European Court of Human Rights.[33] The complaint of the Behramis concerned the right to life under Article 2 European Convention on Human Rights (ECHR) and related to the failure of the French Kosovo Force (the NATO Force) personnel to clear undetonated cluster bomb units. With regard to Saramati the complaint concerned his detention by UNMIK (the UN Interim Administration Mission in Kosovo) on suspicion of

---

[29] *Interpretation of the Agreement of 25 March 1951 Between the WHO and Egypt* [1980] ICJ Rep 73, 89–90.
[30] Tomuschat, 'International Law: Ensuring the Survival of Mankind on the Eve of a New Century: General Course on Public International Law' (1999) 281 *RdC* 9, 34–5.   [31] Ibid, 129–30.
[32] *Waite and Kennedy v Germany* (2000) 30 EHRR 261, para 67.
[33] *Behrami and Behrami v France; Saramati v France, Germany and Norway* (2007) 45 EHRR SE10.

attempted murder. The question of whether these acts were attributable to the relevant states or to an international organization arose before the Court.

The Court engaged in a detailed examination of the respective responsibilities of UNMIK and KFOR and concluded 'that issuing detention orders fell within the security mandate of KFOR and that the supervision of de-mining fell within UNMIK's mandate'.[34] The Court held that it could not attribute any responsibility to the states that provided the relevant units to these peace operations. The implication of the judgment is that the remedy lies at the level of the UN and the Security Council that had authorized both operations. However, whether or not these acts should be attributed to the UN or to NATO, there is no reason the acts should be *solely* attributable to such an organization. As a Special Rapporteur of the International Law Commission, Giorgio Gaja, put it: '[O]ne may argue that attribution of conduct to an international organization does not necessarily exclude attribution of the same conduct to a State, nor does, vice versa, attribution to a State rule out attribution to an international organization.'[35]

The idea that international organizations have human rights obligations has been reinforced by the UN human rights treaty bodies. For example, general comments prepared by the Committee on Economic, Social and Cultural Rights on topics such as the right to health, the right to food, the right to water, and the right to work, now include the duty of states to protect individuals from non-state actors that might infringe on the enjoyment of these rights. The Committee has a chapter at the end of its general comments entitled 'Obligations of Actors Other than State Parties'. This includes, for example, in the context of the right to work, recommendations for 'individuals, local communities, trade unions, civil society and private sector organisations'.[36] Special attention is given to 'private enterprises—national and multinational'. The general comment goes on to address the role of 'the ILO [International Labour Organization] and the other specialized agencies of the United Nations, the World Bank, regional development banks, the International Monetary Fund, the World Trade Organization and other relevant bodies within the United Nations system'.

Now that it is plain that international organizations have human rights obligations, the question arises of how to build accountability mechanisms that would help to influence their behaviour and provide redress for victims. One option is to ensure that human rights treaties allow for international organizations to become contracting parties. This is currently the case for both the Convention on the Rights of Persons with Disabilities and its Optional Protocol. The Convention explains that it allows for 'regional integration organizations' to become parties where those organizations are 'constituted by sovereign States of a given region, to which its member States have transferred competence in respect of matters governed by this Convention'.[37] The European Community has so far only signed the Convention. In the same way, Protocol No 14

---

[34] Ibid, para 127.

[35] Special Rapporteur, Second Report on Responsibility of International Organizations, A/CN.4/541 (2 April 2004) para 7 (footnotes omitted).

[36] CESCR, General Comment 18, HRI/GEN/1/Rev.9 (Vol I) 243.   [37] Arts 42–4.

ECHR allows for the European Union to become a party to the Convention and its Protocols so that complaints could eventually be brought against the Union before the European Court of Human Rights.[38]

5 INTERNATIONAL CRIMINAL RESPONSIBILITY OF NON-STATE ACTORS

It is more and more likely that international criminal law will become primarily concerned with non-state actors as opposed to state officials. The Statute of the International Criminal Court provides that its jurisdiction can be triggered by a state party that refers a situation in which relevant crimes appear to have been committed.[39] Three states have referred their own situations to the court. In all three situations— Uganda, Central African Republic, and the Democratic Republic of the Congo—the government concerned is cooperating in order to see non-state actors tried before the Court. Thus, the first trials before the International Criminal Court will be for acts committed by rebel leaders rather than for acts committed by state actors.[40]

Similarly, the only prosecution in the UK for the international crime of torture concerned an Afghan, non-state, warlord who had been fighting the government.[41] Attempts to try government officials for international crimes in foreign courts have been met with multiple jurisdictional and immunity-based hurdles. Belgium and Spain both came under serious political pressure when they attempted to exercise national jurisdiction over foreign governmental officials. Although this migration of international law from state actors to non-state actors has mostly been observed at the level of individual criminal responsibility, there is no convincing conceptual reason why it should not be extended to cover corporate actors and rebel groups as such.[42]

6 CORPORATE SOCIAL RESPONSIBILITY AND THE MOVE TOWARDS ACCOUNTABILITY

Some activists have drawn a distinction between corporate responsibility and corporate accountability. According to the NGO CorpWatch: 'Corporate responsibility refers to any attempt to get corporations to behave responsibly on a voluntary basis,

---

[38] For a discussion on how this might work, see Parliamentary Assembly of the Council of Europe, AS/ Jur (2007) 53 (12 October 2007).   [39] Art 14.

[40] See Chapter 24, above.

[41] *R v Zardad*, Central Criminal Court (7 April 2004). See Clapham, n 14, 342–3.

[42] For a debate on this issue, see (2008) 6 *JICJ* 899–979; Nollkaemper and van der Wilt (eds), *System Criminality in International Law* (CUP, 2009).

out of either ethical or bottom-line considerations.'[43] Corporate accountability (or compliance), on the other hand, 'refers to requiring corporations to behave according to societal norms or face consequences'.[44] Christian Aid now states that it 'is advocating giving "teeth" to the ethical commitments of companies by moving beyond corporate social responsibility, which does not and cannot go far enough, to corporate social accountability, to ensure that companies have a legal obligation to uphold international standards'.[45]

Some businesses have been expressing human rights commitments from a desire to: protect reputation; reduce risk of disruption through strikes, protests, and boycotts; enhance their attractiveness for future and current employees; and because it is the 'right thing to do'. Major companies now have human rights policies as a matter of course and few now claim openly (as they used to do) that 'human rights are none of our business'. In fact in some sectors the move towards developing principles to guide the companies in fulfilling their responsibilities and developing accountability has led to innovative studies such as the ones undertaken by Paul Hunt, the UN Special Rapporteur on the right to health. His reports take us beyond a generalized claim that companies have human rights responsibilities into the detail of what sort of measures they are expected to take, for example 'to make medicine as accessible as possible' subject to the 'capacity' of the company at issue.[46]

Three further factors are forcing greater attention to the human rights implications of corporate activity. First, the decision by some governments to link export credit guarantees to human rights impacts.[47] Second, studies and mechanisms being developed by international organizations such as the UN, the ILO, and the Organisation for Economic Co-operation and Development (OECD) are reinforcing the notion that companies have international responsibilities. Worthy of particular mention are the multiple studies produced by the Special Representative of the UN Secretary-General, John Ruggie, and the possibility of complaining to an OECD National Contact Point that a company has failed to respect human rights.[48] Third, human rights compliance is increasingly factored into investment decisions, in particular by funds which

---

[43] Karliner and Bruno, 'Responsibility vs. accountability', *International Herald Tribune* (1 July 2002) 14.

[44] Ibid.

[45] Christian Aid, *Behind the Mask: The Real Face of Corporate Social Responsibility* (2004) 56.

[46] Report of the Special Rapporteur on the right of everyone to the enjoyment of the highest attainable standard of physical and mental health, A/HRC/11/12/Add.2 (5 May 2009) para 37; Report of the Special Rapporteur on the right of everyone to the enjoyment of the highest attainable standard of physical and mental health, A/63/263 (11 August 2008) paras 8–18; Human Rights Guidelines for Pharmaceutical Companies in relation to Access to Medicines, A/63/263, Annex.

[47] See eg UK Export Credit Guarantees Department, *Mission and Status Review 1999–2000* (HMSO, 2000) Cm 4790.

[48] See Report of the Special Representative of the Secretary-General on the issue of human rights and transnational corporations and other business enterprises, A/HRC/8/5 (7 April 2008); Rights and Accountability in Development in association with the Corporate Responsibility Coalition and the Trades Union Congress, *Fit for Purpose? A Review of the UK National Contact Point for the Organisation for Economic Co-operation and Development (OECD) Guidelines for Multinational Enterprises 2008* (2008). See generally, Clapham, n 14.

advertise an ethical investment dimension. Perhaps the most interesting process in this respect is the Norwegian Council on Ethics for the Government Pension Fund— Global. Under the Council's ethical guidelines, '[u]pon request of the Ministry of Finance, the Council issues recommendations on whether an investment may constitute a violation of Norway's obligations under international law'.[49] While the concern is expressed as a question of Norway's obligations under international law, in effect it is a review of a company's respect for international human rights or humanitarian law, and recommendations for disinvestment may be made even in the absence of a violation of international law.[50]

The concept that has become central to understanding the expectations on companies in this context is that of complicity. Three factors can be said to have combined to reinforce the importance of this concept.

First, since the late 1990s, human rights NGOs have become more interested in reporting on the behaviour of multinational corporations. They found themselves, however, confronted with a legal conundrum. Unlike ethical investors or those in the corporate social responsibility movement, international human rights organizations were starting from a position of cataloguing violations of international human rights law. These violations were usually expressed in terms of violations of human rights treaties which the relevant state had ratified. The legal methodology did not seem suited to complaining about the behaviour of corporations. Accordingly, Amnesty International formulated 'Human Rights Principles for Companies' (1998), which included a policy recommendation that companies should establish procedures to ensure that all operations are assessed for their potential impact on human rights and safeguards are put in place to ensure that company staff are never complicit in human rights abuses.[51] Similarly, without radically altering the traditional understanding of human rights law, groups such as Human Rights Watch argued that, although corporations did not have obligations as parties to human rights treaties, the states in which they were operating did have such obligations, and the behaviour of the corporations could be seen as contributing to violations by those states. As such, it made sense to talk about the corporations being 'complicit' in such violations.[52]

Second, in 1999, the then UN Secretary-General Kofi Annan launched what became the Global Compact with a speech in Davos. He addressed business leaders in the following terms:

You can uphold human rights and decent labour and environmental standards directly, by your own conduct of your own business. Indeed, you can use these universal values as the cement binding together your global corporations, since they are values people all over the

---

[49] Section 4.3.

[50] Recommendation concerning whether the weapons systems Spider and Intelligent Munition System (IMS) might be contrary to international law (20 September 2005).

[51] See also Irene Khan, 'Understanding Corporate Complicity: Extending the Notion beyond Existing Laws' (2006).

[52] See eg Human Rights Watch, *Oil Companies Complicit in Nigerian Abuses* (1999); Human Rights Watch, *The Enron Corporation: Corporate Complicity in Human Rights Violations* (1999).

world will recognize as their own. You can make sure that in your own corporate practices you uphold and respect human rights; and that you are not yourselves complicit in human rights abuses.[53]

The Global Compact was developed the following year and operates within the UN as a 'policy platform and a practical framework for companies that are committed to sustainability and responsible business practices'.[54] Its first two principles are: 'Principle 1: Businesses should support and respect the protection of internationally proclaimed human rights; and Principle 2: make sure that they are not complicit in human rights abuses.'[55]

Third, the growing number of cases being litigated under the Alien Tort Statute has focused attention on the scope of corporate complicity in human rights violations.[56] In 2009, one of the longest running cases, the complaint against Shell for complicity in human rights violations in Nigeria, was settled for the sum of US$15.5 million. This result is now seen as emblematic of the liability of corporations for human rights violations and according to one of the plaintiffs, Ken Saro-Wiwa Jr, 'this historic case means that corporations will have to be much more careful'.[57]

In sum, businesses are increasingly expected to comply with a broad range of human rights obligations. The UN and the OECD offer a certain degree of analysis and the prospect of monitoring, while there is an emerging sense of accountability due to the Alien Tort Statute. These legal developments should, however, be seen for what they are: simply the beginnings of an awareness that companies have human rights responsibilities.[58] It would be naive to believe that human rights law has already met the challenge of preventing and punishing human rights abuses committed by companies. The challenge to translate the obligations, develop the monitoring and accountability mechanisms, and overturn assumptions remains ongoing.

7 ARMED OPPOSITION GROUPS

While international humanitarian law is now seen as 'obviously' applicable to the non-state party to an internal armed conflict there is an apparent problem with the application of human rights law to such armed groups. This is for two main reasons. First, because in contrast to international humanitarian law, human rights law is seen as applicable only to states. Human rights treaties only rarely address non-state armed

---

[53] Press Release, SG/SM/6881 (1 February 1999).

[54] *UN Global Compact: Corporate Citizenship in the World Economy* (UN, 2008) 1.

[55] UN Global Compact Office and OHCHR, *Embedding Human Rights in Business Practice* (2004), available at: <http://www.unglobalcompact.org/docs/news_events/8.1/EHRBPII_Final.pdf>.

[56] Alien Tort Statute, n 16.

[57] 'Shell agrees to settle rights case for $15.5million', *International Herald Tribune* (10 June 2009) 19.

[58] For a rejection of the notion that all international human rights obligations apply to corporations, see Vásquez, 'Direct vs Indirect Obligations of Corporations Under International Law' (2005) 43 *Columbia J Trans L* 927.

groups.[59] In contrast, international humanitarian law is considered to apply to the non-state party to the conflict. In 2004 the Appeals Chamber of the Special Court for Sierra Leone simply held that 'it is well settled that all parties to an armed conflict, whether states or non-state actors, are bound by international humanitarian law, even though only states may become parties to international treaties'.[60] Second, there is a perception that engaging with rebel groups on human rights issues lends them a certain legitimacy. This is in part related to the first issue: by claiming that a group has violated human rights one is implying that they are a state-like entity because it is presumed that only states have human rights obligations.

Both these obstacles are being eroded. As with corporations, the human rights monitoring mechanisms are starting to include reporting on non-state armed groups in their range of activities. Although several commentators insist that only states have human rights obligations in this context[61] and that the non-state actors are exclusively bound by international humanitarian law, this is being challenged. The challenge comes in the form of increasing demands by the Security Council for armed groups to respect human rights, in the reports of the various truth commissions (such as those in Guatemala and Sierra Leone) which detail the human rights violations committed by non-state actors, and the failure to explain why international humanitarian law has the theoretical potential to bind non-state actors while human rights law does not.[62]

Let us turn to three practical applications of human rights obligations to armed non-state actors: first, the work of the Security Council with regard to children's rights; second, the work of the UN special mechanisms; and third, the work of one NGO, Geneva Call.

7.1 THE UN SECURITY COUNCIL ON CHILDREN AND ARMED CONFLICT

The UN's work on children and armed conflict has led to an innovative approach which details violations by non-state actors. Reports by the UN Secretary-General to the Security Council on certain situations now list the non-state actors concerned and whether they are involved in any of six grave violations:

(1) Killing or maiming of children;
(2) Recruiting or using child soldiers;
(3) Attacks against schools or hospitals;
(4) Rape or other grave sexual violence against children;

---

[59] The exception being the Optional Protocol to the CRC on the involvement of children in armed conflict.

[60] *Prosecutor v Sam Hinga Norman*, Decision on Preliminary Motion Based on Lack of Jurisdiction (Child Recruitment), SCSL-2004-14-AR72(E) (31 May 2004) para 22.

[61] Moir, *The Law of Internal Armed Conflict* (CUP, 2002) 194; Zegveld, *Accountability of Armed Opposition Groups in International Law* (CUP, 2002) 53.

[62] See Clapham, 'Human Rights Obligations of Non-State Actors in Conflict Situations' (2006) 88 *IRRC* 491, 495–508.

(5) Abduction of children;

(6) Denial of humanitarian access for children.

The UN Secretary-General's initial report explains that these violations are based on international norms, commitments that have been made by the parties to the conflict, national laws, and peace agreements.[63] Subsequent reports on various country situations have detailed the 'grave violations of children's rights' committed by the non-state actors concerned.[64] These reports dedicate as much, if not more, space to the violations committed by the non-state actors as they do to addressing the states concerned. The mechanism vis-à-vis the non-state actors works not only through naming and shaming but by encouraging them to submit an 'action plan' to the Security Council. In this way, the groups can be removed from the list of violators. One non-state armed group that has supplied such an action plan and claimed to no longer be a violator is the Forces Nouvelles (FAFN) in Cote d'Ivoire. It was delisted by the Security Council in 2008.[65] The Security Council also has in mind that it could adopt:

country-specific resolutions, targeted and graduated measures, such as, inter alia, a ban on the export and supply of small arms and light weapons and of other military equipment and on military assistance, against parties to situations of armed conflict which are on the Security Council's agenda and are in violation of applicable international law relating to the rights and protection of children in armed conflict.[66]

Although the focus started with the recruitment of child soldiers, the Security Council has requested the Secretary-General to include in his reports 'those parties to armed conflict that engage, in contravention of applicable international law, in patterns of killing and maiming of children and/or rape and other sexual violence against children, in situations of armed conflict'.[67] Even if the reports refer in general terms to the rules of international law that are actually being violated, the prospect of follow-up sanctions by the Security Council is premised on the idea that these groups have violated international law and not simply a set of moral or political imperatives.

This activity is complemented by the Special Representative of the Secretary-General on children and armed conflict whose work not only feeds into the reports to the Security Council but also relies on country visits, engagement with non-state actors, and facilitation of commitments by those armed groups.[68] Let us look, however, at the work of the UN special procedures more generally.

[63] Report of the Secretary-General on Children and Armed Conflict, S/2005/72 (9 February 2005).

[64] See eg Report of the Secretary-General on Children and Armed Conflict, S/2009/158 (26 March 2009).

[65] See Conclusions on Children and Armed Conflict in Côte d'Ivoire, S/AC.51/2008/5 (1 February 2008). [66] SC Res 1612 (26 July 2005) para 9.

[67] SC Res 1882 (4 August 2009).

[68] See eg Report of the Special Representative of the Secretary-General for Children and Armed Conflict, A/63/227 (6 August 2008).

7.2 UN SPECIAL PROCEDURES

The UN's Special Rapporteur on extrajudicial, summary or arbitrary executions, Philip Alston, has grappled with the question of the human rights obligations of armed non-state actors in the context of his report on Sri Lanka. He concluded in the following terms:

25. Human rights law affirms that both the Government and the LTTE [Liberation Tigers of Tamil Eelam] must respect the rights of every person in Sri Lanka. Human rights norms operate on three levels—as the rights of individuals, as obligations assumed by States, and as legitimate expectations of the international community. The Government has assumed the binding legal obligation to respect and ensure the rights recognized in the International Covenant on Civil and Political Rights (ICCPR). As a non-State actor, the LTTE does not have legal obligations under ICCPR, but it remains subject to the demand of the international community, first expressed in the Universal Declaration of Human Rights, that every organ of society respect and promote human rights.

26. I have previously noted that it is especially appropriate and feasible to call for an armed group to respect human rights norms when it 'exercises significant control over territory and population and has an identifiable political structure'. This visit clarified both the complexity and the necessity of applying human rights norms to armed groups. The LTTE plays a dual role. On the one hand, it is an organization with effective control over a significant stretch of territory, engaged in civil planning and administration, maintaining its own form of police force and judiciary. On the other hand, it is an armed group that has been subject to proscription, travel bans, and financial sanctions in various Member States. The tension between these two roles is at the root of the international community's hesitation to address the LTTE and other armed groups in the terms of human rights law. The international community does have human rights expectations to which it will hold the LTTE, but it has long been reluctant to press these demands directly if doing so would be to 'treat it like a State'.

27. It is increasingly understood, however, that the human rights expectations of the international community operate to protect people, while not thereby affecting the legitimacy of the actors to whom they are addressed. The Security Council has long called upon various groups that Member States do not recognize as having the capacity to formally assume international obligations to respect human rights. The LTTE and other armed groups must accept that insofar as they aspire to represent a people before the world, the international community will evaluate their conduct according to the Universal Declaration's 'common standard of achievement'.[69]

Alston goes on to include specific human rights recommendations addressed to the non-state actor.[70] This approach was also applied in the joint report on Lebanon and Israel by a group of four Special Rapporteurs.[71]

---

[69] Report of the Special Rapporteur on extrajudicial, summary or arbitrary executions, Philip Alston, Mission to Sri Lanka, E/CN.4/2006/53/Add.5 (27 March 2006) (footnote omitted).

[70] Ibid, para 85. See also the letter addressed directly to the LTTE concerning prevention of killings, lack of investigations, and the application of the death penalty: 'Allegation letter sent 21 November 2005', E/CN.4/53/Add.1 (27 March 2006) 320.

[71] Report of the Special Rapporteur on extrajudicial, summary or arbitrary executions; the Special Rapporteur on the right of everyone to the enjoyment of the highest attainable standard of physical and

Calling for a group to respect human rights is one thing; engaging with the group over why it has not respected such human rights or even assisting the group to come into compliance raises a whole new set of problems. The issue is less whether the standards apply, but the perceived sense of legitimization of the group through the act of engagement. To the extent that the group is proscribed under national law, association with, or assistance to, the group carries with it the risk of being considered to have aided or abetted terrorism. While governments have usually understood that the International Committee of the Red Cross has to engage such groups in a dialogue about the laws of war, human rights monitors have been wary of engagement, and humanitarian workers are becoming cautious regarding their dealings with such armed groups.[72]

Alston's report on Afghanistan illuminates the dilemma. Having recalled the demand from some quarters for more pressure to be brought on the government of Pakistan, he continues:

Others argued that there was a need for international actors to engage directly with the Taliban to understand the rationales for its abusive tactics and to apply targeted pressure for change. Prominent elders in the South told me directly that the problem with visits by international envoys was that they only spoke to one side. An international military commander expressed surprise that I was not speaking with Taliban representatives. In general, when I conduct country visits and fact-finding missions, I speak with armed opposition groups, but I did not speak with any formal representatives of the Taliban or other armed groups during my visit.[73] In retrospect, this was a mistake. Taking account of information provided by such sources would permit a more nuanced understanding of Taliban and other AGE [anti-government elements'] strategies. While some of the explanations and justifications provided for engaging in abusive tactics would be self-serving and deceitful, there is no reason to assume that the Taliban could never be persuaded to modify its conduct in ways that would improve its respect for human rights. And purely humanitarian contacts have had a positive impact in the past.[74]

7.3 NGOS AND THE EXAMPLE OF GENEVA CALL

Engagement with such groups is not, however, limited to UN human rights mechanisms. NGOs increasingly report on human rights abuses committed by armed non-state actors. Recent Human Rights Watch reports on Hamas and Fatah have built on the approach developed by the Special Rapporteurs and emphasize the commitment

mental health; the Representative of the Secretary-General on human rights of internally displaced persons; and the Special Rapporteur on adequate housing as a component of the right to an adequate standard of living, A/HRC/2/7 (2 October 2006) para 19.

[72] Thorne, 'Terrorist Lists and Humanitarian Assistance' (2007) 37 *Humanitarian Exchange* 13.

[73] 'Initially, I assumed that security concerns, largely of the armed groups' own making, would make doing so impossible. I was also aware that various actors had reservations about the political implications of doing so. Ultimately, I felt I had no option but to abide by these reservations despite the fact that realistic opportunities were presented to me' (footnote in the original).

[74] Report of the Special Rapporteur on extrajudicial, summary or arbitrary executions, Mission to Afghanistan, A/HRC/11/2/Add.4 (6 May 2009) para 42.

of the Palestinian Authority to human rights and the fact that these groups are seen to be in control of territory.[75] In other situations, human rights law is transposed from the state-based treaty provisions in ways that allude to customary international law. In one case where a non-state actor's justice system was found wanting, the report stated: 'The fairness of any justice system should be tested against international human rights law criteria that include independence, impartiality, and competency of judges, presumption of innocence, right to legal counsel and adequate time for preparation of defense, and the right to appeal.'[76] Amnesty International's reports similarly address its concerns to the armed non-state actors in terms which go beyond the strict obligations found under the laws of war.[77]

The International Campaign to Ban Landmines, having recognized the limits of the Ottawa Treaty to address the possession and use of landmines by non-state actors, set up its own working group which led eventually to the establishment of the NGO, Geneva Call.[78] Geneva Call has engaged armed groups in 'Deeds of Commitment' regarding a 'total ban on anti-personnel mines and for cooperation in mine action'.[79] Having negotiated the signature of the Deed, Geneva Call receives the armed non-state actors' regular reports, monitors compliance with the Deed, and helps arrange mine action including demining and destruction of stocks. It is worth inquiring at this point what might be the incentives for a non-state actor to bind itself to such a Deed.

First, rebel groups realize the advantages of being seen to abide by international norms in the context of moves towards peace negotiations. Second, it is much easier to criticize governments and their armed forces for committing international crimes if the group has policies in place to avoid and punish such crimes. Third, factions may be able to distinguish themselves from other armed groups and thus 'get ahead' in terms of dialogue with the government or other actors. Lastly, in some circumstances, entering into such commitments will facilitate access to assistance from the international community in the form of mine clearance.

Such explicit recognition of specific obligations by the groups themselves helps to transform the debate about the human rights obligations of non-state actors. If armed groups are prepared to take on such obligations, arguments about their non-applicability under international law lose much of their force. States may fear the legitimacy that such commitments seem to imply, and international lawyers may choose to accord them no value, but from a victim's perspective such commitments may indeed be worth more than the paper they are written on.

[75] Human Rights Watch, *Internal Fight: Palestinian Abuses in Gaza and the West Bank* (2008); Human Rights Watch, *Under Cover of War: Hamas Political Violence in Gaza* (2009).

[76] Human Rights Watch, *'Being Neutral is Our Biggest Crime': Government, Vigilante, and Naxalite Abuses in India's Chhattisgarh State* (2008) 98. Compare Sivakumaran, 'Courts of Armed Opposition Groups: Fair Trials or Summary Justice?' (2009) 7 *JICJ* 489.

[77] See eg Amnesty International, *Haiti: Abuse of Human Rights: Political Violence as the 200th Anniversary of Independence Approaches* (2003).

[78] See Busé, 'Non-State Actors and their Significance' (2001) 5 *J Mine Action*, available at: <http://maic.jmu.edu/Journal/5.3/features/maggie_buse_nsa/maggie_buse.htm>.

[79] For the Deed of Commitment, see <http://www.genevacall.org/resources/deed-of-commitment/deed-of-commitment.htm>.

The extension beyond the issue of antipersonnel mines into human rights obligations for non-state actors is foreseen in the Statute of Geneva Call, which states that its aim is to be:

dedicated to engaging armed non-State actors to adhere to a ban on landmines and to respect humanitarian and human rights norms, in particular, through the signing of deeds of commitment to a total ban on: the use of anti-personnel mines; the enrolment and/or the use of child soldiers; the practice of torture and other cruel, inhuman or degrading treatment.[80]

At the time of writing it looks likely that a similar Deed of Commitment will be developed to address the issue of the participation of children in armed conflict.

8 CONCLUSION

This chapter has covered three challenges posed by non-state actors. First, there is a need to find ways to translate existing norms to create appropriate obligations for non-state actors. This work has started in that it is now clear that individual non-state actors will be prosecuted for certain international crimes. Furthermore, corporations and armed groups are increasingly expected to respect not only international criminal law but human rights obligations as well. The second challenge concerns the development of monitoring and accountability. As we have seen, while the jurisdictional state-centric limits of the traditional human rights courts and bodies remain, the UN and NGOs have developed their own ways of monitoring non-state actors.[81] Lastly, it is suggested that a further challenge is to question our own assumptions about what it means to talk about human rights and who has these obligations. It is hoped that those readers who have reached this point may be starting to meet this last challenge.

FURTHER READING

ALSTON (ed), *Non-State Actors and Human Rights* (Oxford University Press, 2005).

BIANCHI (ed), *Non-State Actors and International Law* (Ashgate, 2009).

CLAPHAM, *Human Rights Obligations of Non-State Actors* (Oxford University Press, 2006).

DE SCHUTTER (ed), *Transnational Corporations and Human Rights* (Hart Publishing, 2006).

HESSBRUEGGE, 'Human Rights Violations Arising from Conduct of Non-State Actors' (2005) 11 *Buffalo Human Rights Law Review* 21.

---

[80] Art 3.

[81] It is worth noting that two recent proposals for a World Court of Human Rights both foresee applications against non-state actors (international organizations, corporations, and non-state armed groups). The proposals by Martin Scheinin and Manfred Nowak and Julia Kozma are available at: <http://www.udhr60.ch/research.html>.

JOSEPH, *Corporations and Transnational Human Rights Litigation* (Hart Publishing, 2004).

OECD WATCH, *Guide to the OECD Guidelines for Multinational Enterprises' Complaint Procedure: Lessons from Past NGO Complaints* (2006).

OLIVER and FEDTKE (eds), *Human Rights and the Private Sphere* (Routledge-Cavendish, 2007).

USEFUL WEBSITES

Business and Human Rights Resource Centre: <**http://www.business-humanrights.org/Home**>

Geneva Call: <**http://www.genevacall.org/**>

OECD Watch: <**http://oecdwatch.org/**>

Rule of Law in Armed Conflicts Project: <**http://www.adh-geneva.ch/RULAC/**>

Transnational and Non-State Armed Groups Project: <**http://www.armed-groups.org/home.aspx**>

26

TERRORISM

Martin Scheinin

SUMMARY

Terrorism, and measures to combat terrorism, pose major challenges to the international protection of human rights. Those challenges relate to both the substance of human rights norms and their scope of application. While the focus of attention has been on a number of specific human rights and the rights of those who are suspected of involvement in terrorism, everyone's human rights are, to a lesser or greater extent, affected by counter-terrorism measures. Acts of terrorism, in turn, constitute a serious form of crime and often result in the destruction of human rights.

1 INTRODUCTION

Particularly in the era after the atrocious terrorist attacks in the USA on 11 September 2001 ('9/11'), a whole wave of counter-terrorism measures have been introduced. While human rights are not absolute, and public security therefore may form a legitimate ground for introducing certain limitations, it would be a mistake to conclude that security generally trumps human rights. A more nuanced legal analysis is required in order to respond to the challenges of complying with human rights while at the same time effectively combating terrorism. Those challenges appear not only at the level of domestic law, where increased security has often been the justification for measures that restrict human rights. At the international level the UN Security Council has identified international terrorism as a threat to peace and security, and resorted to its far-reaching powers under Chapter VII of the UN Charter. Shortly after 9/11 it adopted Resolution 1373, imposing a whole set of legally binding counter-terrorism obligations upon states, and established a new subsidiary body, the Counter-Terrorism Committee (CTC).[1] Another subsidiary body, the 1267 Sanctions Committee,

---

[1] SC Res 1373 (28 September 2001).

administers a regime of listing individuals and entities for targeted sanctions for their association with al-Qaida or the Taliban.

Section 2 of this chapter addresses the question of whether terrorism constitutes a violation of human rights, or whether the notion of human rights violations can only be applied to action by states. Section 3 deals with challenges to the applicability of human rights law in the fight against terrorism, particularly since 9/11. Section 4 focuses on the notion of terrorism and in particular the risks created to human rights protection by vague or over-inclusive definitions of terrorism. The main section of the chapter, Section 5, deals with some of the major challenges posed by counter-terrorism measures to substantive human rights protections. While all human rights are affected by a global wave of new counter-terrorism laws and measures, some human rights have been at the forefront. Section 6 addresses the issue of listing of terrorists by the UN, which poses a challenge of an institutional nature. Is the Security Council bound by international human rights standards, and how can the sanctions resulting from its listing of terrorists be made subject to judicial or other independent review? The final section, Section 7, suggests that the unprecedented wave of counter-terrorism laws and measures that infringe upon human rights has already started to calm down and that governments and intergovernmental organizations are increasingly recognizing that full compliance with human rights in the fight against terrorism is not only morally and legally correct but in the long term also the most effective way of combating terrorism.

2 IS TERRORISM A VIOLATION OF HUMAN RIGHTS?

Human rights are usually seen as vertical norms between the state and a private beneficiary (in most cases an individual person). However, changes in the world order, often referred to as globalization, have resulted in an awareness of the existence of other public and private actors that are equally as powerful as states in their capacity directly to affect the enjoyment of human rights.[2] Terrorism is one such challenge emanating from non-state actors. It is generally defined as deadly or otherwise serious violence against 'civilians', that is, members of the general population or a segment of it, for the purpose of spreading fear amongst the population, or to compel the authorities to do, or refrain from doing, something. Acts of terrorism adversely affect several human rights, including the right to life, the right to physical integrity, the right to health, the right to property, in cases of hostage-taking the right to liberty, and so on. Terrorism has, therefore, been rightly described as the destruction, or the antithesis, of human rights.

---

[2] See Chapter 25, above.

However, this does not necessarily mean that terrorist acts amount to a *violation* of human rights. Resolutions adopted by intergovernmental organizations in response to the threat of terrorism apply different approaches to the issue of whether the perpetrators of acts of terrorism may be described as violating human rights. Variation in the wording of such resolutions reflects different doctrinal and political positions on the question of whether only states may commit human rights violations, or whether such violations can also be attributed to non-state actors. For example, the resolution of the then UN Commission on Human Rights creating the mandate of the Special Rapporteur on human rights and counter-terrorism referred in its preamble to acts, methods, and practices of terrorism being 'aimed at the destruction of human rights', while deploring the occurrence of human rights 'violations'—by states—in the context of their fight against terrorism.[3] However, the same Commission on Human Rights had on other occasions adopted resolutions that speak of human rights 'violations' committed by terrorists.[4]

Although the general public may feel perplexed by such inconsistencies and by the insistence of many human rights experts to reserve the notion of human rights violations to states alone, there is good reason for maintaining the distinction between terrorism as *destruction* of human rights and a more straightforward reference to human rights *violations* by states, at least for the time being. The legally binding normative framework of human rights law is established in human rights treaties. Those treaties are clearly based on human beings as their beneficiaries and states parties as bearers of the corresponding obligations. Further, all the monitoring mechanisms under human rights treaties are geared towards making *states* accountable for human rights violations. When human rights treaty bodies find a human rights violation, this represents the end result of the application of the treaty in a concrete case or situation and includes an attribution of state responsibility for a breach of its obligations. Under other, non-treaty-based procedures, such as the special procedures of the Human Rights Council, a finding of a human rights violation entails a pronouncement that a state has acted in breach of its obligations under international human rights law.

No similar treaty-based or other monitoring mechanisms generally exist in respect of *non-state* actors. Hence, even assuming that the notion of human rights violations could meaningfully be applied in respect of terrorists, there are no mechanisms through which the actors in question could be made accountable. To a limited extent, the development of international criminal law has come to serve as a substitute for the inability of human rights mechanisms to address the destruction of human rights by non-state actors. For instance, many of the crimes for which an individual can be prosecuted and punished under the Rome Statute of the International Criminal Court have a direct destructive effect on the enjoyment of human rights. In some

[3] CHR Res 2005/80 (21 April 2005).
[4] See CHR Res 2004/44 (19 April 2004). In the preamble, the Commission expresses serious concern 'at the gross violations of human rights perpetrated by terrorists'.

instances, the Rome Statute may be applicable in respect of specific acts of terrorism.[5] In addition, several international conventions and protocols address particular forms of terrorism—such as hostage-taking, or hijacking of an airplane—and require states parties to criminalize the acts in question.[6]

If, in the future, a mechanism such as a World Court of Human Rights,[7] with jurisdiction over both states and non-state actors, was established, then it will make more sense to speak about terrorist organizations being responsible for human rights *violations*.

3 APPLICABILITY OF HUMAN RIGHTS LAW IN THE FIGHT AGAINST TERRORISM

The applicability of human rights law to the fight against terrorism has been challenged in two ways. First, some states have argued that this fight amounts to an armed conflict or that it justifies the proclamation of a state of emergency. Second, some states have argued that international human rights law does not apply to counter-terrorism measures taken outside the state's own territory.

3.1 TIMES OF ARMED CONFLICT OR EMERGENCY

Some governments have sought to justify their unilateral exceptions to international human rights norms by referring to a 'war' against terrorism which triggers the application of international humanitarian law.[8] Such a position is usually factually incorrect, since acts of terrorism on their own constitute neither an international armed conflict between two or more states, nor a non-international armed conflict between a state and a non-state actor capable of conducting armed hostilities. Instead, terrorism should primarily be seen as a serious form of crime and fought within a law-enforcement paradigm. Therefore, the full applicability of human rights law as the proper legal framework for the rights of terrorist suspects or other persons affected by counter-terrorism measures should be the point of departure.

It is possible, however, that for a limited period of time and in respect of a specific geographic area, non-state actors referred to as 'terrorists' may be engaged in an armed conflict. The prime example is Afghanistan in late 2001, when members of al-Qaida

---

[5] See eg Rome Statute of the International Criminal Court, Art 7(1) (listing eg torture and disappearance as crimes against humanity).

[6] For a summary of the 13 major conventions and protocols dealing with terrorism, see <http://www.un.org/terrorism/instruments.shtml>.

[7] For two versions of a statute for such a court, see Nowak and Kozma, *A World Court of Human Rights* (June 2009) and Scheinin, *Towards a World Court of Human Rights* (June 2009) available at: <http://www.udhr60.ch/research.html>.

[8] For international humanitarian law and its relationship with human rights law, see Chapter 23, above.

were engaged in an armed conflict against the USA, siding with the local Taliban that constituted the de facto government of Afghanistan.[9] But even in such rare circumstances human rights law remains applicable, although it may need to be interpreted in the light of more specific rules contained in international humanitarian law.[10]

Major terrorist attacks, or another situation in which a terrorist organization manages to destabilize public order in a state, may constitute a threat to 'the life of the nation' in the sense of the derogation clauses contained in many human rights treaties. Consequently, a state may officially proclaim a state of emergency and introduce measures that derogate from certain human rights.[11] For instance, declaring a curfew for a city, introducing checkpoints on major roads, restrictions on mass demonstrations, and closer inspection of postal packages may, within the exigencies of the situation, constitute lawful derogations in respect of the normal scope of freedom of movement, the right to peaceful assembly, and the right to privacy as guaranteed by the International Covenant on Civil and Political Rights (ICCPR). Such measures must be temporary and their aim must be the restoration of normalcy, including the protection of human rights.

As has been elaborated by the Human Rights Committee in its General Comment on states of emergency, the power of a state to derogate from some provisions of the ICCPR does not mean a power to suspend completely the application of these provisions. Rather, any derogation is subject to the requirements of necessity and proportionality. Not only must there be full respect for non-derogable human rights, but also the rights that are subject to derogation must remain protected as far as possible and may include non-derogable dimensions.[12]

3.2 EXTRATERRITORIAL APPLICABILITY OF HUMAN RIGHTS LAW

A separate, but in practice often simultaneously presented, challenge to the applicability of human rights in the counter-terrorism context is the argument that human rights obligations are territorial in scope, limited to a state's own territory where it exercises full jurisdiction. For example, governments may establish detention centres abroad and argue that constitutional guarantees or human rights treaties do not apply there.

While this argument has some support in the text of Article 2(1) ICCPR,[13] consistent practice by the Human Rights Committee demonstrates that a state must comply with the Covenant wherever it factually exercises powers that affect the enjoyment of

---

[9] See Report of the Special Rapporteur on human rights and counter-terrorism, A/HRC/6/17/Add.3 (22 November 2007) in particular para 9.   [10] Ibid, para 7. See Chapter 23, above.

[11] See Chapter 6, above.

[12] HRC, General Comment 29, HRI/GEN/1/Rev.9 (Vol 1) 234 (27 May 2008). See also Chapter 6, above.

[13] ICCPR, Art 2(1) provides: 'Each State Party to the present Covenant undertakes to respect and to ensure to all individuals within its territory and subject to its jurisdiction the rights recognized in the present Covenant...'

the rights enshrined in the ICCPR.[14] Thus, even if that provision were to be taken as excluding the obligation to 'legislate' for other countries or their population,[15] this cannot form a justification to engage extraterritorially in outright human rights violations such as arbitrary detention, torture, or other cruel, inhuman, or degrading treatment.[16]

In summary, human rights law continues to apply during situations of armed conflict or a state of emergency, and it applies also to a state's conduct abroad. Closer analysis may be needed as to how the norms of human rights law and international humanitarian law inform the proper interpretation of each other during times of armed conflict, what derogations from certain human rights norms may be permitted as necessary and proportionate within the exigencies of a state of emergency, and what the exact scope of a state's human rights obligations is when its agents are operating outside its own territory. These considerations, however, do not change the basic rule that human rights law continues to apply in any of these circumstances.

4 THE NOTION OF TERRORISM AND ITS MISUSE

'One man's freedom fighter is another man's terrorist' is an often heard and somewhat cynical reference to the degree of opportunism employed when using the word 'terrorism'. Although the UN has adopted a whole series of international treaties related to specific forms of terrorism, such as hostage-taking, nuclear terrorism, or terrorist bombings,[17] work towards a comprehensive convention against terrorism is still underway. Governments have not been able to agree on the definition of terrorism. Differing views persist, inter alia, with regard to whether states can commit acts of terrorism and whether the quest for self-determination precludes an act from being a form of terrorism.

Particularly in the aftermath of 9/11, governments have increasingly resorted to vague and broad definitions of terrorism. While this may have been triggered partly by a desire to respond to an unspecific threat, all too often governments intended to target individuals or groups that do not deserve to be labelled as terrorist, such as political opposition groups, radical trade unions, vocal but non-violent separatist movements, indigenous peoples, religious minorities, or even human rights defenders. At least for a while, the global consensus about the imperative of combating terrorism

---

[14] See eg *Lopez Burgos v Uruguay*, CCPR/C/13/D/52/1979 (29 July 1981); *Gueye et al. v France*, CCPR/C/35/D/196/1985 (6 April 1989); HRC, Concluding observations: Israel, CCPR/C/79/Add.93 (18 August 1998); HRC, Concluding observations: Israel, CCPR/CO/78/ISR (21 August 2003); HRC, General Comment 31, HRI/GEN/1/Rev.9 (Vol I) 243 (27 May 2008) para 10. See further Chapter 7, above.

[15] This was the expression used in 1950 by the US representative, Mrs Eleanor Roosevelt, in the drafting of the ICCPR. See Third Periodic Report of the US to the HRC, CCPR/C/USA/3 (28 November 2005) annex I.

[16] Report of the Special Rapporteur on human rights and counter-terrorism, A/HRC/6/17/Add.3 (22 November 2007) para 8.

[17] For a list of these treaties, see <http://www.un.org/terrorism/instruments.shtml>.

was so compelling that authoritarian governments could get away with their repressive practices whenever they renamed their opponents as 'terrorists'.

Of particular concern to the international protection of human rights is that in the aftermath of 9/11, and in the absence of a universal and comprehensive definition of the term, repeated calls by the international community, including the Security Council, for action to combat terrorism, could be understood as leaving it to individual states to define what is meant by the term 'terrorism'. This aggravates the potential for unintended human rights abuses and even the deliberate misuse of the term. There is a clear risk that the international community's use of the term of 'terrorism', without defining it, results in the unintentional international legitimization of conduct undertaken by oppressive regimes, through delivering the message that the international community wants strong action against terrorism however defined. Besides situations where some states resort to the deliberate misuse of the term, there is reason for concern about the more frequent adoption in domestic anti-terrorism legislation of terminology that is not properly confined to the countering of terrorism.[18]

Legal definitions of terrorism should refer to the methods used, not the underlying aim. What transforms political or ideological aspirations into terrorism is the decision by one or more morally responsible individuals to employ the morally inexcusable tactics of deadly or otherwise serious violence against 'civilians'. With the qualification that hostage-taking entails a threat of serious violence and should therefore be included in the definition, terrorism and terrorist crimes should always be defined so that such violence forms a mandatory element of the definition.[19]

Amongst Security Council resolutions calling for action against terrorism, Resolution 1566 comes closest to defining terrorism by including the following three cumulative conditions:

(1) acts, including against civilians, committed with the intention of causing death or serious bodily injury, or the taking of hostages; and

(2) irrespective of whether motivated by considerations of a political, philosophical, ideological, racial, ethnic, religious, or other similar nature, also committed for the purpose of provoking a state of terror in the general public or in a group of persons or particular persons, intimidating a population, or compelling a government or an international organization to do or to abstain from doing any act; and

(3) such acts constituting offences within the scope of and as defined in the international conventions and protocols relating to terrorism.[20]

---

[18] See eg Reports of the Special Rapporteur on human rights and counter-terrorism, A/HRC/4/26/Add.2 (16 November 2006) paras 11–18; A/HRC/4/26/Add.3 (14 December 2006) paras 12–17; A/HRC/6/17/Add.2 (7 November 2007) paras 23–4; A/HRC/10/3/Add.2 (16 December 2008) paras 6–14.

[19] Report of the Special Rapporteur on counter-terrorism and human rights, E/CN.4/2006/98 (28 December 2005).   [20] SC Res 1566 (8 October 2004) para 3.

As to the third cumulative element, that only acts constituting offences within existing terrorism-related conventions may fall under the terrorism definition, there is a qualification to be made. Where a state is responding to an international call to suppress terrorism, this third cumulative element is essential in determining what type of conduct is to be suppressed. However, states may feel compelled to implement additional counter-terrorist measures according to regional or domestic threats. Where there is evidence that a state must respond to domestic or regional terrorist threats, it may therefore have genuine reasons to proscribe acts that fall outside the scope of offences under the existing universal terrorism-related conventions.

However, any national definitions of crimes must meet the requirement of legality, enshrined in the non-derogable provision of Article 15 ICCPR. In the absence of an internationally agreed definition of terrorism, this provision has come to serve, together with the prohibition against discrimination, as the basis for a checklist for the conformity of definitions of terrorism or terrorist crimes with human rights. Besides the obvious element of a prohibition against the retroactive application of the criminal law, Article 15 ICCPR also includes the requirements of *nullum crimen sine lege* (all elements of a crime must be defined by the law), *nulla poena sine lege* (all punishments must be defined by the law), accessibility (the law must be publicly available), precision (the line between permitted and prohibited conduct must be clear), and foreseeability (the law must enable an individual to anticipate the consequences of his or her conduct). The safest way to secure compliance with these requirements is to base any definitions of terrorist crimes on an exhaustive list of already defined serious violent crimes. Criminalization of terrorist intent as such, or circular definitions that refer back to the word 'terror', or definitions that generally cover crimes against the state, regularly fail the test under Article 15 ICCPR.

5 SUBSTANTIVE CHALLENGES TO HUMAN RIGHTS LAW IN THE FIGHT AGAINST TERRORISM

Governments have often felt tempted to depart from ordinary laws, normal procedures, or the fundamental rights of the individual when confronted with acts of terrorism or the threat of them. Since 9/11, an unprecedented wave of special legislation or special powers has emerged all over the world, and practically all human rights have been under attack or 'reconsideration'. While most human rights are not absolute but allow for some limitations to protect public security, in many cases governments have gone beyond these permissible limitations, resulting in human rights violations. This section gives an overview of some of the most frequent areas of problematic practices.

As a graphic illustration of the effects of counter-terrorism measures upon human rights, reference can be made to a pyramid. At its top, a relatively small number of individuals—in many cases real or suspected terrorists—are subjected to grave human rights violations, such as torture or extra-judicial execution. At the bottom of the pyramid, all members of society are confronted with new interferences with some of their human rights because of counter-terrorism legislation. Typically, everyone's right to privacy is affected by new rules on interception of communications, databases and data retention, and exchange of personal information across borders.[21] Between the top and the base of the pyramid, certain groups of individuals are affected more than the average citizen by counter-terrorism measures, and many of these interferences easily escalate into violations of human rights law.[22] Immigrants or ethnic or religious minorities are often targeted by counter-terrorism measures affecting a broad range of human rights. Persons fleeing persecution in their own country are confronted with tighter controls of international borders in the name of countering terrorism, effectively preventing them from exercising their human right to leave their own country.[23] Even human rights defenders may find themselves targeted, as associations, public gatherings, and fundraising are subject to tighter control by the authorities.

By using the metaphor of a pyramid, it is made clear that the perception that insistence on the importance of human rights in the fight against terrorism would seek to defend the terrorists is wrong. Everyone's human rights are affected to a lesser or greater degree by counter-terrorism measures, and keeping all counter-terrorism legislation under careful public scrutiny is the best way to ensure that measures justified as targeting the 'real terrorists' do not result in the erosion of human rights in general.

5.1 FREEDOM FROM TORTURE AND CRUEL, INHUMAN, OR DEGRADING TREATMENT

The prohibition against torture or any other form of cruel, inhuman, or degrading treatment or punishment is an absolute human right that allows for no exception, even during times of emergency.[24] Accordingly, it is very rare that states would actually legislate to allow for torture. Proposals of legalized forms of torture, such as courts being empowered to issue 'torture warrants' in order to administer lawful torture in a 'ticking-bomb scenario' (which assumes that the police have captured a terrorist who refuses to reveal the location of a time bomb that will soon detonate and kill thousands of innocent people), have remained hypothetical.[25] Furthermore, governments will normally deny that extra-legal torture is used by their law enforcement or intelligence agencies or military forces. Nevertheless, the practice of subjecting terrorist suspects or their presumed associates to torture or related practices became widespread after

---

[21] See Report of the Special Rapporteur on human rights and counter-terrorism, A/HRC/13/37 (28 December 2009).

[22] For an assessment of the gender impact of counter-terrorism, see Report of the Special Rapporteur on human rights and counter-terrorism, A/64/211 (3 August 2009).

[23] See Report of the Special Rapporteur on human rights and counter-terrorism, A/62/263 (15 August 2007).   [24] UNCAT, Arts 1 and 2(2); ICCPR, Arts 7 and 4(2). See also Chapter 10, above.

[25] For a critique of a broad interpretation of what constitutes a 'ticking bomb', see Report of the Special Rapporteur on human rights and counter-terrorism, A/HRC/6/17/Add.4 (16 November 2007) paras 20–1.

9/11 and many long-term patterns of using torture against terrorist suspects were also revealed.[26]

There are various ways in which many governments have ended up compromising the absolute prohibition against torture. First, denial of the extraterritorial applicability of the Convention against Torture (UNCAT) and the ICCPR has been used as an argument by the USA to cover the engagement in torture of military forces or intelligence agencies abroad. Second, some states, such as the UK, have relied on information obtained by torture 'for operational purposes' and various forms of cooperation with states that practise torture to circumvent existing rules about torture. Third, by using notions such as 'enhanced interrogation techniques' (USA) or 'moderate physical pressure' (Israel) some governments have tried to shift the barrier between what is prohibited and what is permitted. Fourth, some governments have tried to relax the standard for sending a person to another country under the risk of torture or other ill-treatment, by proposing the replacement of an absolute prohibition in situations of 'real risk' with a 'balancing test', a 'more likely than not' standard, or shifting the responsibility to the receiving state through the use of diplomatic assurances.[27] Finally, there has been a lack of investigation and accountability in cases where allegations of torture of terrorist suspects were made, for instance in Spain, where the authorities have maintained that allegations of ill-treatment follow the 'manual' of terrorist organizations and are therefore prima facie unfounded.

In a report dealing with the role of intelligence agencies and their oversight bodies in countering terrorism, the Special Rapporteur on human rights and counter-terrorism applied the principles of state responsibility and concluded that any form of collusion in torture or other prohibited treatment by intelligence agencies amounts to a human rights violation.[28]

5.2 RIGHT TO LIBERTY AND RIGHT TO A FAIR TRIAL

In the counter-terrorism context, practices breaching the prohibition against torture are often coupled with, and shielded by, secret or arbitrary detention and the denial of a fair trial. The right to liberty of the person and the right to a fair trial are guaranteed, respectively, by Articles 9 and 14 ICCPR.[29] Resort by governments to emergency powers while countering terrorism constitutes a major challenge to these guarantees, as neither of these provisions is on the list of non-derogable rights contained in Article 4(2) ICCPR. Only the requirement of legality in the field of criminal law of

---

[26] See eg Amnesty International, Saudi Arabia: Assaulting Human Rights in the Name of Counter-Terrorism (22 July 2009).

[27] While many states, including Canada and the USA, demonstrate elements of this trend, the most systematic effort towards 'reconsidering' the rule of *non-refoulement* was made by the UK and several other states in *Saadi v Italy*, App no 37201/06, 28 February 2008. The Grand Chamber of the European Court of Human Rights maintained its position that the rule is absolute. Ibid, paras 137–9.

[28] Report of the Special Rapporteur on human rights and counter-terrorism, A/HRC/10/3 (4 February 2009).   [29] See Chapter 14, above.

Article 15 ICCPR, including the principles of *nullum crimen sine lege* and the prohibition against retroactive criminal laws, is explicitly listed as non-derogable. However, in its General Comments on states of emergency and the right to a fair trial, the Human Rights Committee has clarified that the rights to liberty and a fair trial nevertheless include dimensions from which there can never be derogation.[30] Arbitrary detention and denial of court review over any form of detention are prohibited at all times. The fundamental principles of fair trial, including the presumption of innocence and the requirement that only a court can order a criminal punishment, must equally be respected during a state of emergency.

As a consequence, laws and practices that are applied in the name of combating terrorism may be in violation of the rights to liberty and a fair trial. Secret or unacknowledged detention automatically violates the prohibition against arbitrary detention and in some cases also amounts to prohibited disappearance of the person.[31] Even narrowly crafted provisions on *incommunicado* detention, or on delays in effective court review over the lawfulness of detention, easily end up in breaches of Article 9 ICCPR. This risk can be demonstrated by a reference to Spain, which despite international criticism continues to apply a regime of *incommunicado* detention, denying terrorist suspects contact with a freely chosen lawyer during the initial period of detention. Instead, detainees are represented by a state-appointed lawyer whom they will usually not meet. The compatibility of such a regime with international human rights law is doubtful and will depend on the merits of the reasons given for denying freely chosen legal representation and the ability of the appointed lawyer to independently and effectively protect the rights of the detainee, including against any form of torture or other prohibited treatment.[32]

The US detention facility at Guantánamo Bay has become a notorious symbol of practices of long-term detention of terrorist suspects without trial. Many other states continue also to detain terrorist suspects or their presumed associates without trial or even any criminal charges. Hence, the first fundamental dimension of the right to a fair trial, access to a court, is denied and as a consequence the persons concerned cannot exercise any of their fair trial rights. Some governments, including the US administration, have referred to the war paradigm as the framework for their counter-terrorism measures, seeking to justify long-term detention without trial as long as the 'war against terrorism' continues. Under a law-enforcement paradigm that treats terrorism as a serious crime, however, it is evident that the purpose of detaining terrorist suspects must be the investigation of their alleged crimes in preparation of a criminal trial.

Even in countries in which terrorist suspects *are* brought before a court for trial, there may be serious deviations from international human rights standards. Through

---

[30] HRC, General Comment 29, n 12, in particular paras 12–16; HRC, General Comment 32, HRI/GEN/1/ Rev.9 (Vol 1) 248 (27 May 2008) in particular para 6.

[31] See International Convention for the Protection of All Persons from Enforced Disappearance, Art 2.

[32] See Report of the Special Rapporteur on counter-terrorism and human rights, A/HRC/10/3/Add.2 (16 December 2008).

special legislation, terrorism cases may be dealt with by military or special courts. The trying of civilians by a military court as such is problematic under the right to a fair trial. Moreover, outright violations of Article 14 ICCPR may result from the lack of independence and impartiality of the judges of a military or special court and from undue interference by the executive in deciding that a case will be tried by a military or special court, in the worst cases even after acquittal by an ordinary court. In addition, trials before military or special courts may involve restrictions on the rights of the defence, including in respect of secret evidence, denial of full communication between client and counsel, and breaches of the principle of equality of arms, for instance through restrictions on access by the defence to exculpatory evidence. As to the last-mentioned example, terrorist trials often involve a huge amount of primary material such as transcripts of intercepted telephone calls. If only the prosecution has access to the full records and if it presents to the court only a carefully selected sample, this may result in bias against the defence who may wish to contest the value of the excerpts as evidence by putting them into a broader context. However, this may only be possible if access to exculpatory evidence not presented by the prosecution to the court is provided to the defence, under terms that allow its proper examination.

A general solution to the challenges related to the detention and trial of terrorist suspects can be identified in the principle of normalcy. Terrorism should be treated as a serious form of crime, which is subject to ordinary laws on criminal procedure and dealt with by ordinary courts. This is a recommended course of action for avoiding the temptation to engage in practices that violate international human rights law.[33]

5.3 RIGHT TO NON-DISCRIMINATION

As indicated with the pyramid metaphor referred to above, not everyone's human rights are equally affected by counter-terrorism measures. An alarming trend in the post-9/11 era has been the increased use of 'terrorist profiling' as a significant component of states' counter-terrorism efforts.[34] The European Union recommended in 2002 to its member states to develop 'terrorist profiles', defined as 'a set of physical, psychological or behavioural variables, which have been identified as typical of persons involved in terrorist activities and which may have some predictive value in that respect'.[35]

Profiling has been applied, for instance, in the context of data-mining initiatives, that is, searches of personal data sets according to presumed characteristics of suspects. But it also occurs in less explicit forms. For example, law-enforcement agents often rely on sets of physical characteristics when deciding whom to stop and search

[33] For a systematic assessment of the right to a fair trial in the context of countering terrorism, see Report of the Special Rapporteur on counter-terrorism and human rights, A/63/223 (6 August 2008).
[34] Report of the Special Rapporteur on human rights and counter-terrorism, A/HRC/4/26 (29 January 2007).
[35] Council of the EU, Draft Council Recommendation on the development of terrorist profiles, 11858/3/02 REV 3 (18 November 2002).

for counter-terrorism purposes. Even when there are no explicit instructions to target specific groups, stop-and-search powers may disproportionately affect persons of a certain ethnic or religious appearance.

When law-enforcement agents use broad profiles that reflect unexamined gener-alizations, their practices may constitute disproportionate interferences with human rights. In particular, profiling based on stereotypical assumptions that persons of a certain 'race', national or ethnic origin, or religion are particularly likely to be involved in terrorism may lead to practices that are incompatible with the principle of non-discrimination. Such profiling is also ineffective. An illustrative case is the so-called *Rasterfahndung* programme, initiated by the German authorities in the wake of 9/11 to identify terrorist 'sleepers'. The German police forces collected personal records of several million individuals from public and private databases. The criteria for the search included: being male, age 18–40, current or former student, Muslim denom-ination, and a link through birth or nationality to one of several specified countries with a predominantly Muslim population. Approximately 32,000 persons were iden-tified as potential terrorist sleepers and more closely examined. In none of these cases did the *Rasterfahndung* lead to bringing criminal charges for terrorism-related offences. The programme was eventually found to be unconstitutional by the German Constitutional Court.[36]

In the UK, police forces have relied on profiles based on a person's ethnic and/ or religious appearance when conducting stops, document checks, or searches for counter-terrorism purposes. Accordingly, stops and searches under section 44 of the Terrorism Act 2000, which authorizes the police in designated areas to stop and search people without having to show reasonable suspicion, have disproportionately affected ethnic minorities. Between 2001–2 and 2002–3, for example, the number of persons of Asian ethnicity subjected to section 44 searches rose by 302 per cent as compared to a rise of 118 per cent for white people. By 2003–4, Asian people were about 3.6 times more likely, and black people about 4.3 times more likely, to be stopped and searched under counter-terrorism legislation than white people. Yet the measures resulted in only a handful of arrests, all of which were white persons.[37]

At worst, terrorist profiling is not only legally and morally wrong and ineffective, it may even be counterproductive. Terrorist organizations can easily evade the profiles employed by the authorities and adjust their tactics accordingly, for instance when recruiting suicide bombers and choosing them for a mission. Profiling may also have negative effects on the targeted minorities. Their stigmatization may result in a feeling of alienation and end up facilitating recruitment to terrorism from within the group.

The Special Rapporteur on human rights and counter-terrorism has therefore rec-ommended abandonment of profiling based on group characteristics and its replace-ment with a combination of universal controls affecting everyone equally, genuinely

---

[36] Bundesverfassungsgericht, 1 BvR 518/02, 4 April 2006.

[37] Report of the Special Rapporteur on human rights and counter-terrorism, A/HRC/4/26 (29 January 2007) para 37.

random searches coupled with proper monitoring to secure that they do not transform into unregulated de facto targeting of specific groups, and profiling based on
individual conduct instead of group membership.[38]

5.4 OTHER HUMAN RIGHTS

The above examples all relate to well-known and widely discussed human rights
impacts of counter-terrorism measures. However, it is important to understand that
all human rights are affected, to a greater or lesser extent, and in respect of a smaller
or larger group of individuals, by counter-terrorism measures.

An under-explored issue relates to the effect of counter-terrorism measures upon
economic, social, and cultural rights.[39] While the equal status, indivisibility, and interdependence of all human rights has been broadly acknowledged,[40] the discourse on
human rights and counter-terrorism has tended to focus on civil and political rights.
Even among the UN human rights treaty bodies, the Human Rights Committee and
the Committee Against Torture have been much more systematic than the other treaty
bodies in questioning and assessing states' compliance with human rights while countering terrorism. The Committee on Economic, Social and Cultural Rights has very
rarely given attention to counter-terrorism measures.

A prime example that demonstrates the need for a systematic assessment is the construction of a wall or barrier into the Occupied Palestinian Territory (OPT) by Israel,
the occupying power. Explained as a security measure against the risk of suicide terrorists trying to enter Israel or to attack Israeli settlements inside the OPT, the wall or
barrier has resulted not only in the construction of a major physical barrier between
Israel and the OPT but also in a whole architecture of associated obstacles, barriers,
walls, checkpoints, and so on within the OPT.[41] As a consequence, Palestinian individuals find their everyday life devastated through multiple forms of hardship, many of
which are directly related to their enjoyment of economic, social, and cultural rights.
For instance, access to hospitals, schools, water resources, olive groves, and other
places of work are all adversely affected and in many cases to a degree that amounts
to a violation of, respectively, the right to health, the right to education, the right to
water, the right to an adequate standard of living, and the right to work. In its advisory
opinion on the Israeli wall, the International Court of Justice concluded that Israel
was in breach of international law, including of the Covenant on Economic, Social and
Cultural Rights, through the construction of the wall.[42]

---

[38] Ibid, paras 83–9.
[39] See Report of the Special Rapporteur on human rights and counter-terrorism, A/HRC/6/17 (21
November 2007).   [40] See Chapter 8, above.
[41] See Report of the Special Rapporteur on human rights and counter-terrorism, A/HRC/6/17/Add.4 (16
November 2007).
[42] *Legal Consequences of the Construction of a Wall in the Occupied Palestinian Territories* (Advisory
Opinion) [2004] ICJ Rep 136, para 116.

The case of the Israeli wall illustrates that economic, social, and cultural rights must also be taken into account when societies design their security infrastructure, including their measures against terrorism. But economic, social, and cultural rights also have another important role in ensuring responses to terrorism conform to human rights. Violations of human rights in general have been identified in the UN Global Counter-Terrorism Strategy as one of the conditions conducive to the spread of terrorism.[43] Amongst the other identified conducive conditions there are many that have direct links with economic, social, and cultural rights. Hence, long-term work for the promotion of the full enjoyment of economic, social, and cultural rights can be seen as an important element in building societies without terrorism.[44]

6 AN INSTITUTIONAL CHALLENGE: TERRORIST LISTING BY THE SECURITY COUNCIL

While states are responsible for many violations of human rights in the name of countering terrorism, the listing of terrorist individuals or entities is one of the rare occasions where the UN itself engages in action that has a direct effect upon individuals. Therefore the question of the UN's compliance with human rights arises.[45]

In Resolution 1373, the Security Council identified the terrorist attacks of 9/11, 'like any act of international terrorism', as a threat to international peace and security. Acting under Chapter VII of the UN Charter, it imposed upon all member states a range of legally binding obligations to counter terrorism, including an obligation to report on their measures to a new body, the CTC. This Committee is composed of the diplomatic representatives of the 15 states that at any given time serve as members of the Security Council.

Despite its fundamental role in UN action against terrorism, Resolution 1373 did not result in the blacklisting of terrorists by the UN. The UN is not involved in any general listing of terrorists. Instead, the listing system in place is based on the earlier Security Council Resolution 1267 of 1999 and is limited to individuals or entities belonging to or associated with al-Qaida or the Taliban. The consolidated list of al-Qaida and Taliban terrorists maintained by a separate Security Council committee, the 1267 Sanctions Committee, includes hundreds of individuals and entities.[46] As Resolution 1267 was also adopted under Chapter VII of the UN Charter, the implementation of the resolution and the listing decisions by the 1267 Committee is often perceived by states as a Charter obligation that under Article 103 of the Charter trumps competing treaty obligations, including those emanating from human rights treaties. Article 103

[43] GA Res 60/288 (20 September 2006).
[44] For a broader discussion on the role of economic, social, and cultural rights in the context of countering terrorism, see the Report of the Special Rapporteur on human rights and counter-terrorism, A/HRC/6/17 (21 November 2007).   [45] See also Chapter 25, above.
[46] For the consolidated list, see <http://www.un.org/sc/committees/1267/pdf/consolidatedlist.pdf>.

proclaims the primacy of Charter obligations over any other agreement to which a state is party. As a consequence, many governments take the view that national authorities enjoy no discretion whatsoever in implementing the sanctions but must without hesitation freeze the assets, and prevent international travel, of any person put on the 1267 terrorist list. Some governments, as well as many scholars and human rights experts, however, argue that as long as there is no effective independent review of listing and delisting decisions at the UN level, member states must secure such review in respect of their own measures implementing the UN-imposed sanctions.[47]

Against this background it is natural that there is growing concern that the Security Council must comply with human rights when listing or delisting persons. Several rounds of improvement have already been made, so that the current version of the regime, contained in Security Council Resolution 1822 of 2008, includes a duty to inform the person of the reasons for his or her placement on the list, as well as a mandatory two-year review by the 1267 Committee of all the entries in the list.

However, these piecemeal improvements have not remedied the main shortcomings of the 1267 listing procedure. Decisions are taken by a political body composed of diplomatic representatives of the 15 member states of the Security Council. States do not necessarily disclose the real reasons for a listing proposal even to each other but may use vague references to existing intelligence information. There is no judicial or other independent review of the listing and delisting decisions by the 1267 Committee. Instead, all forms of review are in the hands of one and the same Committee. On top of this, the delisting of an individual requires a consensus decision by the 1267 Committee. For all these reasons, the terrorist listing procedure of the 1267 Committee fails to meet the requirements of a 'fair and clear procedure', a notion used to describe the level of procedural guarantees that one can expect an intergovernmental organization to deliver, not to speak of full compliance with the right to a fair trial, as would be required if a state were to impose criminal sanctions.

In October 2008, the Human Rights Committee concluded that Belgium had violated Articles 17 (right to privacy) and 12 (freedom of movement) ICCPR in respect of a Belgian couple, because it had initiated their listing as terrorists by the 1267 Committee, and was subsequently unable to have them delisted even though no case had been proven against them.[48] On 20 July 2009, the 1267 Committee finally removed the couple from its list. This decision by the 1267 Committee is indicative of a broader acknowledgment that there is a need for judicial or other independent review of terrorist listing. Although Belgium was unable to reach a delisting decision earlier, it managed to obtain consensus within the 1267 Committee, after the Human Rights Committee had concluded that because it initiated the listing, Belgium was responsible for a human rights violation. The subsequent decision to delist these individuals can be seen as a recognition of the Committee's possibility to conduct indirect

---

[47] See Report of the Special Rapporteur on human rights and counter-terrorism, A/61/267 (16 August 2006) in particular para 39.

[48] *Sayadi and Vinck v Belgium*, CCPR/C/94/D/1472/2006 (29 December 2008).

quasi-judicial review over the consequences of the listing by the Security Council, as long as a state that has ratified the Optional Protocol to the ICCPR can be shown to have had a strong enough role in initiating (or implementing) the listing.

Other indications of the broader trend of calling for judicial or other independent review are the earlier *Kadi* ruling by the European Court of Justice, quashing EU-level implementation of sanctions imposed by the 1267 Committee due to insufficient procedural guarantees,[49] and a UN General Assembly resolution of 2008, urging states 'while ensuring full compliance with their international obligations', to include 'adequate human rights guarantees' in their national procedures for the listing of terrorist individuals and entities.[50] This statement should be seen as an appeal to states to implement UN-imposed sanctions against terrorists not blindly but subject to adequate human rights guarantees. Equally importantly, in Resolution 1822 the Security Council itself acknowledged that the UN should comply with human rights when listing individuals.[51]

7 CONCLUSION: IS THE PENDULUM ALREADY SWINGING BACK?

The terrorist acts of 9/11 have led to the worst backlash in the international protection of human rights since the inclusion of the notion of human rights in the UN Charter, in the aftermath of the Second World War. In this sense, terrorism can be seen as the antithesis of human rights. Still, one needs to remember that what constitutes the backlash is the reaction and overreaction by governments that have introduced a whole wave of retrogressive measures in respect of human rights in the aftermath of 9/11. Furthermore, the terrorist attacks were more a triggering cause than a structural one. Many of the human-rights-hostile practices employed by governments in the name of countering terrorism existed prior to 2001 in some parts of the world, albeit that those practices have now become much more widespread.

What has been disheartening in the backlash is the ease by which governments that were known as champions of the international concern for human rights have changed course and become generators of legal arguments and doctrines that seek to deny the applicability or substantive contents of human rights law when they engage

---

[49] *Kadi and Al Barakaat International Foundation v Council of the European Union*, Joined Cases C-402/05 P and C-415/05 P, European Court of Justice (Grand Chamber), 3 September 2008.

[50] GA Res 63/185 (3 March 2009) para 19.

[51] See SC Res 1822 (30 June 2008) ('Reaffirming the need to combat by all means, in accordance with the Charter of the United Nations and international law, including applicable international human rights, refugee, and humanitarian law, threats to international peace and security caused by terrorist acts, stressing in this regard the important role the United Nations plays in leading and coordinating this effort...'). See also ibid, para 27 (reiterating the importance of all states using 'adequate procedures' when implementing the sanctions).

in measures against terrorism. Such constructions try to turn the clock back by more than 60 years, to times when human rights were not yet recognized as a matter of concern for the international community. Even worse, some Western governments, such as the Bush administration of the USA and the Blair-Brown government in the UK, appear at times to try to turn the clock back by 200 years, to times before Immanuel Kant, by reducing a human person to a mere means, instead of treating every individual always as an end. Mass murderers are recognized as an end in the traditional criminal law system, which aims at establishing the facts, the culpability of the person, and the punishment. But suspected terrorists—or even persons only suspected of knowing something of relevance—are reduced to a means when they are tortured to extract information, without any intention to bring them before a court for their possible crimes. Whether a government itself tortures or whether it is complicit in creating an international industry of torture for the production of intelligence information does not matter.

However, there are many signs that the pendulum is swinging back and the damage triggered by the terrorist acts of 9/11 is being assessed and the process of repairs started. For instance, both in the USA and the UK there are important steps away from earlier human-rights-hostile practices and towards accountability of those who engaged in such practices. The Attorney-General in the USA and Parliament in the UK appear to have taken the lead in this process. Within the Security Council and other important engines of counter-terrorism measures, it is gradually understood that violating human rights in the name of countering terrorism is not only wrong in legal and moral terms but also counterproductive for any effective strategy against terrorism, as respect for, and promotion of, human rights are acknowledged as important elements in building societies without terrorism.

If it took ten years to turn the clock back by 60 or 200 years, it may take 30 years to repair the damage and to reach a situation where the commitment to respect the human rights of each and every human person in any situation is again universally accepted. But once that is achieved, we will not be in the same situation as before 9/11. We will be wiser than then, and conscious of the fact that much of the seeming universal acceptance of human rights was mere lip service.

FURTHER READING

CAMERON, 'UN Targeted Sanctions, Legal Safeguards and the European Convention on Human Rights' (2003) 72 *NJIL* 159.

DUFFY, *The 'War on Terror' and the Framework of International Law* (Cambridge University Press, 2005).

FARER, *Confronting Global Terrorism and American Neo-Conservativism: The Framework of a Liberal Grand Strategy* (Oxford University Press, 2008).

INTERNATIONAL COMMISSION OF JURISTS, *Assessing Damage, Urging Action: Report of the Eminent Jurists Panel on Terrorism, Counter-terrorism and Human Rights* (Geneva, 2009).

MOECKLI, *Human Rights and Non-discrimination in the 'War on Terror'* (Oxford University Press, 2008).

SAUL, *Defining Terrorism in International Law* (Oxford University Press, 2006).

UNITED NATIONS, Reports by the UN Special Rapporteur on the promotion and protection of human rights and fundamental freedoms while countering terrorism, UN documents A/60/370, E/CN.4/2006/98, A/61/267, A/HRC/4/26, A/62/263, A/HRC/6/17, A/63/223, A/HRC/10/3, and addenda, 2005–2009.

USEFUL WEBSITES

Reports by the UN Special Rapporteur on human rights and counter-terrorism: <**http://www2.ohchr.org/english/issues/terrorism/rapporteur/reports.htm**>

Blog related to the mandate of the Special Rapporteur: <**http://legalift.wordpress.com**>

Blog related to the mandate of the Special Rapporteur, with focus on Russia and other former Soviet countries: <**http://eurasialift.wordpress.com**>

UN website on terrorism: <**http://www.un.org/terrorism**>

Website on terrorism by the UN Office on Drugs and Crime: <**http://www.unodc.org/unodc/en/terrorism/index.html**>

Website of EU Framework Programme 7 project on detection technologies, counter-terrorism ethics, and human rights: <**http://www.detecter.bham.ac.uk/**>

27

POVERTY

Stephen P Marks

SUMMARY

This chapter addresses the challenge posed by poverty to the protection of human rights. Human rights define the entitlements considered necessary for a life of dignity in society, including the right to an adequate standard of living, that is, the right to be free from poverty. At this high level of abstraction, the elimination of poverty and realization of human rights are similar in that both clarify what needs to be done so that all human beings enjoy minimal standards of a decent existence. The context for this inquiry is the consensus regarding the imperative of poverty reduction and human rights realization, and the contested interpretations of the impact of globalization and financial crises on poverty and human rights. This context will be set out first, followed by a discussion of how international legal discourses on human rights and poverty issues diverge and, finally, how they converge.

1 INTRODUCTION

People who have thought about the relationship between poverty and human rights sometimes see poverty as a challenge for human rights and ask how these rights can have meaning for the one-fifth of humanity living in misery. Thus, they may see the elimination of poverty as part of the human rights struggle. There are deep political and even ideological issues involved in the relationship between poverty and human rights. It has been argued that 'the present global institutional order is foreseeably associated with such massive incidence of avoidable severe poverty, its (uncompensated) imposition manifests an ongoing human rights violation—arguably the largest such violation ever committed in human history'.[1] Others have argued that development of the middle class exercising economic freedoms under competitive capitalism without

---

[1] Pogge, 'Severe Poverty as a Human Rights Violation' in Pogge (ed), *Freedom from Poverty as a Human Right: Who Owes What to the Very Poor?* (OUP, 2007) 52.

state interference comes first and then political freedom and democracy follow. A recent survey of attitudes of lower and middle class people in 13 countries confirms the hypothesis that '[e]conomic well-being is linked with support for democracy'[2] and '[m]iddle-class respondents often assign a higher priority to free speech than do those in the lower income group'.[3] Although it may appear tautological, the survey found that 'lower-income respondents were more likely than their wealthier fellow citizens to prioritize avoiding hunger and poverty'.[4] Are the poor indifferent to human rights? Is the way out of poverty to provide economic freedoms under competitive capitalism to favour the middle class on the assumption that it is on that class that the affirmation of human rights must rely and that a rising tide lifts all boats? Or is it the responsibility of the state to redistribute wealth so as to eliminate poverty and guarantee human rights to all, including the poor?

This chapter addresses the relationship between human rights and models of development in response to these questions. If, as the classical liberal model might suggest, human rights is a luxury that comes to people who have risen out of poverty, then it is likely to be limited to what Karl Marx called 'bourgeois freedoms', those that protect the interests of the middle class and the rich against those of the poor. The first challenge regarding the relationship between poverty and human rights is therefore to explore whether, and to what extent, human rights is a regime hostile to the interests of the poor.

While that understanding may still have proponents today, the more widely accepted understanding of human rights is that they are supposed to empower the poor in their struggle against the obstacles to their liberation from misery. From this perspective— and this is the real challenge raised by this chapter—poverty is a human rights issue in terms of ends and means. The end of human rights is to ensure for all—rich and poor— equal rights, including those called 'economic, social and cultural rights'. The means of human rights—awareness by rights-holders through learning and accountability of duty-bearers through laws, policies, and enforcement mechanisms—provide anti-poverty campaigns tools for mobilization and action. Unless and until these ends and means guide popular awareness and the functioning of institutions, poverty will pose a serious challenge to the protection, and perhaps the very concept, of human rights.

2 HUMAN RIGHTS AND POVERTY IN THE GLOBAL ECONOMY

At the outset, it is necessary to define the meaning of 'poverty' and explore its relationship to human rights, development, and social justice. Equally important as background to the topic of this chapter is the context of globalization.

---

[2] Pew Global Attitudes Project, *The Global Middle Class: Views on Democracy, Religion, Values, and Life Satisfaction in Emerging Nations* (Pew Research Center, 2009) 2.   [3] Ibid, 14.
[4] Ibid, 15.

2.1 POVERTY AND ITS SIGNIFICANCE FOR HUMAN RIGHTS

Extreme poverty, measured as the number of people living on an income below the current threshold set by the World Bank at US$1.25 per day, declined from 1.90 billion people in 1981 (51.8 per cent of the world population) to 1.38 billion in 2005 (25.2 per cent). When one uses a US$2.00 threshold of poverty, the total number increases for the same years from 2.54 billion to 2.56 billion, although as a percentage of the global population the share decreases from 69.2 per cent in 1981 to 47 per cent in 2005. Regional differences are considerable. For example, in Sub-Saharan Africa the number of people living below US$2.00 per day went from 294 million in 1981 to 557 million in 2005, although that represents a change from 74 to 73 per cent of the population. In contrast, in the East Asia and Pacific region, including China, those living below US$2.00 decreased from 1.28 billion (95.4 per cent) in 1981 to 0.73 billion (38.7 per cent) in 2005.[5] However, the global financial crisis, which began in 2008, stalled this progress, especially for poorer countries. The UN estimated that in 2009 '55 million to 90 million more people will be living in extreme poverty than anticipated before the crisis'.[6] As the authors of a World Bank publication on absolute poverty measures note, 'the developing world outside China has seen little or no sustained progress in reducing the number of poor, with rising poverty counts in some regions, notably Sub-Saharan Africa'.[7]

Poverty can be measured according to absolute poverty lines or relative poverty lines. Absolute poverty lines set a floor of, say, US$1 per day (the current threshold used by the World Bank is US$1.25) as the minimum amount required to secure the necessities for life, or a level of per capita caloric intake. Relative poverty lines measure, for example, the bottom 10 per cent of the income distribution or a certain fraction of median income, such as the 40th percentile. The Human Poverty Index ranks countries according to an index of several factors, which differ between developing and developed countries. While calculating the number of people living on extremely low income is a convenient way of identifying poverty, it is widely acknowledged that the definition of poverty is broader than income data. As the Nobel prize-winning economist Amartya Sen put it, '[the] identification of poverty with low income is well established, but there is, by now, quite a substantial literature on its inadequacies'.[8] He notes four types of contingencies that determine variations in the impact of (low) income and that cause us to appreciate that poverty is more than just low income: individual physical characteristics, environmental conditions, social conditions, and behavioural expectations within the community.[9] These characteristics vary by individual, family, and society such that a given level of income may result in one person living in poverty in terms of their capability to lead a life they value, compared

---

[5] Chen and Ravallion, *The Developing World is Poorer than we Thought, But no Less Successful in the Fight Against Poverty* (World Bank Development Research Group, 2008) 41–3.

[6] UN, *Millennium Development Goals Report 2009* (2009) 4.

[7] Chen and Ravallion, *Absolute Poverty Measures for the Developing World, 1981–2004* (World Bank Development Research Group, 2007) 1.

[8] Sen, *The Idea of Justice* (Allen Lane, 2009) 254.   [9] Ibid, 255–6.

to another with the same income but whose functionings (the term used by Sen for what you actually do) provide a higher level of happiness or well-being. In sum, 'real poverty (in terms of capability deprivation) can easily be much more intense than we can deduce from income data'.[10]

UN human rights bodies, in particular the Committee on Economic, Social and Cultural Rights, share the critique of a statistically determined definition of poverty. In its statement on poverty, the Committee endorsed a 'multi-dimensional under-standing of poverty, which reflects the indivisible and interdependent nature of all human rights' and defined poverty 'as a human condition characterized by sustained or chronic deprivation of the resources, capabilities, choices, security and power necessary for the enjoyment of an adequate standard of living'.[11]

Whether measured in relative or absolute terms or in terms of capabilities, the prob-lem of global poverty is staggering in its magnitude and affects both developing and developed countries. It has attracted the attention of the human rights community for decades.

Even before the adoption in 1948 of the Universal Declaration of Human Rights (UDHR), the UN Educational, Scientific and Cultural Organization (UNESCO) con-vened a Committee on the Philosophical Principles of the Rights of Man to reflect on an eventual declaration of human rights, which stated, 'one group of rights is essentially connected with the provision of means of subsistence, through [one's] own efforts or, where they are insufficient, through the resources of society'.[12] In 1968, on the occasion of the twentieth anniversary of the UDHR, the International Conference on Human Rights proclaimed that '[t]he widening gap between the economically developed and developing countries impedes the realization of human rights in the international community'.[13] Thus the basic idea that poverty and underdevelopment are human rights concerns has been part of the rhetoric of human rights since the founding of the contemporary human rights movement and even before. The UN High Commissioner for Human Rights declared in 1998 that extreme poverty was the worst violation of human rights[14] and the Assistant-Director General of UNESCO (himself a former Secretary-General of Amnesty International) launched a programme on poverty as a violation of human rights.[15]

---

[10] Ibid, 256.

[11] CESCR, Statement on Poverty and the ICESCR, E/C.12/2001/10 (10 May 2001) para 8.

[12] UNESCO, *Human Rights: Comments and Interpretations: A Symposium Convened by UNESCO*, UNESCO/PHS/3 (rev) Appendix II (25 July 1948) 11. The published version of the work of the Committee appears in Maritain, *Universal Declaration of Human Rights: Comments and Interpretations* (UNESCO, 1949).

[13] Proclamation of Teheran, Final Act of the International Conference on Human Rights, Teheran, A/CONF. 32/41 at 3 (13 May 1968) para 12.

[14] 'I am often asked what is the most serious form of human rights violations in the world today, and my reply is consistent: extreme poverty.' UNDP, *Poverty Reduction and Human Rights: A Practice Note* (UNDP, 2003) iv.

[15] UNESCO's project on poverty was launched in 2002 under the title 'Ethical and Human Rights Dimensions of Poverty: Towards a New Paradigm in the Fight Against Poverty'. See Pogge (ed), n 1, vii–viii.

2.2 DEVELOPMENT, SOCIAL JUSTICE, AND HUMAN RIGHTS

Poverty and human rights are related in the context of development, whether defined as an increase in aggregate production of goods and services (economic growth) or in more social terms of improvement of the well-being and quality of life for a community (human development). Definitions vary across the spectrum of development as more wealth in material terms and development as greater freedom to be and do what one values, to use the concept in Sen's book *Development as Freedom*. Development strategies have evolved from earlier formulations focusing on modernization, industrialization, and growth, to the current view that even growth-based strategies must prioritize poverty reduction.

Another definitional issue that should be clarified at the outset is the overlap and distinction between human rights and 'social justice'. While social justice is part of the vocabulary of both development and human rights, the focus of much of the social justice movement is to challenge unjust structures (structural violence); support communities of poor, vulnerable, and marginalized people, using methodologies of community development and empowerment; and challenge the processes of international economic integration ('globalization') by which the rich get richer and the poor get poorer. A human rights approach to addressing poverty may well find merit in such approaches but would focus more on an accountability framework for pursuing social justice and refer to explicit human rights norms rather than a broad appeal to notions of redistributive or egalitarian justice.

Human rights are claims on those in authority with respect to protection of the dignity and well-being of the human person. Human rights approaches, especially when applied by courts of law, tend to focus on claims of individuals anchored in binding law rather than redressing broader injustices and concern for the welfare of the poor. The latter are regarded as policy matters to be determined by other branches of government. In one sense, human rights is narrower than the general commitment to social justice in that it is based on specific norms agreed upon as enforceable human rights. It is at the same time more general insofar as it protects rights for all, not just the poor. Therefore, social justice, as described here, is fundamentally oriented towards eliminating poverty, whereas human rights is concerned with poverty among other problems that affect people's capacity to lead meaningful lives. The two tend to overlap when addressing the consequences of globalization.

2.3 THE CONTEXT OF POVERTY AND HUMAN RIGHTS: GLOBALIZATION

The term 'globalization' is often used to refer to the increased interconnectedness of people across borders and, in economic terms, to those features of the global economy that favour liberalization of trade in goods and services, the operations of giant transnational corporations, deregulation and privatization, virtually unrestricted capital flows, and the macroeconomic policies of international financial institutions. Globalization also suggests the dominant 'neo-liberal' model of development, that is, one that relies on the self-correcting and wealth-generating power of markets.

The term 'globalization' in the economic sense has proved to be highly controversial. Ferocious opposition has come from pro-poor anti-globalization movements outraged by the motivating force of greed behind the behaviour of the economically and militarily powerful and by the devastating impact of the process in terms of widening economic and social disparities, destruction of non-renewable resources, ecological devastation, and homogenization of culture. The violence of their opposition was felt in Seattle, Geneva, Washington, Hong Kong, Mexico City, and other locations of World Trade Organization (WTO) ministerial meetings and annual sessions of the G-20 and the Bretton Woods Institutions (the International Monetary Fund (IMF) and the World Bank), which are seen as icons of the harm brought about by globalization. The economic analyses supporting anti-globalization build on older neo-Marxist analysis of the global class struggle, dependency theory seeing the 'centre' as exploiting the 'periphery', and similar frameworks for pinpointing the injustice inflicted on the poor by the rich.

Many mainstream economists argue that globalization 'works' and is eventually an antidote to poverty. Some argue that 'the cure for poverty is economic growth'[16] or writing off debt and vastly increasing aid from donor to poor-country governments. What is interesting from the perspective of human rights and poverty is that human rights tends to be part of the strategies contesting globalization and to be absent from the discourse of its supporters. This preference is symptomatic of a deeper divergence of poverty reduction and human rights agendas.

3 DIVERGENCE OF POVERTY REDUCTION AND HUMAN RIGHTS AGENDAS

To a certain extent, the divergence in perspective between the human rights and poverty reduction discourses can be explained by the dominance of law, political science, and philosophy among those who theorize about and develop policies on human rights and the dominance of economics among those who theorize about and develop poverty reduction strategies. Some of these divergent ways of thinking are explored in Section 3.1, which examines how economists think about poverty and human rights. Section 3.2 analyses the thinking of governors of central banks and ministers of finance.

---

[16] Coyle, *The Soulful Science: What Economists Really Do and Why it Matters* (Princeton University Press, 2007) 72.

3.1 RESISTANCE TO HUMAN RIGHTS DISCOURSE
IN ECONOMIC THINKING

Economists and economic decision-makers only rarely invoke human rights concepts, although many are open to related concepts. Some economists tend to consider their professional role as value-neutral, offering the tools of analysis to be applied to policies set by others. Other economists address moral dimensions of economic issues, but avoid human rights language. Jeffrey Sachs proposed to end extreme poverty by 2025 through a nine-step programme that he places in the historical trajectory of the ending of slavery, colonialism, segregation, and apartheid. Although all of these were human rights movements, he does not call them that.[17] He does not explicitly make the link between the human rights causes of the past and the current cause of poverty elimination. Economists often apply notions of minimum standards, transparency, participation, and the like in the context of development policy, without relating them to a human rights framework. Thus, in the economics literature on international trade, there has been much discussion about appropriate mechanisms to promote labour standards, including addressing child labour in developing countries.[18] Likewise, the literature on public services has highlighted how a lack of transparency, insufficient accountability, and corrupt government officials will increase social wastage and distort economic and service delivery outcomes.[19] Other research has focused on matters of 'process', correlating economic performance with democracy and the rule of law.[20]

These analyses are illustrative of the divergence between human rights and economic thinking insofar as the authors grapple with many of the same concerns as are used in human rights (fairness, accountability, transparency, labour standards, child labour, democracy, rule of law) without reference to the respective standards contained in international human rights instruments. Nobel prize-winning economist Joseph Stiglitz, in his influential book *Making Globalization Work*, contrasted how at the national level 'we argue for and against different policies on the basis of whether they are just, whether they hurt the poor, whether their burden falls disproportionately on those less well off', whereas in the international arena, 'not only do we fail to do the analysis, we almost never argue for a policy on the basis of fairness'.[21] He does allude in his conclusion to the UDHR but only as something the founding fathers of the USA would be pleased with, rather than as the inaugural document to a rather extensive set of international instruments relevant to reducing what he calls the 'gap between economic and political globalization'.[22]

Furthermore, there are many points of tension between mainstream economic thinking and human rights-centred approaches when it comes to defining

---

[17] Sachs, *The End of Poverty: Economic Possibilities for Our Time* (Penguin Press, 2005) 360–8.

[18] eg Edmonds and Pavcnik, *International Trade and Child Labor: Cross-country evidence* (National Bureau of Economic Research, 2004).

[19] eg Shleifer and Vishny, 'Corruption' (1993) 108(3) *Quarterly J of Economics* 599.

[20] eg Rigobon and Rodrik, *Rule of Law, Democracy, Openness and Income: Estimating the interrelationships* (Kennedy School of Government, Harvard University, 2004).

[21] Stiglitz, *Making Globalization Work* (WW Norton, 2006) 278.   [22] Ibid, 292.

development goals or implementing anti-poverty policy. One such point of tension is that growth-oriented economic analysis tends to disregard the impact of income on the realization of such human rights as the rights to health, education, and cultural and political freedoms. Economic analysis and policy interventions are fundamentally about making *choices* among alternatives in a world of limited resources. In contrast, the language of human rights (and associated *obligations* towards bearers of rights) appears less forgiving about choices and options. Rights language tends to be used by economists when it enhances, rather than limits choices. As Sen has said:

In economics the concept of rights is often invoked...however...[n]o intrinsic importance is attached to the existence or fulfilment of rights, and they have been judged by their ability to achieve good consequences, among which the fulfilment of rights have not figured.[23]

Indeed, human rights principles are quite different from rankings of social arrangements based on utilitarian and Rawlsian principles that are favoured by economists. Part of the appeal to economists of John Rawls, one of the leading rights theorists of the twentieth century, is probably the use of the fiction of a 'rational' person making choices, which is typical of economists.[24] In his influential *A Theory of Justice*, Rawls imagines such a person choosing behind a 'veil of ignorance' the fairest social arrangement in assigning rights and duties and distribution of advantages in society. He hypothesizes that such a free and rational person would choose, first, a principle of equal enjoyment of basic liberties (civil and political rights in international human rights language, language which Rawls does not use) and, second, equality of opportunity to occupy offices and positions under a social arrangement that provides the greatest benefit to the least advantaged members of society. This hypothetical and ahistorical reasoning is not unlike models that are developed in economics and it is not surprising that the economics literature draws on Rawls and uses rights language without reference to the human rights that, in historical fact, have been agreed upon. There is certainly value in economic analysis using a model of a society of only two individuals deemed to act rationally in order to isolate choices, before extrapolating to social arrangements, without considering the messier arrangements that actually exist. This démarche of Rawls and other rights theorists is appealing to economists but often pays no heed to the actual human rights that have been defined through historical social processes.

When, almost 30 years after his *A Theory of Justice*, Rawls does allude to 'human rights', he does so in a somewhat idiosyncratic way. In *The Law of Peoples*, he explains that human rights 'set a necessary, though not sufficient, standard for the decency of domestic political and social institutions', but only Articles 3 to 18 UDHR (those relating to civil and political rights) contain 'human rights proper'; while economic, social, and cultural rights, which 'presuppose specific kinds of institutions', presumably are not 'human rights proper'.[25] Elsewhere, he enumerates human rights as the

---

[23] Sen, *On Ethics and Economics* (Blackwell, 1988) 49.
[24] For a detailed discussion of Rawls' theory, see Chapter 2, above.
[25] Rawls, *The Law of Peoples* (Harvard University Press, 1999) 80, n 23. See also Chapter 2, above.

rights to life (including 'the means of subsistence'), liberty, and 'formal equality as expressed by the rules of natural justice'.[26] This interpretation is quite remote from the human rights that are guaranteed by international law and reinforces the tension between human rights and a concern for poverty. Mainstream human rights thinking and international human rights instruments adopted by the UN and regional organizations have no hesitation in regarding health, education, work, social security, and housing as 'human rights proper' and therefore of direct value to promoting poverty elimination, which the Rawlsian framework does not.

Another point of tension between human rights and economic thinking is that, even when the importance of goals other than that of economic growth is recognized in economic analysis, there is a temptation to consider civil and political rights as optional goods that can await a sufficient level of economic growth. The holistic human rights approach would not accept such a trade-off. Economic literature has come down on both sides of this issue. There are scholarly articles, both theoretical and empirical, that suggest that priority attention to political rights, for instance, can make a positive contribution to economic growth.[27] Others suggest that economic growth is more likely to pave the way for institutional, including political, development—and that prioritizing political freedom may not be the best strategy for developing countries to pursue economic growth.[28] There seems to be little doubt that political freedoms are positively related to economic growth and that rising living standards foster democratic freedoms, while declining living standards subvert them. However, as Benjamin Friedman has said:

That there is usually more freedom in countries with higher per capita incomes does not by itself reveal whether having a high income leads a society to value and therefore provide these freedoms, or whether having widespread rights and liberties enables a country to achieve a higher level of income—in other words, whether a high material standard of living fosters freedom, or freedom facilitates economic success.[29]

The more interesting question is how adherence to human rights principles can instrumentally contribute to the effectiveness of economic policy interventions, including those aimed at growth and efficiency.

Thus, there is no simple answer to the question of how economists think about poverty and human rights. Some attempt to be value-neutral; some favour eliminating poverty through redistribution; some apply the concept of development as freedom; but most favour raising the condition of the poor through market-based growth. The latter group tends to dominate in high-level decision making among central bankers and treasury departments.

---

[26] Ibid, 65.

[27] eg Kaufmann, 'Human Rights, Governance, and Development: An Empirical Perspective' (2006) 8 *Development Outreach* 15–20 and references cited therein.

[28] eg Glaeser, La Porta, Lopez-de-Silanes, and Shleifer, *Do Institutions Cause Growth?* (National Bureau of Economic Research, 2004).

[29] Friedman, *The Moral Consequences of Economic Growth* (Alfred A Knopf, 2005) 314.

3.2 THE PERSPECTIVE OF CENTRAL BANKS
AND MINISTRIES OF FINANCE

The divergence between human rights and poverty reduction agendas is perhaps best represented by the G-20.[30] Founded in 1999, it claims to represent around two-thirds of the world's population and 90 per cent of world gross domestic product. It describes itself as 'an informal forum that promotes open and constructive discussion between industrial and emerging-market countries on key issues related to global economic stability',[31] which does not include human rights. The G-20 finance ministers and central bank governors meet once a year. At its meeting in Berlin in 2004, members agreed to the G-20 Accord for Sustained Growth (the Accord) and the G-20 Reform Agenda, setting out guidelines for economic growth and development, both nationally and globally.[32]

The meeting of ministers and governors held in China in 2005 adopted the G-20 Statement on Global Development Issues. Neither 'human rights' nor 'human development' are mentioned in that document and 'good governance' is only mentioned in relation to sound economic policies and accountability. The statement does say, 'we are committed to strengthening the dialogue on varying development philosophies, strategies, and policies, from which all countries can benefit'.[33] Human rights did not fare any better at the meeting in Australia in 2006, which adopted a set of country-specific actions to implement the Accord, none of which mentions directly or indirectly human rights, equity, human development, or good governance. Similarly, the final communiqué of the meeting of ministers and governors held in South Africa in 2007 makes no mention of 'human rights' or even 'right', and the word 'human' is never attached to development (it is used once in 'human capital'). Development is mentioned 11 times, usually next to growth, which is mentioned 18 times. The essence of the communiqué is expressed in the 'collective determination to achieve balanced and sustainable growth'. In the immediate aftermath of the 2008 financial crisis, the G-20 met in London and adopted the Global Plan for Recovery and Reform of 2 April 2009. Once again, there was no reference to human development or human rights. Only the following rather feeble acknowledgement was made: 'We recognise the human dimension to the crisis. We commit to support those affected by the crisis by creating employment opportunities and through income support measures.'[34] This

---

[30] The members of the G-20 are the finance ministers and central bank governors of 19 states: Argentina, Australia, Brazil, Canada, China, France, Germany, India, Indonesia, Italy, Japan, Mexico, Russia, Saudi Arabia, South Africa, South Korea, Turkey, the UK, and the USA. The European Union is also a member and senior officials of the IMF and the World Bank participate in G-20 meetings.

[31] See <http://www.g20.org/about_what_is_g20.aspx>.

[32] 'G-20 Accord for Sustained Growth: Stability, Competition and Empowerment: Mobilising Economic Forces for Satisfactory Long-Term Growth' (Berlin, 2004) and 'G-20 Reform Agenda: Agreed Actions to Implement the G-20 Accord for Sustained Growth' (Berlin, 2004). Both available at: <http://www.g20.org/Documents/2004_germany.pdf>.   [33] Ibid, para 3.

[34] 'The Global Plan for Recovery and Reform', para 26, available at: <http://www.g20.org/Documents/final-communique.pdf>.

was echoed in the Pittsburgh Summit the same year with its reference to 'collective responsibility to mitigate the social impact of the crisis' and the pledge to cooperate 'to improve access to food, fuel, and finance for the poor'.[35] The underlying philosophy of the summit is expressed in the statement: 'the only sure foundation for sustainable globalisation and rising prosperity for all is an open world economy based on market principles, effective regulation, and strong global institutions'.[36] Critiquing the London communiqué of the G-20, two human rights scholars noted:

> The crisis, its human impact, and the proposed solutions are also issues of international human rights law—and in particular of state obligations to take collective action to create a global economic system amenable to the fulfilment of basic rights to subsistence, security, and freedom.[37]

A similar focus on growth and markets as the solution to poverty characterizes the pronouncements of the G-8 and the Davos Economic Forum. These settings and the G-20 illustrate an ambiguity regarding human rights and poverty. The confrontation is not between the morally indignant voices of the poor against a band of greedy capitalists meeting in some boardroom in Washington or London. Many in the anti-globalization movement do indeed claim to speak for the poor, but so do the representatives of the G-20 governments, which include India and China, as well as Argentina, Mexico, South Africa, and the European Union. These are not the forces of evil against the forces of good. They are the principal actors in the global economy and they send contradictory messages about the proposition that human rights have anything to do with poverty. It is little wonder, therefore, that human rights do not figure prominently among the approaches to poverty in vogue in international financing of development.

However, the situation is changing progressively as human rights specialists learn more about the economic analyses of poverty and development economists learn about the compatibility of their goals with those of human rights and the instrumental value of human rights for poverty reduction. These trends have opened the space—still fairly restricted—for the convergence of human rights and poverty reduction agendas.

4 CONVERGENCE OF POVERTY REDUCTION AND HUMAN RIGHTS AGENDAS

The previous section illustrated several ways in which human rights concerns diverge from those of development and poverty reduction. This section addresses the convergence—or at least the trends that demonstrate mutually reinforcing relations—between

---

[35] 'Leaders' Statement: The Pittsburgh Summit', paras 34 and 38, available at: <http://www.g20.org/Documents/pittsburgh_summit_leaders_statement_250909.pdf>.   [36] Ibid.

[37] Fukuda-Parr and Salomon, 'A Human Rights Analysis of the G-20 Communique: Recent Awareness of the "Human Cost" Is Not Quite Enough', Carnegie Council online, available at: <http://www.cceia.org/resources/ethics_online/0033.html>.

human rights and anti-poverty agendas, beginning in Section 4.1 with some economic thinking that is congruent with human rights and continuing in Section 4.2 with policies to combat poverty using human rights tools.

4.1 TRENDS IN ECONOMIC THINKING CONGRUENT WITH HUMAN RIGHTS

Apart from the economic studies referred to above which deal with fairness, transparency, and participation, there is another strand of development economics that acknowledges human rights as providing goals for development: the development ethics movement. The International Development Ethics Association (IDEA), for example, defines its members as 'a cross-cultural group of philosophers, social scientists, and practitioners who apply ethical reflection to global development goals and strategies and to North/South relations'. They advocate a normative approach to development-based theories 'that appeal to social justice, human rights, basic needs, and theological understandings of the human condition'.[38] In 1989, IDEA adopted the Mérida Declaration, which enumerates among their guiding ethical principles 'the absolute respect for the dignity of the human person, regardless of gender, ethnic group, social class, religion, age or nationality'.[39] Leading development economists, such as David A Crocker, Paul Streeten, and especially Denis Goulet, spearheaded this movement. The centrality of their concerns to human rights and poverty should be evident, although human rights as such is rarely an operative concept in their work.

The principal exception to the divergence between human rights and economic thinking, however, is the 'human development and capabilities' approach, theorized primarily by Amartya Sen and Martha Nussbaum. This approach has been embraced by the UN Development Programme (UNDP) in its Human Development Report and is promoted by an association of academics and practitioners called the Human Development and Capability Association (HDCA). The openness to human rights of this perspective is due to the centrality of the concept of development as freedom and expanding choices. In the words of the Human Development Report:

Human development shares a common vision with human rights. The goal is human freedom. And in pursuing capabilities and realizing rights, this freedom is vital. People must be free to exercise their choices and to participate in decision-making that affects their lives. Human development and human rights are mutually reinforcing, helping to secure the well-being and dignity of all people, building self-respect and the respect of others.[40]

The farther one moves from trade, finance, and treasury departments of governments, including in their multilateral settings of the WTO and the G-20, and the closer one gets to bilateral and multilateral fora for addressing poverty, the more relevant human rights considerations become. This continuum runs from the G-20 to

---

[38] See <http://www.development-ethics.org/what_is>.
[39] See <http://www.development-ethics.org/merida_declaration>.
[40] UNDP, *Human Development Report 2001*, 9.

the World Bank Group and regional development banks to broad-based deliberative bodies (such as the global conferences and summits, and the UN Economic and Social Council), to development aid agencies and programmes (such as the UK Department for International Development (DFID) and UNDP), to UN human rights bodies (such as the Human Rights Council and the Third Committee of the General Assembly), to human rights treaty regimes. To illustrate the gap, compare the various G-20 communiqués discussed in the previous section with the statement of the Committee on Economic, Social and Cultural Rights on poverty. In this statement, the Committee regretted 'that the human rights dimensions of poverty eradication policies rarely receive the attention they deserve. This neglect is especially regrettable because a human rights approach to poverty can reinforce anti-poverty strategies and make them more effective.'[41]

The World Conference on Human Rights, in its 1993 Vienna Declaration, stated that '[t]he existence of widespread extreme poverty inhibits the full and effective enjoyment of human rights; its immediate alleviation and eventual elimination must remain a high priority for the international community'.[42] It further affirmed:

[E]xtreme poverty and social exclusion constitute a violation of human dignity and . . . urgent steps are necessary to achieve better knowledge of extreme poverty and its causes, including those related to the problem of development, in order to promote the human rights of the poorest, and to put an end to extreme poverty and social exclusion and to promote the enjoyment of the fruits of social progress. It is essential for States to foster participation by the poorest people in the decision-making process by the community in which they live, the promotion of human rights and efforts to combat extreme poverty.[43]

4.2 HUMAN RIGHTS APPROACHES IN POVERTY REDUCTION POLICIES

Human rights have become part of the international development agenda, including poverty reduction, through the introduction of human rights approaches into UN development cooperation, poverty reduction strategies, the Millennium Development Goals, and bilateral development programmes. Each of these is examined below, before the most systematic approach to integrating poverty and human rights, namely by considering development itself as a human right, is explored.

4.2.1 UN development cooperation

In 2003, representatives from across the UN system met in Stamford, USA, and defined a Common Understanding on a Human Rights-based Approach to Development Cooperation.[44] This document has become a standard reference for translating

---

[41] CESCR, n 11, para 2.

[42] Vienna Declaration and Programme of Action, A/CONF.157/23 (25 June 1993) para 14.

[43] Ibid, para 25.

[44] UN Development Group, The Human Rights Based Approach to Development Cooperation: Towards a Common Understanding Among UN Agencies (7 May 2003), available at: <http://www.unescobkk.org/fileadmin/user_upload/appeal/human_rights/UN_Common_understanding_RBA.pdf>.

normative human rights commitments of member states into development cooperation policies and projects of UN agencies, funds, and programmes. In his report *Strengthening of the United Nations: An Agenda for Further Change*, the UN Secretary-General called human rights 'a bedrock requirement for the realization of the Charter's vision of a just and peaceful world'. He listed, among 36 actions to realize this vision, 'Action 2' on joint UN efforts at the country level, which was based on the Action 2 Plan of Action, adopted by 21 heads of UN departments and agencies.[45] This Plan, which ended in 2009, integrated human rights into humanitarian, development, and peacekeeping work throughout the UN system. The Action 2 Interagency Task Force, consisting of the Office of the High Commissioner for Human Rights (OHCHR), UNDP, the UN Population Fund (UNFPA), the UN Children's Fund (UNICEF), and the UN Development Fund for Women (UNIFEM), worked towards clarifying, and training staff in, this approach, including through launching the Action 2 Global Programme. In 2007, the Working Group on Training, in collaboration with the UN System Staff College, issued the UN Common Learning Package on Human Rights-Based Approach (HRBA), building on the experience of all agencies.[46] In the four years of its operation, Action 2 supported over 60 UN country teams and their national partners in capacity-building to integrate human rights into their work.[47] In late 2009, the OHCHR was preparing a follow-up mechanism 'aimed at further strengthening system-wide coherence, collaboration and support for human rights mainstreaming'.[48]

4.2.2 Poverty reduction strategies

Since the Asian financial crisis in the 1990s, there has been a rethinking in the World Bank and the IMF of their earlier policies of structural adjustment, sometimes taking into account the human rights impact of such policies, but mostly to avoid social impacts that reduce the productivity of workers and the stability of regimes. Health and education are frequently cited as suffering the most from structural adjustment programmes. More recently, the focus of these institutions has been on the Poverty Reduction Strategy process to reduce the debt of Highly Indebted Poor Countries (HIPC) that have submitted to the Poverty Reduction Strategy Papers (PRSPs). Launched in September 1999, the PRSP approach 'results in a comprehensive country-based strategy for poverty reduction' and reflects 'a recognition by the IMF and the World Bank of the importance of ownership as well as the need for a greater focus on poverty reduction'.[49]

In a concept note, the High Commissioner for Human Rights drew the World Bank's attention to the following:

In linking a Poverty Reduction Strategy to a universal normative framework and State obligations emanating from the human rights instruments, the goals of the Poverty

[45] Strengthening of the United Nations: An Agenda for Further Change, A/57/387 (9 September 2002).
[46] Available at: <http://www.undg.org/index.cfm?P=531>.
[47] Report of the UN High Commissioner for Human Rights, A/64/36, para 93.   [48] Ibid.
[49] IMF Factsheet, available at: <http://www.imf.org/external/np/exr/facts/prsp.htm>.

Reduction Strategy could be sustained with enhanced accountability of the relevant stake-holders. The universal nature of human rights, their mobilization potential and their emphasis on legal obligations to respect, protect and promote human rights, while encouraging national ownership and people's empowerment makes the human rights framework a useful tool to strengthen the accountability and equity dimensions of the Poverty Reduction Strategies.[50]

The issue had already been raised by the Commission on Human Rights, which in 1990 requested its Sub-Commission to consider the relationship between human rights and poverty.[51] The Sub-Commission appointed a Special Rapporteur on human rights and extreme poverty, whose report was published in 1996, followed in 1998 by the appointment of an Independent Expert on human rights and extreme poverty. In a related development and in direct response to a request from the Chair of the Committee on Economic, Social and Cultural Rights, the High Commissioner commissioned in 2001 guidelines for the integration of human rights into poverty reduction strategies, a 60-page document setting out basic principles of a human rights approach to: (1) the process of formulating a poverty reduction strategy; (2) determining the content of a poverty reduction strategy; and (3) guiding the monitoring and accountability aspects of poverty reduction strategies.[52]

4.2.3 Millennium Development Goals

Following the commitments made by heads of state at the Millennium Summit in 2000, all governments and international institutions have set specific targets for poverty reduction in the Millennium Development Goals (MDGs). While these goals are important to development planning, they have tended to ignore commitments made by states to human rights and the rule of law. The MDGs define the priorities for the international community and guide much of the technical cooperation and assistance provided by bilateral and multilateral donors. They are a set of eight goals with 18 numerical targets and over 40 quantifiable indicators, most of which are to be met by 2015. These MDGs are:

- eradicate extreme poverty and hunger;
- achieve universal primary education;
- promote gender equality and empower women;
- reduce child mortality;
- improve maternal health;
- combat HIV/AIDS, malaria, and other diseases;

---

[50] OHCHR, Comments on the Concept Note: Joint World Bank and IMF Report on Poverty Reduction Strategy Papers—Progress in Implementation 2005 PRS Review, available at: <http://siteresources. worldbank.org/INTPRS1/Resources/PRSP-Review/un_ohchr.pdf>.

[51] CHR, Human Rights and Extreme Poverty, E/CN.4/Res/1990/15 (23 February 1990) 5.

[52] Hunt, Nowak, and Osmani, *Draft Guidelines: A Human Rights Approach to Poverty Reduction Strategies* (OHCHR, 2002). See also Hunt, Nowak, and Osmani, *Human Rights and Poverty Reduction Strategies: Human Rights and Poverty Reduction: A Conceptual Framework* (OHCHR, 2003).

- ensure environmental sustainability; and
- develop a global partnership for development.

The High Commissioner for Human Rights has focused attention on the relationship between the MDGs and human rights by disseminating to governments charts on the intersection of human rights and the MDGs and has published *Claiming the MDGs: A Human Rights Approach*, which is an exhaustive analysis of how human rights can contribute to the MDGs.[53] Similarly, the UNDP has published a primer called *Human Rights and the Millennium Development Goals: Making the Link*,[54] and various national development agencies have published their own human rights approaches to MDGs.[55]

4.2.4 Bilateral development cooperation

The trend of national development agencies to adopt human rights approaches has been studied by the Organisation for Economic Co-operation and Development (OECD), which has determined that 'human rights offer a coherent normative framework which can guide development assistance'.[56] The advantages identified by the OECD relate to adaptability to different political and cultural environments, the potential for operationalizing human rights principles, relevance to good governance and meaningful participation, poverty reduction, and aid effectiveness.[57] The growing trend among scholars, development NGOs, and international institutions to use the human rights-based approach to development and poverty reduction both integrates concepts that already had currency in development theory, such as accountability and transparency, in the context of good governance, and adds a dimension with which development practitioners were less familiar, especially the explicit reference to government obligations deriving from international human rights law.

Efforts to integrate human rights have been less successful in relation to the Paris Declaration on Aid Effectiveness, adopted in 2005 by ministers or senior officials of some 85 developed and developing countries and heads of 20 bilateral and multilateral development agencies. The Declaration seeks to reform the delivery of aid and outlines the five overarching principles of ownership, alignment, harmonization, managing for development results, and mutual accountability, with agreed upon indicators, targets, timetables, and processes to monitor the implementation up to 2010. Each of these

---

[53] OHCHR, *Claiming the MDGs: A Human Rights Approach* (2008).

[54] UNDP, *Human Rights and the Millennium Development Goals: Making the Link* (Oslo Governance Centre, 2007).

[55] See eg the Swedish International Development Agency (<http://www.sida.se/English/About-us/Organization/Policy/>); the UK's DFID (<http://www.dfid.gov.uk/mdg/>); the US MCC (<http://www.mcc.gov/mcc/bm.doc/mcc-report-fy2010-selection-criteria-and-methodology.pdf>); Canada's CIDA (<http://www.acdi-cida.gc.ca/INET/IMAGES.NSF/vLUImages/HRDG2/$file/HRDG-Policy-nophoto-e.pdf>); and Denmark's DANIDA (<http://www.danidadevforum.um.dk/en/menu/MonitoringAndIndicators/MDGAndPRSPAlignment/>).

[56] OECD, *Integrating Human Rights into Development: Donor Approaches, Experiences and Challenges* (2006) 58. [57] Ibid, 58–68.

principles has been examined critically from the human rights perspective in a paper commissioned from the Overseas Development Institute by the OECD, which argues for using human rights to broaden the scope and content of the Paris Declaration commitments and indicators on mutual accountability.[58] Many see the Paris Declaration as donor-driven, with insufficient local ownership or mutual accountability with respect to implementation and the assessment of its effectiveness. More important from the perspective of this chapter is the very minimal attention given to human rights in the context of using aid to address poverty.

4.2.5 The right to development

One of the greatest challenges for an economic approach to poverty is to accept the proposition that development itself—essentially an economic process—can be regarded as a human right—an essentially legal and governance concept. The challenge from the beginning has been to translate the hopeful but ambiguous language of the UN Declaration on the Right to Development (1986) into concepts that are meaningful to economists and useful to the rethinking of the development process and poverty reduction strategies. Most developing states use the right to development to voice their concerns about the negative impact of certain aspects of international trade, unequal access to technology, and the crushing debt burden; they promote the idea of an international convention to establish binding obligations to facilitate development. In contrast, most donor states see the right to development as a way of improving the governance and rule-of-law performance of recipient states.

The real test is whether the right to development can help define a middle ground between these two contrasting positions, on which consensus can be sustained and practical outcomes achieved. The right to development embodies three components or attributes, which not only clarify the meaning of the right but specify how it can be instrumental in responding to poverty. The first is a holistic approach to development that integrates the realization of all human rights into the process. The second is what is called an 'enabling environment', by which is meant fairer terms for developing countries in international economic relations and respect by those countries of principles of the rule of law and good governance. The third is social justice and equity, which involves participatory development and fair distribution of the benefits of development, with a special attention to marginalized and vulnerable populations. The principles of participation, non-discrimination, transparency, and accountability, which permeate these attributes, are already reflected in official policy of most international financial and development agencies and, except for the integration of human rights into development, do not seem to make economists uncomfortable. Taken with human rights, they constitute a framework for a serious dialogue on the implementation of the right to development. Such a dialogue holds the promise of removing the

[58] Foresti, Booth, and O'Neil, *Aid Effectiveness and Human Rights: Strengthening the Implementation of the Paris Declaration* (Overseas Development Institute, 2006).

right to development from the realm of controversy and allowing the claims on which it is based to inform development practice to combat poverty.

5 CONCLUSION

There are two reasons why those who favour the growth model of development resist what they see as the well-intentioned but misguided intrusion of human rights into pro-poor development work. The first is the conviction that economic progress suffers as a result of advancing human rights before a sufficient level of prosperity has been reached. However, the examples of countries that developed rapidly under conditions of human rights deprivation and that liberalized later (for example, Brazil, Chile, South Korea, and Taiwan) are far too complex to be probative, and counter-examples can be found. The second is that those who have responsibility over the economy—ministers of finance, corporate executives, shareholders, and academic economists—often assume that human rights are merely matters of legal disputes or strident claims of the political opposition to the government of which they are part or with which they cooperate.

However, in response to the challenges posed at the beginning of this chapter, there are compelling reasons why human rights are both definitional of and instrumental to anti-poverty objectives. The first is the common purpose of both human rights and development, which specialists in either field rarely articulate. The second is the relationship between human rights and forms of empowerment that make anti-poverty measures sustainable and equitable.

A powerful justification for human rights in the anti-poverty agenda relates to the proposition that human rights define the same objective as pro-poor development, for which human development is a convenient proxy. From the capability perspective, both human development and human rights increase freedom. From the utilitarian perspective, both enhance human well-being. However, the similarity is diminished if development is defined merely in terms of growth in goods and services, which is the case in particular of the G-20 process discussed above. Growth is desirable but not as an end in itself; it is a means towards various ends. If the end is the enrichment of the few at the expense of the many and of the planet, then it will not help the poor. If it is a means toward sustainable development, then it must be governed so as to reach that end. As has been pointed out, '[e]conomic growth is often promoted as a means to alleviate poverty; yet even when growth does materialize, its benefits are unevenly distributed and rarely accrue to the poor'.[59]

Thus, the first step in clarifying in practical terms the meaning of poverty in the context of human rights is to note that pro-poor human development, like human

[59] Millen, Irwin, and Yong Kim, 'Conclusion: Pessimism of the Intellect, Optimism of the Will' in Yong Kim, Millen, Irwin, and Gershman, *Dying for Growth: Global Inequality and the Health of the Poor* (Common Courage Press, 2000) 383.

rights, is a process that enables choices by people to lead a life they value and thus enhance their well-being. Human rights are also about creating an environment in which people can develop their full potential and lead creative lives by, in the words of the UDHR, assuring 'the dignity and worth of the human person' and promoting 'social progress and better standards of life in larger freedom'.[60] The ultimate objective of both human development and human rights is, therefore, well-being as understood in both fields. The greatest obstacle to those choices is poverty, which is both capability deprivation and a measure of the denial of human rights.

The G-20 Accord mentioned above notes—albeit in a sort of afterthought in the final paragraph—the following: 'Mobilising all productive forces of a society requires empowering individuals and enhancing economic participation. Equal economic opportunities allow people to better provide for themselves and their families, thus helping to reduce poverty and social tensions.'[61] Although the word is overused, empowerment has a special significance in this context. Thus, to conclude, a brief explanation is offered here of why and how human rights is a strategy for empowerment understood as social and economic transformation by and for the poor, bringing the human rights and anti-poverty agendas together. This transformative strategy sometimes goes by the name of human rights education and learning. The UDHR was proclaimed 'to the end that every individual and every organ of society, keeping this Declaration constantly in mind, shall strive by teaching and education to promote respect for these rights'.[62] When education and learning are transformative, poor people take charge of their own lives and become subjects rather than objects of history; they build on human rights obligations of states to challenge unjust power relations and claim their rights. Where contrary interests are entrenched, this struggle is difficult but it targets the root causes of poverty, which is where the struggle belongs.

These empowerment outcomes of human rights education and mobilization are surprisingly consistent with the empowerment strategy of the World Bank, insofar as it seeks 'the expansion of assets and capabilities of poor people to participate in, negotiate with, influence, control, and hold accountable institutions that affect their lives'.[63] As noted by its former Vice President, Gobind Nankani, 'much of the poverty work of the World Bank and other donors is informed by the same notions of equality and non-discrimination that are central to human rights and empowerment approaches to development'.[64] The economic empowerment of people to be subjects rather than objects of their own history, to know, claim, and realize the full range of their human rights is both morally desirable and the principal means to realize the right that Article 28 UDHR refers to, namely that to 'a social and international order in which the rights and freedoms set forth in this Declaration can be fully realized'. The combats against poverty and for human rights come together in the vision of such a social and international order.

---

[60] UDHR, preambular para 5.   [61] n 32.   [62] Preambular para 8.

[63] Narayan (ed), *Empowerment and Poverty Reduction: A Sourcebook* (World Bank, 2002).

[64] Foreword in Alsop (ed), *Power, Rights, and Poverty: Concepts and Connections* (World Bank and DFID, 2004) 8.

FURTHER READING

ALSTON and ROBINSON (eds), *Human Rights and Development: Toward Mutual Reinforcement* (Oxford University Press, 2005).

COLLIER, *The Bottom Billion: Why the Poorest Countries Are Failing and What Can Be Done About It* (Oxford University Press, 2007).

HUNT, NOWAK, and OSMANI, *Human Rights and Poverty Reduction Strategies: Human Rights and Poverty Reduction: A Conceptual Framework* (OHCHR, 2003).

MARKS (ed), *Implementing the Right to Dev elopment: The Role of International Law* (Friedrich-Ebert Stiftung and Program on Human Rights in Development of the Harvard School of Public Health, 2008).

OHCHR, *Claiming the MDGs: A Human Rights Approach* (UN, 2008).

POGGE, *World Poverty and Human Rights* (Polity Press, 2008).

SALOMON, *Global Responsibility for Human Rights: World Poverty and the Development of International Law* (Oxford University Press, 2007).

SEN, *Development as Freedom* (Alfred A Knopf, 2000).

UVIN, *Human Rights and Development* (Kumarian Press, 2004).

USEFUL WEBSITES

Freedom From Want/Freedom From Poverty: <**http://www.everyhumanhasrights.org/ freedom-from-want-freedom-from-poverty-0**>

International Network for Economic, Social and Cultural Rights: <**http://www.escr-net. org/**>

International Centre on Economic, Social and Cultural Rights: <**http://www.esc-rights. org/**>

World Bank: <**http://www.worldbank.org/**>

MDG Gap: <**http://www.un.org/esa/policy/mdggap/index.html**>

UN Development Programme, Millennium Development Goals: <**http://www.undp.org/ mdg/resources2.shtml**>

28

ENVIRONMENTAL DEGRADATION

Malgosia Fitzmaurice

SUMMARY

This chapter investigates the challenges environmental degradation poses for human rights protection. Two human rights approaches to combating environmental degradation are discussed. First, the idea of substantive environmental human rights is examined. Such rights are explicitly provided for in the African Charter on Human and Peoples' Rights as well as in the San Salvador Protocol to the American Convention on Human Rights. Other efforts to imply substantive environmental human rights are critically analysed. There are, however, concerns with the development and use of substantive environmental human rights. Therefore, there have been efforts to develop procedural environmental human rights. Such efforts include the Aarhus Convention, environmental impact assessments, as well as the creative approaches of the European Court of Human Rights to imply that such a right exists within the framework of existing rights. Procedural environmental human rights provide the best way forward for meeting the challenges of environmental degradation.

1 INTRODUCTION

This chapter addresses the challenges environmental degradation poses for human rights protection, examining whether substantive and procedural environmental rights can overcome them. The main issue is whether human rights constitute an efficient and practical tool that can be used to combat environmental degradation.

The link between the enjoyment of human rights and the environment in which we live was addressed for the first time in 1972 at the UN Conference on the Human Environment. The Declaration of the Conference (Stockholm Declaration) recognizes that 'man's environment [is] essential to his well-being and to the enjoyment of basic human rights', such as the right to life. It is clear that:

The harm caused to individuals and communities by degraded environments—from unsafe drinking water to disappearing wild life—is increasingly seen by many people as a question of 'rights' being violated... Protection of the environment can no longer be seen as simply a policy choice.[1]

Degradation of the environment, by which we mean the deterioration in environmental quality from ambient concentrations of pollutants and other activities and processes, such as improper land use and natural disasters,[2] can cause violations of human rights. For example, the Office of the UN High Commissioner for Human Rights has investigated the varied effects of climate change on the enjoyment of human rights. In a 2009 report to the Human Rights Council, the impact of climate change on several human rights, including the rights to life, adequate food, water, adequate housing, health, and self-determination, was examined.[3] The report notes that the effects of climate change, including heatwaves, floods, and other natural phenomena, will pose direct and indirect threats to the right to life and the closely related rights to food, water, health, and housing. Climate change will have disastrous effects on the right to food as its production will decrease, particularly at lower latitudes. It is estimated that 600 million people will face malnutrition. It will cause a shortage of water supplies, adversely impacting on the availability of drinking water and resulting in an increase in water-related diseases. Therefore it may be said that climate change also constitutes a grave challenge to the right to health. The report also details the impact climate change will have on the right to adequate housing. For example, rising sea levels and the erosion of livelihoods will result in increased migration to cities and a corresponding increase in the number of hazardous dwellings. Finally, climate change will adversely affect the right to self-determination, especially for indigenous peoples, whose traditional livelihood depends on access to land and natural resources. Women and children, who constitute the most vulnerable groups during natural disasters and whose health and livelihoods are the most endangered, will be disproportionately affected.

The threat to the enjoyment of human rights posed by environmental degradation has also been considered by the Committee on Economic, Social and Cultural Rights. In its General Comment 14, the Committee observed that the steps that should be taken to realize the right to health, and in particular 'the improvement of all aspects of environmental and industrial hygiene' include 'preventive measures in respect of

---

[1] Kravchenko and Bonine, *Human Rights and the Environment: Cases, Law, and Policy* (Carolina Academic Press, 2008) 3.

[2] OECD Glossary of Statistical Terms, available at: <http://stats.oecd.org/glossary/detail.asp?ID=821>.

[3] Report of the OHCHR on the relationship between climate change and human rights, A/HRC/10/61 (15 January 2009).

occupational accidents and diseases; the requirement to ensure an adequate supply of safe and potable water and basic sanitation; the prevention and reduction of the population's exposure to harmful substances such as radiation and harmful chemicals or other detrimental environmental conditions that directly or indirectly impact upon human health.[4] Comparable comments have been made in relation to the right to water.[5]

Similarly, the effect of dumping of toxic waste on the enjoyment of human rights has been widely acknowledged. In 1995, the Commission on Human Rights established a Special Rapporteur to investigate this link. In 1996, the Rapporteur reported that environmental degradation following the dumping of toxic waste would impact on the enjoyment of the rights to self-determination, life, health, food, safe and healthy working conditions, housing, information, participation, and freedom of association, as well as cultural rights.[6] These adverse effects have been repeatedly emphasized in Commission on Human Rights and Human Rights Council resolutions.[7]

There is clearly a negative link between environmental degradation and the enjoyment of human rights. The question then arises, can human rights be used as an effective tool to deal with environmental degradation? How should, and indeed does, human rights address this challenge? One answer is through the use of substantive environmental rights, that is, the right to a clean and healthy environment. A different approach is to use procedural environmental rights which guarantee access to information, participation in decision making, and access to justice in environmental matters. Each of these approaches and their merits will be discussed in the rest of this chapter.

2 SUBSTANTIVE ENVIRONMENTAL RIGHTS

There are very few human rights treaties that grant a direct right to a clean and healthy environment. Only the African Charter on Human and Peoples' Rights (ACHPR) and the San Salvador Protocol to the American Convention on Human Rights in the Area of Economic, Social and Cultural Rights (San Salvador Protocol) do so. Despite this, there has been some progress at the UN level in drafting 'soft law' documents that suggest that there might be a substantive human right to a clean and healthy environment. Furthermore, the European Court of Human Rights has found that such a right can be derived from the prism of existing human rights.

---

[4] CESCR, General Comment 14, HRI/GEN/1/Rev.9 (Vol 1) 78, para 25.

[5] See CESCR, General Comment 15, HRI/GEN/1/Rev.9 (Vol 1) 97. See also Fitzmaurice, 'The Human Right to Water' (2007) 18 *Fordham Envm LR* 537.

[6] Preliminary report of the Special Rapporteur on the adverse affects of the illicit movement of toxic and dangerous products and wastes on the enjoyment of human rights, E/CN.4/1996/17 (22 February 1996) para 132.   [7] eg HR Council Res 9/1 (5 September 2008).

2.1 AFRICAN CHARTER

The first treaty to accord a direct right to a clean and healthy environment was the ACHPR. Article 24 provides peoples with a right to 'a general satisfactory environment favourable to their development'. This provision was one of the bases of a claim in the *Ogoniland* case before the African Commission on Human and Peoples' Rights.[8] The complainants alleged that the Nigerian government had directly participated in unsustainable oil development practices in Ogoniland. It was also claimed that the state-owned oil company had caused environmental degradation, including widespread contamination of soil, water, and air, the destruction of homes, the burning of crops, and the killing of farm animals. These actions, in turn, had led to health problems amongst the Ogoni people. As such, violations of the rights to health, a healthy environment, housing, and food were alleged.

The African Commission held that the right to a satisfactory environment as set out in Article 24 requires states parties to adopt reasonable measures to prevent pollution and ecological degradation, to promote conservation, and to pursue the concept of sustainable development and use of natural resources. Furthermore, a satisfactory environment is one which is clean and safe and promotes health. Similarly, the right to health imposes obligations on states to 'take the necessary measures to protect the health of their people'.[9] In the view of the Commission, states must *respect* these rights by refraining from directly threatening the health and the environment of their citizens, as well as *protect* them by adopting measures to prevent pollution and ecological degradation. Concluding that although Nigeria had the right to make use of its natural resources, including oil, the Commission held that Nigeria had breached its human rights obligations in relation to those living in the Ogoni region and that 'the pollution and environmental degradation to a level humanly unacceptable has made living in [Ogoniland] a nightmare'.[10] The Commission not only saw environmental degradation as leading to the violation of other rights, but as a human rights violation in itself because of its impact on the quality of life. It further stated that 'an environment degraded by pollution and defaced by destruction of all beauty and variety is as contrary to satisfactory living conditions and development as the breakdown of the fundamental ecologic equilibria is harmful to physical and moral health'.[11]

Although the decision in the *Ogoniland* case is truly remarkable, particularly as it confirms the justiciable nature of Article 24, the Commission's restricted regulatory powers and the poor record of compliance with its recommendations limit the practical usefulness of its attempts to remedy environmental degradation in the African region.

---

[8] 155/96, *Social and Economic Rights Action Center and the Center for Economic and Social Rights v Nigeria*, 15th Activity Report of the AcommHPR (2001–2002) ('*Ogoniland*'). See Shelton, 'Decision Regarding Communication 155/96 (Social and Economic Rights Action Centre/Centre for Economic and Social Rights v Nigeria). Case No ACHPR/COMM/A044/1' (2002) 96 *AJIL* 937; Coomans, 'The Ogoni Case before the African Commission on Human and Peoples' Rights' (2003) 52 *ICLQ* 749.   [9] ACHPR, Art 16.
[10] *Ogoniland*, n 8, para 67.   [11] Ibid, para 51.

2.2 SAN SALVADOR PROTOCOL TO THE AMERICAN
CONVENTION ON HUMAN RIGHTS

Article 11 San Salvador Protocol provides for a right to a healthy environment:

1. Everyone shall have a right to live in a healthy environment and to have access to basic public services.
2. The States Parties shall promote the protection, preservation, and improvement of the environment.

However, the Inter-American human rights institutions have limited powers in respect of this right. They can only receive annual reports from states on their observance of this right as there is no provision for individual applications to the Inter-American Commission or Court regarding alleged violations of the San Salvador Protocol. Despite this, the Commission and the Court have linked environmental degradation and human rights on numerous occasions when deciding cases regarding indigenous rights.[12] In such cases, the Commission has stressed that the importance of economic development should not override environmental considerations. However, it is questionable whether these decisions will have an impact beyond the particular context of indigenous peoples' rights to their traditional lands.[13]

2.3 PROGRESS AT THE UN

Several 'soft law' instruments have been adopted by the UN which suggest the possibility of a substantive environmental human right. The first suggestions of such a right can be traced to Principle 1 Stockholm Declaration, which provides that:

Man is both creature and moulder of his environment, which gives him physical sustenance and affords him the opportunity for intellectual, moral, social and spiritual growth. In the long and tortuous evolution of the human race on this planet a stage has been reached when, through the rapid acceleration of science and technology, man has acquired the power to transform his environment in countless ways and on an unprecedented scale. Both aspects of man's environment, the natural and the man-made, are essential to his well-being and to the enjoyment of basic human rights the right to life itself [sic].

Many saw this as an incipient environmental human right. However, although '[t]his grand statement might have provided the basis for subsequent elaboration of a human right to environmental quality,... its real-world impact has been noticeably modest'.[14]

In 1992, world leaders met again at the UN Conference on the Environment and World Development. There were great expectations that this conference would produce

---

[12] Case 7615, *Yanomami v Brazil*, IACommHR Res 12/85 (5 March 1985); *Mayagna (Sumo) Awas Tigni Community v Nicaragua*, IACtHR Series C No 79 (31 August 2001); Case 12/053, *Maya Indigenous Community of the Toledo District v Belize*, IACommHR Report No 40/40 (12 October 2004).

[13] Boyle, 'Human Rights or Environmental Rights? A Reassessment' (2007) 18 *Fordham Envm LR* 471, 476.   [14] Ibid, 473.

a document which included an explicit human right to a clean environment. However, these hopes were dashed as no compromise could be found as to its content. Instead, the Rio Declaration 1992 maintained the position taken in Stockholm, that: 'Human beings are at the centre of concerns for sustainable development. They are entitled to a healthy and productive life in harmony with nature.'

In 1989, in preparation for the Rio Conference, a Special Rapporteur on environment and development was appointed by the Sub-Commission on Prevention of Discrimination and Protection of Minorities. The Special Rapporteur, Fatma Zohra Ksentini, addressed the link between human rights and environmental degradation in her 1994 final report. She stated that the environment, development, democracy, and human rights are the fundamental building blocks of modern society. Endorsing the view that environmental rights are protected by existing human rights, she reported that there was universal acceptance of the right to a satisfactory environment at national, regional, and international levels. The Special Rapporteur recommended the adoption of the Draft Declaration of Principles on Human Rights and the Environment, which had been drafted by academics and NGOs.[15] Presuming that environmental human rights exist, the Draft Declaration builds on the Stockholm and Rio Declarations and provides that:

1. Human rights, an ecologically sound environment, sustainable development and peace are interdependent and indivisible.
2. All persons have the right to a secure, healthy and ecologically sound environment. This right and other human rights, including civil, cultural, economic, political and social rights, are universal, interdependent and indivisible.

Containing a wide range of both substantive and procedural environmental rights, the Draft Declaration includes rights to freedom from pollution, environmental degradation, and activities that adversely affect the environment, threaten life, health, livelihood, well-being, or sustainable development within, across, or outside national boundaries. There are also rights to the protection and preservation of the air, water, soil, sea ice, flora, and fauna, and the essential processes and areas necessary to maintain high biological diversity and ecosystems. The Declaration also proclaims the right to safe and healthy food and water, a healthy working environment, as well as adequate housing. The Declaration was not adopted by the Commission on Human Rights and, to date, has not been considered by the Human Rights Council.

2.4 INDIRECT SUBSTANTIVE ENVIRONMENTAL RIGHTS

As the Special Rapporteur on environment and development reported, rights to a clean and healthy environment may be drawn from other human rights: civil and political, as well as economic, social, and cultural rights. Some favour civil and political rights

[15] Report by the Special Rapporteur on environment and development, E/CN.4/Sub.2/1994/9 (6 July 1994).

as more useful in realizing a healthy and clean environment as '[i]nternational courts and tribunals are likely to be more easily persuaded that civil and political rights are capable of creating practical and enforceable obligations in relation to environmental and related matters'.[16] Recourse to existing political and civil rights gives individuals, groups, and NGOs access to existing information as well as tried and tested remedies and political processes. Others argue for the mobilization of second generation rights, that is economic, social, and cultural rights, over first generation rights in the protection of the environment as many of these rights have a direct bearing upon environmental conditions. However, the translation of economic, social, and cultural rights 'into specific environmental standards will never be an easy task'.[17] Although he prefers this approach, Anderson has stated that '[d]espite their advantages, the existing system for implementing and monitoring second generation rights construe these rights rather narrowly, and continue to approach environmental questions only indirectly'.[18]

The European Court of Human Rights has been very active in determining a right to a clean and healthy environment within existing civil and political human rights, and this approach will be examined in the next section.

2.4.1 European Convention on Human Rights

The European Convention on Human Rights (ECHR) does not contain a direct substantive environmental human right and the first few cases regarding environmental degradation were regarded as inadmissible. For example, *X and Y v Federal Republic of Germany* was the first 'environmental' case to come before the Council of Europe institutions, and was deemed inadmissible by the European Commission on Human Rights on the basis that the ECHR did not include a right to the preservation of nature.[19]

However, more recently, the jurisprudence of the European Court has undergone a fundamental change regarding environmental issues. The Court has given effect to environmental rights indirectly through its interpretation of the protections accorded to other rights set out within the ECHR, including Articles 2 (right to life), 3 (freedom from torture), 8 (right to respect for private and family life), and 10 (freedom of expression), as well as Article 1 Protocol 1 (right to property). Dealing with environmental degradation in this manner is particularly challenging as there is competition between those rights explicitly protected by the ECHR and the protection of the environment which is not.

Most cases have been brought under Article 8 ECHR, the right to respect for private and family life, home, and correspondence. This right is qualified and may be restricted if this is 'necessary in a democratic society', understood as requiring that

---

[16] Sands, *Principles of International Environmental Law* (Manchester University Press, 2001) 297.

[17] Ibid.

[18] Anderson, 'Human Rights Approaches to Environmental Protection: An Overview' in Boyle and Anderson, *Human Rights Approaches to Environmental Protection* (OUP, 1996) 6.

[19] 15 DR 161 (1976).

'the interference corresponds to a pressing social need and... is proportionate to the legitimate aim pursued. The reasons given to justify the interference must be "relevant" and "sufficient".'[20] The first 'environmental' case brought before the European Court concerned noise pollution from aircraft arriving and leaving London airports. In *Powell and Raynor v UK*, the Court balanced the competing interests of the individuals who were disturbed by flights to and from Heathrow airport and those of the community at large, including the economic importance of the airport as a source of employment and the development of trade and communications. The European Court concluded that although the quality of life of the applicants had been disturbed, this was necessary for the well-being of the community.[21]

Lopez Ostra v Spain is considered to be a ground-breaking case.[22] In 1988, a tannery company erected a waste treatment plant on municipal grounds (with state subsidies), without a licence for activities which may be classified as causing a nuisance, 12 metres from the applicant's apartment. The applicant alleged the impairment of both her health and that of her family due to fumes generated by the tannery. She had to be re-housed. The European Court held that environmental pollution, even without causing serious damage to health, could affect the well-being of individuals and impede enjoyment of their private and family life. Spain had not struck a proper balance between the well-being of the applicants and the general economic benefits brought by the waste treatment plant. Although the plant was privately owned, there was a positive obligation to regulate private actions carried out on state territory in order to protect private and family life and the home. This was the first time that the European Court had found a violation of the ECHR on the basis of environmental pollution.

The case of *Hatton v UK* also concerned state responsibility for pollution caused by private industry. This case was a disappointment from the point of view of environmental protection and human rights. The European Court adopted a very restrictive approach to the link between environmental degradation and human rights, exhibiting a more deferential attitude towards states than in the *Lopez Ostra* case. The case concerned night flights to and from Heathrow Airport which, it was argued by the applicants, disturbed their sleep. The UK government had introduced the use of noise quotas in order to minimize the disturbance caused by night flights.

The case was first heard by a Chamber of the Court in 2001.[23] Referring to the 'fair balance' which must be struck between the competing interests of the individual and the community as a whole, the Chamber admitted that the state enjoyed a certain margin of appreciation in determining the steps to be taken to ensure compliance with the ECHR. The Chamber found that despite the margin of appreciation left to the UK government, the implementation of the noise quota scheme failed to strike a fair balance between the country's economic well-being and the applicants' effective enjoyment of their right to respect for their homes and family lives, therefore violating Article 8

---

[20] *Olsson v Sweden* (1988) 11 EHRR 259. See Chapter 6, above.   [21] (1990) 12 EHRR 355.
[22] (1994) 20 EHRR 27.   [23] (2002) 34 EHRR 1.

ECHR. The UK government requested the referral of the case to the Grand Chamber. The Grand Chamber stated in no uncertain terms that 'there is no explicit right under the Convention to a clean and quiet environment' and that only 'where the individual is directly and seriously affected by noise or other pollution' may an issue arise under Article 8.[24] Finding that there was no violation of Article 8, the Grand Chamber reiterated the fundamentally subsidiary role of the Court: national authorities have direct democratic legitimacy and are better placed than an international tribunal to assess local needs and conditions. In matters of general policy, which may involve different opinions contained within democratic society, the actions of domestic policy-makers to ensure compliance with the ECHR should be given a wide margin of appreciation.

A minority of judges appended a powerful joint dissenting opinion.[25] The dissenting judges argued that the 'evolutive' interpretation of the ECHR leads to the construction of an environmental human right on the basis of Article 8. They asserted that the European Court has confirmed on several occasions, including in *Lopez Ostra*, that Article 8 embraces the right to a healthy environment: 'the Convention and the Court have increasingly taken the view that Article 8 embraces the right to a healthy environment, and therefore to protection against nuisance caused by harmful chemicals, offensive smells, agents which precipitate respiratory ailments, noise and so on'.[26] They felt that, unfortunately, the Grand Chamber's judgment in *Hatton* appeared to deviate from these developments, appearing to take a step backwards, and that the UK government had not sufficiently substantiated the economic importance of Heathrow Airport for the country.

The European Court adopted a very restrictive and deferential view towards the state's position regarding environmental human rights and the possibility of redressing environmental degradation through this means in *Hatton*. The Court took into consideration the fact that the UK government had acted in conformity with national laws concerning night flights. By contrast, in *Lopez Ostra* the authorities had failed to comply with domestic law as there was no licence for the tannery.

This line of reasoning was also present in *Fadeyeva v Russia* in which the Court noted the breach of national laws by the defendant state. The European Court clarified in *Fadeyeva v Russia* that not every instance of environmental degradation will constitute a breach of Article 8 ECHR.[27] The case concerned air pollution from a Soviet steel plant which had been privatized. In order for pollution to raise an issue under Article 8, the Court reiterated the principles it had set out in its earlier cases. First, the deleterious effects of the pollution must directly affect the applicant's home, family, or private life; and, second, the adverse effects must have reached a certain minimum level if they are to fall within the scope of Article 8. The minimum level to be reached is not general but relative and depends on all the circumstances, including the intensity and duration of the nuisance, its physical or mental effects, and the general environmental

---

[24] (2003) 37 EHRR 28, para 96.
[25] Joint Dissenting Opinion of Judges Costa, Ress, Türmen, Zupančič, and Steiner, ibid.
[26] Ibid, para 2.   [27] (2007) 45 EHRR 10.

context (for example, there would be no claim under Article 8 if the harm complained of was negligible in comparison to the environmental hazards inherent to life in every modern city). The Court held that the emissions from the industrial plant had affected the applicant's health, making her more vulnerable to various diseases, as well as affecting the enjoyment of her home. Taken together, the effects of the pollution were of a level to bring it within the scope of Article 8. A violation of Article 8 was found as the state had made no efforts to provide the applicant with an effective solution to the dangers of the steel plant's emissions.

The European Court has also examined the obligations of states under Article 2, which protects the right to life, where environmental pollution has had, or may have, lethal effects. So, for example, in *Öneryıldız v Turkey,*[28] and *Budayeva and Others v Russia,*[29] the Court found a causal link between gross negligence attributable to the state and the loss of human lives which resulted from environmental degradation. In both cases the relevant states had failed to fulfil their positive obligations to protect the right to life. The Court held that where 'dangerous activities' are embarked upon which may have potentially lethal consequences, including those which cause environmental degradation, there must be enhanced national regulation. National authorities must govern the licensing, setting up, operation, security, and supervision of such activities and make it compulsory for all concerned to take practical measures to ensure the effective protection of citizens whose lives might be endangered by the inherent risks. These preventive measures include the public's right to information. Appropriate procedures, considering the technical aspects of the activity, for the purpose of identifying shortcomings in the processes concerned and any errors committed by those responsible at different levels must be established. The Court also stated that in the context of dangerous activities, the scope of positive obligations under Article 2 largely overlaps with those under Article 8. As in many other cases concerned with environmental issues, the choice of measures to be taken falls within states' margin of appreciation. The Court stressed in the *Budayeva* case that, where environmental disasters have occurred, the scope of the positive obligation imputable to the state depends on the origin of the disaster and whether its risks were susceptible to mitigation. Furthermore, the Court observed that if the infringement of the right to life or physical integrity is not caused intentionally, the positive obligation to set up an effective judicial inquiry does not necessarily entail criminal proceedings and may be satisfied if impartial civil, administrative, or even disciplinary remedies are at the disposal of victims.

The above discussion demonstrates a willingness of the European Court of Human Rights to remedy environmental degradation through human rights, despite the lack of a specific environmental right in the ECHR. However, the numerous requirements which 'an environmental claim' must fulfil to fall under the scope of Article 8 ECHR are challenging. It would be overstating the case to consider that there is a substantive environmental right under the ECHR. Rather, as the Court said in *Kyrtatos v Greece,*

---

[28] (2005) 41 EHRR 20.   [29] App nos 15339/02, 21166/02, 20058/02, and 15343/02 (16 October 2003).

no provision of the European Convention is designed to protect the environment itself, unless the rights of individuals are directly affected.[30]

2.4.2 Other international treaties

There are other treaties which grant indirect substantive environmental rights. One such treaty is the International Labour Organization (ILO) Convention No 169 concerning Indigenous and Tribal Peoples in Independent Countries. Of particular importance are Article 14, regarding ownership and possession of land, and Article 15, regarding the right to participate in the use, management, and conservation of natural resources. These provisions were the main reason for the lack of widespread ratification of the Convention. These indirect environmental human rights should be viewed from the perspective of the culture and religion of indigenous peoples for whom the link with land and the environment and natural resources is frequently part and parcel of their identity as human beings. They are also linked to the question of self-determination. Therefore, environmental rights are at the heart of protections for indigenous populations.

2.5 SUBSTANTIVE ENVIRONMENTAL RIGHTS AT THE NATIONAL LEVEL

Although at present more than 100 national constitutions contain a right to a healthy, decent, or good environment, the role these provisions play in remedying environmental degradation is not altogether clear. Formulations regarding such a right vary considerably. They may refer to the duty of authorities to provide a healthy and balanced environment or go further and impose a duty on citizens to cooperate in the protection of the environment for present and future generations. For example, Article 24 of the Constitution of the Republic of South Africa provides that:

Everyone has the right to an environment that is not harmful to their health or well-being; and to have the environment protected, for the benefit of present and future generations, through reasonable legislative and other measures that prevent pollution and ecological degradation; promote conservation; and secure ecologically sustainable development and use of natural resources while promoting justifiable economic and social development.

Constitutional rights may be a very useful tool in challenging regulations and executive action which negatively impact the environment, but only if such rights are justiciable. For example, a case was brought before the Supreme Court of the Philippines regarding commercial logging agreements which had a deleterious effect on the rainforest. In *Oposa v Factoran*, 44 children argued that their right, and the rights of generations yet unborn, under the constitution to a balanced and healthful ecology was being violated.[31] The Supreme Court held that:

---

[30] (2005) 40 EHRR 16.   [31] GR No 101083 (30 July 1993).

Each generation has a responsibility to the next to preserve that rhythm and harmony for the full enjoyment of a balanced and healthful ecology.... the minors' assertion of their right to a sound environment constitutes, at the same time, the performance of their obligation to ensure the protection of that right for the generations to come.[32]

The Supreme Court was of the view that the children had standing before national courts on the issue and thus confirmed the justiciable nature of the environmental right.

A progressive approach to environmental rights based on a broad interpretation of the right to life has been taken by the courts of India. In 1991, in the case of *Subhash Kumar v State of Bihar*, the Supreme Court of India observed that the 'right to life guaranteed by article 21 [of the Constitution] includes the right of enjoyment of pollution-free water and air for full enjoyment of life'.[33] In this case, the Supreme Court also recognized the right to a wholesome environment as part of the fundamental right to life. It held that municipalities and a large number of other governmental agencies must take adequate steps to prevent pollution. This approach has since been followed by courts in Bangladesh,[34] Pakistan,[35] and Colombia.[36] In addition, the Constitution (Forty Second Amendment) Act 1976 has explicitly incorporated environmental protection and improvement as a part of state policy so that Article 48A Indian Constitution, a directive principle of state policy, provides that '[t]he State shall endeavour to protect and improve the environment and to safeguard the forests and wild life of the country'.

2.6 IS THERE A NEED FOR A SUBSTANTIVE ENVIRONMENTAL RIGHT?

Do we need a substantive environmental human right? This is a highly controversial issue which has attracted much debate.[37] One of the main critics of this approach, Handl, has argued that it is far from clear that environmental human rights and environmental protection share common objectives.[38] Handl raises several concerns regarding the use of a substantive environmental human right as a solution to the problem of environmental degradation.

---

[32] Ibid. However, Judge Feliciano in his Separate Opinion forcefully argued that such a right is too general and vague to constitute a ground for a legal action. [33] AIR 1991 SC 420, para 7.

[34] eg *Dr M Farooque v Secretary, Ministry of Communication, Government of the People's Republic of Bangladesh and 12 Others*, WP No 300 of 1995.

[35] eg *The Employees of the Pakistan Law Commission v Ministry of Works*, 1994 SCMR 1548.

[36] eg *Victor Ramon Castrillon Vega v Federacio Nacional de Algodoneros y Corporacion Autonoma Regional del Cesar* (1997) Case No 4577.

[37] See eg Boyle and Anderson (eds), n 18; Boyle, n 13; Handl, 'Human Rights and Protection of the Environment: A Mildly "Revisionist" View' in Cançado Trindade (ed), *Human Rights, Sustainable Development and the Environment* (Instituto Interamericano de Derechos, 1992); and Handl, 'Human Rights and Protection of the Environment' in Eide, Krause, and Rosas (eds), *Economic, Social and Cultural Rights* (Kluwer Law International, 2001) 303. [38] Handl in Eide, Krause, and Rosas, ibid, 309.

First, he argues that, to date, the normative content of such a putative environmental human right has not been defined. Any definition is likely to be qualitatively different from, for instance, the right to health.[39] A clean environment would be difficult to conceptualize as an inalienable right, as environmental protection measures are subject to the reordering of national socio-economic priorities to meet public policy objectives, such as ensuring continued 'development' or 'saving jobs'.[40] Environmental rights will also differ according to the area where they arise, that is, whether they relate to the North or the South.[41]

Second, he argues that any attempt to establish criteria for the evaluation of state compliance with obligations stemming from generic environmental human rights would encounter political and technical difficulties. Where would the division of labour between human rights and environmental institutions lie? What would be the appropriate locus of decision making: the international or national level? However, others maintain that adhering to a strict division of labour between environmental and human rights institutions, which deal with similar or at least comparable issues, is to duplicate efforts and leads to the depletion of available resources.[42]

Third, Handl expresses concern regarding the democratic legitimacy of a human rights-based approach to environmental issues. A generic environmental human right would serve as a powerful tool for socio-economic engineering by human rights decision-making bodies. Implementation of the right could lead to internationalized decision making in sensitive areas that traditionally belong to the state. However, it may be noted that many other human rights share this characteristic. Therefore, it does not appear that this feature sets apart environmental human rights from other human rights.

Handl looks to the regional human rights systems for evidence that the relationship between environmental degradation and human rights either remains not fully accepted as an operational normative concept (ECHR), or is formulated in ambiguous language, due to inherent conflicts with economic development (ACHPR).[43] He also notes that there is little evidence that states will be willing to use Article 11 San Salvador Protocol as a vehicle to push the environmental agenda.[44]

Others have also been critical of adopting a generic environmental human right. They argue that such a right is only human-oriented and does not consider the intrinsic right of the environment itself for protection.[45] Boyle has noted that the implications of the argument for anthropocentricity are essentially structural. They imply a need for the integration of human claims to a decent environment within a wider spectrum

---

[39] Ibid, 315.   [40] Handl in Cançado Trindade, n 37, 117–42.

[41] Handl in Eide, Krause, and Rosas, n 37, 126.

[42] Taillant, 'Environmental Advocacy and the Inter-American Human Rights System' in Picolatti and Taillant (eds), *Linking Human Rights and the Environment* (University of Arizona Press, 2003) 118.

[43] Handl in Eide, Krause, and Rosas, n 37.   [44] Ibid.

[45] Boyle, 'The Role of Human Rights in the Protection of the Environment' in Boyle and Anderson, n 18, 43 and 51–3; Handl in Cançado Trinidade, n 37, 138. See also, Redgwell, 'Life, Universe and Everything: A Critique of Anthropocentric Rights' in Boyle and Anderson, n 18, 71.

of decision-making processes that is based on balancing of the interests of human beings, the environment, and authorities through international cooperation and supervisory institutions. Boyle submits that such decision-making processes should take into consideration the competing interests of future generations and other states and the collective interest in common spaces and wildlife preservation. The right to environment and the right of the environment are two concepts that are impossible to reconcile. Therefore, the question remains

should we continue to think about human rights and the environment within the existing framework of human rights law in which the protection of humans is the central focus— essentially a greening of the rights to life, private life, and property—or has the time come to talk directly about environmental rights—in other words a right to have the environment itself protected? Should we transcend the anthropocentric in favour of the eco-centric?[46]

Some would argue that the 'eco-centric' approach is the only proper way to consider environmental rights.[47]

A further unresolved issue is the classification of such a putative environmental human right. Such a right is 'understood to represent aspects of a first generation, a second generation right, or to represent a mix thereof' and this indeterminacy is based upon the ambiguity of the content of the right.[48] Whilst some have argued that to classify the right to a clean environment in the group of social, economic, and cultural rights would give it a normative quality,[49] in general the right has been categorized as a so-called 'third generation' human right.[50] Third generation rights are said to include the rights to development, peace, and co-ownership of the common heritage of mankind and are primarily viewed as being collective in nature with regard to both their object and subject. Human rights experts consider them immensely vague[51] and it has been argued that they are so vast they encompass anything and anybody.[52] Therefore some have argued that a generic environmental human right 'would scarcely be a "human" right in an orthodox sense'.[53]

As indicated by the serious criticism and doubts presented above, it is clear that substantive environmental human rights are not a straightforward means to remedy environmental degradation. In the following sections we will examine another approach to dealing with the problem of environmental degradation: procedural environmental rights.

---

[46] Boyle, n 13, 473.

[47] Rodriguez-Rivera, 'Is the Human Right to Environment Recognised under International Law? It Depends on the Source' (2001) 12 *Colo J Intl Envm L and Policy* 1, 11–12.

[48] Handl in Eide, Kraus, and Rosas, n 37, 313.

[49] Merrills, 'Environmental Protection and Human Rights: Conceptual Aspects' in Boyle and Anderson, n 18, 25.

[50] Alston, 'A Third Generation of Solidarity Rights: Progressive Development or Obfuscation of International Human Rights' (1982) 29 *Netherlands ILR* 307, 309; Vasak, 'For the Third Generation of Human Rights: The Right of Solidarity', Inaugural Lecture to the 10th Study Session of the International Institute of Human Rights, Strasbourg (2–27 July 1979).   [51] Boyle, n 45, 46.

[52] Alston, n 50, 317.   [53] Boyle, n 45, 48.

3 PROCEDURAL ENVIRONMENTAL RIGHTS

The definition of procedural environmental rights is included in Principle 10 Rio Declaration 1992:

Environmental issues are best handled with participation of all concerned citizens, at the relevant level. At the national level, each individual shall have appropriate access to information concerning the environment that is held by public authorities, including information on hazardous materials and activities in their communities, and the opportunity to participate in decision-making processes. States shall facilitate and encourage public awareness and participation by making information widely available. Effective access to judicial and administrative proceedings, including redress and remedy, shall be provided.

Procedural rights are based on three pillars: a right to information, a right to participate, and a right to access to justice. They can be 'understood as a refinement of established political or civil human rights or as novel human rights'.[54] They are an expression of democracy, where democracy concerns 'the role of people in governance'.[55] Although it may be premature to claim that such rights are binding on states as part of customary international law, it appears that there has been a gradual expansion of the participation of civil society in environmental matters.[56] Procedural environmental rights are of fundamental importance in the protection of the environment as they bestow on individuals and civil society rights that can be used, through various ways, to influence, shape, and evaluate state activities which may have an adverse impact on the environment. Through the participation of civil society, a degree of transparency in environmental matters can be achieved.

Procedural environmental rights have been realized in a number of ways. There is the Convention on Access to Information, Public Participation in Decision-making and Access to Justice in Environmental Matters (Aarhus Convention) which develops the three pillars of a procedural environmental right. In addition, environmental impact assessment (EIA) procedures have been developed, whilst the European Court of Human Rights and African Commission on Human and Peoples' Rights have found violations of an indirect procedural environmental right.

3.1 THE AARHUS CONVENTION

The Aarhus Convention was drafted within the UN Economic Commission for Europe (UNECE).[57] Any UN member state can accede to the Convention; at the time of

---

[54] Handl in Eide, Kraus, and Rosas, n 37, 318.

[55] Franck, *Fairness in International Law and Institutions* (OUP, 1995) 83.

[56] International Law Association, 'Final Report on the Status of the Universal Declaration of Human Rights in National and International Law' (1994) 546, 548. See Fitzmaurice, 'Some Reflections on Public Participation in Environmental Matters' (2002) 2 *NSA and IL* 1.

[57] The UNECE was set up as one of the five regional commissions of the UN in 1947 by the Economic and Social Council. For more information on the UNECE, see <http://www.unece.org/about/about.htm>.

writing, it has been ratified by 44 states. The Convention links the substantive right to a clean environment with a procedural one, guaranteeing all three limbs of the right: the right to information, the right to participate in environmental decision making, and the right to access to justice. The preamble of the Convention states that everyone has the 'the right to live in an environment adequate to his or her health and well being', and the Convention recognizes that this can only be realized with the broad participation of civil society acting in the public interest.[58]

3.1.1 Right to information

The Aarhus Convention provides a very broad definition of environmental information. The general public is entitled, without proving a special interest, to access to information regarding the state of the environment, public health, and other factors impacting on the environment. This right is to be realized by both public authorities and private entities that exercise public responsibility in the field of conservation. Article 4 grants the right to request and obtain information and Article 5 imposes an obligation on states to collect and disseminate it. However, Article 5(3) Aarhus Convention limits the right to information by according states a much-criticized discretion to refuse to disseminate information if it is not available in electronic form. The right to information has been implemented extensively by states parties to the Aarhus Convention.

3.1.2 Right to participate in environmental decision making

Article 6 Aarhus Convention provides a very far-reaching participatory right in environmental decision making, with a focus on certain industries, such as the energy sector, production of metals, mineral extraction, chemical processing, and waste management. Public participation during the preparation of plans and programmes relating to the environment is provided for in Article 7, while Article 8 provides that states 'shall strive to promote effective participation at an appropriate stage, and while options are still open, during the preparation by public authorities of executive regulations and other generally applicable rules that may have a significant effect on the environment'. However, it has been noted that this second pillar of public participation has not been implemented as extensively as the right to information.

The adoption of the 2003 Kiev Protocol on Strategic Environmental Assessment was an attempt to further develop Articles 7 and 8 Aarhus Convention. However, the Protocol does not address public participation generally,[59] but only information and public participation within the context of an environmental impact assessment. EIAs traditionally involve the procedural rights of information and public participation in relation to certain activities which would impact on the environment. They have their roots in the USA where they were first used in 1968. Historically, they were seen as

---

[58] For a good outline of the Aarhus Convention, see Redgwell, 'Access to Environmental Justice' in Francioni (ed), *Access to Justice as a Human Right* (OUP, 2007) 153.

[59] Kravchenko and Bonine, n 1, 285.

part and parcel of environmental law and not treated as part of a procedural human right. Even in 1991, the Espoo Convention on Environmental Impact Assessment in a Transboundary Context, another UNECE initiative, treated the EIA as a tool of environmental law. However, since then the rights realized by EIAs have begun to be viewed as part of a procedural human right, not purely an environmental procedure.

3.1.3 Access to justice

Article 9 Aarhus Convention grants the right of access to national courts to challenge decisions relating to the provision of information and public participation. Such a right is based on the assumptions of wide participation of civil society in environmental affairs and a balancing of interests between the government and society. This right has found its expression, and is already well established, in civil and political rights.[60] Access to justice, as defined by the Aarhus Convention, is a means of correcting erroneous administrative decisions on environmental issues by a court or another independent and impartial body established by law.[61] The right to access to justice may be triggered (1) by any person if her/his request for environmental information has been ignored, refused, or not dealt with in accordance with the Convention (Article 9(1)), or (2) by any member of the public who has a sufficient interest or maintains impairment of a right (Article 9(2)).

Article 9(2) provides that what constitutes 'a person with a sufficient interest' and the 'impairment of a right' is to be determined in accordance with the requirements of national law, bearing in mind the objective of giving broad access to justice. Standing should be granted to NGOs and they are to be considered in national law as persons with 'a sufficient interest'. Thus, public interest litigation in access to environmental justice is of a particular importance. Certain jurisdictions allow *actio popularis* to be used in civil claims, such as those concerning consumer and environmental protection, whilst in some jurisdictions the existence of the right to life in national constitutions is interpreted as granting standing in *actio popularis* proceedings.[62] However, it is worth noting that in some states there has been a movement backwards to the traditional practice of standing based on interest.[63] Thus, this pillar of the Aarhus Convention is still not fully implemented. Considering how national laws stand at present, such a state of affairs, at least in some states, will continue for a considerable period of time.

---

[60] Franck, n 55, 98, states that the conception of democratic entitlement may be dated from the General Assembly's adoption of the UDHR. See also Ebbesson, 'The Notion of Public Participation in International Environmental Law' (1997) 8 *YIEnvmL* 62.   [61] Aarhus Convention, Art 9(3).

[62] *Drustva Ecology Slovenje*, Case No U-I-30/95. See Bruch and King, 'Constitutional Procedural Rights: Enhancing Civil Society's Role in Good Governance' in Burch (ed), *The New 'Public': Globalisation of Public Participation* (Environmental Law Institute, 2002) 36.

[63] See eg Verschuuren, 'The Role of the Judiciary in the Environmental Governance in the Netherlands' in Kotze and Paterson (eds), *The Role of the Judiciary in Environmental Governance: Comparative Perspectives* (Kluwer Law International, 2009); Tolsma, de Graaf, and Jans, 'The Rise and Fall of Access to Justice in the Netherlands' (2009) 21 *JEnvmL* 315.

3.1.4 The Aarhus Compliance Committee

A Compliance Committee, a quasi-judicial body, further strengthens the procedural right of access to environmental justice within the context of the Aarhus Convention. It consists of independent experts who decide on alleged breaches by states parties of provisions of the Convention. There is a requirement that national remedies have been exhausted before the Committee can examine complaints. The unique feature of this compliance mechanism, which sets it apart from similar mechanisms set up under environmental agreements, is that environmental NGOs can bring complaints of alleged violations of the Aarhus Convention to the attention of the Committee.[64] However, the decisions of the Compliance Committee are not binding, and so the effectiveness of this procedure is rather weak. Nevertheless, the public nature of these proceedings can put considerable pressure on a state that is not in compliance.

An example encompassing all relevant characteristics of this system is a case concerning Turkmenistan, which was initiated by a Moldovan NGO on behalf of the population of Turkmenistan. The communication alleged that Turkmenistan's new Law on Public Association was in breach of the Aarhus Convention provisions relating to recognition and support of environmental NGOs, and non-discrimination as to citizenship, nationality, and domicile of the members of the public.[65] The communication observed several restrictions that the law of Turkmenistan imposed on freedom of public association and noted the possibility for a public association to be liquidated by a court decision with no right of appeal. It was further alleged that the legislation provided the basis for the Ministry of Justice to abolish the majority of environmental NGOs in Turkmenistan, leaving only the NGO led by the Turkmen Deputy Prime Minister. The Compliance Committee made a preliminary decision on admissibility and the communication was forwarded to Turkmenistan for a reply. No response was received.

The Compliance Committee adopted a decision that Turkmenistan was in breach of certain provisions of the Aarhus Convention. It also found that Turkmenistan had failed to comply with the general requirements of establishing a clear, transparent, and consistent legal framework to implement the Aarhus Convention. It adopted a set of recommendations, which were submitted to the Meeting of the Parties of the Aarhus Convention. These included amending the Act on Public Associations with a view to bringing all its provisions into compliance with the Convention, immediately taking appropriate interim measures to ensure compliance with the Convention, carrying out these measures with the involvement of civil society, and submitting a report to the Compliance Committee on the measures taken to implement the recommendations. The proceedings, which were open and involved all parties concerned, related, inter alia, to the development of the awareness of the public as to the use of the

---

[64] Fitzmaurice, 'Environmental Justice through International Compliant Procedures? Comparing the Aarhus Convention and the North American Agreement on Environmental Matters' in Ebbeson and Okowa (eds), *Environmental Law and Justice in Context* (CUP, 2009) 211.

[65] Aarhus Convention, Arts 3(4) and 3(9).

rights granted by the Convention, which include inquiries about the progress made. Turkmenistan was also granted the possibility to address the Compliance Committee for assistance. This case clearly indicates the constitutive elements of justice: very strong, if not crucial participation of NGOs, transparency for all parties involved, and openness and fairness.

3.2 INDIRECT PROCEDURAL ENVIRONMENTAL RIGHTS

The practice of the European Court of Human Rights in relation to procedural environmental rights is based on an interpretation of Articles 8 and 10 ECHR. Recent developments of the jurisprudence of the Court indicate that the content of these rights is similar in scope to the rights granted by the Aarhus Convention. The right to receive information has been interpreted by the Court in several cases: *Guerra and others v Italy*,[66] *Taskin v Turkey*,[67] *Tatar v Romania*,[68] *Öneryıldız v Turkey*, and *Budayeva v Russia*. In each of these cases the European Court stressed the essential duty of a state to provide environmental information, broadly understood, concerning environmental hazards, as well as environmental procedures which are necessary to initiate and conduct projects such as EIAs. In *Guerra* the Court was of the view that providing relevant information to the applicants, all of whom lived in the vicinity of the factory, could have a bearing on their private and family life and physical integrity protected under Article 8 ECHR. Furthermore, the Court reiterated that Article 10 ECHR 'basically prohibits a government from restricting a person from receiving information that others wish or may be willing to impart to him'.[69] However, that freedom was interpreted restrictively and cannot be construed as imposing on a state, in circumstances such as those in *Guerra*, a positive obligation to collect and disseminate information of its own motion.

In *Taskin*, the European Court took the view that 'whilst Article 8 contains no explicit procedural requirements, the decision-making process leading to measures of interference must be fair and such as to afford due respect to the interests of the individual as safeguarded by Article 8'.[70] As such the participation of those affected by environmental issues in the decision-making process will be essential for compliance with Article 8 ECHR, as well as Article 6 Aarhus Convention.[71] In *Tatar*, the Court explicitly referred to the rights of information and participation guaranteed by the Aarhus Convention. The Court stated that these were breached by prohibiting interested persons from obtaining information and participating in environmental decision making. However, this right of participation in decision making is only available to persons whose Convention rights have been affected and not to everyone. The European Court also alluded to EIAs as a necessary requirement to evaluate the effect of a proposed activity on the environment and the rights of the individual.

---

[66] (1998) 26 EHRR 357.   [67] (2006) 42 EHRR 50.   [68] App no 67021/01 (18 October 2007).
[69] n 66, para 41.   [70] n 67, para 118.   [71] Boyle, n 13, 496.

There is no express procedural environmental right under the African Charter. However, in the *Ogoniland* case, the African Commission on Human and Peoples' Rights drew such a right from Article 24 ACHPR, which grants a substantive environmental right. The Commission gave the substantive right a meaningful content by supporting the rights of the public to information and participation in environmental matters.[72] In particular, it decided that states should follow certain environmental procedures such as EIAs, involve the public in a manner that encompasses the three limbs of the procedural environmental right, and monitor potentially harmful activities. According to Shelton, such a comprehensive approach should become a blueprint 'for merging environmental protection, economic development, and guarantees of human rights'.[73]

4 CONCLUSION

This chapter has analysed the challenges posed by environmental degradation to the realization of human rights. Substantive and procedural environmental human rights were explored as possible solutions to the problem of environmental degradation. It is clear that the human rights approach to environmental degradation faces many challenges. The normative content of a substantive environmental human right is not well defined and its global acceptance is doubtful. Environmental rights can be derived from other existing human rights. Such an approach, however, as developed by the European Court of Human Rights, has been limited to cases of direct harm to individual interests and states are given a wide margin of appreciation.

The way forward, it appears, lies in reliance on procedural environmental human rights, which are not nearly as controversial as the substantive right and widely accepted and implemented. A cross-fertilization of ideas between various human rights systems might mean that the approach to environmental information and participation, as professed by the European Court of Human Rights in *Taskin*, may acquire global acceptance.[74] Similarly, the very broadly conceived participatory rights in the Aarhus Convention may gain worldwide acceptance,[75] especially as they impose on states parties a duty to spread the ideas therein at international fora. Application of procedural rights is steadily growing, even in institutions traditionally criticized for their inadequate respect for the environment and human rights, such as multilateral development banks. The use of a participatory right, however, is not devoid of challenges, as procedural rights alone are not sufficient to counterbalance a presumption in favour of development and economic interests.[76]

---

[72] Shelton, n 8, 939.   [73] Ibid, 942.   [74] Boyle, n 13, 504–5.
[75] The Aarhus Convention does not exclude participation of non-UNECE states as parties. The amendment to the Espoo Convention also provides for such a possibility.
[76] Hayward, *Constitutional Environmental Rights* (OUP, 2005) 180.

Generally, it appears that within the domestic context, environmental procedural rights have the potential for successful implementation in practice, as they can be enforced by NGOs and individuals, and may be used to influence the shaping of domestic policy. Public law litigation may help to overcome the intrinsic anthropocentricity of environmental rights, 'to the extent that rights can be exercised on behalf of the environment or of its non-human components, and not solely for human benefit'.[77]

FURTHER READING

BOYLE and ANDERSON (eds), *Human Rights Approaches to Environmental Protection* (Oxford University Press, 1996).

FITZMAURICE, 'Some Reflections on Public Participation in Environmental Matters as a Human Right in International Law' (2002) 2 *NSA and IL* 1.

—— and MARSHALL, 'The Human Right to a Clean Environment—Phantom or Reality? The European Court of Human Rights and English Courts Perspective on balancing Rights in Environmental Cases' (2007) 76 *Nordic JIL* 103.

HANDL, 'Human Rights and Protection of the Environment' in Eide, Krause, and Rosas (eds), *Economic, Social and Cultural Rights* (Kluwer Law International, 2001) 303.

MOGERA, 'An Update on the Aarhus Convention and its Continued

Global Relevance' (2005) 14 *Review of European Community and International Environmental Law* 138.

OHCHR, Report on the relationship between climate change and human rights, A/HRC/10/61 (15 January 2001).

PALMER and ROBB (eds), *International Environmental Law Reports, Vol 3: Human Rights and Environment* (Cambridge University Press, 2001).

SHELTON, 'Human Rights, Environmental Rights and the Right to the Environment' (1991) 28 *Stanford JIL* 103.

STEC, "Aarhus Environmental Rights" in Eastern Europe (2005) 5 *YEnvmL*.

TURNER, *A Substantive Environmental Right: An Examination of the Legal Obligations of Decision-Makers Towards the Environment* (Kluwer Law International, 2009).

USEFUL WEBSITES

OHCHR, climate change and human rights: <**http://www2.ohchr.org/english/issues/climatechange/index.htm**>

UNECE, Aarhus Convention: <**http://www.unece.org/env/pp/welcome.html**>

---

[77] Birnie, Boyle, and Redgwell, *International Law and the Environment* (OUP, 2009) 298.

INDEX